A Youthful Diary

A Youthful Diary

ONE MAN'S JOURNEY FROM
THE BEGINNING OF FAITH
TO WORLDWIDE LEADERSHIP FOR PEACE

DAISAKU IKEDA

World Tribune
Press

Published by World Tribune Press
606 Wilshire Blvd., Santa Monica, CA 90401

Hardcover edition: © 2001 Soka Gakkai
ISBN: 978-0-915678-68-6

Paperback edition: © 2006 Soka Gakkai
ISBN: 978-1-932911-19-0

Cover design by Alma Orenstein

10 9 8 7 6

Library of Congress Cataloging-in-Publication Data

Ikeda, Daisaku.
  A youthful diary : one man's journey from the beginning
of faith to worldwide leadership for peace / Daisaku Ikeda.
     p. cm.
  ISBN-13: 978-1-932911-19-0 (pbk. : alk. paper)
  1. Ikeda, Daisaku—Diaries. 2. Soka Gakkai Buddhists—
Japan—Diaries. 3. Soka Gakkai International—Biography.
I. Title.
  BQ8449.I387A3 2006
  294.3'928092—dc22
  [B]
                                                    2006023394

CONTENTS

PREFACE

I MET JOSEI TODA, WHO BECAME MY TEACHER, IN AUGUST 1947, WHEN for the first time I attended a Soka Gakkai discussion meeting in Tokyo's Ota Ward. Two years had passed since the end of the Pacific War, and the city was just beginning to recover from the ravages of the bombing raids.

Mr. Toda was forty-seven at the time; I was nineteen. I remember that I asked a number of rather bold questions. Though it was our first meeting, Mr. Toda, at times with an austere expression on his face, at other times in a more relaxed manner, explained his views, speaking like a kind father giving instructions to his son. His remarks seemed to glow with the light of profound conviction. I remember being deeply impressed by the fact that, though imprisoned during the war by government authorities because of his religious beliefs, he had adamantly refused to give in to the pressures brought to bear on him.

Some ten days later, I expressed a desire to join the Soka Gakkai. It was during the lingering heat that marked the close of summer. Since then, as though guided by destiny, my life has followed one fixed course: While struggling to overcome my own health problems, I have given myself wholly to the great task of propagating the Buddhist teachings.

Around the beginning of 1949, a year and a half after I became a Soka Gakkai member, I began working for the publishing company headed by Mr. Toda. Working for him day after day, I came to realize that he never for a moment forgot his teacher, Tsunesaburo Makiguchi, the first Soka Gakkai president. Mr. Makiguchi had been sent to prison along with Mr. Toda and died there during the war at the age of seventy-three. Mr. Toda saw himself as the heir to his teacher's faith and convictions, firmly dedicated to carrying out Mr. Makiguchi's unfulfilled hopes for widespread propagation of Nichiren Daishonin's teachings. The fervency with which he devoted his life to the realization of that goal made him in my eyes a figure of shining nobility.

A Youthful Diary was begun in May 1949, the year I started working for Mr. Toda, and continued over the ensuing eleven years, ending shortly after May 3, 1960, when, after Mr. Toda's death, I took office as the Soka Gakkai's third president. It is an unadorned record of my life from age twenty-one to age thirty-two, the events in it constituting, as it were, a single dramatic narrative. The entries were not set down after long and careful thought, nor are they in polished literary form. During those years, I was racing here and there with hardly a moment to catch my breath, and the diary is thus made up of disconnected jottings, often as not written very late in the evening.

Perhaps for that reason, however, these jottings clearly reflect my thoughts at the time. I was pondering how best I could assist my mentor in the task of propagating the Buddhist Law, while at the same time I had my own youthful worries, my vows for the morrow. There were days when sickness dragged me down, when I was so exhausted that I seemed to hover on the brink of death. Mr. Toda's business ventures did not fare well, and I berated myself for failing to be of greater assistance to him, at times going to bed bathed in sweat from my tubercular condition. Sometimes I even secretly prayed I might die a martyr's death, offering up my short life in the service of faith.

Those youthful years, when I was striving day by day to advance in my undertakings, seem no further away than yesterday. I served my teacher for some ten years — in one sense a long time, in another sense a mere instant — and those ten years contained my entire future.

Deep in my heart was one single thought — how I could best help to fulfill my teacher's goals and ambitions. I saw myself as the vessel of Mr. Makiguchi's and Mr. Toda's hopes. This meant working tirelessly on a practical level to protect the precious Soka Gakkai membership.

At the same time, the years spanned in my diary represent a period when my own life as an individual was taking shape. These were the years of my marriage, the births of our children, the blessings of a happy home life; so I could fortunately pursue the fight for my religious convictions without doubt or distractions.

But I must stress here that the diary was never written with the thought that it might be read by others. In Japan, in response to requests from a number of persons, it has come out in printed form. I hope that, in this form, it may lend encouragement to those who share my dedication to the cause of Buddhism; however, it was originally intended for my eyes alone.

The present English translation is published here in response to earnest requests from the SGI-USA Publications Center and youth division members. It was serialized earlier in the *Seikyo Times*, the SGI-USA monthly magazine, now renamed *Living Buddhism*, and appears here as a single volume.

This past September, the SGI-USA Youth Grand Culture Festival was held in Los Angeles, a symbol of the remarkable growth achieved by these young people of America who will play a key role in the world of the twenty-first century. I was deeply gratified by this event and, thinking of the brave faces of the youth who took part in the festival, I happily agreed to their request to publish the diary in book form.

If, through this English version of the diary of a single individual, they may respond to the spirit that was stirring in me at that time and gain some measure of encouragement in the business of living, I will count myself most fortunate. And if the diary can somehow hasten the progress of the movement for peace and cultural development in America, which constitutes a vital key to the happiness and prosperity of all humankind, I will be doubly gratified.

The coming year, 2000, which will mark the beginning of a new millennium, has special meaning for several reasons. First, it will be forty years since I first visited the United States and began my journeys in the cause of world peace. Second, it will be twenty-five years since the founding of the SGI. At the same time, it will mark the seventieth anniversary of the founding of the Soka Gakkai itself and the hundredth anniversary of the birth of my teacher, Mr. Toda.

The twenty-first century waits for the youth of America to grow and soar to new heights.

DAISAKU IKEDA

EDITOR'S NOTE

A YOUTHFUL DIARY IS THE COMPILATION OF A SERIES BY THE SAME NAME that appeared in the SGI-USA study journal *Seikyo Times* (currently *Living Buddhism*) from May 1983 to October 1996. Over the thirteen years of its appearance in the magazine, conventions in translation have changed. The translation of this new volume reflects those changes, and the text has been reedited for clarity.

Also, please note that the people referred to by initials are not necessarily the same from entry to entry. For example, "S." in one entry may not be the same person as "S." in another entry. The author used these initials to maintain the subjects' anonymity.

Finally, the citations most commonly used in this book have been abbreviated as follows:

- GZ refers to the *Gosho Zenshu*, the Japanese-language compilation of letters, treatises, essays and oral teachings of Nichiren Daishonin.
- LS refers to *The Lotus Sutra*, translated by Burton Watson (Columbia University Press: New York; 1993). The citation usually appears as (LSXX, xx), where XX refers to the chapter number and xx is the page number.
- WND refers to *The Writings of Nichiren Daishonin* (Soka Gakkai: Tokyo; 1999).

IN MAY 1949 WHEN THIS diary begins, Daisaku Ikeda was twenty-one. A year and nine months had passed since he had taken faith in Nichiren Daishonin's Buddhism and joined the Soka Gakkai. Since April of the previous year, he attended the night-school extension of Taisei Gakuin (now Fuji Junior College) in the economics and political science department. In January, he began working for the Nihon Shogakkan, a publishing firm owned and managed by his mentor, Josei Toda, then the Soka Gakkai general director, who would later become its second president. The young Ikeda was at first assigned to help edit the monthly children's magazine *Boys' Adventure*, and in May became its chief editor. During this period the Soka Gakkai was still in the first phase of its postwar reconstruction but had already regained its peak prewar membership of 3,000 families. Its study magazine, *The Daibyakurenge* (Great White Lotus), would soon be inaugurated in July.

In 1949, an economic policy called the Dodge Line was enacted to help check runaway inflation. As a result of this ultrastringent measure, initiated by the general headquarters (GHQ) of the Occupation, the economy did an about-face into rapid deflation. Medium-sized and small businesses went bankrupt one after another. As the ranks of the unemployed swelled, labor disputes broke out nationwide. The Tokyo Joint Federation of Labor Unions held a retaliatory strike on June 2 to protest the death of a participant in a demonstration a few days earlier against the Tokyo public safety regulations. A two-day strike followed, on June 10 and 11, by Japan National Railways workers. Railway strikes became so widespread that the GHQ had to intervene.

Another threat soon became evident. On June 13, in connection with the problem of the return of Japanese prisoners of war from the Soviet Union, hostility between the United States and Russia surfaced at a United Nations Security Council meeting, and the intensification of the Cold War cast its shadow over Japan.

The mass dismissal of workers resulting from the implementation of the Dodge Line provoked a series of bizarre incidents between June and September. On July 6, the Japan National Railways president was found dead on the tracks between two busy railway stations, just days after major layoffs were announced. On July 16, an unmanned electric car in the car barns at Mitaka Station suddenly moved, apparently by itself, and crashed into neighboring homes, killing six and injuring thirteen. Such occurrences seemed to symbolize postwar confusion. In the midst of this, on August 31, a typhoon struck Kanagawa and

swept across eastern Japan, leaving sixty-eight dead, thirty-nine missing and 10,000 homes destroyed. Causing the worst storm damage in eleven years, it was a severe blow to a nation still in the throes of reconstruction.

The Daibyakurenge was first published in September 1949. Before the war, the Gakkai had published a magazine known as *Value Creation*, but in 1942 it was suspended due to pressure from military authorities. In June 1946, a single issue was published as a mimeographed copy. To fulfill the needs of a rapidly increasing Gakkai membership, the monthly *The Daibyakurenge* was born, beginning as a standard-size, thirty-two—page magazine of basic Buddhist theory.

The final, December issue of *Boys' Adventure* (renamed *Boys' Japan* from the August issue) was ready on October 28, 1949. Young Daisaku Ikeda had been deeply involved with the editing. Along with the general economy, Josei Toda's business was experiencing a decline, and his company, the Nihon Shogakkan, suspended magazine publication in October. In December, Nihon Shogakkan employees became the staff of Toda's new business venture — the Tokyo Construction Credit Association.

Tuesday, May 31. Light rain.

One meets too many hypocrites in this world. Youth especially must revere the truth. Whoever pursues the truth throughout life is a great person.

Half a year has passed already since I went to work for Mr. Toda's company. Stormy and eventful days. All I can do is steel myself to meet hardships cheerfully. Must advance toward the dawn, never wavering in my conviction, following my lifelong—no, my *eternal* mentor.

Finished the July issue of *Boys' Adventure*. My maiden work. I advance in the cultural vanguard, in company with pure-hearted children. Will develop my editing to the limits of my ability, treating it as my dearest friend, or as my lover.

"Fulfill your mission for today"—for by doing so, you will make the future glorious.

Saw a movie at Shinbashi on my way home. Up at 7:00, to bed at 12:00.

Through faith, youth must cultivate a wealth of spirit, a vast tolerance.

Wednesday, June 1. Clear.

"To lie is the basest act in life." But in reality, all live under false pretenses, and truth is lost to expediency. How pitiful! Must remember to think seriously about my own future and carry through the supreme mission throughout my life. The road to hell and the gallant road of a significant and truthful life are both at the feet of youth.

Received guidance and advice from Mr. Toda about the logical system of "main point, outline and development" in terms of both work and public relations.

June, month of fresh green and summer breezes, wafting a thousand miles. Must advance without regrets in the time of my passionate youth.

Skipped tonight's lecture on the Lotus Sutra to help Mr. Kodaira proofread *The Daibyakurenge*. I pray earnestly for the development of *The Daibyakurenge*, the vanguard of kosen-rufu.

My room is so cramped, I feel that I insult the Gohonzon. It makes me quite apologetic. Disrespect for the Gohonzon is the same thing as contempt for one's own life. As soon as possible, I want to enshrine my Gohonzon in a place of dignity.

What a magnificent moon tonight! Without the moon and the stars twinkling above us, how empty and desolate the world would be!

Life demands confidence. Life demands effort. Life demands compassion. To live without confidence is to live without meaning, like a stagnant puddle, never knowing what it means to risk or dare. To live without effort is to live on cunning, like some despicable and insolent thief. To live without compassion is to be like contemporary scholars and politicians. People of the limelight, masters of seeking their own advantage, ignorant of life's subtle beauty.

Strength and conviction of a life lived confidently. Noble figure of a man of heroic effort, meeting troubles and hardships head on. A man filled with unfathomable mercy and dignity—Mr. Toda. How wondrous is the perfection of life!

Thursday, June 2. Clear.

Days of youth wet with tears. Through tears, I sense the surge of new power. Through tears, I experience unutterable emotion welling from my innermost heart. Youth, rich in poetry. Youth, who live with passion and effort. Now in the precious moments of youth, I wish to express the pinnacle of art in my way of living.

In literature, in poetry, in music.

I pray that youthful impulse will not lead me to follow the wrong road.

To break through hardships, to fulfill one's purpose in life, to carry out the great task of human salvation—ultimately, there is no other way but to cherish absolute faith in the Gohonzon.

I must live always conscious of the supreme mission. Must advance, toward the glorious dawn.

All men strive to impress, and I'm no different. Leaders of the future, however, must be men of real capability. Must remember the spirit of our forebears, the men of old.

The times advance, day by day. I want to be someone who can keep pace with that advance—no, who can lead it!

I love children, those new arrivals who will fulfill the future's dreams. I love all my countrymen. I long to embrace and shake hands with everyone, at any time, anywhere, but the rules of society forbid it.

I love the whole human race like a lover. But even if I cry out my love at the top of my voice, they cannot hear me.

People of the world! The time has come to embrace the true religion, to follow Nichiren Daishonin's teachings.

I strike the golden bell and shatter the dawn's silence. I drown out the noisy clamor of leaden bells.

Friday, June 3. Cloudy.

Cool since morning. Threatening to rain since afternoon, but none fell.

Busy days, but I grapple squarely with the tasks assigned to me. That gives my work meaning. Even when I'm suffering, I'm truly happy. Must make Mr. Toda's company the best in Japan. Must create the finest magazine in the nation.

I am deeply stirred by the Gakkai's growth and struggles.

Must persuade my father to take faith as soon as possible. I have to change my family's destiny fundamentally. I keenly feel this to be my mission.

Nothing is achieved in life without decisiveness. Am I a coward? Or a young man who will truly carry out religious revolution? In the true spirit of youth, wake up! In the true spirit of youth, advance!

At night, read from the Gosho:

> Scholars of the Latter Day, how can you judge Buddhism without reading this? Three principles you should closely study: the sudden teaching (which corresponds to the truth of nonsubstantiality), the gradual teaching (corresponding to the truth of temporary existence) and the round teaching (corresponding to the Middle Way). These are the three truths revealed in the lifelong teachings of Buddha. He expounded the sudden and gradual teachings for forty-two years, and the round teaching for eight. Together they total fifty years. There is no Buddhism apart from these. Why are you confused about this? They are called the three truths while one remains a common mortal; when he attains Buddhahood, they are called the three enlightened properties. These are but two names for a single thing. That which clarifies them is the lifelong teachings of Shakyamuni. When one realizes and manifests their perfect unification within himself, he becomes a Buddha.
>
> —(GZ, 573)

Oh, vast motion of a boundless universe! History being endlessly created. People rushing about in confusion, as though imprisoned in a burning house. Lives surrounded by conflict after conflict. Ordered flux of the great cosmos that no human intellect can fathom. Where shall sensitive youth turn for an answer? As I read the Gosho, I tremble with delight.

Buddhism, clearly expounding the origin and basis of all, offering true happiness.

Who can doubt it? Here is the ultimate, the guiding principle for all humanity. Politicians, men of letters, scientists! Awake! Believe in the Great Pure Law.

Saturday, June 4. Clear.

Progress and revolution involve all forms of opposition. Those who overcome it are worthy to be called youth. Like seeds that endure through winter and sprout from the earth in spring.

Youth! Abandon wishful thinking. Reality is harsh. Youth is the time to advance, to grow, to battle against corruption. A youth is most worthy of respect when advancing earnestly toward a goal. But don't forget to smile. Be cheerful always.

Editorial conference at 2:00. Discussed renaming *Boys' Adventure*. No matter what, somehow, it must become the best boys' magazine in Japan. That is my mission and the way I can repay Mr. Toda.

Youth division meeting at 6:00. K. and I announced our religious debate to refute the erroneous Butsuryu sect. Surprised at our seniors' lack of enthusiasm.

Has my hour finally come to advance on the front line? For the sake of kosen-rufu, armed with the Daishonin's supreme philosophy.

Monday, June 6. Cloudy.

Exhausted, both mentally and physically. Heavy assignments every day.

Youth amid the storm: profound, remote, mysterious. Youth, like the surging strains of Beethoven. Youth, brimming with poetry as wildly impassioned as Dante's. Valiant young trees that bear up in the storm. The mysterious beauty of forests lit by lightning storms. Same old familiar scent of the earth, though the soil is plowed up again and again. Irrepressible motion of a soul that, even when drenched by rain and buffeted by wind, does not forget remote and timeless beauty. Youth in the storm! Advance, never forgetting the blazing sun soon to rise.

Cloudy since morning. We were warned by the chief accountant that we'd better start coming to work earlier to get everything set up. I feel sorry for the female clerks. The gulf between management and labor is glaringly obvious.

I wait for the day when employees at every company can work happily together in mutual trust. No, better not wait. We must create it ourselves, with our own hands.

Three chapters of the Tokyo Railway Workers' Union went on strike in Meguro, Hiro'o and Yanagishima.

The strike was in demonstration against public safety regulations. A man named Kinji Hashimoto died. Days of violence go on and on.

Pray, pray. That's all I can do.

For kosen-rufu to come even one day sooner.

Worked at the office till 9:40. Everyone went home; I stayed on alone. Working hard makes me happy, even if no one sees.

Home by 11:20. It's so far to go!

Ate a bowl of noodles before bed.

Tuesday, June 7. Light rain.

The rainy season seems to have started. A gentle drizzle since morning. Asian peoples, especially the Japanese, have a strong, poetic feeling for nature. I hope our nation, now recovering from the ravages of war, will never lose this.

But the reality of it is that average working people's nerves are on edge during the rainy season, and emotional outbursts are all too frequent. It's a shame. I am physically exhausted. I can't seem to stop over-sleeping in the morning.

Human revolution is the goal of faith. Must strive harder.

I can feel my body growing stronger year by year. To self-indulgent youths, to suffering senior citizens, to all stubborn-minded people, I must show the true joy of faith, a strong body brimming with ardor and a youthful spirit striving in a great mission.

"Stand up in the cause of justice and your strength is doubled" (Schiller).

Talked for nearly two hours with the artist Ichiro Ikebe about French politics, art and society.

Raining harder toward evening.

Read alone in the quiet editorial room. Will study hard. Must not be defeated. Especially must study politics and economics.

Wednesday, June 8. Rain.

Raining again, and almost cold.

The layout for the August issue of *Boys' Adventure* is almost finished now. What a relief. This issue has to show great results.

Buddhism is a battle. We of the Nihon Shogakkan who embrace a correct view of society will never knuckle under to other companies.

I meet lots of artists and writers through my work, many of them considered to be masters. It's disappointing once I actually talk to them. Those of character are the only great people in the world.

How many people in the arts today are truly worthy of respect? Maybe artists have a right to be eccentric, but how often they make me run after them, wasting such valuable time!

Dropped by a shoe shop near Kamata Station on the way home. Bought a pair of old shoes. Society holds too many contradictions. Some people are poor, though they live and work honestly. Others live by deceit and never lift a finger, but they lack for nothing. All kinds of people in the world.

Is the one who amasses material possessions the final winner in life? Absurd! Must examine my own situation and then leap beyond, to show great proof in the future. Isn't that what faith teaches?

Youth, never be envious. Never lose heart.

Thursday, June 9. Rain.

Rainy season. Walked to Umeyashiki Station.

The passers-by all got drenched in the summer rain. Rain makes the female students' white dresses stand out even more brightly. Young girls, in your future…you may have nothing special in mind, yet you feed others' imaginations. You have in you all the elements of great art. Perhaps you are art personified. Without your fresh presence, this town, society, the world itself—how cold and forbidding they would be! Like a house without flowers, or the night sky without the twinkling stars. May your futures be blessed—and the future of young girls in America, in France, in Spain—everywhere.

Got home in the rain about 10:50. Soaking wet all the way. Thoroughly miserable. I feel lonely but can still weep tears of joy in hopes of a future dawn.

Supper tonight—a hunk of bread.

Monday, June 13. Cloudy.

Had a headache since morning. Have to take better care of myself. My mind changes from one moment to the next. I know what my goals are, but I waver all the same. Pathetic. One moment I'm in high spirits, bursting with youthful intensity, and the next moment I'm as petrified as though I were standing on the edge of a cliff.

One moment I contemplate high ideals and religious revolution, but in the storm of my actual situation, I tremble. It's pitiable.

Youth, stand up! Advance! Otherwise there will be no human revolution.

Plunge into the whirlpool of reality and fight. Fear nothing. Remember your great mission.

Bought three books at Kanda: Pascal's *Pensees*, *The Book of Passion* and one more. Altogether, spent ¥120.

Leaders meeting today. How valiantly the Gakkai forges ahead. I must not be left behind. My sole frustration and regret is that because of work, I can't do Gakkai activities the way I want to. What joy it must be to offer one's whole life to the Daishonin!

I must carry out propagation. I'm falling behind in my studies, too. Hope I can go back to night school tomorrow. I've been gone so long my classmates probably wonder what happened to me.

Tuesday, June 14. Cloudy.

A refreshing morning. My physical condition is not good. Got to work at 9:30. Everyone else was already working, and I felt self-conscious, embarrassed. Resolved to get to work earlier, starting tomorrow.

Thursday, June 16. Rain.

Scolded by Mr. Toda. Agonizing. All my fault. Must reflect on myself.

I believe in Mr. Toda, and I'll strive till the bitter end. I've got to recognize my weak points and change them...otherwise I'll be miserable all my life.

Must advance again, with all my might. Remember the childhood and youth of great men of the past.

Friday, September 2. Typhoon.

Typhoon Kitty was here. Streets flooded with muddy water. Pouring rain since morning. It is a stifling feeling.

Those awakened to their mission must, day by day, purify their lives, more than those around them.

Never be hypocritical. Never be weak. Even a person of public acclaim should not glory in superficial praise or formal honors. Those who seek such distinctions are to be pitied more than beggars.

Youth! Squarely challenge your difficulties and advance. To live a great existence with belief in justice, for your country and for the happiness of humankind!

Don't ever be defeated by external pressure. Cherish hope and ambition in your heart.

History will definitely prove the righteousness of those who wield the sword of justice.

Nichiren Daishonin is watching your efforts, so never be afraid of anything, and never be cowardly.

Forge on courageously and boldly, because you are young.

Always grow.

Never forget to go beyond the limits.

Must take a good look at myself again today.

Am I lying to myself? Am I committing some offense? Have I true compassion or not?

My life until now has been like a play, a dream, already a thing of the past. Now is what counts. From this moment on. The future is my arena, a training ground where I can make up for my shortcomings.

Read from "The Record of the Orally Transmitted Teachings":

> Concerning the "peaceful and comfortable practice" of Myoho-renge-kyo: In the Latter Day of the Law, in terms of the practice which Nichiren and his disciples now carry out, to meet obstacles in the course of one's practice of Myoho-renge-kyo should be regarded as "peaceful and comfortable." (GZ, 750)

Sunday, September 4. Cloudy.

What is today's task? To fulfill my mission for today. What is my mission for today? To struggle in my own circumstances. What is that struggle? To advance, to the limits of my strength.

What is tomorrow's problem? Is tomorrow a moment-by-moment extension of today? No matter how hard today may be, when we dream of tomorrow, hope returns.

When we do our best today, the future sparkles, and flames of joy leap high. Reality consists of our actual feeling at this moment, and this moment continues eternally. There is no choice but to pursue the human revolution.

What is life's ultimate problem? The problem of death. What is death? Countless saints and sages have appeared in the 5,000 years of human history, yet have any of them found a conclusive answer? Has anyone come back to prove their theories?

The Mystic Law is the only path by which one can resolve the problem of death. Must clarify and resolve this problem and show proof of it.

Without this Law, two billion human beings would be lost in the abyss of misery.

The Mystic Law is the only principle for human salvation. How sharply I feel its fundamental significance!

Listen, self that is so weak: Advance! Have you no courage to keep forging ahead? Stand up and do something significant this year, as the Daishonin's disciple.

Monday, October 24. Clear.

The fourth Soka Gakkai general meeting was held yesterday. Fine refreshing autumn weather continues.

Department Chief O. discussed our company's future this morning.

Three months have passed already since *Boys' Adventure* was renamed *Boys' Japan*. We seem to be in severe straits, pressured by competition from larger companies. But management's not my role. All I can do is carry out the task assigned to me.

Boys' Japan—what a broad and powerful phrase! Boys growing toward the future, motions lighthearted as spring. Eyes clear as autumn skies. Hopes boundless as a prairie. Innocent boys deserve our respect. We must consider them the treasures of our nation, for they are builders of the society to come.

This year I strive beside these pure-hearted children. Want to be confident that our work is of high quality.

Boys of Japan! Boys of the whole world! Each of you, be forever cheerful and courageous, like a messenger of heaven.

At noon, I visited the author M. and the artist I. I want them to depict the dreams of youth for our New Year's issue.

I. lives in Minami-tama, a newly developed area. I got the good-natured man to understand my idea. It's quiet where he lives. I emerged from the twilight of the still woods and caught the Odakyu Line at 6:20. I. is said to be a Christian. He has drive but doesn't truly know himself. There was nothing I could learn from him.

A new moon hung brilliantly in the open sky. Back to work at 7:30. Talked over several matters with senior coworkers. Home at 10:00.

Tuesday, October 25. Rain.

Cloudy skies in the morning. Later, the autumn rains. Gloomy day.

It was announced that we would stop publishing *Boys' Japan*. Utterly discouraged. Nothing to do all morning but deal with visitors in the editorial room or in the office.

If the Earth were to stop turning on its axis, the reaction would be overwhelming. If an engine suddenly broke down while a plane was in flight, the result would be tragic. Up until now, I poured my whole life into that magazine, and now it's been discontinued. Naturally, it's a shock.

My only fear is that people will misunderstand. I know Mr. Toda's character. I know his supreme mission.

Under his guidance, I'll devote myself wholeheartedly to the next project, whatever it may be. When I see it in that light, the others' flurry and panic seem almost laughable — even the ones with faith. Mr. Toda is not one to be swayed by storms or raging billows. The victory of his great character will be decided by his final undertaking. Surmounting tempests and towering waves, his strength and noble influence will in the end remain like a monument, engraved in gold characters, of the people's respect and admiration.

The public are fools, they say, and history, too, often forgets great people. But Mr. Toda is a man of true character, and I believe his shining influence will never die.

Went in the autumn rain to visit the artist A. An unhappy man.

I told him about the Daishonin's philosophy, wanting him to find happiness as soon as possible. Went to the Ginza library this evening for I.'s pen-and-ink drawing of Magellan discovering the Pacific. Went to a movie in Shinbashi on the way back. Feel keen remorse about missing the discussion meeting.

Well, there's tomorrow. Tomorrow brings hope.

Wednesday, October 26. Fine and clear.

Fresh, clear autumn weather. Went to work in high spirits.

Tied up the loose ends of *Boys' Japan*. Will finish as soon as possible. I look forward eagerly to Mr. Toda's next enterprise. Also want to spend a glorious autumn.

Visited the artist H. this afternoon. Perhaps we said goodbye for the last time. Friendships based on profit are hollow ones. The great artist doesn't understand the soul of youth.

Took my shoes to be repaired. Cost a hundred yen.

Physically exhausted. Night school begins to seem impossible.

Things seem very hard for Mr. Toda, too.

What is your purpose? Religious revolution.

What is religious revolution? The straight road to human happiness.

What are the means to win religious revolution?

Carrying out the supreme philosophy myself.

Grasping and mastering the basis myself.

創立90周年へ
創価勝利の年

Year of Soka Victory—
Toward Our 90th Anniversary

創価学会総本部へようこそ!
Welcome to the Soka Gakkai Headquarters complex!

Thursday, October 27. Rain.

Dreary autumn rain. Chitchatted till noon in the editorial room. A storm is reportedly on the way. It's rare to have as many storms as we've had this year. Why is that? Natural phenomena alone cannot account for it.

Went to see I. at the Ministry of Health and Welfare. Happy to see my friend cheerful as always. He seems to be absorbed in the dance. I'm afraid he'll overdo it.

He was busy, so I left after a brief visit. The wind was rising and the rain fell harder. I'd promised to meet Y. at 5:00 at Omori. He showed up at 5:30.

Went with him to a discussion meeting at H.'s place at Kominato in Yokohama. The streetcar was delayed because of the rain, and it was past 7:00 when we arrived. About fifty people were there, a fruitful meeting. Over at 10:00. I went back as far as Kamata with I. The typhoon was mustering force. Got home through the storm, chanting daimoku to myself.

12:00.

Friday, October 28. Rain, clearing later.

The typhoon's over. Clear autumn skies since 10:00.

Finished up the remaining business. Sat and read at my desk all afternoon. The last issue of *Boys' Japan* came off the press. Is this our company's final effort? Hardly great workmanship. It's really a shame. Both the paper quality and the printing make me feel disappointed.

Had some noodles at 5:30. I hear some of the staff are going to leave the company. I suppose it's to be expected.

I'll fight again, from tomorrow, with a strong, cheerful energy. I'm young. A youth.

Went to the baths tonight for the first time in quite a while. Feel sorry for my aging mother.

Saturday, October 29. Cloudy.

Got to work at 8:00.

Took a brief walk with some co-workers down Kanda Avenue. Everyone is discouraged.

It rained a little on the way.

Had a meeting at 3:00 to discuss new projects.

Listened with bursting excitement to Mr. Toda's views on economics. Among other things, he talked about capitalism, communism and their bearing on credit associations.

He also related some of his business experiences. I don't know how the others felt, but to me, the stories of his lifelong efforts, his passions and his agonizing struggles were all precious.

At 6:00, we received part of our salary. Our wages are being paid in installments.

Went to the barber's. Our wages are low. Hard times for me, for everyone.

Sunday, October 30. Clear.

Lots of sleep last night. Got up at 9:00. Clear autumn skies.

Chanted vigorous daimoku. Played with my niece till lunch. Lovable children are like oases in our lives.

If everyone really were to care about these precious children, I think that in itself would automatically put a brake on war.

Went to work in the afternoon. En route, three times I passed runners from the All-Japan Athletic Competition, carrying flags. Their pure white uniforms suggested a vigorous strength.

Worked on unfinished business till evening in the editorial room. Read for a while.

At night, visited K. Talked frankly about a number of things.

Came home and found my mother fast asleep. My mother is great.

Sunday, December 4. Clouds and light rain.

My physical condition is quite bad. Health above all. Gongyo is the only way to improve it.

Disagreeable weather. Clouds in the sky, and I feel like there are clouds in my heart, too. Small creature that I am, the elements play with me at their will.

Started preparing for a new project today.

In the evening I met professors K. and I. on business.

There are so few truly great educators.

Home at 11:00. Read.

1 9 5 0

THE BEGINNING OF 1950 saw new political directions for the nation: General Douglas MacArthur, commander-in-chief of the Occupation forces, stressed the right of the Japanese to self-defense in his New Year's address; new ¥1,000 bills bearing the image of Prince Shotoku were printed; tobacco rationing by family was abolished and so on. On the other hand, in March, casual laborers demanding full employment staged sit-ins at the public employment security offices in Tokyo and Hachioji. Similar incidents occurred throughout Tokyo, demonstrating that postwar economic difficulty continued to cast its bleak shadow over the country.

Josei Toda, however, did not slacken in the least in his kosen-rufu efforts as then Soka Gakkai general director. On April 19, he began his tenth Lotus Sutra lecture series. Daisaku Ikeda had left his parents' home the year before and was living in a one-room, six-tatami—mat apartment in Omori, Tokyo. While working desperately to help Mr. Toda with their faltering business, he devoted himself to discussion meetings and other Soka Gakkai activities almost every night.

The Occupation ended in 1950. That year, the Japan peace treaty problem came to a head. Argument raged over whether Japan should sign a general treaty with all the nations it had fought against in World War II or conclude separate treaties with individual nations.

Economic issues facing Japan at this time included affiliation with the International Monetary Fund (IMF), the introduction of foreign capital, etc. Finance Minister Hayato Ikeda visited the United States to discuss these problems and returned on May 22. The "four-power conference" referred to in the May 24 entry was a summit conference involving England, France, the United States and the Soviet Union, proposed by the U.N. secretary-general in hopes of resolving the Cold War. No significant progress was achieved. General MacArthur, who once hoped Japan would be the Switzerland of Asia, now voiced a need to maintain American Air Force bases in Asia to counter the Communist threat. Clearly Japan was now expected to play a role advantageous to the West in the international standoff.

Following World War II, Japan was bombarded almost annually by typhoons and other heavy rains leaving considerable storm damage in their wake. During the 1950 summer rainy season, devastating rains fell in many areas. In Nagano Prefecture, a train was derailed, causing some casualties, and streets were flooded. In Tokyo, 880 homes were flood damaged.

Nearly five years after the war, food shortages persisted and rice was still strictly rationed. Except in cafeterias where patrons used ration tickets, the serving of rice in restaurants was considered a violation of rationing laws. On June 21, testifying to the drastic food shortages of the times, some sushi shop managers in Tokyo's Yurakucho area were apprehended on suspicion of serving rice, and authorities announced that henceforth, ration violators would be arrested and detained.

A government economic report issued on June 30 claimed that the standard of living had risen to only seventy-six to seventy-eight percent of its prewar level. People spent on clothing only thirty percent of what they did before the war, making do with the items they had on hand.

The straitened economy bankrupted many smaller companies. The Tokyo Construction Credit Association, established by Josei Toda to recoup his earlier business venture losses, had to suspend operations on August 22.

On September 3, a typhoon struck Kobe and swept across Japan toward the northeast, leaving one thousand injured or dead and some six-thousand homes and businesses destroyed, chiefly in the Osaka–Kobe area.

The severe flood damage on top of an already suffering economy demoralized many.

October 24, United Nations Day, commemorated the formal establishment of the U.N. charter five years earlier. Japan, still under Occupation government, did not yet belong to the United Nations, but the anniversary was nevertheless observed in several commemorative events, including a large Tokyo rally and the ceremonial presentation of a United Nations flag sent by the U.N. headquarters. Prime Minister Yoshida, addressing the rally, stressed the need to understand the U.N. spirit.

The seventh memorial service (marking the sixth anniversary) for the first Soka Gakkai president, Tsunesaburo Makiguchi, and the fifth Soka Gakkai general meeting were held in the Kyoiku Hall in Kanda, Tokyo, on November 12. At the general meeting, Josei Toda officially resigned as general director, determined that his business failure should not adversely affect the Gakkai. In his lecture, however, he affirmed that "kosen-rufu is the Buddha's will and the Buddha's mandate," making clear that he had in no way faltered in his resolve to achieve kosen-rufu. He then turned his attention toward training Daisaku Ikeda and other youth division members for the future, pouring his energies into Gosho lectures and other developmental efforts. In particular, he made time early each Sunday morning to instruct young Daisaku in politics, economics, law, science and other fields. These private lessons continued for several years. SGI President Ikeda would later say of them, "They turned into invisible possessions that have been literally engraved on my life."

Sunday, January 1. Rain.

Slept until 10:00 this morning. Was awakened by the lady next door, who treated me to *zoni* [rice cakes in soup, a traditional New Year's dish]. Feel carefree, living in an apartment by myself, but it's rather lonesome.

Hurriedly did gongyo and went to Mr. Toda's house.

Clustered around him were Miss K., I., Y., I. and several others. He offered us refreshments and gave guidance on a variety of subjects until evening. A memorable New Year's. He also lectured on "On Dispelling Delusions and Observing One's Mind" [a lecture by Nichio, the fifty-sixth high priest].

New Year's Day sun—shed your light on me this year!

Day by day, I am renewed. Today, I am born again.

—FROM AN ANCIENT CONFUCIAN TEXT

Monday, January 2. Cloudy.

Got up early, at 4:40 a.m. So cold!

New Year's pilgrimage to the head temple. Walked vigorously to Omori Station. The train leaves Tokyo at 6:00; I boarded from Shinagawa at 6:12.

Met the others there. Everyone in high spirits.

Remember to live confidently, with dignity.

Morita and I sat next to Mr. Toda. He talked to us about Hall Caine's *The Eternal City*.

Chanted to the Dai-Gohonzon at 2:00.

This year, I'm determined to live powerfully.

On the train home, we sang the "Song of Disciples" and other Gakkai songs at the top of our lungs from Numazu all the way back to Shinagawa.

Tuesday, January 3. Clear.

Rested all morning. All alone here and tired. I wish I'd visited my parents.

I'm concerned about my mother.

Read in the afternoon. Spent the evening talking with some friends. Work starts again tomorrow.

Tuesday, May 9. Fine and clear.

Ah, how happy I am!
Serving under my master
for eternity…

Overslept this morning. Running behind schedule. Wolfed down two helpings of breakfast at the K. restaurant. A bachelor is such a casual creature! Inevitably disorder creeps into his life and causes him trouble.

Already a year since I left home.

My parents, mysteriously bound to me by cause and circumstance, joined in a single moment of our eternal lives. They raised me to manhood at the cost of much pain and anxiety. I can never forget them, not even for a moment. Must be filial. Wait and see.

Wednesday, May 10. Light rain.

On the path of attaining Buddhahood, chant Nam-myoho-renge-kyo without arrogance or attachment to biased views.

> —"How Those Initially Aspiring to the Way Can Attain Buddhahood through the Lotus Sutra" (WND, 888)

I must not get so tired. Only daimoku will help. In this oppressed frame of mind, went on business with my department chief to O. School. Also to O. Elementary School. Business is like drama or warfare.

Came home a little earlier than usual. Played with the children next door and some of their friends. A pleasant, lighthearted evening. Must find a way to save these poor children through Buddhism.

Thursday, May 11. Cloudy with rain.

In the past, all men have been our fathers and all women have been our mothers. Thus through lifetime after lifetime and world after world we have become indebted to all living beings, so we should pray that they all attain Buddhahood.

> —(GZ, 1527)

A youthful life. What a powerful expression!

How to spend my life, how to consume it? Dedicate it to the worthwhile practice of Buddhism.

At 6:00 my department chief and I invited O. and Miss T. to the G. Chinese restaurant. Enjoyed a leisurely supper for the first time in quite a while.

Youth, let us live for tomorrow!

Don't be prisoners of the past. The past is nothing but a dream.

Friday, May 12. Cloudy.

When a man leaves his parents and home and becomes a monk, he should always have as his goal the salvation of his father and mother.

> —"The Opening of the Eyes" (WND, 228)

Hot today. A little tired from our grueling struggles.

How noble, how beautiful is the image of youth, marching on to proclaim the supreme philosophy to all humanity.

Business is like drama or warfare. How wonderful to take an active, adult role on so significant a stage, to participate to my heart's content!

Discussion meeting at K.'s tonight.

Came home at 11:30. Prepared for tomorrow's campaign and went to bed early.

Saturday, May 13. Cloudy.

Copper mirrors reflect the body but not the mind, while the Lotus Sutra mirrors not only people's faces but their minds as well.

—(GZ, 1521)

We've put up a good fight for half the month, but today another serious defeat. Walked on errands all day with my department chief. It hurts me to watch the old man. He has made an indelible impression. To me, he is invaluable in managing the business because he protects Mr. Toda.

Am I tired from all our struggles? My physical condition is extremely bad.

Shall a disciple of Nichiren Daishonin be defeated? Never! Burn with great conviction! Faith, arise!

Points to remember from today on:
1. Study Buddhism.
2. Cut down on expenses.
3. Live productively.

Sunday, May 14. Fine and clear.

The Buddha will not dwell in a woman of no faith, but a woman who embraces the Lotus Sutra is like clear water in which the moon of Buddha will be reflected.... The same holds true with the teachings of the Lotus Sutra. When you believe Nam-myoho-renge-kyo in your heart, the Buddha will be conceived there. You may not realize it at first, but as the months pass, the Buddha in your heart will gradually appear in dreams and bring you immense delight.

—(GZ, 1395)

A most meaningful day. Chanted daimoku to my heart's content at Kankiryo temple [now Shorin-ji']. Feel as though I'd been purified. I told T., the elementary school teacher, about Nichiren Daishonin's Buddhism.

Went to visit my family for the first time in a long while. Delighted to see my mother in good health.

On the way home, met some friends from my old neighborhood. Before I left, I encouraged them and told them about Buddhism. None of them have any convictions or sense of purpose. They seem sad and pitiable now.

Home at 10:30. I. was waiting for me at the door. He wanted to consult me about his business failure. Feel sympathy over the sorrow of this once-prosperous businessman, who has no faith to sustain him.

1. -ji: temple.

Monday, May 15. Clear.

The mind is as restless as a monkey in flight, never still, even for a moment. If you wish to spread the Law, recite this Mahayana sutra earnestly and meditate on the Buddha's supreme enlightenment, on his power and fearlessness.
— SUTRA OF MEDITATION ON BODHISATTVA UNIVERSALLY WORTHY

A mind that perceives life to be as vast as the universe. A heart that pursues eternal beauty. Unshakable conviction that glows like red-hot iron. I shall strive to acquire them all. To serve humanity and the world. To love and guide the nation.

Let people laugh if they wish to. Let them rage if they so desire. Their abuse means nothing.

What matters is to carry out the true practice of Buddhism. That demands unusual effort. Those efforts, moreover, will surely lead to the great way of happiness.

Another desperate battle today. I must not be defeated. To be weak is to be unhappy. Defeated ones, your name is misery.

Fight! Win! Save the weak and the vanquished. Isn't that a victor's sense of justice?

Tuesday, May 16. Cloudy.

Where there is water, fish dwell. Where there are woods, birds gather. On the mountain island of P'eng-lai there are many jewels, and on Mount Malaya sandalwood trees grow. There is gold in the mountains from which the river Li-shui flows. Now this place, too, is like that. It is the place of the cluster of blessings where the Buddhas and bodhisattvas dwell. The blessings of the Lotus Sutra, which I have recited over these many years, must be vaster even than the sky.
— "THE PLACE OF THE CLUSTER OF BLESSINGS" (WND, 1070)

Home early for a change. Only 8:00.

Paid my rent. Mr. Toda is facing terrible battles. He is called upon both to attack and defend...I must resolve to stand up soon.

The time has come when a son of the revolution must arise!

Some day this shabby six-tatami–mat room will be a precious memory. Youth must fear nothing.

No flaw is worse than cowardice in a young man.

Youth! In whatever drama life may cast you, play your part well.

Wednesday, May 17.

Do society's brutal conflicts spring from the instinctive struggle to survive? Are they inevitable if one is to live and prosper? How base it all seems! It saddens me.

But with us it is different. Ultimately we must discern the nature and essence of such conflicts and discover the laws in operation there. Great thought and great statesmanship will spring from that understanding. Clearly, a supreme philosophy will resolve the dissension.

Thursday, May 18. Cloudy.

If the three powerful enemies predicted in the Lotus Sutra did not appear, then who would believe in the words of the Buddha? If it were not for Nichiren, who could fulfill the Buddha's prophecies concerning the votary of the Lotus Sutra?

—"THE OPENING OF THE EYES" (WND, 243)

Summer has begun. Each day we toil harder. Each day demands greater fortitude.

Told I. about Nichiren Daishonin's Buddhism.

Yesterday, I heard Mr. Toda lecture from "The Record of the Orally Transmitted Teachings" on the passage concerning "the one great reason" why the Buddhas make their advent. Read it again later on.

Thought seriously about my work. I am so happy I can protect Mr. Toda.

Great achievements are the extension of smaller ones. Must remember that a succession of small achievements leads to great success. Victory is won only by building patiently, step by step, in the present moment.

Plain, honest work, day by day, unknown to anyone — that is important. Time alone will reveal my actions to the world.

Will embrace the True Law and strive day by day. Will hold no task beneath me.

Friday, May 19. Clear.

"Though the baby fish are many, there are few that grow up to be big fish. Though the flowers of the mango tree are many, there are few that turn into fruit. In like manner, there are many people who set their hearts on enlightenment, but only a few who continue their practice and in fact attain the true way."

— "The Fourteen Slanders" (WND, 758)

The weather has gotten warmer. Today feels like the hottest day so far this year. Right now I'm concentrating on public relations as Mr. Toda's advance guard. Public relations is a trying task, but it will let us test our abilities to the utmost.

National politics also demand wise and capable diplomats. A nation with no outstanding diplomats cannot take its place on the stage of global affairs, nor can it make a historic contribution to peace.

Today each individual nation must play a direct role in international affairs as an integral part of the world community.

Diplomacy is necessary to individuals, families, society and the nation. It depends not upon wealth or military might but upon individual ability.

Only through diplomacy can we be schooled in courage, wisdom and sincerity. Mr. Toda once said that those with no ability in public relations are not qualified to hold top positions in a company.

Discussion meeting at K.'s. A memorable evening.

Returned home late at night.

Saturday, May 20.

Appreciation for one's parents is so fundamental that one scarcely need speak of it, but I particularly respect the kindness of my mother, which is indelibly etched upon my heart. Birds raise their nestlings and beasts suffer for their young; at the sight, men are put to shame and are deeply moved. Thinking of this, too, I cannot forget the debt I owe my mother.

—(GZ, 398)

Courage is a special talent of youth. To make my mother and father happy, rebuild our business, establish my own foundation and save the nation—courage is the root of it all.

Moved to tears by the Daishonin's concern for his mother.

How many filial sons in ancient times wrote poems about their mothers? They too must have praised their mothers and wept for them.

Read until late at night. Distressed by my empty stomach.

Sunday, May 21. Clear.

If a man builds a road for others and someone loses his way on it, is that the fault of the roadbuilder? If a skilled physician gives medicine to a sick person but the sick person, repelled by medicine, refuses to take it and dies, should one blame the physician?

— "THE SELECTION OF THE TIME" (WND, 539)

Spent a leisurely Sunday for a change. Went to the baths with a friend and had breakfast at a cafeteria where you pay with ration tickets.

Bought some toys for the children in my apartment building at a store in front of Omori Station. They seemed very pleased with them.

The manager of the building came by to make some unpleasant remarks about my faith. The I.'s next door also criticize me harshly. People are always ready to find fault.

Must take a firm stand. No choice but to forge ahead and have the courage to survive. No matter what anyone may say, advance, under the Daishonin's compassion.

Read until midnight. To bed at 1:00.

Monday, May 22. Clear.

Felt unwell all day. Must chant daimoku.

An outstanding person knows what it is to weep, knows when to admonish, knows how to endure patiently, knows others' suffering. Wish to perfect myself as Nichiren Daishonin's disciple and become an outstanding person.

Youth must not be timid. Also, it is important to study great figures' biographies. Must never be content with what I've achieved so far.

Worked hard all day. To work is noble. He who only does enough to get by is no better than a thief or a beggar.

Am now crawling into bed at 1:00, drenched in sweat.

Tuesday, May 23. Cloudy.

Youth, be messengers of the Buddha!
Youth, be fighters in the revolution!
Because I love humanity,
*   no hardships, no angry waves can move me.*

Home at 10:00.
Read the Lotus Sutra. Quite difficult.
There are six difficult and nine easy acts.

"The Emergence of the Treasure Tower," the eleventh chapter, states:

> "The other sutras
> number as many as Ganges sands,
> but though you expound those sutras,
> that is not worth regarding as difficult.
> If you were to seize Mount Sumeru
> and fling it far off
> to the measureless Buddha lands,
> that too would not be difficult.
> If you used the toe of your foot
> to move the thousand-millionfold world,
> booting it far away to other lands,
> that too would not be difficult.
> If you stood in the Summit of Being heaven
> and for the sake of the assembly
> preached countless other sutras,
> that too would not be difficult.
> But if after the Buddha has entered extinction,
> in the time of evil,
> you can preach this sutra,
> that will be difficult indeed!"
>
> —(LS11, 178–79)

Our practice demands great courage.
Went to bed at 1:00.

Wednesday, May 24. Cloudy.

I, Nichiren, was born in this land, so how could I not care about its welfare?

—(GZ, 183)

Early summer.
Each day is a fierce and significant battle.
The world's raging currents dash against me; their roar echoes in my heart.
The June 4 senatorial election campaign is now entering the final stretch. Finance Minister Ikeda returned to Japan and conferred with the prime minister. The four-power conference seems to have made the situation even tenser. Cold War darkness weighs upon people. War is a crime. No matter how just the cause, war must never happen again!

What defines justice? Neither power nor authority. True justice must stem from the supreme Law of the universe.

In the future, numbers of great leaders and statesmen must emerge from the Gakkai's ranks.

To bed at 1:00.

Thursday, May 25. Cloudy.

Nichiren Daishonin. I am the true Buddha's disciple! As the Buddha's disciple I must fear nothing. All I need do is accept and uphold his great compassion and dash ahead. Contemplation alone accomplishes nothing. Whoever merely contemplates is not a true disciple. Am I free from illusion? Do I display the great life force that springs from faith and practice or not?

The arrogance of "ignorant lay people," as the sutra calls it, is flourishing among my neighbors. The people in my apartment building do nothing but criticize my faith without understanding. How pitiable they are! They move fearfully from one dream to another.

How to awaken them? Our mission is great. My trials, too, will be greater and greater.

Friday, May 26. Light rain.

If I praise myself, people will think that I am boastful, but if I humble myself, they will despise the sutra. The taller the pine tree, the longer the wisteria vine hanging from it. The deeper the source, the longer the stream. How fortunate, how joyful! In this impure land, I alone enjoy happiness and delight.

— "A SAGE PERCEIVES THE THREE EXISTENCES OF LIFE" (WND, 642)

Physical condition extremely bad. Has my life force waned? All I can do is chant more daimoku.

Shouldn't reformation begin with life's fundamental problems? Must reflect on myself again and again and again. Otherwise, no progress.

Youth must never fall. Forge on. Forge on. Forge on until death. In the cause of kosen-rufu. In order to grasp life's eternity.

Saturday, May 27. Rain.

More valuable than treasures in a storehouse are the treasures of the body, and the treasures of the heart are the most valuable of all.

— "THE THREE KINDS OF TREASURE" (WND, 851)

Don't feel well at all. It was 9:50 by the time I got to work. Lost today's battle from the beginning.

May has been a month of grueling struggles, both personally and at work. Only four days left. Must strive till the last moment. Mr. Toda also seems to be weathering great hardships.

I am a man now. It's been twenty years already since I set out on the voyage of life. This must be a time of joy and hope. A time to burn with ideals.

Advance. Only advance.

Time will tell.

Daishonin and Mr. Toda, my wonderful mother and my fellow believers—keep your eyes on me. Watch this young man, this individual that is myself. My activities, my conviction, my ideals, my practice.

Starting tomorrow, must write more legibly.

Discussion meeting at Mr. Kodaira's.

Home at 12:00. To bed at 1:00.

Sunday, May 28. Cloudy with rain.

Up at 8:30. Went to Kankiryo temple.

Forced to consider more deeply the attitude of one who studies Buddhism.

I am a follower of the true Buddha; I share a bond with Nichiren Daishonin. I must never topple.

Pondered the grave mission of one who embraces Buddhism's supreme teachings and strives for kosen-rufu. It forced me to reflect on my faith.

Arouse the great desire. Advance smiling in the face of hardship for the sake of your noble mission.

I am young. I will advance courageously, bursting with joy.

Watch me, Gohonzon, a youth of the future, convinced that kosen-rufu will be achieved.

Monday, May 29. Clear.

They will spread favor extensively, grant mercy to all suffering beings, and lead them into the Way.

—SUTRA OF INFINITE MEANINGS

Twenty years since my life began. Now this year is already halfway over. This year is proving to be enjoyable.

Youth—what a promising word! I'll live up to its promise and spend my own youth in a worthwhile and memorable way.

What is my mission? To strive to my utmost in becoming capable for kosen-rufu. Maybe I'll make my contribution as a man of letters, an influential statesman or a successful businessman. Any of these would be fine. What counts is to be active and to meet today's challenges and advance to the limits of my youthful energy

Let people criticize me if they wish. Let them laugh if they want to. What does it matter?

Only the Daishonin sees me for what I am.

Don't die for small virtues. Live for the great ones!

For people. For the world. For the Law.

Tuesday, May 30. Light rain.

Devote yourself single-mindedly to faith with the aim of reaching Eagle Peak.

Money serves various purposes according to our needs. The same is true of the Lotus Sutra. It is a lantern in the dark or a boat at a crossing. At times it is water and, at times, fire. This being so, the Lotus Sutra assures us of "peace and security in our present existence and good circumstances in future existences."

— "THE SWORDS OF GOOD AND EVIL" (WND, 452)

Went to the barber's for the first time in quite a while.

Mr. Toda's business seems in serious difficulty. It tears me apart inside.

Life is eternal, without beginning or end. Whether we suffer, weep or rejoice, regardless of our state of mind, it is the same life still.

I will march forward, out of the burning house. No doubt powerful foes will arise, but I shall confront them resolutely.

That is the only road for me to follow. Gohonzon, watch me.

Concerned about my mother.

Wednesday, May 31. Light rain.

"All of you with a single mind should don the armor of diligence and determine to be firm in intent."

— (LS15, 218)

May, with its fresh green of spring, has passed already. A cool day. Physically, I'm a little better. I will strive at this pace with all my energy.

June begins tomorrow. Scent of young leaves and new buds. Green month of mysterious rhythms. I, too, am in the springtime of life. My heart leaps. My spirit soars. A month for youth to be active.

The past is a dream, and the future is a dream, too. Dreams of the past, still and empty as the moon, excite no fires of passion. Dreams of the future, like the sun—the morning sun—giving birth to dawn and dreams that thrill with emotion.

Youth must pursue dreams of the future.

Bought all eleven volumes of the *Selected Writings of the Fuji School*. Cost me ¥3,500.

Thursday, June 1. Rain.

June opens with fragrant breezes.
1. Take care of my health.
2. Study hard.
3. Live productively.

Looking forward to a month of progress and fulfillment, grounded in faith. Will advance confidently in the vanguard of justice and the highest good.

How wonderful! How rewarding!

Attended a discussion meeting at M.'s. Home at 1:30.

Friday, June 2. Rain.

It is my earnest desire that all priests and lay believers will distinguish false doctrines from true, embrace the True Law and pray for enlightenment in their lives to come. What will it serve to lose the opportunity of human existence and fall into the three evil paths to regret it later on?

—(GZ, 70)

Went to Takashimaya Department Store in Shinbashi with my department chief, en route to visit A. Was amazed at the bustle of the department store, stocked with all the latest top-quality goods. How many wealthy people there must be! Throngs of shoppers, cosmetic fragrances, piles of displayed goods that dazzle the eyes!

Does business create and motivate the times? Is business the best arena for a stalwart youth? There are so many kinds of business. Which is the most important? It must be a business linked to establishing eternal peace for the happiness of humanity.

Saturday, June 3. Light rain.

> More than twenty years have passed since I, Nichiren, in accordance
> with the sutra's teachings, mustered the great cohorts of the Buddha.
> Not once since then have I even thought of retreat.
>
> .   —(GZ, 1224)

The pain of self-scrutiny and the drive to progress, extremes of suffering and hope, worldly thoughts and pure ideals—these are what torture youth. Youth must possess sharp, critical minds, a strong sense of
justice and the passion to forge ahead.

What can the smooth talk of middle age accomplish? Must not be influenced. Only young people's zeal for reformation can open our
decrepit society's eyes.

Youth must never be like spiritless, cowardly old men. Otherwise
they will soon find themselves leading wretched, lonely existences of
cunning and compromise.

Youth, be lighthearted! Advance seriously toward your ideal.

Youth division meeting at 6:30. Held a productive joint planning
session.

Mr. Toda, please keep your eyes on me. I will definitely fulfill your
expectations.

Sunday, June 4. Rain.

> There were bodhisattvas and mahasattvas, eighty thousand of them....
> [They] had trained themselves in compassion, were good at entering
> the Buddha wisdom, and had fully penetrated the great wisdom and
> reached the farther shore.
>
> —(LS1, 4)

Abstained from voting in the senatorial election.

What is life's purpose? How should good and evil be judged? These
are grave questions for all people everywhere. Whoever could answer
them clearly and conclusively would be a truly great person.

To practice and study the supreme Buddhism and possess in myself
both confidence and conviction—those are the most important things.

Is there any error in my present way of life? Or perhaps youth
shouldn't hesitate and ponder over every detail.

Youth has only to advance—with justice, passion and conviction.

Hardship dogs the footsteps of revolutionaries and pathfinders.

Suffering is youth's constant companion. But to break through those hardships and suffering and forge on — that is revolution.

Monday, June 5. Clear.

> Everyone in Japan, from the sovereign on down to the common people, without exception has tried to do me harm, but I have survived until this day. You should realize that this is because, although I am alone, I have firm faith.
>
> — "THE SUPREMACY OF THE LAW" (WND, 614)

Work pressures piling up at the office. Is it because I'm inexperienced?

Each day, a fierce struggle. Youth go to do battle, with all their might.

> *Noble and beautiful are they.*
> *Eyes look up from their weariness.*
> *There, hope is kindled and future is born.*
> *There, the music of the heavens resounds.*

> *Fight, for the sake of justice!*
> *Struggle, toward the highest good!*
> *Now the eyes of the people are closed.*
> *But someday they are bound to open.*
> *No. I must open them myself.*

Held a discussion meeting here in my tiny room. K. attended. Not many people came. A desolate feeling, but these efforts are all part of our practice.

Tuesday, June 6. Clear.

Somebody once said that people's minds are smaller than beans, and only a hero knows a hero's heart. Someone else said: "Let those who laugh, laugh. Let those who slander you say what they will."

Fools cannot possibly grasp the great principles of the Daishonin's Buddhism. You who criticize, go ahead and criticize if you wish. Because of you, I can attain my enlightenment.

Twenty-four Japan Communist Party central committee members were purged.

Political views intensify here and abroad.

Finally, the time has come for youth to arise.

Poets! Reformers! Youth of the religious revolution!

Friday, June 9. Light rain.

Discussion meeting at K.'s. Home at 11:30.

The summer rain falls endlessly.

Where else does a religion of supreme compassion reach out to save people groaning in misery? Society and politics are so irrational.

A whole lifetime passes like a dream. Fifty years go by.

To strive to the utmost as the Buddha's envoy — as the true Buddha's disciple — that is my greatest pride.

Saturday, June 10. Rain.

> Though one might point at the earth and miss it, though one might bind up the sky, though the tides might cease to ebb and flow and the sun rise in the west, it could never come about that the prayers of the practitioner of the Lotus Sutra would go unanswered.
>
> —"On Prayer" (WND, 345)

More tired than ever. My health grows worse and worse. My family held a memorial service in their home tonight for my older brother. More than five years already since he was killed in the war. How tragic to die unmarried at twenty-six! Will send him my most sincere prayers from here in my room.

Bought *Goethe and Schiller* and the *Complete Works of Chogyu Takayama* [a modern writer] in Kanda.

Out of all the billions of years past and the hundreds of billions to come, how are people joined together in the present moment as mentor and disciple or as parent and child? It awes me to think about it.

Sunday, June 11. Rain.

Losing weight. I can see it myself. Never will I yield to the demon of sickness.

A pure life, a face flushed with health and joy — faith will achieve that state. Impatient to see myself after I've conquered my own weakness.

This morning went to Kankiryo temple in Nakano. Stopped by S.'s home with some friends on the way back.

The rains fall incessantly. Must take care of my health.

Gohonzon, that's all I ask. Let me recover my health!

Monday, June 12. Rain.

Went to my parents' home at 7:00. Overjoyed to find everybody in high spirits. Especially glad to see that my mother has gained some weight. Bought her a pair of geta in Kamata.

Went with H. and Y. to Toho Medical College to urge several people to take faith.

A state of mind in which one can tell another about the supreme Buddhism with no other desire but to see that person happy—surely there can be no nobler spirit, no more admirable action, in all this world.

Must advance tomorrow, too. No other way but to struggle and forge ahead.

Tuesday, June 13. Rain.

I pray that before anything else I can guide and lead the ruler and those others who persecuted me. I will tell the Buddha about all the disciples who have aided me, and before I die, I will transfer the great blessings deriving from my practice to my parents who gave me life.

— "ON THE BUDDHA'S PROPHECY" (WND, 402)

How weak and dull my faith is! It is inevitable that my father and mother will die before I do. Cannot neglect my efforts for their eternal happiness. Must enable them to attain Buddhahood as soon as possible.

Rained in torrents all day. It's inconvenient not owning an umbrella.

Wednesday, June 14. Rain.

Rained heavily again. Bought an umbrella. It cleared up around evening.

The newspapers report flood damage throughout the nation.

"The wind will no longer buffet the branches, and the rain will no longer break the clods of soil" (WND, 392)—when will that day of kosen-rufu come? When will we see the utopia for which humankind has hungered waking and sleeping—the peaceful world where bright laughter never ceases?

Youth, live powerfully, for the sake of tomorrow. With the help of the Gohonzon's power.

Thursday, June 15. Cloudy.

One step forward.

Effort. I advance on the great path, step by step, traversing mountains and valleys.

Patience. Weather the storms of criticism with a smile. Await the time. Create the opportunity. Step by step.

Confidence. Whatever the battle, no weapon can compare. Continue to set great waves in motion, with the full power of 'three thousand realms in a single moment of life.'

Conviction. Amid the succession of hard struggles, how truly wonderful to survive, win and show proof of victory! History books are filled with errors. But in our own history, the history written only in our hearts, we cannot record a single falsehood or embellish anything.

Friday, June 16. Clear.

Beautiful weather for a change. Home at 11:30.

How delightful to work under the warm, bright sun! One appreciates it only after a long rainy spell.

Discussion meeting at K.'s tonight. He lectured on compassion. Remarkable lecture. A remarkable man.

I respect him.

Faith — a crucial word, one that many people know and practice. But there are also reasons why many try to avoid it. What most people do not know is that no faith is valid without an object of devotion. Nor is it valid if its object of devotion is false or inferior.

Only chanting daimoku to the Gohonzon of the Three Great Secret Laws can be considered faith in the true sense. When one practices this teaching, all the phenomena and occurrences of daily life will be experienced as happiness. Faith must apply equally to everyone, irrespective of time and place. It must be based on a living Law.

Home at 11:30. Irritated at the dampness of my apartment.

Saturday, June 17. Cloudy.

What was the result of today's campaign?
I just did my best, as I always strive to.
Any regrets about today's campaign?
Yes, in one sense. No, in another.
Nothing to be ashamed of in today's campaign?
I am certain mine was not a coward's battle.
Are you prepared for tomorrow's advance?
I am prepared. On a thousand-mile journey, we must
forge on, or we will not reach our destination.
Have you the confidence for tomorrow's ascent?

I have the confidence. Without climbing the mountain,
we cannot gaze out from the peak.
Have you conviction for tomorrow's efforts?
Yes, that I do. Nothing is completed without day-by-day effort.
Are you faithful to life's purpose?
I do my utmost. I can do no more.
You have not forgotten life's ultimate mission?
I have not forgotten. Should I forget that, what else would remain?

Department Chief O. treated me to dinner in Kanda.
Home at 11:00.

Thursday, June 22. Light rain.

There are countries where stones are exchanged for gold, and lands where earth is sold for rice. Even a person with a thousand pieces of gold may die of starvation. He would then be inferior to someone with only a single bowl of rice. A sutra states, "Where there is famine, rice is precious." All is determined by the country and the time. In Buddhism, one should understand this principle.

—(GZ, 1579)

The times, society, the world and ideas—along with human history, all have entered an era of unparalleled complexity.

How will Japan and the world develop in the future? Can anyone tell? Does anyone know?

Worldwide tension mounts daily. Am I the only one so anxious about it?

Overslept this morning. Was warned by my department chief.

Tonight I'm going to bed early, by 11:30.

Friday, June 23. Clear.

Leaders conference at Mr. Koizumi's from 8:00 till 11:00. Afterward, saw Mr. Kodaira to his home. He is a good senior to me.

Back home at 1:00.

Tonight's participants: K., K., T., U., R., S.

Saturday, June 24. 90° F. Clear.

Hot all day.

In the morning, met my friend O. at Omori Station and gave him a little money, with the thought of somehow sharing his hardship. A troubled man. I worry about his family. A pitiful end for this poor schoolmaster.

Discussion meeting at 8:00 at K.'s. Extremely tired.

Home at 11:30 and to bed.

Today's battle is over. Tomorrow, will fight wholeheartedly again.

Monday, June 26. Clear.

Common mortals are deluded to the nature of their mind; they do not perceive it nor are they awakened to it. Buddhas are awakened to it and the expression of their enlightenment is called "mystic power" (*jinzu*), meaning that it penetrates without obstacle all the phenomena of existence. This unrestricted mystic power dwells in the mind of all sentient beings.

—(GZ, 563)

War finally broke out between North and South Korea. Anxious that it might trigger another world war.

The world moves, moment by moment. The planet Earth has already become like a small battlefield or a stage.

Is humanity to be plunged again into a whirlpool of grief and suffering, loneliness and torment?

"There is no safety in the threefold world; it is like a burning house" (LS3, 69).

The time has come for us to rise to action.

First, prayer. Then, practice. For the sake of kosen-rufu.

Behold, humanity, our gallant image: our love for humanity, our aspiring toward peace.

Wednesday, June 28. Rain.

World crisis looms.

Will it come to that? Must people steel themselves to do battle to the end?

I yearn for peace. The flames of war must not spread.

My resolution is as firm as Mount T'aishan.

I have nothing to fear.

But I think of the weak, and my heart aches.

I pray that all may live long and dwell in peace.

Saturday, July 1. Cloudy.

Meaningful youth division meeting at the Kanda Gakkai headquarters. Twenty participants, both young men and young women.

The youth division has set sail toward the future's storms and raging waves.

I, too, will advance, to the limits of my strength.

Sunday, July 2. Clear.

Fine weather. Slept until 10:00.

K. came by. Lent him some of my hard-earned money.

My younger brother and my sister visited for the first time in quite a while. She's my only sister. I want to guide her well, to make her happy.

Held a discussion meeting in my room. Very few came. Many tasks and hardships lie ahead.

Monday, July 3. Cloudy.

The Shinjikan Sutra states, "All living beings are born and reborn continually in the six paths, like the turning of a wheel that never stops, becoming now father and mother, now husband and wife, mutually indebted in lifetime after lifetime and world after world."

—(GZ, 471)

Saw the movie *Listen, the Waves* at the Globe Theater. Much to think about.

War is a crime. Must avert it, no matter what. Keenly aware of the need for valid religion.

Must carry out propagation. When the time comes, I wish to die with dignity.

Back to my room at 10:30.

Tuesday, July 4. Cloudy.

Put up a good fight all day. I have no regrets.

Am truly grateful for being in the happiest of circumstances.

I rejoice with all my heart that my efforts and dedication will bear fruit.

I regret only that I cannot study in a settled atmosphere.

Distressed that I cannot convince my parents, brothers, sister and relatives to take faith.

Wednesday, July 5. Cloudy.

Strove vigorously all day. Mr. Toda seems in grave financial troubles.

Pressured by work, I cannot freely take part in Gakkai activities. It makes me feel lonely.

I caused trouble for K. and H. on account of work.

Friday, July 7. Clear.

This year made record-high temperatures.

A thoroughly hot, miserable day. Discussion meeting at K.'s. Home at 11:00. Returned with T. and the others.

Reflected on these points:

1. Don't be conceited.
2. Don't speak ill of others.
3. Don't get entangled with weak-spirited people.
4. Don't waste money.
5. Don't talk too much.

To bed at 1:00.

Saturday, July 8. Fine and clear.

Evening, went to Kankiryo temple in Nakano. Gongyo and daimoku there. Sweltering weather continues. Totally exhausted. Surprised to find my weight has dropped below 110 pounds. But when people see me five years from now, after I've overcome these trials and hardships and made real strides in my human revolution, who will recognize me?

Home at 12:00. T. came by and gave me a back rub. Appreciated it very much.

Sunday, July 9. Clear.

Cool all day today.

Mr. Toda and I keep struggling desperately. The business is obviously failing day by day.

Anxious about Mr. Toda's health deteriorating.

No one but I can succeed my teacher, Mr. Toda.

I must not die. I must not fall.

> *Billows grow in power*
> *as they buffet the immovable.*

Friday, July 14. Clear.

Meeting at K.'s.

Studied the "Orally Transmitted Teachings" with K. and M. Can only weep with emotion at this profound and mysterious doctrine.

Do life and society decree that powerful people are virtuous? Are the defeated always condemned as evil? It's frightful to contemplate.

Tomorrow we enshrine the Gohonzon at I.'s. I'm so happy for him.

Sunday, July 16. Cloudy.

Mr. Toda's business seems to be in grave difficulty. I see bad signs both inside and outside the company.

Went to work today, too. Rested a little in the morning.

It tears my heart to see my co-workers leaving the company.

Who is going to stand up and take responsibility both in the business and in the Gakkai?

My mission grows heavier and greater.

Thursday, July 20. Cloudy.

The times bring about vast changes.

People's minds change as easily as water flows. Lashed out fiercely at Department Chief O. for criticizing Mr. Toda.

The company is in desperate straits. It pains me to see Mr. Toda in this condition.

The devils are mustering forces. Must advance more carefully. Real comrades are few. Friends and neighbors turn into devils, one after another. Will break through and forge ahead.

Great evil augurs great good.

Stand your ground, no matter what may happen.

Whoever will not bow before the raging storm
is the youth who carries Japan's destiny.

Saturday, July 22. Clear.

The struggle intensifies moment by moment. I hear that our company is in grave danger. Those who bestir themselves at a time of crisis are truly admirable. That's the kind of person I must become.

Discussion meeting at K.'s. Home at 12:30. Must strive harder in both personal and business affairs.

Tomorrow is Sunday. No doubt several people will visit.

I want to put Mr. Toda's mind at ease. At least I am young. I will fight for all I'm worth.

> Suffer what there is to suffer, enjoy what there is to enjoy. Regard both suffering and joy as facts of life, and continue chanting Nam-myoho-renge-kyo, no matter what happens.
>
> —"HAPPINESS IN THIS WORLD" (WND, 681)

Tuesday, July 25. Fine and clear.

Scorching heat wave continues. Briefly refreshed by merciful showers that fell in the morning and evening as though to heal my heart.

Convinced our company needs drastic reforms in structure, personnel and management. I'm in no position to initiate it. How can I help? What shall I do?

No matter what the situation:

1. Keep striving to improve myself.
2. Study Buddhism diligently.
3. Remember to study other subjects, too.

Monday, July 31. Light rain.

> At the time when the Law has spread far and wide, the entire Japanese nation will chant Nam-myoho-renge-kyo, as surely as an arrow aimed at the earth cannot miss the target. But now you must build your reputation on the Lotus Sutra and give yourself up to it.
>
> —"THE TRUE ASPECT OF ALL PHENOMENA" (WND, 385)

I'm returning home after midnight each night. The effect is beginning to tell on me a little.

Next month we'll hold the summer course at the head temple. I've been looking forward to it all year. I'll definitely go, no matter what.

A sweltering July. Somehow I've managed to struggle through this month, too. Tomorrow is the first day of autumn. August is our month. I'll strive again, with all my youthful passion. As befits a youth who lives in pursuit of an ideal, a youth burning with great joy.

High and fierce are the waves of life, the waves of society. Steep are the mountains that rise before us. But one way or another, people advance.

Youth who embrace the True Law must advance no matter what.

I will go on, bravely. I will pioneer the world to come.

Wednesday, August 2. Light rain.

Talked with Mr. Toda for about an hour. He seems to be facing extreme difficulty. It's prolonged torture for me, too. He places great hope in his future plans. It's too bad that things haven't gone as he wished.

I will keep fighting, displaying all the ability and character I possess.

Thursday, August 3. Rain.

Society is harsh. Keenly aware of the importance of trust. Fought well today. A stern battle amid anguish, effort and the rain.

I have a mission to protect Mr. Toda throughout life. I have no ties with the other department chiefs.

It saddens me that Mr. Toda cannot immediately perceive what I'm trying to accomplish. I've never seen him stare at me with more displeasure than he did today. Feel totally miserable.

All I can do is devote myself faithfully to my work. I'm just an employee. Mr. Toda expects more from me than from the directors. An awkward position I'm in now.

Mr. Toda, no matter what, I will fight till the last moment. Please, wait just a little longer. Please don't misjudge me — you'll see. I will seize the rudder of the mighty ship and steer her safely over the angry waves. I will set sail in high spirits.

Watch this Ikeda!

Many people admire flowers, but few truly understand their beauty.

Thursday, August 10. Rain.

A month of bitter struggles. Wherein lies the cause of such misery? Few days in my life, I think, will be as painful as today has been.

I'm ill. The business is failing. Our finances are at the point of bankruptcy. People are losing faith in our company.

Mr. Toda is in a dreadful position. I'm fighting with grim determination but nothing works out the way I hope. Mortified at my co-workers' complaints.

> *Do not fear, though obstacles surround you,*
> *You, a Bodhisattva of the Earth.*

> *The youth who pledged his oath before the Buddha*
> *Arises to carry out his heavy mission.*

> *Mighty waves that tower on high,*
>   *Break with all your fury. Test your power against mine!*

Friday, August 11. Rain.

I feel truly sorry for Mr. Toda. He was badly scolded by A. So was I, for that matter. This is all training for me. Our company's affairs grow worse and worse.

I want to protect Mr. Toda. Somehow, in any way I can.

I am myself. I am what I am.

He who seeks to learn my name does not know me. Don't ask my name. Touch me, life to life.

Sunday, August 13. Thunderstorm.

Study meeting this evening on "The Object of Devotion for Observing the Mind."

Talked for a long time with K. about Mr. Toda's situation and the comeback he will make in the future.

Left at 11:30.

Exhausted but in much better spirits.

Tuesday, August 15. Fine and clear.

Anniversary of the cease-fire. My heart flooded with a thousand emotions.

Cherry trees blossomed and red leaves fell, snow lay on Mount Fuji and the summer sun beat down — so quickly, five years have passed.

Hard times for the company. We have reached a crisis. The directors conferred until 10:30. More employees seem to be leaving. My responsibilities are heavy, heavy indeed.

Who will build the coming era? Who will be its driving force, who will set its direction?

Read Tolstoy's *Confessions*.

The World-Honored One of Great Enlightenment is a great leader for all living beings, a great eye for them, a great bridge, a great helmsman, a great field of good fortune.

— "THE OPENING OF THE EYES" (WND, 223)

Saturday, August 19. Clear. Broiling heat.

The directors conferred this morning. In the afternoon, they held what seemed to be an even more serious meeting. I pray it will all conclude successfully.

Burdens of illness, spiritual torment and financial crises are piled on my shoulders.

This evening, read "The Object of Devotion for Observing the Mind" with others.

Must not forget faith and study, no matter how badly the business goes.

Home at 12:00. Walked alone on the road bathed in moonlight. Much to think about.

Sunday, August 20. Light rain.

Each and every one of you should be certain deep in your heart that sacrificing your life for the Lotus Sutra is like exchanging rocks for gold or dung for rice.

— "The Actions of the Votary of the Lotus Sutra" (WND, 764)

Relaxed at home for the first time in a long while. Extremely tired. My head aches when I think of tomorrow's struggle.

1. Study.
2. Be victorious at work.
3. Regain my strength.

Visited N. this afternoon. Home at 11:00.

Sometimes I long to drift on the lake of sentiment. Other times I hunger for the intense emotions of struggling amid the violent whirlpools of reality.

Must believe in yourself. Faith will awaken you to who you are.

Tuesday, August 22. Clear.

Our company has decided to suspend operations.

Exchanged parting cups with Mr. Toda. He shared with us his great hopes and his profoundly touching resolution in the face of defeat.

I felt as though my heart would break. How mortifying! How tragic!

I, however, will advance with Mr. Toda toward our next effort. Nothing else matters. Forward. Eternally forward. Those who truly know me will know my destiny.

Saturday, August 26. Cloudy.

> The fact that her prayers have gone unanswered is like a strong bow with a weak bowstring, or a fine sword in the hands of a coward. It is in no sense the fault of the Lotus Sutra.
>
> —"THE ROYAL PALACE" (WND, 489)

Ran around all day on business. Returned to the office in the evening. Mr. Toda was waiting for me. We had a planning session until quite late, after which I went home with Mr. Toda. Mrs. Toda seemed rather surprised.

How calm and self-assured he is, even in defeat! In the middle of the night, we played two games of *shogi* [Japanese chess]. Afterward, he urged me to sleep beside him on his mat. I excused myself, went downstairs to where his son was sleeping and silently crept in beside the boy under his quilt.

A night of profound memories.

Sunday, August 27. Cloudy.

Did gongyo with Mr. Toda in the morning and also ate breakfast with him. Mrs. Toda seemed very tired, too. He sternly told her that one or two business failures are no reason to be discouraged.

Rode the train with him to the office in Kanda.

A memorable but gloomy Sunday. While putting things in order at the office, an irate letter from my brother arrived, complaining about my faith. I seem to be the target of everyone's mistrust. My physical condition is terrible. It looks like tuberculosis. Went to the barber's late at night.

Tuesday, August 29. Thunderstorm.

My sister-in-law brought me some ration tickets and clean clothes, which she had washed. I was deeply grateful to her. I hear my family are all quite worried about me. I feel bad about causing them so much anxiety.

Mr. Toda told me, "I'm depending on you." Powerful and encouraging words. Delighted that he trusts me and expects more from me than from anyone else. In response to his encouragement, I will sound again the bell of the century. Let those who wish to leave him, leave.

Must become a young hero, a young warrior. I will carry out Mr. Toda's will.

My handwriting has become completely illegible. It seems I can't stop scribbling.

Wednesday, August 30. Light rain.

Day by day, as things settle down, the full gravity of our company's debts is beginning to be felt. I know nothing whatever about the details, but I sense that the future is dark.

My heart aches when I think of what Mr. Toda must be feeling or when I think of my parents' anxiety.

Those who fall to the ground have no choice but to stand up from where they fell.

Rebuilding from our present circumstances will be the best proof of my efforts. Above all, I want to make Mr. Toda rejoice. I will bestir myself with all the fury of an *asura* demon to:

1. Arrange finances for the coming term.
2. Fully accomplish our plans.
3. Promote guidelines for liquidation.

Also to:
1. Not work with Department Chief O.
2. Start working directly with Mr. Toda.
3. Have W. pay us back as soon as possible.
4. Train new department staff.

Tomorrow will go with N. to the tax administration bureau.
Finished reading *Les Miserables*.

Thursday, August 31. Clear.

Autumn has come.
Crickets shrill in the moonlight. Emotion wells in the poet's heart.
Autumn is hushed and still.
No turmoil, no raging currents can disturb the poet's mind.
Autumn is noble.
A season clear as a mirror, a time to advance, with a benevolent mind, in the struggle for justice.
Autumn is serene.
Deep in the poet's heart is a great clarity that distinguishes good from evil.
Autumn is a time for thinking.

Friday, September 1. Clear.

Every day seems like the night before a storm. Moment by moment presses us hard.

I'm twenty-two, in the springtime of my life. Is this bond between mentor and disciple my destiny?

Come to grips with small matters and don't be swayed by large ones. Another sharp complaint letter arrived from my brother.

Mr. Toda seems in a truly painful situation. My eyes fill with tears of vexation, and also with tears of gratitude for being allowed to share his suffering.

Remember the plans that will endure a hundred years. Must lay them without error.

Saturday, September 2. Clear.

> Among my disciples, those who think themselves well versed in Buddhism are the ones who make errors.
> —"The Teaching for the Latter Day" (WND, 903)

This week is over.

Many voices of criticism and slander are raised, within and without.

Went to Omiya with Mr. Toda and other company directors to investigate ways to break our business deadlocks. I sense the directors do not trust Mr. Toda.

What I believe in is the Gohonzon alone.

Solitude lets us know ourselves deeply and, at the same time, make our minds sincere. Only those who love their country can understand the hearts of other patriots.

Monday, September 4. Clear.

Our company liquidation progresses slowly. It saddens me that staff members' minds have been so greatly swayed by our misfortune. As we are all human, I suppose it cannot be helped.

Visited S. for the first time in about a month. A painful experience. When things are going well for me, he is all smiles; now that I'm undergoing hardships, he treats me like a stranger.

The September moon shone on my way home. I often feel inclined to drift into the poetic world of fantasy. The whirlpool of reality, however, will not permit me to dwell in fantasy.

My heart pounds with excitement. Hopes. Great ambitions. Setting sail anew in life. I am ready to meet any storms.

Saturday, September 9. Cloudy.

When a nation becomes disordered, it is the spirits which first show signs of rampancy. Because these spirits become rampant, all the people of the nation become disordered.

— Benevolent King Sutra

My physical condition is extremely bad. If I ruin my health, I cannot achieve anything. Must be careful.

Slept profoundly, as though I'd slept for a year.

Chanting daimoku is the only way to break through deadlocks, whether of the body or the mind.

I believe in my eventual victory. Daimoku will be its driving force.

I am young.   I will advance. Straight ahead, on the road I must follow.

I am young.   I will fulfill what the heavens have ordained.

I am young.   I will muster my courage, convinced that all struggles under my teacher's guidance will lead to the good.

I am young.   I must keep my spirits up, whether I win or lose, even during painful or lonely times.

Monday, September 11. Clear.

Home at 11:30.

Today, too, I fought to the limits of my strength.

This, however, is only the calm before the storm — both in the company and according to the weather report.

Went with Director O. to Omiya. There, K. has totally lost his composure. He is the last person we should rely on.

The Gakkai leaders conferred with Mr. Toda at the company office about the future.

Tuesday, September 12. Cloudy.

Every day, an opportunity for human revolution.

Every day must be a time to advance.

Mr. Toda deeply encouraged me about my health. He prayed to the Gohonzon at the headquarters for me. He was severe with me regarding my weak life force.

I was startled at how serious he was. I felt moved, terrified, awed.

Returned to Omori Station with K.

Home at 11:00. I should sleep well from tonight on.

Saturday, September 16. Fine and clear.

A hot day.

Attended a discussion meeting at Mr. Toda's and listened to him speak on philosophy. Everyone seemed delighted.

Mr. Toda is still only the Soka Gakkai general director. I wonder why he does not assume the presidency.

T. came to see me. We talked for nearly an hour about faith and about our company. He is a good person.

To bed at 12:30.

Reality and ideals. Ideals and reality. Whoever avoids reality is a coward. Whoever holds no ideals is the same as a living corpse.

Sunday, September 17. Clear.

Slept until 9:00. Stayed in my room all day. Today was the first day I've ever done that. No one came.

Mapped out tomorrow's plans.

Washed my laundry. The lady who lives next door on the right upbraided me for doing gongyo late at night and disturbing others' sleep.

The man who lives next to her told me I should come home earlier and took me to task for "hanging out" until late every night.

The young building manager also admonished me about something or other, on account of my having the Gohonzon.

Early in the evening I went alone to a cafeteria and ate enough for two meals. As I had skipped both breakfast and lunch, it tasted wonderful.

Cleaned my room for the first time in quite a while.

To bed shortly before 10:00.

My room is quiet.

Monday, September 18. Thunderstorm.

Read Tolstoy's *Diaries*.

Though Tolstoy was a great literary master, his life was a succession of troubles. This caused me to think deeply.

In any event, those who pursue the highest path in life must exert boundless effort. We have, however, already come to know the absolute and ultimate principle, the Mystic Law. This is a fortunate and wonderful thing.

The sooner we know the Mystic Law, the sooner we can attain happiness and peace. Even a day's hesitation will cause a day's delay of happiness and peace.

No matter how prominent we may be or how great our scholarship, we cannot solve life's problems fundamentally without embracing the Mystic Law. Therefore, ultimately, we will be unhappy.

Home at 11:30.

Alone, listened to Rentaro Taki's "Moonlight Over a Ruined Castle."

"In the spring, a flowery banquet on a high terrace...." The changes of history and the images of brave individuals rose forlornly in my mind.

Tuesday, September 19. Thunderstorm.

Arrived at the office at 7:40. It feels as though the crowded trains double my fatigue.

To deceive oneself is a great evil. Ours should be a society in which all can properly carry out their duties and enjoy their rights. It is a bitter thing to be unable to act openly on your ideas or do what you think is right. There is too much deceit. It is a sad thing.

Too much ugly strife. What destiny creates the difference in individual personalities? Adults should at least take the responsibility for children and young people to grow up freely and correctly, for the sake of the future.

Home at 11:00.

Read the Gosho. It is extremely difficult.

Thursday, September 21. Light rain.

Fish want to survive; they deplore their pond's shallowness and dig holes in the bottom to hide in, yet tricked by bait, they take the hook. Birds in a tree fear that they are too low and perch in the top branches, yet bewitched by bait, they too are caught in snares.

—"LETTER FROM SADO" (WND, 301)

After the meeting, I gave Mr. Toda a poem I had written. He was extremely happy and immediately composed two poems for me in return:

> *Often I stand*
> *on the field of battle*
> *with you as my sword,*
> *at my side, always.*

> *My glory as king fades,*
> *and my power is failing:*
> *I will leave behind, however,*
> *you, my crown.*

Boundless are my youthful emotions.
I overflow with greater resolve.

Friday, September 22. Cloudy.

The autumn breeze feels refreshing to the skin.

A cool, clear, exhilarating day. It became almost cold toward evening.

Lecture at the headquarters on the "Orally Transmitted Teachings." About fifty people attended. Walked back to Omori Station with K., talking of various things.

I want to lead a just and honorable life, transcending the fluctuations of the passing years and the times. I want to advance with a humble yet courageous spirit. I want to lead a noble life, shouldering grave responsibilities.

Back home after 11:00. Fortunately, the mosquitoes have become fewer.

Saturday, September 23. Clear.

A cool day. Returned home at 12:00. Physical condition improving.

Some days I can work in high spirits. Other days I must struggle on in spite of suffering. But because I have striven so earnestly, I will have absolutely no regrets, even if I should fall or if no one notices my efforts.

Only the Gohonzon enables us to solve everything. All I must do is reflect on my faith and whether I am committing any slander.

Discussion meeting at K.'s.

I composed a poem:

> On the desolate plain
>   I will stand alone, resolutely
> Holding aloft the light,
>   as the child of a great forerunner.

1. Don't neglect self-reflection.
2. Remember to advance step by step.
3. Don't be swayed by things.
4. Be strict in faith.

Thursday, September 28. Cloudy.

"This sutra can cause all living beings to free themselves from suffering and anguish. This sutra can bring great benefits to all living beings and fulfill their desires."

—(LS23, 286)

Arrived at work at 7:30.

It has become rather cool. I am a young man with a single white shirt. I wish I had an overcoat. All the people on the train were wearing overcoats.

I was completely taken in by I. An evil man. To deceive others and put on pretenses is the basest form of human conduct.

Labor with a purpose is worthwhile. Those who toil and die to no purpose are like slaves.

Attended Mr. Toda's lecture on "The Threefold Secret Teaching"[1] by Nichikan (the twenty-sixth high priest).

It rained on the way home. Thoroughly cold. Returned to Omori with T. He is an honest man.

1. "The Threefold Secret Teaching": A component of the *Six-volume Writings* by Nichikan that, elaborating on a passage of the "Life Span" chapter of the Lotus Sutra, makes a clear distinction between the Daishonin's Buddhism and Shakyamuni's Buddhism.

Monday, October 2. Rain.

In the evening, I went with Mr. Toda to visit K. in Koiwa. Discussed various business matters on the train.

On the way back, Mr. Toda treated me to sushi near Koiwa Station.

On the train home, we talked enthusiastically about Rousseau's *Emile* and other aspects of literature. Saw Mr. Toda off at Meguro Station.

Back home at 11:00. I regret that I did not see him all the way home.

Though one may appear to believe in the Lotus Sutra at the beginning, it is difficult to carry out one's faith to the end. The mind changes as easily as wind ruffles the water or as dew alters the hue of cherry blossoms. That you have somehow maintained your faith until this time must be solely due to merit accumulated in past lifetimes, and moreover, to the protection of Shakyamuni Buddha. How reassuring !

—(GZ, 1395)

Wednesday, October 4. Rain.

The mystic principle that is the essential nature of phenomena possesses two aspects, the defiled aspect and the pure aspect. If the defiled aspect is operative, this is called delusion. If the pure aspect is operative, this is called enlightenment. Enlightenment constitutes the realm of Buddhahood. Delusion constitutes the realms of ordinary mortals.

—"The Entity of the Mystic Law" (WND, 417)

Self-awakening is most important. Those governed by circumstance, with no self-awakening, will be overwhelmed by life's storms. Can we not say that self-awakening is the basis of ideology?

In society we find those who win and those who lose. Fortune and misfortune cannot be calculated. Even if we win, however, our elation will not last indefinitely. But a person of self-awakening, even if temporarily defeated, can go on to built a future vaster, broader, deeper and greater than that of the person who originally won. As long as we are not defeated fundamentally, we should continue to advance step by step, confident of our eventual victory.

Those who have tasted defeat can truly appreciate the joy of victory. Arrogance in victory and sorrow in defeat are both ultimately comic. What are we striving for and how great is our self-awakening? These are what matter. This self-awakening is possible only through faith.

Visited the homes of S., K. and H. with the directors. Home at 12:00.

Saturday, October 7. Fine and clear.

Up at 6:30.

Vexed at my dilapidated shoes and worn-out clothing.

> *Youth!*
> *You are young.*
> *Your youth itself makes you stronger than anyone.*
> *We should practice without forgetting*
>   *our self-awakening.*
> *If we do not live joyfully*
>   *then where is the joy of humankind?*
> *Our bewilderment and fear*
>   *are mere illusion, like young shoots*
>   *trembling in the air.*
> *Young leaves are fragrant. They endure*
>   *through heat and cold.*
> *We must remember their image.*

Our thinking, effort, devotion and practice:
All these will become our flesh and
    blood; remember this.
Society is not a playground.
Develop a self that can endure, whatever the times and
    society may bring.

Home at 11:00. Read the Gosho. Tired.

Sunday, October 8. Fine and clear.

Up at 8:00. Skipped breakfast.

Washed clothes in the morning. They didn't come completely clean, but I hung them up in the room to dry just as they were.

In the afternoon, I read and listened to music by myself.

In the evening, I took a walk in the neighborhood. Drank milk and coffee at Shop B.

Composed a poem called "Look Up and Behold the Sky."

Later Mr. Toda telephoned. I went to see him immediately and received guidance on various matters.

Home at 12:00.

Monday, October 9. Cloudy.

Arduous responsibilities every day. I'm physically exhausted.

When I think of the sufferings Mr. Toda faces in his efforts to accomplish the noble cause, however, I cannot complain. It is a bad disciple who seeks to live more comfortably than his teacher.

Youth!
    Know the stately swells of the Pacific.
    Know the blazing passion of the sun.
    Know the solemnity of the mountain recesses.
    Know the graceful scarlet of the autumn maples.
Youth!
    Live without forgetting these.
    Advance with them in your hearts.
Youth!
    Be courageous in today's battle.
    Celebrate tomorrow's ideal.
    Forget the dreams of the past.
    Arise, for the dreams of the future!

Youth!
 Advance, advance,
 Onward and eternally.

To bed at 1:00.

Wednesday, October 11. Rain.

A still, autumn night. A light rain fell.

Life is ultimately a battle with oneself. It is also a struggle against external forces. Nothing is more pitiable in life than to be defeated. Do effort and wisdom distinguish the victors from the vanquished? Or is it fortune or something akin to destiny? Even after a major defeat, it is vital that we begin striving again with that experience as our foundation. How well we grapple with stern realities, using the whole of our beings and experience, how deeply we think of our own lives and society in the struggle and how noble the goals we cherish — these are what create value in life, which is something for which youth should be thankful.

1. Will
2. Courage
3. Sincerity

These three are vital.

I don't even have one sock left without a hole in it. I'll have to darn a pair for tomorrow.

Believe in yourself, in your conviction and responsibility.

Friday, October 13. Clear.

"I am always here,
but through my transcendental powers
I make it so that living beings in their befuddlement
do not see me even when close by."

       —(LS16, 229)

Home at 11:00.

S. returned all my letters trying to convince him to take faith. It is sad that so few people seek the True Law.

The battle intensifies daily. No other choice but to forge ahead, cherishing the desire to win.

Work is important, but we must not neglect regular study of the Gosho.

I must be active, to my heart's content.

Advance, raise the cry, fight!

I am young, I am young.

If I do not strive now, then when again shall I have my days of youthful struggle?

To bed at 12:30.

Thursday, October 19. Fine and clear.

If people should try to weaken your belief in the Lotus Sutra, consider that your faith is being tested.

— "THE WORKINGS OF BRAHMA AND SHAKRA" (WND, 800)

Few people prove reliable in a crucial moment. Most turn out to be selfish. It is, however, a matter of utmost joy that I have found the Mystic Law, as well as a teacher, who observe my actions.

Mentally sluggish all day today.

Tomorrow, must strive for further development.

I will not rely on any of my fellow employees but display my own ability and do my best.

Whoever is strong when standing alone is a true hero.

1. Think about plans for developing O. Company.
2. Expedite liquidation of the T. Credit Union.
3. Establish a financial base as soon as possible, so that Mr. Toda can act freely.

Saturday, October 21. Light rain.

History never stops. It is created continuously, day by day and year by year.

The past several thousand years now carve out the present—no, rather they mark the first step toward the next five thousand years.

This is a great truth.

Mr. Josei Toda spoke to me entrusting to me in detail various matters for the future. His will reverberates in my heart.

You who are weeping, you who are rejoicing! Humanity, the time has come! Do not forget the awesome echo of the bell heralding a new century.

Sunday, October 22. Light rain.

Went to Kankiryo temple in Nakano for the first time in two months. T. accompanied me.

Friendship based on the Law is noble. Friends are precious indeed.

My mind has been slow all day. Is this my lack of faith?

A full three years have passed since my conversion. I will make this a starting point toward the next stage. I need a renewed self-awakening in faith.

I must chant daimoku to open the curtain on the next scene. I shall spur on my weak self.

Attended a discussion meeting at M.'s house on the way back from the temple.

Home at 11:30.

1. Remember the spirit of untiring practice.
2. Love the truth.
3. Live in the way that's right for me.

To bed at 1:00.

Thursday, October 26. Cloudy.

Up at 6:30.

Read from the essays of Francis Bacon. Found them meaningful.

Visited I.'s home in Ito, as Mr. Toda's representative. My mission there all but completed. We feel happiest when our dreams and mission are fulfilled.

Lately I've been extremely tired mentally.

Home shortly before 12:00.

Friday, October 27. Fine and clear.

What matters most is that we honor the Buddha's words. As a rule, people in the world value what is distant and despise what is near, but this is the conduct of the ignorant. Even the distant should be repudiated if it is wrong, while what is near should not be discarded if it accords with the truth. Even though people may revere [their predecessors' doctrines], if those docrines are in error, how can we employ them today?

—"REPLY TO HOSHINA GORO TARO" (WND, 155–56)

Personal and family troubles cause people to suffer. These are the most immediate and the most important of problems. Politics, science, institutions, education and so forth all represent attempts to solve certain issues, but for the personal and family problems closest at hand they offer no actual solution. The only fundamental answer lies in a correct faith.

Those who embrace the True Law are few. Perhaps, as the sutra states, this is because people are content with small pleasures and, being carried away by them, do not desire the supreme happiness.

Let those who laugh, laugh. Let those who slander us do so if they wish. Let them mock us freely if they so desire.

If Buddhism is true, then the law of causality must also be strict.

Watch the Soka Gakkai and me, ten years from now.

Keep your eyes on the Soka Gakkai, and on all of us, twenty years hence.

Even though I may be suffering, I will continue to advance single-mindedly for the religious revolution.

Saturday, October 28. Fine and clear.

To work at 7:30. Home at 11:00.

Saw a movie in Shinbashi around 7:00 in the evening. I was tired and slept through more than half of it.

Listened to Beethoven's Fifth Symphony for about half an hour before going to bed.

Sunday, October 29. Light rain.

This morning at Mr. Toda's house I discussed our company's future with him and one of the department chiefs. In the afternoon, talked with Mr. Toda and his wife about various things. A meaningful day.

Mr. Toda treated me to both lunch and dinner.

Home at 7:30.

Read from Whitman's *Leaves of Grass*.

I seem to feel colder, perhaps because my room faces north.

My bedding has not been aired for more than half a year now. It's not good for one's health.

To bed at 11:30.

Monday, October 30. Rain.

Spent the whole day on business in the Omiya area with my department chief.

Home at 12:00. Took a pedicab from the station on account of the rain.

Youth. Youth has many dreams. Fearful dreams. Beautiful dreams. Dreams of yearning. Dreams of hardship.

Impressionable youth. My dreams expand daily; both suffering and joy have their significance. Dreams of youth, chasing after rainbows. Turning the wheel of effort, progress, perseverance and hope, we must pursue our dreams.

We must strive with the courage to confront and break through society's corruption and guile. Then our path will surely open a step further, and our minds will be purified of regrets.

Tuesday, October 31. Rain.

Farewell to a memorable October. A month of sufferings and pleasures, of disagreeable experiences and joyful ones.

A month of strife, of the rough billows of reality, of lakes of lyrical emotion and hopes like rainbows in the sky.

The curtain falls on the drama of this precious month.

The blue sky is clear, the air is pure.

Heaven and earth are beautiful in the moonlight at dusk.

On a vast stage, against the backdrop of nature, appalling scenes of human creation unfold, one after another.

Neither victors nor vanquished know the destiny at work backstage.

Some people's lives are like aimless ships.

Others face life courageously, like battle cruisers of small purpose.

Others meet the high waves like warships of great ambition.

Some have no ships at all. Some are in danger of drowning and sinking.

Some travel about with confidence, though they ride in small boats.

Others overload their tiny boats and do not realize they will capsize.

I want my life to be of the highest purpose, aboard the greatest vessel.

Wednesday, November 1. Light rain.

Those who call themselves my disciples and practice the Lotus Sutra should all practice as I do. If they do, Shakyamuni, Many Treasures, Shakyamuni's emanations throughout the ten directions, and the ten demon daughters will protect them.

— "ON ESTABLISHING THE FOUR BODHISATTVAS AS THE OBJECT OF DEVOTION" (WND, 978)

The clear autumn sky deepens; chrysanthemums spread their fragrance.

Just two months from now I will be twenty-two.

This afternoon, I went to the wedding of S., an elementary school friend.

The marriage of a friend my age prompted me to reflect on my own circumstances.

Home at 10:00. Read for a while. Disturbed at my lapses of memory.

Saturday, November 4. Clear.

Monthly youth division leaders meeting at 6:00. About twenty people attended. Though all appear in earnest, no powerful youth division renewal seems in sight.

The meeting ended at 8:00. Went with my friends as far as Suidobashi Station. Regret that I somehow seem not to fit in with them.

> There are three categories of people that all human beings should respect. They are the sovereign, the teacher, and the parent.
>
> —"THE OPENING OF THE EYES" (WND, 220)

Tuesday, November 7. Light rain.

1. Live up to the promise of youth and advance as a pioneer for kosen-rufu.
2. Make clear judgments about the Soka Gakkai top leadership.
3. Thoroughly study the Gosho and reflect seriously on how to put it into practice.
4. Make the chapter I am assigned to develop and swiftly consolidate its organization.
5. Think about how to develop Mr. Toda's business.
6. Reflect on the depth of my conviction.
7. Resolve my financial problems, and think about when to establish a family.

Financially, I am in serious straits. Mr. Toda's family also seems to suffer privations. I hope life will be tranquil for them as soon as possible. All I desire is that Mr. Toda can take the lead in the vanguard of kosen-rufu.

Wednesday, November 8. Clear.

Rice plants change and become seedlings. Seedlings change and become stalks. Stalks change and become rice. Rice changes and becomes a person. And a person changes and becomes a Buddha.

—"REPLY TO ONICHI-NYO" (WND, 1089)

Went to the home of Y., a friend and fellow employee, to celebrate his recovery. Stayed till 11:00. A beautiful, lofty gathering of young friends and kindred spirits.

Recited poetry aloud, three times, something I haven't done in quite a while. K. and U. seemed deeply moved.

Dropped by M.'s on the way home.

Friday, November 10. Cloudy.

The Lotus Sutra is the staff that helps all the Buddhas of the three existences as they set their minds on enlightenment. However, you should rely on Nichiren as your staff and pillar. When one uses a staff, one will not fall on treacherous mountain paths or rough roads, and when led by the hand, one will never stumble. Nam-myoho-renge-kyo will be your staff to take you safely over the mountains of death. The Buddhas Shakyamuni and Many Treasures, as well as the four bodhisattvas headed by Superior Practices, will lead you by the hand on your journey.

—"THE SWORDS OF GOOD AND EVIL" (WND, 451–52)

Up at 7:30. Home at 11:30.

I worry a little as it grows colder, since I have no other shirts to wear.

As Mr. Toda's representative, visited several of our customers with my department chief. Regardless of time or place, trust is the most vital thing.

Sunday, November 12. Cloudy.

The fifth Soka Gakkai general meeting held at Kyoiku Hall.

Although perhaps slow, the Soka Gakkai's efforts seem substantial. How many of our present membership will remain in the world of the Gakkai by 1960, ten years from now?

My resolution to follow Mr. Toda has grown firmer. It is vital to reflect on ourselves while observing the progress and growth of our companions. If we don't try to learn from others, we cannot understand the real meaning of progress.

Mr. Toda, keep your eyes on me. Without fail, I will carry out your will. This resolution arose in me during his lecture.

Monday, November 13. Clear.

Even medicine compounded from a hundred or a thousand herbs will not cure illness if one fails to take it. It is like starving while having treasure in a storehouse and not knowing how to open the door, or dying with medicine in one's pocket and not knowing that one should take it.

—(GZ, 416)

Home at 10:00.

Put in order my record of Mr. Toda's speech yesterday. It took me until midnight. It gave me a solemn feeling.

I am determined to follow after Mr. Toda.

When, and to whom, can I tell what is in my heart?

Mr. Toda temporarily relinquished the general director position to Y. at yesterday's general meeting. He is waiting for the next opportunity. No matter who may lead the Soka Gakkai, my only teacher is Mr. Toda.

Tuesday, November 14. Fine and clear.

Went again to I.'s in Ito as Mr. Toda's representative. Arrived at 7:00 p.m. A cold, windy evening. I left his home at 9:00 and stayed at the M. Inn. A good, quiet inn. Took a hot-spring bath and read Oscar Wilde's *De Profundis* until nearly 12:00.

Physically overtired. Troubled that I cannot make my body respond as I want it to.

My first experience staying alone at an inn. Paid ¥430 altogether.

Wednesday, November 15. Clear.

Is not the meaning of the sutra and the commentary that the way to Buddhahood lies within the two elements of reality and wisdom? Reality means the true nature of all phenomena, and wisdom means the illuminating and manifesting of this true nature.

— "THE ESSENTIALS FOR ATTAINING BUDDHAHOOD" (WND, 746)

Took the 7:14 for Atami. Transferred at Atami Station, where I waited forty minutes, and arrived in Tokyo at 10:30. A cold morning. I slept well on the train, perhaps because I am so tired.

Reached the office at 11:00. Reported everything to Mr. Toda.

Started working at noon. Cannot help feeling tired. On the way home, saw the movie *Les Miserables* in Shinbashi.

Thursday, November 16. Fine and clear.

To bed at 12:00. My room is so cold. No warmth whatsoever.

Special discussion meeting at M.'s. Strongly refuted the mistaken beliefs of a participant who furiously opposed our faith.

Had lunch with Mr. Toda at the Nihon University cafeteria.

He gave me guidance on ethnic issues, the Gakkai's future, economic trends, establishing a university someday and other matters.

A memorable page in my life.

Friday, November 17. Clear.

A fire burns higher when logs are added, and a strong wind makes a kalakula grow larger. The pine tree lives for ten thousand years, and therefore its boughs become bent and twisted. The votary of the Lotus Sutra is like the fire and the kalakula, while his persecutions are like the logs and the wind. The votary of the Lotus Sutra is the Thus Come One whose life span is immeasurable; no wonder his practice is hindered, just as the pine tree's branches are bent or broken.

— "THE DIFFICULTY OF SUSTAINING FAITH" (WND, 471)

Left Gakkai headquarters with Mr. Tsuji at 8:00.

Read "On Practicing the Buddha's Teachings."

Deeply realized the necessity of courageous faith.

Nam-myoho-renge-kyo.

In the end, our powers of faith and practice determine everything. The Gohonzon possesses the powers of the Buddha and the Law. Only by our own faith can we prove, test and acquire the great power of the supreme Law embodied in the Gohonzon.

To bed at 1:00.

Sunday, November 19.

The treasures bestowed by a single wish-granting jewel equal those bestowed by two such jewels or by innumerable jewels. Likewise, each character in the Lotus Sutra is like a single wish-granting jewel, and the innumerable characters of the sutra are like innumerable jewels.

— "LETTER TO THE SAGE NICHIMYO" (WND, 323)

Went to Mr. Toda's house at 6:30 and listened to him lecture. He spoke on the "Oral Commentary on 'On the Enlightenment of Plants'" and "On Attaining Buddhahood in This Lifetime."

I renewed my determination, seeing his passion to foster Soka Gakkai leaders for the next era.

Miss Kashiwabara and several others were present.

Treated to supper. Home at 10:30.

Monday, November 20. Fine and clear.

On inquiring into the nature of the mind, one finds that there is no mind. It arises from distorted thoughts. The mind that has some defin-able aspect stems from delusion. It is like the wind in the sky which has no abode.

—SUTRA OF MEDITATION ON BODHISATTVA UNIVERSALLY WORTHY

Discussed our company's reconstruction all day with Mr. Toda. Many things to do and many hardships to overcome. Many passionate thoughts and emotional feelings.

With my common mortal's wisdom, I can accomplish nothing. But confident of the teaching that because our wisdom is inadequate, we substitute faith, I chant daimoku single-mindedly and exert myself to the utmost in the cause of construction.

Am I truly loyal to Mr. Toda?

Home at 11:00.

My room is so cold. Yet when I chant daimoku, my entire being seems to warm up. It is most strange, indeed.

Wednesday, November 22. Light rain.

"I am the father of this world,
saving those who suffer and are afflicted."

—(LS16, 231)

Out of the office with M. all day on business.

Thoroughly exasperated at Department Chief O.'s cowardice. Mr. Toda comforted me, comparing my situation to that of the bold young officers during the war who suffered under fainthearted generals' leader-ship.

I deeply feel that this year is vital for the company, for myself and for the Soka Gakkai. Each of us, as a gear in the kosen-rufu process, must strive to the utmost to lead the organization to victory.

Went to a discussion meeting at the O.s' home. No new faces.

Home at 12:50.

A still moonlit night. Recited poetry to myself on the way home, for the first time in a long while. My thoughts are many.

I read somewhere that if our hearts are light, our tasks will be light as well, and that prudent actions are more important than wise thoughts.

Friday, November 24. Light rain.

Went to Ito again as Mr. Toda's representative. Met with I. and S. Bewildered by the change in their position. I cannot grasp the subtleties of these older men's conversation.

Boarded the train after 4:00. At the sight of the still eastern sea with its waves gold and silvery under the moonlight, I felt as though transported briefly from reality to a dreamlike world of sacred art. Reached Tokyo at 7:00.

Returned to the office and then went immediately to Mr. Toda's house.

I reported everything to him in detail. He was in an extremely foul mood.

Home at 11:50.

Sunday, November 26. Light rain.

Up at 10:00. A cold morning. The season is turning wintry. I have no overcoat. This winter, too, I will have to make do without one.

Went with T. to M.'s house to encourage M. to take faith. He declined. To convert even one person is extremely difficult. No other action, however, is nobler, greater or more worthy of respect.

Even if not one person takes faith at present, hundreds of millions are waiting for us in the future. The two of us returned home confidently.

Went alone in the evening to Omori and saw the Western film *The Babe Ruth Story*.

Home at 10:30. It's cold. I wish I at least had some tea. I suppose not having anything will be a good memory in the future.

Monday, November 27. Light rain.

Light rain beginning in the evening. Returned home slightly after 9:00. After gongyo, read *Mystery of the Universe* until midnight.

My physical condition is improving slightly, to my great joy.

Even though I came home early, I cannot help feeling somehow unsatisfied.

Today I was promoted to business department chief.

1. Must study economics.
2. Must assume more responsibility for the company's future development.
3. Must not fall behind the advance of the Soka Gakkai.

Tuesday, November 28. Light rain.

When one shakes his head, his hair sways, and when his mind works, his body moves. When strong winds blow, the grasses and trees do not remain silent, and when the earth quakes, the sea is agitated. When one moves Lord Shakyamuni, can grasses and trees remain unmoved, can any waters remain still?

—(GZ, 1187)

A cold day. Each day grows colder. My physical condition is improving steadily. I am confident this is a benefit of my faith.

My salary has been delayed three months. Today I received a little. Bought some shirts in Omori on my way home. Cost ¥160.

Home at 9:30.

Finished volume seven of *Collected Works of World Literature*.

Wednesday, November 29. Sleet.

Rainfall from morning. A cold wave is upon us. The coldest weather so far this year.

Spent half the day talking with Mr. Toda. He thoroughly instilled in me that I must carry on and fulfill the task that he, my teacher, has begun.

In the afternoon, he went to the Ministry of Finance and returned shivering. He smiled and said, "How cold the world is!"

"Daisaku," he told me, "I am not defeated. I lost a battle, but that is past. The real fight starts from now."

Resolve blazed up anew within me that I must strive never to let anyone so much as point a finger at Mr. Toda or at the Soka Gakkai.

Must keep an eye on I. He pretends to be on our side but maneuvers against Mr. Toda behind his back.

Home at 11:00. Tomorrow I must go to the Omiya area.

Thursday, November 30. Light rain.

The month of November has finally drawn to a close. Tomorrow, the decisive battle of the last month of the year awaits me.

Left for Omiya in the afternoon. Home 10:30. Must remember that business is an activity we experience for fifty years or so, but the Buddhist practice is most fundamental, as it effects our lives eternally.

Read Tolstoy's *Boyhood*. Became immersed in thought, contrasting the tyrant's boyhood with my own.

Friday, December 1. Rain.

The last month of 1950. I will soon complete my twenty-second year. Arrived at the office in high spirits before anyone else.

Away from the office all day on business. Worked to my heart's content.

Read Takiji Kobayashi's *Solitary Cell*. Keenly sensed the young leftist writer's agonies.

Pondered the strict fate that awaits one mislead by wrong ideas.

Reality is filled with contradictions and misery. I hate when the innocent are punished. Ultimately, we must be strong.

Home at 11:30. My room is cold.

Saturday, December 2. Clear.

It is rare to be born a human being. The number of those endowed with human life is as small as the amount of earth one can place on a fingernail. Life as a human being is hard to sustain—as hard as it is for the dew to remain on the grass. But it is better to live a single day with honor than to live to 120 and die in disgrace.

—"The Three Kinds of Treasure" (WND, 851)

Departed with Mr. Toda at 12:50 on the *Pine Island* train on a business trip to Ito. We went to see I. On the train, Mr. Toda lectured to me on "The Object of Devotion for Observing the Mind."

Stayed at the I. Inn. The two of us took a leisurely dip in the hot springs. Talked about several things. Mr. Toda seems to be pondering various matters.

I. came to see us again in the evening.

I am to call on him tomorrow morning.

The regular youth division meeting was held in Tokyo tonight. This is the first time I've missed it.

Tuesday, December 5. Cloudy.

M. and N. visited me early in the morning. Had a brief talk with them. Ran to the bus stop so as not to be late for work.

Struggles and hardships!
  In their midst, you will develop true humanity.
  In their midst, you will forge an iron will.
  In their midst, you will know real tears.
  In their midst, know that there lies the human revolution.

Home at 11:00.

Thursday, December 7. Clear.

Small waves and light winds cannot damage a large vessel, but high
waves and strong winds can destroy a small boat. Errors in the secular
law are like small waves and light winds; they cannot ruin a great
nation or great men. But errors in Buddhism are like strong winds and
high waves smashing a small boat; without doubt, they will destroy the
country.

—(GZ, 1521)

Up at 6:00. In high spirits. Off to a vigorous start.

In the evening, I invited the couple who found me this apartment
and their daughter to the Yurakuza Theater. We saw a first-run showing
of *Wuthering Heights.* Deeply moved by the sorrows of Heathcliff and
Catherine on parting from each other. On the way home, treated my
guests to *chirashi-zushi* [vinegared rice with a variety of ingredients] in
the basement of the Nichigeki Theater. Returned home happily.

Inviting people out is fine, but I cannot help feeling that saving them
by convincing them to take faith is the only real way to express thanks.

Home at 10:50.

Saturday, December 9. Rain.

Even if a man is blessed with a strong body, his talents will be useless
if he lacks a sincere heart.

Met with the reporter K. at the metropolitan police headquarters
press club. Discussed news reporting at a Toranomon tea shop.
Interesting.

Read from the Gosho at the office until midnight—"On the
Enlightenment of Plants," "On Attaining Buddhahood in This Lifetime,"
and "The Heritage of the Ultimate Law of Life."

Home at 2:00.

Sunday, December 10. Fine and clear.

In the morning, did my laundry and other chores. In the afternoon, went to Mr. Toda's house. He lectured for me on "The Heritage of the Ultimate Law of Life.'" Received guidance from him on various matters until late at night. Feel chagrined at my inability to fully grasp his guidance, even though I seem to have understood it at first.

Monday, December 11. Clear.

A philosopher once declared, "Life is another name for struggle." Truly, life is like warfare, severe and bewildering. I fondly recall my boyhood days when I knew nothing of life. But I cannot retreat a step.

Life is a struggle.

Yet, even in the midst of struggles, rest is necessary.

And in rest, we can dream of the next ideal.

That ideal must encompass the greatest good for the individual and society.

Then, while striving to realize it, we must arouse the full power of our bodies and minds.

For that purpose, rest is necessary.

After all, we must fight to the end in life —

For the highest ideal, the realization of kosen-rufu.

Tuesday, December 12. Clear.

In propagating this supreme Law, one should make the sacred teachings of the Buddha's lifetime his basis and familiarize himself with the commentaries of the eight sects.

—(GZ, 1038)

Nothing is more changeable than the human mind. Friends who were as close as fish and water until yesterday may become enemies brandishing arms at one another today. A person deeply in love in the morning may change his or her mind by evening, as easily as water flows. A visitor with whom one conversed intimately a few days ago may flare up in anger in response to a moment's shift of mind.

My heart does not change, but my circumstances are intimidating.

Though youth may be trampled upon and assailed by their surroundings, they must grow straight and powerfully, like young shoots emerging from the black soil. They must live with pure and youthful vitality.

Youth is the highest and greatest privilege in the universe.

Society is in chaos. Yet to be defeated would be tragic. Defeat could all too easily be the first step toward a miserable life.

Home at 11:00.

Saturday, December 23. Clear.

Only one week remains of this year.

This year truly has been a succession of misfortunes. Yet the Mystic Law's power will transform great evil into great good.

Until the last day, I shall fight, brandishing the sword of the Law—for Mr. Toda, for myself, for the Gakkai, for the company, for the Japanese people and for humanity.

Both our company and the Soka Gakkai are like the morning sun—now about to rise and dispel the darkness.

Went in the evening to M.'s house on a business errand. About twenty people were gathered there. Made various explanations.

Home at 11:30.

Wednesday, December 27. Fine and clear.

Clear skies. A refreshing morning.

My physical condition good.

Worked vigorously all day. Bitter criticism leveled at Mr. Toda. I will fight resolutely.

I am confident I understand Mr. Toda's great mission better than anyone else. I alone truly understand what is in his mind. Blazing with righteous anger, I will fight with all my life.

Home at 1:20. To bed at 3:00.

Thursday, December 28. Fine and clear.

Life is a succession of struggles. But I think the important thing is what we struggle for and what foundation underlies our striving.

The purpose of my own battle being sublime, as long as I have not the slightest particle of regret, it will be a battle of supreme happiness. Now I realize there will be no regrets. Therefore, I have only to march ahead with a smile.

I wish to adorn the finale of my battle with splendid efforts that are truly worthy of me. Whether I win or lose is secondary. I must make it my first priority, however, to display ability, power of action, firmness and responsibility in this struggle.

Napoleon won in battle, and then, after a crushing defeat, won again, but in the end, he was a defeated hero.

Pestalozzi's fifty-year struggle seemed a total defeat, yet in the end, he emerged victoriously as a great educator.

The important issue for me now is how to strive, how to crown my life's finale with victory.

Ultimately, there is no other way but to base one's life to the end upon daimoku.

Home at 11:30. To bed at 1:30.

Sunday, December 31. Fine and clear.

In the morning, went to clean up the office.

Returned in the evening. Straightened my room a bit. Went to the baths for the first time in a while. Ate alone at a sushi shop on the way home.

Next year, I want to go to night school again.

Next year, I want to study to my heart's content.

I cannot foresee what turn my destiny will take next year.

Next year, too, my whole life will be to act as my teacher guides me.

The twenty-second year of my youth is ending, etching in my heart its history and memories in the workings of cause and effect.

To bed at 12:50.

THE YEAR DAWNED AMID a worsening of the Cold War. In his New Year's address, General MacArthur, Allied Forces commander, stressed the need for collective security and hinted at possibly rearming Japan. Meanwhile the Korean War intensified, and on January 4, the North Korean army captured Seoul. Thus the new year opened amid an extremely strained international situation. Yet, on January 3, Japan National Radio broadcast a singing contest, and on the same day, Kabuki theaters reopened their doors, indicating that people's lives were slowly returning to normal after the war.

The tight controls over rice were being relaxed. In March, it became legal to sell rice on the open market. Although more available than before, food was generally still in short supply. The government therefore set goals for a ten percent increase in rice production, and newspapers held contests for the highest production in the nation. Consequently, rice became the prime factor in increasing Japan's overall food production.

Japan's political arena comprised three political parties: the Liberal Party, the Democratic Party and the Socialist Party. On January 19, a joint conference of top leaders from each party was held. The greatest debate over public funds allotment concerned "military rearmament."

To further peaceful Japan–U.S. relations, the secretary of state under U.S. President Harry S Truman, John Foster Dulles, visited Japan to meet with Prime

Minister Yoshida and leaders in various areas of society. His purpose was to discuss the restoration of Japan's national sovereignty. The visit heralded an end to American forces occupation of Japan.

Possession or operation of airplanes by Japan's airline industry had been forbidden by the Allied Forces' Far East Commission. On February 5, however, the Ministry of Transportation requested and received permission from the GHQ to resume airline operation using Japanese capital. Although, at first, both planes and pilots had to be borrowed from overseas, a reestablished domestic airlines industry was soon under way.

Despite his difficult business situation, Josei Toda poured his entire being into training the youth to whom he would entrust the future of kosen-rufu. Discussing the Gosho and important literary works, he conducted a series of meetings that lasted about six months, from fall 1950 until spring 1951, in which he instilled in these youths his dynamism and ideal for kosen-rufu. These meetings produced a core of capable youths who would form the nucleus of the youth division (established later that year) and set a precedent for the

1952 formation of the Suiko Group.

February 19, 1951, marked the passing of the famous French writer Andre Gide, winner of the Nobel Prize for literature in 1947 and well known for works such as *Strait Is the Gate*, *The Immoralist* and *The Vatican Swindle*. Other foreign works then read widely in Japan were *The Stranger*, by Albert Camus, and *The Wayward Bus*, by John Steinbeck. *The Stranger* became an especially popular bestseller and a topic of heated debate among Japanese literary critics.

As the March 17 entry suggests, preparations for launching the *Seikyo Shimbun*, the Soka Gakkai's newspaper conceived by Josei Toda, were well under way. On March 20, the first issue was published. The *Seikyo Shimbun* was then a thrice-monthly, two-page tabloid with a circulation of 5,000. In general, most daily papers were then published in four-page editions on weekdays and two-page editions on Saturday and Sunday. After the war, the GHQ had little choice but to impose censorship and other controls upon the Japanese press. In May 1956, however, such restrictions were removed.

On April 3, 1951, the second

nationwide local elections under Japan's new constitution were announced. Unlike the previous election, community and city leaders who had held office during the war were allowed to run, but an endless stream of unopposed candidates made for a rather dull election. The general tendency was for the reformists to retreat, losing seats in the Diet, while the Liberal and Democratic parties, actually Japan's political conservatives, predominated.

On April 11, an event of major importance occurred. President Truman removed Douglas MacArthur as the Supreme Commander of the Allied Occupation forces. Citing MacArthur's failure to support the U.S. government and U.N. policy, Truman replaced MacArthur with General Matthew Ridgeway. Underlying the move was friction between Truman and MacArthur over how to deal with the forces of communism in East Asia. MacArthur favored escalating the Korean conflict into an all-out war against the Chinese communists, while Truman wished to avoid another large-scale East–West confrontation.

By 1951, most aspects of daily life had been restored at least to a prewar level of quality. This was not true, however, for telephone service. In 1951, demand for service outweighed supply. Out of 7.1 million requests, only some eighty thousand phones could be installed. And an average of one call was completed for every 2.5 dialing attempts.

With Josei Toda's inauguration as second Soka Gakkai president on May 3 came a great surge in propagation. In May, 284 households were converted, and in June, the number rose to 440. In a short time, the monthly organization growth rate climbed from five to nine percent.

Saturday, January 6. Cloudy.

Went to Mr. Toda's at 11:30. A slightly cold New Year's season. Put the company's business documents in order together with Mr. Toda.

Helped with various matters all evening at his house. He also gave me guidance and instruction. I keenly sense his extraordinary resolve.

Mr. Toda is like Masashige, while I am like Masatsura.[1] His wife wept. Never throughout my life will I forget the emotion, solemnity, tears, sense of mission, of karmic bonds and of life's worth that I have experienced today. It has been decided that I will be his successor.

A stormy year has dawned, and it advances moment by moment. Overcoming all sufferings, I will strive throughout this year as a man and as a youth.

Let this be the year of dawn for the Soka Gakkai and for our company.

1. Masashige…Masatsura: Kusunoki Masashige (?-1336) was a warrior chieftain of Kawachi province who supported the short-lived Kemmu Restoration (1333–35) of Emperor Go-Daigo, following the collapse of the Kamakura regime. He is regarded as a personification of the virtues of courage and loyalty. Masatsura, his son, supported him in his committed struggle.

Sunday, January 7. Cloudy.

Spent the entire day at Mr. Toda's house. My spirits soared doing gongyo with him. We continued yesterday's task of organizing various documents.

He is so perfectly composed. His life-state is inconceivably great.

No matter what sufferings may await me, I will always count as my highest, greatest happiness the honor of having studied under this man.

Cold all day.

Home at 11:00. Opened the Gosho, but my brain utterly refuses to function.

Monday, January 8. Clear.

You, why do you suffer so?
Why do you weep so much?
Why do you worry thus?
Suffer as you must,
*   for the young shoots to break through the fragrant earth*
*   and shoot up straight.*
Weep as you will,
*   for you cannot help weeping,*
*   until the day that you behold the sun*
*   beyond the rainy season.*
Worry as you must,
*   for until the darkness of midnight passes,*
*   you cannot behold the solemn breaking of the dawn.*

Home at 10:00. Read from Milton's *Paradise Lost*.

Wednesday, January 10. Snow.

It is spring.[1]
Spring, when youth are full of life and their fighting spirit dances.
Spring!
Spring, when a warm and golden breeze touches the icy snow of
   youth's suffering.
Nature, vibrant with life.
The season heralds blessings.
A stage adorned with dreams of joys and sorrows.
It is spring.
Green leaves, flowers and birds live to their utmost.
The philosopher smiles, even gloomy hearts are pierced by the
   sunlight.
Spring, spring of freedom.
The joy of life dances in the heart of youth.
Spring is near. Spring of the earth. Spring of humanity.

1.   Spring: This is a reference to the lunar calendar, which was followed in Nichiren
   Daishonin's time. According to the lunar calendar, spring arrives much closer to the
   beginning of the year.

Thursday, January 11. Light rain.

FAITH
Because I have faith,
   I am capable of comprehending life,
   eternal and mysterious.
Because I have faith,
   amid the ugly struggle for survival,
   I can stride, maintaining purity,
   through a victorious life.
Because I have faith,
   amid humanity bound by iron chains
   and imprisoned in the burning house,
   I can walk, in peace and tranquility,
   through a life of freedom.
Because I have faith,
   I can grasp life as the reality of
   eternity, happiness, true self and purity,
   and not illusory dreams born of transient phenomena.

Because I have faith,
> *even in a society filled with contradictions and irrationality,*
> *I can advance boldly, confident in the law of cause and effect.*

Because I have faith,
> *I will not be moved even in the least by huge waves,*
> *for I have boarded the great ship of eternity.*

Because I have faith,
> *I can experience value, major good and vital life force,*
> *and the happiness of human revolution.*

Friday, January 12. Cloudy.

My acute bronchitis of the last three days has improved slightly.

At 10:00, went to visit Mr. Toda and planned various matters.

At 11:00, encouraged his wife and left for the office. The office is depressing when he is not there. Felt dreadfully lonely and spiritless.

My throat and head ached all day. I feel terribly exhausted. But what worries me is Mr. Toda's health.

In the evening, met with W., K. and O. on business. I must win in my present battle. Win—opening the way with faith and courage.

Saturday, January 13. Cloudy.

Even the most selfish person, when drunk on wine, will unexpectedly arouse a mind of generosity, and desire to give others whatever he has. This is because, even though he may be destined to fall into the realm of Hunger due to his lifelong avarice, under the influence of the wine, he manifests the bodhisattva nature.

—(GZ, 1417)

Up at 7:00. Extremely fatigued.

Victor Hugo, great master of literature. Finished reading his great work of revolutionary poetry, *Quartre-vingt-treize*. Many thoughts and feelings. Earnestly hope that many great literary figures of his caliber will appear in our country as well. Ah, when will we see the emergence of great literary masters who base themselves on this great philosophy, thought and religion. Ah, great authors who burn with passion, revolution and profound ideals! Your appearance could not come a day too soon! Though Sensei's health seems to have improved somewhat, he has grown thinner. Delighted to see him come to work.

To the area near Tsurumi in the evening on business. Visited the homes of S., Y. and T. A very cold night. Home at 12:00.

Sunday, January 14. Fair.

Though it has mind, a painting of a demon looks dreadful. A lady will hate the picture of a mistress, though it has no power to allure her husband. No one wants to wear even the finest brocade quilt if it has the design of a snake embroidered on it. A warm wind is disagreeable to one's warm body.

—(GZ, 1417)

Up at 10:00. Very cold. Visited Kankiryo temple for the first time in two months. Chanted daimoku to my heart's content. Strangely, I began to feel fresh and vigorous, and the spirit to fight rose up within me. How wonderful! It must be because the battle begins tomorrow.

Arrived at Mr. Toda's house at 5:30 in the evening. The lecture was at 6:30. Covered were:
1. "Reply to Lord Matsuno," written by Nichiren Daishonin in December 1276.
2. Discussion of the Gakkai's mission, etc.

Excused myself from Sensei's residence at 10:30. The coldest day so far this year.

Monday, January 15. Clear.

Stones are split open for their hidden gems, deer are slain for their hides and meat, fish are caught for their flavor, the kingfisher is killed for its gorgeous feathers, and a beautiful woman is envied for her beauty. This is the case with me. Because I am the votary of the Lotus Sutra, I have suffered all manner of persecution at the hands of the three powerful enemies.

—"THE SWORDS OF GOOD AND EVIL" (WND, 451)

Extremely cold.

Feeling exhausted since yesterday. Heavy feeling—not well.

Remained in bed until 11:00 a.m. Out of tea. Out of food. Out of clothing.

I don't mind that no one has come to call.

In the afternoon I visited the homes of S. and W. and later, around 4:00 p.m., called on Y.

Home at 10:30.

Tuesday, January 16. Snow.

Even if a good priest sees someone slandering the law and disregards him, failing to reproach him, to oust him, or to punish him for his offense, then that priest is betraying Buddhism.

— NIRVANA SUTRA

The Gosho states, "Exert yourself in the two ways of practice and study." There is no true value in life apart from Buddhist practice.

Took the day off of work because of illness — the first time I've done so. When I think of Mr. Toda working so hard, I feel miserable. Laying in bed, I tried to reflect on my activities and practice over the past year. I also contemplated my goals and objectives in practice for the coming year. S., Y., T. and M. stopped by in the evening to inquire about my health. I appreciate having such friends as them.

1. Carry out a consistent practice of morning and evening gongyo.
2. Visit the temple at least once every month.

Wednesday, January 17. Clear.

All disciples and lay supporters of Nichiren should chant Nam-myoho-renge-kyo with the spirit of many in body but one in mind, transcending all differences among themselves to become as inseparable as fish and the water in which they swim. This spiritual bond is the basis for the universal transmission of the ultimate law of life and death. Herein lies the true goal of Nichiren's propagation. When you are so united, even the great desire for widespread propagation can be fulfilled. But if any of Nichiren's disciples disrupt the unity of many in body but one in mind, they would be like warriors who destroy their own castle from within.

— "THE HERITAGE OF THE ULTIMATE LAW OF LIFE" (WND, 217)

The sun is warm today, but my physical condition is particularly poor. Worked hard all morning trying to catch up with work I missed yesterday. Went to S.'s house on business.

Mr. Toda has begun to hold lectures for Gakkai members on "On Establishing the Correct Teaching for the Peace of the Land." My youthful heart soars ever higher.

Went with K. to visit O.'s home in Ogikubo in the evening. We discussed various matters until midnight. On the way back we stopped by Mr. Toda's house. I was invited to stay the night. K. also slept over.

Each historic day leaves a meaningful impression in my heart.

Thursday, January 18. Clear.

Women support others and thereby cause others to support them. When a husband is happy, his wife will be fulfilled. If a husband is a thief, his wife will become one, too. This is not a matter of this life alone. A husband and wife are as close as a form and shadow, flowers and fruit, or roots and leaves, in every existence of life. Insects eat the trees they live in, and fish drink the water in which they swim. If grasses wither, orchids grieve; if pine trees flourish, cypresses rejoice. Even trees and grass are so closely related.

— "LETTER TO THE BROTHERS" (WND, 501–02)

When winter comes, spring cannot be far off. Although it is the dead of winter, my heart races to think of spring close at hand. Whatever hardships I must face, I must never give up hope. I once heard of a certain man, who, in the midst of a series of hardships, kept a painting of a springtime scene that he looked at day and night in order to encourage himself. When "spring" finally did come to his family he kept the painting, which became a cherished family treasure. How much more does this principle hold true for one who embraces the Mystic Law, not to mention for youth who devote themselves to upholding and protecting the Daishonin's Buddhism!

Life — human beings must survive, powerfully. Youth, scattered like so many fallen flower petals by the Pacific War. When I think of them, I feel unending gratitude for living out my youth today.

Think of the young men who marched onto the battlefield, rifles in hand.

Think of the young men who, grasping the controls of their aircraft, battled enemy planes.

In any nation, youth should be treasured above all else — for the sake of that nation's future and for humankind.

Even if we die in our twenties, death comes in an instant. This is true also if we die in our fifties or in our eighties. Death is a juncture through which one passes in but a single moment.

To live a life without regret is truly difficult. It is even more difficult to die an honorable, dignified death. I feel keenly aware that the path toward solving such problems lies nowhere but within the realm of Buddhism.

Is life a drama? Is it a solemn reality?

To bed, 11:30 p.m.

Friday, January 19. Overcast.

Mr. Toda arrived at the office around 10:00 a.m. It was warm all day. Whenever I carry out propagation activities, I am criticized without fail. It's almost uncanny. Some people call us arrogant, while others say we are irrational. Still others become so enraged that their faces turn bright red. Pride or arrogance based on the Lotus Sutra is permissible. Arrogance in this sense means the confidence and conviction of one who spreads the Mystic Law.

Although some may call us senseless, such people cannot fathom what it means to have a seeking mind toward Buddhism. They cannot grasp it with their everyday, shallow reason. Seeing people's faces flush with anger, I cannot help feeling that they lack reason, conviction and open-mindedness, despite whatever previous impression they may have given.

Youth! Advance, no matter what anyone says. Carry out propagation like Nichiren Daishonin's disciples and Mr. Josei Toda's followers. Spreading the Law!—the supreme battle for a youth.

Visited K. in the evening. Returned home, 11:00 p.m. Want to carry on with burning faith throughout my life.

Saturday, January 20. Light rain.

The old fox never forgets the hillock where he was born; the white turtle repaid the kindness he had received from Mao Pao. If even lowly creatures know enough to do this, then how much more should human beings!

—"On Repaying Debts of Gratitude" (WND, 690)

King Ashoka reigned in India about a hundred years after the Buddha's passing. He devoted himself to the large-scale propagation of Buddhism.

Mr. Toda's health is not at all good. I am deeply worried about him. Today he scolded me for letting myself become too exhausted. He sternly warned me not to let my resolve for construction be shaken. Spent the night thinking deeply about my teacher, Mr. Toda—more so than ever before. Lecture tomorrow.

Sunday, January 21. Clear.

At 6:00 p.m. Mr. Toda lectured on "The True Aspect of All Phenomena" at the Gakkai headquarters. He thoroughly explained the Gakkai's mission and the correct manner of propagation.

Worried about my teacher's health.

As one close to Mr. Toda, I reflected seriously on my past careless remarks.

1. Make the way of mentor and disciple the eternal way of the Gakkai.
2. In the next three years, perfect the Soka Gakkai's foundation and our company's as well.

Entering the coldest time of year. Today was especially cold.

The height of the narcissus is reflected in its shadow.

— CHIGETSU

Monday, January 22. Fine and clear.

A sword is useless in the hands of a coward. The mighty sword of the Lotus Sutra must be wielded by one courageous in faith. Then one will be as strong as a demon armed with an iron staff.

— "REPLY TO KYO'O" (WND, 412)

Physical condition very poor. The cold wind penetrates my entire body. Went out on business in the afternoon. Spent nearly two hours at Y.'s house, where I could rest, but my fever didn't subside.

Returned to the office in the evening and received strict guidance and a scolding from Mr. Toda on various matters. My head aches— could this be a result of slander?

Rested alone in my four-and-a-half-tatami-mat room. Tomorrow will probably be cold again. The thought chills both my body and my mind. Home at 11:00, to bed, 1:00 a.m.

Tuesday, January 23. Clear.

Up at 8:00 a.m., beautiful weather. Left for work in a hurry. Physical condition, poor. It is difficult to work hard while in such poor health. My first priority is to fight to establish good health. Only through faith can I change my physical condition and develop a robust constitution. Will do my utmost, in any way I can.

Left on business to Kanagawa in the afternoon. Returned home directly, without stopping at the office. To bed a little before 10:00.

Wednesday, January 24. Clear.

Missed work today because my temperature rose to 104° F. Felt delirious all day and experienced nightmares when I slept. In the afternoon, K. stopped by to look after me. Our company's situation pains me deeply.

Can rely on no one but myself. At any rate, all I can depend on is my faith. Today more than any other, I can profoundly sense the greatness of this faith. Nam-myoho-renge-kyo. Nam-myoho-renge-kyo.

1. Resolutely carry out a great propagation campaign during the coming year.
2. Carefully read the Gosho.
3. Read "The Record of the Orally Transmitted Teachings" and Nichikan's *Six-volume Writings*.[1]
4. Solidify business for our company.

1. *Six-volume Writings*: (Jpn Rokkan Sho) The masterwork of the twenty-sixth high priest, Nichikan (1665–1726), which distinguishes the correct interpretations of the Daishonin's teachings from misleading ones; contributed to Nichikan's restoration and prosperity of Nichiren Shoshu. The six treatises are: "The Threefold Secret Teaching," "Meanings Hidden in the Depths," "Interpretations Based on the Law," "Teaching for the Latter Day," "The Practice of This School" and "The Three Robes of This School."

Thursday, January 25. Clear.

Fine weather.

Spent the day in bed again. Passed the time listlessly. K. stayed with me and cared for me again today. I am deeply grateful to him.

Miss T. visited me in the evening wanting to consult with me about her marriage. She seemed delighted when I expressed my support. Many unhappy people are becoming happy. I can see the power of the Mystic Law clearly reflected in the lives of other believers.

Spent an uninteresting evening reading magazines.

Friday, January 26. Clear.

Failure in business. The pure-hearted will of youth. Great, bright future hopes become clouded. Friends draw distorted conclusions. Associates level criticism. Energy exhausted—my mind is a raging storm.

The human mind is complex. It is vital to live strongly, courageously. This is especially true for maintaining correct faith.

The eternity of life, the simultaneity of cause and effect, fate, destiny, the moment—when I consider these realities of life's continuum, I lament over my own lack of ability. I know of no other way but the power of strong faith.

The battle. The drama of life. Victory. Defeat. Effort. Resignation. Hell. Dreams. Transient attachments. Good and evil. Sincerity, truth and falsehood. There are many courses we may take in life, but, ultimately, is there any other way to tap the essence of our humanity and lead a correct way of life than to devote ourselves to the Gohonzon?

Saturday, January 27. Clear.

Myogaku—literally "mystic awakening," the Buddha's enlightenment. It is so called because it is ultimate, perfectly endowed and impossible to fathom. This is why the term *myogaku* always represents the Buddha.

Left for the office after chanting daimoku with a robust voice. The sun felt warm. Visited S. in Tsurumi in the afternoon. At 3:00 p.m., I accompanied Mr. Toda to Shinjuku to meet with K. We discussed various future business arrangements. Had dinner at 7:00 with N. and others, stopping by N.'s house on the way home. Back home at 9:30.

Sunday, January 28. Clear.

Our head is the head of our father and mother; our feet are our father's and mother's feet. Our ten fingers are the ten fingers of our parents, and our mouth is our parents' mouth. We and our parents are inseparable, just like a seed and its fruit, or a body and its shadow. When Shakyamuni attained the Way, so did his parents, Shuddhodana and Maya, and when Maudgalyayana attained enlightenment, [his parents] Kissen Shishi and Shodainyo simultaneously attained enlightenment.

—(GZ, 977)

Up at 9:30 a.m. A warm Sunday. B., his wife and S. came to see me. It's troublesome to have visitors first thing in the morning. Ate a meal at noon—breakfast and lunch combined, then went to S.'s house on business. Since it was Sunday and he was off work, I could talk with him at length.

At 7:20 I arrived at Mr. Toda's for a lecture and was scolded for being late. It was totally my fault. Mr. Toda completed his lecture on the *Sozai Ichinen Sho*. I must devote myself completely to this great teaching.

Returned home at 11:00. Had a multitude of thoughts.

Monday, January 29. Fair.

Felt tired from the time I awoke—perhaps because of nightmares. It was warm and pleasant all day.

Received strict guidance from Mr. Toda. I've nearly come to understand the weak points in my own faith.

Propagation!… I will pour my whole life into working vigorously for kosen-rufu. Mere ideology or speculation is fruitless. For youth, life should be based on nothing but practice and action.

Faith is the foundation of my life.

Pure faith, the root of my existence.

My weak self—low-spirited and agonized by troubles. Ultimately, the only way to solve these problems is to chant daimoku. Is faith's ultimate purpose to prove myself to myself?

Visited N.'s and S.'s in the evening.

Tuesday, January 30. Light rain.

It is very difficult to know oneself. It may be that all troubles and failures spring from the inability to know oneself.

Destiny, fate, personality—at times, I feel I can do nothing to control these aspects of my life. Must become stronger. A good environment is important, and a capable leader or teacher is also necessary. Most important, however, is the Gohonzon and my faith.

I think there are excellent people in the world with many enemies. I also believe some gain others' enmity of because of their own bad nature or misdeeds. One sees fine people with many friends, while, at the same time, some who appear attractive and who are well liked by many are actually nothing but riffraff.

Am considering the correct way for a human being to live. To bed, 11:50.

Wednesday, January 31. Light rain.

One month has already passed. Time goes so quickly. There will only be one "today" throughout eternity.

I want to live with a state of life as vast as the Pacific Ocean.

I want to struggle throughout my life, with a life force as powerful as the raging waves of the Pacific.

I want to live with passion and vigor, like the swirling Pacific current.

Thursday, February 1. Clear and pleasant.

The fine weather brightens my heart. Having trouble patching my worn-out clothes because I lack skill at sewing. To bed, 11:20.

Friday, February 2. Clear and pleasant.

No practice is as deep, far-reaching or powerful as this faith. Isn't good advice harsh to the ear? Doesn't good medicine taste bitter? If we carry out propagation, we will undoubtedly incur opposition. It is certain that whoever practices faith now will be truly filled with fortune and gain absolute happiness in the future.

Those carrying out their faith now are pioneers. Doubtlessly, they also will be praised by Nichiren Daishonin.

Tonight, Mr. Toda lectured on the "The Record of the Orally Transmitted Teachings."

A warm evening. I began to feel sentimental.

12:00. Drifting off to sleep. The wind is blowing harder. Tomorrow, again, I must do my best — in high spirits.

Saturday, February 3. Clear.

In poor physical condition. Having difficulty getting up on time in the morning.

In winter, I will train my body and train my mind.

Then, the warm sunshine of spring awaits me.

My dreams must not become scattered, along with the falling cherry blossoms. Toward my long-cherished mission, I will forever hold today's awakening in my heart.

> No one has ever set eyes upon such words [which declare the Lotus Sutra to be a heretical, non-Buddhist teaching] in any of the numerous sutras. Though the Lotus Sutra contains phrases which refute the other sutras, none of the other sutras contains even a single phrase refuting the Lotus Sutra. After all, the statement which refutes the provisional teachings by declaring the Lotus Sutra to be supreme among all sutras formerly preached, now preached or to be preached in the future, is no arbitrary assertion of the sage Nichiren. These are the golden words of Shakyamuni Buddha, and the reason for his appearance in this world.
>
> —(GZ, 848)

Home at 10:30.

Sunday, February 4. Clear and fair.

It's almost miraculous that such fine weather has continued for so long.

The monthly youth division meeting was held today. Feel miserable because I did not attend.

Visited N., the schoolteacher. We discussed education until 10:00.

Decided to drink a small glass of whiskey from now on before I go to bed each night, for my health.

Feeling tired.

> But disgrace in this life is nothing. Of far greater concern is the disgrace that appears in the next life. Proceed to the place of practice of the Lotus Sutra, bearing in mind the time when you must face the wardens of hell, and the garment-snatching demoness and the garment-suspending demon will strip off your clothes on the bank of the river of three crossings. The Lotus Sutra is the robe that will keep you from disgrace after this life. The sutra reads, "It is like a robe to one who is naked."
>
> —"LETTER TO JAKUNICHI-BO" (WND, 994)

Returned home, 12:00. To bed, 1:30.

Monday, February 5. Clear and pleasant.

Ate two portions of breakfast this morning at a restaurant that honors food coupons. Continuing to live immoderately. It seems I'm always doing something to make my health worse.

Bad causes bring bad effects, while good causes bring good effects. No one knows the reasons for my situation better than I do. In the end, no one else is to blame. It is no one's responsibility but my own.

Went to Mr. Toda's in the evening. He finished lecturing on the comparison of provisional Mahayana with the true Mahayana teachings (the Lotus Sutra), as expounded in the Gosho "On the Teaching Affirmed By All Buddhas Throughout Time" (GZ, 558). A truly difficult concept. After the lecture, he reprimanded me about several things. Strongly reflected that ultimately, I was being admonished for my own conceit and arrogance.

Home at 11:00. Finished reading the book *Yoritomo*. Mr. Toda never leaves my mind.

Faith, human revolution, kosen-rufu: I must stand up!

Tuesday, February 6. Clear.

Felt terrible all day long. Could it be from lack of sleep? Worked inefficiently. It was a bad day.

Held a discussion meeting at my place in the evening, but not one

A YOUTHFUL DIARY (1951)   87

new person came. The only participants were K., T., H. and myself. A truly lonesome gathering.

Some are violently passionate, while others appear more reasonable. Which are happier?

Promised myself I would try my best during the next ten years. To bed, 12:30.

Wednesday, February 7. Fair and pleasant.

Up at 7:30. Finished three prayers of gongyo, then left for work in high spirits. Made little progress at work. What is the cause? I can attribute it only to my own lack of progress or growth.

Treated N. and some others to dinner in the evening. Ended up paying ¥600. It really hurt my finances. Home at 11:20. It's cold.

Thursday, February 8. Fine weather.

A youth division meeting was held at I.'s in Koiwa. At 7:00, fourteen young religious revolutionaries gathered boldly under the leadership of our teacher, Mr. Toda. Solemn and vibrant, tonight's meeting lasted more than three hours. All participants were serious. Finally, Mr. Toda's superb Gosho lecture on "The Three Great Secret Laws" filled my heart with furious resolve. Mr. Toda defined for us the 'kosen-rufu of substantiation' during the Latter Day of the Law.

Next, the participants discussed the book *The Eternal City*. I asserted that revolutions can be divided into three major categories — political, economic and religious. I said I thought this book describes a political revolution similar to Japan's Meiji Restoration. Communist revolutions are economic in nature. The revolution we are solemnly striving to achieve is more fundamental — a religious revolution. In other words, it is a truly peaceful, bloodless revolution.

How will we fourteen youths gathered today be living ten years from now, on February 8, 1961? I pray that not one will have fallen by the wayside, that all will be healthy and working vigorously.

Returned with U. and others, through the cold streets, in a cold train car.

Saturday, February 10. Clear.

Conviction — we often repeat the word. Firm conviction, however, is extremely difficult to grasp. How many times must we emerge from the brink of death, or cross raging rivers of hardship to acquire it? Faith — faith alone leads to lives of supreme conviction. Can we not ultimately acquire true conviction through the valiant and untiring practice of faith?

Sunday, February 11. Clear.

Up at 10:00. Awakened by B. Pleasant weather continues. Went to a small restaurant for a leisurely brunch. A single person is a free spirit.

After noon, I went to the Kankiryo temple. M. and U. broke our appointment to discuss Buddhism. Troubled. I am young, however. Must never become mean-spirited.

If I consider that everything is a reflection of my faith in the Gohonzon, then life is truly bright. On the other hand, it is also strict.

Visited Mr. Toda's home at 6:00. He began the second stage of his lecture on "On the Teaching Affirmed By All Buddhas Throughout Time" (GZ, 558). Determined all the more to advance toward kosen-rufu with my teacher.

Today was Mr. Toda's birthday. Sadly reflected that I did not offer him my best wishes.

Home just before 11:00.

Monday, February 12. Clear.

I lied to Mr. Toda. Felt terrible all day long. I apologize from the depths of my heart. My physical condition is not at all good. Could my lie have been the agonized cry of a person suffering from illness? Suffered miserably because of my weakness and lack of fortitude.

Went to Kanagawa in the afternoon and then on to Koiwa. Visited N.'s home where I spoke with him and another about various matters.

Concluded that my only course is to perfect myself. Then, illuminated by the Mystic Law, I will have no cause to be ashamed; I will be swayed by nothing.

> *Always carry out propagation,*
> *For faith is for oneself and for others.*

> *Never neglect the practice of gongyo*
> *For it is the motivating force for all of life's activities.*

> *Never forget construction and growth.*
> *For they are youth's most valuable asset.*

Tuesday, February 13. Clear.

Already the middle of February. Visited S., bringing him a bottle of whiskey I bought along the way.

Cut short my work so that I could attend a discussion meeting at M's. Waited for I. and others at Keihin Kamata Station for fifty minutes. They never showed up. Keenly realizing the difficulty of propagation.

After the discussion meeting, K. and Miss Y. together advised me to reflect on my attitude. It was concerning work and faith. It is regrettable to think that even K. understands neither my situation nor the depths of my heart, to say nothing of Miss Y. She is a blind and conceited woman who flatters her seniors. I have not the slightest bit of regret concerning the recent activities to which I have been assigned. I must advance, absolutely, along my own path. I am a disciple of Mr. Toda. All my activities, my mission and my practice center around Mr. Toda.

Back home at 1:30 a.m. Y. came over, and we talked until 2:00. He's a good person—a comrade in faith.

Wednesday, February 14. Snow.

Awoke at 8:00.

Left for work in a great rush after completing only three prayers of gongyo. Strange weather. I stayed in the office until 2:00. Discussed a pressing matter with Mr. Toda concerning his home mortgage. If the problem is not solved by tomorrow it will be foreclosed. I myself must solve this problem. Daimoku—with the power of daimoku!

The third snowfall of the year—snowflakes began to dance in the air. I wish the snow would cleanse my troubled mind, as well as my heart and body, which have been muddied by many battles within society. The golden saying "faith as pure as snow" flashed before my mind. But perhaps from lack of sleep, I walked on as if in a dream.

Went to Y.'s in the evening. He has worked so hard together with me. I am eternally grateful. Will remember his family as long as I live—a humble family, like a stone by the roadside. I think of them as unknown comrades even more precious than the valiant, capable people now in the spotlight. I love them from the bottom of my heart; I trust them dearly.

At 7:30, I returned home. Had some vague thoughts. The important thing is not to let my life force drop. Must never let myself be defeated.

Thursday, February 15. Snow.

The heaviest snowfall in fifteen years. National Railways has been forced to shut down. On the other hand, the snow has created a splendid world of silver. Stayed home from work to research a solution to yesterday's problem [concerning Mr. Toda's mortgage]. Made various arrangements over the phone. Went to visit O. at noon. I must reflect adequately on my own bad points. Must never become arrogant.

A meeting was held with fourteen youth division members at Ishida's in Koiwa. Most regrettably, however, our teacher Mr. Toda could not attend. Together, we read the Gosho "The True Aspect of All Phenomena," finishing at 9:20. Y. accompanied me to my place. He is my comrade in faith.

1. Help T. to grow steadily and dynamically.
2. Self-reflect on the last six months.

Friday, February 16. Overcast.

Rushed off to work after three prayers of gongyo. Such an impetuous nature—reflects the state of my life. Regret that I could not attend the lecture on the "Orally Transmitted Teachings." Spent the entire day in Koiwa, meeting with K. and discussing various matters.

Why are people so foolish?

Why are people so unhappy?

Why are people so arrogant?

How can people be so selfish?

Life's ultimate purpose, the simultaneity of cause and effect, happiness—Nam-myoho-renge-kyo. Home at 11:00.

Sunday, February 18. Clear.

Mr. Toda lectured on the following passage from "On the Teaching Affirmed by All Buddhas Throughout Time," "When Shakyamuni was a common mortal at the time of numberless major world system dust particle kalpas..." (GZ, 568). Heard the essence of the Daishonin's teachings. I want to have real power and ability. I want my mind to become clear.

1. Make certain that, until I am twenty-five, I can dedicate my life solely to kosen-rufu.
2. Until I am twenty-five, I must polish my ability as a leader and solidify my determination to carry out the will of my teacher, Mr. Toda.

Monday, February 19. Clear.

Awoke at 6:45. Left quickly with Y. for Omori Station. It was early and the train car was empty, but the cold was unbearable.

Spent the morning visiting O.'s family in Waseda. All I can do for the sake of my work is to offer my deep, heartfelt prayer to the Gohonzon each day. Nam-myoho-renge-kyo. Returned home at 10:30—went to bed early.

Tuesday, February 20. Clear.

Warm all day. My physical condition has taken a turn for the better —the power of daimoku. I am overjoyed. Because of 'the oneness of body and mind,' it is only reasonable for one's body to become healthy.

This faith is correct and absolute. Today's religious world has become defiled. World conflict has spread far and wide, and communism has greatly expanded its influence. How should we deal with this force that denies all religion? The ultimate solution lies only in the selfless, courageous and untiring advance of the Bodhisattvas of the Earth. How many true bodhisattvas exist today? I must read "On Establishing the Correct Teaching for the Peace of the Land" and "The Three Great Secret Laws" until I am ready to shed blood and tears.

Keenly aware of my mission in the vanguard of kosen-rufu. Throughout life, throughout eternity, the important thing is to raise capable people for the future. This is extremely vital. And to find capable people, one needs the eye of wisdom—that is the eye of faith.

Raising capable people requires time. There is no other way but to have them fuse their lives with the Gohonzon through the power of faith. To bed at 10:40.

Wednesday, February 21. Clear.

Fight again today, in high spirits!

Today again, advance vigorously!

I am young. Still young.

Spring—spring will soon arrive, a season aglow with hope. My passion and great conviction will grow like the trees and grass.

Spring—spring reminds us of the joy of living. Ultimately, I believe in the Gohonzon—the profound, eternally unchanging truth. Also myself. Because the self is the subjective reality, my comrades in faith who represent the environment will follow powerfully and boldly.

Youth, arise!

Youth, advance!
Youth, move!
Onward, ever onward!
Unafraid of towering precipices or raging waves.
Like Bruno or Rossi.[1]
Like Napoleon, Alexander, Whitman or Dante.
Home at 11:00. To bed at 1:00.

1. Bruno…Rossi: Characters from *The Eternal City*, by Hall Caine.

Thursday, February 22. Light rain.

A youth division meeting at Mr. Toda's Shinjuku office. Fourteen gathered for a lecture on "The True Aspect of All Phenomena." Mr. Toda asked us several questions concerning the relationship between the first and second parts of "Expedient Means," the second Lotus Sutra chapter. Pained by my own lack of study. Must learn by watching my seniors.

Deeply sense the growing strictness with which Mr. Toda trains his disciples. My heart aches as the one destined to represent all other Buddhas. I want us all to carry out splendidly our teacher's noble will. Now Mr. Toda and the Gakkai are being slandered and maliciously spoken ill of. But a profound emotion wells up from deep within my heart —just let them see us after ten or twenty years, after we have grown!

We are combatants in a religious revolution, the forerunners of a great social transformation.

We are warriors who fight to propagate a great ideal.

We are the builders of world peace.

Champions who save the people.

Messengers of the Buddha, who love the people.

Why?

Because now is the time for this great Buddhism's essence to spread.

Because humanity awaits a fundamental solution to the impurities of thought, of the people, and of life itself.

Because we possess the great guiding principle that saves the people.

Because we are awakened to the fundamental principle that determines the growth or decline of nations.

Friday, February 23. Rain.

It rained incessantly all day. Slept in. My health is improving. In the early evening I went to Mr. Toda's amid a heavy downpour. There was no lecture, but he gave me an assignment on the topic of the eternity of life.

Utterly perplexed at the difficulty of this problem. T. was waiting for me when I returned, and he will spend the night at my place. Cautioned him not to get sick because of the cold. To bed at midnight.

Saturday, February 24. Cloudy.

Today was warm. Spring approaches step by step. A young man's heart should swell with youthful passion, whether he is happy or suffering. Finished reading the last volume of *The Romance of Three Kingdoms* (an ancient Chinese classic). The grand plot skillfully portrays the human spirit's subtleties. It conveys the feeling of a giant scroll-painting depicting the heat of battles as well as the intrigues of generals and politicians. Schemes, love, tears, high spirits, ability and moral lessons. The main character, Liu Pei Hsüan-te, is a youth of revolution—a man of construction.

My head aches. From exhaustion? Must be careful not to slander. Have been thinking of Kojiya Chapter, which is under my charge. Greatly respect K. who, by himself, is striving vigorously. To bed—12:00.

Monday, February 26. Light rain.

Spring in full bloom—the season of peach blossoms and clear skies. Like youthful children of revolution.

In March, April and May, heaven and earth open wide with life.

Young children of revolution—let us blossom together, like fragrant flowers, you and I, honored to protect our mentor's revered teachings. Let us blossom, leaving our names behind for eternity.

The cheerful, the suffering, the bright, the sorrowful, the wealthy, the troubled—children of revolution living with deep emotion and tears.

Together—we followers of the Mystic Law, children of the great sage, disciples of our revered teacher. Always encouraging one another, we fight until we achieve our purpose. Advancing, we try our best, never retreating.

Wednesday, February 28. Light rain.

Since today was payday, I stopped to buy some sweets before visiting Y.'s in the evening. Ten or so people gathered to discuss business, and we talked of various matters as everyone shared the cakes I brought. Delighted to spend a few pleasant hours.

In any age or society, whether ravaged by war, disturbances or turmoil, we must progress without doubting the Gohonzon and with absolute belief in its great blessings. I think that if we can only do this, we will be splendid individuals—people of great faith. Home at 10:40. February is now over. Just hearing the word *March* somehow makes me feel warm.

Thursday, March 1. Rain.

We have now entered the bright month of March.

Buddhism is a battle. Whether we are victorious or defeated—doesn't this determine happiness or unhappiness, construction and growth or retreat and ruin? This month again, I must conquer myself, conquer my circumstances, and advance victoriously within society.

Want to publish books during my youth. Wish to produce great works.

- A view of politics, science and education based on the law of Buddhism.
- A discourse on life, pointing out the absolute necessity of faith.
- A history of the Gakkai's activities and progress toward kosen-rufu.

Home at 11:00.

Friday, March 2. Overcast.

The warmth of spring, a season of blooming flowers when hearts throb with hope. Want to struggle to establish myself, overflowing with life force. Want to save the people around me through bright, vigorous and cheerful activity.

Mr. Toda declared, "The Law of Buddhism is definitely superior to the law of the land," with conviction based on the concrete evidence of his own experience.

In the evening, I attended Mr. Toda's lecture on the "Orally Transmitted Teachings." This included a lecture on the Gosho, "On the Buddha's Prophecy." We studied the "Orally Transmitted Teachings" portion titled "On the Great Favor of the World-Honored One."

Returning home, I spoke with fellow members. Talking with the members is my greatest joy. We are all pioneering sons and daughters. Went to the barber for the first time in quite a while. Arrived home at 10:20.

Saturday, March 3. Cloudy.

I am now filled with happiness—to the point where I can scarcely desire more. Everything has been coming to fruition, a little at a time, and it is strangely satisfying.

In many cases, youth who struggle against storms of hardship and suffering are likely to sense greater meaning in life. Once again, must face the next storm and advance! This is an expression of the courage and passion of youth undertaking the task of construction.

Thinking about democracy. Cannot help feeling there are many contradictions in the so-called democracy present-day Japan clamors about. Vaguely considered how true democracy might be achieved.

Finished reading fourth volume of *The Complete Works of Leo Tolstoy*.

Returned home, 10:00. To bed 1:30.

Sunday, March 4. Clear.

A youth division meeting of about thirty young men and women. A lively gathering, but somehow it felt as if we accomplished little.

Courageously expand our activities further in society.

Develop young leaders with a revolutionary spirit.

Instill in the youth division the pride, practice and awareness befitting young pioneers of the Gakkai.

I wish to promote the above.

The meeting ended at 8:10. On the way back, I stopped at the Kanda Nikkatsu theater to see my first movie in quite a while.

Monday, March 5. Clear.

Went to Mr. Toda's for an evening lecture—the conclusion of "On the Teaching Affirmed By All Buddhas throughout Time." Afterward, we received detailed explanations of the Ten Worlds and the concept of nonsubstantiality (*ku*). Can only be astonished by the Buddha's great principles.

Troubled because I lost my monthly commuter pass. I don't have enough to buy another one, so for now I'll have to buy a ticket each morning.

Tuesday, March 6. Rain.

Those who sincerely offer food to others will enjoy the reward of a prolonged life, while those who steal food from others will incur the effect of having their life span shortened. Those who will not offer clothing to others will, as a result, be naked in lifetime after lifetime.

—(GZ, 1296)

Read "The True Aspect of All Phenomena" and "Reply to Lord Matsuno" together with members of Kanagawa Prefecture chapters. To study Buddhist doctrines leads to the deepening of our faith. This is truly the greatest of joys.

Home at 11:00. Read *The Count of Monte Cristo*. Had many thoughts.

Wednesday, March 7. Rain.

Day after day, I am filled with gratitude and deep emotion. Gradually, I am comprehending the sublime blessings of the Gohonzon. Because this teaching is infinitely profound and immeasurable, I can only exert myself untiringly and wholeheartedly. Who can fathom the actual proof, the reality of what we experience through this faith? Could there be a more magnificent principle, manifesting itself in our lives and in our daily affairs? Such phenomena—such power—cannot be denied. To do so would be the same as denying that which can be scientifically proven.

The Gosho "Conversation between a Sage and an Unenlightened Man" reads:

> The sage said: "The human heart is like water that assumes the shape of whatever vessel it occupies, and the nature of beings is like the reflection of the moon undulating on the waves. Now you insist that you will be firm in this faith, but another day you are bound to waver. Though devils and demons may come to tempt you, you must not allow yourself to be distracted. The heavenly devil hates the Buddha's Law, and the non-Buddhist believers resent the path of the Buddhist teachings."
>
> —(WND, 134)

Prepared for bed, thinking over tomorrow's plans. Half past 12:00.

Thursday, March 8. Clear.

We are by far the most fortunate of people. This is because we are developing under our mentor's deep, compassionate consideration. I must grow, replying to his expectations. This is my responsibility and obligation.

1. Firmly establish my faith.
2. Build a splendid foundation for our company.
3. Cultivate my ability as a disciple and successor to Mr. Toda.

Attended an evening discussion meeting at A.'s. Quite a few participated. It was a lively gathering, but I returned home, by myself, feeling lonely.

A person gives utterance to speech on two occasions: On one occasion, it is to tell other people what one does not oneself believe in an effort to deceive them. That person's voice in this case "accords with other's minds." On the other, it is to voice what one truly has in mind. Thus one's thoughts are expressed in one's voice. The mind represents the spiritual aspect, and the voice, the physical aspect. The spiritual aspect manifests itself in the physical. A person can know another's mind by listening to the voice. This is because the physical aspect reveals the spiritual aspect. The physical and spiritual, which are one in essence, manifest themselves as two distinct aspects; thus the Buddha's mind found expression as the written words of the Lotus Sutra. These written words are the Buddha's mind in a different form. Therefore, those who read the Lotus Sutra must not regard it as consisting of mere written words, for those words are in themselves the Buddha's mind.
— "OPENING THE EYES OF WOODEN AND PAINTED IMAGES" (WND, 86)

1. Never neglect daily self-reflection. Must understand that the basis for such reflection is nothing other than faith.
2. If our life forces are strong, then we can be happy under any circumstance. Must realize that the only basis for this is faith.

Hope to see:
1. A fresh restructuring of the Gakkai organization, as soon as possible.
2. A dramatic reorganization of the company staff, which is also necessary.

Sunday, March 11. Clear.

Up at 7:00, ate a quick breakfast and then took off for the Hall of Education where the Soka Gakkai was holding its general meeting. My greatest delight was seeing my teacher, Mr. Toda, participate in high spirits.

No one knows how much I have been quietly protecting him. My tears flow. Delighted to hear my teacher's bold declarations. He lectured on a passage from the Gosho "Remonstration with Bodhisattva Hachiman." I must study harder. Several hundred attended.

Monday, March 12. Overcast.

Once again, my health has taken a turn for the worse. It's agonizing. Must take good care of myself.

Went to Josen-ji at 7:00 to attend a memorial service for the mother of F., a friend of Mr. Toda. It was the second anniversary of her death. Offered prayers for her enlightenment, together with Mr. Toda. The temple was filled with people. A cold, blustery wind blew, at a reported velocity of about 40 mph. On the way home, stopped with K. for pork cutlet. Discussed foreign policy.

Tuesday, March 13. Clear and pleasant.

Must regain and improve my health.
Went to T. company in Kyobashi with Mr. Toda.
Stopped by my parents' house. All seem to be getting along well.
Will study the Gosho more seriously.
Bought a briefcase. Cost ¥6,500.
Feeling fatigued. To bed early at 9:40.

Thursday, March 15. Clear.

Water as it grows colder turns into ice. Snow which accumulates over the years changes to crystal. Evil deeds, when amassed, will lead one to hell, while an accumulation of good deeds will lead to Buddhahood. If a woman's jealousies mount up, they will turn her into a poisonous serpent. If you accumulate the blessings of devotion to the Lotus Sutra, will you not attain Buddhahood, just as the dragon king's daughter did?
—(GZ, 1547)

My character: Is it good or is it bad? I myself cannot know. Recently I have been pondering which profession I am best suited to, the field in which I can make the best use of my character.

How the youthful mind changes from moment to moment! Why does it shift and flow so, endlessly vacillating? Is it only me, or is it the same with others?

Fourteen youths gathered in Koiwa, at Ishida's home, for Mr. Toda's lecture on "The Heritage of the Ultimate Law of Life."

Saturday, March 17.

A severe headache. Troubled, as I wonder what slander I may have committed to cause it. Inquired about the condition of those whom I introduced to the Gohonzon. Six families in all—S., K., K., T., M. and I.

Went to a Shinjuku coffee shop with Miss Y. and K. during my lunch break. Discussed love, among other things, spending about an hour.

It is growing warmer, warm enough to do without an overcoat—quite a relief.

At 4:30, conducted a planning meeting at Mr. Toda's to discuss publication of the *Seikyo Shimbun*. There were four of us in all—M., Miss K., I. and myself. Sincerely resolved to develop it into the greatest newspaper in Japan—no, in the world.

Our battle for kosen-rufu is finally about to begin. Preparations for the decisive struggle are complete. The responsibilities of the position "chief of general staff" have become more crucial.

Keenly aware of the importance of technical ability based on faith, study based on faith, knowledge based on faith, diplomacy and struggle founded on faith.

Sunday, March 18. Clear.

In poor physical condition all day. Remained in bed until 5:00 in the evening. My brother visited me—I am very fond of him. Cannot help feeling sorry for him, as there is little I can do to help him out.

At 5:30, I prepared to leave for Mr. Toda's. His lecture covered up to the middle section of "Remonstration with Bodhisattva Hachiman." Having difficulty remembering the material. Must study all the harder.

The Lotus Sutra reads:

> If a person....
> on seeing those who read, recite,
> copy and uphold this sutra,
> should despise, hate, envy,
> or bear grudges against them,
> the penalty this person must pay....
> When his life comes to an end
> he will enter the Avichi hell,
> be confined there for a whole kalpa,
> and when the kalpa ends, be born there again.
> He will keep repeating this cycle
> for a countless number of kalpas.
> —(LS3, 74).

It also states:

> If there is someone who seeks the Buddha way
> and during a certain kalpa
> presses palms together in my presence

and recites numberless verses of praise,
because of these praises of the Buddha
he will gain immeasurable blessings.
And if one lauds and extols those who uphold this sutra,
his good fortune will be even greater.

—(LS10, 164).

Climbed into bed after chanting daimoku in earnest—11:50.

Monday, March 19. Clear.

Propagation is truly difficult. Those women members who live among the people and continue propagation, converting many, are hundreds of times more worthy of respect than we are.

A spring breeze from a thousand miles afar. Will build a life in which I can fully enjoy the feeling of spring in both body and mind, year after year.

In the evening, a discussion meeting in Gotenyama. Several participants; no newcomers.

The Lotus Sutra reads to this effect:

If there should be those who cause trouble to a votary of this sutra, then may their heads be split into seven pieces.... Those who protect and make offerings to this sutra will amass good fortune surpassing the ten honorable titles [of the Buddha.]

—(LS26, 310–11)

Returned home, 9:50.
Read *Scaramouche*.

Tuesday, March 20. Clear.

If one were to read the sutra in reverse order, beginning with the "Peaceful Practices" chapter and proceeding through the "Encouraging Devotion," "Devadatta," "The Emergence of the Treasure Tower" and "The Teacher of the Law" chapters, it would become apparent that these chapters were preached primarily for those who would appear after Shakyamuni Buddha's passing, and secondarily for those during his lifetime. To explain this in terms of the period after Shakyamuni's passing, the thousand years of the Former Day of the Law and the thousand years of the Middle Day of the Law are secondary, while this period of the Latter Day of the Law is primary. And in the Latter Day of the Law, Nichiren is the primary subject of the Lotus Sutra.

—(GZ, 333–34)

My physical condition is poor. This vicious cycle of disharmony in my life, a miniature universe, must definitely be due to some deficiency in my faith.

Must perform morning and evening gongyo completely and correctly. Herein lies the basis for a clear understanding of the cause of my problem.

To dedicate this ordinary, five-foot body to serving the Mystic Law, a fundamental spirit of appreciation is most essential.

Those absorbed only in their personal affairs cannot achieve anything great. Without developing ourselves, however, it would be equally impossible to achieve anything of importance. In Buddhism, there is no such thing as sacrifice. With the goal of attaining enlightenment, we strive for kosen-rufu, and awakening to our mission for kosen-rufu enables us to attain Buddhahood. Perhaps this relationship is like that of the earth's revolution around the sun and its rotation on its own axis.

Met Executive Director T. and Business Advisor O. at the Kyobashi office. Can only marvel at these old business world foxes' craftiness — never allowing others even a pinhole of a chance to take the advantage. All this contending over personal interests makes me feel disagreeable.

The courage to fight. The courage to love the peaceful and the ordinary. Perhaps capable youth can be called truly courageous only when they possess both these qualities.

Home at 11:00.

Wednesday, March 21. Overcast.

The vernal equinox. A beautiful, balmy spring day. Slept until about 9:00. Leaving home at 10:40, visited Mr. Toda. Discussed various matters and received guidance.

A *Seikyo Shimbun* editorial staff meeting at 6:00. As a leader, I myself will shoulder an important part of this battle for the Law. How delightful! How rewarding!

A passage from "On Chanting the Daimoku of the Lotus Sutra" reads: "The blessings of those who believe in this sutra are expounded in the 'Distinctions in Benefit' and 'The Benefits of Responding with Joy' chapters. Slander means to go against, and joyful acceptance (*zuiki*) means to sincerely follow" (GZ, 4).

Home at 10:30. Read for a while.

Friday, March 23. Light rain.

A lecture on the "Orally Transmitted Teachings," on the part dealing with the fifth Lotus Sutra chapter, "The Parable of the Medicinal Herbs." Also, a lecture on the "Letter to Jakunichi-bo."

My only desire is that Mr. Toda can, as soon as possible, take his stand as the leader on the front lines of kosen-rufu. This is the fervent wish of all sincere members. Must wait a bit longer for the right time to come.

There are good members and bad members, reliable members and those somehow unreliable. Does Mr. Toda recognize them for what they are, or does he not? In any event, nothing is concealed when reflected in the Mystic Law's clear mirror. Time will resolve everything and reveal it clearly.

A passage from "How Those Initially Aspiring to the Way Can Attain Buddhahood through the Lotus Sutra" states: "To illustrate, in kindling a fire, three things are needed: a good piece of steel, a good flint, and good tinder. The same is true of prayer. Three things are required—a good teacher, a good believer, and a good teaching—before prayers can be effective and disasters banished from the land" (WND, 880).

Sunday, March 25. Overcast.

Went to Mr. Toda's house. He completed his lecture on the Gosho "Remonstration with Bodhisattva Hachiman." Received guidance on various matters. I am quite an emotional person. Mr. Toda let me spend the night at his house. A memorable evening.

Monday, March 26. Rain.

Getting warmer, day by day. Spring has definitely arrived. Whether people suffer or rejoice, regardless of political shifts and of what accidents may occur, spring arrives precisely on time, embracing all.

With this body, I have been born into this world—this is an undeniable reality. As a youthful Bodhisattva of the Earth, I wish to live and die nobly, protected and watched over by all Buddhas and bodhisattvas throughout time and space.

Home at 11:00. To bed at 12:50.

Tuesday, March 27. Clear.

Growing warmer, bit by bit.

Buddhist practice—this is the way to attain Buddhahood. This is why Buddhist practice means the happiest, the supreme way of life. How refined! How ideal! How valuable a practice it is!

It is natural that we should meet hardships and criticism along the way. How can one go fishing yet fear the ocean breeze or the waves? What would the mountains be like without steep paths and boulders? In the end, how empty are the lives of those without faith!

Home at 10:50. Tomorrow I will go to a discussion meeting.

Saturday, March 31. Clear.

March, too, is now over. As we repeat the cycle of emotions, life passes by in an instant. I cannot help feeling that the next ten, twenty or thirty years will pass by in the space of a moment. Must value my time every day. Again, the problem is how to spend these precious hours.

This is a society in which people with no conviction and no basis, who do nothing but criticize others, are considered wise. Must remember that although people with conviction and ideals may appear passive at first glance, they are ultimately the strong and happy ones.

Whoever advances with an ideal is strong. Fiercest of all are the winds and waves that buffet the sails of a king's ship. Never falter or be afraid.

A Kamata area leaders meeting was held at the K.s'.

Home at 12:30. Received word that T.'s baby had died.

Saturday, April 7. Rain, then overcast.

In the evening, the regular monthly youth division meeting was held. Several dozen participants — both men and women. Disappointed at the foolish and pretentious leaders. They seem to think this is simply a neighborhood youth organization. I'm thoroughly dissatisfied with the frivolous attitude of two or three leaders. Mr. Toda seems to put his full trust in the youth division. For the Gakkai to fulfill its true mission, many outstanding leaders who deeply grasp Mr. Toda's true intention must emerge one after another.

The leaders lectured and gave guidance concerning kosen-rufu and faith. The meeting finished at 8:30. Home at 10:00.

Sunday, April 8. Cloudy.

Up at 10:00. K. visited, a weak but truly good-natured young man. Next, Y. came over. The three of us went out for breakfast, soaking up the sun along the way. Went to the baths in high spirits.

After gongyo, the three of us waited for S. at Omori Station. Arrived at Kankiryo temple at 2:30. Sutra recitation and sermon until 5:00.

Together with M., I enshrined the Gohonzon for S. Words cannot express the great joy of enshrining the Gohonzon for even one new member. It gives me the greatest sense of happiness.

Visited N.'s at 9:30.

A passage from "The Supremacy of the Law" reads:

> No matter whom you may marry, if he is an enemy of the Lotus Sutra you must not follow him. Strengthen your resolve more than ever. Ice is made of water, but it is colder than water. Blue dye comes from indigo, but when something is repeatedly dyed in it, the color is better than that of the indigo plant.
>
> —(WND, 615)

Neighbors accuse us of being half mad. They do not understand, however, that when viewed from the fundamental standard of the universe, those who criticize are themselves mad. This is the true aspect of our society—everything is completely backward. What can I say to them?

Home at 12:00.

Monday, April 9. Rain.

Rained all day long. Visited N.'s in Urayasu in Chiba Prefecture. It was my first time in Urayasu, a simple, poor fishing port. Here, too, the Mystic Law's torch has been kindled. Delighted to see that N. is also becoming more high-spirited. Regretted I could not visit K.'s this evening as planned.

To bed, a little after 9:00.

Tuesday, April 10. Overcast.

Rained all morning, but cleared in the afternoon. Discussed several matters with Mr. Toda until 2:00. Polished various plans for the future.

At Koiwa, beginning at 6:30, Mr. Toda lectured on the "The Four Stages of Faith and Five Stages of Practice." The lecture was attended by fourteen enthusiastic youth division members. K. did not attend.

Deeply impressed by Mr. Toda as a great philosopher. His is not mere knowledge. A fresh stream of principles, reason, conviction, determination, theory and foresight well forth like a spring arising out of his sagacious wisdom. Returned home just after 10:30.

Began to read from a collection of Walt Whitman's poetry:

> When I peruse the conquer'd fame of heroes and the victories of
>   mighty generals, I do not envy the generals,
> Nor the President in his Presidency, nor the rich in his great house,
> But when I hear of the brotherhood of lovers, how it was with them,
> How together through life, through dangers, odium, unchanging,
>   long and long,
> Through youth and through middle and old age, how unfaltering,
>   how affectionate and faithful they were,
> Then I am pensive—I hastily walk away fill'd with the bitterest
>   envy.
> —"WHEN I PERUSE THE CONQUER'D FAME," LEAVES OF GRASS

To bed, 1:30. It's warm.

Friday, April 13.

> Suppose there is a young couple. The husband is so in love with his
> wife, and the wife thinks so tenderly of her husband, that they com-
> pletely forget about their parents. As a result, the parents go about in
> thin clothing, while the bedroom of the young couple is warm and
> snug. The parents have nothing to eat, while the young couple's stom-
> achs are full. Such young people are committing the worst kind of
> unfilial conduct, and yet they fail to see that they are doing wrong. A
> wife who would deliberately turn her back on her own mother and a
> husband who would go against his own father—are they not guilty of
> an even graver offense?
> —"LETTER TO THE LAY PRIEST ICHINOSAWA" (WND, 529)

A balmy day. The cherry blossoms have already fallen. Will I have
regrets about my youth? Clearly engraved in my memory is a portion of a
song we sang during the war when I was working at N. Iron Works:
"Falling cherry blossoms. The remaining blossoms shall also fall." The
verse expresses a youthful, Japanese spirit, and a gallant way of life. In
Buddhism, life is ultimately considered most precious. Once again considered how to live, reevaluating my view of life and death.

Admonished on many points by Mr. Toda. Every time I am scolded, I
feel as though I am falling into the pit of hell. I am completely at a loss.
No one encourages or helps me.

Will visit the head temple the day after tomorrow. Will resolve once
again to make a fresh start.

Took a walk with K. and Miss Y. during our lunch break. The fine

April weather is bright and refreshing. Deeply feel that those who can experience the changes of the four seasons are fortunate and happy.

Home at 11:00.

Friday, April 20. Light rain.

> If a common mortal of the latter age should hear this teaching, he will not only attain Buddhahood himself, but will also lead his parents to enlightenment. This is the greatest form of filial piety.
>
> —(GZ, 984)

Drizzle in the morning. Cleared up in the afternoon. Warm all day.

Went to Kanagawa in the afternoon. Visited the homes of M., N., S., Y. and M. Wish to move powerfully, even though I feel uncomfortable in some situations. Cannot become a winner unless I strive powerfully.

In the evening, Mr. Toda lectured on the "Letter to Akimoto."

1. Wish to raise the sacred torch of propagation in my community.
2. It is agony to know that I am a disciple of the Daishonin yet cannot propagate the Law.

To bed at 12:30. My room is warm.

Saturday, April 21. Light rain.

A monotonous day. My health is extremely poor. A real disappointment. Came home at 8:00 to get to bed early. To fight without resting is a cause for defeat. I must rest today for tomorrow's battle. Resting, then, becomes part of the battle.

Sunday, April 22. Overcast.

> Many kings, ministers, court nobles and other officials, thinking that there is no greater pleasure than to have attained such positions, are content with such trivial gain. The Buddha compared this to prosperity gained only in a dream, or to the pleasures of an illusion, teaching that one should instead embrace the Lotus Sutra and quickly attain Buddhahood.
>
> —(GZ, 386)

Attended an evening discussion meeting at M.'s in Ota ward. It was quite successful, several guests deciding to join at once. Carried out the dignified practice of propagation. Extremely delighted.

Regret missing Mr. Toda's lecture.

Returned home just after 10:00. Put on a record and read poetry by Walt Whitman:

> *Proud music of the storm,*
> *Blast that careers so free, whistling across the prairies,*
> *Strong hum of forest tree-tops — wind of the mountains,*
> *Personified dim shapes — you hidden orchestras,*
> *You serenades of phantoms with instruments alert,*
> *Bending with Nature's rhythmus all the tongues of nations;*
>   — "PROUD MUSIC OF THE STORM," LEAVES OF GRASS

Tuesday, April 24. Clear.

Growing warmer, day by day.

My apartment is now also a scene of activity and much commotion.

Left home at 7:30, stopped for breakfast, then on to the office.

Read from *The Complete Works of Torahiko Terada* while on the train.

Because I was tired and it was quite late, I spent the night at Y.'s. My first night away from home in a while. Read and discussed "The Opening of the Eyes" with the other youths halfway through the night. Although this Gosho is difficult to comprehend, the Daishonin's conviction resounds in my heart. In these troubled times, how worthy of respect it is for youths in such strained circumstances to meet in such a shabby house to study Nichiren Daishonin's philosophy.

All are serious. All pure-hearted. The Daishonin's great mercy will strongly and deeply penetrate the unsullied hearts of these youths.

After the discussion, we went out onto the balcony, which was bathed in moonlight. One young man talked about the future, while another related his hopes and still another proclaimed his resolution with a poem. Youths of poverty, destitute sons of revolution! You are to be congratulated on the path that lies ahead of you! A few slices of pickled radish, served in large bowls, became our evening meal. Ten years from now, this chance encounter will be our precious memory.

Wednesday, April 25. Clear.

Attended Gohonzon-enshrining ceremonies with Mr. Toda at the homes of Y. and M. My teacher's determination is becoming more and more sublime. He seems in deep contemplation. The Soka Gakkai's progress is decided entirely by Mr. Toda's determination and progress.

Met priests Hosoi and Chigusa. Thinking of the prosperity our religion will enjoy ten years in the future fills me with joy.

Late at night, my brother came to visit me. Shed tears when I saw him.

To bed, 1:30.

Thursday, April 26. Clear.

Say these things mildly but firmly in a quiet voice with a calm gaze and an even expression.

—"The Teaching, Practice and Proof" (WND, 478)

The five characters of Myoho-renge-kyo, the heart of the essential teaching of the Lotus Sutra, contain the benefit amassed through the countless practices and meritorious deeds of all Buddhas throughout the three existences.

—"The Teaching, Practice and Proof" (WND, 481)

My physical condition is quite bad. Pondered deeply whether this is caused by some slander I may have committed.

Visited T. in Tachikawa. An evil man. Regret having maintained faithful friendship with him, not realizing him to be such a schemer. I was misled by his status as a senior graduate from the same school.

An evening youth division meeting. Discussed "On the Four Stages of Faith and Five Stages of Practice." Given an assignment on the 'three assemblies in two places' by Mr. Toda.

Must deeply ponder the Daishonin's teachings and study them systematically. Must undertake my study based upon faith.

Ashamed of my shallow Buddhist study. I can only forge ahead.

Encouraged U., whom I met looking downcast at Koiwa Station. The image of his joyous expression lingers in my mind.

Home at 11:30.

Friday, April 27. Clear.

Could observe, for the first time, the behavior of a court bailiff. Clearly witnessed the strictness of the legal system, or rather, the miserable state of the weak. Can only pity them—is this reality? Feel that I now know a bit more about society's harshness and complexity. Aware that I have been too innocent and idealistic until today.

The Soka Gakkai is advancing faster and faster. Our district must also try its best. Must make the propagation spirit and our organization's solidification the fundamental causes for our development. In any case, I myself must strive, I must be responsible.

The wind blew all day. Read a little from the complete works of Kyoson Tsuchida (1891–1935).

The "Letter from Sado" states, "When an evil ruler in consort with priests of erroneous teachings tries to destroy the correct teaching and do away with a man of wisdom, those with the heart of a lion king are sure to attain Buddhahood. Like Nichiren, for example"(WND, 302).

To bed, after 2:00.

Saturday, April 28. Cloudy.

A sultry wind blew all day. Not feeling quite well. An empty day.

A meeting with T. Construction Company lasted through the morning.

Attended an evening discussion meeting at S.'s. No guests came. A spiritless meeting.

> In the same way, the renegade disciples say, "Though the priest Nichiren is our teacher, he is too forceful. We will spread the Lotus Sutra in a more peaceful way." In so asserting, they are being as ridiculous as fireflies laughing at the sun and moon, an anthill belittling Mount Hua, wells and brooks despising the river and the ocean, or a magpie mocking a phoenix.
>
> —"LETTER FROM SADO" (WND, 306)

Read for a while. To bed, after 3:00.

Sunday, April 29. Light rain.

Stayed in bed until 10:00. Feel as if this fatigue has been building up daily in my exhausted body. Could this be the accumulated fatigue of the past several years? Visited by N. and B. Strongly debated with them.

Went to the barber for the first time in a while. Stopped by the baths on the way home. A hot and humid day—my physical condition is not good at all. For our district's progress, I visited the home of W. of Magome District, a place that brings back fond memories. Lost two precious hours, since he was not home. Will visit M.'s on the fifth of next month, to introduce him to the Daishonin's teachings. Returned home dispirited. Sensei, please forgive me, for I will definitely make our district advance next month.

Read before going to bed, after 2:00.

Thursday, May 3. Clear.

The second Soka Gakkai president, Mr. Josei Toda, was inaugurated. The place — Josen-ji in Mukojima.

Fine weather. The ceremony began at 2:00, and the day's events ended at 9:00, after a celebration.

At last, Mr. Toda has become president. This was the long-awaited, common wish of all his disciples. I will remember this day for the rest of my life. A thousand and some several hundred must have attended.

Advance! Holding high the banner of the Mystic Law, toward attaining kosen-rufu. Two billion people await us, await the Soka Gakkai's bold advance.

The leaders' faces were clear and bright as the new organization implementation was announced. Everyone was in high spirits, each determination, lecture and resolution statement filled with dynamic vigor. I sat by myself in the center of the meeting, quietly listening to my mentor and the other senior leaders, thinking that no one but Mr. Toda is aware that a lone youth's sights are firmly set on the Soka Gakkai's path ten years into the future.

An unforgettable memory — to see my mentor joyfully tossed into the air after the ceremony. Cannot forget the eyes of H., who always ponders so deeply the Soka Gakkai's future. Before returning, stood at the temple door to gather donations for the Gohonzon that will be bestowed on the Soka Gakkai. Home, a little before 11:00.

Sunday, May 13. Clear.

Only Nam-myoho-renge-kyo. Coming to feel that, ultimately, there is no other way but faith. Plans, methods, efforts or wisdom alone don't always yield expected results. Without embracing the Mystic Law, we cannot lead a free and magnanimous life, nor can we establish happiness.

Saw a play at the Mitsukoshi Theater at 11:00 along with all the company's employees. Went to Mr. Toda's house where he began to lecture on Nichikan's commentary on "The Entity of the Mystic Law." Extremely difficult. Must remember to listen carefully, without asking useless questions.

From "Letter to the Mother of Oto Gozen":

> There was once a woman who traveled a thousand miles to see the man she loved, at various times transforming herself into a rock, a tree, a bird or a snake.

—(GZ, 1223)

Must try my best again from tomorrow. The only way is to be strict with myself and advance throughout my life. Read, then to bed at 3:00.

Monday, May 14. Cloudy.

A Gohonzon-enshrining ceremony for Miss Y. of Kamata Chapter at 7:00. Mr. Toda attended, and I accompanied him.

The S. family is bright and happy. It is easy to see that Mr. Toda cares for them dearly. Even among those who practice faith, there are people or families who give us good feelings, as well as those who make us uncomfortable. It seems to me that the people or families who leave us with a good impression are those with pure faith, who are sincere and happy.

Read until midnight. Had many thoughts.

I would like, someday, to write a long poem titled "Religious Revolution."

Sunday, May 20. Cloudy.

M. and S. came by. As soon as they left, Y. came over. Together, we went to Omori for propagation activities. Really troubled over my own inability to introduce others.

Returned to my room early in the evening. Spent the day feeling vaguely lonely. What a miserable day it was.

Rested and read a magazine. To bed, 11:00.

Monday, May 21. Clear.

Truly fine weather.

My head aches. Fatigued.

Could this exhaustion be caused by last night's nightmare? Felt empty all day. Defeated in battle.

Visited M.'s in the afternoon. Though weak, they are a good family. On the way home, visited Y.'s. Engaged him in dialogue, taking a dauntless attitude. He seems to have felt something.

Character determines destiny. The stouthearted may be strong but may still suffer greatly.

"Questions and Answers on Embracing the Lotus Sutra" reads:

Now, if you wish to attain Buddhahood, you have only to lower the banner of your arrogance, cast aside the staff of your anger, and devote yourself exclusively to the one vehicle of the Lotus Sutra. Worldly fame and profit are mere baubles of your present existence, and arrogance and prejudice are ties that will fetter you in the next one. Ah, you should be ashamed of them! And you should fear them, too!

—(WND, 58–59)

Tuesday, May 22. Cloudy.

A warm day. Things are not going smoothly at work. Troubled. There is an expression "Advance one step and retreat two." Faith is absolutely the only way to a solution.

This year we conducted the first Omori District discussion meeting. Only four guests attended. Shocked, as this truly was not what I had expected. Why do so few people seek this faith, this True Law? Felt alone, dejected. All I can do is fight with all my might until the end. The motion of a single wave yields two, then a thousand and ten thousand waves. Through the power of the Mystic Law, the day will definitely arrive when people beg us to be allowed to take faith. Until then, I will try my best. I must do my best. If I try my best, this is enough. The members are all fighting hard. They are truly admirable. Fellow members, I congratulate you! Let the flower of happiness blossom—for this, I feel like praying.

Wednesday, May 23. Light rain.

A great day.

Spoke with M. about various matters for about two hours in the afternoon. He is really trying hard. I appreciate him from the bottom of my heart.

Lectured in the evening to a dozen or so members at I.'s house on "The Opening of the Eyes" and "Reply to Hakiri Saburo." Everyone looked delighted. Nothing makes me happier than to see members' spirits raised even a little.

Returned home at 8:50. Tried working on copy for *The Daibyakurenge* but could make no progress. Felt discouraged. When will the day come that I can satisfactorily express my thoughts in writing? Prayed to the Gohonzon to convince U. and T. to take faith this month so that they may be saved from unhappiness. To bed, 12:00.

Friday, May 25. Clear.

In the evening, fourteen eager youths gathered for a lecture from Mr. Toda. It was on "Letter from Sado." Must try my best.

Regret that I cannot progress as I desire. Some days I feel so miserable I want to cry. I keep worrying about Omori District. Will pray to the Gohonzon for it to become a perfect district.

Why are youth's minds always changing? Inspiration, despair, joy, suffering, the desire for improvement, dejection, high spirits, worry, optimism, caution.... In any event, I must be youthful. Must live as befits a young man. To bed 3:00.

Saturday, May 26.

In the evening, Mr. Toda gave a Gosho lecture at the headquarters. Tomorrow, I will accompany the youth division chief, T. and three other youths to the Tochigi area for propagation, staying overnight. Delighted, as it will be my first expedition to campaign in an outlying area.

My district has many points that need improvement. U. and T. came by late in the evening. Inwardly, I feel some Gakkai members could use a little more common sense. Spontaneity deserves respect. Nonetheless, it should be appropriate. Actions that cause trouble for others can in no way be called spontaneity. Rather, we could conclude that those who act in such a way are taking advantage of Buddhism.

Qualities like courtesy and common sense should serve to enhance spontaneity. They should not exist merely for their own sake.

When each individual understands the True Law, and it becomes the driving force, the fundamental principle for that age, how deep the nation's foundation will be! How reasonable and splendid a society will be established! People will then lead lives free from contradictions and deadlocks.

The True Law: Understand it deeply!
The True Law: Spread it widely!
The True Law: Apply it powerfully to your daily life!
The True Law: Praise it highly!
The True Law: Let it flow, purely, to the depths of your life!

Returned home, 11:30. To bed, 2:00.

Wednesday, May 30. Clear.

India is called the land of the moon because it was there that the Buddha made his appearance. Japan is called the land of the sun; now could a sage fail to appear there? Just as the moon moves from west to east, the Buddhism of India has spread toward the east. The sun rises in the east. This is a sign that the Buddhism of Japan will one day return to India. The feeble light of the moon [of Shakyamuni's Lotus Sutra] illuminated this world for a mere eight years. The brilliance of the sun far surpasses that of the moon. This indicates that [the Buddhism of the sun] will illuminate the long darkness of the fifth five-hundred years. The Buddha did not cure those who slandered the Lotus Sutra, for they did not appear in his lifetime. But in the Latter Day of the Law, powerful enemies of the one vehicle will abound. The blessings [which result from propagation in such an age] will be the same as those of Bodhisattva Fukyo. You who are my disciples must exert yourselves thoroughly.

—(GZ, 576)

More and more like summer every day.
First, believe in the Gohonzon.
First, never doubt the Gohonzon.
First, continue to pray to the Gohonzon.
First, never leave the Gohonzon.
First, proclaim the greatness of the Gohonzon.

Home at 11:00.

Thursday, May 31. Light rain.

May is over. The greater the hardships we encounter, the more courageous and passionate we must become.

Youth who live to propagate the Great Pure Law, this is your destiny, your mission. Advancing toward kosen-rufu, determined youth. How many true comrades in faith are there? My true friends, who are they? Does my heart know them? My faith is only in the Gohonzon. Aren't those who fully believe in the Gohonzon truly reliable? And truly reliable comrades—aren't they those who truly believe in the Gohonzon?

To bed, 1:30.

Wednesday, June 6. Clear.

Awoke at 6:50. Did gongyo, feeling refreshed both in body and spirit. Not to be filled with vitality and burning with passion during the precious years of youth would be a waste. *Advancement*—what a youthful word, filled with possibilities for the future. I will, throughout my life, use and practice this word both in name and in reality. *Advancement*— this word implies growth, hope, courage, youth and justice.

1. Finish copy for the article to be used for propagation by the 15th.
2. Exert myself to make my district prosper.

Discussed various matters with Miss M. at Y.'s.

Revolutionaries, poets, thinkers, politicians, educators—aren't their endeavors all included within Buddhism's essence? Alone, thinking deeply about Mr. Toda. Read a book.

The greater the man, the deeper his love. To bed, 3:00.

Friday, June 8. Light rain.
1. Write a poem titled "Forward, White Horse!"
2. Reflect on myself for not compiling President Toda's guidance.
3. Strictly and seriously refrain from overestimating myself.
4. Be clear about what I do and don't know.
5. Take people's good qualities to heart and make them a model for myself.

Saturday, June 9. Light rain.

None of you who declare yourselves to be my disciples should ever give way to cowardice. Neither should you allow concern for your parents, wife, or children to hold you back, or be worried about your property. Since countless kalpas in the past you have thrown away your life more times than the number of dust particles of the land for the sake of your parents, your children, or your lands. But not once have you given up your life for the Lotus Sutra. You may have tried to practice its teachings to some extent, but whenever you were persecuted, you backslid and ceased to live by the sutra. That is like boiling water only to pour it into cold water, or like trying to strike fire but giving up halfway. Each and every one of you should be certain deep in your heart that sacrificing your life for the Lotus Sutra is like trading rocks for gold or dung for rice.

—"THE ACTIONS OF THE VOTARY OF THE LOTUS SUTRA" (WND, 764)

A dinner party with business acquaintances at the F. restaurant in Shinjuku, near Tsurumi. Attended with Mr. Toda at 7:00. Later, attended a discussion meeting at a Suginami school. A few guests participated. All joined. Participated in propagation activities and gave guidance in high spirits before returning home, feeling exhilarated.

It is now mid-1951. How quickly the time has gone! How will I, the company and society change in the next ten years? No one can know.

Those who can continue to advance boldly, according to their own convictions, without being swayed by others, are great. Without being stubborn or narrow-minded, they must have firm conviction in the fundamental truth.

Many appear to be great individuals. But looking more closely, they lack compassion. For myself, all that remains is to follow Mr. Toda. Must seriously caution Miss Y. and K.

Sunday, June 10. Light rain.

Before the Gohonzon, I must make a vow and deeply apologize. Also I must reflect on the following points:

1. Take action for propagation and practice for others.
2. Awaken to a sense of responsibility for the sake of my district.
3. Be careful about my speech.
4. Deeply reflect on my tendency to insist on my own viewpoint.
5. Be careful to show proper courtesy to senior members.

My language and actions with regard to Y. were clearly wrong. Must reflect. There is truly no end to my problems.

When we reflect, we can advance. Resolutely, determinedly. Nothing else suits my nature.

Saturday, June 30. Light rain.

A busy month of fierce struggles. The first half of the year is now over. Tomorrow, or rather now, July begins.

Read the newspaper on the train. Reading the international news, I feel a strong urge to travel to various countries as soon as possible. Seriously thinking about studying English.

In the afternoon, visited the homes of S., Y., M. and O. Talked about many things. They are all good people.

Met S. at Omori Station in the evening. We ate dinner together. Had a small meeting with K., I. and M. in my apartment. Apologized for not having met with them in such a long time. To bed, 2:00 a.m.

1 9 5 2

THE GAKKAI BEGAN THE year with a membership of 5,727 families. Converting 16,597 families in the course of the year, it reached a membership of 22,324 families in 1952, surpassing its goal of 20,000. In February, under the leadership of Kamata Chapter senior staff member Daisaku Ikeda, the chapter accomplished an unprecedented conversion of 201 households. That historic month paved the way for the Soka Gakkai's traditional February propagation activities. Kamata Chapter's 1952 result was the highest of any of the sixteen chapters throughout the nation.

On May 3, Daisaku Ikeda married Kaneko Shiraki.

The year 1952 might be called a major turning point in Japan's postwar history. On April 28, Japan's independence was restored with the enactment of the San Francisco peace accord. At the same time, a security agreement went into effect between Japan and the United States. The same year also saw movements for the enactment of an Anti-Subversive Activities Act, the reestablishment of a police reserve security force, and a strong push for remilitarization and for implementing a public security system. The response to such government trends was an explosion of anger, particularly among laborers and metropolitan center residents. This resulted in a number of violent protests, the most tragic of which occurred on May 1 and was remembered as the "bloody May Day incident."

Friday, December 5. Clear.

We have now entered the last month of 1952. What a year of unforgettable memories this has been.

Home at 10:00. The brilliant moon shining in the cold night sky makes me temporarily forget the whirlpool of intense struggle I am in the midst of. How it calms my agitated mind, affording a respite to prepare me for tomorrow and the future! This is the Buddhism of 'the oneness of body and mind.' I have never before been as keenly aware of this principle, in my body, my spirit and my life, as I have this year. Rather, this year I sensed it so deeply I often felt alone or in anguish.

President Toda's physical condition is extremely poor. I, too, am in poor health.... How discouraging! Sensei, please take care of yourself!

Gohonzon! Watch over my destiny also! I must stand up for my great mission and fight.

Read from the *Tale of the Heike*.

Saturday, December 6. Fine weather.

The clear sky is more precious than ten thousand gold pieces. There are days when I feel deep gratitude and appreciation for the sun. From the perspective of the great workings of nature, how trivial matters of human conflict or political unrest appear to be! How limited and narrow people are!

A religion like the sun — no, greater, as the universe itself. This is the Daishonin's Buddhism. No philosophy or religion other than this Buddhism can illuminate the darkness of the ten thousand years of the Latter Day of the Law.

From 2:00, prepared for tomorrow's seventh Soka Gakkai general meeting at the Gakkai headquarters — K., I., K. and myself. Finished at 8:00. After gongyo, went to Chuo University Auditorium with ten youth division members to make final arrangements. Grateful for these youths' devoted attitude.

Very tired. Returned home at 11:20. My faith is entirely in the Gohonzon.

To bed, 1:00.

Sunday, December 7. Clear and pleasant.

The seventh general meeting was held. Fine weather. Awoke at 6:30. Took a taxi directly to the meeting place, arriving at 7:30.

At 9:10, the historic meeting began. Some five thousand people completely filled the auditorium. I was the master of ceremonies. The meeting ended at 3:45, a complete success. After the meeting, a dinner party. On the way back home, I bought a muffler for my wife to commemorate today's meeting. Went to the baths for the first time in awhile. Alone in the bath, I contemplated the Gakkai's future. Mr. Toda seems somewhat dispirited. I'm worried about him. To bed, 1:30.

Monday, December 8. Clear, then high clouds.

My health has improved. The final battle of the seven-hundredth anniversary year of Nichiren Daishonin's Buddhism. In the evening, met with Mr. Giichiro Shiraki. Together, we visited S. in Yaguchi and were treated to sukiyaki. It was very tasty.

A little over twenty days left to the year. To bring in a splendid year, I wish to spend the remaining days of this year meaningfully. Next year, my twenty-fifth, ought to be a most brilliant and dynamic year. This year has been a succession of battles with obstacles and devils. But it was also a year of splendid victories. I want next year to be the same.

Read some Chinese poetry before going to bed.

Tuesday, December 9. Rain and sleet, first snowfall.

Snow fell from noon. A cold day. Rain, wind and snow in nature, as well as the rain, wind and snow that exist within our lives, all become a stage setting for developing and polishing ourselves.

The great universe possesses the Ten Worlds. My life, too, contains the Ten Worlds. So there should be nothing in the world to fear.

Gave a lecture at Kawagoe District, in Saitama Prefecture. Finished at 8:00. Talked with T. for almost twenty minutes.

Visited Mr. Toda's a little before 10:00. Spoke with his wife for nearly an hour.

Since the end of the war, the word *revolution* has come to be used quite frequently. It has even become somewhat fashionable. The term *human revolution*, however, has real meaning. Have come to realize that this revolution, in other words the transformation of our destiny, can only be accomplished through faith.

Wednesday, December 10. Overcast.

Warmer today. Work went smoothly. Stopped by my father's company around 11:30. Deeply pleased to see him working so hard in such high spirits. He treated me to sushi for lunch.

Attended a discussion meeting at 6:30 in the evening at Kigetsu in Kawasaki. Overjoyed to see the members' fresh and lively spirits. Headed for home, praying they will all still be striving in such high spirits five or ten years from now.

Home at 11:30.

Having my own family has changed my life in many ways from the days when I was single. There are good sides and troublesome sides to married life. On one hand it has been a real help to me, while on the other, I sometimes feel as if my freedom has been curtailed.

Convinced that the direct path, the shortest route to a happy life for oneself and one's family, in a spiritual, physical and material sense, is absolutely nothing other than faith.

Sunday, December 14. Clear.

Slept through the morning. I wish I could say I slept well, but I was disturbed by a succession of bad dreams. In the end, I was still tired.

Went to Omori with my wife to look for a suit. Evening, met with leaders in Yaguchi to discuss various matters and make preparations for upcoming activities. Decided to start tomorrow to make year-end preparations for Gakkai activities and for the company.

1. Detailed planning.
2. Well-organized administration.
3. Ability to take broad-minded action.
4. Unyielding progress.

Many thoughts. Such is the heart of a youth who embraces a great ambition. Read *The New Tales of Heike*, by Eiji Yoshikawa[1]. Very interesting. To bed, 1:30.

1. *The New Tales of Heike*, by Eiji Yoshikawa: (Jpn *Shin Heike monogatari*) Considered to be the lifework of Yoshikawa. Written following the trauma of Japan's defeat in World War II. Depicts the tumultuous power struggles of the late twelfth century as seen through the eyes of a groundskeeper in the Imperial Palace. Portrays the arrogance of power and the indomitability of the common people.

Tuesday, December 16. Rain.

A Suiko Group meeting at 6:00. Those who met were the president, the secretary-general, the guidance division chief, as well as the corps chiefs, corps staff and one representative group chief from each YMD corps.

Read from the preface of *Tales of Suiko*. Mr. Toda then discussed the Suiko Group's significance, mission and conviction. Thirty-eight attended. Young phoenixes, resolutely carrying out their revolution in the realms of religion, politics and society. Each, overflowing with a fighting spirit that seemed to soar into the heavens. Their conviction and courage are strong enough to move the ocean. I trust them deeply. I can picture them ten years from now.

Must:
1. Exert myself in study.
2. Excel in my specific areas of responsibility.
3. Carry out my activities with courageous resolve.
4. Become a considerate and decisive leader.

The meeting adjourned at 9:00 with the spirited singing of the Sendai Chapter song.

Wednesday, December 17. Cloudy.

Warm all day. My head aches. Shopped at Mitsukoshi Department Store for New Year's gifts for my family and others. Attended R.'s corps discussion meeting at 7:00. A successful meeting—about eighty people attended. The youth division is growing day by day. The foundation of kosen-rufu, the pillar of the Soka Gakkai, lies nowhere but in the youth division.

Never seek others' approval. My actions are witnessed by the Gohonzon. Have I no regrets? I do—many, but I must forge ahead.

Returned home at 11:00. Read from *Tales of Suiko*.

Thursday, December 18. Clear.

The New Year's holiday atmosphere is reaching a fevered pitch. Went to Keihin Department Store to look for New Year's gifts, then to S.'s and K.'s to give my best wishes, and then to Mr. Toda's in the evening to wish him a happy New Year. Received guidance on various points for about an hour.

The S. Press stubbornly persists in slandering the Soka Gakkai with a series of unfounded, malicious articles. We cannot suppress our anger. Decided to visit them with several others to negotiate a retraction.

I am realizing all the more that our Soka Gakkai is a religious organization correctly carrying out the Buddha's will. So many other religious bodies in Japan today are merely businesses that, without efforts in propagation, focus on hiding their weakness behind the power of money. The Gakkai is pure. It will never compromise with authority, financial power, or evil or diabolical influences. The function of a devil is to deplete one's life of Buddhahood.

Will protect President Toda to the best of my ability—as long as I live. I have but one reason. That is, to protect President Toda is to protect the spread of faith in the Gohonzon. In the way of mentor and disciple, the two must be of one mind. I have only to advance straight ahead along this highest path.

Mr. Toda's majestic image never leaves my mind, not even for a moment.

Read *Tales of Suiko* before going to bed at 1:30.

Friday, December 19. Partly cloudy.

A severe day. Began negotiations with the S. Press. From 3:00, a general staff meeting. H., Miss K., K., B., T., U., H., I., R. and myself. Finished at 5:30, then to a youth division leaders planning meeting. At 7:00, a lecture by President Toda on the "The Entity of the Mystic Law." After the lecture, I met with the five research division members, one representing each corps, instructing them on various matters. Left with T. and U.

Purchased a suit for ¥12,000.

Faith. Will spend my life establishing my faith. When viewed from the perspective of life's eternity, that should be the objective of this life. Those around us may criticize us. But no one else teaches the answers to the fundamental questions of life. When it comes to these fundamental questions alone, it is unnecessary to ask others' opinions. The correct way is simply to practice as Nichiren Daishonin taught. Next year, I will further exert myself in faith and advance in practice. I will apply myself thoroughly to studying Buddhism. I will gain trust and respect as a youth.

Read *Tales of Suiko*.

Sunday, December 21. Fog.

A chilly Sunday. Slept until noon. T. came by. I really pity him, but I can do nothing except encourage him to take faith.

At 6:00, the research committee met at the headquarters. Advance! Advance! Must hasten the establishment of a reliable communication network.

At 8:30, I invited some of my seniors and fellow members over for sukiyaki. Everyone ate well. My wife later told me we almost ran out of beef and rice.

Monday, December 22. Clear and fine.

The last district chiefs meeting of the year was held at 7:00, at the headquarters, in conjunction with a year-end party. Very dull. Very few among the senior leaders really consider the youth. In fact, none do. Can they think only of their own affairs? I wish each would reflect that without raising capable juniors to shoulder the responsibilities of the coming era, we cannot secure the foundation of kosen-rufu after Mr. Toda dies.

I am seriously concerned, since they are people whose positions should be deeply respected from the standpoint of faith.

Returned home, 11:30.

Happiness is not to be found in material wealth alone, nor in the pursuit of fame or pleasure. Ultimately, it lies only in tapping the world of Buddhahood through faith. This is accomplished through ceaseless activity, practice and action. To bed, 12:30.

Tuesday, December 23. Clear.

A warm day. Mr. Toda is back in high spirits. Sensei! As long as I am here, please don't worry. Please rest assured!

I. is a fine senior, a man of great ability. I will protect him.

Rested in my apartment for about two hours, then attended a chapter leaders meeting at 7:00 p.m. — two hundred gathered. Our chapter converted 430 families this month. Such growth is truly astonishing. Next year we will boldly accomplish an unprecedented five hundred new members in one month.

Have no regrets about this year's struggle. Think I have fought well. I say this not out of self-satisfaction or arrogance.

Wednesday, December 24. Overcast.

T. received the Gohonzon. Faith is his only hope. Cannot help pitying him. Shall never forget him, as long as I live.

A headquarters leaders meeting from 7:00 at Myoko-ji. Afterward, went with a few others to G.'s Gohonzon-enshrining ceremony. The image of his grandmother heartily participating in enshrinement preparations deeply impressed me.

Profoundly moved by Mr. Toda's constant concern for my parents and my brothers.

Stand up! Advance, like a young warrior! I shall boldly sound the bell of glory, in my own heart, and for all humankind.

Thursday, December 25. Overcast.

T. came over in the morning. He is sincerity itself. Just a few days remain in this seven-hundredth year since the establishment of Nichiren Daishonin's Buddhism. Constantly thinking about next year. Today, again, I worked to my heart's content.

Short of money. Now in utter poverty. What shall I do?

Attended a Dragon Corps leaders meeting. Deeply delighted to see such spirited youths. In business, revolution, labor, politics, education or science — in any age or endeavor, one cannot achieve victory without making an ally of youth. The key to every battle, to victory or defeat, lies in whether one wins the allegiance of or makes an enemy of youth.

Returned home, 11:30.

Many problems plague individuals, families, society and the world. Absolutely none is more important, however, than the problem of death.

My physical condition is poor. Even speaking is a burden. May have a fever. Had my wife give me an innoculation.

To bed, 1:50.

Friday, December 26. Cloudy, then rain.

A cold morning. I consider enduring the cold wind as training for both my body and mind. Must grow strong, to become someone on whom others can rely. I am now embraced by my mentor and protected by my parents. I have excellent comrades in faith. Society, too, enjoys better times.

Wish to become a leader who will never be swayed, who can always protect my juniors no matter what adversity I might encounter. Praying strongly that my fellow members and my family will spend the year-end enjoyably and safely. Wish to read many books next year. I will read and read and read. Next year will be my year of study. This is so I will not fall behind the Gakkai's advancement.

Sunday, December 28. Clear and pleasant.

Slept in. Feel a bit recovered from my fatigue. Y., N. and K. came by at 12:30. We ate, talked and sang until 4:00. Polished plans for next year's activities.

In the evening, visited Mr. Toda with my wife. Received guidance and warnings on various matters. Very happy. Left at 10:30.

I. is an excellent leader. I respect him deeply. Wish my fellow members, my friends, my seniors and juniors to be people of whom I can be proud.

To bed at 12:30.

Tuesday, December 30. Clear and fine.

For me, it has been a peaceful year-end. Went alone to O.'s house in Kanagawa to pay my respects and give them a New Year's gift. Was not feeling well. Returned home at 3:00 and immediately took my temperature: 102° F. To bed early in the evening. Leafed through some magazines.

Wednesday, December 31. Cloudy.

Today is the finale of 1952, the final glorious day of the seven-hundredth year of the history of Nichiren Daishonin's Buddhism.

For me, too, it is one of the few remaining days I will spend as a twenty-four-year-old youth.

At 4:00 we had a year-end company gathering. Everyone surrounded President Toda as he gave guidance to each individual, one by one. To some he was strict, while to others, he spoke of the next ten years to come. He also spoke of problems with the economy and foreign policy. Sometimes he would mention the importance of Buddhist study, while to others he spoke of his own childhood and youth. I ate until my stomach hurt. Everyone ate and drank well. Returned home a little before 8:00, put on a record, and spent a quiet, peaceful evening. A happy and harmonious family. Grateful that I can enjoy the greatest, supreme sort of happiness, illuminated by the Mystic Law.

THE SOKA GAKKAI YOUTH division organization at the outset of 1953 consisted of four *butai* or corps for the young men's division and five for the young women's division. Each corps was composed of youth from several of the Soka Gakkai's sixteen chapters. The First YMD corps, to which Daisaku Ikeda was appointed chief, was made up of youth from the Koiwa, Mukojima and Joto chapters. By the latter part of November 1952, this corps had some 316 young men, and 1953 saw YMD activities centered around vigorous propagation. As reported at the March 3 youth division meeting, YMD propagation results were: First Corps, 515 households; Second Corps, 217 households; Third Corps, 19 households; and Fourth Corps, 20 households.

The lyrics to "Gojogen" are taken from a poem by the same name from the anthology *Tenchi Ujo*, by Bansui Doi, the famous Japanese poet. The composer is unknown. The song tells the story of Zhu-ge Kong-ming and his unyielding loyalty to Liubei Xuan-de, the minister of the kingdom of Shu, during the period of the Three Kingdoms of China (220–80). This song, which Daisaku Ikeda led during the New Year's party mentioned in the January 5 entry, resounded within President Toda's heart, and from then on, the song was sung throughout the Gakkai. A detailed account of the "Gojogen" story, taken from the Chinese semifictional historical work *The Romance of the Three Kingdoms*, can be found in the "Flight" chapter of volume 7 of Daisaku Ikeda's *The Human Revolution*.

Japan began 1953 in the midst of an economic recession. In spring there was a shift in the world of education. Many school-age children in Japan could not attend classes for some time or could not attend school at all because they were forced to work during the day to help support their families. Schools in Katsushika, Sumida, Ota and other Tokyo wards began holding night classes for middle-school–age students. According to a February 1 *Asahi Shimbun* (daily newspaper) report, the night-school students were not in the least inferior to daytime students when it came to intelligence and physical or emotional development, and they seemed to have a far greater desire to learn than did their daytime counterparts.

Soviet Premier Joseph Stalin died on March 6. He was succeeded as premier by Georgi Malenkov. Other significant events of 1953 included the first successful hydrogen bomb test and the first ascent of Mount Everest, by a British climbing party. In Japan, television broadcasting began.

The Friday lecture mentioned in the March 6, June 12 and June 19 entries was a weekly lecture by President Toda directed toward newer members. To accommodate a rapid increase in participants, the lectures were moved to Toshima Civic Auditorium in Ikebukuro, Tokyo. Each week, members flocked in from throughout the city and adjoining prefectures to hear the president's lecture, fully packing the auditorium and leaving about two hundred people to listen from outside, many pressing their noses against the windowpanes as they eagerly absorbed President Toda's lecture.

On June 16, about a year after the Suiko Group was formed, the group was severely reprimanded by President Toda for having a too-easygoing attitude. Unable to formulate their next goal, they found themselves deadlocked. Deeply troubled by this, Daisaku Ikeda drafted three pledges or oaths to clarify the Suiko Group's purpose as heirs to the task of kosen-rufu. These consisted of (1) a pledge to the Gohonzon, (2) a pledge to President Toda, and (3) a pledge to fellow believers. On July 21, the newly reformed Suiko Group met once again with President Toda and together signed and affixed their thumb prints to this "Oath of Suiko."

On April 28, Daisaku and Kaneko Ikeda's first son, Hiromasa, was born.

In September, the *Seikyo Shimbun*, became a weekly publication, coming out every Sunday. The circulation was then 21,000. Also, in October, pilgrimages to the head temple were increased from one to two a month. As a result, the number of pilgrimage participants in October grew to about 4,000. A powerful advancement rhythm pulsated through every corner of the organization and from September 1953 on, the number of households converted each month never fell below 5,000.

The standard of living returned to a level comparable to that before the war, and the shortage of basic necessities abated. In autumn, however, inclement weather and flooding resulted in the most meager postwar rice harvest. Since government-rationed rice was far from enough to meet nutritional needs, most city dwellers had to buy rice on the black market. The price of this illegal rice almost doubled by the year-end, directly affecting every kitchen. Many supplemented their diet with wheat or rice mixed with other grains to make "artificial" rice. As Japan's main staple ran out, people survived on bread and other flour products, like noodles.

Incidents in which the Butsuryu (Erect Buddha) sect either attempted to or successfully confiscated and destroyed Gohonzon began in spring. By fall, twenty such incidents had been reported. As members of their sect increasingly switched to Nichiren Daishonin's Buddhism, fearful Butsuryu priests and lay leaders visited the homes of these new converts. There, they would illegally confiscate the Gohonzon and burn or destroy it in some manner. On October 15, 1953, Soka Gakkai youth division members met with Butsuryu sect representatives at their main temple in Tokyo. Confronting them on the issue, the Gakkai youths obtained a promise from the sect's leaders to prohibit further attacks.

Thursday, January 1. Clear and pleasant.

Awoke at 7:00.
New Year's morning.

A flower blossoms on the road to battle.

The first sunrise.
In my heart, too, the sun rises anew.

To the Gakkai headquarters at 10:00 for the year's first gongyo. A few dozen leaders gathered. I led the others in singing the "Song of Comrades" and the Sendai Chapter song. The meeting adjourned at 12:40. Took the first step in my human revolution for this year.

President Toda left for the head temple. I saw him off at Tokyo Station. He appeared to be feeling quite well. Overjoyed.

Had visitors in the evening. Chatted until 7:00.

The Gosho "On Prayer" reads:

> It makes no difference if the practitioner himself is lacking in worth, defective in wisdom, impure in his person, and lacking in virtue derived from observing the precepts. So long as he chants Nam-myoho-renge-kyo, they will invariably protect him. One does not throw away gold because the bag that holds it is dirty; one does not ignore the sandalwood trees because of the foul odor of the eranda trees around them; and one does not refuse to gather lotuses because the pond in the valley where they grow is not clean. If they ignore the practitioner of the Lotus Sutra, they will be going against their vow.
>
> —(WND, 345)

It is fitting that those who bravely uphold the Mystic Law, warriors who take the lead in the struggle for kosen-rufu, should advance with this conviction.

Friday, January 2. Cloudy.

My birthday today. I am now twenty-five. Lately, I deeply sense my destiny to carry on the struggle for kosen-rufu after my mentor is gone. Thankful that I can stand up, be active and fight without being confined to a sickbed.

Left for the year's first head temple pilgrimage on the 11:00 train from Tokyo. At the Rikyo-bo lodging house, President Toda announced my appointment as chief of the First YMD Corps. New Year's was the first step in the battle, as though it symbolized the rest of the year. Must take my stand as a brave young man, lead the youth, fearing nothing.

Saturday, January 3. Clear and pleasant.

Morning gongyo at the Rikyo-bo. 7:30. Mount Fuji soars brilliantly. Rather than calling it a sacred peak, I would call it a magnificent mountain of sublime masculine beauty. From amid its stoic solemnity floats a brilliant culture's fragrance. A truly fine mountain. Incomparable Mount Fuji. It is wondrous that this mountain exists in Japan. This mountain bears a profound relationship to the Daishonin's Buddhism. If an inanimate mountain could characterize Nichiren Daishonin, I think it would have to be Mount Fuji.

We chanted before the Dai-Gohonzon at 9:00. Offered many prayers toward next year's first ceremony of chanting before the Dai-Gohonzon. Departed the head temple at 3:00 on a very crowded train. Arrived home at 8:00. The S.s came over for a pleasant dinner.

Sunday, January 4. Clear and pleasant.

Stayed in bed until noon. Had many afternoon visitors. Saw them all, since I was well rested.

Treated my friends to sukiyaki. There were seven of us in all. We talked and ate until 12:00. The members are truly great. How wonderful it is to have friends!

Tomorrow, the decisive battle begins.

Monday, January 5. Overcast, then rain.

The first work day of the new year. Got to work at 9:00. A new year's banquet from 12:00, at the N. Chinese restaurant. We sang "A Star Falls in the Autumn Wind over Wu Zhang Yuan" for Mr. Toda. He had us sing it over and over again as he listened with tears in his eyes. Finished at 4:30.

At 5:30, I attended a ceremony at Josen-ji in Mukashima to appoint the new Koiwa Chapter chief. Intensely moved by Mr. Toda's profound consideration for his beloved disciples. Today will become an important day in Gakkai history. I was keenly aware of President Toda's leadership as we took a concrete step toward kosen-rufu.

Returned home, 11:00. Countless stars in the heavens shine for us! For the strong members and for the weak. For the troubled members and for the joyous.

Tuesday, January 6. Fair.

In the morning, Mr. Toda lectured on principles of law. Morning study is now in full swing. Must be clearheaded every morning so that I can absorb the lecture.

Indomitable spirit. Guts. Stubborn determination—these may not be elegant terms, but I believe they are necessary qualities for a man's life. Must fight hard now to ensure victory ten years from now. Will study hard and work hard, looking ahead ten years into the future.

At 6:00, a ceremony to appoint new corps chiefs was held at Jozai-ji in Ikebukuro. President Toda had us sing "A Star Falls in the Autumn Wind over Wu Zhang Yuan" again and again, as he wept openly. Why does he weep? Is it because he is troubled by this immature disciple?

I am disgusted with my own immaturity. I am twenty-five. Must study. Must discipline myself. Must develop. Amazed at my own shallowness.

Returned home, 10:30.

Wednesday, January 7. Clear, then cloudy.

A warm day.

Could not see President Toda all day long. Very lonesome. Went to a movie with some co-workers in the early evening. Saw *Duel* and *Scaramouche* at the Yurakuza. Later, attended a discussion meeting at I.'s. Determined to read at least fifty books this year. Began today—off to a great start.

Thursday, January 8. Fair, partly cloudy.

Went to R.'s at 2:00. Paid him ¥80,000—compensation for a traffic accident he was involved in. He showed no signs of gratitude. A disagreeable person. There is nothing more pitiful than a self-centered or authoritarian member.

The year's first corps chiefs conference was held at the headquarters. Our activities are becoming more vigorous. Our responsibilities are heavier than ever. The meeting ended at 9:00.

Thursday, January 15. Fair.

Coming-of-Age Day. Corps chiefs met at 4:00 at the G. restaurant in Shinjuku. President Toda was extremely upset with us. He scolded us severely, like a violent storm. The responsibility rests completely with me. Sensei, please forgive me.

Have decided to reflect on myself more seriously from now on. The path I must follow with respect to my mentor demands the greatest self-awakening. Deeply regret my thoughtlessness, having presumed upon President Toda's profound consideration. My own lack of realization is as clear as if reflected in a mirror. To trip over the same stone twice is indeed foolish. Will reflect, and then advance once again, cheerfully and boldly.

Representing all of us, I saw Mr. Toda home. Dismayed to find that not one person remained when I returned.

Friday, January 16. Fair.

Mr. Toda, suffering from a cold, stayed home all morning. Visited him to apologize for what happened yesterday. He told me: "So, it's sunk in deeply. Now you must act with conviction!" His words were filled with strict compassion. Reflecting more and more on my own shallowness. Must reflect deeply and sincerely on my frivolous attitude.

Mr. Toda gave his first Friday Gosho lecture of the year, finishing his lecture on "The Entity of the Mystic Law." Have now commenced this year's battle for kosen-rufu. Will charge forward, hoisting the First Corps banner.

Thursday, January 22. Cloudy, then fair.

Fine, springlike weather. Went with K. to Totsuka on business. Filled my lungs with the pleasant Tokai ocean scent.

Held this year's first First Corps leaders meeting at 7:00. The spirit of those who gathered soared into the heavens. Went to bed thinking about Mr. Toda. Have I served him well until today, or have I not? Have I acted sincerely? Have I traveled the path of mentor and disciple honorably? Ashamed of my incompetence as a disciple.

At 2:00, put down my pen to go to sleep.

Friday, January 23. Clear and fine.

The fine weather continues. Many problems trouble the world. The newspapers are devoid of any encouraging news. A dreadful world. It pains my youthful heart. The only security is to advance with bold determination, without begrudging my life.

Mr. Toda's lectures on the principles of law progress steadily. His lectures, his ideas are loftier than a mountain, deeper than the sea.

Went with Y. to Tsurumi for the first business dealings of the year. Like a young warrior on horseback, wherever I go, I will crown myself with victory.

Sunday, January 25. Clear, then overcast.

Received a report that Mr. Toda is not feeling well. Feeling quite bad myself. Rested until 10:00.

Thought about the other day's spiritless leaders meeting of Koiwa chapter, held at Masui's house. There were about sixty participants. They lacked joy and appeared to have lost confidence. Decided in my heart to charge forth with tremendous passion into this desertlike area. I am worried that these leaders, however, who lack spirit or an understanding of their mission, cannot accept my spirit and intent.

Whatever the chapter and whomever the members, I want them to become happy. Dreaming of making the Gakkai, with vigor and unity, a nationwide, even a worldwide organization. Convinced this can only be achieved through all the members attaining happiness. Disturbed by the shallowness and bias of two or three top leaders who do not understand President Toda's will. Visited Mr. Toda in the afternoon. He was delighted. It seemed he hadn't had visitors for some time.

Returned home, 10:30.

Monday, January 26. Overcast.

Worked vigorously all day. Gave a lecture for the first time this year. Feel I must study harder and harder. Had friends from work over for dinner late in the evening. Talked to our hearts' content about our dreams for the next twenty years.

Mr. Toda is not well. He stayed home from the office again today. Deeply resolved to fight joyfully by his side, whatever the battle. Strongly determined that I must absolutely redeem myself after having been such an unworthy disciple.

To bed, 12:30.

Tuesday, January 27. Rain, then snow.

A cold day. Mr. Toda was absent again. I think it best that he gets a good rest.

Snowflakes fell. Led a study session on the book *The Principles of Law*. We've made quite a bit of progress. Returned home at 8:00; went to bed early.

Ichinen, single-minded determination—this is what enables the arrow to pierce the rock, as the saying goes. Mr. Toda's frequent statement that "there is no power stronger or greater than faith" has gradually come to touch my heart.

Wednesday, January 28. Overcast.

Conducted my first district-level study lecture of the year. Spoke in high spirits, lecturing to my heart's content.

Following President Toda's advice, I began today to read *Eighteen Short Histories*, a novel of ancient China. Visited Mr. Toda's home late in the evening. He seems to have recovered. "I'll be going out from tomorrow!" he declared joyfully.

Thursday, January 29. Fair.

Sensei has regained his health. How splendid! In the evening, attended a Study Department lecture at the headquarters. On each such occasion, I keenly feel the need to study. A corps chiefs conference was held after the lecture. Treated the corps chiefs and the division chief to dinner at S. restaurant. Home at midnight. Want to advance, singing a triumphant song of life and youth!

Friday, January 30. Clear.

The Gakkai headquarters leaders meeting. Sensed the strict and solemn atmosphere. All were serious and filled with a fighting spirit. Felt it to be miniature world of Buddhas and bodhisattvas who have passionately arisen to achieve kosen-rufu. It is apparent, however, that steep mountains and violent storms await us. Will it be possible to achieve kosen-rufu in our time? Or will it be 50, 100 or 200 years from now? In the end, there is no other way for me but to devote this life, until I die, to the battle for propagation, with a determination, conviction and dream for two hundred years from now. January has already passed. Home at 10:30.

Sunday, February 1. Clear, then partly cloudy.

Youth division members came to receive guidance in twos and threes. Attend the monthly youth division meeting at 6:00 p.m. Witnessed their bold departure toward the coming year. How splendid! Someday, want Sensei to see the result of our behind-the-scenes unity and growth. I talked about the importance of study. I, myself, however, must first take the initiative and serve as example. Personally resolved to take a great leap forward during the coming year. The February campaign has begun, both officially and personally. As a young man, my foremost desire must be to roll up both sleeves and fully display my power and ability.

Monday, February 2. Clear.

A Study Department lecture. Warm all day. Have come to the part about the Hogen Civil War in *New Tales of Heike*. Deeply moved. Rise and fall, prosperity and decline — human history filled with discord and misery. I believe the greatest person is one who strives to attain a bloodless revolution, based on a correct view of humanity, the world and the universe. This is a standard that transcends commonly held views of right and wrong. Invited K. to drop by my home after the lecture.

Together with this senior and companion in study, studied the life of Nikko Shonin in *The Daibyakurenge* magazine. Home at 10:20.

Tuesday, February 3. Cloudy.

A district lecture on the Gosho "On Establishing the Four Bodhisattvas as the Object of Devotion." About forty attended. Feel sorry for those sincere members, since I lack capability as a lecturer. After the lecture, I gave personal guidance. To grasp people's true suffering, to hear their true voices and guide them, enabling them to find the solution, is the noblest work we can undertake in life. I only worry that I lack the power to do so.

Wednesday, February 4. Overcast, then clear.

Feeling wretched, as if a hot iron plate has been inserted into my back or a burning wooden pole driven into my chest. Once I recover my health and strength, there will be nothing to fear. Faith is the only solution.

Koiwa Chapter leaders meeting held at Josen-ji. Very successful. I, too, will stand up with a strong resolution. After the meeting, I accompanied Mr. Toda to the I.s' home. Witnessed the strict guidance of Buddhism and the Gakkai concerning I.'s problem. Felt as if I had been cut with a sharp sword. Saw Mr. Toda home. It was already 1:00 in the morning. This will become a historic evening, one filled with profound memories. Must study. Must become an excellent individual of fine capability.

Sunday, February 8. Clear and pleasant.

Fine weather. Can sense the fragrance and color of spring.

Made a pilgrimage to the head temple with Mr. Toda's wife. A day's journey. Left Tokyo on the 7:36 train to Hamamatsu.

Mr. Toda's health has not improved. Keenly feeling my determination for the Gakkai's future. Sensei, please live long!

I, too, am in poor health. But I am young. Must defeat the Devil of the Sixth Heaven. Felt exhausted in the train on the way home. Slept.

Tuesday, February 10. Clear and fine.

Physically and spiritually fatigued.

Gave a lecture at Kawagoe District in Saitama Prefecture on "Letter from Sado." About fifty gathered. Seems as if many capable people, as well as individuals of excellent character, have gradually appeared. Troubled about the conflict between the world's two armed camps — the communist nations and the free world. The progress of our movement will be a first step in building a bridge between these two world powers. We are powerless, however, to do anything as we are members; the people; humankind. We must wait for the right time.

Sunday, March 1. Overcast.

Springlike warmth. March has now begun, a season resplendent with life's hopes and ideals. This month, I will strive to the limits of my youthful ability. Will fully express myself as a youth.

Yesterday, visited S. and Miss H. to give guidance and to carry out propagation. Though it may seem impertinent of me since they are older, I had no choice but to do so.

S. lost his small, portable Gohonzon. He must deepen and purify his faith throughout his life. Only in this way can he apologize. I don't believe the Daishonin would allow someone with a sincere, pure mind to suffer over such a thing throughout his life. Ultimately, it is a matter of the individual and his sincerity.

At 4:40, Mr. Toda's wife stopped by. At 7:00, attended a leaders meeting of Koiwa Chapter.

Monday, March 2. Cloudy, then rain.

A meeting of new Study Department members was held at the headquarters. About fifty attended. Touched by the participants' sincere attitude toward the study of Buddhism. Ten or twenty years from now, these people will splendidly take the lead within the Gakkai and in the professional or academic world.

Light rain fell as I returned from the headquarters. T. and S. accompanied me home. Began to study Nichikan's "Commentary on 'The Object of Devotion for Observing the Mind.'"

1. Must exert myself in study.
2. Must approach it in a scholarly manner.

Talked until after 12:00.

Tuesday, March 3. Cloudy.

A youth division meeting at 6:00 at Jozai-ji. The First Corps was the best by far. Other corps members seemed struck with admiration.

The other day, I wrote a poem for each group chief, which I presented to them individually. Today, I wrote fresh words of encouragement for each corps chief.

I pray that, from among the members of my corps, men of power and ability for kosen-rufu will appear in rapid succession.

Members of my corps! I pray you will each develop into men who surpass me in capability.

Members of my corps! I pray not one of you will discard your faith.

These days, I deeply sense the tremendous mercy of the Gohonzon.

Wednesday, March 4. Clear and pleasant.

Heard President Toda is suffering from tonsilitis. Saw him in the office later in the day. Hope he will take good care of his health. To make this possible, we, his disciples, must mature all the more quickly.

Heard a report that Soviet Premier Joseph Stalin is in critical condition. The world is entering an era of great change. At 7:30, studied "The True Aspect of All Phenomena" with about twenty youth division members at my place. Adjourned at 10:30.

Feeling a little better.

Spring is coming, with its brightness and fragrance. Spring is on the way!

Hearts of youth! Resound! Take to the sky!

To bed, 12:30.

Friday, March 6. Clear and pleasant.

My physical condition has taken a complete turn for the worse. Last night, at a general staff meeting, President Toda gave guidance and scolded me harshly. Thought about it a great deal.

Tonight was the Friday lecture. Had trouble fighting off the urge to sleep in the middle of the lecture. It was the first time this has happened.

My wife's parents, S. and T., visited us. We talked until late. Everyone said they enjoyed coming over. It was after 11:00 when they left.

Reflected on many things. To bed, 1:30.

Sunday, March 8. Morning rain, clearing, then overcast.

Heavy morning rain. Awoke at 7:00. Hurried to Shinagawa Station. Set out to the head temple with Youth Division Chief T. and others.

12:00: Arrived at the head temple.

1:00: Met the high priest.
2:30: Chanted before the Dai-Gohonzon.
5:00: Departed from the head temple.

It is now six years since I began to practice this faith. So far, I have visited the head temple each month this year. This makes me truly happy. What good fortune I have! Truly pleased I could act to my heart's content for the people, for the Law and for society. This is the direct path to changing one's karma.

Georgi Malenkov will be the next premier of the Soviet Union.

Monday, March 9. Clear and pleasant.

A lecture for Study Department seniors at the headquarters. Mr. Toda's strictness and the earnestness of those attending remind me of the severe training of master swordsmen. Whenever I participate in a study meeting, I feel I have not studied enough. Profoundly aware of the importance of study. Left with U., the YMD chief. Wish I had good health.

Gakkai leaders must protect and encourage from the bottom of their hearts those who show promise for the future as well as those who are alone and those who are sincere.

Will deeply self-reflect. Must never be conceited. Must never lose the spirit of construction, training, effort and study throughout my life.

Returned home after 11:00.

Tuesday, April 7. Cloudy.

Physical condition poor all day. A miserable day. If only my health would improve!

The world is changing acutely. To the rest of the world, the Gakkai may still seem as insignificant as a particle of dust. But look at us ten, twenty, or rather, thirty years from now! There is no doubt the Daishonin's great philosophy will shine brilliantly throughout the world. Until then, we must fight. Until then, we must advance, we who possess a sense of responsibility and mission.

Finished reading *The Romance of the Three Kingdoms* for the third time.

Wednesday, April 8. Clear.

A corps chiefs conference. Lasted until 9:30.

Prepared for the general meeting on the 19th. Gradually, all plans seem to have come to completion.

April
> *Flowers blossom randomly,*
> *And scatter with the breeze.*

April
> *Youthful hearts, blossom fragrantly,*
> *And dance, to a youthful song of progress.*

April
> *Month of youth,*
> *Month of the young.*

April
> *The month when youth*
> *Sing of the joy of life.*

April
> *The month when Whitman, Goethe,*
> *Milton and Dante each sang from his*
> *heart, fought, suffered and advanced.*

Read a book in the evening.

Friday, June 12. Cloudy.

Proofread President Toda's lecture on "The Opening of the Eyes" with several other members from 6:00 p.m. at the Gakkai headquarters annex. It reminded me of my early days on the editorial staff.

The Friday lecture was conducted at 7:30 at Toshima Civic Auditorium. I participated. Delighted to see the attendance grow each week. To listen to Mr. Toda's excellent lecture and hear his conviction make me truly happy.

My health steadily gets worse. It's really pitiful. Met over dinner with K. and some associates at the I. restaurant at 9:00. I have no vitality. It's agonizing.

Sunday, June 14. Cloudy.

A summer storm of the rainy season. Pained, both physically and spiritually. Sensei left on the *Tsubame* express to attend the Kansai general meeting. Saw him off at the station.

I am already twenty-five. When the first president, Mr. Makiguchi, was thirty-two, he wrote his innovative work, *Human Geography*, which is known worldwide. And, beginning with *Guidelines to Math*, Mr. Toda, my revered teacher, while still in his thirties, published many books popular throughout Japan. What will I have accomplished when I am that age?

Attended a general meeting of Hashimoto District. A great success. Returned on the 10:09 train. Exhausted—the most exhausted I've been this year.

Monday, June 15. Rain, then cloudy.

Completely exhausted, both physically and spiritually. Slept until 10:30. Totally disgusted with K. The rain grew harder. It is as if my entire being were in pain. Don't they speak of "a sound mind in a sound body"? Rather, both body and mind must be healthy simultaneously. This is an ultimate principle of faith.

Must complete the following:
1. Accomplish my chapter's goal.
2. Accomplish my mission at work.
3. Pursue the study of Buddhism.

In the evening, attended Musashino District's general meeting. No spirit whatsoever. It's a shame.

Lately I feel my mind becoming dull. No other fundamental solution than to "substitute faith for wisdom."

To bed at 12:00.

Tuesday, June 16. Fine and clear.

From today, I can stop wearing my overcoat. The weather has become warm like summer.

In the afternoon, I went to K.'s house. We spoke for a long time about many things. Things have improved with him. I'm happy.

The Suiko Group met in the evening. Sensei was furious. We were at fault. Reflected on our complete lack of spirit and fortitude. Sensei left the meeting after only an hour or so. We stayed and went over our attitude and behavior until 10:00. My heart is like a dark cloud.
1. Take care to be on time.
2. Unity among the corps chiefs.
3. The Suiko Group's purpose, determination and passion.

Strictly reflected that I, alone, am responsible for Sensei's anger.

Faith will change everything. The power of faith is the only way to a solution and further advancement.

Late at night, my brother came by. He seems to be having a very hard time.

Wednesday, June 17. Clear.

A corps meeting at M.'s in Koiwa.

Arrived at 8:00 after getting lost. There were about a hundred participants. Pleased to see everyone in high spirits, filled with hope, determination and vitality. In the future, how many Shinsaku Takasugis or Genzui Kusakas[1] will appear from among them? Soiled clothes, wrinkled shirts, unkempt hair—they have, however, the precious eyes of youth, looking toward and living for the future. Furthermore, though not apparent on the surface, theirs is a gathering of young pioneers of the Mystic Law.

Resolved deep in my heart to develop them into a group of a hundred, a thousand, or ten thousand youth. Will take good care of my juniors. Must make them better than myself. This is the mission of a leader or senior in faith.

After 10:00, I was summoned by the police about a matter of giving notice of our intention to hold a meeting. Alone, I went to Koiwa police headquarters. The situation has become more and more interesting. After explaining everything thoroughly, I returned home late at night.

In anything, whoever continues to fight on will be a winner in the end. To bed at 3:00 a.m. Exhausted.

1. Shinsaku Takasugi (1839–1867) and Genzui Kusaka (1840–1864): Young samurai warriors who contributed to the overthrow of the Tokugawa Shogunate (1603–1867) and the achievement of the Meiji Restoration (beginning 1867), which ended the feudal, shogun-led system and created the modern state of Japan under Emperor Mutsuhito.

Thursday, June 18. Overcast, with rain later in the day.

At 6:30, a corps chiefs conference was held at the headquarters. All shared a solemn intensity.

Topics of discussion:

1. Refuting the K. sect.
2. Debating the B. school.
3. The problem at Myofuku-ji (the priests and the membership had been ostracized by the rest of the community).
4. The purpose and attitude of the Suiko Group.
5. Promoting the study of Buddhism.

The rain of the wet season continued. Was caught in a downpour near Omori Station.

Feeling ill.
To bed a little before 2:00.

Friday, June 19. Cloudy, occasional rain.

Physically and mentally exhausted. All day long, I feel like a person suffering from a serious illness. How regrettable, how sad! Could this be the result of my past misdeeds or karma? How bitter my destiny. Must not allow it to defeat me. Because I have a mission, I must win! There are many things I must accomplish. Will dedicate this life to my mentor, Josei Toda. Shall I allow my will to be broken? How frightening. Must reflect on my selfishness and frivolity. Can only apologize to my mentor for all my shortcomings.

The Friday lecture — "Letter to the Wife of Shijo Kingo" and "Reply to Shijo Kingo." It left me deeply impressed. Boundlessly happy to follow such a great teacher. Treated several fellow members to sushi. Fatigued.

Sunday, June 21. Cloudy, occasional rain.

A light shower in the evening.
Got up a little after 9:00 a.m. K. came by. I am quite angry with him. S. came over.

At 2:30, I attended the Kamata Chapter general meeting at a Hoshi Pharmaceutical College lecture hall. A large meeting. Pray the members will continue to advance without becoming overburdened or arrogant. Gave congratulatory words as a guest speaker.

Afterward, had dinner with H. in Gotanda. My friend! Advance cheerfully, in high spirits! Arrived at the home of the chapter chief, T., at 6:30.

A chapter leaders meeting began at 7:00. To date, the chapter has introduced 114 households. This is the largest number of new families since the chapter was formed. Resolved together to introduce 200 families next month. Steadily, the Gakkai ranks are advancing. The Buddha's armies, astride white stallions, must transcend the raging waves of adversity.

Monday, June 22. Cloudy, occasional rain.

Physical condition very poor, Missed the fourth-level lecture in the evening and went home early. Imagined my friends listening to the lecture in high spirits. So this is how painful it is to be resting when I should be advancing.

Thought about tomorrow's work. Felt lifeless. Decided to chant many daimoku. To bed, 11:00.

Thursday, October 1. Rain.

Met the S.s at Yaguchi in Kamata District. Congratulated him on struggling boldly in the Kansai area. "Our propagation efforts in September were beaten by Bunkyo Chapter," he said regretfully. Pray for the happiness of this good fellow and good friend. Set out for Chapter Chief T.'s home in the evening. He was away, but I stayed and chatted with some women's division leaders.

A youth division leaders meeting at 6:30. Gave strict direction toward a goal of one thousand members for each corps, and regarding religious debates with the Butsuryu sect. Regrettable that I could not see Corps Chief I. on the way back.

Friday, October 2. Rain in the morning.

A steady autumn rain. Appreciative in many ways for my circumstances, which allow me to grow while fighting courageously day after day and night after night. How fortunate that I can dedicate myself heart and soul to my job, my mission and my activities during this active time of my youth. Next year I'll be twenty-six. Construction, improvement, fierce struggle, devotion—with these I will live, fight and advance under my mentor, in a way befitting a youth and a disciple.

Met with Y. on business in Yaguchi. In the evening, talked over various matters with the chapter chief. Concluded these should be our two main objectives—to build an excellent chapter and raise capable people.

The Friday lecture. Sensei seemed to be suffering from a throat pain. Pray and pray that he will live until the day kosen-rufu is achieved.

Saturday, October 3. Fair.

A fine autumn day. Clear blue skies. The morning sun glistened over earth and sky. October is calm, deep and expansive. The great aspirations, hopes and ideals of youth should be the same. To Kogane City in Yokohama with K. on business. Things did not turn out too well. Reflected that faith equals work. Sensei's morning lecture passed the midpoint in our astronomy study. My heart leaps when I consider the relationship between Buddhism and the study of the cosmos.

Home after 1:00. Is life a cross between comedy and tragedy?

Sunday, October 4. Cloudy.

Stayed home all morning. Have grown exhausted. Only wish to become healthy.

To Hashimoto in Kanagawa Prefecture with Chapter Chief T. in the afternoon to conduct a Gohonzon-enshrining ceremony for H.

Had dinner in Shinjuku afterward. Discussed many things, including our mentor, the Gakkai's future and the chapter reformation.

Home at 11:00. It is natural young pioneers are seldom at home — we are working to construct our happiness. Nothing — not the earth, the sun's flames, the cells of our bodies or the growth of plants — is ever stagnant. Our guidance and faith toward realizing kosen-rufu must also never cease. I think of my mentor, the Gakkai and my fellow members.

Monday, October 5. Fair.

A fine autumn day. There are days of rain, days of snow and overcast days. Similarly, there are days when we feel spirited, days of worry and days of sadness or regret. Traveled to the Joto area. My work is not going as planned. A youth's mind is intensely restless. Must be strong, upright, untiring and self-disciplined.

The general conference began at 6:00 and ended at 8:00. Received guidance from Sensei on various matters.

Walked home along the Ginza with some fellow employees. Surprised at the difference in this main thoroughfare at night since I was last here.

Wednesday, October 7. Clear.

Bright sunshine. The sky, a stage in a dreamlike play. I want my life, too, to shine in a spirited dance of "happiness in this world" on the stage of this earth.

Completed my astronomy study. Great nourishment for the future. Deeply thankful to President Toda.

Read a book on Oda Nobunaga[1] — a courageous general. A sharp mind. He acted in the spirit of male ambition. Toyotomi Hideyoshi[2] was also fascinating. He was an individual of great friendliness. Many times, Mr. Toda has encouraged me to read books on history. One's view of history is important.

In the evening, I gave a lecture at Musashino District. About eighty attended. Back home a little after 11:00.

1. Oda Nobunaga: (1534–1582) The prime mover of Japan's sixteenth-century reunification after a hundred years of strife. Nobunaga deserves his reputation as a brutal warlord, but it should not be permitted to obscure his accomplishments, which were cultural as well as institutional.
2. Toyotomi Hideyoshi: (1537–1598) Warlord of humble origins who, in 1590, completed the work of national reunification begun by Oda Nobunaga. A brilliant strategist and shrewd politician, he usually showed a generosity toward his enemies untypical of his time. His story is recounted in the work *Record of the Taiko*.

Friday, October 9. Light rain.

In physical and spiritual anguish all day. My only choice is to improve my faith. Must make myself practice strictly. Went in the rain to Yokohama to help negotiate the construction of a new home for M.'s relative. I enjoyed a meal on the way back.

The Friday lecture was on "The Opening of the Eyes." Could not absorb it because I was suffering from a headache. But Mr. Toda's courageous spirit brought tears to my eyes. Sensei! Please live another thirty years! For Japan, for Asia and for world peace. I will not begrudge my meager efforts. I can only pray and pray.

After the lecture, held a First Corps group chiefs meeting for the first time in quite a while. Brave generals stood up resolutely once again.

Saturday, October 10. Clear.

A clear autumn sky. Talked with M., a fellow employee, until past noon about the company's future. A fine man. My physical condition is quite poor.

Went shopping with my wife in the Ginza in the evening. Exhausted. Returned home early and fell into bed.

The faith that can change destiny cannot be carried out easily. Must not doubt. The fundamental cause lies in my own determination and faith.

I have a mission. Without a mission, a Bodhisattva of the Earth has no reason to exist. Human beings must never forget their mission. Since this is the case, my only choice is to courageously carry out powerful unyielding, indomitable faith.

Sunday, October 11. Clear.

Awoke at 6:30. Set out on a daylong visit to the head temple. Slept well on the train. Keenly pondered the importance of carrying on my studies.

Met with the high priest at 1:00.

Chanted before the Dai-Gohonzon at 2:00. Prayed for good health and about pressing matters at work, as well as for my YMD corps development. Returned home after 8:00. Really exhausted. Will this impossible schedule continue?

Monday, October 12. Rain.

Gentle rain throughout the day.

The ashen sky resembles my state of mind.

Skipped the senior lecture.

Went to S.'s to discuss M.'s upcoming marriage. On the way home, stopped to eat in Meguro. Being where I had lived until last year brought back memories.

In the evening, a few members from my YMD corps came by for guidance. I feel great affection for them. Sincerely hope they will never abandon their faith. They are all great. Each courageously battling his own obstacles in order to save the people, each struggling with his own difficulties. How praiseworthy! Must pay heartfelt attention to each individual. In society, how many irresponsible youths live only for momentary pleasure? How does the government intend to reward or punish these two different kinds of youths? How foolish are politicians who have no gauge to measure good or evil!

To bed, 12:00. Tired.

Tuesday, October 13. Clear with scattered clouds.

Read the book *Hana no Shogai*.

No matter what, I must deepen my study of Buddhism. Must master the Daishonin's Buddhism.

A group chiefs meeting at my house at 7:00. Lectured on "The True Aspect of All Phenomena." Important that I reflect on my own lectures. Everyone left in high spirits. My dear members, my juniors, my friends, with whom I share bonds deeper than those of brothers or relatives, I pray for your great happiness. I pray for your uninterrupted growth.

Ah, how time passes. A new time must come. I await that time. I live for that time. Must make meaningful progress during my youth. Whether in suffering or sadness, must remain youthful like a child of the Gakkai—fresh and alive.

Must reflect on myself. Arrived at work after Mr. Toda. Disappointed at my total incompetence as a disciple.

Thursday, October 15. Clear.

7:00. Jozai-ji, Ikebukuro, Tokyo. Confronted the erroneous Butsuryu sect in a meeting with four of their representatives, led by U., and eight Gakkai youth division representatives. Met to negotiate a halt to incidents, which began last spring, of that sect's confiscating Gohonzon from the homes of ex-members of their sect who had newly converted to practicing the Daishonin's teachings. The meeting continued until 10:00. Infuriated at their cowardly attitude to the end.

To the public baths late in the evening. Have lost about 8 lbs. Surprised. Though this is the season of bright blue skies, a time to eat and drink heartily, my health is not as it should be. Must challenge myself.

Tomorrow evening, Mr. Toda will travel to Sendai for guidance. He leaves from Ueno on the 10:45 train. I will see him off at the station. As his secretary, it is only natural that I do so. To bed after 2:00.

Saturday, October 17. Cloudy, then rain.

Autumn rain.

How swiftly the days pass! Like the flow of a great river. How much have I developed? Must strictly reflect. Accompanied Mr. Toda, his wife and his son to the Kokusai Theater in the evening. A dance of autumn. A memorable, lively maidens' dance, their sure-footed figures surging with life. Returned home after 10:00. Two leaders came by to discuss plans for tomorrow's district chiefs meeting.

Sunday, October 18. Cloudy.

Read all morning. In the afternoon, visited my chapter chief. A district chiefs meeting began at 5:00. Delighted to see everyone in high spirits. I just can't stop worrying about each of their living situations. But each face is aglow with benefit. They have really grown. They have truly fought along with me. I am forever indebted to them. Those faces, those people and their accomplishments will forever be illuminated by the light of the Mystic Law. I will never forget them.

At 10:00, we met to plan for the upcoming general meeting. Also solidified plans for the chapter leaders meeting.

Came home at 1:00. Fight, and the devil will retreat. Advance, and break through the clouds. Then the morning sun of Buddhahood will definitely appear.

Thursday, October 22. Clear.

Out of bed at 6:30. Arrived at work, 8:00. Went to Katsuura, in Chiba, on business.

Arrived back in Tokyo at 8:00. Met with Study Department freshmen to study from 9:00.

Y. has become a bit conceited. It's become necessary for him to receive strict guidance. If I act humbly toward him, he's all the more arrogant. I seem to be the only one who can scold him or guide him correctly.

We are at the last two months of the year. I, too, have reached a stage where I must move with a fresh determination and awareness. Must not revert to my shallow way of thinking from when I was single. I must now proceed responsibly in everything I do.

Ultimately, I must advance, step by step, with faith as my basis, never yielding or losing sight of my goal. Then, the Gohonzon will resolve everything.

Monday, October 26. Clear, then cloudy.

Thirty of us, including the *Seikyo Shimbun* staff, took a company trip to Shiohara Hot Springs.

President Toda could not attend due to illness. Truly disappointing.

Left from in front of the Ichigaya Building on the morning of the 25th. Arrived at the Tamaya Inn in Shiohara at 2:00.

Left Tamaya Inn at 10:00 on the 26th. Arrived in Kidogawa at 2:00.

Left for Tokyo at 4:30, arriving at Ueno at 8:00.

Went directly to Mr. Toda's home in Meguro to report. He still seems to have a slight fever. Told him that all had enjoyed themselves in high spirits. He was extremely pleased. Received guidance on various matters concerning the Gakkai and business. Glad to hear he will come to the office tomorrow.

Home after 12:00.

Wednesday, November 4. Clear.

Feeling bad, physically and spiritually. Having sad thoughts, as if my life were about to end.

Twenty-five years along this journey of life.

Will I fall now?

It seems like Mr. Toda's physical condition has gradually gotten worse.

Sensei! Please persevere!

I, too, will strive determinedly.

Bunkyo Chapter has made steady progress. What fine people in our chapter! This is my great fortune.

Returning home from a lecture in Toshima, I stopped at the chapter chief's house. Deeply appreciate his family, which welcomes me brightly any time I stop by. Worked out various future plans with my chapter chief. In the future, this family's fortune will rise as high as a mountain.

Tuesday, November 10. Cloudy.

Winter begins. It will soon be necessary to burn coal.

Visited Miss K. and Sugimari Fifth Elementary School. Talked about President Toda. Returned together as far as Ichigaya. A wise senior.

In the evening, I gave a lecture at the Tsurumi Market. Finished the fourth part of the "On Establishing the Correct Teaching for the Peace of the Land." Continued from 9:30 until 11:00 with a question-and-answer session at S.'s home. Want them to become more like the Bunkyo Chapter leaders.

Read *Princess Kazunomiya*. To bed, a little after 1:00.

Tuesday, December 22. Rain, then overcast.

Drizzle. It's gradually gotten colder. The morning lecture has progressed from law, to politics, to economics, to science, to Chinese literature. How can I ever repay my debt of gratitude to my mentor, who has striven to raise this disciple without regard even for his own health? Now is the time to accumulate my power and ability. Must develop my capability in preparation for the time to come.

Walked through Adachi to Kameto for our company's year-end gathering. Returned by way of the Nihonbashi. Met my chapter chief in Ichigaya, Tokyo, to make plans for next year.

Returned home early, not feeling well. Relaxed as my wife and I ate sukiyaki together. Rested a little after 9:00.

DURING THE FIRST gongyo of the new year at the headquarters, President Toda recited a *waka* poem he had written: "If I go forth in the robe of this precious Law, I need not fear even the peaks of the Kun-lun Mountains."

The Kun-lun Mountains were legendary sacred peaks west of China. Through his poem, one can sense President Toda's passion to spread the Daishonin's Buddhism throughout Asia. To further establish the Gakkai's solid progress of the previous year, Toda devoted himself in 1954 to formalizing and systematizing a new Study Department, reorganizing the youth division and fine-tuning the entire organization. As a result, the Gakkai surpassed the membership goal of 150,000 households Toda had set for the year, reaching more than 160,000 by the end of 1954.

On March 1, a Japanese tuna boat named, ironically, *The Lucky Dragon*, was exposed to radioactive fallout from an American hydrogen bomb test blast at Bikini atoll in the Marshall Islands. Upon returning home, the twenty-three–member crew was found to have been exposed to near-lethal radiation doses. The men were hospitalized and received ongoing treatment but one crew member died in September. The incident sparked protest cries from Japan, calling for the complete abolishment of atomic and hydrogen bombs.

In each locality the pace of Buddhist study was on the rise. The graduate exam for professor level required that each examinee submit a thesis on one of three topics: "The sacred teachings on the eternity of life," "Prophecy and conviction for kosen-rufu," and "On [the Buddhist concept of] sowing, maturation and harvest." The results were announced in June. Out of the seven candidates who passed, six, including Daisaku Ikeda, were youth division leaders.

Great plans were implemented for youth division advancement and the organization's development as a whole. At a March 30 headquarters leaders meeting, the seven YMD and YWD corps spread among fifteen chapters, were expanded to fifteen corps per division, one in each chapter. In addition, a youth division staff office was established and Daisaku Ikeda was appointed chief. The youth division staff was created to come up with campaign strategies, ideas and suggestions aimed to further youth division development. Later, under Chief of Staff Ikeda's leadership, this body became responsible not only for the youth division growth, but provided the driving force for the entire Gakkai organization's advancement.

In April 1954, the *Seikyo Shimbun* celebrated its third anniversary by expanding from two to four pages. The price was ¥12 per issue. Also, to keep pace with the rapidly expanding membership, a second printing of *The Complete Works of Nichiren Daishonin* (Gosho Zenshu) was decided upon at the end of the previous year.

The vacuum tube, a principal component of electronic equipment including radios, televisions and electronic calculators, was now being challenged by a new device, the transistor. With American engineering help, transistors came under full-scale production in Japan during spring 1954. Transistors were smaller, lighter and consumed less power than vacuum tubes. They also were more durable, having a far greater operational life expectancy. Japan first put transistors to use in radios, paving the way for the portable transistor radios that became a leading Japanese export during the late '50s and early '60s.

In 1954, the Japanese economy experienced a continuing foreign trade surplus. This was brought about by a steady increase in exports that accompanied postwar reconstruction. Goods exported from Japan, however, were criticized by other countries, the label "made in Japan" symbolizing cheapness and inferior quality. In particular, foreign trade partners continually charged that shipments of machinery, sundry goods, textiles and agricultural and marine goods were of inferior quality or short in quantity, and many demanded compensation for claimed losses.

According to the July 25, 1954, *Seikyo Shimbun*, membership figures for various areas of Japan as of May that year included (numbers indicate households): Kanto, 65,519; Hokkaido, 510; Tohoku, 10,114; Chubu, 4,910; Kansai, 6,353; Chugoku, 578; Shikoku, 317; Kyushu, 1,213, — approximately 90,000 households in all. Although eight prefectures, including Ishikawa and Yamaguchi, had less than ten Soka Gakkai households, members now appeared in every prefecture of the nation. Thus in the three years since President Toda took office, the membership had tripled.

The summer training course was held July 30 – August 3 at the head temple. Participants totalled 4,500. Activities included Gosho lectures and question-and-answer sessions with President Toda, meetings for Study Department members, and various activities for each division, all designed to allow members to train and develop themselves in the areas of practice and study. In particular, the YMD and YWD members planned and carried out on their own a dynamic study meeting and a youth division rally.

From the end of October through the beginning of November, the youth division conducted a series of large-scale events, including a 10,000-participant general pilgrimage to the head temple and the first youth division sports festival. Held on the Nippon University grounds, it was designated the "Century Festival" and featured several athletic competitions. Later, spirited youth festivals were held in each area, eventually giving rise to major sports and culture festivals.

Saturday, January 9. Overcast.

Worked on the second Gosho proofreading in Hatake, under the direction of Nichijun, the retired high priest. A noble task. A sublime and important undertaking. All were amazed at the pleasant, springlike weather.

Must deepen my study of Buddhism. Must likewise strengthen my understanding of philosophy. The reason is that study is unquestionably the Gakkai's cornerstone. It is therefore a leader's most essential qualification. Enthusiasm and practice are also vital. In this connection, study becomes all the more important.

Spent the night at the T. inn in Hatake. We bathed in the mild waters of the famous spring located there. The entire party of Study Department professors seemed to enjoy themselves.

Monday, January 11. Overcast.

Very cold all day.

The first youth division leaders meeting of the year was held in the Hall of Education in Kanda at 6:00. About nine-hundred youths participated. There was no end to their joy as they welcomed President Toda.

A New Year's celebration was held in an adjoining room for about an hour after the meeting. Sensei's guidance to us was that the Gakkai's foundation and future lay with the youth division. He is entrusting everything to us. Someone energetically sang the Tokyo University dormitory song. Finally, we ended the evening's festivities by singing "Moonlight Over a Ruined Castle," our voices joining in a solemn, resolute chorus.

In his final words, President Toda stated: "I am striving resolutely ahead to carry out a revolution. My revolution, however, is a bloodless revolution, based on compassion and reason." His words resound in my mind.

Tuesday, January 12. High clouds.

A cold day.

My heart leaps with joy to see Sensei's health has returned. Sensei! So long as you are alive and well I am filled with courage. I have nothing in the world to fear.

Held a group chiefs meeting at our chapter chief's house at 6:00. I scolded the leaders. Feeling sorry for them, I apologized in my heart. Sometimes, however, this cannot be helped if everyone is to advance.

After the group chiefs meeting, we held a senior leaders meeting until 11:00. The men's division leaders looked tired. On the way home, I thought to myself that more consideration should be given to the participants' age when planning late meetings.

Thursday, January 14. Overcast.

Covered a fair amount of ground in the morning Japanese history lecture. My heart feels as vast as the boundless blue sky. Continuing to proofread the Gosho a little each day.

At 6:30, I turned over the proofreading task to another committee member.

At 9:00, a small New Year's celebration in the second president's room. Everyone seemed to enjoy themselves, singing songs. President Toda could not attend, and I found it completely uninteresting. I doubt their sincerity. Just what did they think they were doing in the president's room?

Returned home, 11:30.

Friday, January 15. Clear.

Adults' day.

Went for a morning bath, then to Sensei's house in the afternoon. He talked cheerfully with me until late. Left at 7:30.

K. and some others stopped by at 10:30. Talked seriously with them for about an hour. Shocked at how easily people's minds change. Also, surprised at my own strict reprimand.

Saturday, January 16. Cloudy.

At 6:00, a children's group meeting at the N. Chinese restaurant. President Toda had invited us. Each of this group of married people focused on President Toda's words. The group has really grown since its first meeting last year. Everyone seemed happy and enjoyed some Peking-style food.

Couldn't help being moved to tears at our mentor's warm consideration and compassion.

Sunday, January 17. Cloudy, occasional rain.

Light rain.

Went to the headquarters in the afternoon. Ate with M. and R. prior to getting to work. Visited Mr. Kunio Yanagida[1] to present him with a copy of President Makiguchi's work, *The Philosophy of Value*. Unfortunately, he had gone out to visit the Seijo School.

Administered the first study exam for group chiefs from 6:00 until 8:30.

1. Kunio Yanagida (1875–1962): Scholar, poet and government bureaucrat. Yanagida founded the field of folklore studies in Japan.

Monday, January 18. Intermittent rain.

The first joint young men's and young women's division district leaders meeting was held at 6:00 in the president's office.

President Toda attended. His strict guidance applies especially to me.

1. Come up with a plan for twelve corps chiefs by April.
2. Be rigorous in proofreading the Gosho.
3. Be thorough in studying Buddhism.

The above points are vital.

Tuesday, February 9. Clear.

Yesterday evening, President Toda had a bout of ill health. Heard that his condition was extremely poor. There is no excuse for my absence at such a crucial time. When I heard that he called out my name two or three times my heart ached. I wonder what he was thinking. He seems a little better today. My only hope is that he lives long. I am not the only one repeatedly amazed by his tremendous life force, which resurges like a great immortal Phoenix.

At 6:00, a Suiko Group meeting. Finished the ninth volume of *Tales of Suiko*. Seventy-six members attended. I was master of ceremonies.

Met with Sensei in the president's office at 10:30. He is completely unshaken by yesterday's episode. My noble mentor! "Study! Study!" he told me. Returned home after midnight.

Wednesday, February 10. Clear.

Saw President Toda in his office at 1:30. Reported on various matters. Greatly appreciate Sensei's passion to instruct me in many areas, as ignorant as I am.

Gave a lecture in Ikebukuro this evening. Visited President Toda again afterward, bringing him two boxes of strawberries. He was extremely happy. Received guidance for an hour together with H. Truly amazed at his life force and boundless wisdom. Got home around midnight.

Thursday, February 11. Fine weather.

Today is President Toda's fifty-fourth birthday.

In the morning, I gave him a white shirt and a necktie as a gift. He seemed quite fatigued.

At 2:00, I helped administer the Study Department oral examination, along with Secretary Y. About forty candidates took the exam. Ashamed about my own lack of ability. Must study. Must not be defeated.

Must burn with a youthful passion to learn. Must advance with a seeking spirit, like one truly seeking the Way. This is the most important requisite for becoming an excellent leader.

To Josen-ji at 8:00 for a YMD First Corps meeting, three hundred attending. In accord with the principle of 'the simultaneity of cause and effect,' I think of this meeting as a model of the future for these young leaders. Got home just before midnight.

Friday, February 12. Cloudy.

A mild winter day. A harbinger of spring.

Hope and a fighting spirit—both well forth as spring approaches.

The Friday lecture on *The Philosophy of Value* began at 6:30 at To-shima Civic Auditorium. A great success. I alone, however, am aware of Sensei's illness. I am pained to think of how he must have suffered through the lecture. The crucial time approaches; day by day, year by year. A disciple must strive to his utmost. An absolute truth, reality.

At 8:30, I attended a group chiefs meeting for Bunkyo Chapter at S.'s. Got home at 11:30.

I don't feel so well. Very tired. Angry seniors, jealous friends and those who are full of hostility. A person with a goal and a mission will forge directly ahead, facing any difficulty with a smile.

Saturday, February 13. Overcast.

At 12:30, took the *Niagra Express* to Niigata District for propagation activities, arriving around 6:00. This is the first time I have ever set foot in this snow-covered country. A historic place. Also, a memorable page in the history of my life. It is warmer than I had expected. A friend who accompanied me thinks it is even warmer than Tokyo.

7:00. A guidance meeting at O.'s. About a hundred attending. After the meeting, talked until late with eleven youth division members, encouraging them. Praying that many capable future leaders will arise one after another from this area. Yet how many fellow members will truly trust and follow me?

Must not think people are attracted to me due to my own power or ability. They are following the power of the Mystic Law. The members will advance on account of the Gakkai's power. Disgusted with my tendency to ignore my own lack of ability and pretend to know more than I do. Must seriously reflect. Spent the night at O.'s with the other members.

Sunday, February 14. Cloudy with occasional snow.

Stayed in Niigata. Light snow fell. The Mukojima Chapter leaders spread out among the chapter's eight groups and plunged into propagation activities. As we resolutely carry out propagation in this outlying area, I sorely miss the presence of many capable leaders. First and foremost, leaders must fully apply themselves to finding and raising capable people.

A group chiefs meeting at 7:00. Poured all my energy into giving guidance.

Faith and guidance must be carried out with the realization that "now is my last moment."

Can I visit this area again one day?

I believe some can become happy as a result of the guidance they received during these two days.

At the end, I composed a poem and presented it to E., a youth division unit chief:

> *In that land connected*
> *To the Daishonin's struggle,*
> *Holding high the banner of the Law,*
> *Each of you, arise!*

Boarded the night train, the 10:00 express to Tokyo.

Monday, February 15. Clear.

Arrived in Tokyo's Ueno District on the night train from Niigata just before 6:00 in the morning. Exhausted, I went with K. and others for a morning bath. Arrived at work after 8:00. The morning lecture on Japanese history is making good progress. Reported to Sensei about our activities in Niigata. All he said was, "Thank you."

Tuesday, February 16. High clouds.

Sensei struggles relentlessly against the devil of sickness.

I, too, continuously battle the same devil.

Where there is passionate faith, there must be victory. I am young; my life begins from now. If only I can be the engine that turns President Toda's plans and ideas into realities.

Spent the entire day at work. Returned home after midnight. Life is nothing but struggle and advancement. Such is my destiny.

Thursday, February 18. Cloudy, occasional rain.

Gentle rain. Finished reading *The Count of Monte Cristo* at the office. Reading develops wisdom and allows us to accumulate knowledge. It also enhances our ability to read and understand the Gosho. Someone once said: "Read throughout your life, even if only thirty minutes each day. In the course of a lifetime, this will add up to a tremendous amount of reading."

7:00. A Bunkyo Chapter leaders meeting at Jozai-ji. A spirited meeting. These people are truly honest, sincere and pure-hearted people. They are leaders who deserve the highest degree of respect and praise, as they represent the people. Got home just before midnight.

Saturday, February 20. Fine weather.

Rode the 9:00 express to Osaka along with President Toda to attend a youth division meeting in the evening.

Sunday, February 21. High clouds.

Met with Sixth Corps (the Kyushu Corps) members in the morning. Everyone was in good spirits. In Osaka, in Kyushu and in the Shikoku area, young Bodhisattvas of the Earth are gathering. Look ahead! Ten or twenty years into the future!

At noon, a joint general meeting of Osaka, Sakai and Yame chapters was held at Yuhigaoka Hall. The room was completely filled—standing room only. The meeting ended at 5:00, with a banquet meeting at 6:00. Boarded a night train back to Tokyo at 8:00 along with fifteen leaders from the headquarters.

Monday, February 22. Fine weather.

Arrived at Shinagawa Station about 7:10 in the morning. Secretary Y. and I saw President Toda to his home in Meguro. Sensei treated us to breakfast and gave us guidance on various matters for about forty minutes.

Went to Meiwa Printing Company at 7:00 in the evening to proofread the Gosho. Returned home at midnight.

Tuesday, February 23. Fine weather.

Did not see Sensei in the morning. Felt somewhat melancholy all day. A Suiko Group meeting at 6:00. Sensei seemed extremely tired. He ended the meeting at 7:00. Deeply ashamed that I couldn't answer when he asked me a question.

My own growth is the growth of the youth division. Self-awakening and growth are my absolute duty! Youth of Japan! Youth of the Gakkai! Try your best!

Stopped for dinner on the way home with the youth division chief, T. Returned home around 11:30. Went to bed at 2:00.

Thursday, February 25. Clear.

Warm all day.

Stopped by K.'s home during business hours. His faith seems to have gotten stronger. Glad my work is going smoothly. The ultimate objective in life, the culmination of our hopes and dreams, can be found in the life-condition we attain through faith.

Proofreading at Meiwa Printers in the evening. Afterward, attended a group chiefs meeting with H. at T.'s in Ikebukuro.

Friday, February 26. High clouds.

A warm day. To Meiwa Printers for proofreading. Home at 10:30. A light rain falling. My son is growing up healthy and strong. A happy family—isn't this the greatest treasure? Went to the public baths. Put on some music when I got home. The small streets in the evening in early spring are so pleasant.

Monday, March 1. Light clouds.

Warm.

Spring has arrived at long last.

Gentle breezes, budding greenery, mist—my life absorbs them all.

At 6:00, a lecture for the Study Department's fifth level on Nichikan's "Commentary on 'The Object of Devotion for Observing the Mind.'" We studied the commentary on the passage, "Shakyamuni's, however, is the Buddhism of the harvest, and this is the Buddhism of sowing" (WND, 370).

Beginning at 7:30, President Toda lectured for one hour to all Study Department members on methods of teaching. A truly interesting and profound discussion, one that should be digested thoroughly. During his lecture, Mr. Toda cited the teaching methods employed by Utako Shimoda in her lectures on *Tales of Genji*.

From 9:00 until 11:30, T., U., H., M., R. and myself met to discuss the formation of a new YMD corps. Earnestly went over youth division plans for the next ten years.

Tuesday, March 2. Light rain, then thinly overcast.

Many warm days so far this year.

Read an essay on Goto Shinpei (1857–1929), a powerful statesman with a progressive spirit, a man of foresight and practice and a leader of great capability. Nevertheless, he had many points that deserve criticism. I, however, love to see such excellent achievement by a youth. There is no need to elaborate on his ideas or his actions.

5:30. Discussed the selection of a new YMD corps chief and studied plans for a new YMD corps organization with the youth division chief and four corps chiefs at the Gakkai headquarters.

7:30. A new members' guidance meeting at T.'s home in Ikebukuro.

9:45–10:30. Went over public information division plans with Y.

Thursday, March 4. Cloudy with snow later in the day.

My fever has not yet subsided.

It's awful.

6:30. A YMD leaders meeting at the Hall of Education in Kanda.

Went to Meiwa Printers at 9:00 to proofread the Gosho. The train wasn't running due to a heavy spring snowstorm. Took a taxi home, finally arriving after midnight.

Tuesday, March 9. Clear.

August will mark my seventh year of practice. Will this be a time of great change for me?

I still have a slight fever. My physical condition is rather poor.

6:00. A Suiko Group meeting at the headquarters.

Studied *The Count of Monte Cristo*. Second- and third-year group members are standing up one after another as excellent, capable young people. I hold great expectations for them. Truly amazed by Mr. Toda's profound insight, wisdom and understanding.

Returned home just before 11:00.

Wednesday, March 10. High clouds.

Mr. Toda seems to have regained his health somewhat. This makes me truly happy.

The Japanese history lecture is drawing to a close. I found the sections on the Kamakura and Ashikaga periods particularly interesting.

Went to the president's second conference room at 11:00. Spoke with Sensei for about an hour.

Received guidance on the following points:
1. Discussion on life — Sickness and death are not the same thing.
2. The third president and general director.
3. Direction for the Gakkai and for myself for the next three years.
4. Important points to ensure the Gakkai's eternal flow.

My mentor's deep love and consideration for this incapable disciple makes me weep heartfelt tears of appreciation.

Discussed the next issue of *The Daibyakurenge* with K.

Thursday, March 11. Rain.

Rained all day long. Spoke one to one with about ten people. Giving personal guidance is difficult. President Toda and the other senior leaders are truly skilled at it. They can grasp thoroughly the nature of the other person's problem and what he or she is seeking, leading that person to a solution. Though it might seem simple, it is really vital. The guidance given by a senior in faith can determine the course of a person's entire life.

Went to Meiwa Printers at 6:00 for proofreading. Worked with eleven Study Department members.

Sunday, March 14. Clear and pleasant.

At Taiseki-ji. Up at 7:00.

Though I am in this sacred place — this "Eagle Peak" — my spirits are somehow low. Visited President Makiguchi's grave at 8:00. Recited the sutra and chanted daimoku.

Chanted before the Dai-Gohonzon at 9:00. Prayed about many things.

Left Fuji for Tokyo at 1:30, becoming just another train passenger.

At 6:30, we held a YMD First Corps general meeting at Josen-ji. Spirited youth; shining eyes and happy faces. I trust them deeply.

Thursday, March 18. High clouds.

Early morning — worked on a thesis titled "On the Sacred Teachings Concerning the Eternity of Life." Fifteen pages. My graduate thesis for the Study Department. Thoroughly reflecting on my lack of deep insight.

A Bunkyo Chapter leaders meeting at Josen-ji at 6:00. Spirits seemed rather low. Poured all my energy into giving guidance.

A *Daibyakurenge* editorial staff meeting at 8:00. Out of ten expected participants, only three showed up. President Toda was furious, as could only be expected.

He spoke to us about the third Tokugawa period shogun. Saw Sensei off as far as the inside of the train car. Deepening my determination to strictly protect my only mentor.

Sunday, March 21. Clear.

> The Buddha wrote that one should become the master of one's mind rather than let one's mind master oneself. This is what I mean when I emphatically urge you to give up even your body, and never begrudge even your life for the sake of the Lotus Sutra.
>
> —"LETTER TO GIJO-BO" (WND, 390)

Accompanied Mr. Toda and twenty-seven other staff members on a spring tour. An enjoyable trip—three days and two nights, beginning on the 19th. Spent one night at the hot springs at Rendai-ji in Ito. On the second day, we visited Shuzen-ji, staying over in Minamiya. Sensei looked tired. Everyone was completely exhausted. Ate dinner at I. restaurant and everyone returned home from there.

Tuesday, March 23. Partly cloudy.

Worked on manuscripts in the morning. The Suiko Group met at 6:00. Have gradually come to sense my heavy responsibility.

Stopped by the chapter chief's house on the way home. Seriously discussed the chapter's future development. Emphasized that good communication among top leaders is fundamental to effectively managing the chapter.

> No matter how sincerely one believes in the Lotus Sutra, if one is guilty of failing to rebuke slander of the Law, one will surely fall into hell, just as a single crab leg will ruin a thousand pots of lacquer. This is the meaning of the passage in the sutra, "Because the poison has penetrated deeply and their minds no longer function as before."
>
> —"THE ESSENTIALS FOR ATTAINING BUDDHAHOOD"
> (WND, 747)

Tuesday, March 30. Clear.

At 6:00, a headquarters leaders meeting at Toshima Civic Auditorium. Have been assigned by the headquarters to function as public information department chief advisor and youth division general staff chief. Step by step, I am coming closer to the Gakkai's core — to being responsible for the progress of kosen-rufu. This is my personal mission. Flowers and grass exist together, but only the flower blossoms — this is its mission. I, myself, must accomplish propagation of the Mystic Law. This is my mission.

After the meeting, went for sushi with Chapter Chief M. and others.

> Even if they pray to the gods, the Buddha, or the Lotus Sutra, these calamities will only be aggravated. But it is different when the votary of the Lotus Sutra offers prayers to the essential teaching of the Lotus Sutra. In the final analysis, unless we succeed in demonstrating that this teaching is supreme, these disasters will continue unabated.
>
> — "THE TREATMENT OF ILLNESS" (WND, 1114)

Thursday, April 1. High clouds.

A warm spring day.

Can sense the return of spring, the season of progress.

There are pleasures and sorrows; they blend together in a complex poem of youth.

A youth division leaders meeting at 6:30 in the Hall of Education. The pace is now truly set for youth division development.

Considering the next stage, I pour my heart and soul into the task. This person — this youth — will definitely stand upon the grand stage of the future, ten or twenty years from now.

> Life is the most precious of all treasures. Even one extra day of life is worth more than ten million *ryo* of gold. The Lotus Sutra surpasses all the other sacred teachings because of the "Life Span" chapter. The greatest prince in the land of Jambudvipa would be of less consequence than a blade of grass if he died in childhood. If he died young, even a person whose wisdom shone as brilliantly as the sun would be less than a living dog. So you must hasten to accumulate the treasure of faith and quickly conquer your illness.
>
> — "ON PROLONGING ONE'S LIFE SPAN" (WND, 955)

Friday, April 2. Rain, then overcast.

Saw President Toda with I. in the morning. Went to Jozai-ji at 5:00 to discuss T.'s betrayal. Several participated, including the top directors. A youth division general staff meeting at 8:00 at S.'s. President Toda stopped by after his lecture. He severely rebuked us—like an atomic bomb going off. Calling us naive, he trembled with rage as he spoke. Completely unable to understand his intentions. Severely reproached myself, reflecting deeply.

I, Nichiren, am the only person who is aware of this. If I should begrudge my life and thus refrain from speaking out, not only would I be failing to repay the debt of gratitude I owe to my country, but I would also be acting as an enemy of Shakyamuni Buddha, the lord of teachings. On the other hand, I knew from the outset that, if I set aside my fears and declared things exactly as they are, I would be sentenced to death.

— "LETTER TO THE LAY PRIEST ICHINOSAWA" (WND, 529)

Saturday, April 3. Clear.

Visited President Toda at home to apologize for the other evening. Arrived at 5:45. He was still in an unpleasant mood. Escorted him to Tokyo Station where he took the 7:37 to Kansai. My heart is clouded as he did not forgive me. In the evening, a banquet celebrated the appointment of new chapter leaders. Everyone was in extremely high spirits.

In the Latter Day of the Law, no treasure tower exists other than the figures of the men and women who embrace the Lotus Sutra. It follows, therefore, that whether eminent or humble, high or low, those who chant Nam-myoho-renge-kyo are themselves the treasure tower, and, likewise, are themselves the Thus Come One Many Treasures.

— "ON THE TREASURE TOWER" (WND, 299)

Sunday, April 4.

Stayed home all morning. Visited Myoko-ji in the afternoon. Many people came to chant. Can truly sense the great prosperity of the Daishonin's school of Buddhism.

Various meetings at the headquarters at 7:00. One or two leaders have been fighting with confidence and courage. Can the day be far off when millions of excellent leaders will appear, valiantly advancing to put the finishing touches on kosen-rufu?

Monday, April 5. Cloudy.

My physical condition is extremely poor. Went to the Namamugi area on business. Felt ill all day.

Must chant daimoku, first and foremost. There is no other way to challenge and overcome my destiny than to chant daimoku. Practice — concrete action with a bold, unyielding spirit. Not even partial reform can be accomplished through mere theory. To the headquarters in the evening for a *Daibyakurenge* editorial staff meeting.

A lecture for the fifth level of the Study Department. Returned home, 9:00. Went to bed early. The intense pain continues. Studied Nikko Shonin's "Twenty-six Admonitions":

> "Those of insufficient learning who are bent on obtaining fame and fortune are not qualified to call themselves my followers."

> "Followers of this school should engrave the teachings of the Gosho in their lives and thereby inherit the ultimate principles expounded by the master. Then, if they have any leisure time, they should inquire into the doctriness of the T'ien-t'ai school."

Tuesday, April 6. Rain.

Rained all day long. A gloomy day. Have recently deeply realized that life force is the greatest fundamental requirement for happiness.

Live and move within society. Eventually I will die.

For 10,000 people, 10,000 unique lives. Simply amazing. What does equality really indicate? Have come to understand the law of causality inherent in life.

Stayed at the headquarters in the evening. The atmosphere was exciting. Unless the staff is properly trained and given excellent guidance, however, and steps are taken to place the right person in the right position, I'm afraid we will face a stalemate in the future. I worry their pride in working so closely to President Toda will make them haughty and bureaucratic. Mr. Toda knows this. Then again, he may not. The most important thing is that the disciples who work closely with him awaken to their mission and maintain a 'many in body, one in mind' spirit based on faith.

Returned home around 10:30. Not in the best of spirits tonight for some reason.

Sunday, April 11. Partly cloudy.

Attended Kamata Chapter's general meeting at 10:00. Hold great hopes for their pure, dynamic growth. Met with the leaders for a meeting review from 4:30 to 6:30.

7:00 at Josen-ji—my last meeting with the First Corps. They seemed sad to see me go.

You have fought well. I am grateful to you.

You have followed me closely. I thank you deeply.

You have endured many hardships. Well done!

I will protect you steadfastly throughout my life.

Home after 11:00. On the way back I treated a few corps leaders to skewered chicken at Shinbashi. Presented them with copies of *The Eternal City*.

Monday, April 12. Rain.

Heavy rain all day.

Went for sushi with H. at noon. Discussed many things. Enjoy talking with friends. Talked endlessly about the chapter, the Gakkai, work, the members. Fortunate to have a lifelong friend in faith—a fellow revolutionary.

To the headquarters at 8:00 for the first editorial conference of *The Daibyakurenge*. Earnestly hope the staff members will freely and unhesitatingly exchange their opinions. In the evening, gave direction to each youth division corps. Afterward, met over dinner with the division chiefs and the youth division staff.

Wednesday, April 14. Overcast.

Argued with a visitor in the morning. It was my fault. Must reflect on my tendency to be satisfied with trivial successes.

Stayed at the headquarters in the evening, together with H. President Toda was serenely tossing food to the carp in the pond. Afterward, we sat together and received guidance on various matters.

A chapter promotion planning meeting at S.'s at 2:30.

Gave a lecture to Musashino District in the evening.

At times I think of the organization as a hindrance. But I know that without an organization, the Gakkai, the individual members and their faith would become disordered and confused, ultimately resulting in the greatest unhappiness. Those who despise the organization appear to be self-centered and arrogant; ultimately they will fail in the world of faith.

The most excellent principle of organization is none other than that of many in body, one in mind.

Since childhood, I, Nichiren, have never prayed for the secular things of this life but have single-mindedly sought to become a Buddha.
— "THE HERO OF THE WORLD" (WND, 839)

Friday, April 16. Overcast.

Physically very ill. Pitiful. A young revolutionary with a great mission and dream for the future must never die young!

I must live so I can show actual proof of my faith by changing my destiny.

Took the 2:19 from Tokyo to Ito on business. Called on I. On the train, read from the collected works of Nobuaki Makino.

Returned home around 10:30. Chapter members were waiting to receive guidance. All were suffering from grave daily-life problems. It made me truly appreciate the life-condition and circumstances I am blessed with.

To bed at 1:00.

Sunday, April 18. Rain, then clearing.

A Koiwa Chapter general meeting. Left the house at noon. Heavy morning rain but clearing in the afternoon to become a warm spring day. The meeting was held in the Chuo University auditorium. Felt it was a bit too formal. Finished at 5:30.

The evaluation meeting was over at 7:30. Feel as if I am about to die of exhaustion. In great pain.

Together with Director H., stopped by Jozai-ji where there was a cheerful, hope-filled chapter leaders meeting.

Need capable people. Raise capable people. Find capable people.

Read *Diary of Santaro* by Jiro Abe.

Monday, April 19. Intermittent overcast.

Few friends know me.

Few members trust me.

Few seniors sincerely look after my development.

Few truly protect me.

No — such a spoiled attitude will not do.

Everything derives from my determination. Before judging others, remember to look strictly at myself. Must take a good look at my own faith. The Gohonzon watches over and protects me. My mentor watches over me and guides my growth.

> If a person cannot manage to cross a moat ten feet wide, how can he cross one that is a hundred or two hundred feet?
>
> —"The Actions of the Votary of the Lotus Sutra" (WND, 766)

Must never forget that my mentor has led me from miserable circumstances to the state of growth and happiness I now enjoy. To bed 1:25.

Thursday, April 22. Cloudy.

Warm today. Arrived at the headquarters at 6:30. The first corps chiefs meeting, with new corps chiefs attending. Gave strict guidance.
1. Take responsibility.
2. Give accurate direction and communication.
3. Do away with criticizing fellow believers.
4. Never behave in an authoritarian manner.

Talked with Miss K. from 10:00 regarding President Toda's illness as well as various problems within the Gakkai.

> "First of all, when the god of the sun rises in the morning and sheds his great light from the east, he opens his heavenly eye and views the world below. At that time, if he sees a votary of the Lotus Sutra, he is delighted at heart. If, however, he sees a country that despises the votary of the Lotus Sutra, he will glare down furiously upon that land with his heavenly eye, and if the people of that land continue to ignore or persecute the votary, internal strife will break out of its own accord and the country will be destroyed by foreign invasion. This is clear in light of the sutra."
>
> —"Letter to Lord Matsuno"

Thursday, April 29. Clear then cloudy.

Clear in the morning, turning to light afternoon cloudiness. Awoke around 8:00. Spent the morning writing my speech to the joint young men's division and young women's division general meeting. A ceremony will be held to present corps flags to the new corps formed on March 30 under the one chapter/one corps system.

Rehearsal was held at Chuo University Auditorium at 11:00. My heart leapt at the dynamic sound of the marching band.

The meeting began at 1:00 with about thirty-five–hundred young men and women participating. Everything was over by 4:05.

From 5:00 to 6:30 we met with President Toda. He left early, looking very tired. Felt quite lonely without him.

The youth division has been growing steadily. The youth division members' pure faith and conviction should be the Gakkai spirit. On the way back, accompanied friends first to Kanda, then to Shibuya where we ate sushi and discussed the Gakkai's future and its personnel. Began to rain shortly before 10:00.

Monday, May 3. Overcast with rain later in the day.

The tenth annual Soka Gakkai general meeting. Arrived at Nihon University Auditorium at 9:30. Surprised at the huge crowd—perhaps twenty-thousand participants. Profoundly sense the Gakkai's sublime mission. At 12:25, the curtain opened for this historic general meeting. From the opening ceremony to the finale, it was a dynamic four-hour gathering, overflowing with powerful life force. Pondered the smallness of my own existence. Keenly feel the tremendous power of unity among the members.

The clean-up was completely finished by 8:00. I bow my head in respect to those nameless individual young men and women who stayed behind, working quietly to clean up after the meeting. Felt unworthy to be directing them. Resolved in my heart that I shall never forget the feelings of those who toil inconspicuously behind the scenes.

Returned to the youth division staff office at the headquarters at 8:40. Expressed my deep appreciation for the unseen, intense struggle of the youth division members. Briefly met High Priest Nissho in the second floor president's office. Quickly excused myself. Met informally for about an hour-and-a-half with T., U., H., M., R. and others at H.'s apartment next door to the headquarters.

During the next three years, I must pour extra effort into studying Buddhism. I have a fierce disposition—like a roaring waterfall. Whether this leads to good or evil will depend on my faith. Must prepare my mind for the next advance. Arrived home close to midnight.

Thursday, May 6. Cloudy with rain later in the day.

Home from work with a severe headache. Even at home, I could not relax. Left the house at 3:30. Saw Mr. Toda in the president's office at the headquarters. Reported to him on my physical condition. He gave me guidance: "You are engaged in a battle with the 'three obstacles and four devils.' There is no other way to break through than to pray, shedding tears before the Gohonzon."

Must live powerfully!

Must stand up powerfully!

Must fight powerfully!

This is a battle between me and the devil of sickness.

Worked on plans with the top youth division leaders until late in the evening. Got home just before midnight. My wife has been worrying about me.

Saturday, May 8. Fair.

To the headquarters to plan the upcoming joint youth division pilgrimage. A hectic day. Gongyo with the leaders at 7:00. All were filled with enthusiasm and vigor.

Arrived at the Meiji Shrine Outer Garden to direct bus staging for the head temple trip. The buses, scheduled to depart at midnight, were late. Final departure at 3:40 a.m. Firmly negotiated with the bus company. Participants numbered fifty-three hundred.

Sunday, May 9. Rain.

Arrived at the head temple at 9:00 a.m. in the rain. Distressed to see rain on the day of such a memorable, grand ceremony. President Toda prayed in front of the Treasure House.[1] I wept inwardly.

The ceremonies began at noon before the Sanmon Gate. The schedule went as follows:

1. Gakkai song.
2. Speeches by the chiefs of both divisions.
3. Direction from the youth division chief.
4. Guidance by the president.
5. Closing procession.

The heavy rain fell incessantly. Pounded by the rain, President Toda wore an expression of strict love for the members. After the ceremony, he presented me with the gold pin he was wearing. He could not have picked a more appropriate time to bestow such a memorable gift upon me. My life has been much like this storm.

Afterward, went to the Rikyo-bo lodging to thank him. Mr. Toda was deeply worried some people might catch cold, and he directed me to hand out newspapers so the members could cover themselves as protection. Accompanied top leaders for an audience with the high priest. Departed the head temple as evening set in. As the rain let up and the sky cleared, a completely changed world of portraitlike beauty opened before us.

1. Treasure House: (Jpn Gohozo). At the time of this diary entry, the building at the head temple where the Dai-Gohonzon was enshrined. The Dai-Gohonzon was later moved to the Hoan-den and finally, in 1972, to the Sho-Hondo.

Tuesday, May 18. Fair.

Wore my brand new suit to the office. Met with I. at the headquarters. Discussed various matters concerning the Gakkai's future. Regret that there are but a few truly stouthearted individuals.

Attended a chapter leaders meeting at S.'s in the evening. To Jozai-ji afterward for a meeting of the Fourth Corps. Gave my utmost. The Gakkai is advancing rapidly. The chapters and the youth division are seeing victory as well.

Want to live undefeated until the end. Want my life to be a succession of victories.

Wednesday, May 19. High Clouds.

A warm, humid day.

Physical condition very poor.

Could I be suffering from tuberculosis? Or perhaps I have stomach trouble or diabetes. How I wish I was healthy.

If the principle 'the oneness of body and mind' is true, then my spiritual determination should spur me on, and there is no reason my body cannot be restored to health. Reflecting, I realize I must firmly establish powerful faith.

A battle with my destiny. A battle with myself. Nothing could be more valuable and appropriate for my lifelong practice of faith.

Went to Tsurumi in the evening to give a lecture. Every time I lecture, realize that I must study harder.

Tuesday, May 25.

Physical condition extremely poor. Have been pondering deeply my severe destiny. Pained over the complexity of my own feelings.

The Suiko Group met at 6:00 at the headquarters. My spirits were not especially high. Like a brave soldier who has just entered a peaceful forest. The other members, though, were quite inspired. This is as it should be. Received strict guidance from President Toda. Felt as if I had been stabbed in the chest. Faith. Nothing but faith. Faith with passionate resolve.

Thursday, May 27. Clear.

My slight fever and poor health continue unchanged. Recalled Takuboku's poem "A Cloud is Genius." A youth division staff meeting at 7:00. H. and T. attended as well as S., Y., I. and H. of the young women's division. Worked out details for implementing YMD and YWD activities for the latter half of the year.

9:30—a chapter leaders meeting at O.'s. This month resulted in 420 new families. Worried that the chapters may get too caught up in the propagation numbers alone. My hope is that we will advance steadily, amid warm bonds of unity, without one person discarding faith or disrespecting the Gohonzon. But can such a large-scale movement be free from a little overzealousness; can we help becoming result-oriented? As of now, I cannot clearly answer these questions, even for myself.

Wednesday, June 2.

An empty day. It seems as though part of me despises peace and quiet. Perhaps I prefer to boldly face life's onslaught of trials and tribulations. Tonight, we wrapped up the end-of-month accounting for May. Held a joint staff conference at the W. Gardens restaurant. Feeling quite ill. Fatigued. For the sake of the Gakkai's future, must not die, must survive until I can raise many excellent juniors. Sensei is not well either. Cannot help shedding tears when I think of the Gakkai's prospects after he is gone.

Thursday, June 3. Cloudy.

My illness seems to gradually get worse. Tonight, a YMD leaders meeting at Shibuya Civic Auditorium. The room was completely packed. Everyone was bathed in sweat; spirits soared. Trust them deeply. Afterward, met with several leaders over dinner in Shinjuku. Never have I felt so loathsome and disagreeable as I have tonight. A night I hope I soon forget.

Sunday, June 6. Rain.

Had planned to take the 6:00 a.m. train from Tokyo to Taiseki-ji. Finally left at 7:30. Physical condition, extremely poor. Feel like death. Disappointment, agony — it even hurts to breathe.

11:30 a.m. — finally arrived at the head temple. Was granted an audience with the high priest at noon. He offered me a cup of sake. Extremely grateful. I and several other leaders invited about thirty young acolytes to engage in a friendly discussion at the Rikyo-bo lodging. At 2:00, we chanted before the Dai-Gohonzon. A light rain continued to fall. Kneeling behind the high priest, I poured my entire life into gongyo. Prayed from the bottom of my heart for my health to return. Left the head temple after 3:00 p.m., hurrying to Fuji Station by taxi with my mother, my wife, S. and others. Took the *Genkai*, the second-class express, back to Tokyo. Exhausted. Going to bed early.

Monday, June 7. Cloudy, then rain.

My physical condition has become serious — but I cannot take time off from work.

Read *Wind and Waves*, a book that describes the life of Teisuke Akiyama.[1] Though it seems his life was truly interesting, I cannot sympathize with his way of thinking. Each has his or her own way of living, so as not to have any regrets. Akiyama took his course and I shall take mine.

A ceremony to congratulate new Study Department professors from 6:30 p.m. Participants numbered nearly 130, but the meeting somehow lacked spirit. Was this because of Mr. Toda's fatigue, or was it due to my own poor physical condition? Throughout the meeting, kept thinking that senior leaders should be more considerate of their juniors. Cannot help feeling the seniors are selfish.

Worried about the Gakkai's future. To allow the youth to grow freely, to carry out their activities with peace of mind — is this not our mentor's true intention? Top leaders should advance with the same broad mind as their mentor. Unless this happens many pure-hearted youth with boundless potential may have their growth stunted. Without ever perceiving their mentor's heart, they will fall by the wayside. Am I the only one who grieves over this? Cannot help feeling there is something lacking when I consider the future.

Stand alone, young king, yet uncrowned!

1. Teisuke Akiyama (1868–1950). Politician and publisher of the Meiji-period newspaper *Niroku Shimpo*. He and his newspaper won popularity by carrying out exten-

sive campaigns to expose the injustices of Japanese monopolies and later to abolish prostitution.

Tuesday, June 8. Cloudy with showers.

A cool, dreary day. My finances are marginal—like today's weather. Felt uninspired all day.

Scolded severely by Mr. Toda in the evening. The leaders closest to him were also scolded. A day that starts out wrong, ends up the same.

Carp try again and again to climb a waterfall. Grass and flowers that have been trod upon, blossom again. Surmounting many adversities, people achieve greatness. Must youth be a time of such emotional turmoil?

"The Record of the Orally Transmitted Teachings" states:

> "Ultimately, Shakyamuni's four great disciples of average capacity represent the four phases our lives: birth, aging, sickness and death. Kashyapa represents birth; Katyayana, old age; Maudgalyayana, illness; and Subhuti, death."
>
> —(GZ, 730–31)

Strangely, I sense the dark portent of my own death. Is this what is called 'the devil of death.' My faith has reached the seven-year point. Am I about to face my greatest and most difficult trial? Feel especially tormented and lonesome tonight.

Now, with no close friend or assistant, I feel as if my energy is waning, moment by moment. Tears flow in torrents. I do not want to die now. I am only twenty-six. It would be too miserable to die now without fully understanding the depth of my life, without having made any great contribution to humankind or society, or without repaying my debt of gratitude to my mentor. To allow myself to die now would be equivalent to committing suicide. It would be pitiful to die, still mocked by others.

Wednesday, June 9. Cloudy.

Discussed various matters with Mr. Toda in the president's room for three hours beginning at noon. He is worried about my loss of weight. Told him that I worry about his health. "I am overjoyed at your sincere concern," he told me.

No one loves the youth division more than I do. Must enable them to someday become active on the grand stage of world affairs, not to mention Japan. The final stage of kosen-rufu will not be accomplished by my seniors [the disciples of President Makiguchi].

A meeting in the president's room from 5:00 to 6:30. Questions were posed regarding the guidance and information departments.

A district lecture in Ikebukuro at 7:30.

Worried about the weak spirit of the division chief, Z. Can't help thinking a leader who intimidates his juniors is weak at heart.

Thursday, June 10. Cloudy. Rain later in the day.

National Time Day. Very fatigued.

7:00—a meeting of outlying groups at Jozai-ji.

At 9:00, a youth division staff conference at the headquarters. The attendants were Chief T.; U. and M., YMD and YWD chiefs, respectively; and the rest of the staff.

This was the largest conference since the youth division was inaugurated.

A final conclusion was reached regarding the entire operation and function of the youth division. Management, programs and activities were unanimously approved by all present. The meeting closed at 10:30.

Talked with H. until 11:30 p.m. He is a fine friend.

Ten years from now, I think the Gakkai will be playing an important role at the core of society; active in the fields of politics, economics, culture and education. Now is the time to encourage youth division members to study earnestly, specializing in one of these specific fields. To this end, I must master many things myself.

The leaders should have ability and power. They should never be sly or conniving. Without earnest study, they are not qualified to be leaders. As part of my responsibility, I will study, little by little. Reason and passion—intellect and conviction.

My wife met me at Omori Station. Together, we ate tempura in San'no. A happy memory.

Saturday, June 12. High clouds.

Though early summer, today was like a bright, fresh spring day. For me, however, it was somewhat empty.

Talked about law with H. at I. restaurant in the morning.

In the afternoon, we went to T. Company in Mitaka. Deeply impressed with the employees, all working together in earnest, burning with the spirit of construction. Praying for their success. Praying for their development—as a castle of kosen-rufu. Deeply sense the difference between workplaces located in the dirty urban soot of Tokyo and those of the open plains of Musashino. People in the cities forget the greatness of nature; this is equivalent to forgetting their humanity. I myself never want to become such a man, living like a cog in a giant machine.

Attended an evening Twelfth Corps meeting. Everyone was somewhat subdued.

Read *Parallel Lives* by Plutarch. Late to bed. Will read again tomorrow.

Sunday, June 13.

Stayed home in the morning. Went to the public bath, despite a headache.

In the evening, met with 130 old First Corps members at the W. Hall in Den'enchohu. My constant hope—that they fight throughout their lives, that they be future able leaders of society, and that they be capable individuals for kosen-rufu.

Read to about 3:00 a.m. My wife cautioned me to go to bed earlier.

Monday, June 14. Rain.

My physical condition has improved slightly. This really makes me happy. But the rainy season continues. To Mr. Toda's in the afternoon. Studied Buddhism. In the evening, Mr. Toda, his wife, and I invited the branch manager from M. Company to dinner at K. restaurant in Kudan.

Tuesday, June 15. Cloudy.

A cool day. Periodically, ideals and reality mix and my mind becomes very complex. There are times I want to blame others, while overlooking my own faults. Must not forget to self-reflect and consider my own shortcomings.

Want to live powerfully and righteously throughout my life—to become respected and trusted by the people of society. If I cannot accomplish this, I would like to be recognized by history after I die. No, I think I would rather be a true disciple whose actions are recognized by the Mystic Law and who is praised by the Daishonin. Should this not be my ultimate perspective on life?

A chapter secretaries meeting at the chapter house at 5:00. H. also attended. Completely lacking in spirit. When their senior lacks spirit and conviction, juniors really suffer.

A youth division staff conference at 9:00. Disappointed we could not come to a consensus. T. came late to the staff room. Has he no sense of awareness as a leader? Strictly cautioned him on his error, pointing out that important strategies for the future are conceived here; this is where great plans for the next hundred years of kosen-rufu are laid. YMD Chief U. was in quite high spirits.

> When we revere Myoho-renge-kyo inherent in our own life as the object of devotion, the Buddha nature within us is summoned forth and manifested by our chanting of Nam-myoho-renge-kyo. This is what is meant by "Buddha."
> — "HOW THOSE INITIALLY ASPIRING TO THE WAY CAN ATTAIN BUDDHAHOOD THROUGH THE LOTUS SUTRA" (WND, 887)

Wednesday, June 16. Clear.

My physical condition has again taken a turn for the worse. Went home in the afternoon and rested for a while.

The organization is vital. It has even been said the organization has a life of its own. Therefore, nothing is more terrible than a thoughtless or foolish leader in the organization. I burn with rage when I hear of inconsiderate leaders who try to lord it over their pure-hearted and sincere members.

Gave a lecture at S.'s in Tsurumi this evening. Happy that, perhaps because I've gotten a little rest, I could give a powerful, inspiring lecture. Personal guidance after the lecture. A few members accompanied me to Tsurumi Plaza Station on the Keihin express line. Filled with deep gratitude. Though we use the term *members* to describe our comrades in faith, when compared to the members of a labor union, of the communist or socialist parties, or even of conservative political groups, how much more profound, powerful and praiseworthy are the bonds we share — bonds of unity without prejudice or class distinction.

Nothing is more beautiful or worthy of respect than the human mind. But, on the other hand, nothing can be so ugly. However much our technological society has progressed in the nineteenth and twentieth centuries, this truth about the human mind never changes. This is because the principle 'three thousand realms in a single moment of life' illustrates the essence of life.

First, I must firmly establish this as my perspective on life. Then, I must perform a dance on the grand stage of kosen-rufu. Will overcome the storms of my youth.

Thursday, June 17. Overcast.

My physical condition is somewhat better. Whenever my health improves, my voice becomes more resilient. The Gosho teaches that one's voice expresses the 'oneness of body and mind.'

Talked over various matters for about an hour with Senior Director M. At 7:00, a unit chiefs meeting was held for Bunkyo Chapter—at the headquarters.

Shared my thoughts on the following topics:
1. The meaning of faith as freedom from doubt.
2. Doing our best in our present positions.
3. Never being passive; instead taking the initiative in faith activities.

A bright, pleasant meeting. Faith, study, work—these I must repeat throughout my entire life.

Friday, June 18. Cloudy.

Chilly all day.

9:30—to Kobayashi on business. Feeling ill. Talked with H. for about two hours over lunch. He seems dispirited. Poured my whole life into encouraging him. I wonder how much he understood. Heard Mr. Toda is not feeling well. He was absent from the office this morning.

In the evening, he conducted the Friday lecture at Toshima Civic Auditorium. Heard he began lecturing on the Gosho "The Actions of the Votary of the Lotus Sutra."

Met with Corps Chief A. and thirty leaders at S.'s. Discussed politics and economics. Truly enjoyable. When I think of these young pioneers' future, however, I realize I must convince them how important it is to study many different fields.

Returned home after 11:00. Fatigued. Tomorrow, I want to meet with President Toda.

Saturday, June 19. Rain.

Light rain all day, a cool day.

Met with President Toda at the headquarters all morning. Though he was ill, and quite busy as well, he seemed in especially good spirits throughout our meeting. Received careful guidance and counsel on matters both public and private. My heart was brimming with passion.

The second proposal for the youth division staff conference passed. Feel a load has been lifted from my shoulders. The staff conference is still a matter for the youth division to decide upon. But unless it can become a forum for discussing all sorts of problems — such as politics and education, both foreign and domestic — kosen-rufu will not be perfected. The magnitude of responsibility for such a staff conference will be immeasurable.

Had dinner with Mrs. Toda in the evening. Raining. Looks like the rain will continue all night.

Sunday, June 20. Rain.

Rain in the morning, then overcast. Stayed home in the morning. A Mukojima Chapter general meeting began at 12:30 at the Shutoku School Auditorium in Katsushika Ward.

I was scheduled to offer congratulatory words, but urgent business prevented me from attending. It pains me to think how S. must feel. No words can express my apology. If we believe that "this is my last moment," we can earnestly and sincerely discuss the essence of Buddhism. Words spoken with such pure, sincere determination can warmly and deeply touch anyone's heart.

Returned home a little before midnight.

Discussed the family budget with my wife. When I look at the difficult times my brothers have been facing, my family seems very happy and fortunate.

Monday, June 21. Clear.

If I don't take care of my health, I cannot fulfill the important task of kosen-rufu. The morning lecture, on East Asian history, is making steady progress. How great Sensei is! Only praying that the day will soon come when he can actively take his place as a world leader.

Hot and humid in the afternoon. A planning meeting for Bunkyo Chapter at the chapter chief's house at 6:00.

Through propagation, we can save many suffering people. The next important matter is raising capable people. We must develop several thousand capable leaders. Thinking about the Gakkai's progress. Senior leaders should be deeply concerned about this point.

Because of his illness, President Toda spent the night at the headquarters. H. and I looked after him until late. Started for home, feeling reassured about his condition after he chatted with us cheerfully.

On the way home, thought over and over about what Sensei had talked about. He had given guidance on the following topics:

1. Ethnic migration.

2. The newspaper business.
3. Theories on life.

Awestruck at his sharpness, spirit and intellect. If Sensei were to fall, the Gakkai would amount to nothing. The company and my family would be as good as ruined. No, it would mean all East Asia would be on the verge of darkness. His lecture on the difference between the view of life as expounded in Theravada Buddhism and the theory of life based on the principle of 'eternity, happiness, true self and purity' as taught in Mahayana Buddhism remains vivid in my mind.

H. accompanied me as far as Gotanda. A lonesome-looking man. Is he fully confident of his own ability? Want to protect this brave individual's future. To bed, 1:50.

Tuesday, June 22. Cloudy.

Chilly. Is this really the rainy season?

There are days when the sun shines and others when it remains hidden. There are days my faith is dynamic and others when it seems somehow weak. Is it fitting to compare the two? What great effort is required to continue throughout life with faith like flowing water. My deepest respect goes to those who have assiduously persevered in their faith for ten or twenty years, though they may be aged or living a mundane life.

Went for a haircut at lunch time. It's been a while. To Omiya on business with N.

A Suiko Group meeting in the evening. Mr. Toda emphasized the importance of establishing an organization of Asian states. He said the people of Asia should unite as soon as possible.

He seemed extremely fatigued.

How fortunate are the Suiko Group members. In the future, a sparkling stage awaits them as great heroes. As Suiko Group members, they bear a tremendous responsibility. They must thoroughly carry out our mentor's guidance. Many hardships lay ahead.

After the meeting, I and three other staff members shared our concern over our young men's division chief. I sometimes feel indignant over the rapidly changing nature of people's minds. Ultimately, the important thing is that I, myself, live on strongly. Must stride on, boldly and freely, across the land. Returned home after 11:00. Read a book.

Wednesday, June 23. Rain.

Rained heavily from the morning. Changed into winter clothes. Seriously reflected on my morning lack of daimoku. Went to Tsurumi on business. Visited S. at his home. He is very impudent. I will endure it. But three years from now, who will be the victor?—this I pondered on the way home.

In the evening, a lecture and guidance meeting in Ikebukuro. Finished at 10:30. Would like to develop the habit of reading, even if only a little, every morning. Will go to Hokkaido in August. Boundless plains; land that I adore! I will deeply breathe the fresh air. Feel almost choked by the hustle and bustle of Tokyo. When can I travel to the United States, Australia or Europe? For me, it may be in the distant future. But I must definitely go, to carry out my mission for kosen-rufu. Thought until midnight about many things. My mind is clear.

Thursday, June 24. Cloudy.

My health has gotten a little better. Relieved.

Thinking on my own about renovating the Gakkai's secretariat section. It is likely that I alone will present this view. Visited T. Company in Mitaka in the afternoon. Musashino in the early summer is really pleasant. Can almost taste the air's sweetness. Talked until evening with the staff, including the president, H.

7:00—a youth division staff meeting.

Discussed the following:

1. The summer training course.
2. The *Seikyo Shimbun*.
3. A formal protest to the *Tokyo Times*.

Spoke to Y. for the first time in a while. An unfortunate person. Hope H. and M. will grow more. Don't know what to make of someone who lives in the world of faith with such a haughty mind. I dislike that attitude more than anything.

Friday, June 25. Cloudy, then rain.

Awakened by a nightmare. A dream of death—a dream of demons; it was a long, long dream of death.

Seriously reflecting on my inability to do a perfect gongyo. Went to K. School and stayed there all morning. The summer rain continues.

A Study Department professors meeting beginning at 5:30. Everyone devoted themselves to their study with serious expressions. Must not fall behind the others. As a future leader, must never neglect study. Talked with Professor H. after the meeting.

A chapter leaders meeting commenced at 8:30. Worried that if I did not get home early enough, I would be too tired at work tomorrow to get anything done. Home just before midnight.

Saturday, June 26. Rain.

Haven't shaved for four days. Not in good spirits. Arranged with Mrs. Toda to go to the T. Theater someday soon.

4:00 — at the headquarters; prepared to welcome thirty young priests and acolytes. From the Gakkai, the president and top leaders attended. Chanted from the bottom of my heart for the healthy growth of these young phoenixes who will shoulder the priesthood's future. A light rain fell after the meeting. Strolled around the grounds in front of the Imperial Palace, talking with friends about the future.

Home late. Tired. Don't want to think about anything else today.

Sunday, June 27. Rain.

Slept until 10:00. Feverish.

T. came over. Could not do gongyo before leaving for Hoshi Pharmaceutical College Auditorium in Gotanda to attend the Suginami Chapter second general meeting. The meeting seemed a relative success. Sensei, who loves Suginami Chapter the most, looked delighted.

Evening — accompanied H. to the Education Hall in Kanda.

The rainy season continues. Sang songs with and encouraged the Bunkyo Chapter members until 9:00, then returned home. My bright, warm family.

Approaching the end of June.

Monday, June 28. Rain.

The rain of early summer continues; yesterday, today.

Missed seeing Sensei in the morning. A lifelong mentor makes me profoundly happy. No honor in the world compares to that of having a lifelong mentor.

To Setagaya in the rain. K. appears to be taking faith. Seems that an elementary school teacher has many worries. A group discussion with the chapter chief in the evening. At times the discussion progressed as we wanted it to, but at other times it did not. Afterward, hurried to the

S. restaurant for the monthly executive committee meeting. Finished at 8:00. Back to Kamata by taxi with the elderly S.

Read until midnight.

Tuesday, June 29. Rain.

Morning, scolded by Sensei. For me, scolding is frequent.

My younger brother visited for the first time in a year. We ate together at I. restaurant. Feel so sorry for him. As a memento of our meeting, I gave him a fountain pen, a carrying case for his monthly train pass and some spending money.

To my chapter chief's house in the afternoon. Administered a practice exam for our chapter members taking the Study Department oral exam this evening. Wonder how many from our chapter will pass. Those who have studied tirelessly and acquired real ability will do well on the test. Must emphasize that those lacking in study will not be qualified future leaders. I think tests are unnecessary. The times, however, demand a system of examinations. Are the only excellent people those who can pass university exams? Are the members who pass Gakkai study exams not happier than they? Ultimately, this will be clearly proven through lifelong experience.

6:00, at the headquarters—the oral exams were held. I was responsible for the examinees from Suginami and Osaka chapters, who numbered twenty-six in all. At the last professors meeting, I was scolded severely by President Toda with regard to my grading of Assistant Professor S.'s test. I had tried to be fair and accurate, but Sensei told me that to become a great leader, I must become more generous in my grading. Am I too strict? Had taken my way of grading for granted. Returned home, feeling lonesome. It was after 11:00

Wednesday, June 30. Cloudy with occasional showers.

Hot and humid. Changed into a shirt with an open collar. An open-necked shirt befits action. Think it would be truly great if the National Diet, the United Nations and all government offices adopted the open collar as acceptable attire. From now on, year by year, formality will become less important worldwide. I, too, must take another step in my growth. Must not have a childish, easygoing attitude. It is clear that the world of the future will be more complex. Since this is the case, I must take great pains to train myself and devote myself to strict practice.

Echoes from the objective world, waves of my own anguish — drifting; I am liable to lose my conviction. Still young, immature; green.

Extremely tired; missed the senior leaders meeting. Will be scolded, most likely. Rebuked myself for being the most self-centered person in the Gakkai. Went to the public baths. Stopped for sushi on the way home. Talked with the owner about many things. He seems to want to take faith. Got into bed early; read Yonejiro Noguchi. Tomorrow, July begins. Will advance with a greater resolution.

Thursday, July 1. Cloudy, occasional rain.

Hot and humid.

Went to Surugadai Library at 1:00 p.m. Absorbed myself in reading the biographies of the world's three great men until 5:00. Surprised at my own lack of patience. Seeing the students' serious attitude makes me smile. Worry they may push themselves too hard and ruin their health. In Kanda, bought a copy of *Japan's Economic History* for ¥2,000. Have to study.

To the chapter chief's house at 6:00 for a chapter staff meeting. It was reported that the number of families converted through June propagation activities was 503. Everyone has fought well. The foundation is now complete. In high spirits, gave guidance until 10:00 about propagating the Gohonzon and the strictness of faith. For everyone's great benefit, I alone summoned the courage to scold and to encourage those present. Extremely grateful to them, as they are delighted to follow. Tonight Mars shone with mysterious brilliance and clarity. Cannot help pondering the wonder of the universe and its heavenly bodies.

Fluctuations, centripetal force, gravitation; light-years, atmosphere, distance, circular form; living beings, life and death — how mysterious! Must come to understand it by living my entire life based upon the Mystic Law. Never have I thought so seriously about life after death as I have tonight. Rather, I have never been so worried about it.

Hiromasa stayed with my wife's parents. Talked quietly with my wife until late at night. Hope she will never become old. Want her to be eternally youthful.

Friday, July 2. Cloudy.

The sun shone for the first time in quite a while. A bright morning. Nevertheless, could not absorb this morning's Western history lecture. Must not be lazy. Whoever fails to study deeply will regret it for a lifetime.

Discussed the company's accounts and administrative structure with M. until after 2:00, then talked about making home visits and other subjects.

Met S. just before 3:00 at Tokyo's S. restaurant. Offered my opinions regarding his company's personnel structure and sales network. He seemed overjoyed to hear my views. Will pray for his benefit.

6:00 — A Bunkyo Chapter leaders meeting at S.'s. Composed a song for the Tenth Corps. Putting my own determination into the lyrics, I presented it to them.

> *Surging before the storm of the five impurities,*
> *Raging waves arise,*
> *Young warriors! Brandishing the sword of justice,*
> *Advance for the sake of your homeland!*
>
> *Marching on, toward Kun-lun Mountain,*
> *Astride white horses, you fight!*
> *Valiant, noble, loyal;*
> *You proudly live up to your name as protectors.*

A. and the others have been fighting hard. Will take good care of those chapter and corps leaders who have been really striving. The joy of seeing my friends in Bunkyo Chapter prosper — the pain that I feel when they are suffering.

Stopped by at the headquarters afterwards. President Toda was still in his office. Seeing my mentor's dignified figure moves me to tears.

Saturday, July 3. Rain, then overcast.

A hot day. The heat in the office was torturous. Couldn't help feeling exhausted. Felt like going home before the day was half over. Next month is the summer training course. Applications to participate will be accepted August 1–3. Each year, must use this training course as a steppingstone to train myself to my fullest ability. Must do away with my spoiled egoism.

Arrived at the headquarters at 3:00. Sitting before the Gohonzon at the headquarters, a sense of solemnity, vastness and power naturally wells up within me.

Went to the president's office to report to Sensei. When I see his compassionate and merciful eyes, I feel strangely peaceful and secure. Only pray that he lives long.

This evening, took my wife and child to a movie. My son slept through more than half the picture. My wife seemed very happy. Want to take her again. Tomorrow, I will go to the head temple.

Sunday, July 4. Cloudy.

Buddhism is truly strict. Was one minute late to an audience with the high priest. Severely scolded by Sensei. Felt awful. The ceremony of chanting before the Dai-Gohonzon was at 1:30. When I see people escorting their parents to the head temple to chant to the Dai-Gohonzon, I am envious. Those who can carry out this ultimate act of filial devotion are the greatest of human beings. Must visit this "Eagle Peak" once each month. As a direct disciple of President Toda, I must carry out such a practice if I am to be a person of genuine faith in any sense of the term. Took a bus to Fuji Station, then a train to Numazu Station where we all boarded the express back to Tokyo. Fell asleep inside the train, exhausted. Must have snored terribly.

This evening, did gongyo and chanted daimoku to my heart's content. Reported that I could pray to the Dai-Gohonzon of the High Sanctuary of True Buddhism. Cannot forget about world kosen-rufu. My heart leaps when I think of setting out to accomplish kosen-rufu throughout the world after carrying out propagation in Japan.

Monday, July 5. Overcast, with rain later on.

Light rain again today. Society's dark reverberations and the tide of the times are gradually encroaching. Voices of fear, brutality; savagery! This is the evil age of the Latter Day of the Law. Must live powerfully. The only way is to have courageous faith. After lunch, bought gifts for our company's business associates for the summer season.[1] Though they will be presented on the company's behalf, paid for them all with my own money.

6:30 — a lecture for the Study Department's fifth level on "The Object of Devotion for Observing the Mind." Beginning in September, must pour my entire heart and soul into study. Was warned by Sensei during the morning study meeting about certain bad habits I've developed in reading the Gosho aloud.

A meeting at the headquarters to plan local propagation activities. The planning, focused on the board of directors, progressed very slowly. Expecting a great change in the board of directors. The Gakkai's spirit and ideals should be put into practice more deeply, more powerfully, more fairly and more rapidly. Ate *soba* [buckwheat noodles] afterward with my chapter chief. Met three or four Gakkai members on the train home. Each was energetic. Rely on them for the future. The current of the next era has begun to flow. Ten or twenty years from now, society will be astonished at our progress. Moreover, I think they will come to trust us.

1. Summer season: A traditional midsummer visiting and gift-giving period.

Wednesday, July 7. Cloudy with periodic showers.

Chilly all day. Nature's movements follow the sublimest principles of science, do they not? Rather, they are functions of the universal life, the very workings of the Mystic Law. Therefore, it is absolutely certain and extremely reasonable that whoever embraces the Mystic Law will lead the ultimate, supreme life.

In good physical condition. Overjoyed. As usual, talked with staff members all morning. Seems that those who lead leisurely, uneventful lives become unhappy, while those who courageously challenge many waves of adversity find meaning in their lives.

Went to Hodogaya by train in the afternoon. Attended a discussion meeting at the M. residence. A dynamic meeting of more than two hundred people. Eight guests decided to join. Nothing is more pleasurable than propagation activities.

We are truly happy. This is because we have met the greatest person in the world, President Josei Toda.

If we forget the debt of gratitude we owe our mentor, from then on we will be lower than animals. Those who devote their entire lives to the mentor — these are true disciples.

My wife is three months pregnant. Feeling my responsibility growing heavier each day. As a man of responsibility, I will courageously fight to open the way, no matter what hardships I may face, for my wife and for my children.

Thursday, July 8. Cloudy.

Cool all day. Reflected on the ultimate importance of making daily efforts to build a foundation. A Tokyo native must not be impatient. Must train myself to be more composed and to develop the power of patience.

Went to a used bookstore in Kanda this evening. The book I wanted was too expensive; disappointed that I could not buy it. Bought seven books in all. Kanda is a powerfully appealing place.

7:00 — to Tsurumi Chapter to lecture on "The Opening of the Eyes."

Put my whole life into it. Returning home, thought of how sorry I will feel for the members who come to my lectures if I do not grow more. True ability. Must always nurture and strive to develop my true ability.

Friday, July 9. Partly cloudy.

This afternoon, it was my turn to give guidance at the headquarters. Talked with more than thirty people. Wonder whether each person could accept and understand my guidance. Still green — must grow and improve rapidly.

From 6:30 to 10:00, a youth division general staff meeting. Discussed the following topics, among others:

1. Strengthening the corps.
2. Buddhist study.
3. Expanding the organization.

Met with K. in Nakano after the meeting.

Saturday, July 10. Cloudy.

Woke up early in the morning and read a book by Kikuchi Kan.[1] Ate breakfast hastily and left for work.

Visited Sensei's home in the evening for summer season greetings. Imposed on them until late in the evening. They fed me well — feel ashamed. Mrs. Toda taught me something about women's kimonos, cooking, important things women must be aware of and other subjects. Left for home a little before midnight. Each year the automobile traffic in front of my house gets heavier. In a few years it will become unbearably noisy.

1. Kikuchi Kan (1888–1948): Author, journalist, playwright and founder of the influential literary magazine *Bungei Sunju*. His contributions have had a major influence on Japanese writing and journalism.

Sunday, July 11. Rain.

Light rain from morning. The refreshing coolness is a true relief. Accompanied Sensei and his family to the Imperial Theater at 3:00. On the way back, we stopped for dinner in Shinbashi. An enjoyable afternoon.

In the evening, the youth division general staff met — until midnight. The staff members, all excellent individuals, will become the center of the Gakkai and of Japanese society, ten or twenty years from now. In the mountains or on the plains, they will leap courageously into action.

Afterward, took everyone out for sushi. They ate well. Rely on them. To campaign, they must have bodies like iron.

Tuesday, July 13. Cloudy with scattered showers.

Caught a glimpse of the moon tonight for the first time in a while. It fills the youthful poet's heart with joy. Good and evil, right and wrong; theory and practice, reason and emotion, material and spiritual, present and future; power, position, authority; the people. Many ideas come and go. From day to day, I sometimes feel I am being drawn into a muddy swamp. Other times I feel I am soaring in the sky. The human mind is a mysterious thing, never stopping, even for a moment. I wonder what dire circumstances my life would be in by now if I did not have faith or a mentor in life. A frightening prospect.

Copyedited the guidance in Mr. Toda's notebook until shortly before 1:00 a.m.

Wednesday, July 14. Clear, then cloudy.

The sun shone brightly. Filled my lungs with fresh air. Rather cool in the afternoon. Sensei seemed busy with the transcript of his ten major lectures. Disappointed that I could not speak with him for quite some time. Can distinctly sense the power of his wondrous ability.

Must accomplish the following:
1. Support T. Chapter until the very end.
2. Help K. Chapter from the side.
3. Allow S. Chapter to grow and develop until it is the same as our chapter.
4. Make plans for the youth division to advance several more steps.

Must always arrange things in my mind, then put them into practice.

Thursday, July 15. Rain.

The summer rainy season continues. Feeling very fatigued.

Went to T.'s for summer greetings. The family was not at all in good spirits. Miss M. was there. She is a very bright woman. She, however, bears no relationship to me.

I am twenty-six. I have awakened to the determination to be ready to give my life at any time for Buddhism. I have been fighting to my heart's content. If I think about it deeply, however, haven't all my actions been carried out under President Toda's warm protection?

Was invited once again by Sensei to attend a play. The performance began at 5:00 at the Shinbashi Theater. Sensei's family, my wife and I watched a passionate performance. After the show, we separated in front of the theater. My wife and I went to Uraku-cho, then walked home. A peaceful evening.

Friday, July 16. Cloudy.

Left home in the morning wearing a new open-necked shirt. Dislike formal attire—find it inconvenient. As society grows more complex each year, clothing styles will become more practical. Went to B.'s home in the afternoon with summer season gifts. Such formal obligations should be abolished. Don't think this sort of custom exists in the workplaces of Europe or America. Must these customs remain to preserve the quality of Japanese culture or for mere tradition?

Ultimately, the well-to-do become more arrogant, while poor people must continually rack their brains to buy suitable gifts for their superiors. What a vicious cycle.

Met at 6:00 at S.'s to finalize plans for the upcoming general meeting. Until 10:00, poured my whole heart into grappling with the details. My oldest son, Hiromasa, is becoming quite a raucous child. What destiny awaits him? Can only pray he becomes a healthy, upstanding individual, a man of pure faith, a believer in the Daishonin's Buddhism.

Saturday, July 17. Cloudy with occasional sunshine.

Was sent to Jonan and Kanagawa on business. Though midsummer, chilly weather continues. So far, it has been a disappointing year, a year of foreboding. The currency exchange rate is ¥765 to the American dollar; concerned about Japan's economic future. Politicians! Leaders! I want to cry out—do your best! Discard your hunger for fame and wealth and donate your lives for the suffering people!

Visited Sensei's home in the evening. Received guidance on various matters. Was also severely reprimanded. This could not be helped; it was totally my fault. Disciples will forge on and grow, no matter how many times they are scolded. Must never become arrogant. For me to think that I, who lacks ability and a solid foundation, am something great—this is arrogance.

Lifelong advancement; lifelong study; lifelong effort; lifelong construction.

Sunday, July 18. Cloudy.

Our long-awaited Bunkyo Chapter general meeting. Not hot, and no rain—a perfect day. Some twenty-five hundred members gathered at Toshima Civic Auditorium. Overjoyed. An impressive day. The opening ceremonies, and the closing ceremonies as well, were full of vigor. The meeting was charged with a fighting spirit. A follow-up meeting at Josen-ji. Everything went excellently. Everyone did well; they fought extremely hard. No face showed any sign of regret. All were bright. Truly fond of these members. They are truly dear to me. When I think of them, tears well up in my eyes. Sensei seemed even happier than I. Will this be my last general meeting? As times progress, will I fight on new battlefields to build castles of the Law? Pondered alone about the next road that kosen-rufu will take.

Monday, July 19. Cloudy, occasional rain.

Monday—a day on which I tend to lose my rhythm and feel off-balance. Since it's the first step for the week, must make a healthy start on this day. In the afternoon, a special staff conference to determine summer propagation activities. The meeting was somewhat restrained; dull. How self-serving I am. Strictly reflected that this is my greatest weak point. Then again, I am also obstinate.

Highly value my great teacher, excellent seniors, fine friends and good neighbors! Must care for and respect them.

Tuesday, July 20. Cloudy.

Deep agony day after day. Could finally see the sun break through the clouds. The daily papers are filled with articles about the atomic and hydrogen bombs. My head hurts from reading them. This is an age in which science's pure essence has been defiled by the worlds of Anger and Hell. In this period of threatened crop damage due to unseasonably cool weather, we can strongly sense the validity of the "On Establishing the Correct Teaching for the Peace of the Land" prophecies.

Went to S.'s in Mukojima in the evening. The downtown area needs a little more cultural growth. S. must awaken and determine to create value and build a new environment through his political efforts.

Returned home alone, immersed in thought. Besides President Toda, I shall bow my head to no one. After Sensei dies, I must act in a pivotal role, taking on heavy responsibilities. Let storms and raging waves come as they may! Resentment, criticism and trickery mean nothing!

Nothing in the universe surpasses the strict law of Buddhism. Later, there was a group chiefs meeting and congratulatory banquet at O.'s. The thoroughly enjoyable meeting finished after 10:00 amid storms of laughter.

Seniors! Lead your juniors by example, through your own growth. Juniors! Continue to follow your seniors and advance!

Wednesday, July 21. Partly cloudy.

Saw a very dignified young woman this morning at Omori Station. She must come from a fine family. Quietly enjoyed her presence. Newspaper reports on the crop damage resulting from the cold weather are frightening. Praying for an end to the food shortage. Waiting to hear of a workable plan by government officials.

The morning Western history lecture continues. Sensei gave earnest guidance, ignoring his own fatigue. Feel ashamed. To Tsurumi in the afternoon for a banquet with women's division members at T. restaurant. Greatly indebted to them for all their hard work. Thanked them. Lectured at Tsurumi Chapter in the evening. Each time I lecture, think that I must make courageous progress; must continue to study.

Thursday, July 22. Clear.

Opportunities to talk with Sensei are few. Feel a sense of solitude. Cannot comprehend his life force and sublime state of mind. He is truly awakened to the mysterious law of Buddhism. Passionate, quiet, cool, insightful, composed, domineering, severe, compassionate....

Want only to purify my faith, step by step. Deeply ashamed of my lack of ability, my tendency to rely on shallow understanding.

A lecture in Ikebukuro between 7:00 and 8:00. Centered on a passage from "The Opening of the Eyes" but did not finish. Beginning this fall, I must exert myself even harder in studying Buddhism.

After 8:00, attended a Kamata Chapter leaders meeting at Toshima Civic Auditorium. Filling the hall, the meeting was a great success. I spoke briefly, saying how splendid it is to awaken to the Gakkai's fundamental mission, the mission to accomplish kosen-rufu. This mission only has meaning when we stand up together to take the lead in each area. Afterward, went for sushi with some of the leaders. Had a dull time. Leaders must not be small-minded.

Friday, July 23. Cloudy.

Today passed quickly. This week, too, has gone by swiftly—it's already Friday. Keenly feel that the fundamental power behind every campaign is one's life force. A cool day. Want to carry out my faith, strictly and nobly advancing along the true, great path throughout my life. 7:30—to Jozai-ji in Ikebukuro to attend an M. Corps meeting. Spoke about:

1. The importance of unity.
2. The relationship between Gakkai activities and the workplace.
3. The ideals and implementation of Buddhist study.

9:30—Escorted Sensei to Ueno Station where we left for a general meeting in Akita. About three hundred members gathered, mostly of the young women's division. Surprised at their success, but they lack unity. When I think of social status and popularity, I realize they merely obstruct kosen-rufu. I, alone, worry over these things. More substantial training is necessary for the Gakkai to advance. On the way home, walked with Sensei's family near Shinobazu Pond in Ueno. This peaceful pond has recently turned into one of terror. If average, honest people, or women in general cannot walk through such a park with peace of mind, how can we call our country a democracy? Enraged thinking about irresponsible and crafty politicians. Dinner at the S. Chinese restaurant. A happy day, a happy evening. And lately, every day has been a happy one.

Saturday, July 24. Cloudy.

Spent the morning in Kanagawa on business. O., M. and Y. are typical common citizens. At times, however, each speaks more wisely than any statesman or scholar. When I talk with them and others like them, I can't help feeling I am hearing the voices of heaven.

Become a lifelong ally of the people.

Live my entire life together with the masses.

Beginning at 5:00, spent about an hour watching the Ryokoko fireworks festival with my family. Thought about how fireworks resemble life's changes.

To the headquarters at 7:00. A Bunkyo Chapter unit chiefs meeting.

In his speech, one leader quoted Taiko Hideyoshi,[1] saying, "People are at once the greatest and the smallest thing in the world." Thought what great words these are. Home just before 11:00.

1. Taiko Hideyoshi: Toyotomi Hideyoshi. *Taiko* is an honorific title meaning "grand minister of state." See note on p. 146.

Sunday, July 25. Cloudy with showers.

Spent all morning cutting out newspaper articles and fixing my bookshelf. At noon, took Sensei's family to see a Kabuki play, which we all enjoyed watching until 4:00. In the evening, a Bunkyo Chapter leaders meeting. The chapter has made magnificent progress.

Must heed the following points:

1. Give thorough guidance on propagation.
2. Assign the most capable people as group and district chiefs as soon as possible.
3. Always consider how to put the right person in the right place.
4. Show heartfelt respect to the unity of members and unit chiefs; give them confidence.
5. Let them know that all have their own individual missions as Bodhisattvas of the Earth.

Monday, July 26. Cloudy, then clear.

Have now practiced this faith for almost seven full years. A long time; yet, it has passed swiftly. Today was the first summerlike day of the season. Worried if the low temperatures continue, the rice crops will suffer. Praying for an abundant harvest. Afternoon, went to T. Company to lend my support. Everyone is working hard. Always awaiting the day they will overcome this difficult situation and conduct their business happily, with peace of mind.

In this world, economic collapse means the end of everything—the nation, the individual and the family. Is this the way it should be? No, the ultimate problem lies in preventing the environment from sapping people's determination, in other words, their resolution to defeat devillish forces. Either our determination is destroyed by the environment or we develop a condition of life powerful enough to reconstruct the environment. Must ponder deeply the relationship between life and its environment.

Wednesday, July 28. Cloudy.

A hot day. Bought two Japan Airlines tickets, one for Sensei and one for myself. Feel a childlike excitement at flying for the first time. Went to the headquarters at 6:30 to discuss problems and lay plans for a Study Department general meeting. Late in the evening, received a phone call from Sensei. Was scolded severely. This has deep meaning. Had no time to offer an explanation.

Thursday, July 29. Clear, then cloudy.

In the evening, a staff meeting at the G. Chinese restaurant. Surprised to see the G. so run down. I felt especially disappointed because I had thought it an elegant establishment.

President Toda gave guidance on various topics including:
1. The question of stock prices.
2. The increased issuance of bank notes by the Bank of Japan, and this year's national budget.
3. Praiseworthy individuals who embraced faith in the past.
4. Kosen-rufu in East Asia and the economy.

Visited S.s on the way back. A bright family, filled with good fortune.

Friday, July 30. Cloudy.

Went to Omiya on business. Resent K.'s insolence. Wait another five or ten years, then we will see who is victorious. Exhausted, returned home just after 8:00. Bored. Must take care of my health. Sat quietly at my desk, scribbling notes in my notebook.

Sunday, August 1—Tuesday, August 3.

The summer training course.

Spent a meaningful time at the training course. Visited Shiraito Falls and even went under the falls. Strove to further develop my state of life at this training course. At next year's training course, I will have been practicing this faith for eight full years. Must do my best.

Thursday, August 5. Clear.

10:50. Boarded a Japan Airlines plane with Mr. Toda. The weather was fine. A perfect day for flying. Arrived at Osaka's Itami Airport at 12:30, ten minutes early. S., with about twenty others, greeted us. Went directly to Hanazono Inn. Upon arriving, Sensei earnestly gave guidance.

From 6:30, there was guidance, a lecture, and a question-and-answer session at Yuhigaoka Hall. Finished at 8:00. I, too, delivered a lecture as the chief of staff.

At 8:00, a special corps chiefs meeting was held. Prayed from the bottom of my heart for the development of Kansai, the next bastion of kosen-rufu outside Tokyo—a place with which I share a deep karmic bond. Sensei did not attend the follow-up meeting. I went alone. The meeting was interrupted by a power failure.

Friday, August 6. Cloudy.

Awoke, 6:30. Extremely tired.

Greeted Sensei in his office. He was immersed in sublime contemplation. Such a dignified countenance; that of a great leader, solemn and awe-inspiring. "Daisaku, if I were to die today, would you keep your composure?" he asked. "Do you have confidence enough to become the next prime minister of Japan?"

Left Osaka on the *Swallow*, the 9:00 express to Tokyo.

Hot all day.

Saturday, August 7. Clear.

Very hot, more than 90° F. Everyone in the company is doing well; trust them deeply. Talked with the managers until noon. Visited the chapter chief's home in the evening. Want him to become more serious about the chapter members, the Gakkai and kosen-rufu.

Sunday, August 8. Clear.

Another hot day. Must be more concerned about the family finances.

A meeting, beginning at 10:00, to map out the upcoming summer propagation campaign for each locality. Will throw my entire life into this weeklong activity. I am scheduled to go to Sapporo.

When I think about the path that lies ahead of the Gakkai I am awestruck. Must protect Sensei, since it is my destiny to be the child of such a great leader. A warm evening. Visited a nearby public bath. A beautiful moonlit night.

Monday, August 9. Clear.

The highest temperature of the year. Over 93°. Spent all day in the office. Fatigued, drenched in sweat. Thinking of the members throughout the country diving into the summer propagation activities. Hoping they will take care of their health and avoid accidents.

Returning from Kyushu, Sensei arrived at Haneda Airport at 4:30. He seemed tired. Several people came to greet him. I drove with him to the headquarters. Tomorrow, we go to Hokkaido.

Tuesday, August 10 — Friday, August 20.

Departed Haneda Airport, August 10, 2:20 p.m. — arrived, Chitose, 5:20 p.m.

Departed Chitose, August 20, 7:45 p.m. — arrived, Haneda, 10:30 p.m.

Campaigned in Hokkaido, centering in Sapporo, for ten days.

Created many profound memories at the Marushin Inn, our base of operations. A large field, lined with poplar trees. Flowers blooming in Odori Park. Peaceful houses, peaceful people, peaceful streets. Savored Hokkaido's fragrant scents, which have colored my youth with a thousand emotions. Atsuta Village, Sensei's youthful home, left a particularly deep impression. A refreshing drive along a straight road through the mountains. Sensei, too, seemed delighted. Stayed three days with one of his relatives near his birthplace. To serve my mentor is my supreme honor. Standing alone on a promontory at Atsuta Bay, I faced the Asian continent and voiced my personal determinations. I will never forget the exquisite taste of the *ishikari-nabe* [a seafood and vegetable broth] we ate that evening. Will record the historical events of this trip someday soon. Keenly aware of the deep sense of mission.

Wednesday, August 25. Cloudy, occasional rain.

A cool day. Feeling physically healthy. Must never forget faith. Must remember to maintain strict practice and training. I, myself, am weak. On my own, I am timid and cowardly. Strong faith is important. Need a strong senior; rather, a strong mentor in life. Then, I must become a strong disciple. Went to T. Company in the afternoon. There seems to be a severe problem with management. Hope they will grow into a large company as soon as possible. Met M. in Shinjuku for dinner just after 6:00.

Sunday, August 29. Partly cloudy, then thundershowers.

Glad my physical condition has improved. With this as a turning point, must further my human revolution. Stayed home all morning. The children are noisy, but it's good they are in high spirits. Amazed at how quickly they are growing. Never want to grow old. Wish to live out this century as a youth. Both corps chiefs, Akiya and Suzuki, and later, S. and others, came by. Heavy rain in the evening. Thunder and lightning. Went to S.'s in Yaguchi-no-watashi. Will fight again tomorrow.

Monday, August 30. Cloudy.

Sensei seems healthy and in high spirits. This makes me truly happy. Made a trip to Yokohama on business in the afternoon. A Study Department professors meeting from 5:00. I am now being dispatched to Osaka Chapter each month to give a lecture. Must study.

A general staff meeting from 7:00. Returned home early after a pleasant meeting. Must not neglect gongyo.

Tuesday, August 31. Cloudy, occasional rain.

Another cool day. Everyone has been warning me to eat more vegetables. Agree with them. It stands to reason that a good daily diet is more important to my health than medicine.

6:30—a headquarters leaders meeting at Toshima Civic Auditorium. Afterward, the top leaders met at Jozai-ji. Worried that the senior leaders are not listening carefully enough to the other leaders' views and ideas. Can only await the board of directors' further growth. On the way back, talked carefully with Z. Think he understood a little. A weak and wretched character. I truly misjudged him. Home at midnight.

Tomorrow is September. The Japanese autumn has quietly arrived. Like the coming of spring, I savor autumn's arrival. It gives a true, aesthetic sense of Japan. Autumn seems to epitomize the Japanese spirit.

Wednesday, September 1. Cloudy.

At long last, we have entered the battle of the last part of the year. Must finish this autumn, and this year, with no regrets. Talked with Sensei all morning about many things. Deeply pleased and overjoyed that he trusts me so. He said he wishes to hire another administrative clerk. Will take care of the matter quickly.

An evening lecture in Tsurumi. "On the Buddha's Prophecy." When I have truly prepared myself, my lectures go very well. This is how it should always be. Met with M. at a sushi shop until 11:00. He had visited Miss I. during lunch. Dinner was ready when I returned home. My wife reminded me that when I left for work in the morning I had promised her to be home in time for dinner. No excuse.

Thursday, September 2. Cloudy, occasional showers.

Light rain. Attended the Thursday lecture on the "Expedient Means" and "Life Span" chapters of the Lotus Sutra. Definitely want to attend every week. Went to President Toda's home afterward. Sensei, the general director and I discussed the Gakkai's future progress. Stayed late, until 11:00. Sensei's demeanor was serious. Must reply to his trust in me.

1. On November 3, we will hold a headquarters general meeting. In general, the tempo of propagation activities will be eased, and the focus will be toward steady growth.
2. Establish a substantive membership of twenty thousand for the youth division. Once and for all, discontinue visiting erroneous sect temples to refute their doctrines.

Ask Sensei about the difference between the theoretical and actual teaching of 'never begrudging one's life.'

Friday, September 3. Cloudy, occasional rain.

Sleepy all day. It's gotten cooler. Lacking sleep, especially the past several days. A life that lacks common sense will definitely come to an impasse. Must be careful.

Attended a general meeting of Toshima District, Bunkyo Chapter, at Jozai-ji in the evening. Returned home extremely disappointed. Arrived at home a little before 11:00. Read *Heroes of East and West*.

Saturday, September 4—Sunday, September 5.

At 3:00 p.m. on September 4, boarding a bus in front of the head-quarters building, we departed for the first Suiko Group outdoor training meeting. Sixty participated, including Sensei. Building a campfire along a mountain stream in Hikawa, we prepared dinner. The atmosphere was elated, everyone filled with the highest spirits. Finally, President Toda asked that we meet once again in the same spot ten years from now. He ended his mysteriously prophetic speech saying that at that time there will be something he will ask of us.

Behold! The real power of the Suiko Group twenty years from now.

Behold! The dynamic action of the Suiko in twenty years to come.

Spent the night in a bungalow with Sensei. A memorable two days.

Wednesday, September 15. Clear.

Had dinner with Sensei and his wife at the N. Chinese restaurant. Sensei's physical condition is extremely poor. Was scolded severely. Certainly, what I said was wrong. Can only reflect seriously.

Received guidance about the future responsibilities of the president and general director. Very strict. Sensei is truly a fearsome teacher. Must study! Must remind myself again and again to study! Accompanied Sensei as far as his house, then returned home. It was close to 10:00.

Saturday, September 18—Sunday, September 19.

Saturday, there was a storm. I am twenty-six, the departure point for the journey of my life. Soon, this coming year, I will be twenty-seven. I end each year in the midst of a battle with myself. Sad—disappointing. Why can't I become a youth who is praised by his brilliant teacher?

There are times I think about death and times I am filled with the joy of living. At times I give guidance, overflowing with profound gratitude and appreciation for the Mystic Law; at other times I only go through the motions, giving guidance and carrying out propagation out of obligation. At times I want to run to Sensei's side, while at others, I feel in the depths of my heart like avoiding him.

A lonesome youth. A young man gripped by myriad emotions. Fateful days of youth. I can only advance with all my might. In any event, whether joyful or suffering, I must advance, as a child of the Gakkai.

Friday, October 8. Cloudy, then rain.

The moon shone clearly in the evening sky, reflected in the clear mirror of my heart. On this night, I keenly sense the severity of the way of mentor and disciple. Without Sensei, I do not exist — if mentor and disciple are truly one. At times I envy some of my friends' free lifestyles. Ten years from now, however, the difference in our power and capability will be strikingly apparent. Every day, I live with determination, advancing toward a new goal. Today, too, I will exert my full energy and effort. This is the only way for me, no matter what mountains I may have to cross.

White clouds soar, great rivers flow on and on.

Have been entering verses of poetry on nature in my notebook.

Chapter leaders met in the evening at S.'s. Just after 7:00, a youth division general staff conference convened in the president's room at the headquarters. Topics of discussion were as follows:

1. Public grants.
2. A 10,000-participant pilgrimage.
3. A headquarters general meeting.
4. Sports rally.

With the successful completion of these events, my mission for the seven-hundredth anniversary of Nichiren Daishonin's Buddhism is complete.

Saturday, October 9 — Monday, October 11.

Departed on the night train from Ueno Station at 10:50 p.m. on the 9th. A guidance trip to Sendai. Slept well on the train. The Sixth Sendai Chapter General Meeting was wonderful. Worry that Chapter Chief S.'s unreserved behavior may cause a future problem. Was told that some five thousand attended. The sports center seemed completely full.

President Toda, the general director, Chapter Chief F., Miss I., M., A. and I also attended. Was directed by Sensei at the follow-up meeting to lead the song "Young Men of Japan." Felt exhausted after leading two rounds. Later, I learned that Sensei had sadly related to the other senior leaders his concern for my health, saying, "Because Daisaku is physically weak, he will not live long if he continues to exhaust his energy as he has been." Can only chant daimoku and change my destiny.

Met privately with corps leaders all morning on the 9th. On the 10th, under an autumn sky, the Thirtieth Corps held a sports meet beside the Aoba Castle ruins. In the afternoon, President Toda lectured on the Lotus Sutra. Wonder how deeply the thousand Gakkai members could absorb the profound essence of Buddhism contained in his lecture. Afterward, walked alone through the Sendai shopping district before returning to the inn where we were staying. Surprised at the scarcity of products.

At 11:28, boarded the express for Tokyo. Sensei gave me a sleeping car ticket and told me to get some rest. Took the liberty to rest by myself.

A gentle rain fell in Ueno in the morning. Saw Sensei home to Meguro, then went directly to work. Arrived at the office too early. The activities of the last three days will remain in history.

Wednesday, October 13. Clear.

A clear autumn day. Beautiful, cloudless skies. A fierce flood of criticism has been raised against me both from within and from outside the Gakkai. Speak forthrightly! Never fear or panic. Just forge ahead, for the sake of justice and my own conviction — in a way befitting a youth and a Gakkai pioneer; like a true prince of the orient; like a youthful revolutionary and a foremost disciple of President Toda.

Met Sensei in the afternoon. He did not scold me as I had expected. Disappointed. At 5:30, I went with T., M., R. and others to the grounds of Nihon University in Shimotakaido to inspect the upcoming sports festival site. On the way back, we all stopped to see a movie in Shibuya. Not very interesting. Walked home alone from Kamata Station. The autumn moon shone brilliantly. The heartbeat of youth — pristine, praiseworthy. One who protects the Mystic Law must become like the lotus, blooming amid the muddy swamp of our complicated society. Even if we find ourselves lonely, heartbroken, afflicted with sadness or in the midst of a trying or difficult time, we still have the Mystic Law. Never forget the moon and the greenery of nature. They are good friends.

Thursday, October 14. Clear.

It was my turn to give personal guidance at the headquarters in the afternoon. Discharged my responsibility in high spirits. To enable even one person to fundamentally solve his or her problem is a respectable and sublime act, one I am truly grateful I can carry out. It surpasses even a billion excellent theories, or a great politician's speech before the national assembly. It is called propagation.

The ten-thousand–participant pilgrimage, the headquarters general meeting and the gymnastics festival—whether these three important events are successful is entirely up to me. Will chant to the Gohonzon for their great success.

On the way home from the station, the light of the moon in a cloudless sky brightens my heart. Feel like praying to the god of the moon.

Monday, October 18. Rain.

Yesterday was the monthly pilgrimage. Afternoon, visited S.'s in Koganei, bringing along F. and W. Later, spoke intimately with the chapter and youth division corps leaders from Bunkyo Chapter. Listened patiently to all their questions concerning faith, life, daily living and work. Occasionally, there was an important problem. Where do these people's problems lie? When a river's flow is impeded, it may be blocked by accumulated refuse. Without knowing the subtle details of a person's life, guidance in faith will not get through.

Confucius taught that one should think nine times before uttering a single word. I, too, must choose my words carefully before speaking. Though all wish their actions would match their words, few can make that happen. I must follow through on this account.

Tuesday, October 19. Cloudy, then clear.

5:00. A Shiki Chapter general meeting at Toshima Civic Auditorium. Attended as a guest, with M.

Met with T., an A. newspaper reporter, in Shinbashi until after 11:00. The Gakkai must take its first step into the realm of society. Returning home, the autumn night made me feel peaceful and refreshed.

Wednesday, October 20. Overcast with rain later on.

Another peaceful autumn evening. The chrysanthemums have wilted and fallen, however, and the cold of winter is close at hand.

Discussed the reconstruction of T. company with H. all morning. To Jonan on business in the afternoon. Stopped in Shinjuku afterward to look at stopwatches for the upcoming sports festival, then went to the headquarters.

The sports festival; the Information Department; the chapter; the Public Relations Department; the Awards Department; the Accounting Department; worn out from discharging my many varied responsibilities. Home at midnight.

Thursday, October 21. Clear.

A clear autumn day. Spent the morning in Surugadai Library doing research. Surprised to see the library so filled with people.

6:00. A senior leaders meeting at the headquarters. Finished at 7:30. Went to my chapter chief's home after 8:00. Finalized the appointments of district chiefs and other leaders. When we finished, he let me take a bath—it has been quite a while. Returned home feeling refreshed. Arrived after midnight. Had better take care of my health.

Wednesday, October 27. Cloudy with rain later on.

Light rain. Sensei traveled to Atami. His physical condition seemed poor. I, too, am in an awful state of health. Must do something. Met with W., an A. newspaper reporter. Disappointed that the reporter, I., did not come. Truly regrettable.

The youth division general staff met in the evening. Not much was accomplished; everyone clung strongly to their opinions, personal views and prejudices. The powerful character, conviction and foresight of the central figure is vital.

Thursday, October 28. Rain, then clearing later in the day.

From light rain to clear autumn weather. Arrived at the headquarters twenty minutes after noon. Talked with President Toda for two hours. He seemed to be feeling a little better. "You'd better develop your physical health so that you can live long," he warned me. A meeting to plan upcoming guidance and direction was conducted in the second president's room. The participants' views and opinions did not mesh. A problem. Would like to see the directorate develop a step further. If the senior leaders fail to develop their life-condition, how can their juniors feel any joy or happiness?

Live powerfully, to become an ally of people of the future. Fight powerfully, to become the friend of sincere and honest people. Advance powerfully, to break through conservatism and create reform.

Saturday, October 30 — Sunday, October 31.

Boarded busses at 9:30 on the evening of the 30th in front of the Meiji Art Museum in Shinano-machi and departed for the head temple. The ten thousand youth division members arrived at Taiseki-ji at 5:00 the next morning.

At 7:30 a.m., the weather was clear and bright. Opening ceremonies were held for the ten thousand young men and women participating in this pilgrimage, on the grounds of a high school near the head temple. Sensei seemed truly pleased. In his address, he mentioned: "Economics, culture, education and science must all be grounded in an excellent philosophy. This supreme philosophy is none other than Nichiren Daishonin's teachings, and it is our mission to spread it widely, accomplishing kosen-rufu." Afterward, we marched in a group to the head temple. An intensely satisfying day. Here are the new era's models for youth, the youthful leaders of the new age, brilliant symbols of tomorrow's youth.

At 4:00 p.m., all participants departed. On the way home, we stopped to visit Squad Chief A. of Nippon University in Mishima. Home at 11:30. Fulfilled my heavy responsibility, without incidents or accidents.

Monday, December 20. Clear.

A warm, springlike day. Physical condition poor. Troubled by my deep karma. A frightening thing, this destiny. Physically, I feel like I have aged beyond my fifties. How much longer will I live? Some days I become too sentimental. Spent the morning visiting S., the Yaguchi middle school principal.

Yesterday, a YWD general meeting was held at the Meiji University Memorial Auditorium. During the meeting, I was formally appointed as divisional advisor. Felt no special joy or excitement, since I have been fulfilling this responsibility every day for some time now. With its more than three thousand participants, the general meeting was a great success.

At 4:00, representing President Toda, I attended installment ceremonies for the M. Bank's new president at their main offices. A cocktail party was held in a third-floor hall. About four hundred people from the worlds of finance and politics attended. These key society members must advance as one toward national reconstruction. Many thoughts filled this young pioneer's mind. In the evening, I accompanied H. to Chapter Chief T.'s home. We then attended a Tenth Corps general meeting at Jozai-ji. Completely exhausted.

Monday, December 27. Clear.

Yesterday, I visited Sensei at home to offer my year-end respects. He scolded me severely. Like the strict anger of a father, the intensity of his voice made me want to cringe.

Ah, I was at fault. It is exactly as Sensei said. His strict love aims to prevent me from becoming a failure in life. He admonishes me so I will not become a general defeated in battle. Over the past several days, I have looked hard at my negative karma—my destiny. I have shed tears, felt frustration and pondered deeply. Determined to reply to Sensei's expectations.

Sensei's power is like that of the Buddha. His eyes are like the eyes of the Buddha. Now, a real sense of mentor and disciple deeply penetrates my heart. Beg his forgiveness. I will offer my life, standing at the front lines of kosen-rufu. A wintry wind blew all day. It was cold and dark, like the depths of my heart.

Tuesday, December 28. Clear.

Only two or three days left to the year. I feel like the roc, a magnificent bird of legend who has flown and fought all year. Now, returning to his nest, he rests. This year of my youth, my twenty-sixth, is now over. Time passes. A new time approaches. History has been made and is now behind us. We shall make history from now on. How should one live? This is truly a difficult question. The right teacher, the correct faith. Beyond these, the strength of my determination is what's vital, is it not?

In the afternoon, I visited the S. Bookstore in Hongo, in front of Tokyo University's Red Gate. Wanted a book on Buddhism as a gift for the *Seikyo Shimbun*. Utterly surprised at the small number of books available.

An evening year-end gathering. Sang the second part of the "Kuroda Bushi." Sensei exploded with indignation—wasn't it the militaristic spirit contained in this song that killed his revered teacher, President Makiguchi? His eyes brimmed with tears. Very sorry.

With a heavy heart, I think how foolish I am. I thought I knew my mentor's mind, but I know nothing. Arrived home, 11:30.

Wednesday, December 29. Cloudy, then clearing later on.

Overcast and cold in the morning, clearing a little in the afternoon. Read a Chinese poem in the morning. My physical condition is extremely poor. An agonizing day. Dined with K. and others at 1:00 p.m. (a year-end meeting), then from 4:00 p.m., with M. at the O. restaurant.

From 7:00, visited my family home—the home of my father and mother who raised me—for the first time in six months. Hope and pray their lives may be extended even a single day. Excused myself after a short while.

To R.'s home at 8:00 with a friend from the youth division staff. An impudent family. Was particularly irritated with his wife.

Returned home, 11:30. Decided on various aspects of my schedule for next year. Read a slanderous article about the Gakkai. What a shallow argument! What irresponsible criticism! Can only be amazed at the arrogance of such critics. In ten or twenty years, correct and fair commentary will determine who is the victor.

To bed after 1:00 a.m. Tired.

Friday, December 31. Clear.

Left the office at 2:00 p.m. Had a haircut. It made me feel refreshed. On such occasions, I can truly feel that mind and body are one.

4:00 p.m. —the year's final general committee meeting. Sensei reminisced about his childhood, his youth and his adulthood. He has led a tumultuous life. There have been many great individuals and many pioneers. Absolutely no one but President Toda, however, stands by the common people and inspires youth to construct a new era. Without power, wealth, background or status, all he possesses is the raw power of humanity, the power of faith gushing forth from his entire being, and the wisdom to see ten years, no, two hundred years into the future. Had profound thoughts. Did evening gongyo with the members at the headquarters. Afterward, left on a long-awaited trip to Taiseki-ji with eighteen-hundred friends in faith.

ON JANUARY 4, WHILE helping members returning from a New Year's pilgrimage to the head temple, a Traffic Control Group member (precursor to today's Soka Group), Toshihiko Yamanouchi, fell between the platform and a departing train at Fuji Station. He had been directing a young child away from danger. Yamanouchi died on the 5th, as his parents and fellow traffic control members stood at his bedside. The last word to pass through the lips of this eighteen-year-old youth who had taken faith only eight months before was simply, "kosen-rufu." Memorial services were solemnly held on the 9th by Nakano Chapter.

On January 28, Daisaku and Kaneko Ikeda's second son, Shirohisa, was born.

In 1955 the United States produced sixty-seven percent of the world's automobiles, followed by England, France and West Germany. Japan accounted for less than one-tenth of a percent of the world's new cars. By 1986, with total worldwide production 3.5 times greater than in 1955, Japan produced twenty-seven percent of the world's autos, making it the number one car-manufacturing nation.

At the February 28 headquarters leaders meeting it was announced that some 11,475 households had taken faith that month.

Around the same time, a debate unfolded between a Soka Gakkai group chief and Minobu Nichiren sect priests in the town of Otaru, on Hokkaido. Minobu priests, greatly underestimating the

Gakkai members' faith and understanding, demanded what became the famous Otaru Debate. On March 2, the Otaru Group chief signed a written agreement to publicly debate the Minobu priests. The youth division rallied to support. Youth Division Chief of Staff Ikeda, master of ceremonies for the Gakkai side, proclaimed, "Through this debate, the Minobu sect's doctrinal errors will be made absolutely clear before one and all." The Gakkai, from the start, focused on Minobu's erroneous doctrine and distorted historical view. Minobu was forced into embarrassing confusion by the Gakkai's pointed questions and insistence on documentary evidence. It was an overwhelming victory.

President Toda had been racking his brains over how to develop the Culture Department—which had just been established the previous November—with the hope that as the frontiers of kosen-rufu broadened, many members would appear who could make solid contributions in various fields. On March 8, thirteen new members were appointed, among them educators and other professionals from the forefront of society.

On May 3, the Spring Headquarters General Meeting was held at the National Sports Hall in Ryogoku. A drive to achieve a membership of 300,000 households before the end of the year was announced.

The Treaty of Paris was implemented on May 5, releasing West Germany from its occupied status and allowing it to emerge as an independent, autonomous nation. From the fifteen nations represented at the treaty signing the previous October, the Western European Alliance was formed. At the same time, West Germany was given independence and allowed to re-arm. NATO was also established. Almost simultaneously, the Soviet Union and the seven nations of eastern Europe concluded the Warsaw Pact on May 14. Both events solidified the division of Germany into separate states of East and West.

On May 29, 1955, 10,360 YMD members participated in a pilgrimage to Taiseki-ji amid heavy rains.

In 1955, the last summer outlying-area propagation campaign was conducted. August 16–25, more than six hundred leaders were dispatched to forty-five cities to launch vigorous propagation activities. Daisaku Ikeda was assigned to Sapporo, on the northern island of Hokkaido. Sapporo topped the nation, surpassing its three-hundred–household goal. Nationwide, 5,558 families joined through those activities, and the total households receiving the Gohonzon in August was 28,450.

Japanese and American officials met in Washington, both sides agreeing that major reductions in U.S. military forces on Japanese soil should be planned. Demonstrations erupted protesting that U.S. military bases in Japan violated the spirit of Japan's postwar constitution.

The Tenth U.N. General Assembly opened in New York on September 20. Included on the agenda were arms reduction and the peaceful use of nuclear energy. More than sixty nations participated (Japan would be admitted the following year). On the first day, the Soviet Union proposed that the People's Republic of China be admitted to the United Nations. A majority of delegates, however, voted that the motion be shelved.

On October 19, the U.S. Department of Defense made public documents pertaining to World War II, which included information on the dropping of the atomic bomb. Thus the Japanese people learned for the first time that the bomb was ordered to be dropped without any special warning, with the objective of demonstrating this new weapon's destructive power. The report also suggested that a committee be appointed to study the bomb's effects. Potential targets had included Kyoto, Hiroshima, Kokura, Nagasaki and Niigata. Nagasaki was eventually selected for the second attack because weather conditions at Kokura, the primary target, were less than adequate on the day of the bombing, and Niigata's distance from the base of attack made a mission there too risky.

Capping off the year's activities was the December headquarters leaders meeting held at Toshima Civic Auditorium on the 23rd. At that meeting, it was announced that over the year the Gakkai membership had grown by some 194,000 households, well exceeding that year's overall 300,000-household membership goal.

Saturday, New Year's Day. Clear and bright.

At the head temple, Taiseki-ji.

Taho Fuji Dainichirenge-zan — Fuji, Treasure Mountain of the Great Sun-Lotus.

From today onward, throughout eternity,
Devoted wholeheartedly to serving the Buddha.

A springlike day. Chanted to the Dai-Gohonzon to advance through-out the year with a youthful spirit, like a child of the Gakkai. Also prayed for my health, for my family, for my mother and father and for my work.

President Toda arrived at the head temple at 6:00 in the evening. He was greeted by all the corps chiefs, the youth division staff and the division chiefs. He spoke for about an hour at the Rikyo-bo lodging. Then, each person sang a New Year's song.

Though the journey toward the kosen-rufu of myoho is long,
Let's set out together, encouraging one another.

A corps chiefs meeting on the Kujo-bo lodging second floor, at 8:00. Spent an enjoyable evening with my dear friends. Spent the night at the Kujo-bo with youth division staff members.

Sunday, January 2. Clear.

At Taiseki-ji. My twenty-seventh birthday.

There are people of the past, of the present and of the future. Want always to be a man of the future. Departed the head temple at 2:30. Back to my small, cramped house. Home before 7:00 in the evening. Went to bed early, exhausted.

Monday, January 3. Clear.

A cold New Year's season. Slept all morning. Feeling ill. My family life is happy. Perhaps more so than I deserve. All of this is due to Sensei's warm consideration. Must never forget what he has done for me, throughout my life. In the afternoon, paid my respects to Chapter Chief T. The chapter leaders had gathered. We ate together, and everyone seemed happy. Wrote a poem and presented it to the senior leaders. A meaningful evening. Although it was a New Year's gathering, everyone was simply dressed.

The Lotus Sutra is the robe that will keep you from disgrace after this life. The sutra reads, "It is like a robe to one who is naked."

—"LETTER TO JAKUNICHI-BO" (WND, 994)

Returned home after midnight. The house was quiet.

Tuesday, January 4. Intermittent cloudiness.

Remained home all morning. Physically ill. It's terrible. Had several visitors. Happily offered my New Year's greetings. Visited T.'s home with the chapter chief in the afternoon. Many chapter and corps leaders had gathered. Made various plans. Everyone listened to classical music, then we recited poetry. On the way home, the stars glittered brightly, as if reminding me not to forget my tremendous debt of gratitude and admonishing me not to get too caught up in trivial matters.

Wednesday, January 5.

In the world of the Gakkai, that is, the world of Buddhism, those who are sincere and earnest will win in the end. It may be said that the same principle applies in any aspect of society.

I have now turned twenty-seven; I am no longer a child.

Before I die, I want to grow into a splendid and powerful person under my revered teacher.

Before I die, I want to be an excellent capable person for kosen-rufu.

Before I die, I want to be a splendid example of a President Toda disciple.

Before I die, I want to be praised as an excellent person of great faith.

I do not fear worldly opinion. Nor do I fear others' criticism. What I do fear, however, is Buddhism. The Daishonin and my mentor are truly fearsome. Saw a movie with my wife in the evening.

Thursday, January 6. Partly cloudy.

The year is now fully under way. From 10:00, a meeting with Sensei; made various plans. Sensei seems to be aging rapidly.

Evening gongyo with the members at the headquarters. Afterward, attended a meeting at T. Company. The employees worked resolutely, moving at a hectic pace.

The members are young; vigorous. The nature of the Gakkai is eternal. We are inexperienced, but the elements necessary to complete our great task lie far beyond mere experience. Daringly and courageously, we cast off the old and open the way for the new.

> Because I have expounded this teaching, I have been exiled and almost killed. As the saying goes, "Good advice grates on the ear."
> —"THE ESSENTIALS FOR ATTAINING BUDDHAHOOD" (WND, 748)

To bed, just before 1:00 a.m.

Friday, January 7. Clear.

The annual children's group meeting was held at 6:00 this evening. The meeting place the N. Chinese restaurant. Many couples attended with their children. Everyone seemed to enjoy themselves. President Toda gave strict guidance to one couple who was late. Feel that this was only proper. Pained when I think of those who couldn't attend. Whenever people are enjoying themselves, others are definitely sad or lonely. Want never to forget this throughout my life. Want to be a man of fairness, that is, an ally to those who work behind the scenes, to those who are lonely, who are suffering. Joyfully sang Gakkai songs, "Gojogen," "Dainanko," and "Young Men of Japan." These couples and their children, without exception, are responsible for forming the Gakkai core.

Saturday, January 8. Fair, with scattered high clouds.

In the evening, a New Year's dinner with the Y. shop employees. Afterward, M. and F. joined me in visiting the family of the Traffic Control Group member Y., who was killed over the New Year's holiday. Presented his father with a gift of ¥200,000, a sincere expression of heartfelt condolence from youth division members. Returned home concerned about whether his father will persevere with splendid faith.

Can imagine that with the passing of each year, the kosen-rufu battle will become more intense. Must take the lead with fresh determination, in a way that befits a young leader.

> This life is like a dream. One cannot be sure that one will live until tomorrow. However wretched a beggar you might become, never disgrace the Lotus Sutra.
> —"A WARNING AGAINST BEGRUDGING ONE'S FIEF" (WND, 824)

Sunday, January 9. Cloudy.

A chapter memorial service for Y. Services began at Jozai-ji at 1:00 p.m., with about six hundred in attendance. Offered a eulogy on the youth division chief's behalf. Witnessed everyone moved to tears with emotion, out of love for their fellow member. To the extent that such pure unity exists, nothing can obstruct our limitless advancement.

At 6:30, youth division group chiefs met at the headquarters. It impressed me as a gathering of future corps chiefs and senior leaders. Deepening my sense that, as a saying goes, "Future generations are truly promising."

K. visited late in the evening. A fine youth. I sense, however, that he lacks backbone. Concerned about him.

Monday, January 10. Partly cloudy.

Attended a New Year's celebration by invitation from our bank at 6:30. Found it uninteresting, as I do not drink. Seemed like a waste of time. "Is this the nature of our society, of the world in general?" I thought. I often have the opportunity to deal with people older than me. This is my destiny, isn't it? The key society leaders all seem to be in their forties and fifties. For me, still in my twenties, they seem a bit too far removed in age. Returned home, 9:30. Read.

Tuesday, January 11. Fair.

A group of priests were invited to dinner at the N. Chinese restaurant. I was the master of ceremonies. My teacher, President Toda, has fully devoted himself to the development of the priesthood. Hope that the priests will soon understand his tremendous spirit, like that of King Utoku [who sacrificed his life to protect a Buddhist monk]. The Gakkai is protecting the priesthood and striving hard to fulfill the Daishonin's prophecies. Therefore, it is clear from the principles of Buddhism that the Gakkai is performing the function of King Utoku. Must never forget that we of the Gakkai are not merely vassals or humble servants of the priesthood, but instead possess a profound mission.

Wednesday, January 12. Fair.

At 3:30 p.m., a "Friends of the *Seikyo Shimbun*" meeting at the headquarters. Priest Horigome attended, along with a number of representatives from each division. The discussion proceeded in a friendly manner. President Toda seemed pleased. Awaiting the growth of the Seikyo Press as a pioneer of journalism. It must set the pace for kosen-rufu's progress.

The paper began with just one or two amateurs and has now grown to a circulation in the tens of thousands. People laughed. "What can amateurs accomplish?" they asked. But Sensei replied, "In five years' time, even amateurs will turn into professionals."

Expressed my concern for Priest Horigome's health.

Thursday, January 13. Fair.

Met with a group of young acolytes at 5:30 in the headquarters building reception room. Went to T.'s home for a study meeting. All were serious. Ashamed at my own lack of study. No matter how high our leadership positions, if we fail to study seriously, our juniors will eventually surpass us. Frightening. The Daishonin's words, "Exert yourself in the two ways of practice and study," apply equally to everyone. I am no exception.

Saturday, January 22. Fair.

At 9:00, left for Osaka on the *Swallow* express. Sensei, Priest Hosoi, Director I., women's division committee member Mrs. I. and myself— five in all. Fine weather. On the train there was discussion of the Gosho and much guidance. Spent the night in Osaka.

Sunday, January 23. Clear.

Boarded a Far-East Airlines plane at Itami Airport along with S., A. and T., and flew to Kochi. 9:30—Landed at Kochi Airport, which seemed nothing more than an empty field. Heard it was used as a naval air base during the war. Drove to Sansuien in three cars that greeted us at the airport.

The Kochi District general meeting was held at 1:30. Sensei lectured on revolutionaries like Itagaki Taisuke and Nakae Chomin, who stood up for the people's right to freedom, basing their ideas on Rousseau's *Social Contract*. The great philosophy for bringing about peaceful revolution in these times, he said, is none other than Nichiren Daishonin's Buddhism. Speaking as Public Relations Department chief, I mentioned that kosen-rufu in the Kochi area is being built through the efforts of each person present. A dinner celebrating the meeting's success was held at 7:00, with Nichiren Shoshu priests from throughout the entire Shikoku area, more than ten in all, attending.

Left for Osaka at 11:30 on the *Midnight* express. Tired. As long as I live, I will probably never forget that long ride on the night train.

Monday, January 24. Clear.

Stood on the train-car platform in the morning, refreshed by the breathtaking view of the Inland Sea with its sparkling silver wavelets. Spectacular scenery; limitless movement; a slight morning breeze. A moment when this sentimental youth blended into the cosmos. Arrived in Osaka at 12:10 p.m. Left later in the afternoon to attend the Osaka general meeting. A tremendous success. Spent the night in the Hanazono Inn. Strict guidance from Sensei. I. and I went out for dinner together.

Tuesday, January 25. Clear.

Returned to Tokyo on the *Swallow*. A nationwide corps chiefs meeting at the headquarters. Sensei left early. Must be more aware of Sensei's deep consideration. Feel we are becoming too spoiled.

Must sincerely and patiently strive to establish something in the areas of my daily responsibilities.

Must seriously exert myself in study; if I neglect to do so now, I will regret it later.

Must carefully and steadily establish my finances.

Of course, all of my material possessions are dedicated for kosen-rufu and for the Gakkai.

Wednesday, January 26. Cloudy.

Heard there would be a meeting at President Toda's home at 5:30 this afternoon. What kind of meeting, I did not know. Attending were K., I., H., T., U. and myself. Wherever or whenever the meeting, I always take the last position. Sensei's profound guidance was fascinating. The storms of criticism directed toward the Gakkai are becoming stronger each day. Each senior leader is fighting hard.

In his heart, Sensei has taken a step beyond these waves and is thinking about the Gakkai's stability and dynamic advancement during its next growth period. Wonder if everyone present clearly understands Sensei's heart and mind. A difficult question.

Daisaku—the son of a poor seaweed vendor. But the Mystic Law can transform filth into gold. Why, then, should I begrudge my life. When we are truly prepared to offer our lives, magnificent power wells forth.

Thursday, January 27. Clear.

A chapter leaders meeting at Jozai-ji.

Appointment of a new chapter chief was announced. The meeting was a joyous welcome for the new chapter chief. This will be a fresh new step for the chapter. Times change like a raging torrent. I have been pouring all of my energy and effort into this chapter. This is an occasion of profound significance. Can report to the Gohonzon, free from any regret. Afterward, we had a small banquet with the chapter leaders. Deeply aware of the Bunkyo Chapter members' goodness.

Personnel placement is vital. I hope, however, that based on their faith, the former chapter chief and the new chapter chief will enjoy their change of responsibility. Those responsible for personnel decisions must handle them fairly and objectively, being careful to place the proper person in the proper position. If we do this in accord with Sensei's guidance, we cannot go wrong.

In the middle of the night, my wife felt the beginnings of labor. Took her by taxi from our apartment in Omori to her parents' house in Yaguchi. Just when I feared we may not find a taxi, one passed by. It seemed as though we were protected. Spent the night in Yaguchi.

Friday, January 28. Cloudy.

At 4:20 in the afternoon, my second child was born. Relieved to see he is healthy and normal. Feel great appreciation to the Gohonzon.

The mystery of life. Scholars, medical doctors, scientists, politicians or diplomats—none can solve, with even the slightest confidence, the indeterminable question of this child's destiny. Ultimately, life's fundamental questions can be answered nowhere but within Buddhism's essence. From today, my awareness of my responsibility as a parent, and for my entire family, has deepened. Must have strength. Must protect my children and my family and bring them happiness.

Returned home just before 11:00. Read a book by myself.

Saturday, January 29. Rain.

Drizzle. The day had a grayish cast. The scheduled afternoon visit to Tanjo-ji in Chiba Prefecture was cancelled due to rain. Went to the headquarters at 3:30 to work on public relations matters. It seems others are not given much responsibility. Cannot help feeling that the responsibility always falls on me. Am I complaining?

Sunday, January 30. Clear, then cloudy.

A balmy day. Got out of bed at 10:00. My brain is exhausted. Did gongyo late. Feel so much better when I do gongyo early.

Went to a contribution division[1] meeting at 1:00, only to find I was mistaken; it was actually scheduled for 6:00. Miscommunication can be frightening.

A leaders meeting and a contribution division meeting were held at 6:00. Representing the chapter chief, I conducted a ceremony to transfer the chapter flag to the new chapter chief.

On the way home, I spoke with a friend about the Chinese classic, *The Romance of the Three Kingdoms*: Cao Cao's courage, Xiang Yu's great valor, Guan Yu's character, Zhang Fei's strength, Kong-ming's[2] wisdom and Sun Quan's youthfulness. Talked a lot about the concepts of right and wrong, good and evil.

Be a person who follows the way of kings, not of tyrants;
—a king among the people, not an authoritarian general.
—a friend of the masses, not a slave to wealth.
—a man of benevolent wisdom, not of evil intellect.

1. Contribution division: A group of members formed by Josei Toda to secure the financial base of the Soka Gakkai. It consisted of volunteers who desired to make a regular monetary contribution to the Gakkai.

2. Kong-ming: Zhu-ge Kong-ming. A heroic figure in *The Romance of the Three Kingdoms*. Dies heroically in the battle of Gojogen. A favorite literary character of President Josei Toda.

Monday, January 31. Clear.

To Tokyo University at 1:00. Held a discussion meeting with Assistant Professor O. and four Tokyo University students on the study of religion. At 6:30, a joint conference. Exhausted. Suffering from relentless, extreme fatigue. Got home early and went to bed.

Tuesday, February 1. Fair.

A 6:00 unit chiefs meeting at Shibuya Civic Center. A full house. Filled with passion. Depending on them.

Saw S. Once a neighborhood ruffian, he has undergone a splendid transformation. Overjoyed. How satisfied his parents must be.

Spoke about comparative ways of practice during the lifetimes of Shakyamuni, of T'ien-t'ai[1] and Dengyo[2], and of Nichiren Daishonin. Further, discussed phases of our struggle to accomplish the 'kosen-rufu of substantiation' (the ideal of peace and happiness prevailing throughout the world based on the propagation of the Daishonin's Buddhism). Reflected that I should have been a little clearer about the significance of establishing the high sanctuary and the process by which it will come about. Afterward, we gathered at a Chinese restaurant for a corps chiefs meeting. A light rain began falling. Returned home, feeling somewhat melancholy. Arrived at 11:50.

1. T'ien-t'ai: (538–597) Also, Chih-i. The founder of the Chinese T'ien-t'ai school and commonly referred to as the Great Teacher T'ien-t'ai. He refuted the ten major Buddhist schools of his day and established the supremacy of the Lotus Sutra. He also expounded the theory of 'three thousand realms in a single moment of life.'

2. Dengyo: (767–822) Also, Saicho. The founder of the Tendai (T'ien-t'ai) sect in Japan and commonly referred to as the Great Teacher Dengyo. In opposition to established beliefs, Dengyo maintained that all people have the Buddha nature and the supreme vehicle of Buddhahood expounded in the Lotus Sutra is the true teaching.

Wednesday, February 2. Clear.

A mediocre day. Feel it unpardonable to spend even one day in leisure during this crucial period of construction. Admonished myself in this regard.

Read "The Meeting of Hong Men" and "Surrounded on All Sides." The tragic Red Poppy fills my heart with a poetic sense of history. A Study Department professors meeting at 6:00. Extremely tired. Tomorrow, will ask President Toda for instruction on Nichikan's *Six-volume Writings* and the following Gosho:

1. "One Hundred and Six Comparisons"
2. "The Mystic Principle of the True Cause"
3. "The Record of the Orally Transmitted Teachings"
4. "The Object of Devotion for Observing the Mind"
5. "The Opening of the Eyes"

Thursday, February 3. Clear.

A cold day. At times I am frustrated by certain aspects of my nature, while at others I think it is fine the way it is. Ultimately, no matter what criticism or slander I encounter, I will follow my mentor and, while invoking the Mystic Law, shall continue each day with patience and perseverance, carrying out my Buddhist practice so that I will have no regrets.

Attended a beginning-level lecture at Toshima Civic Auditorium. Few leaders attended. Want to master the wonderful, mysterious Lotus Sutra doctrines and principles while President Toda is still alive.

Friday, February 4. Rain, overcast.

6:00—an emergency leaders meeting at the headquarters to discuss the R. temple problem.[1] Sixty representatives were dispatched to visit seventy-seven different temples. Finished at 11:00. It was decided that tomorrow I will visit Butsugen-ji in Sendai. Heavy fatigue. I look tired.

1. R. temple problem: In early 1955, the chief priest of Renge-ji temple in Osaka refused to support the Soka Gakkai's efforts to propagate Nichiren Daishonin's Buddhism. Not only did he refuse to bestow the Gohonzon on Gakkai members, he also demanded the return of the Gohonzon from those Gakkai members who had received it at Renge-ji. The temple eventually seceded from Nichiren Shoshu.

Saturday, February 5. Clear.

Left for Sendai at 9:50 on the *Michinoku* express. Accompanied Sensei. Also traveling with us were K., Y., Mrs. B., Y. and A. Sensei's guidance is strict; his actions, compassionate. Will serve him earnestly. Arrived in Sendai at 3:49. Quite a few people greeted us. Very cold. Troubled by pain in my chest. Having faith in the Lotus Sutra is like being in the midst of winter. Winter never fails to turn to spring. My life is the same.

At 4:30, President Toda was interviewed by the news announcer Kojima at the Tohoku Broadcasting Company. I was the only other person present. Noticed that Sensei's talk was being recorded on tape. A lecture on the "Expedient Means" chapter at 6:00 at the labor union hall.

Sunday, February 6. Clear.

10:00 — a continuation of yesterday's union hall lecture. The discussion turned to the "Life Span" chapter. A third lecture was scheduled for 1:00. Stood in for Sensei, who was two hours late because of either business or his health.

During that time, gave guidance to all members dispatched to the various temples. I talked about the concepts of life force and punishment and reward in Buddhism.

A youth division group chiefs meeting at 4:30 at S.'s residence. Impressed with them for having tried so hard, in spite of their difficult circumstances. From among them, great leaders will definitely emerge, I said. Guts, patience, the perfection of strong youths. Such is this spiritual climate, this environment.

Visited Priest S. at Butsugen-ji at 6:30. Asked his opinion on various matters concerning Chief Priest S. He was kind enough to give me a surprising amount of information. Departed from Sendai Station on the 11:28 train. Gave President Toda a detailed report on the way back to Tokyo. Sensei sat silently in profound contemplation. He gave the impression of one who has accomplished his mission.

Monday, February 7. Cloudy, with rain later on.

Arrived in Ueno at 6:35 in the morning. Sensei went directly to the headquarters. I went for a haircut and arrived at work at 8:10. A light rain fell; the first in a while. With each rain, I get a stronger sense of the coming warmth of spring. Deeply aware of the need to record Sensei's guidance and speeches in writing for posterity.

To the headquarters at 5:30. Reported to Sensei all details of the results obtained by youth division members dispatched to individual temples. Sensei's serious demeanor became frightening. Afterward, accompanied Chapter Chief T. and the chapter women's division chief to Gotanda where we dined on eel. The rain did not let up.

Tuesday, February 8. Rain, then overcast.

A quiet day. Reflected, must sincerely consider my societal obligations and responsibilities without ever becoming arrogant.

From tomorrow, must further intensify my determination and deal with everything that arises. Inertia and construction; obligation and privilege; negative and positive. Also, discipline and self-indulgence; confidence and self-contempt. What fine qualities and superior points do great people hold in common? Ultimately, isn't it that they have successfully challenged and overcome their own weaknesses and persevered until they achieved their desired goals?

1. Thoroughly exert myself in Buddhist study.
2. Read books, as a source of future nourishment.
3. Never forget to develop myself.

A 6:00 corps chiefs meeting at the headquarters. Hoped to give guidance until satisfied everyone was fine. Severely scolded by President Toda in the president's room concerning T. Industries. It could not be helped. It came about because I helped and protected a friend. Before the Gohonzon, I am unashamed.

Stopped by S.'s on the way home. His father's strong, domineering personality was bothersome. It's too bad. No matter how old we get, we are often easily influenced by those around us. Arrived just before midnight. It was deserted and lonely.

Wednesday, February 9. Clear, then cloudy.

Remained in the office all morning. Must apologize to President Toda for many things. Must spur myself on. Youth must not be caught up in the past. Isn't the Daishonin's teaching that of 'for the present and the future'? If people become too caught up in the past, their hearts will age and their spirit will die. Must forge ahead, even if laughed at or scorned.

At 6:30, a Culture Department meeting. I am an uncrowned, common person. They are blessed as pioneers leading the way to kosen-rufu. Hope they will never lose their way, as they construct a strong, broad and sturdy path for their juniors to follow.

Later, a staff meeting. Everyone looked tired, including myself.

Thursday, February 10. High clouds.

Fatigued throughout my body. An agonizing day. Is it my evil karma? I am reading with my life the passage from a sutra that states, "The people's sins are like frost or dew, which vanish in the sunlight of wisdom." At noon, shopped for birthday gifts for President Toda at Mitsukoshi and Isetan department stores. Purchased a dress shirt, two neckties, pearl cuff links and a shoehorn. Confident these gifts express my sincere feeling.

At 2:00, I was responsible for giving personal guidance at the headquarters. Regret my exhaustion made it difficult to give spirited guidance.

From 7:00, attended a beginning-level lecture.

To Jozai-ji at 8:30 to request a written opinion. A group chiefs meeting at 9:30. Exhaustion forced me to spend the night at T.'s.

Friday, February 11. Partly cloudy.

Today is President Toda's fifty-fifth birthday. I am twenty-seven. Han-tsu took his own life when he was thirty-one. Alexander the Great united the world at thirty-one. Napoleon became emperor at thirty. Who is truly a great person? What ideas do they have as their basis? What value is in their great accomplishments? Is it their destiny? Do these people possess some sort of inborn ability?

I am satisfied being just a common person. I shall live my entire life, however, spreading the Mystic Law, the fundamental power of the universe itself. Whatever wind, waves or misunderstandings I face, I shall offer this life for this great benevolent principle throughout the ten thousand years of the Latter Day of the Law and forever. Society's stormy seas, the rise and fall of fortunes, are no more than the epitome of transience, an illusion. Only a life lived strictly protecting the Law possesses the essence of reality, and herein lies the truth. Such people will definitely prosper. Twenty-seven years of life—I do not want to lose.

Saturday, February 12. Fair.

A cold day. Woke up late in the morning. Extremely tired. Am constantly thinking I must pour my energy into studying Buddhism. To the headquarters at 6:00. Did gongyo. Troubled that my voice was not quite right while chanting daimoku.

At 6:30, a corps chiefs conference in reception room #1. Discussed

Culture Department business. Before returning home, met with Z. and two others over dinner at Omori Station.

Sunday, February 13. Cloudy, then clear.

Out of bed at 9:00. A cold morning. Went by myself to take a morning bath. Around noon, S. and Miss M. came by to congratulate us on the birth of our new child. Sorry we were out of tea.

Kamata Chapter's fifth general meeting was held at 1:00. Was told that four- to five-hundred people attended. Trust them dearly. Gave a two- or three-minute speech as Public Relations Department chief.

At 6:30, met at S.'s for a celebration that became forlorn and unexciting. Afterward, accompanied H. to a chapter meeting. Received a report that President Toda's condition had taken a turn for the worse. Hurried to the headquarters.

Monday, February 14. Fine, with high clouds later in the day.

In the evening, visited Sensei at his bedside; asked him to lecture on the Gosho "One Hundred and Six Comparisons." He cheerfully gave guidance and lectured to me from his bed. Grateful. Attended a graduate-level lecture. A little surprised at the professors' and assistant professors' beautiful progress. Simple, unpretentious people steadily come to possess real ability. Truly happy; must not let up in my efforts.

On the way back, treated M. and H. to dinner.

Tuesday, February 15. Fair.

President Toda gave severe guidance from the morning on. My heart feels as if I am standing on an icy mountain peak, naked before the cold wind. No excuse. Spiritual age, physical age: must revolutionize both simultaneously. Actual proof will result from my Buddhist practice, due to the principle of 'the oneness of body and mind.' In the evening, gave guidance and lectured on "One Hundred and Six Comparisons." Making steady progress. Afterward, a unit chiefs meeting at Jozai-ji. Tremendous success. A joyful gathering of common people, devoid of motives like profit, fame or power. Only here can true democracy be found. Future historians! Watch us with all your heart! Arrived home, midnight. Read alone.

Wednesday, February 16. Fair.

Nichiren Daishonin's birthday. Chanted daimoku with satisfaction.

To the president's room at noon. His strict guidance is painful. Went with Y. and A. to the Y. newspaper office to protest an article critical of the Gakkai in the February 9th issue of that paper's Saitama edition. Pressed them to take responsibility for reporting unsubstantiated and fabricated information. Chief editor A. was extremely resistant. He did not conceal his anger as he insisted that the article was a fair commentary. Next we proceeded to the Urawa bureau office, where we met with bureau chief K. to request a retraction. Finally got him to concede that the paper was at least partially at fault. We returned, our mission accomplished.

A district chiefs meeting in the evening. Responding to their sincerity, gave guidance in earnest. All have been fighting hard. My eyes brimmed with tears. Went directly to the headquarters after the meeting. Reported to Sensei on our newspaper office protest. He was delighted with our efforts. Relieved.

Thursday, February 17. Clear, with clouds later on.

Lately, have been seriously pondering the problem of life and death. Went to the president's room in the afternoon. Severely admonished by Sensei about the R. temple matter. I am always the one scolded. The general director and other directors are not scolded very often. When I think about it, if I am to boldly take the lead in the future, this is as it should be. My back is to the wall.

An emergency meeting of the board of directors and the staff was called. Continued with a planning meeting afterward. Seriously considering strategy and organization. Home at midnight. Made phone calls concerning Osaka.

Friday, February 18. Cloudy.

Up at 6:00. The early morning air is more precious than gold—a morning I want to last. Received a phone call from Sensei. Strictly scolded for not knowing about the newspaper article concerning R. temple. Went quickly to his home to apologize. Received guidance on various matters. While on the train, read "Reminiscences," a Chinese poem by Wei Zheng:

> Returning to Jong Yuan, like a deer to pasture,
> I toss away my pen and take up the sword.
> All strategy comes to naught,
> But, still burning with righteous fury,

I reveal our battle plans in the audience of the Emperor.
Mounting horses we ride, out of the city gates,
Our request for special permission to bring
*   peace to Yue (southern China)*
*   granted by the Emperor.*
Grasping the Emperor's written decree,
*   we ride to subdue the Eastern clans.*
A long and arduous journey, passing in and
*   out of the steep mountains.*
From the dark ancient forest, a lonely bird calls;
At night, the chatter of monkeys echoes
*   through the mountains*
Gazing ahead a thousand miles, we sense the
*   sadness of war;*
Mostly we fear for the common people.
Our journey is treacherous, but we never give in
Because of our deep reverence for our countrymen.
Kwai Pui never made two promises;
Hou Ying always honored a single word;
If one feels this way about life,
Then who needs to speak of fame?

My favorite poem. Very enjoyable.

Saturday, February 19. Fine Weather.

Sensei left on a pilgrimage in the morning. Sorry I could not see him off. Lately, been thinking about my own stupidity. Nothing to do but stick with the Gohonzon. Boarded an 11:00 train for the head temple. Accompanied by division chiefs T. and U., as well as youth division staff member M. Slept well in the train.

Arrived at the head temple at 3:00. Visited the resident priests at each lodging to discuss several matters and to inform temple administrators of the situation with R. temple.

Built a bonfire at midnight. Severely admonished by Sensei about the youth division pilgrimage participants. It is frightening when someone close invents stories.

Sunday, February 20. Cloudy.

On the head temple grounds. About 4:00 a.m., the wind began to blow more than 45 mph. Stormy.

At 10:00, attended funeral services for Y. Sensei placed Y.'s ashes in the grave. Our mentor's mercy is deeper than the ocean. Everyone felt this way, seeing someone who lost his life along the road to kosen-rufu laid to rest, embraced by his mentor.

Left from Fuji Station just after 11:00 on the night express to Osaka, together with twenty-four members. As we approached Kyoto, pure white snow fell intermittently. An impressive sight. Outside was bitterly cold. Arrived in Osaka at 8:16 in the morning. Amid the cold, we immediately divided into two groups, one of which went to R. temple and the other to a meeting of that temple's parishioners. This parasite within the bowels of a lion, the lion in this case being Nichiren Shoshu, is a truly fearsome thing. Grateful to see the pure-hearted action, based on strong faith, of these senior members, in spite of any difficulty. Like a beautiful painting.

Monday, February 21. Clear.

Extremely cold. Up at 5:30. Split into four groups and carried out various assignments. Met with the priest responsible for one section of Osaka. Also met with the chief priest of Shoren-ji. Even visited the police station. In light of Buddhism, our actions are absolutely correct. Evil people are always disrespectful and cowardly, possessing a kind of corrupt wisdom. A confrontation between the Buddha's army and the army of the devil. Between the friends of Buddha and the friends of Devadatta. Will such scenarios exist for eternity?

Tuesday, February 22. Fair.

Arrived in Tokyo at 9:24 on the third-class train. Immediately went to report to Sensei. Disappointed that I could not meet him, as he had gone to the doctor. Came back to the headquarters to report after a little more than an hour. It was difficult, as he would not give me his full attention. Have no idea why. Excused myself, feeling embarrassed. Perhaps what we accomplished did not meet with Sensei's expectations. Certainly, he seemed worried about something. Or was it that he felt disappointed about our immaturity and lack of development?

Wednesday, February 23. Fair.

Today's warm sunshine reminds me of spring. Spent an uneventful morning. My head was filled with incoherent thoughts. The character *myo* signifies the head. Could this confusion in my head arise from slander of the Law? No choice but to chant daimoku.

Left the office at 3:00. Took a walk with some fellow employees down a small path in the springlike sunshine. Walked from Gotomachi to Ueno. The people we came across varied widely in appearance. It seems that, since the war, people's appearance in particular has gotten worse. Could this be because of the world of Anger or Animality? Returned early to my home in Omori. Intend to sleep soundly.

Thursday, February 24. Fair.

Skipped the lecture on "The Formalities of This School." Have had few opportunities to talk with Sensei. A desolate feeling.
1. Want to have unreserved faith in the Gohonzon.
2. Want to become a disciple praised by his mentor.
3. Want to become trusted and respected by my fellow members.

In the evening, went to the home of the general administrator of Nihon University. Came late to a leaders meeting at Jozai-ji. Got home early. Sat alone at my desk.

Friday, February 25. High clouds.

The days have been warm. Somehow I lack composure. Have come to understand this thing called faith. Went to Sensei's home in Meguro at 1:00.

At 3:30, to the M. newspaper offices with A.

Arrived at the headquarters at 6:00. Met with Sensei. Reported to him directly. Feel somewhat annoyed at T., though he is a senior. Such a shallow person.

Attended a Shiki Chapter leaders meeting. Stayed late, giving personal guidance before going home. To bed around 1:30.

Saturday, February 26. Cloudy, then clearing.

The weather seems to be turning for the worse. Some days I feel little hope or joy; others, I sense progress and advancement. Ultimately, no matter how bad I feel, I must continue my training. Especially within the realm of Buddhist practice, which enables us to grasp the eternity of life.

This year's second joint leaders conference. Sensei gave guidance on the following topics, among others:
1. Life force and the power needed for daily living.
2. How to live each day.
3. The definition of a capable leader.

When the meeting was over, went to A. City to visit my wife's younger brother's university instructor. Next, went to S.'s in Yaguchi. Accompanied by the general director and H. Shocked to see how small and thin S.'s father is.

My salary is now not quite enough to cover living expenses. Capitalism; communism; socialism. Lately, I have been thinking about what would be the ideal economic system.

Sunday, February 27. High clouds.

Up at 8:00. While I am young, I do not want to live with reservations. It is vital that I act with conviction, life force and responsibility.

10:00—a funeral service was held for a Second Corps member at Kuon-ji in Yokohama. Attended with T., the corps chief. To Josen-ji in the afternoon for N.'s wedding. Wish them happiness.

Sensei spoke about benefit and gave guidance about the importance of determination. A stern talk. Exhausted. Felt like collapsing when the day was half over. Afterward, attended a joint district discussion meeting in Katsushika Ward. Was told 230 people attended. Courageously carried out propagation—for the first time in a while. Refreshed.

Monday, February 28. Rain, then clearing.

Slept until 8:00. Could not do gongyo.

A 6:00 leaders meeting at Toshima Civic Auditorium. A senior leaders meeting afterward at Josen-ji. As might be expected, Sensei's guidance to the senior leaders was strict. I, myself, will fight to the best of my ability.

> The wisdom of the world of Buddhahood manifests itself in the objective reality of the nine worlds, and the wisdom of the nine worlds is inherent in the reality of the world of Buddhahood. When reality and wisdom are thus fused, Buddhahood equals the nine worlds and the nine worlds equal Buddhahood. This is what is known as "attaining enlightenment in a moment." When one realizes that the "three paths" equal the "three virtues," all evil will be transformed immediately into goodness. This is what is meant by "attaining Buddhahood through half a verse."
>
> —(GZ, 876)

My living situation is more strained with each passing day. Must chant daimoku. Home at 2:00.

Tuesday, March 1. Clear, then cloudy.

Intense back pain—suffered all day. Could this be the work of the Devil of the Sixth Heaven? Can only chant to the Gohonzon for the protective functions of Bodhisattva Medicine King and the gods Bonten and Taishaku to become manifest. Received a lecture from President Toda in his office on "One Hundred and Six Comparisons." Keenly aware of my own lack of intelligence. Attended a combined discussion meeting in Adachi Ward. Reported attendance was 250. Lacked energy; could not contribute as I had wished. For me, it was a regrettable meeting.

Wednesday, March 2. Cloudy.

With A., visited the Y. newspaper's Urawa Bureau office to meet with M. for further negotiations. Our meeting ended in apparent success.

Next, a meeting in Katsushika Ward at the public health center behind the government offices. The meeting was held to support candidate N. for ward assembly. About 350 attended. His election seems inevitable. Miss M. accompanied me to Omori Station. She talked about many things, expressed her opinions and asked many questions.

> Worthy persons deserve to be called so because they are not be carried away by the eight winds: prosperity, decline, disgrace, honor, praise, censure, suffering and pleasure.
>
> —"THE EIGHT WINDS" (WND, 794)

Some friendships are shallow; others are deep. My relations with some are superficial, while others share my pleasures and my pains. Many people believe only in themselves, but they are egoistic and self-centered. Is this instinctual? Only the Gakkai tries to realize profound and powerful unity based on the principle 'many in body, one in mind.' In all the world, we are the only ones to do so.

Thursday, March 3. Clear, then cloudy.

How sad to be weakened by illness while trying to grow. How miserable, how pitiful. What great things I could accomplish if healthy!

Attended a gathering for W. to present betrothal gifts to the T. family. Hope both families will be happy.

To the headquarters in the evening. Sensei seemed in high spirits, saying he felt refreshed after seeing the barber. "You and I have been carrying out many a battle together," he said, offering warm words of encouragement.

To Katsushika after. Several block members gathered. Today, I gave resolute guidance and encouragement.

Live! For kosen-rufu. Survive! For the eternal prosperity of the Law, for the Gakkai, for the members and for my wife and children. Rather, I must survive to attain Buddhahood in this lifetime and thus avoid falling into the state of Hell. Arrived home after midnight. Exhausted, both physically and spiritually.

Friday, March 4. Cloudy.

Gakkai criticism has become fierce. The weak will retreat and the strong will be overjoyed. This is just as the Daishonin says, "The wise will rejoice and the foolish will retreat" (WND, 637). Emotional criticism; slander based on ignorance! For the time being, rather, for the rest of my life, if I am truly the Daishonin's disciple, I will encounter criticism. When I think of the Daishonin's golden words, my conviction is firm.

Though Sensei opposed the military during the war, they call him a militant. How absurd! Because we correctly point out misleading religions' errors, we are labeled "self-righteous." It is vitally important to proclaim, with great confidence and based upon an accurate standard, what is correct and what is false. In this world of selfishness and cowardice, such criticism should not be surprising.

The moon shone brilliantly. The autumn moon is splendid, as is the spring moon. The gods of the moon and the stars reside together in my heart. How wondrous, I thought. The cosmos is a mystery; life, too, is a mystery.

Saturday, March 5. Cloudy, with snow later on.

Late. Inexcusable. At 1:35, left on a train for the head temple. Pondered while alone on the train. Must spur myself on, powerfully, strictly. This is a battle with myself. Must not hold anyone else responsible.

Sunday, March 6. Clear.

Awoke at 7:00 on the head temple grounds. Had a long, serious discussion last night with the Rikyo-bo lodging chief priest. Discussed the Gakkai's mission, the Daishonin's prophecies and the priesthood's role. Citing the Gosho, we shared our passion and sincerity. Other top leaders engaged in similar activities at their respective lodgings. The priesthood is also coming to realize that the dawn of kosen-rufu is at hand. At 8:00, welcomed Sensei to a Suiko Group meeting. Studied *Romance of the Three Kingdoms*.

The ceremony of chanting before the Dai-Ggohonzon was held at 10:30. Afterward, we were granted an audience with the high priest. Also met with the retired high priest, Nichijun Hori.

At 4:00, an opening ceremony for the new Sessen Lodging. Over at 6:00. We sent off Nichijun with the song, "Young Men of Japan." He appeared extremely happy.

Left the head temple at 7:00, returning by way of Numazu. Always thinking I must make study a part of my life. I am not a scholar, but real practice must be thoroughly backed by great ideas.

Monday, March 7. Fair.

Faith, confidence, conviction—These thoughts arise, somehow, in the midst of practice: What is life's fundamental energy?

Fate, destiny, karma—what determines the course of one's life? What is the most powerful influence? Thought about how it relates to my efforts in this life.

Met over dinner with H. A relaxing break. Yet, I had thought of him as a more trustworthy friend. Is it his nature to succumb to seeking honor and profit? Must wait and see about him.

At 6:30, an emergency chapter chiefs meeting. Everyone was tired and spiritless. Sorry for them.

When a general is rich in humanity, those under him will be happy. When a general becomes political and authoritarian, no one will be unhappier than his subordinates. The Soka Gakkai leaders still have a long way to go. They must experience more hardship.

Home at 11:00. My home and my family are what I enjoy.

Tuesday, March 8. Cloudy, occasional rain.

An emergency conference in the president's office. A youth division corps chiefs meeting. Campaign strategies and plans were announced. Discussed the Otaru Debate with the Minobu sect in Hokkaido. The way Sensei pours his energy into this event is extraordinary. The advance group left immediately for Otaru on the night train. The responsible Study Department professors selected are to be K., T., L., R. and myself.

Friday, March 11. Clear.

Left for Hokkaido on Japan Airlines. Arrived in Chitose at 11:30, a bit late. Four of us: Sensei, K., T. and myself.

Took a train from Sapporo to Otaru. Arrived at 3:00 p.m., checked into an inn across from the station and immediately worked on our strategy. Went to Otaru Civic Auditorium. Upon arriving, I met with the advance youth division party waiting for me there. For all practical purposes, I was in charge. Met with I. from the Minobu sect and discussed the order in which the debaters would take the rostrum, as well as points of debate and questions to be presented. Happily, everything was decided according to my original plan. In response to guidance and encouragement from the advance leaders party, about 750 members gathered from Asahikawa, Hakodate, Sapporo and Otaru.

The historic debate began at exactly 7:00. To begin, the master of ceremonies for the Minobu side, Mr. Matsui, spoke for about three minutes. Next, I gave my opening words.

The order of speakers was as follows: Giichi Hasegawa, followed by Takehisa Tsuji, then Ichimyo Murozumi, followed by Yoshihei Kodaira. Each had twelve minutes to speak on behalf of his side. Next, Hasegawa, Tsuji, Murozumi and Kodaira each followed with a five-minute rebuttal. Next was a question-and-answer session lasting twenty minutes. Questions were addressed to any of the four debaters. Finally, the two sides faced off, each with seven minutes to address four questions. Of particular importance were questions pertaining to the object of devotion and the identity of the true Buddha. These topics caused sparks of debate to fly

All was over at 9:10. A magnificent Gakkai victory from the standpoints of both theory and actuality. Sensei seemed extremely pleased.

Saturday, March 12. Snowy.

Snowy Hokkaido, of the poetic beauty I love. Got up at 8:30. Left Otaru for Sapporo on the 9:50 train. Went directly to the M. temple in Sapporo, where we had been invited to meet with High Priest Nissho Mizutani, in Hokkaido on a lecture tour. There were nineteen in our party, including Sensei, the top leaders and some youth division members.

At 6:30, a meeting with several dozen members of Sapporo Group at the Grand Hotel. After greetings from the various leaders present, President Toda answered a few questions. A lonesome, spiritless group.

Sunday, March 13. Cloudy.

Awoke at 8:00 in the Grand Hotel in Sapporo. Went to say good morning to Sensei. He seemed extremely happy. I was overjoyed.

Representing President Toda, went to Sapporo Station to send off the high priest, who left on the 9:40 train for Asahikawa, the next scheduled stop on his lecture tour. "Please take care of your health," I told him.

Set out on the snowy streets to a meeting at O. Industries, where I was scheduled to give guidance. Seemed like more than twenty group members were present. Youth Division Chief T. accompanied me.

At 4:00, we waited in front of the Japan Airlines business office. Our flight departed at 5:55 and arrived at Haneda Airport in Tokyo at 9:35. Tired. Sensei seemed in relatively high spirits. Spoke to several members who greeted us at the airport, then accompanied Sensei to his house.

Monday, March 14. High clouds.

Have been feeling extremely tired since morning. Arrived at the headquarters at 5:30.

Listened to a tape of the Otaru Debate at 6:30, to review what really took place. Study Department professors and assistant professors listened together. Thinking of the next time I will have an opportunity to be a master of ceremonies, I reflected on various aspects of my performance. Must be more courageous. More fast-paced.

Left for an emergency youth division leaders meeting at T.'s house. Everyone seemed spiritless. Were they tired? Or do they lack initiative? It's all right. I will stand up by myself. Returned home close to midnight. Passion and sentimentality, wisdom, reasonableness, compassion, courage, capacity, fortune, ability.... What is human revolution? Religious revolution? Social revolution? Political revolution? Cultural revolution? Vaguely wondered about these topics.

Tuesday, March 15. Partly cloudy.

My physical condition is very poor. Thought about how long I will live. About my destiny. My back hurts; it feels heavy. Attended a Bunkyo Chapter unit chiefs meeting in the evening. Spiritless, sad.

After 8:00, I attended a joint discussion meeting of a district of Tsukiji Chapter in Hasunuma. Approximately three hundred participants. An extremely difficult meeting. The general director and the statistics department chief also came. The meeting was over at 10:00.

The Gosho states:

> You surpass others in your resolve, and it is because of your devoted support that I have been able to survive. The heavens are certainly

aware of this; the earth surely knows about it, too. If any misfortune were to occur to you, it could only mean that heaven wanted my life itself. Wherever one may be, whether in the mountains, on the seas, in the skies, or in the cities, one cannot escape death. Nevertheless, a sutra explains that even one's fixed karma can be changed. T'ien-t'ai's commentary also states that one can prolong one's fixed span of life.

— "PROPAGATION BY THE WISE" (WND, 753)

My life, both inside and out, is like a storm. Must do battle with the devil of illness. Must do battle with those jealous of me as a youth and as President Toda's closest disciple.

Wednesday, March 16. Cloudy.

Physical condition extremely poor. Is it destiny? Karmic retribution? The result of past slander?

No spirit, no will. I am like someone on the brink of death. The cherry blossoms of the springtime of my youth have now fallen and scattered. How sad! Must devote myself to chanting daimoku consistently. My only choice is to spur myself on powerfully, to show actual proof of Buddhism's strictness and of the strict power of my own determination.

After fulfilling my mission to spread the Great Law, wish to die an honorable death. Then, I would like to rest for eternity. Quietly, deeply.

Life and death. Formation, continuance, decline and disintegration. Birth, aging, sickness and death. Eternity, happiness, true self and purity. Life from the remotest past. Life that continues eternally. Eternity in a moment. The oneness of life and death. The oneness of body and mind. The three existences — past, present and future.

Without understanding, I deeply sense how pitiful it would be, as a follower of the correct faith, to die now. Must fight! Must strive!

Thursday, March 17. Fair.

Physical condition poor. My wife said I look pale. Forced myself to leave for work. Began to feel ill on the train. At 7:00, went to a rally in support of O.'s ward assembly election. About 450 gathered at Jozai-ji. His election seems assured.

Thursday, April 7. Fair.

Warm today. My physical condition was poor all day. Was given an injection. Took the 2:15 Kurihama-bound train to Yokosuka, with chapter staff members Y. and K., YWD Corps Chief M., and Miss U. Felt sorry

I caused trouble for everyone by not feeling well. It was my first visit to Yokosuka, a town with rich international flavor.

The meeting began at 7:00. A tremendous success. After words from the district chief and a determination from the corps chief, I spoke. Left the meeting quietly after speaking for about fifteen minutes.

Sunday, April 10. Clear then overcast.

Slept past 9:00. Feeling unsettled.

Went to K.'s campaign office at 11:00. Something seemed strangely offensive. The Gakkai's cultural and social battle has begun. Sensei appointed me in charge of the Jonan and Yokohama areas. Have many strong feelings about this election campaign, being held to promote the Gakkai's fusion of Buddhism with society. People of faith, people of ability, people who sincerely care about the common people, in other words, the purest, most capable people will be sent into society through this election. Must be strongly on guard against those who are conceited or self-serving or those who desire recognition. My responsibility is heavy. Must be particularly careful about those who try to flatter or kowtow to the top leadership.

Beginning at 1:00, went out to the streets to campaign. Continued until after 4:00. Some leaders brazenly parade about with a typical politician's air. Relying on only worldly ways, such candidates are in danger of forgetting faith and forgetting the Gakkai. How foolish, how stupid! Some among them are likely to open their eyes.

Monday, April 11. Fair and clear.

The spring sunlight dazzles my eyes. To the headquarters in the evening. Chanted daimoku for a long time. Never retreat. Persevere with valiant and untiring faith. Afterwards, stopped by the home of I., an election campaign headquarters. Told them not to be overly optimistic. Seems like everyone has become serious. Was told everyone has been noisily exchanging opinions, and they have yet to reach a conclusion. President Toda also seemed extremely concerned. I said the key to final victory is unity. Strongly urged them to organize as I had instructed. Aware of a fresh breath of progress. Satisfied for the moment. From tonight, I will realistically take the lead. Many difficulties.

Wednesday, April 27. Overcast with rain in the morning.

Physical condition poor. Went to Hashimoto in Kanagawa after 5:00.

Spoke at a campaign gathering for Miss I. Left after pouring my whole soul into speaking passionately on her behalf. Confident of her victory.

Want everyone to win. If anyone were to lose, that person and his or her family and many supporters will suffer. Suffice it to say that victory or defeat is determined by that person's fortune or destiny at the crucial moment. On the way home, I discussed with Chapter Chief T. my concerns about the other chapter ward assembly candidates.

Returned home close to 1:00. Tired. May this family be protected!

Monday, May 2. Clear, then cloudy.

My health has been growing steadily worse. Feel my life gradually coming to an end. How sad. How vexing. Sensei is extremely concerned about my health. Very sorry. Must train myself and practice with bold dignity. If I am pretentious or affected, my faith and daily life will eventually be ruined.

All Culture Department members were elected, with the exception of I. from Akita. Sensei seems happy. Everyone's face was filled with joy. From the standpoint of 'consistency from beginning to end,' this is a good omen for future Culture Department campaigns. Victory, however, is just the beginning. Want to emphasize that we must not forget this is a departure point in our activities to spread kosen-rufu throughout Japanese society.

The sky is dark; my heart, too, is in the shadows. If my health deteriorates any more, I feel I am destined to fall into a deep abyss.

Entering a struggle with the devil of illness, a battle with the demon of death. The end equals a beginning. Must summon up my determination in faith like a raging blaze, and rely only on the Gohonzon.

In the evening, took charge of preparations for tomorrow's headquarters general meeting. Finished after 11:00. Preparations seem to be splendidly complete.

Pushing my sick body beyond reason. Must fulfill my responsibilities. T. escorted me home. Sorry to trouble him.

Tuesday, May 3. Overcast, then rain.

Light rain beginning in the afternoon.

At 12:30, the twelfth Headquarters General Meeting, sponsored by Koiwa Chapter, was held. Heard that the number of participants broke the fifteen-thousand mark. This is an indication of great progress, a model for the limitless progress to come. Heard that a large number of people returned home, disappointed they could not enter the meeting place. Feel sorry for them. Satisfied that everything was completed as planned, without accident. Sincerely appreciate the youth division members who helped behind the scenes. Hope none of the top leaders will forget the efforts of those who always work behind the scenes. Deeply concerned, for the future as well.

A follow-up meeting began at 5:30 at the N. Chinese restaurant. All the top leaders attended, as well as several priests. I and another youth division member acted as masters of ceremonies.

Feeling ill. The most agonizing day of my life. As if dying, I fell into bed at midnight.

Wednesday, May 4. Cloudy with occasional light rain.

My physical condition has not improved in the least. Met with Sensei at the headquarters. Together, we went to pay our respects to the high priest. Sensei also seems very tired. He told me that last night he had a vomiting bout. Sensei's efforts over the last several years would equal hundreds of years of effort by the average man. Like a human projectile, he has thrown himself into the lead for kosen-rufu and for developing his disciples. Meanwhile, other society leaders amuse themselves by playing golf, mah-jongg, or relaxing at the hot springs. The average person may think a leader like President Toda is crazy while the others are wise.

Thursday, May 5. Clear.

Clear skies all day. The beautiful weather permeates heaven and earth. Today the office was closed.

Awoke at 9:00. Went to the public baths. To Sensei's home in the afternoon—the H.s, the M.s and my wife and I. Sensei treated us to plenty of food, then offered his guidance. Thankful. Returned home a little before 10:00. Adjusted the book shelf, then went to bed early.

Friday, May 6. Clear skies.

My health has slightly improved. I envy others' healthy vigor. My wife also seems tired from pushing herself beyond reason. Lately, she seems dispirited.

Must become healthy. I have been causing everyone to worry and am not completing my own work. First, chant daimoku. Second, sleep well. Third, take care of my health. Must be especially careful, put these things into practice and have patience. After all, "Buddhism is common sense."

Sunday, May 15. Light rain in the morning, then cloudy.

Stayed home all morning. My first day off in a while. Ms. M. came by in the afternoon. Following her, Corps Chief H. and three other leaders came over. Together we enjoyed Beethoven's Fifth Symphony. This melody, which portrays an ongoing battle with suffering, resembles the contents of my heart.

In the evening, went to S.'s home in Yaguchi. Was treated to dinner. Spoke for about two hours to one of his relatives, who is a socialist. It turned into an opportunity for propagation. A pitiable person. He is pale, lacks confidence and seems to lead an empty life.

Monday, May 16. Clear.

Felt fine this morning. My health has more or less returned. My wife has also regained her spirits somewhat. Sensei returned from his trip at 2:00. Quickly went to greet him and returned with him to the headquarters. Reported about various matters. He responded with two or three questions, which I could not answer clearly. Began to sweat, feeling miserable. A lecture by retired High Priest Horigome on the "Orally Transmitted Teachings." The moon shone pristinely as I returned home. Feel like singing "Moon Over a Ruined Castle" [a famous Japanese song]. Opened a collection of poetry by Walt Whitman.

> I turn but do not extricate myself,
> Confused, a past-reading, another, but with darkness yet.
>
> The beach is cut by the razory ice-wind, the wreck-guns sound,
> The tempest lulls, the moon comes floundering through the drifts.
>
> I look where the ship helplessly heads end on, I hear the burst as
>   she strikes, I hear the howls of dismay, they grow fainter and
>   fainter.
>   —"THE SLEEPERS," LEAVES OF GRASS

Read a bit from Jiro Abe's *Diary of Santaro*. Not very interesting. To bed early.

Tuesday, May 17. Clear.

Sensei was absent all morning. Went to his home to make various reports. Fine weather. My health seems to have improved. Happy. On the way home, recited Tao Yuan-ming's poem, "Homeward Bound":

> I am homeward bound.
> The fields and gardens will soon be
>   overgrown with weeds,
> So how can I not return?
> My boat rocks gently as my robes
>   flutter in the breeze.

To Jozai-ji at 7:30 to attend a Sixth Corps meeting. A weak showing. What's lacking is a strong foundation of each person's faith, a solid organization and substantive guidance. Afterward, I attended a farewell gathering for S. at Myoko-ji in Shinagawa. Forthrightly expressed my opinion. Quite annoyed at the jealousy of T. and others. They are weak young men.

Wednesday, May 18. Light rain.

Growing a little more fatigued.

In the afternoon, went to an international trade fair in Tsukijima. Looking forward with hope toward great advancement and development in industry, science and manufacturing. Afterward, everyone met over dinner. In the evening, a scheduled Study Department professors meeting was changed to a planning meeting to decide on Seikyo Shimbun branch offices. Received strict guidance on a variety of matters from Sensei. My heart ached. Read *A Disqualified Critic* and *On 'Crime and Punishment'* by Haruo Kobayashi with great interest. Any book I read seems to be saying that what is great, surpassing all, is the "self."

Read poetry by Walt Whitman:

> Of the progress of the souls of men and women along the grand roads
>   of the universe, all other progress is the needed emblem and
>   sustenance.
> Forever alive, forever forward,
> Stately, solemn, sad, withdrawn, baffled, mad, turbulent, feeble,
>   dissatisfied,
> Desperate, proud, fond, sick, accepted by men, rejected by men,
> They go! they go! I know that they go, but I know not where they go,

But I know that they go toward the best — toward something great.
— "Song of the Open Road," *Leaves of Grass*

2:00 a.m. — Growing sleepy. What is my dream? To be a poet? A businessman? A great politician? An ordinary philosopher? An able revolutionary? Or an uncrowned king of the common people?

Thursday, May 19. Clear and fair.

My physical condition is improving. In the afternoon met with K., the marketing manager of Y. Mutual Bank in Yokohama, as Mr. Toda's representative. It's been quite some time since we've met. Sense, with each passing day, society's growing impurity and confusion. This is just as might be expected in the evil Latter Day of the Law. Acutely aware of how fortunate I am to embrace Nichiren Daishonin's Buddhism. To the headquarters at dusk. Reported to Sensei that I delivered his message to K., then met with National Railways officials and travel bureau representatives to discuss transportation and pilgrimages to the head temple.

As the Gakkai continues to grow and advance, day by day and month after month, developing a motivated public relations organization is urgently needed. Discussed various plans with leaders at the chapter chief's home. Home after midnight.

Friday, May 20. Fair and clear.

Sensei does not seem at all well. He took an injection of medication, after which I gave him a thorough massage.
1. Want to advance without error along the path of mentor and disciple.
2. How much do we really understand Sensei's mercy toward us?
3. How much have we absorbed his ideals? Have we been truly practicing as he has taught us?

Pure and honest people who embrace Buddhism and are connected to a great teacher will surely emerge victorious. Today, when people usually look out only for themselves, those with power, ability and character are likely to win in society.
1. The purpose of life — to attain enlightenment.
2. Oneness of life and the universe — an absolutely free and confident state of life.
3. Oneness of body and mind — this includes the spirit, the body, wisdom and finances.

I now have two children. Have decided to leave our apartment in Omorisanno. We have no choice, since our lease soon expires. Will buy a house from an acquaintance for ¥1 million. Negotiations were concluded with the agreement that we would borrow half the amount from my father and pay off the rest in monthly installments of ¥10,000. The house is 18 *tsubo* [one *tsubo* equals about 36 sq. ft.], and we were told that the entire plot of leased land is over 58 *tsubo*. We are scheduled to move around the middle of next month. Since I am away from home so much, I am relieved to see we will be living closer to my wife's parents as I had wished.

Saturday, May 21. Clear.

Busy all morning. Left on the 12:30 express to give a lecture in Osaka. Completed lecturing on "How Those Initially Aspiring to the Way Can Attain Buddhahood through the Lotus Sutra." Utterly disappointed at my own lack of study. After the lecture, attended a Sakai Chapter group chiefs meeting. An extremely bright gathering. Afterward, we all watched a film of the youth division pilgrimage from last October, the 702nd year since the establishment of true Buddhism. Some ten thousand young men and women participated. The film will be a national treasure in the future. In the midst of our confused world, this many youth are burning with the spirit to seek the Way of true Buddhism and to establish themselves, while carrying out activities to rebuild Japan. For foolish critics to label this "fanaticism" is nothing short of malicious abuse. Such individuals are immature, arrogant and pathetic.

Sunday, May 22. Cloudy.

Tired from staying up late last night. Out of bed at 7:00. Heavily fatigued, both physically and spiritually. Reflected seriously about the inadequacy of my lecture. The study meeting continued until noon. Afternoon, met with chapter and corps leaders to discuss personnel and organizational matters. Each time I come to Osaka, I think about the growth and development of Kansai. S. treated me to dinner. Returned to Tokyo on the night train.

Monday, May 23. High clouds.

In the afternoon, accompanied M. to I.'s newly built home to offer our regards. Thought it seemed rather elegant for someone whose business is not going so well. In the evening, a lecture at the headquarters for those in the fourth level of the Study Department. Sensei attended. All were serious. In this special world of seeking the Way, we tightened our bodies and spirits. So long as such an attitude and environment exist, the Gakkai will be firm and solid. Not one person was absent.

Summoned by Sensei. He told me a former city councilman in Numazu has been scheming to take advantage of the Gakkai through a joint business venture. I was completely unaware of the situation. He asked me, was I or was I not a member of the general staff? Ashamed. It seems those who would take advantage of the Gakkai are on the increase. To break the harmonious unity of the membership and use the Gakkai to one's own advantage is none other than the function of a devil or an evil demon. It all comes down to a battle between the Buddha and devils. This is Buddhism.

Tuesday, May 24. Clear, becoming cloudy later on.

To Yokohama on business. Beautiful weather. My health is gradually improving. Attended S.'s wedding in the evening. A magnificent ceremony. Gave congratulatory words. I have now reached the age where many of my friends have their own families. This should be a reason to rejoice. Must not forget my original intention. Have recently become more aware of my own foolishness. Must never forget, throughout my life, to make untiring efforts. Must not assume I have attained what I have not yet attained. Must study consistently so that I may write excellent works on religious revolution, politics and religion, science and religion, and culture and religion. Brave men, youth, young warriors, courageous young men. We live amid the times, amid reality. Must never forget my dream, my great objective, my passion.

Wednesday, May 25. Clear, then brief thunder showers.

Attended I.'s wedding at Myoko-ji. A great success. Could such an unhappy family have become this happy? Is it benefit, effort, or just the times? Met with H. and the T.s at a Shinagawa restaurant to discuss chapter business. I was the only one who was serious. A discouraging gathering. Went to see *Swan Lake*. Vivid hues of fantasy and illusion. Fleeting. Chapter leader O. came over to receive guidance. He appeared deeply troubled but left feeling relieved. He is the problem, I feel.

Thursday, May 26. Clear and fair.

Did not feel well all day. Attended a discussion meeting at S.'s.

Overjoyed that two guests joined. A leaders meeting held afterward. This month's results have not surpassed last month's. Everyone is bright and in high spirits. Those who practice faith, the Bodhisattvas of the Earth, youthful revolutionaries of peace, must continue to fight cheerfully, win or lose. Next month, will earnestly take the lead once again. Thought to myself that new renovations must be added to the Gakkai headquarters building sometime soon, so that it may accommodate growing numbers of people. It must be like the main fortress of kosen-rufu. Many chapter meeting places or community centers will also be necessary. Won't there be hundreds of chapters ten years from now? A common mortal cannot know this. But without these, kosen-rufu cannot be realized in accord with our wishes. How many seriously consider these things with a sense of responsibility and vision for the future?

Saturday, May 28 — Sunday, May 29. Rain.

Youth division pilgrimage. Heavy rain.

Everyone got soaking wet. How strict the Gohonzon is. Is it because there are many slanderers among us? Reflecting heavily on my faith.

Monday, May 30. Overcast.

A joint leaders meeting in the evening. Sensei's guidance was particularly strict. It resounded in my heart like thunder. His guidance covered following main points:

1. Essential nature vs. formality.
2. The entity of the Law vs. substantiation.
3. Fame-seeking vs. strong faith.

My wonderful mentor. Can only listen humbly to his merciful guidance. Have been realizing with each passing day that I can never hope to match him. Lamentable.

Tuesday, May 31. Cloudy.

Sensei's guidance from yesterday, etched in the back of my mind, has been with me all day. Every day his guidance and training become stricter. To bear up, I must spend each day wholeheartedly. To Kanda Avenue in the evening. Bought three secondhand books. The books I want to buy can be piled as high as a mountain. Difficult to afford. The white clouds and the foliage on the trees give me the feeling of summer.

Monday, June 13. Clear and fine.

Yesterday, eighty Suiko Group members went with Sensei to Lake Kawaguchi and Lake Yamanaka. Afterward, everyone accompanied him back to his home in Meguro. Became fatigued after yesterday's strict guidance. Reflected again and again. Dispatched to Koto Ward in the afternoon. The summer sun grows warmer with each passing day. Physically exhausted. Summer is the season of youth. Must try my utmost. Attended a lecture for fourth-level Study Department members in the evening.

A deep, far-reaching philosophy. A great, profound principle. My own lack of ability must be apparent. After I returned home, T. came over. Disappointed. Often have difficulty trusting those with unstable family situations.

Sunday, July 17. Clear and fair.

It's already been a month and a half since we moved to our new home. Today I took a long-needed rest. Watered the garden in the afternoon. Recalled Tokutomi Roka's *Nature and Life*. Y. and K. came by. Had dinner together. Relaxed and read the paper. Isn't *society* another word for complexity, and *the world*, another name for turmoil? Went to I.'s home in the evening to give guidance. On the way back, stopped by S.'s to give my summer season greetings. Troubled by back pain. To bed after midnight.

Thursday, September 8. Clear and Fair.

A hot, humid day. Agonized over my physical condition, which has truly worsened. If I cannot reply to Sensei's expectations, his warm consideration and will to me, where does my mission in this life lie? Only through burning faith can I defeat this destiny. Without it, my own defeat will surely come.

To Nihon University Auditorium in the afternoon to prepare for the upcoming general meeting. Must promote kosen-rufu no matter the hardship. This is my destiny. We should believe, as the Gosho teaches, that the Gohonzon inconspicuously witnesses all of our efforts. After finishing, I attended the Thursday lecture (on the "Expedient Means" and "Life Span" chapters) held at Toshima Public Hall. Many new members present. Went home with my wife for the first time in quite a while.

Tuesday, September 20. Clear.

A meeting centering on Sensei, at 6:00 at the headquarters. Strict

questions and training from Sensei. Isn't this just like the training undergone by a master swordsman? Afterward, accompanied the general
director to I.'s home to give guidance. Because Sensei designated me to
visit I., my responsibility is truly heavy.

It's gotten cool.

Will probably have to start a new notebook for my diary tomorrow.

Sensei presented me with this poem in commemoration of the Otaru
Debate:

> Soaring through the skies,
> to the sea off Otaru,
> Your youthful form, engaging the enemy, remains forever.

And he wrote the following poem in my copy of "The Opening of the
Eyes":

> Like the great Phoenix, soaring into the heavens,
> You will live for a thousand years.

Read quietly until midnight. To bed close to 2:00.

Wednesday, September 21. Rain and overcast.

The first page of my new diary notebook.

While life itself is eternal, everlasting, this life is like a dream; like
the morning dew or winter frost that vanish instantly before the warmth
of the rising sun. The record of this period of my life, my activities, and
my future are, for better or for worse, less significant than a microbe.
And yet, I will leave a mark on this earth and in the universe, a mark that
likely will be seen and pondered by someone in the future. Human
affairs are so small, so miniscule when viewed from the standpoint of
limitless space and beginningless time.

To carefully record one's own feelings, thoughts, recollections, secrets
and even resentment in a single work—this, interestingly enough, is significant. It expands one's personal world and promotes interaction, dialogue and encouragement between one's self and the self of another. I
strongly dislike a diary written only as a mere record of events or in an
obligatory manner. Until I spread my yet immature wings, until my incomplete construction is successfully finished, I will maintain my dream
of free skies, a free world and the free realm of action hidden deep within
my heart. It is the fall of my twenty-seventh year.

Thursday, September 22. Clear.

Becoming very cool. The autumn wind deeply penetrates my heart.

O. Company has now been in business for more than ten years. The staff has overcome hardships time and time again, each time establishing a stabler foundation. Feel satisfied. I am astonished to see such dramatic actual proof resulting from the accumulation of inconspicuous benefit.

1. When I reflect on my selfish ways, I break into a cold sweat.
2. Must revise my overly optimistic view of reality.
3. Remember always to train and develop myself.

A youth division staff conference at 2:00.
1. Discussed thoroughly the system for passing on guidance and direction.
2. Laid out a strategy for challenging the B. sect.
3. Decided to take action against the R. society.

Want to achieve a splendid victory in this, the final campaign of the 703rd anniversary of the establishment of true Buddhism. All depends on my own determination in faith. Attended Sensei's lecture on the Lotus Sutra at Toshima Civic Auditorium. Sensei said he was feeling good. Nothing could make me happier. Will spend my life in self-reflection and admonishment — strictly, like autumn frost.

Friday, September 23. Clear, then partly cloudy.

Talked with Sensei in his office for about thirty minutes. Concerned that my report was not detailed enough. The first meeting for Study Department candidates held at 6:30.

Studied through the second part of "On Practicing the Buddha's Teachings." Deeply reflected on the idea of three levels of ability: unskilled, skilled and artistic. My lectures lack the skill to qualify me as a Study Department professor. Must develop genuine ability; must study and polish my skill. No choice but to forge ahead tirelessly, more than others, more than anyone. Twenty-seven years have passed since I began this voyage of life. Must stand up in three years, when I am thirty. Will live powerfully!

Saturday, September 24. Cloudy with intermittent rain.

The autumn equinox. Thinking about my parents. Buddhism is strict. Do not want to be weak or conniving in my practice of faith. Stayed home all morning. Looked closely at photographs of Sensei. He encourages and watches over me with compassion, warmth and strictness.

A Koiwa Chapter general meeting at Chuo University Auditorium at 1:00. Very successful and significant. Praying the chapter members will continue their bold advance. The meeting was over at 4:00. Afterward, met H., the T.s and the O.s in Ochanomizu for dinner.

To Jozai-ji at 6:30. Met with Priest Hosoi to discuss incidents related to the Hokke-ko [a lay society of Nichiren Shoshu members] and families supporting the temple. Priesthood and laity should advance together in unity toward their grand objective of kosen-rufu. Trifling schemes must come to an end. Attended a Bunkyo Chapter discussion meeting for the first time in a while. My favorite chapter. So many wise and talented people have appeared. Returned home just before midnight feeling tired.

Sunday, September 25. Cloudy, then clearing.

Left for the head temple on the 7:46 train from Shinagawa with my wife and both children. As with each time I visit the head temple, thought about the joy of faith, the meaning of life, and the clear vision of reality I have gained through my Buddhist practice. We are like the lotus flower that blooms in a muddy swamp.

Arrived at the head temple at 11:40. A clear autumn day. The temple grounds were filled with fresh vitality.

The ceremony of chanting before the Dai-Gohonzon began at 2:00.

Was granted an audience with the high priest at 3:00. Sensei has been devotedly serving the head temple. Hope all priests will deeply recognize this as soon as possible and offer him their praise. Praying from the bottom of my heart for Sensei's good health and his protection.

Monday, September 26. Cloudy with intermittent showers.

My oldest son had a high fever in the morning. Really suffering physically myself. A gray day. Understand the limits of the physical body. But the power called life force surpasses both physical and spiritual power. It is a mysterious energy that sets into motion functions far stronger than spiritual or physical power alone. Life force arises from the workings of one's determination. Actually it wells forth limitlessly through the power of the Mystic Law and the power of faith. It comes from practice. Will test this through my own experience and show actual proof.

Missed the lecture for Study Department seniors and went by myself to A. Hospital in Yotsuya for a physical exam. Blood test, urine test, X-rays etc. It is now the time of year for earnest study. Had dinner in Kanda after leaving the hospital. Purchased several secondhand books before returning home. Will challenge myself to read and to write.

Tuesday, September 27. Rain.

For me, President Toda is my sovereign, teacher and parent in life. Since I was nineteen, I have been by his side, serving him as he guides and trains me directly. Pondering deeply our mystic bond. My true wish is to be with him for life. This way, I can fulfill my mission for this lifetime. His scolding, his training and his compassionate love are all deeply engraved in my body and mind.

At 6:00, a Suiko Group meeting. Sensei attended. Tonight we finished *Romance of the Three Kingdoms*. Sensei gave guidance on the method for promoting Asian kosen-rufu and completing kosen-rufu in Japan, as if this were his last will to us. Later, attended a First Corps YMD district leaders meeting. Had no choice but to give strict guidance. Returned home, 11:30. Asked my wife to prepare a little something for me to eat. She seemed happy to do so.

Wednesday, September 28. Rain.

Heard a typhoon is approaching, but it will probably miss us. Also heard this year's rice crop produced the first good harvest since the end of the war. The morning lectures on political science are drawing to a close. Have absorbed almost nothing.

Cancelled my plans to visit the hospital in the afternoon. Want to know the results of my tests, but even when I learn them my only recourse will be to cure myself.

In the evening, finished the second of three parts of Nichikan's "Teaching for the Latter Day."[1] Have gradually gained a clear understanding. It cannot be understood without studying it two or three times. The lecture lasted until 11:00. Tired, but I will do my best. Cannot oversleep.

1. "Teaching for the Latter Day": Part of Nichikan's *Six-volume Writings* (see note on p. 82). It clarifies the correct practice of Buddhism and the object of devotion for the Latter Day of the Law.

Thursday, September 29. Rain, then partly cloudy.

Fatigued all day. An all-leaders conference at 6:00. Discussed and planned until almost 9:00. Sensei also seemed tired. Afterward, went with friends and fellow staff members for dinner in the Yuraku area. A dull time. Lamented that I could have spent it better reading a book.

The Gakkai has grown quite large. There are now many members who have neither seen President Toda nor heard his guidance, among them some politicians and businessmen. Fear possible future rifts. For this reason, we must be undaunted. Believe there are a few truly capable people among my juniors and seniors who can protect the Gakkai. Communicated with M. about various matters involving the Traffic Control Group until late in the evening. He is trustworthy and earnest. Wish him a happy future. Awake until after 2:00. Feel like I've somehow grown very old.

Friday, September 30. Clear, then overcast.

A warm, humid day. Weather influences everything. The human body is particularly sensitive.

A youth division staff meeting at 6:00 at the headquarters. Nothing conclusive arose, as everyone promoted his personal viewpoint. They are forgetting their great mission and objective, their ideas stemming only from their own abilities or intellect. Had Sensei been present, they would have reached a conclusion right away. Frightening. The spirit and significance of the youth division staff conference President Toda entrusted to us has already been lost.

To Josen-ji afterward for an emergency traffic control group meeting. They are taking responsibility for the Gakkai from behind the scenes. The top leaders must cherish and care for these people.

Next, attended a district chiefs meeting at T.'s. The human mind is constantly changing. Must be stronger. Nam-myoho-renge-kyo.

Saturday, October 1. Rain, overcast.

A typhoon, officially the twenty-second of the season. A great fire raged in Niigata. Told there are some thousand and several hundred Gakkai households in Niigata, all belonging to Mukojima Chapter. From among them, only one house sustained damage, it was reported. Even at this stage of my practice, I am amazed at the Mystic Law's terrific power.

At 6:00, met with H., an M. newspaper reporter. Strongly refuted claims that we have been forcing people to convert. He seemed persuaded. Was astonished, however, at the prominent five-column story that appeared in the paper. The cynical press exerts a bad influence on society. Employing the brute force of words, the press reigns unchallenged. The weak are always made to suffer. An extremely biased democracy.

At the headquarters, finished lecturing on "On Practicing the Buddha's Teachings." Gave a fairly good lecture. Surprised, however, at the study candidates' shallow level of understanding. Was I the same in the beginning?

Sunday, October 2. Rain.

Slept all morning, but it did nothing to relieve my fatigue. Pitiful. Mine is like a battle with the devil of death. Our destiny, it seems, is to be misunderstood by others. Is this due to our lack of virtue or refinement?

Attended the Shiki Chapter general meeting a little after 1:00. A light rain fell as more than thirty-four hundred members gathered. Though there were some apprehensive moments, the meeting finished without a hitch.

Afterward, went to the chapter chief's home. Together we attended a Keio District joint discussion meeting. Gave guidance and encouragement to the extent of my ability. Before returning home in high spirits, I tried to leave a deep impression on the middle-level leaders there. I am still very young. Were it not for Sensei, who knows what would have become of me. Ah....

Monday, October 3. Rain.

More rain. Physically exhausted. Feel as if I'm sinking in a dark whirlpool of fatigue. Can only strengthen my faith. Break through, shatter, transform. Thought bitterly about my lack of ability and power.

Went to see I. at the postal services office at noon. He is a friend from the Taisei Business School. Was treated to lunch in the basement cafeteria. He seems to be in trouble in terms of faith, chanting only two or three daimoku per day.

Japan Airlines flights were grounded due to the typhoon. Sensei left Tokyo at 10:30 on the *Silver River* night express. Seeing him off, was given guidance at the station entrance. Don't think well of Chief Secretary I.'s sly tactics. She has become rude and demeaning toward me and others, often distorting the truth. She has no reason to hold herself above those around her and should not take advantage of the kindness and consideration shown her by Sensei. Women can be particularly fearsome. Must be very careful in the future. Strictly warned Miss I., the chapter women's division chief, and Miss U., regarding their arrogance. Worried that several people are hesitating to practice their faith freely. Accompanied Dr. H. to Tokyo Station, then returned home. Got back near midnight. Very tired. Exhausted. How maddening! It is deep autumn; the streets at midnight are quiet. Thought about various historical figures: Kong-ming,[1] Masashige,[2] Yoritomo,[3] Kiyomori[4] and Hideyoshi.[5]

1. Kong-ming: See note on p. 219.
2. Masashige: Kusunoki Masashige; see note on p. 74.
3. Yoritomo: Minamoto no Yoritomo (1147–1199). Founder of the Kamakura shogunate, the first warrior government in Japan. As a boy, he fought alongside his father, Minamoto no Yoshitomo, in a coup attempt against Taira no Kiyomori. Kiyomori routed the rebels, and Yoshitomo was killed. Yoritomo wandered aimlessly in the snowy mountains of Mino province (now part of Gifu Prefecture), where he was captured and returned to Taira headquarters. Kiyomori spared his life, and Yoritomo, then only 13, was exiled to eastern Japan.
4. Kiyomori: Taira no Kiyomori (1118–1181). Prominent political figure at the end of the Heian period (794–1185). Of warrior origin, he rose to dominate the court and saw his grandson become emperor. He is the central figure in Japan's greatest war chronicle, *The Tale of Heike*.
5. Hideyoshi: See note on p. 146 (Toyotomi Hideyoshi).

Tuesday, October 4. Clear.

A fine autumn day. Has the whole world been swept beautifully clear by autumn? Must be extremely cautious of M. and W. They lack earnestness and take our organization too lightly. Feel the time has finally come to give strong guidance to Y. and N.

At 6:30, a YMD meeting at Toshima Civic Auditorium. After a lackluster beginning, everyone's spirits seemed to rise steadily during the latter half of the meeting, expressing the power of the Soka Gakkai young men's division. Though we must never be too hasty in our efforts to develop, we must now maintain a strict and alert spirit. For about thirty minutes, gave them guidance about having awareness of their duty and responsibility as leaders and central figures. Lacked energy. Is it due to exhaustion or am I growing old? Attended a YMD Second Corps district leaders meeting. They are young, weak and green. Because of this, they cannot yet contribute to our movement. Training, discipline. Left with YMD Chief T.

Home at midnight. Tired. M. is a splendid individual. A wise person.

Wednesday, October 5. Clear.

A clear autumn day. Can't stop thinking about Sensei, even for a moment. Actually, my lifelong destiny was determined when I met him and will continue to be guided by him until the end. How fortunate! Though I began poor and sick, nothing could be more glorious than to have Sensei watch over me throughout my life. Articles criticizing the Gakkai have appeared in several magazines. Have gradually sensed the presence of the three powerful enemies. Never fear. What is crucial now is the spirit never to retreat or regress in faith.

At 6:00, received a lecture on the "Orally Transmitted Teachings" in the president's room.

At 8:30, in reception room #1, the *Seikyo Shimbun* sponsored a discussion meeting on the condition of the erroneous sects. The writers have grown considerably. Trust their conviction as bold, youthful pioneers. Awakened with indignation to the poisonous nature and the devilish reality of other sects. Strengthened and solidified my resolve to stand alone and fight. Though others do not see, Dosho and Domyo,[1] the guardian deities, know all. When I realize that all is apparent to the Mystic Law, my heart fills with joy.

1. Dosho and Domyo: Two gods said to dwell on a person's shoulders from the time of birth and record all of his or her actions, to report to King Emma, who judges the dead. They represent the law of cause and effect operating within one's life.

Thursday, October 6. Cloudy with intermittent showers.

Missed the Lotus Sutra lecture. Visited a curio shopping center in Ogikubo to encourage the Nakano Chapter Propagation Handbook research group members. Feel I can give spirited guidance once again. But if I were healthy and physically strong, I could fight five or ten times harder. In the evening, led our campaign to challenge the Minobu sect, the final battle of this 703rd anniversary of true Buddhism's establishment. Chanted to the Gohonzon that our campaign would end in great success, and for protection. The freshness of the pure autumn air seems to deepen with each passing day.

1. Must take pains to treat people with compassion.
2. Advance with warmth and tolerance.

Why? Think it is because I am intense and passionately emotional by nature. Want to be first in Japan and then in the whole world. Is having such a desire a cause for happiness or unhappiness? This I must ask myself.

Do not wish to have regrets in this lifetime.

Friday, October 7. Cloudy.

Made many minor mistakes lately. Whatever my past faults or errors, if I can change poison into medicine, I have nothing to be ashamed of.

The headquarters lecture was postponed for lack of a meeting place. Though I had meant to accompany Sensei to the movie *The New Tales of Heike*, regrettably, a suddenly called corps chiefs meeting prevented me from going. Felt that my mentor's invitation was especially significant. Was informed by his wife that he would like me to see it in the future.

Now is the time to begin putting the finishing touches on this year, the 703rd year since the establishment of true Buddhism. The corps chiefs meeting, a secretaries meeting and a Study Department candidates study session—attended all of these beginning at 6:00. When there is a campaign to be waged, my spirits rise. It's mysterious, yet natural. Last, we sang "Song of the White Tiger Corps." Grew melancholy thinking of those poor, pure-hearted and devoted young children whom this song portrays. The Gakkai's fresh, fortunate, crimson-cheeked children and youth, however, shall never have to tread the same path.

Saturday, October 8. Fair, followed by clouds.

Sensei left for Sendai in the morning to give a lecture. I went to lecture in Osaka. Sensei appeared extremely fatigued. I am young. Even if I should die, it would have few repercussions. But Sensei is a pillar of Asia or even the world. Can only pray for him to live long, at least until he reaches his eighties.

Left on *The Dove*, the 12:30 express to Osaka. Alone, I had a quiet trip. Osaka and Sakai are both chapters where I have formed truly deep friendships. Dropped by Y.'s after the lecture. Had a warm discussion with some members from the neighborhood. Stayed the evening.

Sunday, October 9. Clear. Extremely cold.

According to the paper, the first snow of winter fell in the Japan Alps. A lecture at 10:00. "On the Buddha's Prophecy." About four hundred attended. A question-and-answer session afterward.

At 2:00, began to lecture on "The Blessings of the Lotus Sutra." Finished at 4:30.

At 6:00, went to see *The New Tales of Heike* with the chapter chief, the chapter leaders and the corps chiefs. Thought about the dreams, development, glory and decline of Taira no Kiyomori, the powerful ruler whose travels took him throughout Japan. Think we must place particular importance on the period of our youth. It is a time to advance, filled with ideals and courage. Even more important, however, are our final years. Must take this to heart.

Left at 8:30 on the night train *Venus*.

Monday, October 10. Rain.

Arrived in Shimbashi at 7:03 a.m. A drizzle fell in Tokyo. Took a morning bath at a hot springs; went to work feeling refreshed. Could not absorb Sensei's morning lecture; my head felt heavy. Gakkai campaigns will become extremely intense as the months and years go by. Can feel it in my bones.

Awareness of my mission, determination—must not forget these even for a moment. Only when we are resolved to die if need be will our true power emerge.

To the headquarters at 5:00. Reported to Sensei on various matters, including the youth division and my own failure. Severely reprimanded. Fine, I will accept such scolding like a man and fulfill my responsibility.

A youth division general staff conference. Also met with assistant Study Department professors from Kamata Chapter to study "The Entity of the Mystic Law." For the past ten years, I have unreasonably drained myself both physically and spiritually.

Tuesday, October 11.

Sensei seems a little out of sorts. Worried. Is it fatigue? Or, could it be an expression of his strict compassion, guidance to enable us to reflect on ourselves. My mind becomes more composed with each passing day. A corps chiefs conference at 6:00 at the headquarters. Sensei was in a very weak state of health. A special leaders meeting at 8:30. Various instructions given.

Tomorrow, October 12, at 7:00 we will simultaneously distribute, at Mount Minobu and surrounding areas, the special *Seikyo Shimbun* edition that features articles refuting the Minobu sect's erroneous doctrines.

1. The activity must be accident-free.
2. Six hundred youth division members, including division chiefs, will participate. This activity will remain in the indelible history of the youth division and the Gakkai.

Left Tokyo by train at 11:33, our destination, Fuji then Minobu. Stayed at an inn across from Fuji Station.

Wednesday, October 12. Clear, then cloudy.

Up at 5:30.

At 6:00, we boarded two small taxis for Minobu. The area around Minobu is cold, dark and as still as death. Youth division members congregated in front of the Minobu sect's main temple gate as they arrived. Triumphant young pioneers! Strong and resolute. Thought how limitlessly brilliant the Gakkai's future will be.

At 7:30, 250 members of group one entered the temple compound. At the same time, group two and the other corps spread out to five different locations, including Omachi, Hakiri and Shionozawa.

The synchronized plan was completed beautifully by 10:00. The confused look of the Minobu priests remains clearly in my mind. A temple of arrogance. This temple, which rebels against the Buddha, leads its adherents into a state of hell. The purpose of today's battle was to awaken the people through dialogue, severing the roots of this evil influence. Such practice and determination constitute a cause that will most certainly lead to the Minobu sect's demise in the near future. Nikko Shonin must be deeply overjoyed. Departed for Tokyo from Fuji Station at 1:26. Everyone was filled with the joy of a victorious battle. I thought, could they really be this happy over such a minor victory? Reported to President Toda's office at 4:50. I will always be the one to lay out the strategy and put it into practice.

Thursday, October 13. Clear, becoming cloudy later.

Unsettled all day. Gave guidance at the headquarters from 2:00. Talked to thirty people, guiding them with all my heart. To President Toda's office afterward. Sensei is in poor health. Nevertheless, he retains a great teacher's awe-inspiring air. As his closest disciple, I must stand tall and advance. Keenly aware of the importance of the first-level study lecture. Gakkai members, students of the Daishonin's Buddhism, mustn't forget for a moment our mentor's strict spirit to interpret T'ien-t'ai's and Miao-lo's teachings based on the Daishonin's enlightened insight. If not, it will be difficult to avoid committing grave slander. Seriously reflecting on my earnestness as a disciple.

Happy to see that O. Company, T. Chapter, K. Chapter, the youth division, and B. Chapter could all achieve development and victory by carrying out their mentor's instructions.

Friday, October 14. Cloudy, then rain.

My physical condition has improved somewhat. A rare occurrence. I have the bad habit, however, of overdoing it whenever I begin feeling better. Shopped with Mrs. Toda in the evening at I. Had dinner at T. afterward. Skipped the lecture on "The Object of Devotion for Observing the Mind." Felt bad. Talked with G. at my house. Very low spirits. For both G. and myself, next spring's House of Councillors election will be a decisive first battle. If we fail, the pace of kosen-rufu will be impaired.

Want to score a solid victory in my maiden battle, not for myself, not for honor, but to realize the principles of Buddhism within society. My own mission has become all the more important. When viewed from the standpoint of 'consistency from beginning to end,' this battle will be the beginning, and all future elections, the end. If beginning and end are consistent, then this is the key battle, the one we must win.

> It is lack of courage that prevents one from attaining Buddhahood, although one may have professed faith in the Lotus Sutra many times since innumerable kalpas ago.

> There is definitely something extraordinary in the ebb and flow of the tide, the rising and setting of the moon, and the way in which summer, autumn, winter, and spring give way to each other. Something uncommon also occurs when an ordinary person attains Buddhahood. At such a time, the three obstacles and four devils will invariably appear, and the wise will rejoice while the foolish will retreat.

> — "THE THREE OBSTACLES AND FOUR DEVILS" (WND, 637)

Saturday, October 15. Cloudy.

Last night I had a truly awful dream. Felt bad until morning. Visited S.'s home in Ogikubo in the morning. Is it because of the influence of the environment that the people who live here seem to share a certain appearance or lifestyle. Regardless, I sense this family's elegance. Gave a lecture in the early evening on the *Propagation Handbook*. The place: M. Center in Nakano. Very successful. Poured all my energy into the lecture. Happy. Said that from among them, great future leaders will emerge. Met my wife in Shinjuku on the way back, and we returned home together. We walked from Kamata Station, stopping to eat *okonomiyaki* [a dish similar to egg foo young] along the way. Enjoyable.

Sensei made a pilgrimage to the head temple. His image never leaves my mind.

Prince of the Orient
   astride your horse, sword held high.
I strive, awaiting the day,
   when I will take the reins.

Sunday, October 16. Fair.

A clear autumn day. Not a cloud in the sky.

I adore my sons, Hiromasa and Shirohisa. Don't feel at all like their father. Is it because I'm still so young myself or is it due to my spoiled nature? In any case, all I can do is pray from the depths of my heart that these two will become men of justice who can open their golden wings and take flight as capable people for kosen-rufu.

W.'s wedding ceremony began at 5:00 at Jozai-ji. It was the first time I have acted as a go-between and the first time in a long time I have worn a tuxedo. The weight of passing years leaves me sad. Sensei attended, also other honored guests. About sixty people in all.

After the ceremony, a small reception, which ended at 8:30. Extremely fatigued.

Monday, October 17. Partly cloudy.

A headache all day in spite of the fine autumn weather. Using my busy schedule as an excuse for neglecting gongyo of late is a serious offense. Mentally and physically exhausted. How much criticism and opposition I have incurred. It can't be helped. Because I alone boldly advance, it is natural I should arouse my seniors' jealousy and the enmity of my peers. Everything will be determined by the Gohonzon and my mentor in life. How promising, how joyful!

Fear nothing, including others' criticism. Advance resolutely and behold! The youth will lead in the coming century. Advance valiantly again, for religious and political revolution. Let those who laugh keep on laughing. Let those who slander say what they will. They will regret it later.

Evening, a discussion meeting with the *The Daibyakurenge* staff. Discussed study with Study Department Chief K. for about two hours. Afterward, listened to reports in the president's room about our attack on the Minobu sect. Our objective was splendidly fulfilled. Everyone was happy. But I thought about how small a campaign it was; my mind will not be at ease until I achieve a victory tens of millions of times as great.

Wednesday, October 19. Rain.

Drizzled all day. This morning, an announcement was made about national land development policy. Suppressed my illness and went to work. Could not see Sensei. Felt sadly disappointed. Feel like I'm physically dying. Rested at the office until 3:00.

Went to the headquarters at 4:00, then returned home. Suffered all day, immersed in pain. My temperature was 101.3° F. My head hurts, my back hurts. What kind of illness is this? Going to chant a thousand or two thousand daimoku. Must create a wellspring of life force. Must defeat this devilish illness. Must not die.

A seeker of the Way must always be youthful and brave. People who become wrapped up in intellectual pursuits alone, impressed with their own achievements, soon end up living in the past. Wisdom based on the Mystic Law, intellect for the purpose of creating value, is this not the perfect model for youth of the future?

Thursday, October 20. Rain, then continuing overcast.

Body and mind are out of rhythm. Could not see Sensei during the day again. Felt empty and lonesome. Isn't life force the key to happiness? Clearly this is the most important requirement. Over the next several years, I will put this to the test and prove it decisively. Healthy ones, don't forget to appreciate!

To the headquarters in the evening. Missed the lecture on "The Record of the Orally Transmitted Teachings"; discussed the youth division's future with I., a youth division general staff member. Talked with Sensei for about thirty minutes in the president's room. Overjoyed. It seems he's suffering from weight loss. Sad to see him in such a weak condition. A meeting of Study Department sophomores for N. Chapter at the S. Inn in Koenji.

A little after 8:00, when the meeting was over, went to the home of O., the dancer, to attend a YWD Tenth Corps meeting. Really fatigued. Returned by car to Shinagawa. In a world filled with chaos, irresponsibility and self-interest, must pray for the happiness of these pure-hearted young maidens of the Mystic Law, that over the next ten years, not one will forsake her faith.

Friday, October 21. Clear.

A clear autumn day. Quite fatigued. Understand the severe difficulty of changing my destiny and transforming my fate and the strictness of my past slander's effects. Truly sense life's eternal nature with my entire being. Without this, it would be a contradiction to say I understand this life. Remained in the office all day, resting my body and thinking about many things.

This life is like a dream. Since this is the case, I shall be satisfied if I can spend each day, my entire life, fully exerting myself.

Wouldn't mind being a businessman or a politician or even an average person who lives life deeply. A lecture at the headquarters. Keenly feel I must study completely and intensively "The Object of Devotion for Observing the Mind," which contains the core of the Daishonin's Buddhism. A director's conference held with the general director. Plans made for the upcoming autumn general meeting for this, the 703rd year anniversary of the Daishonin's Buddhism. Decided to lecture on the theme "Until the day we make the Buddha's will a reality." Afterward, went for *kushikatsu* [deep-fried meat and vegetables on skewers] with some YMD district leaders. They all seemed happy. Had a good time.

Saturday, October 22. Fine weather.

It's Saturday; the weekend is already here. People in the Meiji period called Saturday *handon*, a combination of Japanese and Portuguese meaning to "rest half-a-day." None can resist the tide of the times, no matter how they may try. A life based on the Mystic Law will be in rhythm with the great power of the natural law. In Europe and America, people have both Saturdays and Sundays off. Will Japan someday follow suit?

The autumn wind blows from a thousand miles afar. The arrival of autumn in particular gives me a sense of the wondrous cycle of nature. Went alone to the Chinese trade fair in the afternoon. Could feel the intense reverberation of hundreds of millions of people's collective will. Quickly glanced through the three thousand and several hundred products on display from the "New China." Left thinking their manufactured goods still leave much to be desired. Appreciate the Japanese people and their devotion to excellence.

Gave an evening lecture to Study Department candidates on "On the Buddha's Prophecy." Want to bow my head in respect to these members who listened so earnestly to the lecture. Ashamed of my lack of lecturer qualifications.

Sunday, October 23. Clear.

Went to Taiseki-ji.

The morning sun rises above the majestic head temple. With Mount

Fuji as its beautiful backdrop, the head temple, the Eagle Peak of here and now.

People of Asia will definitely come. World leaders as well will definitely visit the place where I now stand. Will make each head temple visit a steppingstone for my lifelong growth. Leaving the head temple grounds, I accompanied Division Chief T. and some youth division staff members to visit the homes of I. and company president I. It was almost 8:00 when I got home. The Jonan area has few trees and little water. Is this environment acceptable? Strolled the neighborhood for about an hour with my wife and children. Enjoyed a delicious meal.

Monday, October 24. Rain, then partial clearing.

Each day, I realize keenly the profound magnificence of Sensei's boundless state of life and way of thinking. Seriously reflecting on my own shallowness. Left Tokyo at 1:20 p.m. by train for Numazu. Arrived, 4:10. Accompanied T., R. and A. to visit the businessman and politician T. After having to wait an hour, we talked until almost 9:00.

Exchanged views on national land development, the central highway, economics, politics, etc. Ultimately, he is not a person with whom I can conduct a deeply meaningful dialogue. Though he expressed his viewpoints in a reasonable, scientific and concrete manner, his way of speaking seemed somehow unnatural or overly zealous. Don't think all politicians, scholars, scientists or businessmen became great solely through their own ability. Many gained advantage through personal relationships, surroundings, tradition, cliques, organizations or family background. Can't help thinking some have succeeded simply by accident.

Tuesday, October 25. Cloudy, occasional rain.

Did not see Sensei in the morning. Felt lonely—an emptiness deep in my heart. Spent an uneventful day in the office. Had a splitting headache. Went to the headquarters in the early evening. To the president's room to report on yesterday's visit with T.

A Suiko Group meeting at 6:00. The candidates for this spring's House of Councillors' election were announced. My heart danced with excitement. There will be five candidates: H., the Statistics Department chief; T., the youth division chief; K, the guidance division chief; S., the Osaka Chapter chief; and H., the Culture Department top advisor. [Note: another candidate was added later.] Feel confident these five will make fitting candidates.

Left for a chapter group chiefs meeting at Jozai-ji. A spirited gathering.

I dearly miss these people. Home at 12:00. Must not destroy my health by reckless overexertion. Read until late. Must read books while young so I will have nothing to regret when I grow older.

Wednesday, October 26. Rain, letting up later with continued overcast.

Somewhat chilly all day. The average person's mind always changes rapidly. At times, it expresses the world of Anger; then, the suffering of Hell; and next, the joy of Heaven. With faith as our basis, our lives naturally become attuned to express the virtues of eternity, happiness, true self and purity.

The Gakkai will take a historic leap forward next year with its entry into [national-level] politics. Want, no matter what, to lead the way to victory—a victory that will surely be a great source of future pride. The Gakkai has now blossomed magnificently. I hope that, beginning next year, all leaders will further strengthen their spirit and resolve, awakening to their mission to build a new age.

Carelessness is our enemy. The ecstasy of victory will surely lead to future regret. The ship of the Gakkai has set sail from Tokyo Bay, outward into the vast Pacific. Will it sail upon the Japan Current? Will it be rocked by the raging billows or surmount the approaching waves?

Treated T. and his younger sister to dinner. A loveable pair. Want them to develop into excellent people. Had a severe stomachache afterward. Returned home in the same condition, took some medicine and read a book. The night is calm and peaceful, happy and warm. Grateful.

Thursday, October 27. Partly cloudy.

Should take better care of my health.

Stayed in the office until the afternoon. Society is dismal. Thankful for such fortunate surroundings. Attended the first-level lecture held at Toshima Civic Auditorium. Sensei seemed very fatigued. Thought about the following points:

1. Don't be a person who makes excuses.
2. Feel joy at others' prosperity and happiness.
3. Don't meddle in others' affairs.

Visited S.'s home in Yaguchi after the lecture. Was joyfully welcomed by all present. Home a little after 10:00. My two children are sleeping quietly. They are so cute. Want them to become excellent, capable people for kosen-rufu. Will write poems to capture the autumn moon's myriad faces.

How trivial are worldly conflicts. How empty, the glories and pleasure of this world, vanishing before a single breeze. Fame and riches, too, vanish like a solitary bubble on a mighty river's surface.

Friday, October 28. Rain.

Fall, the season for reading. No, I would rather make each of the 365 days of the year a "day for reading."

1. Must read the Gosho in its entirety.
2. Will thoroughly read Nichikan's *Six-volume Writings*.
3. Will carefully read good books of past and present, East and West.

— especially during the next three years.

The course of my life will be determined over these three years.

Fate, destiny — they are like the flow of a great river.

No one to confide in, no one to blame.

To the dentist in the afternoon. Can everything be this bad? Attended a lecture on "The Object of Devotion for Observing the Mind" in the evening. Must listen to the lectures with faith. Must read and ponder intensively:

Question: The Buddha clearly explained that each of the Ten Worlds has the same Ten Worlds within itself. Nonetheless, I find it difficult to believe that our base hearts could be endowed with the world of Buddhahood. If I cannot believe it, I will become an icchantika. With your great compassion, please help me believe, and save me from the torture of the Avichi hell.

Answer: You have already seen and heard the sutra passage concerning "the one great reason" [why the Buddhas appear in this world]. If you still do not believe, then how can anyone — from Shakyamuni Buddha on down to the four ranks of bodhisattvas or we ordinary people of the latter age who are at the stage of being a Buddha in theory — save you from disbelief? Nevertheless, I will try to explain. After all, some could not attain enlightenment through the direct teaching of the Buddha, but were able to do so later through the preaching of Ananda and the other disciples.

People can attain enlightenment in two ways: by meeting the Buddha and hearing the Lotus Sutra, or by believing in the sutra even though they do not meet the Buddha. Even before the advent of the Buddha, some Brahmans in India realized the correct view of life through the four Vedas. In China before the arrival of Buddhism, some realized the correct view through Taoism and Confucianism.

—"THE OBJECT OF DEVOTION FOR OBSERVING THE MIND"
(WND, 358–59)

At home, I thought about many future plans, about my health and my family. Insufficient action. Need more life force.

Saturday, October 29. Clear.

Excellent weather. The fine autumn morning suggests a sublime artistry. Or rather, isn't it true that various forms of art derive their quality from nature's essence? Received a phone call from Sensei in the morning. He has been calling more frequently of late. At times, he is pleasant and at other times, stern. Whichever the case, I am happy to hear from him. Went to the book distributors on Sensei's instructions, regarding the Sankibo Press publishing of *The Collected Essential Writings of the Fuji School*.

At 4:00, a "Company Friends Group" meeting in reception room #1 at the headquarters. It was terrible of me not to say anything. Met Sensei for dinner at the N. Chinese restaurant. He introduced two people from outside the Gakkai. Sensei got a bit drunk. Escorted him home before returning home myself. Exhausted. My immature habits cause problems for my life.

Sunday, October 30. Partly cloudy.

Slept until 9:00, but it did nothing to relieve my exhaustion. T. came by just when I was about to leave for M.'s 3:00 wedding ceremony. Together, we took a taxi to Ikebukuro. He is a weak person. Feel sorry, even for some of my seniors. A quiet ceremony and reception. It did not seem the participants were that close to the couple. A pity. Though I have shown him much support over the past few years, he has not come to much of an awakening. Wonder if he can feel anything at all?

To the chapter chief's home at 6:00. Together, we attended a general meeting for one of the chapter's districts — Bunkyo. The reported attendance was 270. The place—the new annex at Toshima Civic Auditorium. Gave encouragement for close to twenty minutes. All were in high spirits. How often it is that leaders, myself, for one, are encouraged by the members. Left with H. after the meeting.

Is it detrimental to think about myself too deeply? Or is it absolutely necessary? Some people become negative through too much self-criticism. Others, after deep introspection, can forge ahead boldly. These days, isn't it more important to always challenge our situation with youthful courage instead of being foolishly self-critical? Ultimately, once we embrace the Mystic Law, we should feel free to think, move and advance in a way most natural to us, so long as we do not cause others trouble.

Monday, October 31. Cloudy.

Isn't conservatism a tendency to place great importance upon, or become caught up in, formality? Isn't it also the inclination to cherish only the past while disregarding reform for the future? Reform — not in the commonly understood sense of the word but true reform — is to enable genuine vitality to surge forth from the midst of a society enslaved by formalism. In other words, by invoking the Mystic Law, we bring forth pure, fresh life force, revolutionizing our own lives and thereby transforming our environment.

A headquarters leaders meeting at Toshima Civic Auditorium at 6:30.

Afterward, a top leaders meeting at Jozai-ji.

Sensei spoke deeply on the concept of benefit. We were delighted.

Reflected on several things at home.

Seriously apologized to the Gohonzon.

Worried about next spring's House of Councillors election. This battle will determine my destiny. My only recourse is to believe in the Buddhist gods' protection. No, rather than simply parroting Buddhist terms, I must first dedicate my entire spirit, my essence. Only then can I expect protection from the Buddhist gods. Must strictly avoid using terminology to support my own sense of value or my personal view of faith. Using Gosho terms irresponsibly will only impede the progress of kosen-rufu.

Tuesday, November 1. Fair.

A clear autumn day.

Not feeling well. I look like an old soldier. Must become healthy. Must take pains to care for my health.

An evening YMD meeting at Nakano Civic Auditorium. Before the meeting, I treated the general director and Department Chief U. to eel. Ate my fill.

The meeting began just after 7:00. One thousand and several

hundred truly capable young men attended. I genuinely trust them. Thought deeply that many of those seated on stage surpass me in ability. Delighted. This morning Sensei gave guidance on conservatism and reform, as well as on the organization and prevalent Japanese trends.

The meeting was a great success, ending a little before 9:00. Afterward, I went with Chapter Chief S. as far as Shinagawa. Getting home late each night. My wife must be lonely. Can only be myself, boldly and powerfully taking the lead on the front lines of kosen-rufu. Like a youth; like a man; like a person of responsibility.

Wednesday, November 2. Fair.

A run-through for tomorrow's general meeting at Korakuen Stadium at 1:00. Took a central role, giving guidance and direction on various points. Everyone felt tired. No excuse for such feelings in the midst of such a hectic schedule. Each leader must take good care of his or her juniors. It is dangerous to be swayed by organizational matters or position. This must be avoided. Humanism must be the first priority.

Thinking I should buy something, especially for the flag bearers. Sadly there is nothing I can do, since I have no money. Finished at 4:00. Left on foot with M., H., Y. and the corps-level leaders. Went to see Sensei at the headquarters. Received guidance for about an hour. Forgot I had promised to meet my wife in front of Kamata Station. She scolded me for being two hours late. Y. and his wife came by late in the evening to talk about their house. A complex person. Department Chief T. also came by. Not pleasant.

Thursday, November 3. Clear.

The long-awaited thirteenth autumn general meeting. A clear blue sky awash with the fragrance of chrysanthemums. The Soka Gakkai is already a rising force in Japan. A grand general meeting, surging forward with the power of a raging wave.

Arrived at the meeting place, Korakuen Stadium, at 9:20 a.m. The faces of seventy-thousand fellow members were flushed with joy. I believe the beautiful advancement and progress of the Gakkai, the wave of the future, is more than a merely transitory phenomenon—it is a cause for limitless, lasting development. More than a hundred guests attended, including journalists and police officials. The Public Relations Department was very busy. Eighty priests also attended. Learned this was the largest group of priests to attend a Gakkai event thus far.

The dramatic opening ceremonies began at noon. Marching toward the center stage were the youth division general staff, the flags of the young men's and young women's divisions, the corps chiefs, followed by the headquarters flag, the president and the directors, the chapter flags and the chapter chiefs, all to the music of "Young Men of Japan," "Flower of Patriotism" and "Song of the Gakkai." New footsteps, fresh emotion, an unprecedented emergence of philosophy, renewed humanity. This was the first time youth division general staff members were seated on the stage. It made me aware, deep in my heart, that we are, step by step, arriving at the time when we must take the lead. "Until the day that we realize the Buddha's will." Do we hesitate to devote ourselves fully to the Gohonzon? Do we harbor any cowardice?

Lion cubs! Roar!

Lion cubs! Advance boldly!

A follow-up meeting at the N. Chinese restaurant.

I was the master of ceremonies. Exhausted. This morning I received a poem from Sensei commemorating the general meeting, directly over the phone:

> *Though the three powerful enemies appear,*
>   *Lion's cubs are bold, upon their voyage to kosen-rufu.*

> *Hearing the roar of the lion king,*
>   *Courageous young lions stand tall,*
>   *On their journey to kosen-rufu.*

In our case, I feel we still need to "be bold!" or "stand up boldly!"

Friday, November 4. Fair.

2:00 p.m. — went to the Metro Police Headquarters with the general director to express our appreciation to those who helped with the security during yesterday's general meeting. Spoke with Chief Clerk S., Assistant Chief S. and Chief K. Chief Clerk S. said he was "surprised at such frightening power." Assistant Chief S.'s extreme haughtiness is something to beware of. Must make certain the members on the campaign forefront do not violate any election laws. Chief K. seems like a typical bureaucrat. He voiced his fear and concern about the Physicians' Act,[1] lack of respect for authority and the infiltration of communist ideas. Reacted strongly to their condescending words, which revealed their ignorance of the Gakkai's essential nature. Fought valiantly to clear up their misconceptions before leaving.

Spoke for about two hours with K., who purports to be a friend of Mr. Toda. A strange person whom, I think, should be regarded with caution.

1. While he appears to respect Sensei on the surface, it seems he ridicules him deep in his heart.
2. He says the Minobu sect will not lose power as Sensei has predicted.
3. He told me it is no use getting close to people when there is no monetary gain involved.

Ah, how frightening the human mind can be.

Lecture on "The Object of Devotion for Observing the Mind." Keenly feel that the true essence of Buddhist study and of Buddhism itself lies in the doctrine of the object of devotion.

1. Physicians' Act: Japanese laws that govern medical doctors' ethics and permissible medical activities.

Saturday, November 5. Fair.

Stayed in the office all morning. No letup to my physical exhaustion. Better take care. A headquarters lecture at 6:30 p.m., finished "On the Buddha's Prophecy."

Regarding my lectures:

1. Read thoroughly.
2. Interpret accurately.
3. Must be logical and lecture broadly, using my own experience.

The Daishonin stated: "Buddhism is like the body, and society like the shadow. When the body bends, so does the shadow" (WND, 1039). Isn't a real "body" one devoted powerfully to faith? To secure such a body, I will advance throughout life as I am: as a youth—without being swept away by the wind and waves of devilish obstacles. Returned home after 11:00. Several friends came over.

Sunday, November 6. Clear.

On Sundays, never know when I might receive a phone call from Sensei. Stood by at home all morning.

About a dozen youth division members came by—First Corps members, and those connected to Setagaya District. Need capable people. Lacking people of character. Trying to reflect thoroughly on my way of giving guidance.

1. Guidance should be clear and to the point.

2. Guidance should express a purpose or objective.
3. Guidance should be given with the Buddhist spirit of compassion and filled with confidence.

Took my whole family to Tamagawa Park a little after 2:00. Played with the children to my heart's content until around 4:00. Left them along the way home to attend a discussion meeting at Jozai-ji, my first in quite a while. Keenly feel it absolutely necessary for me to attend some kind of Gakkai function at least once each day.

A seeker of the Way experiences suffering as a matter of course. On the other hand, I want soon to lead a life where I can naturally soar into the skies and make mighty strides with a clear, bright spirit. Returned home with my wife from Kamata Station. We stopped to eat *okonomiyaki* along the way. Many poetic feelings.

Monday, November 7. High clouds.

My physical condition has turned for the better. Rest, as well as action, is important for my health. Discussed the company's future plans with Sensei and his wife. An intermediate-level lecture at Nakanotoen Community Center in the evening. Began the chapter in the *Propagation Handbook* on the theory of life. I had a good feeling when the lecture ended. It is important to prepare myself by studying before giving a lecture. Went to Chapter Chief N.'s home afterward.

It's becoming colder, moment by moment. Troubled by my habit of sleeping with a hot-water bottle as a foot warmer, despite my young age.

Tuesday, November 8. Cloudy, then fair.

Nyozekan Hasegawa[1] said that dignity is not a matter of intellect or talent but of that person's fundamental humanity. Doesn't the fundamental solution to all problems, the source of all reform, lie only in the Mystic Law? And human revolution is the greatest model for establishing diligence, sensibility, stability and wisdom.

An evening corps chiefs meeting. Everyone was dispirited. Are they tired? Is it their leaders' lack of ability, or are they suffering from financial difficulties? We must have the mercy and compassion to delve deeper, encourage them and save them from suffering. Forge ahead! Advance to your heart's content! Praying in my heart that they will soar with vitality into the skies of freedom! Want to tell them not to worry needlessly, to stride more boldly into the realm of society.

Our society—its structures and systems stifle youth. An upside-down society that does not allow sincere and genuinely able youth to rise within its ranks. Bad leaders, bad society. But youth who fail to rise up and push such leaders aside are also bad. We practice each day to solve such problems. Youth! Try your best! Remember that you—we—are the strongest in the world!

In the office, became absorbed in a discussion with general staff member I. on the introduction of Buddhism [to Japan]. The theories are endless; some say Buddhism was introduced from the north, and others hold that it arrived from the south. I. has a wonderful depth of scholarship.

Ate skewered chicken in Shimbashi with Youth Division Chief T., M. and others. Was surprised to hear that the price, which we thought would be ¥20 per skewer, was actually ¥50. The total came to ¥880. Fortunately, we had enough cash on hand to avoid embarrassment. Home at 12:30 a.m. Exhausted. I've been late for work for the past two or three days. Am I getting lax?

1. Nyozekan Hasegawa: (1875–1969) Social critic and journalist. Through his writings, which included novels and dramas, this journalist sought to provide a theoretical underpinning for political and social democracy and to combat the growing fanaticism of militarist cliques. He remained true to his principles throughout World War II, and in 1948 he was awarded the Order of Culture.

Wednesday, November 9. Fair.

Overslept again today. Sensei arrived at the office before me in high spirits. Very bad. Media reports about the Gakkai have become quite frequent. They are malicious, distorted and ignorant. Heard some have given up on their faith on account of such reports. What a pitiful lot! Swayed by their surroundings, who do they think will strive confidently to save them? Do they think the magazines or the newspapers or the critics themselves have the answer to liberate them from suffering? How foolish!

In the evening, went with a few friends from the office to see a newsreel. Thought a lot about the state of our society, where people betray their own. Ate sukiyaki together afterward. Fine tasting. Got home early. Worked on an article for *The Daibyakurenge*. The Lotus Sutra reads, "Nothing in this world is lasting or firm / but all are like bubbles, foam, heat shimmer" (LS18, 249). There is also the passage "How can I cause living beings / to gain entry into the unsurpassed way?…" (LS16, 232).

Thursday, November 10. Cloudy then clearing.

Morning gongyo is most crucial. It determines today's victory or defeat, whether this day of life will be one of prosperity or decline. Gongyo is the practical application of the philosophy of 'the simultaneity of cause and effect.'

Getting colder each day. Personal guidance at the headquarters at 2:00 p.m. Everyone has periods when things go well and times when they aren't so smooth. But such distinctions disappear when a person is truly strong and capable. Lament my lack of ability in giving guidance.

Yesterday, Sensei took his son to the head temple. Scheduled return is this evening. Today is the final elementary lecture, concluding a three-month series that covered the "Expedient Means" and "Life Span" chapters of the Lotus Sutra, as well as the silent prayers offered during gongyo. *Mai ji sa ze nen* (this is my constant thought). Went to the chapter chief's home after the lecture. Discussed Nichikan's "Teachings for the Latter Day" with the chapter and YWD leaders. Was called to Sensei's home late in the evening. Received strict guidance on various matters. It resounded in my life like a thunderbolt. At night, composed a poem titled "Human Revolution":

> *All people, in some way, are haunted by evil karma,*
> *Which darkens their lives, and causes them to wander*
> *In the states of hell, anger and savagery.*
> *The effects of karma heaped upon karma*
> *Are felt as intense anguish.*
> *This is society.*
> *This is humanity.*
>
> *Beginningless voyage of life,*
> *Eternal motion of the macrocosm,*
> *As the morning sun soars into the sky,*
> *Life stirs anew among the buds.*
>
> *The power of myoho, fundamental force of nature,*
> *Strong enough to shatter boulders,*
> *Or dispel the darkness of our evil karma.*

Friday, November 11. Fair.

Could not meet with Sensei this morning. Felt forlorn. My life craves excitement—I live for upheaval. It is as if I purposely face the raging rapids or thunderous waves.

What is faith?
What is society?
What is country?
Economics? Politics? Culture?

At times I think randomly. It is important to ponder. I want, however, to live my life earnestly and thoroughly, reflecting on my incomplete self in a way most befitting my growth. Must try hard to develop the insight to perceive other people's true worth, their fortune and their essential nature. Also, will try my best to enable each person to move strongly and bravely, in the direction of the greatest good.

Friday lecture. Can only stand in awe of Sensei's tremendous confidence and his ability in Buddhist study. Wish for him to remain this way forever. On the way back, stopped in Ikebukuro and ate *una-don* [short for *unagi donburi*, charbroiled eel in a bowl over rice] with some friends.

> Aside from these people, there are also those who appeared to believe in me, but began doubting when they saw me persecuted. They not only have forsaken the Lotus Sutra, but also actually think themselves wise enough to instruct me. The pitiful thing is that these perverse people must suffer in the Avichi hell even longer than the Nembutsu believers.
>
> —"LETTER FROM SADO" (WND, 306)

I hear that President Makiguchi often quoted this passage. Doesn't it form the basis for the Soka Gakkai's conviction?

Saturday, November 12. A clear autumn day.

Nowhere to go on this autumn Saturday. Stayed in the office until 3:00 p.m. To the headquarters at 6:00. A lecture for Study Department candidates. Finished "The Blessings of the Lotus Sutra." Everyone was serious. Hold high expectations for them. How many modern scholars can comprehend such classical language? Now, how many millions or tens of millions will grasp it and make it the basis for their lives? How praiseworthy! No form of culture is shallower than that of the weekly gossip magazines. There will definitely sprout forth a new, profound and brilliant form of culture, rising from the soil of the masses as an eternal golden monument.

Today completed my morning studies with Sensei. Topics we have covered include politics, law, chemistry, Chinese literature, astronomy and economics. Must study and remain humble throughout my life. Must never become arrogant in my Buddhist study or my scholarship. Afterward, went with my wife to T.'s in Kanda. Almost midnight when we got home. A quiet home, filled with peace, happiness, devotion, hope and good fortune.

Sunday, November 13. Fair.

Up at 8:00 — cold. Went to help Sensei's relatives move. Took a taxi with my wife. A magnificent home. Exerted myself helping until evening. Was treated to dinner, then left.

Attended a Keio District meeting in Umegaoka. A great success. Spoke for nearly forty minutes. The following is an outline of topics I covered:

1. The meaning of Buddhist practice.
2. The significance of propagation.   .
3. Taking pride in being a Gakkai member.

Home at midnight. Cold all day.

Monday, November 14. Fair.

Lately, I have been more keenly aware of the joy of meeting and receiving guidance from Sensei. In the morning, I requested a lecture on Nichikan's "Interpretations Based on the Law."[1] Keenly sense the importance of his *Six-volume Writings* and his other commentaries. Must study intensively over the next three years. To the headquarters at 5:30 p.m. Spoke with Sensei regarding the newly appointed corps chiefs and preparations for the upcoming House of Councillors election.

A youth division general staff conference began at 6:30 p.m. Discussed:

1. The reorganization of the First Corps.
2. Problems in managing the general meeting.
3. The budget.
4. Strategy toward this spring's election.

Finished a little after 9:00 p.m. Afterward, Director S. and Division Chief T. came over. Must take good care of my body and mind. Reflect on myself, study the Buddhist doctrines and devote myself to the important battle now unfolding.

1. "Interpretations Based on the Law": One of the theses that make up Nichikan's *Six-volume Writings*. It interprets important Lotus Sutra passages from the standpoint of Nam-myoho-renge-kyo of the Three Great Secret Laws and identifies Shakyamuni's Lotus Sutra as serving to explain Nichiren Daishonin's Buddhism.

Saturday, December 17. Clear.

Though this is the most hectic time of year, I feel calm and composed — not the least bit excited. Feel like a spectator, watching others run around frantically. I wonder if this is OK. Awaiting tomorrow's YMD general meeting.

At 2:00, I went to make preparations. Sense some laxness in the youth division. Gave strict direction, with the future course of the youth division in mind. Hope that you, whom I scolded, will understand that I do so out of my concern for your happiness.

The cold is becoming intense. My health has improved a little. Nothing could make me happier. In the evening, I presented President Toda with a formal invitation to our meeting. His eyes are filled with Buddhist compassion.

Went over plans with Director I. for an upcoming short-term guidance tour. Also talked over various matters with Corps Chief M. Next year, want to carry out profound faith, faith that will enable me to build a stable foundation of benefit in my life. This is my earnest hope. Want to strive to carry out faith, practice and study to the letter, remaining unswayed by external influence. Will try hard.

Sunday, December 18. Clear.

The Fourth YMD General Meeting. The place: Kuramae National Sports Arena. Things got under way at 1:25 p.m. Some fifteen thousand members gathered. Thunderous applause. People were overjoyed at this general meeting, which heralds the new era. But my heart aches with sorrow, loneliness and anguish at the sight of my mentor's frail walk and because these thousands of young men are not yet truly capable.

The meeting was over at 4:25. A small banquet with the corps chiefs afterward. Expressing my appreciation for their efforts, I emphasized that we are still far from reaching our youth division ideal. In the depths of my heart, I, too, resolved to mount a fierce struggle.

Monday, December 19. Clear.

I did not see President Toda in the office this morning. Perhaps he is fatigued. I, too, have begun to suffer again on account of my health. Feel helpless. Next year, I will pour all my energy into perfecting the youth division, restructuring its organization and training the members.

Attended a lecture by Priest Horigome on "The Entity of the Mystic Law." Nothing surpasses thorough Buddhist study. Got home after 11:00. My wife is really beautiful.

Tuesday, December 20. Clear.

Felt somewhat restless since morning. Both the young men's and young women's general meetings are over. All of this year's important events are now complete. In the afternoon, I along with I., H. and F., spoke with Sensei in the president's room. Sensei talked about the third president and the Gakkai's future prospects. Some are praised by President Toda, while others try to curry favor with him. But faith based on the Mystic Law is something that, on the deepest level, can never be swayed by sweet words of flattery.

In the evening, met with corps staff members to discuss plans for the upcoming short-term guidance tour. These youths' hearts are pure, their lives, robust and powerful.

Wednesday, December 21. Rain. Later, overcast.

Re-read *Miyamoto Musashi*, by Eiji Yoshikawa.[1] It made me fondly recall my days as a fourth grader. A man of the sword, a man of skill. His determination, his psyche, his lifelong training and practice, his dynamic energy—I think all of these qualities are fitting for the modern man. At 6:30, joined Sensei at a banquet in R. at the invitation of our bankers. Home after 10:00. Thought a lot about the past year—self-reflection, courage, Takasugi Shinsaku,[2] the members, my seniors, and my life ten or twenty years from now.

1. Eiji Yoshikawa: See note on p. 121.
2. Takasugi Shinsaku: See note on p. 142.

Thursday, December 22. Partly cloudy.

Received a necktie from M., a business executive. A welcome gift. After Sensei is gone, it will naturally become evident who will fight to protect our movement throughout their lives. Spent half the day with Sensei. Decided to read a biography he recommended to me. Sensei's physical condition seems to be worsening. "I am really living the passage, 'The teaching which I preach, I practice in my heart,'" he said with a smile. He also told me: "Dai, life means suffering. Only when you suffer can you understand faith and become a great individual." Ashamed of my own shallowness.

To Myoko-ji in the evening. Attended the Third Corps inauguration ceremony. Earnestly gave guidance, my last of the year, until 10:00.

> Because my friends are troubled, I shed tears.
> Because I feel joy, my friends dance.

Hummed these words as I walked to the station with the members.

Tuesday, December 27. Clear.

Today seems like Indian summer. Accompanied Sensei to the head temple on the *Genkai*, the 10:00 train from Tokyo. Solemn and majestic Taiseki-ji is reminiscent of Eagle Peak. Have been practicing now for a full eight-and-a-half years and have gained a fair understanding of this faith. Yesterday, Monday the 26th, I., Z., U., K., H., M. and myself, who form the Gakkai's second pillar, met at Sensei's residence.

Received guidance for more than three hours. Strict, yet warm. "Would like us to have people like Nehru, Zhou Enlai, Chiang Kai-shek or the next generation of world leaders visit us. You [youth division members] will be the future leaders of Asia." This was President Toda's bold and grand direction. Physically and mentally fatigued.

Wednesday, December 28. Clear.

Just a few more days left to the year. Another year closer to the day I bid farewell to my twenties, the prime of my life. Have many mixed feelings—sadness, concern about the future, about the severity of society. I am young, still quite young. Must polish and discipline myself.
  1. Read.
  2. Write.

Tonight, an end-of-the-year party. Sang and danced with friends until after 9:00. In three days, I'll be twenty-seven. In three years, I will reach my thirties. What lies on the road ahead for this youth, this person of destiny and myriad feelings? One philosopher said that personality is a matter of fate.

Thursday, December 29. Clear.

A warm day. Feel refreshed and happy.

Keenly feel this is the benefit of the fight I waged this summer. Must deeply ponder the principle 'the oneness of body and mind' and experience it to make my life genuine. There are times I think about the nature of truth. People's minds are ever-changing. There are times I wonder what the standard for truth should be in our complex, changing society.

A youth division staff meeting began at 6:30 at the headquarters. An enjoyable meeting. Everyone has been fighting hard. Want to proceed next year with the same rhythm. Three friends came over after I returned home. Talked about making the next year a glorious year in our lives.

Friday, December 30. Clear.

A warm, springlike day. Unlike recent years, the final days of this year have been unusually peaceful. Can it be I lack enthusiasm? I am one who loves excitement. In spite of my physical frailness, a quiet, mundane lifestyle would be excruciating. It seems the most fitting kind of life is one in which I can soar free and unrestricted into the skies. I think, however, that it is important to have the wisdom and insight to perceive people's true nature, society's trends and the future of the world. Reflected on my twenty-seven years. I have made good progress up to now. How many crises I have faced. Feel gratitude — to the Mystic Law, my mentor, my parents and my friends. If only my health would improve somewhat. Wish to live until the time of kosen-rufu.

Attended Bunkyo Chapter's year-end meeting in the evening. My bad mood must have been very unpleasant for the members. Reflected. Took a taxi home. My house is so peaceful. Amid the simplicity glows a precious light of happiness. There are flowers in every room. A warm feeling.

N HIS *SEIKYO SHIMBUN* New Year's message, President Toda said that although Japan had thus far achieved a level of economic, political and diplomatic stability, something still seemed to be missing. This emptiness stemmed from people's inability to spend each day with energy, life force and vitality. He stressed the importance of sending forth a retinue of people trusted in society. On the youth division page of the same issue, Daisaku Ikeda, the youth division chief of staff, offered his views on the youth division's mission, urging youth to summon powerful faith and stand up with an awareness that they will shoulder the new era.

In the five years since its first issue in 1951, the *Seikyo Shimbun* had grown from a two-page, thrice-monthly tabloid with a circulation of four thousand, to a four-page weekly with more than 200,000 subscribers. And with the opening of the Kansai Soka Gakkai headquarters building in January 1956, a Kansai *Seikyo Shimbun* office was also established. With three localized editions — Northern, Tokyo metropolitan and Western — then being printed and distributed throughout Japan, so began a new campaign to bring the principles of the Daishonin's Buddhism, guidance in faith and news of the Gakkai's movement to the people.

With the aim of realizing President Josei Toda's cherished membership goal of 750,000 households, the Soka Gakkai set its 1956 target at 500,000. Other goals for the year included establishing local chapters outside metropolitan Tokyo and beginning construction of a Grand Lecture Hall at the head temple. Also, at a January 2 headquarters planning board conference, President Toda announced his decision to personally conduct semi-monthly lectures in the Kansai area. He also announced he would begin short-term guidance tours around the country, starting with Kansai, to foster able individuals for the steady development of kosen-rufu.

From the beginning of the year, the famous Osaka Campaign unfolded under Daisaku Ikeda's leadership. The first step in that campaign was to help thoroughly acquaint the area members with the principles of Nichiren Daishonin's Buddhism through study. In addition, Chief of Staff Ikeda painstakingly met with and encouraged as many individuals as possible through wholehearted faith guidance. With the steady repetition of such efforts, an unprecedented groundswell of faith and practice arose. To wit, 1,101 candidates from the Kansai area (where Osaka is located) passed the March 4 nationwide Study Department entrance exam —a percentage far exceeding the national average. In addition, Osaka Chapter increased by 5,005 households in March, making it unrivaled among its fellow smaller chapters.

In April, toward sending able people into all sectors of society, the Gakkai sponsored four candidates in the national House of Councillors election to be held in July: one candidate each from the electoral districts of Tokyo and one from Osaka. This was the first time the Gakkai had sponsored candidates in a national election, an effort that later led to the establishment of the Komeito, or "Clean Government Party," which grew to be one of Japan's largest opposition parties.

During the headquarters leaders meeting of July 1956, Einosuke Akiya, today the SGI deputy president, was appointed YMD chief. In addition, sixteen new chapters were formed in fourteen cities, doubling the existing number of chapters to thirty-two.

The August monthly headquarters leaders meeting was held at Toshima Civic Auditorium. President Toda gave guidance about the fundamental spirit for unit-level discussion meetings that would commence in September, as well as the proper attitude for leaders. He stated that the traditional Soka Gakkai spirit lay in conducting discussion meetings on the unit level and declared that genuine progress toward kosen-rufu and in each person's human revolution could be achieved not through formality or bureaucracy but through steady and continuous Buddhist practice pulsating with the spirit of faith.

In world events, a joint declaration was issued on October 19 by the governments of Japan and the Soviet Union, ending the state of war existing between them since August 9, 1945, and reestablishing diplomatic relations. The peace declaration marked an important step toward Japan's reentry into the international community after World War II.

The Soka Gakkai held its fifteenth fall general meeting on November 1 at Korakuen Stadium in Tokyo. From across Japan, sixty thousand members participated. In his address, Josei Toda proclaimed, "The problems of our materialistic society, as well as the fundamental problems of life itself, must be solved," and he emphasized the profound importance of experience.

In December, the membership goal of 500,000 households, set at the beginning of the year, was attained. Thus the members welcomed 1957 with a growing passion to fulfill President Toda's pledge to attain 750,000 households during his lifetime.

Sunday, New Year's Day. Clear, becoming cloudy.

Awoke at 6:45. Feel no excitement nor anything special on this New Year's morning. Is this as it should be? Had a *zoni* [a special New Year's dish] for breakfast. Went directly to S.'s house. Accompanied my father to Myoko-ji in Shinagawa. Then, we went with the general director, I., K., H. and I. to Sensei's house in Meguro to offer New Year's greetings. It is only New Year's and Sensei has already begun to give profound guidance on the philosophy of life. It struck me deeply. Will never forget it. I am feeling nauseated, perhaps exhaustion from last night. It's terrible.

Accompanied Sensei to Josen-ji, where we were received by the retired high priest, Horigome. It was already 10:35 when we arrived at the Gakkai headquarters. At a leaders meeting for Tokyo area district chiefs and above we recited the sutra and chanted daimoku to the Gohonzon inscribed "for the accomplishment of kosen-rufu through merciful propagation." After, there were words from Sensei and the general director. Sensei read a poem he had written marking the beginning of the new year.

To the people of Asia
    who yearn only for the moon
    to appear from behind a curtain of clouds
    we shall send you the sun.

Left Tokyo on the 1:35 train to the head temple for the first pilgrimage of the new year. This young revolutionary is totally exhausted on the first day of the year. Firmly determined to establish genuine faith.

Monday, January 2. Clear.

Spent the day at the head temple. Today is my twenty-eighth birthday. The magnificent, energetic atmosphere at this Eagle Peak symbolizes the health and prosperity of our great Buddhist school. The Lotus Sutra is the strategy of generals. Chanted during the new year's first ceremony of chanting before the Dai-Gohonzon to become a capable leader for the new era. Was received by the high priest, who gave a powerful sermon. He said the road that lies ahead will grow increasingly more brilliant. My joy runs deep. Left the head temple a little after 3:00 p.m. Arrived home at 7:30. While our hearts are warm, the house itself is very cold. When I think about my health, I believe it is important to consider making plans for a new lifestyle.

Tuesday, January 3. Fair.

Slept until noon. Several friends stopped by to offer New Year's greetings. Sent them home after talking with them for awhile, as I was running a slight fever. Sorry to disappoint those who had come by with high hopes. Spenser said: "Be bold, be bold; everywhere, be bold!" Alone, I thought the essence of faith also amounts to such determination and practice. Several dozen members gathered in the evening at T.'s house in Bunkyo for a New Year's celebration. I love them as brothers. Wish them the greatest glory. Stopped by the chapter chief's house afterward to offer New Year's greetings. Took a taxi home. My wife looks beautiful in her kimono.

Wednesday, January 4 — Thursday, January 5. Overcast, followed by rain.

Took the *Sparrow*, the 9:00 a.m. express to Osaka. Overcast and severely cold. Truly nasty weather. And a truly unpleasant state of body and mind. At 5:00 p.m., a lecture on "The Entity of the Law" at the

Kansai headquarters. Next, a guidance meeting with group chiefs, both men and women. Offered many prayers to the large, specially inscribed Gohonzon enshrined at the Kansai headquarters.

Gave individual guidance beginning at 10:00 a.m. on the 5th until 6:00 in the evening. Many people came for guidance. Flung myself into giving guidance with all my might.

The final district chiefs meeting began at 8:30. Poured all my energy into giving intensive guidance. Returned home, a solitary, forlorn figure, on the 10:00 p.m. *Moonlight* express. Pondered the concept of 'eternally endowed' on the train home. Lament my lack of intelligence. Deeply aware that when all is said and done, there is no other way for me than to hurl myself into practice that will enable me to 'transform faith into wisdom.' Ah, such is the plight of a common mortal.

Friday, January 6. Cloudy, then rain.

Arrived in Tokyo on the night train — a little after 9:30 a.m. Due to many unscheduled stops, the ride took more than eleven hours. After the exhausting trip, the bustling energy of Tokyo Station was almost shocking. The individual and society! A joint leaders conference at 11:00 a.m. Sensei was quite intoxicated. Nevertheless, the inspiration and energy of his mind were as dazzling as an electric discharge.

1. Discussion of goals for this year.
2. The nature of elitism.
3. Training that accords with the trends of society.
4. Other topics.

At 4:00 p.m., took my wife and my younger brother to a play at the Imperial Theater. Wondered when it will be my turn to take my place on stage.

Saturday, January 7. Rain, then cloudy.

Fatigued since morning. Agonizing.

Heard a report that Sensei is not feeling well. In the evening, he appeared at the headquarters. How sad. My teacher is exhausted and I am exhausted. Is it shared karma? The oneness of mentor and disciple? Shopped in the afternoon at the Isetan department store for items for tomorrow's children's group meeting for which I am responsible. Visited Sensei in the president's room in the evening with I. and H. He talked about the Grand Reception Hall and the Three Great Secret Laws. He also pointed out the original meaning of certain Chinese characters. Regret my lack of study. First and foremost, faith begins with a superb and consistent gongyo.

Sunday, January 8. Clear.

Stayed at home all morning. Had a backache and a slight fever. My temperature was 99.7° F. The pain in my back persists 365 days a year. Want to be healthy. Only then will my life be complete. Both my sons, Hiromasa and Shirohisa, are growing well. What course will their lives take twenty years from now? Only hope they will be healthy, ordinary people with a strong sense of justice, who can be themselves and live with no regrets.

A children's meeting was held at N. Chinese restaurant at 5:00 p.m. About twice as many people gathered with Sensei as last year.

The meeting ended at 8:00. Cannot help feeling sorry for the children who could not attend. I can't stand unfairness. Don't understand Sensei's intent in this case. The meeting should be discontinued.

Went with my wife to visit my mother who is home with a cold. I could tell from her face that our visit made her very happy.

Monday, January 9. Fair.

In the morning, accompanied Sensei to check the property for the Mitaka Community Center. Sensei's physical condition was very poor. In the car he seemed utterly exhausted. Terrible—he couldn't even talk. I saw him directly home after work. He went to prison, was released, and has since been carrying out a great battle to reconstruct the Gakkai. Yet he is only human. I am still young.

At 6:30 p.m., invited I., Y., K. and N. over and treated them to a leisurely sukiyaki dinner.

> *From today onward*
> *Thus begins today*
> *Yet today is already over.*

Contemplated the idea of 'fundamental darkness.' To bed. Don't rest! Advance!

Tuesday, January 10. Fair.

Suffering mentally and physically. Perhaps I am the best physician when it comes to my own life. Because I am young, my heart burns with ambition. I am also unyielding, like a great boulder. On the other hand, my state of life is free and expansive, soaring into the sky like a great bird. I also possess the mind of a naturalist, who wishes to escape from society's harsh realities. I know the futility of seeking worldly fame and fortune and understand what it means to "perceive things exactly as they are." Complex—the psyche of youth. To the president's office just after 5:00 p.m. Talked to Sensei for nearly an hour and a half about a variety of subjects. Regret I could not tell him the truth directly. I am weak. Thought about the 'mystic principle of the true cause.'

Wednesday, January 11. Fair.

Extremely cold—the coldest in decades, I am told. My state of life, too, is now like the depths of winter. Greatly anticipate the arrival of spring, its warm breezes and sunshine. Have been wondering how I should live, how to perfect and complete my life.

At 5:00 p.m. at the N. restaurant, there was a New Year's banquet for Tokyo area priests. Finished at 8:00 p.m. A cordial gathering, the first in quite a while. Happy to see Priest Horigome in such high spirits. Left feeling perturbed about the disunity among the top leadership.

Attended a district chiefs meeting at O.'s house, which lasted until 10:00. Got home a little before midnight.

Thursday, January 12. Fair.

Did not see Sensei at all today. Distressing. Finished reading the novel *Miyamoto Musashi*. Kojiro died—by Musashi's sword. Many thoughts.

Went to I.'s in Shinokubo in the evening. Attended a study meeting for the upcoming Study Department exam. All the participants showed the utmost seriousness. Nevertheless, their eyes sparkled. This is a world of devotion and joy unseen in other organizations.

Studied until 10:30 p.m., covering every subject.

I should worry about my next life. Reflected on my lack of real ability. Study, study! Must pursue the two ways of practice and study.

Saturday, January 14—Sunday, January 15. Clear.

Left Tokyo Station at 12:30 on the *Dove*, the express for Osaka, for the Study Department exam. Thought I would study on the train, but couldn't. It was awful. Couldn't concentrate at all. Practice, training. Recalled Musashi.

Answered exam prep questions until after 11:00. Overly tired. Feel a neuralgia-like pain in my left hand. The result of slander? Stayed at the Kansai headquarters building in the morning. Extremely cold. Recalled the R. temple incident last February, when we battled the early morning deep winter cold. Was invited to take a morning bath.

At 1:20, 423 people took the written exam. There were five questions. The quality of my lecture will be reflected in the examinees' performance. The responsibility is ultimately my own. Finished at 4:30.

Afterward, I attended a secretariat meeting, then a leaders meeting. Firming my determination to take the lead toward this July's great objective. Could this be the real, great maiden battle of my twenties? Turn and face society....

Monday, January 16. A perfectly clear day.

Stayed in Osaka. Bright, like spring. Hope wells up within me. Vast, like the universe, extending to the heavens, my heart wants to cry out! Such a clear blue sky!

This year, I will be sent many times to many places. Made my own schedule for the first half of the year. I tend to be away from home often. Because we live close to my wife's parents' home in Yaguchi, I really don't need to worry. I now understand why Sensei told me to "find a house close to the Shirakis [Mrs. Ikeda's family]." Went with S. to Itami Airport at 1:20 p.m. to meet Sensei. Hadn't seen my mentor for three days. Missed him as if it had been a year.

Sensei gave his first lecture on the "Expedient Means" chapter [of the Lotus Sutra] at Nakanoshima Civic Auditorium at 6:30. Some 7,000 came to hear the lecture. Sincere faces. It seems Kansai is advancing steadily, more so than Tokyo. Left Osaka's Umeda Station at 10:00 on the *Moonlight* to Tokyo. Traveled alone. Couldn't sleep on the train. Does this young poet have fragile nerves?

Tuesday, January 17. Fair, with partial cloudiness.

My wife, Kaneko, met me alone at Tokyo Station in the morning. Mentally and physically exhausted. Went straight home. It was 10:00 a.m.

Health is paramount, together with life force and good fortune. Will establish these with the Mystic Law, through the powers of faith and practice.

To the headquarters at 6:00 to grade the exams. Went to give guidance afterward at a YMD meeting at Nakano Civic Auditorium. My wife looked beautiful when I got home.

Wednesday, January 18. Fair.

A Study Department professors meeting, led by the Study Department chief, at the headquarters at 6:00 p.m. A strict and fair meeting to determine the final results of the written exams. Everyone had hoped the candidates would do well. Many, however, did not pass. Ultimately, faith amounts to belief plus study. Being too easy on oneself in faith is the first step toward complacency. My wife passed. She tried hard, studying while praying pure-heartedly to the Gohonzon. Though frail, she has scored a splendid victory. Went to T. with Y. and N. to get dinner and talk. Did not enjoy myself. Want to establish a rhythm of going to bed early and getting up early.

Thursday, January 19. Fair.

Sensei arrived back in Tokyo at 1:00 p.m. on Japan Airlines. Went by myself to meet him. He seemed in high spirits. Felt assured. Made various reports on the taxi ride back.

A YMD district leaders meeting, 6:30 p.m. at the headquarters. Afterward, took Youth Division Chief T. and the youth division leaders to Shibuya to see the movie *The New Tales of Heike*. Not very interesting.

Friday, January 20. Cloudy.

An executive conference meeting in the president's room at 5:00 p.m. It was decided to add a name to the list of five candidates for the House of Councillors election. Strongly insisted it be Study Department Chief K.

Sunday, January 22. Cloudy (the first snow of the season).

Sleet fell. It was bitter cold. The executive conference began at 11:30. A corps chiefs meeting from 1:30. Then at 3:00, an opening ceremony for the new Kamata Chapter community center. Very busy. The times, the people and the Gakkai rush onward like a raging torrent.

The members seem to be suffering from Chapter Chief K.'s haughtiness. Sensei appears unaware such authoritarian leaders are tyrannizing the members. Very dangerous.

Wait! You who are pure of heart! The day is close at hand when the Gohonzon will strictly reveal all!

"When standing alone, a person of strength will be a true hero"(Schiller).

Tuesday, January 24. Rain.

Roused my tired body out of bed and left the house. Late for the morning lecture. Can only bow my head at Sensei's earnest attitude in waiting for me before beginning. How long can I live with Sensei, like parent and child, mentor and disciple? Things suddenly come to mind. Our precious bond is like a drama, joyous. Ultimately, it is my own fortune, my own ability, my sense of mission and conviction that matter.

Attended a Suiko Group meeting at the headquarters from 6:00 and a chapter chiefs meeting afterward. Worry that as the Gakkai grows larger Sensei's leadership may not prevail. You, who are close to Sensei! Do your utmost! Don't spoil yourselves! Know your responsibility! Brooded alone over these matters.

Wednesday, February 1. Cloudy.

Nichiren Daishonin teaches that the true "palace of happiness" exists nowhere but in the depths of a person's life, in one's determination. This is the eternally unchanging, grand philosophy of life—the great ideal for the twenty-first century, the crystallization of spiritualism and materialism.

The Gosho "The Three Kinds of Treasure" states, "More valuable than treasures in a storehouse are the treasures of the body, and the treasures of the heart are the most valuable of all" (WND, 851). Will spend my life putting this idea into practice and proving its validity.

At the headquarters from 6:00. A Study Department professors meeting. Simply astounded by Sensei's splendid and profoundly philosophical lecture. Discussed plans for the Osaka Campaign with F. and K., a serious dialogue. They do not understand my intent. To multiply by ten times the current membership of more than twenty thousand households will require a monumental campaign. They don't seem to comprehend the implications.

Thursday, February 2. Clear.

Keeping a diary has become a burden.

Tuesday, February 7. Clear.

As a person of average capacity, I have many aspects—I sometimes feel like writing and at other times do not. As a youth, I have many aspects—at times I am swept away by swift currents, and other times I stand fast amid the raging torrents. At times I enjoy solitude, while other times I delight in talking with others. Life has many aspects.

The "Life Span" chapter of the Lotus Sutra reads:

> Abandoning restraint, they give themselves up to the five desires
> and fall into the evil paths of existence.
> Always I am aware of which living beings
> practice the way, and which do not,
> and in response to their needs for salvation
> I preach various doctrines for them.
> At all times I think to myself:
> How can I cause living beings
> to gain entry into the unsurpassed way
> and quickly acquire the body of a Buddha?
>
> —(LS16, 231–32)

A lonely day.

Thursday, February 9. Clear.

Early spring. Nothing is as unpredictable as destiny, the path that lies ahead. No one can know the future. Have recently come to understand faith as something ultimately, absolutely essential.

Sensei returned from Osaka at 2:00. Delighted to see him in such extremely good spirits. The fortress of Osaka is solidifying with each passing year. In July, I will wage the maiden battle to fuse Buddhism with society. This will also be Sensei's first major battle for the Daishonin's Buddhism. Must fight resolutely and repay my debt of gratitude. My determination is profound and vast.

Gave personal guidance at the headquarters in the afternoon. Right before my eyes, I can see people's suffering caused by the poison of misleading religions. True Buddhism versus misguided teachings. Though religions may appear similar on the surface, why can't people understand the fundamental differences in religion lie in whether they lead us to happiness or suffering, to good or evil? Poured all my energy into personal guidance.

An assistant Study Department professors meeting at 6:00. Always thinking that my own study is insufficient. Afterward, stopped in Shinagawa for dinner with friends before returning home.

Friday, March 23. Partly Cloudy.

A warm day. Feel out of sorts all day if I miss gongyo. Met in a headquarters conference room to map out Culture Department strategy. Considering reassigning and reorganizing the Culture Department's able personnel. Concerned that this group will, to a large degree, determine the Gakkai's future growth or its extinction. Faith and politics, society and Buddhism, absoluteness and compromise. Confusing these and similar essential issues would be dangerous.

Want to study and write about the following themes:
1. Nichiren Daishonin's view of the nation and the world.
2. An analysis of the religious community and its future.
3. Culture and religion.

Saturday, March 24. Clear, then cloudy.

A warm, spring day. Spring is our realm, our element. Met with Sensei in the morning. His eyes are filled with stern compassion. He is driving himself too hard, and I, too, am overexerting myself. Together, we consoled each other in our exhaustion.

Left Tokyo for the head temple at 1:35 on a Nagoya-bound train. With my wife and two sons, Hiromasa and Shirohisa. It's been a while since I've made such an excursion. To travel to this Eagle Peak with my family fills me with happiness. Arrived at Taiseki-ji at 6:00.

A question-and-answer session in the Reception Hall. Reported attendance was twenty-two hundred. We were received by the high priest afterward. Sang the "Dormitory Song of High School #1" for High Priest Nissho, the lyrics, "Ah! I have received a flower in my jade cup." This is his last night as high priest; tomorrow, he retires. How profoundly moving! My mentor and I recall many fond and heartfelt memories of High Priest Nissho.

Want to issue a call to the vigorous, robust youth of kosen-rufu. March on toward the future and our beautiful grand dream! Am now making many trips to Osaka. Really want to be on good terms with the people of Osaka. How delightful! Want to call out to my true friends in Osaka!

Sunday, March 25. Rain.

Awoke at 7:00. A top leaders meeting was held immediately with Sensei, at the headquarters set up on the second floor of the Rikyo-bo lodging.

The spring rain fell softly. Discussed propagation for about an hour. Finally, Sensei said, in essence, that *shakubuku* means to live with the great conviction that we ourselves are entities of Myoho-renge-kyo.

We carry out the gentle practice of *shoju* based on the spirit of *shakubuku*. In other words, *shakubuku* naturally includes the practice of *shoju.* In terms of 'offerings of wealth' and 'offerings of the Law,' true *shakubuku* corresponds to an offering of the Law.

Left with Sensei at 12:27 on the *Tokai,* the train back to Tokyo. On the way, he talked about appointing a new youth division chief and expressed his ideas on the future of kosen-rufu. Awesome and fascinating.

Monday, March 26.

Debated whether to attend the level-four lecture, finally deciding not to. Disgusted at my lack of sincerity. Drawn by personal responsibility, I attended the end of a Bunkyo Chapter group chiefs meeting. Felt somewhat appeased.

Mrs. K. met me at Toshima Civic Auditorium. Was it because of her pioneering role in the culture movement? I expressed my opinion that the fusion of Buddhism with society[1] accords with accomplishing kosen-rufu. I believe she has definitely made a resolution toward the campaign.

Attended a district chiefs meeting at O.'s afterward. Poured all of my life force into the guidance. Spoke about the following three general topics:

1. The faith of Abutsubo.
2. The similarities between the cultural campaign during the Daishonin's time and today's cultural campaign.
3. The spirit of propagation, as an offering of the Law.

Left with Mrs. H. Want to better understand each person's situation. Want to summon my faith and remain healthy until the daybreak of kosen-rufu. This exhaustion is aggravating—miserable.

1. Fusion of Buddhism with society: This is a translation of the Japanese term *o-butsu myogo,* which literally means the melding of the principles of Buddhism with government and refers to the ideal of the Soka Gakkai in the political arena.

Tuesday, March 27. Cloudy.

An uneventful morning. An executive conference at the headquarters at 3:00. Sensei did not attend. With the general director as the focus, the meeting made little progress. There is a difference between organizational position and the power of faith. Perhaps it can't be helped. Seeing Sensei is the only thing that gives me hope and resolve.

A Suiko Group meeting at 6:00, the first in quite a while. Met with Sensei for two hours, listening to his perspectives on history and the society of ages past, as well as his views on noteworthy individuals. (My heart ached with passion as I listened. An erudite teacher, a profound and great leader.) The thoughts of Oda Nobunaga and his true nature as a general. The social views of Toyotomi Hideyoshi and Tokugawa Ieyasu and their leadership.[1] An analysis of the causes of victory and defeat in the battle of Okehazama. Left with many deep impressions.

Saw Sensei off, then discussed K.'s strategy in reception room #2. Encouraged him to summon honor and determination as the House of Councillors candidate who will represent the head temple area.

Met my wife late and we had dinner in Meguro together before returning home.

1. The thoughts of Oda Nobunaga ... and their leadership: This is a reference to the work studied by the Suiko Group, *Record of the Taiko*. It is a biography of Toyotomi Hideyoshi (see note on p. 146). Oda Nobunaga (1554–82; see note on p. 146), Hideyoshi's predecessor, was an often brutal warlord who nevertheless succeeded in being the main figure in Japan's reunification in the sixteenth century. Tokugawa Ieyasu (1543–1616), who seized power after Hideyoshi's death, was a warlord who put the finishing touches on Japan's reunification and founded the Tokugawa shogunate, the lineage of shoguns who ruled Japan over the 260-year Edo period. He set up his rule in a small fishing village called Edo, which grew to become present-day Tokyo.

Wednesday, March 28. Cloudy.

Harmony with society is important, as is our challenge to impart justice to that society. Isn't propagation our compassionate challenge toward society? Isn't the political world our first step in achieving harmony with society? Propagation not only allows individuals to reform their essential character and achieve a life of harmony, it is the first step toward a harmonious society, or rather, universal harmony. Only when based upon such harmony can government provide for social order with productivity, prosperity and cooperation.

Dinner with the T.s in the evening. Discussed the future of our precious Bunkyo Chapter. Gave my wife some gifts—a fountain pen and a shawl—when I got home. Today was payday.

Thursday, March 29. Rain.

Overly tired, mentally and physically. Could something be lacking in my gongyo? A Lotus Sutra lecture, the first in quite a while, at Toshima Civic Auditorium. Gradually understanding Sensei's true intention. Very happy.

A near downpour in the evening. Nevertheless, I attended a district chiefs meeting in Ikebukuro. There are some unsavory characters among the district leaders. Appalling. The monthly propagation result did not exceed twenty thousand households. Heard Sensei has been asking those around him about the fundamental cause of the problem. It troubles me. The Osaka area has achieved unprecedented growth, increasing its membership by 5,005 households. Ultimately, this year, the 704th since the establishment of Nichiren Daishonin's Buddhism, will be a historic one.

Year 700 (1952): Built a great foundation for Kamata Chapter.
Year 701 (1953): Tremendous growth in Bunkyo Chapter.
Year 702 (1954): Established the foundation and achieved great progress for the youth division.
Year 703 (1955): Achieved a great victory in the metropolitan and municipal elections.
Year 704 (1956): Will finally lead in earnest in this spring's battle in Osaka.

Young revolutionaries of the Mystic Law! Astride white horses, advance at full speed! Transcending mountains, rivers and valleys. Like the Greek runner Milo!

Your mentor is resolutely watching over you!

Friday, March 30. Rain.

The spring rain falls day and night. Feel like walking among the old castles of the Kiso highway [a major Edo-period land route]. Perhaps due to the relentless campaigns, I feel deeply fatigued, mentally and physically. "On Chanting the Daimoku of the Lotus Sutra" states, "'Slander' means to act against [the True Law]; 'immense joy' means to follow [the True Law]" (GZ, 4)). One need only have pure and unaffected faith in the Gohonzon. The only way is to live knowing that Gakkai activities constitute Buddhist practice. Want to stand up and advance based upon sincerity, courage and truth throughout my life.

Many philosophers and sages of old have elucidated their own theories on the relationship between emotion and intellect. Yet how emotionally obstinate intellectual scholars are when discussing the essential reality of their lives. Is it not wisdom founded on great compassion and magnanimous emotion that makes for real human perfection?

At 6:00, accompanied Sensei and his wife to the K. theater. Watched a play until 10:00. Feel sorry for making him stay so late, knowing his fatigue. Enjoyed watching the tragic lead character. Saw the life of this tragic character reflected in the performance.

Saturday, March 31. Cloudy.

Springlike warmth. Left Tokyo Station alone at 12:30 on the *Dove* to Osaka. As soon as I arrived, attended a squad leaders meeting, a block discussion meeting and then a YWD study meeting. Fully exerted myself with the power of an attacking lion. My friends in Osaka, too, are doing their very best. Feel gratitude, deep in my heart. In the future, the benefit they accrue will rise as high as a mountain. Benefit and faith have nothing to do with organization or position.

Sunday, April 1. Rain.

Rested at Kansai headquarters in the morning. Indebted to Y.'s aunt.

A district chiefs meeting at 1:00 in the third-floor meeting room. Saw many strong-spirited people. Entering the second stage of the campaign—guidance and direction. The decisive battle is close at hand. Pursue the objective, advance. A unit chiefs meeting from 6:30, at the headquarters first-floor meeting room. Discussed the following points:

1. The meritorious record of Chapter Chief S.
2. The vital and significant role of Osaka District.
3. Announced our cultural movement.
4. The process of kosen-rufu.

A memorable battle. Memorable days.

Monday, April 2. Rain, then overcast.

Overslept due to exhaustion and missed morning gongyo. A weak young man. Gave personal guidance all morning. A few dozen people came. Went sightseeing in Nara in the afternoon with H. Saw Todai-ji, the Kegon sect's main temple. As a historic spot, it lacked any feeling of life. The wooden treasure house at Todai-ji and Sarusawa Pond brought back fond memories. Rested for about twenty minutes at Wakakusa-yama, lying on our backs and gazing up into the sky. Recalled my childhood, grade-school field trips.

Back to the headquarters after 5:00.

Guidance to group chiefs at 6:00. Went to H.'s in the evening. Composed poetry together. Realistic, yet idealistic youth.

Saturday, April 7. Overcast, followed by rain.

Got out of bed at long last, after last night's transgressions. My thoughts and impressions after reading were not clear. Left Yokohama Station at 9:35 on the *Cherry Blossom* with I., M., I. and others for a joint chapter meeting in Osaka. Together, we discussed the Gakkai's future and talked about noteworthy people.

Arrived in Osaka at 8:03. Have grown fond of Osaka. Rain. Rain, on the day of our long-cherished meeting? My heart aches.

Sunday, April 8. Rain.

Rain. The rain continues. Miserable. Today is the anniversary of the execution of the three martyrs of Atsuhara.[1] A day of bitter persecution. It touches my heart, makes my body and spirit taut.

At 1:00, opening words at Nanba Baseball Stadium. Some twenty thousand members gathered in an orderly manner. The rain fell hard, in spite of it being spring. There were speeches by the Statistics Department chief, the Culture Department chief, the youth division chief of staff, the Guidance Department chief, and from Director I. Next, there were salutations by both chapter chiefs, a senior on the planning board, the general director and then, finally, a magnificent speech by President Toda. The meeting ended successfully just after 2:00.

Will stand alone, aiming toward July 8. Won't retreat a single step. Nothing interesting took place at the follow-up meeting.

1. Three martyrs of Atsuhara: Today, the Atsuhara Persecution is believed to have taken place on October 5, 1279. Around 1275, after the Daishonin had retired to Mount Minobu, propagation efforts in Fuji district began to advance rapidly under the leadership of Nikko Shonin. Alarmed at the rapidly growing number of followers, authorities responded with a series of threats and violent acts over a period of three years, beginning in 1278, which included the deaths of three followers.

Monday, April 9. Cloudy, then clear.

The sun shone brilliantly. Yesterday's storm seems like a dream. Spent the morning discussing various plans with the Culture Department chief. He is young. I, too, am young. We each have strong opinions. Reflect. We must excuse each other's intrinsic arrogance.

Left for home on the *Dove* at 12:30 from Umeda Station. Couldn't read during the eight-hour train ride. Regret I wasted the time. Must quit smoking if I want to improve my health. My wife and brother greeted me at Yokohama Station. It was comforting. Returned to my pleasant, happy home. Remember Sensei's mercy. Worried those close to him lack compassion.

Tuesday, April 10. High clouds.

My memory is fading, perhaps due to fatigue. Human society is complex. At times, I become disgusted with society. Arrogance, power, scheming.... Fortune, sincerity, conviction.... A baffling mixture of realities. Youth is painful. Heard the Tokyo-area members are facing a difficult struggle in the House of Councillors election campaign. They must not forget that only faith and unity will lead to victory. "Too many cooks...." Leaders! Understand Sensei's intention! There is no other way to victory.

I have decisively taken the lead in Kansai. Hoping for the members' glorious victory in Tokyo as well. Discussed the entire campaign outlook with Sensei in the evening. Will never forget the earnest look in his eyes.

Wednesday, April 11. Rain, letting up with overcast later on.

Reported to Sensei for about an hour in the morning. He praised me, saying I have been making great progress in our morning study sessions. How glorious to take flight under my mentor's tutelage. Mine has been the most wonderful youth in all the world. I have no regrets. I am happy.

Pleased to see Osaka is decisively running ahead of the pack in propagation. A tide is rising in Kansai. Must continue to carefully and commendably lead the campaign. They will probably reach several thousand households.

Got home early. Ate a delicious dinner my wife prepared. Thought, read, then went to bed after midnight.

Friday, April 20. Cloudy.

This morning, Sensei was in very high spirits. I, too, felt like springtime. It's mysterious, the way one's life responds. It's the function of the leader's deep determination. Accompanied Sensei to the head temple. We left on the express from Tokyo Station. Several senior directors came. Had not seen them for a while.

At 2:00, we attended the Ceremony to Report the Transfer of High Priests at the Miei-do on the head temple grounds. A solemn and dignified service. Many Hokkeko representatives were there, but only twenty or thirty top Gakkai leaders.

After reciting the sutra, the high priest gave an address. Next, congratulatory words from Nichiren Shoshu's chief administrator, the chief of propagation activities and the chairman of the Nichiren Shoshu Council. Following this, congratulatory speeches from the chief representative of the Hokkeko, the Soka Gakkai president, a representative of believers around the nation and the mayor of Fujinomiya City.

Sensei said: "As long as I am alive, I, Toda, will dedicate myself to the head temple and to the cause of kosen-rufu."

Everyone present straightened themselves and listened in awe to this genuine pledge, which resounded from the depths of his life. This brief yet eloquent statement, which seemed to transcend mountains, ignited a flame in my heart that will not go out as long as I live. The priesthood here at this Eagle Peak are like the monk Kakutoku, and the lay believers are like King Utoku[1] who protected him. A meeting of top leaders in the Rikyo-bo lodging in the evening. Like a parent with his children.

1. Kakutoku…Utoku: Kakutoku was a monk who upheld the True Law, and Utoku was the king who protected him. The Nirvana Sutra explains that Utoku was reborn as Shakyamuni, while Kakutoku was reborn as Kasho Buddha (Skt Kashyapa).

Saturday, April 21. Clear.

Stayed at the head temple with my mentor. The skies were clear and the sun shone brilliantly, seeming to express the Great Law's real prosperity. A discussion meeting was held, centering on Sensei, beginning at 6:30 a.m.

The topics covered were:

1. Plans for the House of Councillors election.
2. How to go about promoting publications.
3. Promoting a clean election.
4. The importance of putting faith first.

The scroll-airing ceremony was held at 9:00 in the Reception Hall. Listened intently to the high priest's sermon on the Daishonin's transfer documents to Nikko Shonin. In one document, the Daishonin refers to the "Dai-Gohonzon of the High Sanctuary of True Buddhism."[1] I secretly feel deep within my heart that this is my lifelong mission, to help realize the establishment of the High Sanctuary of True Buddhism mentioned in this passage.

My heart leapt at seeing the precious treasures stored at the head temple. The Gohonzon intended for enshrining at the emperor's palace. The Sun and Moon Gohonzon. The Never Aging, Never Dying Gohonzon. The Gohonzon of Transfer. The Gohonzon for Saving and Protecting the People for Ten Thousand Years. And many other Gohonzon, including one bestowed by Nichiren Daishonin to Niko.

The ceremony of chanting before the Dai-Gohonzon was conducted at 2:00. Today the sun shone as if dispelling a little more darkness of the ten thousand years of the Latter Day.

1. Dai-Gohonzon of the High Sanctuary of True Buddhism: Also, Dai-Gohonzon. The
    object of worship that Nichiren Daishonin inscribed on October 12, 1279, as the
    ultimate purpose of his advent in this world. The Daishonin defines the True Law
    in the Latter Day as the Three Great Secret Laws: the object of devotion; the high
    sanctuary and the invocation or the daimoku. The object of devotion encompasses
    all three and is thus called the One Great Secret Law.

Sunday, April 22. Cloudy then clear.

Hot all day. Stifling weather.

Was dead tired since morning from staying up so late the previous
night. Greeted Sensei early in the morning. Accompanied him to ceremony of chanting before the Dai-Gohonzon at 8:00. A memorable pilgrimage. Received word from Sensei that we would return together by
car to Tokyo, though I was originally scheduled to depart at 3:00 in the
afternoon. Drove back to Tokyo with Sensei's family. Enjoyed pleasant
conversation in the car.

Got home after 11:00 after stopping at the headquarters. Today I
thought I would like to spend my entire life as a youth in my twenties.
Reflected on the principle that 'Buddhahood is inherent in the nine
worlds.'

Many obstacles and fierce storms lie ahead. But the genuine glory is
the glory we gain in winning over these, is it not?

Monday, April 23. Cloudy.

Life's ambitions, life's tedium, life's significance. What is the purpose
of my existence? Why must I lead such a difficult life? There are days I
wonder heedlessly about such things. Must challenge society and challenge myself every single day. Many in this society grow weary and are
defeated.

Attended an evening district chiefs meeting. Gave strict guidance.
Wonder if it was appropriate. Lectured on the story of the Dragon Gate
Falls at Mount T'ien-t'ai. The twenty-odd generals of the Mystic Law lis-
tened with open eyes and open hearts.

What is power? It is the energy of faith.

Tuesday, April 24. Clear.

I am an emotional person. Rather, I am a man of flaring passions.
Toward justice, toward myself and toward the battle. Is this correct? Or
am I mistaken? The future will determine whether I am correct. Proof
will most definitely appear. Then it will be decided. Right now, there is
nothing more I can do.

A youth division planning board meeting at 6:30. Pleased to buy *A Collection of the World's Art* by Heibon Publishing. Afterward I met with H. over dinner. I have been spending too much. Got home just after 11:00.

Wednesday, April 25. Cloudy.

Light clouds since morning. Received a report that Osaka Chapter grew by 9,002 households this month. An unprecedented result. We have built a golden tower that will shine brilliantly in Gakkai history. Will decisively challenge and surpass this target in May. The dream of ten thousand households is possible to attain. Like a rising tide, like raging waves, we save suffering people. Enjoy! Leap! Shout! Dance! Sing! Robust youth of the Mystic Law! Comrades in spirit!

5:00 — an executive conference at the headquarters. Sensei did not attend. Truly lonesome and sad when he is absent.

Thursday, April 26. Rain, letting up with clouds.

Tomorrow I go to Osaka, a place with which I share a deep connection and where I have many friends. Kansai and I will flourish together. The Osaka area — site of the great desperate battle. The campaign to elect S. has become the Gakkai's greatest thus far. And I am ultimately responsible. There are times my head reels.

In the evening, a Third Corps YMD district leaders meeting. Lectured on the Great White Ox Cart parable. Talked about the importance of resolving not to backslide in faith, the fundamental way of Gakkai activities, activities in society and other topics. Have high expectations for these future corps chiefs and youth division planning board members. Home after 11:00. Read a magazine for a while.

Monday, July 16. Cloudy.

Summoned to the president's office at 9:00 in the morning.

A senior executive conference, led by Sensei, was held until 11:00 a.m. with the general director, the board of directors and others attending. Accompanied Sensei to meet with A. in the evening. The place was the N. restaurant. I understand he is a man of unrivaled prominence. But what is his true worth when compared to the depth of this great Buddhism? Afterward, I attended a Bunkyo Chapter district chiefs meeting. It lacked spirit. Is it because everyone is exhausted, myself included? Spoke primarily on the importance of Buddhist study and guidance. Afterward, we all went to Mejiro Station.

Tuesday, July 17. Clear.

Feel like I'm getting healthier. Want to do my utmost until the day kosen-rufu is achieved. Work was dull. S. has really improved. The old gentleman S. [a different person] is a victim of his own self-centeredness. Yet he is frightfully energetic for a man his age. Went to the headquarters. Sensei was in a very bad mood.

A youth division meeting at 7:00 p.m. I attended. Spirits were low.

I am enraged. I love the youth. To the high-level authoritarian leaders who mistreat these youth, I wish to ask: "Don't you see what progress the Gakkai is making?" I am incensed to think they have forgotten their debt of gratitude to Sensei. Frightening, truly frightening. I am saddened.

I shall live powerfully for the future of the Soka Gakkai.

Saturday, July 21. Clear.

Did not see Sensei all day. Lonesome. Day and night, the image of his face is often at the center of my thoughts. Is it all right for the relationship between mentor and disciple to be like that of parent and child? There is no one I can ask about this. In the early evening, for the first time in four years, I took my wife and eldest son, Hiromasa, to Atami.[1] We stayed at the F. Inn. Surprised at the sparse accommodations. The three of us thoroughly enjoyed ourselves in town on what some said was the hottest day so far this year. The town was quiet, as few people come to the hot springs in the summer heat. Could only think about how I, how every aspect of the Gakkai and how the climate of Japanese society will change in three years.

The eternity of life, this lifetime, contemplation, practice.... Theory and actuality; wisdom and intellect; stillness and motion; good and evil.

1. Atami: A city on the Izu Peninsula known for its mild winters and numerous hot springs.

Sunday, July 22. Intermittent cloudiness.

Slept until 9:00 a.m. I always feel tired. Cannot tell when I will become exhausted or fatigued. Skipped breakfast, and in the afternoon we boarded a pleasure boat that cruised quickly around Nishikigaura and Iwaogishi. We were told that Nishikigaura is so called because when the waves break on the boulders, in the morning or late afternoon, a rainbow appears that, against the backdrop of the breaking silver or golden waves, creates a pattern like fine Japanese brocaded silk. There are caves just inland from the beach. When Yoritomo[1] was defeated in the

Battle of Ishibashiyama and escaped to Awa by way of Manazuru, he used these caves to hide in along the way. We heard that, tragically, sixty people drowned themselves here this year.

Left for Tokyo at 6:48 p.m. Finished reading *The New Tales of Heike* and *History of the Napoleonic Wars*. Over the next three years, will concentrate my efforts on reading books about history. "Rely on the Law and not upon persons" (Nirvana Sutra). Isn't this an essential principle of faith?

1. Yoritomo: See note on p. 252. The Battle of Ishibashiyama against the ruling Taira clan was Yoritomo's first major engagement. The Tairas were later defeated.

Tuesday, August 28. Rain.

Physical stamina is the basis for one's actions and activities in life. A person who possesses such physical strength will be happy, while one who lacks it will suffer.

A afternoon economics lecture from Sensei. In the evening, I escorted him to enshrine T.'s large, specially inscribed Gohonzon. Sensei seemed tired. He instructed us on the proper way to read a newspaper and on the perspective we should have toward great individuals. Must seriously digest each word from my superb teacher. What a shame that some leaders who are not serious carelessly parrot others' words.

Wednesday, August 29. Rain.

Light rain—autumn begins.

The intense summer heat has gone so quickly. Ah, I must cherish these years of my youth. Could not meet with Sensei all day. Disheartening. A problem occurred with one of the chapter staff. He was sternly cautioned by Director H., T., the chapter chief and myself. Indiscretion by leaders toward alcohol, women and money leads to disruption of the Gakkai. Frightening, truly frightening.

Worried about the haughtiness of some Culture Department members. They did not become Diet members only because of their efforts or abilities. They should strive to deserve the trust and respect of society and the members. Didn't they become politicians to help the people? Place all my hope in Sensei's life. He gives meaning to my life, he is my whole existence.

Director Z. came over. A weak-spirited person. Seems I can only rely on those who feel passionately about kosen-rufu .

Thursday, August 30. Rain.

Light rain again today. Physical condition, poor. Is it due to my lack of ability to concentrate on the Law or a disharmony of the four elements?[1]

At 6:00 p.m., a standing executive conference with Sensei. He said: "Look at your own way of life. Work as a member of the rank and file. How can you be a general if you can't inspire ordinary soldiers to advance?" This he said to admonish the leaders about becoming authoritarian.

Me, I shall stay with this teacher forever, lifetime after lifetime. Went with some friends afterward to see the documentary film, *Japan at War*, which played in Shinjuku. War is a tragedy. It must be avoided at all costs, absolutely. Thought about many things.

1.   Disharmony of the four elements: One of the six causes of illness mentioned by T'ien-t'ai in his *Great Concentration and Insight*, and quoted by Nichiren Daishonin in such Gosho as "On Curing Karmic Disease." The ancient Indians thought the four elements—earth, water, fire and wind—were the basic constituents of all matter. In modern terms, disharmony of the four elements may be equated with the idea of chemical imbalance.

Wednesday, September 5. Clear.

The temperature climbed to almost 90°. The late-summer heat is intense. Had an intimate discussion with Sensei about a variety of matters. Sensei talked about eventually retiring from his business. This way, he can fully assume the Soka Gakkai presidency and the leadership for kosen-rufu in every sense. He indicated that next month, there will be a full-scale propagation campaign in Yamaguchi Prefecture. I will take full responsibility.... I will fight like Yoshitsune[1] or Shinsaku.[2] It will be a battle for the Law that shall go down in history.

In the evening, I went to Hashimoto in Sagamihara to give guidance for the first time in a year-and-a-half. Stopped first at Shokei-ji. It may be due to the nature of the area, or it may be the leaders' responsibility or the people's nature, but there was no joy of faith among the seventy members gathered at I.'s home. Home after midnight. Completely exhausted. Must not complain.

1.   (Minamoto no) Yoshitsune (1159–1189): Warrior of the latter Heian (794–1185) and early Kamakura (1185–1333) periods. A principle figure in the Taira–Minamoto War, he has been immortalized in legend and history as Japan's foremost tragic hero. A younger half-brother of Yoritomo (see note on p. 142), he later found himself at odds with his brother and was forced to take his own life in an attack by a former ally who had been pressured by his brother.

2.   (Takasugi) Shinsaku: See note on p. 142.

Friday, September 7. High Clouds.

The late summer heat is intense. Feel listless. A Study Department lecture at the Labor Administration office in Suidobashi at 6:30 this evening. Studied Nichikan's *Six-volume Writings* and the Gosho "Reply to Yasaburo." Seventy members attended. Many were late. Reprimanded them. Afterward, had dinner in Shinagawa. Heard that Mars has approached within thirty-five million miles of the Earth. I am very fond of astronomy. Today's society is so hectic, people don't have the freedom to look into the sky and ponder the Milky Way. Want to lead a noble life in which I can better contemplate nature.

Saturday, September 8. Clear.

A refreshing morning.

Sternly rebuked my wife for misplacing the badge Sensei gave me.

At 10:00, I accompanied Sensei to Taiseki-ji. Arrived at the head temple at 1:30 p.m. It was hot. Talked with him until nightfall. Without his saying as much, sensed there are many things he feels he must teach me before it is too late. Two question-and-answer meetings were held. Heard more than a thousand participated in this pilgrimage. Attended my first *ushitora* gongyo[1] with High Priest Nichijun Horigome. Keenly aware of the purity and power of his life. Deeply sense his joy of faith and the magnificence of a person with a sense of mission.

Ate *soba* [buckwheat noodles] with Director H., then returned to the Rikyo-bo lodging, gazing at the 2:00 a.m. sky on the way. Will definitely participate in each monthly pilgrimage, making every one as meaningful as possible.

1. *Ushitora* gongyo: Morning gongyo as performed by the high priest. *Ushitora* is the name of the time period between 2:00–4:00 a.m.

Sunday, September 9. Light rain, clearing later.

Though the air is fresh like autumn, it is still hot. Stayed at Taiseki-ji. Extremely fatigued, perhaps because I participated in *ushitora* gongyo. Have become aware my practice of faith is shallow.

Chanted before the Dai-Gohonzon at 10:00 a.m. Understand the benefit and virtue of daimoku with every fiber of my being. Particularly in the mysterious upwelling of life force I feel after the ceremony of chanting before the Dai-Gohonzon. Was received by the retired high priest. During the discussion, Sensei spoke strictly on the meaning of benefit and on sincerity in making offerings.

At 12:00, we were received by High Priest Nichijun Horigome.

Fondly reminded of his abundant compassion. In the afternoon, we received a lecture directly from Sensei on Nikko Shonin's "Twenty-six Admonitions" at the headquarters set up at the Rikyo-bo lodging.

Departed the head temple at 2:30 p.m. Changed trains in Numazu. By the time I arrived home, it was already a little before 10:00 p.m.

Monday, September 10. Intermittent clouds.

Exhausted in the morning, could not get up. Is it laziness? Will I challenge myself—or make excuses?

A windy day—dust laden wind. A gray society, an ashen wind. Have long been awaiting the clear, fresh days of autumn, when the typhoon season has passed. My favorite season. Talked with Sensei in the president's room this afternoon. He was in good spirits. What is he thinking, what is he trying to accomplish? At times, a great person's mind is like a secret compartment. A corps chiefs conference began at 6:35 p.m. at the headquarters. Discussed:

1. The upcoming sports festival.
2. Directions for guidance to student division members.
3. The unity of 'many in body, one in mind.'

Decided to do some remodeling at home.

Monday, October 1. Rain.

Rainy and gloomy all day. The weather continues as if it is the beginning of the rainy season. Decided on the daily agenda for the campaign in the Senyo area to which I have been assigned. It will be two weeks. It will be a historic, pioneering battle. Will advance with great pride.

Important points to be aware of:

1. Act with composure.
2. Carry out propagation in a way that engenders understanding.
3. Be meticulous in giving guidance.

A youth division corps chiefs meeting in conference room #2. Announced new goals and targets.

At 8:30 p.m., attended a funeral vigil for S.'s father. Talked with H. until after 11:00. Congratulated him on reaching adulthood.

Thursday, November 29.

Deep autumn. In this most vital and robust season of clear blue skies, I, too, have gained weight. Now weigh 144 pounds.

A panel discussion for the New Year's *Seikyo Shimbun* issue began at 2:00. The topic, "The five main temples of Fuji." It lasted until 5:00. The dialogue covered Nikko Shonin's six original and six new disciples[1] and the origin of Fuji's five or seven main temples. Concluded with the present status of these temples. Keenly reflected on the importance of ability in Buddhist study and of having a correct historical perspective.

Late in the evening, I went to Shinjuku with Y., N. and K. to see the movie *Shizuka and Yoshitsune*.[2] Dull. Nevertheless, it portrayed beautiful trust between a man and a woman. Got home late. My house is pleasant; filled with joy. Eternal.

1. Nikko Shonin's six original and six new disciples: The six main disciples were the six priests that second high priest Nikko Shonin designated to serve the Dai-Gohonzon and the head temple. The six new disciples were six priests to whom he entrusted future propagation.

2. *Shizuka and Yoshitsune*: This is the story of the tragic warrior hero Minamoto no Yoshitsune (see note p. 302) and his mistress, Shizuka Gozen.

Saturday, December 1. Fair.

The regular headquarters leaders meeting was held yesterday, November 30. Sensei said a few admonitory words. We have not reached the goal of 500,000 households yet, one of this year's three major objectives. Ah, I worry about the Gakkai's future. Regrettable.

Toward next year's Study Department entrance exam, I, too, will exert myself earnestly at study. A leader who lacks power in Buddhist study will definitely suffer in the future and will eventually take a step backward. We do not study to impress others; we study for our own sake.

Came home early. Read a book. My family abounds with happiness. A family filled with good fortune. This, I feel, is a benefit arising from faith. Resolved from today to develop further in faith, practice and study.

Sunday, December 2. Fair.

Awoke around 6:00 from a frightening dream. Boundless agony, even after awakening. Proof that the Mystic Law has not yet permeated the mysterious inner world of my life. It was just a nightmare, but it makes me think of life in the state of hell after death. Want to have sublime and beautiful dreams.

Went to the public baths alone and spent the morning there.

Read while lying down until nightfall. My wife's mother came by. She is always a wonderful mother. Miss my own mother. Promised to buy my wife and her mother each a new obi. This is my greatest gift—to let them be beautiful, be happy and enjoy themselves.

Attended a Guidance Department administrative meeting at 6:00 at the headquarters. It lasted until past 10:00. Hold high expectations for the wisdom displayed by the board of directors. Concerned about self-interest and authoritarianism. For the future, they should humbly listen to able and talented people's opinions. This is the way Sensei thinks, and this has been his direction. Arrived home late. Listened to "The Wanderer" and "Beautiful Nature" with my wife.

Monday, December 3. Clear.

Each day has become hectic. Especially since now is the year end. It seems that without adequate physical, spiritual and mental strength, one cannot accomplish anything great. The unity of body and mind. Life is ultimately a manifestation of its inner reality. This is not merely spiritual. It is the oneness of body and mind. We call this *myoho*, the Mystic Law.

Talked with Sensei for almost thirty minutes in the afternoon. A strict yet kind teacher.

A corps chiefs meeting at 6:30 at the headquarters.

1. Be a driving force toward the goal of 500,000 households.
2. The youth division general meeting format is now decided.
3. Other topics.

Tuesday, December 4. Clear, then rainy.

Unless I strive to cultivate my character, I will not become a great and capable general. I must advance, striving each day in practice and study, based upon faith, to become a person of great insight.

Once again pondered Ieyasu's admonition: "A person faces three turning points in life that one should bear well in mind. The first is around the age of seventeen or eighteen when one may become tainted through the bad influence of friends. The second is around thirty when one may become arrogant about things, failing to show respect even to venerable seniors. Then, around forty, one may grow bored with life and be given to reminiscing about the past, thus growing weak at heart."

I should thoroughly self-reflect. In any event, these words are very interesting.

The father states, "Arrogant people do not last long," to which the son replies with a smile, "People who are not arrogant do not last long either."

I value these words as well.

At 7:00, the last youth division leaders meeting of the year was held. The direction for further development was set for each individual, each corps and the entire youth division, based on the golden words, "Not to advance is to retreat."

Talked informally with youth division staff members in conference room #1 at the headquarters. Went home feeling desolate. People are all conceited, wrapped up only in themselves.

Wednesday, December 5. Fair.

Went to the Diet at 2:00 to listen to the ratification of a motion for holding negotiations with the Soviet Union. It lasted two hours. Went with my wife. While there, I thought about the future setting for kosen-rufu.

A lecture on the *Propagation Handbook* in Nakano. It went fairly well. Talked with many people after the meeting.

> When they know that, unseen by others, the Buddhas and bodhi-sattvas are observing them, how can they fail to be ashamed of such actions! The pains of hell are frightful indeed. Beware of them! Beware of them!
>
> —"Questions and Answers about Embracing the Lotus Sutra" (WND, 61)

Finished reading *Record of the Taiko* for the second time. Thinking about citing it when I write my own novel. Talked with my wife until after 12:00. A beautiful, bright and peaceful family.

Thursday, December 6. Clear, with clouds later on.

Met with Sensei for the first time in a while. He gave me a gold watch and a gold chain for my wife's father. It's really too much. Will bring it to my father-in-law.

A warm, peaceful day. It has been decided that propagation efforts will intensify during the week of the 10–16. If Sensei is the master of propagation, then I am his propagation disciple. If the Gakkai is the only group to carry out propagation, then the most honorable warrior is one of propagation. Must never forget this essential, lofty direction.

Studied the lecture on the "Orally Transmitted Teachings" with H. and others at my house in the evening. Finished the "Life Span" chapter. Thought about what I will be doing three years from now and what I must accomplish.

Friday, December 7. Fair.

Not feeling well all day. Deplore my frail health. It's miserable, sad. How will I accomplish anything great in the future with this health? At what age am I destined to die?

If the principle that 'the ultimate reality of an individual's life pervades the entire universe' is true, then it should be possible to reform my life, including its physical aspect, through determined faith.

Went to a barber shop near Tokyo Station in the late afternoon. Then, attended a (Bunkyo Chapter) unit chiefs meeting at Jozai-ji. It was almost 10:00 when the meeting was over. Afterward, I inquired of Priest Hosoi (later to become the sixty-sixth high priest) about:

1. The first Gohonzon inscribed by Nichiren Daishonin on Sado Island no longer exists. It was destroyed by a fire at a temple on the Minobu temple grounds in the eighth year of Meiji (1876). They strongly assert the Gohonzon they possess is a copy of that Gohonzon [made under the Daishonin's direction]. But nothing in the Daishonin's writings proves such a copy ever existed. There is absolutely no basis for Tanaka Chigaku's[1] self-serving views on this matter.

2. Nichiren Daishonin's handwritten seal exists in three variations, which correspond respectively to the Bun'ei, Kenji and Koan eras. Though they are quite similar, they differ according to the era. This is also true of the Daishonin's signature seals on the Gohonzon. And while the seals that appear on the Gosho exhibit a few additional variations, they do not differ essentially from these three basic categories.

3. Nichiren Daishonin uses the term *shakudai kannin* in his original writings and on the Gohonzon he inscribed. This is a Chinese transliteration of the Sanskrit for the Buddhist god [Indra]. Nikko Shonin and subsequent high priests have changed this to the common Japanese name for the deity, Taishaku.

My wife greeted me at Gotanda Station with my son Hiromasa. The three of us had an enjoyable trip home. May it be this way forever.

---

1. Chigaku Tanaka: (1861–1939) A religious activist who promoted Japan's imperial nationalism based on Nichiren Buddhism. In 1885 he founded the religious organization Rissho Ankoku Kai and advocated the unification of the world under imperial Japan and Nichiren Buddhism as well as the worship of the emperor and the supremacy of the Japanese race. His group was renamed Kokuchu Kai in 1914. After his death, the Kokuchu Kai splintered into several groups.

Saturday, December 8. Scattered clouds.

The young women's division general meeting was held at 6:00 in the evening. The place, Kawasaki Civic Hall. The meeting was over at 8:30. I had gone to the meeting place at 1:00 to make various arrangements. By the time the meeting began, I was completely exhausted. Foolish.

A successful meeting. Spoke for about five minutes, as chief of staff. "The Chinese phoenix chooses a tree in which to live. People as well, should choose a teacher with whom to live their lives." Afterward, talked for a little while with some YWD members. Then had coffee with T. and U. in Kamata. Returned home alone. Tired. Went right to bed.

The past is like a cloud—like a dream. It is something I possess.

Sunday, December 9. Cloudy, then rain.

Got up a little before 6:00—pilgrimage. Mentally and physically exhausted; woke up just in time. Arrived at the head temple just after 11:00. Sensei and I were received by the high priest in his living quarters. It's been two months since the last time. Next, we met the retired high priest at the Onjo-bo lodging.

The light rain gave way to weather that was almost too good to be true. Chanted before the Dai-Gohonzon at 2:00. Gongyo was excruciatingly difficult, but afterward it was as if a dark cloud in my heart had lifted to reveal a clear state of life.

Left Fujinomiya at 3:35 on the Minobu line for Fuji City. Left Fuji City for Tokyo at 4:57.

Monday, December 10. Fair.

An unforgettable day in my life. On December 10, at 8:30 in the evening, my father died. He lived to sixty-eight. The cause of death— heart failure. Heard he died while everyone was watching television. My stern, kind father—the one who raised me—has died. Ah, I regret never being a truly filial son. I am twenty-eight.

My venerable, honest father. My old-fashioned, sincere and magnanimous father. Recall how he always watched quietly, never scolding me, not even once. Ah, as his body lay quietly and peacefully before me, I set out my small, portable Gohonzon, reciting the sutra and chanting daimoku, offering him my prayers for one hour.

Wept at seeing my mother's grief. The love between my father and my mother, between my father and his children, father and child. Saw my older brothers and their families after quite a while.

Received much consideration from Sensei. I thank him.

T. and several members came by to pay their respects. I thank them. Many people from the neighborhood also stopped by. I thank them. It was only the death of a simple seaweed farmer, but....

Tuesday, December 11. Fair.

Slept at my parents' house for the first time in ten years. A dozen or so people — my brothers and their families — stayed over as well. Keenly sense that I must now stop by the house from time to time. The past cannot be helped. But from now on, I must.

In the morning, chanted daimoku for three hours to the small, portable Gohonzon before my father's body. In this way, I believe, I could fulfill my ultimate filial duty. At 2:00, my father's body was placed into the coffin. My mother wept openly. She has traveled the last fifty years of her journey of life with my father. No one can possibly understand my mother's feeling or state of mind. It has been a long, happy and difficult journey. My mother's tears of genuine love transcend everything — intellect, status, affluence or vanity. Ah, my simple, yet extraordinary mother and father. The sorrow of being separated from a loved one. Nam-myoho-renge-kyo.

The grief of eternal separation. The absolute solution to such suffering exists, I believe, only in Buddhism's teachings.

Sensei took a 2:50 flight from Haneda Airport to Osaka. We left early enough to make it to the airport on time. My wife and I saw him off. Without words, he seemed to offer me guidance: "You must solve your personal problems and work out your destiny on your own." It will require strong faith and a fierce, fierce struggle.

Wednesday, December 12. Clear.

Felt empty in the morning. Today I must bid my father a final farewell. Will it be an eternal separation? Or, as the sutra phrase *hoben gen nehan* indicates, is death simply an expedient? This is a crucial point for one who studies Buddhism. I recited the "Expedient Means" and "Life Span" chapters and chanted daimoku for my father one last time, along with my wife and her father, Mr. Shiraki. My greatest supporter will be laid to rest.

The coffin was taken away exactly at noon. A good number of Gakkai members stood by to offer their respects. Thankful. On to the crematorium at Kirigaya, then to Omori Cemetery.

It was 4:00 when I returned to my parents' home. Dined until 8:00 with relatives and others. The last three days have been very painful.

Returned home at 9:00. Got a good night's rest for the first time in a while. Had a striking dream about my father: He enters the bath alone, his face turning red; then, looking very happy, he faces death. A vivid image, I cannot forget it.

Thursday, December 13. Fair.

Was informed the memorial service for the first seven-day period would be held at the temple on the cemetery grounds. Resent this feudalistic, wasteful and uncivilized Japanese custom.

Left for Omori Cemetery in at 11:30. No one else had arrived. Recited the sutra by myself before my father's grave. Everyone else gathered at 12:30. Relieved to see my mother in good spirits. Happy. To President Toda's office at 6:00 with my wife to offer our respects and report everything to him. One top leader stood by and greeted Sensei with us. He's become truly authoritarian and impudent. He does not understand Sensei's heart. Must never become so foolish as to forget that any greatness I possess comes solely from the power of the organization and Sensei. No matter how great I may become, must never be haughty. Must build a life based on reasonableness and compassion toward my seniors and my juniors. If not, then ultimately, capable people will not appear. Decided to go to bed early, for tomorrow's sake.

Friday, December 14. Clear.

I, myself, must rebuild and advance.

To my weak self—be dynamic, do not stop.

Sensei treated me to lunch in his office. Thankful.

Attended an evening district chiefs meeting at O.'s house in Ikebukuro. Everyone is in high spirits, pouring everything into preparing for propagation activities. Lectured on the Gosho "Hell Is the Land of Tranquil Light." Discussed the significance of the benefit associated with the single character *myo* of the Lotus Sutra, to which even an adverse relationship constitutes a cause for enlightenment. Home at midnight. The moonlight entered my house. Refreshing and cleansing to the mind. The stream of history is now swelling.

Saturday, December 15. Fair.

Sensei's health is poor. Concerned he might become exhausted and cold. Heard he will be leaving for Sendai from Ueno Station. Ah, I was not thoughtful enough. I think he had better rest. Ah, I was immature. It would have been better to send a representative. My mentor, solemnly advancing kosen-rufu despite a high fever. To Shokei-ji in Hashimoto in the evening. Guidance in the Sagamihara area. It is as if a storm is raging in my head. The pulse of faith is emerging in this area as well. Ultimately, your environment is determined by your innermost reality, which manifests as both body and mind.

Sunday, December 16. Clear.

Slept well—very well. Completely relieved the anxiety built up over the past week. My wife really has been taking care of things. Sincerely thank her. Now I must face the tempestuous battlefield ahead. My wife lives for the Mystic Law and exerts herself beside this young revolutionary. Believe the Gohonzon warmly watches over her.

What is the meaning of status? What is position? Honor? Popularity?

To S.'s home in the afternoon. As a matchmaker. Was treated to dinner. My wife and I excused ourselves at 7:00. Stopped by the Shirakis' on the way back to offer year-end greetings. Gave my wife's brothers a sports coat and an overcoat as New Year's gifts. Spoke with my in-laws for a while before returning home. My sons' faces are so cute as they sleep .

Monday, December 17. Clear.

The good weather continues. It's been seven days since my father's death—thinking of him.

My father, who always argued with my mother over the children's welfare.

My father, who out of concern for his children would take the train himself to pick us up.

My father, who smiled warmly, even when his children were drafted and sent off to war.

My father, who toiled hard at his work, suffering on account of his stubborn sense of justice.

My father, whose earnest belief was steadfast.

My father, proud of his youthful horsemanship, whose figure loomed tall as that of a great man.

My parents were blessed with many children. My brothers had to go off to war. This must have been a time of great hardship for my parents. Deeply moved. I believe the harmony and peace he enjoyed with our family during his later years made my father happier than any king. As an emissary of the Buddha, I will send him daimoku.

Went to the Kanazawa Library. Attended a unit chiefs meeting for Bunkyo Chapter Area #5. About seventy attended. Gave guidance sincerely for about two hours, praying for the prosperity of the members in that area. By the time I got home, it was a little before midnight.

Intensely cold.

Tuesday, December 18. Fair.

Dined with Sensei at his home. Deeply appreciative. Candidate Tanzan Ishibashi's political views came up. Discussed his campaign strategy toward the final polling day. Amazed at Sensei's insight. Ahh! What a rare teacher! As his disciple, I will surpass the strategist Kongming in the novel *Romance of the Three Kingdoms*. I want to become a valiant and wise general for worldwide kosen-rufu. This I must do if it is my destiny to lead tens of millions of members ten years from now.

An evening youth division staff meeting. Everyone made it.

1. Decided upon next year's activities.
2. Created three regions: Eastern Japan, Tokyo and Western Japan. Each region will hold its own general meeting and sports festival.

Dined with Z. in Shinjuku before going home.

Wednesday, December 19. Fair.

Overslept this morning. This day in my life's battle got off to a slow start. Considered my determination and reviewed our household budget. I have been selfish. Told we are a little short on living expenses. Must think about my personal spending.

This evening there was a directors meeting, a corps chiefs meeting and a general staff conference. Very busy.

1. Want to write a letter to each corps chief.
2. Want the senior leaders to take care of their members sincerely.
3. Guidance should be based on the Mystic Law.
4. Concerned about the living circumstances and financial situations of the corps members.

Confucius said:
"At thirty, I stood tall.
"At fourty, I was free from doubt.
"At fifty, I realized heaven's will."
Yet, as a disciple of Nichiren Daishonin, is not necessary to delineate things in terms of age. This is due to 'the simultaneity of cause and

effect,' the 'three thousand realms in a single moment of life.' This is true so long as I feel my mission and maintain the unity of 'many in body, one in mind.' This should be the absolute basis of everything.

In any event, all I need is to continue my human revolution throughout my life based on faith.

Thursday, December 20. Clear.

In keeping a diary, am I engraving a glimpse of my life for posterity? Will it remain in history? A free dialogue. In any case, I will write on. There are times, however, when I write about the real state of things and times I do not. Sly, people are. Want to get up early these days. My life is becoming stagnant.

In the evening, brought the corps chiefs into President Toda's office. Sensei scolded us, yelling "Get out!" Not understanding why, I feel frustrated. Nevertheless, I can only keep advancing with a sincere spirit. Whatever it is, it will be all right. Tanzan Ishibashi named his cabinet ministers. The times surge ahead violently. Must perfect myself. The Gakkai, too, must advance. Was treated to noodles in Yaguchi before returning home.

Friday, December 21. Clear.

My head felt heavy all day. The youthful mind is prone to intense and abrupt change. Growing colder each day. I am aware, however, that my health has been growing stronger. Very happy.

Don't forget to read the Gosho. And don't forget to read novels. Will soon engage myself seriously in studying economics and politics. Thought about Sensei all day long. The strictness of the way of mentor and disciple. A headquarters leaders meeting at 6:00. The place, Toshima Civic Auditorium.

We successfully introduced 58,694 households, thus gracing the end of this year with victory. As a result, the members of some 500,000 households have now embraced the Gohonzon. My only concern is that spreading the Gohonzon not become disorderly. Attended a banquet at Jozai-ji. My mother and F. came over after I got home. Had a good, pleasant, talk.

Saturday, December 22. Fair.

Tomorrow is the youth division general meeting. Brought year-end gifts to two business associates in the morning. Talked with Sensei for an hour in the late afternoon. Always a profoundly stern teacher.

Went to the dress rehearsal at the Tokyo Sports Arena. It was a cold night. Youth, exerting themselves joyfully. Sparkling eyes. Patiently await what they will be like ten years from now.

In any general meeting, or any important campaign, I am always standing behind the scenes, unknown to anyone, without worrying about pleasing anyone or whether anyone appreciates me; there I pour my entire life into leading the battle and driving a wedge of faith. I smile happily at this destiny. Firmly believe everything is revealed under the light of the Mystic Law. Read until late at night, while lying down. Next year—next year, definitely I must study. This, I promise myself.

Sunday, December 23. Fair.

The time for the fifth YMD general meeting has come at last. Have eagerly awaited this general meeting. The Tokyo Sports Arena, the largest in East Asia. A fitting location for young people of the new century.

9:30 a.m.—Arrived at the arena. Could sense an almost fearsome vibration.

All morning, the gymnastics and music event, dubbed "Grand Recreation," was held. Clean-up in preparation for the meeting took until 11:00 a.m. Sensed some of the youth present did not have strong faith. Can only take the lead through the great power of my own faith.

President Toda arrived at 1:00. The high priest was last to arrive. Attendees numbered twenty thousand.

Sensei's address was titled "The People of Asia Await You." Each speaker was filled with vitality. The meeting ended dynamically. A fantastic general meeting; a fitting entry to decorate another page in Soka Gakkai history. The meeting closed at 4:00 with the singing of "Gojogen," a deeply emotional atmosphere pervading the arena.

At 5:00, treated by Sensei to a Chinese dinner at the N. restaurant. Perhaps due to fatigue, I couldn't eat much. Instead of walking ahead leisurely on a flat road, as a young pioneer I'd rather climb a range of mountains.

Monday, December 24. Fair.

Poor health. Have a slight fever of 100° F.

Have caught a cold—my stomach and chest ache.

When can I enjoy the four virtues of Buddhahood—eternity, happiness, true self and purity—in my faith and in my life? Sin, punishment and karma—these things surely exist in this life. M. took very good care of me. Spoke with I. for more than two hours. He hasn't changed. I think he is a great man. Went to Sensei's house in Meguro in the evening to bring year-end gifts. My poor physical condition persisted all evening.

Tuesday, December 25. Fair.

Did not feel well physically or mentally all day. Frustrated, helpless, lonely. Want to be healthy like everyone else. Heard Sensei became stern and angry at dinner at the N. restaurant the night before last. I am surprised. What was the cause of his anger? After thinking about it, it seems there was indeed a cause. He is always and forever a strict teacher. Must self-reflect. Ultimately felt how shallow I am at not understanding my teacher's intention. Is it his great affection?—for the mentor to draw his disciple into the realm of his heart and his will, to create oneness, 'the fusion of subjective wisdom and objective reality.' Ahh!

Went to Sensei's home in Meguro in the evening, prepared to be admonished.

Wednesday, December 26. Fair.

Out of sorts all day. Feel like death. A deplorable destiny. Faith! Must struggle resolutely against my own weakness. Will this year's suffering be the greatest I shall experience on account of illness?

Ahh! This coming year I will launch the true battle with myself. Will I defeat or be beaten by the devil of my own illness? Will I flourish as a youth, or will I succumb in the end?

At 6:00, went to M.'s with my wife to present a year-end gift.

Returned home around 11:00. Had many thoughts. The room felt cold to my fatigued body. Tomorrow a conference of all divisions and departments will be held. Considering various matters.

Thursday, December 27. Fair.

Went to work today, though I should have rested. Because of my responsibility, I cannot take off even one day. Life is truly mysterious—good or bad aside, sometimes when I push myself beyond apparent reason, my health seems to improve more than when I take time to rest.

Sensei talked about deductive and inductive reasoning. Consciousness as viewed by the Western philosopher Heinrich Rickert of the new Kantian school and the theory of consciousness espoused in Eastern philosophy are diametrically opposed. Western philosophy posits that consciousness begins with the six senses and then arrives at what

Buddhism refers to as the seventh, eighth and ninth levels of consciousness. Buddhism, on the other hand, teaches that consciousness arises out of the "Palace of the Ninth Consciousness of Essential Truth" and permeates the eighth, seventh and first six levels of consciousness. There are deductive civilizations and inductive civilizations. Which surpasses the other? It is important to strike a balance between these two. What will the future hold?...

During the general conference, Sensei talked about his childhood, his youth, and how he served President Makiguchi. Impressed, both mentally and spiritually, by many things: by Sensei's words, by his look of fulfillment as he spoke of protecting his teacher, serving his teacher, and deeply driving the sharp stakes securing the foundation of kosen-rufu.

Next year, I will become more serious in my practice of gongyo. I will discipline myself both physically and spiritually. Train myself, develop my state of life. Build genuine ability in the study of Buddhism.

Next year! Next year! I must reveal my true potential.

Friday, December 28. Cloudy.

Heard a report from the secretary's office that Sensei is in poor health. Concerned. Was told he will be staying home for two or three days to recuperate. This is what I want him to do. The fatigue of this tumultuous year has finally shown itself. Sensei is ill, and I am, too. It's frustrating. Why are others, both within and outside the Gakkai, so healthy? Had been concerned about my year-end finances, but mysteriously, it seems we somehow had enough to see us through until the new year. It is an inconspicuous benefit. Waited for a phone call from Sensei, but none came. Lonesome. Tomorrow, for certain....

POINTING TO THE ideological confrontation taking place across the face of the globe, Josei Toda, in his *Seikyo Shimbun* New Year's message, suggested that if Shakyamuni, Jesus Christ, Karl Marx and others were to gather for a grand conference, they would never quarrel or dispute one another. The foremost desire of sages throughout time has been to rid the world of misery, Toda said, and the fundamental purpose of Buddhist propagation, too, is to save people from suffering.

On January 17, a YMD leaders meeting was held at Toshima Civic Auditorium with some twenty-five hundred YMD representatives. On the same day, seventeen hundred YWD leaders held a similar meeting at Nakano Civic Auditorium. Brimming with vital life force, the youth pledged to one another to carry out their faith with great confidence and dignity. At the YMD meeting, Daisaku Ikeda said: "Please become the kind of youth about whom people will say, 'So long as the young men's division is here, I can rest assured.'"

On February 22, at 6:00 p.m., the February headquarters leaders meeting was held at Toshima Civic Auditorium. About two thousand leaders, district level and above, assembled. President Toda said that the Soka Gakkai is an organization of pure faith and emphasized that its structure and management must be conducted based upon faith. He also strictly warned against taking advantage of one's Gakkai position to act in an authoritarian manner toward the membership.

On May 12, a general chapter was formed on Hokkaido where twenty-three thousand people gathered at Sapporo's Nakajima Stadium for the First Hokkaido General Meeting. At that meeting, President Toda said that "Personal happiness depends on nothing but correct faith."

On May 19, the last day of the Tokyo Coal Miners Union's seventeenth regular conference, union officials made the following statement while announcing upcoming activities: "We will organize and fight certain religious groups who are breaking the unity of our ranks." Based on this, union leaders began to launch emotional attacks on Soka Gakkai activities involving union members. This was the spark that set off the so-called Coal Miners Union Incident, which culminated in the mining town of Yubari on Japan's northern island of Hokkaido.

On June 27, the Hokkaido Coal Miners Union issued directions to "Shut out the Soka Gakkai" and also announced its "Three Month Suppression Plan" aimed at Gakkai activities, and thus began its organized oppression of Soka Gakkai members within its ranks.

The more than two thousand members in Yubari were not only striving in faith, they actively participated in union activities. The directives from the union officials constituted an unjust attempt to suppress its members' freedom of religion. Soka Gakkai members received pressure from their union leaders to quit the Gakkai and were even threatened with loss of their jobs. The resistance from the Gakkai members, however, went far beyond the expectations of the union leaders. Forging solid unity, they refused to retreat a single step.

To counter the union's unreasonable harassment, the youth division pooled their strength in Hokkaido. On July 1, the Sapporo General Meeting was held at the Nakajima Sports Center. There, Chief of Staff Ikeda said: "For the Coal Miners Union to issue such directives [barring their members from participating in Gakkai activities] runs counter to democracy. This is beyond comprehension." The union was urged to repeal its orders. On July 2, about two hundred YMD members marched through Yubari, and at a general meeting in the town's Wakana Theater, the members assailed the union's brazenly unjust tactics. Some Yubari miners union officials also attended the general meeting. Afterward, the officials issued the following statement: "We now understand the Soka Gakkai's position. We will discontinue our unwise course of action." Thus the union had no choice but to rescind its anti-Gakkai measures, bringing the problem to a close.

While Chief of Staff Ikeda was busy in Hokkaido with the union problem, he was summoned to the Osaka Prefectural Police Headquarters to answer false charges of violating election campaign laws. These had been designed to put a damper on the Gakkai's rapid advancement.

Mr. Ikeda thus headed for Osaka where he was incarcerated on July 3, the same date Josei Toda had been released from prison twenty years earlier after having stood up against unjust actions of the authorities. The Gakkai members raised their voices in protest, calling for Mr. Ikeda's immediate release. After two weeks of incarceration, the chief of staff was released from the detention center at noon on July 17 and participated in the Osaka General Meeting that evening. That meeting, held amid rain and thunder, was a grand gathering of more than twenty thousand members. Several thousand more waited outside the auditorium, listening to the proceedings over loudspeakers. The so-called Osaka Incident was resolved some four-and-a-half years later, on January 25, 1962, with a not-guilty verdict on all counts against Mr. Ikeda, who by then had become the third Soka Gakkai president.

On September 8, during closing ceremonies for the Fourth Eastern Japan Youth Sports Festival at Yokohama's Mitsuzawa Sports Grounds, President Toda delivered his historic "Declaration for the Abolition of Nuclear Weapons" before fifty thousand Soka Gakkai members, emphasizing the supreme value and dignity of an individual human life.

On October 4, the Soviet Union successfully launched the world's first artificial satellite, *Sputnik I*, thereby launching in earnest the so-called space race between that country and the United States.

Tuesday, New Year's Day. Cloudy; clearing later on.

Got out of bed a little before 6:00. Listless. Could not sleep last night at all. Mentally and physically fatigued.

This is a day to plan for the entire year—feel the weight of my expectations on this, my New Year's Day. In my thirtieth year of life, I shall finally arise. Must solidify my determination to raise capable juniors. Went to President Toda's home in Meguro just after 8:00, after visiting the S.s' home and paying my respects at Myoko-ji. Nine people gathered at Sensei's house—the general director, the board of directors and myself. Was told Sensei was suffering a hangover. Nevertheless, I felt from him the noble, yet unassuming air of a great man. Learned Mrs. Toda has a cold. At 8:30, we boarded three taxis for Jozai-ji. Chanted daimoku with Sensei for a short time.

Arrived at the Soka Gakkai headquarters at 10:00. The sky gradually became clear. Recited the "Expedient Means" chapter portion, the prose and verse sections of the "Life Span" chapter, then chanted daimoku and read the silent prayers. In Sensei's prayer—for the Gakkai's success in its compassionate propagation campaign; for the fulfillment of the great objective of kosen-rufu; his expression of gratitude for the efforts of the successive high priests—can sense one aspect of the mystic power of his profound faith.

Sensei's first poem of the year—to the youth division:

> Like noble dolphins gathering in the stormy sea
> Youthful assemblage of kosen-rufu
> I place my trust in you.

Delighted Sensei possesses the temperament to love the youth most of all. Gratified. Sensei strictly directed us, "This year, I want all of the top leaders to go out and lend their support in areas such as Osaka, Kyushu and elsewhere." Left with my mentor on the *Nagasaki* express from Tokyo Station at 1:30 for the year's first head temple pilgrimage. In the evening, Sensei and I were treated by the high priest to New Year's dinner. Until late in the evening, contemplated the future on the peaceful head temple grounds. Spring is far off—it was very cold.

Wednesday, January 2. Clear.

My twenty-ninth birthday. I have now been practicing this faith for ten years. Ten years of challenging storm clouds and raging waves. Ten years from now, when I am thirty-nine, what destiny awaits me? What kind of person will I become? Thought of Yomejiro Noguchi's "Ode to New Year's Day."

> The silence of wisdom flows through the heart of the great ocean
> that runs from the North Pole to the South.

The silence of love extends from the sun-kissed East to the mountains that range in the West.
Ah, the silence of this day, January 1!
Celebrate this day, January 1!
Declare without words, "From the aged heart of time, a new king is born! Behold this king, born of the great pain of the people's sorrow."

The year's first ceremony of chanting before the Dai-Gohonzon at 8:30. Sat directly behind Sensei, expressing my many prayers and wishes. A directors meeting with the president lasted all morning. Participants were serious as they decided upon the coming year's direction. Departed the head temple with my wife at 2:30 in the afternoon. A very memorable day. A day of much reflection.

Thursday, January 3. Clear, then cloudy.

Slept soundly, until late. Opened my eyes to the noise of children in the neighborhood. Food, shelter and clothing are below standard in this area. Yet children behave like kings and queens. Happy lowlands. Impartial, cheerful children.

Read a little from Ikutaro Nishida's theses "The Intellectual World," and "Intuitive Knowledge." Leaders from Bunkyo Chapter came by in the afternoon. Pure-hearted people. They left three hours later, after drinking quite a bit. Thinking on my own about developing capable senior leaders. Two new groups, the Dolphin Group and the Elephant Group were formed. Hold expectations for their courageous efforts. Offering profound prayers for the mid-level leadership's growth this year. There is a bit of ill will between the different chapters. Leaders must cooperate based upon a broad view encompassing our entire movement, and strive to create harmony. If not, chapter members will suffer. I am going to pour all of my effort into developing the youth division.

Receiving many New Year's greeting cards.

Friday, January 4. Cloudy, then clear.

I never attend New Year's parties. In the morning, stayed in bed until nearly 10:00. Have a slight fever. Deplore the frailty of my life. Envy those who are healthy. Want to be like the Phoenix.

Took my son Hiromasa for a morning bath. It occurred to me I do not want to leave this child without a father. His life is pure and new. Left the house at 2:00. A Study Department entrance examinees' study meeting at I.'s. Seeing everyone's earnestness, I am naturally filled with admiration. Spent five hours lecturing and answering questions on the first portion of the Gosho "The Teaching Affirmed by All Buddhas Throughout Time." This year, I keenly sense the importance of researching deeply the proper way to conduct lectures. Must cultivate myself in many areas. A New Year's dinner at O.'s with some youth division members. They are pure, fresh and enterprising, ordinary and honest. Afterward, I made two stops to offer New Year's greetings, then returned home, exhausted, around midnight. The moonlight—boundlessly serene. My small, humble, warm house immersed in the golden light.

Saturday, January 5. Clear.

Another fine day. Happy. Rested through the morning—read. Various thoughts about the future arise like gathering clouds. At 2:00, lectured on the latter portion of "The Teaching Affirmed by All Buddhas Throughout Time" at I.'s. Though incapable, I gave it my all. In the evening, attended Shigi Chapter's first meeting of year. Gave guidance sincerely. There are times I hope for people's happiness and other times that feeling does not arise. Strange, the common mortal's mind.

My wife met me at Kamata Station. It was after midnight. In the small, quiet street, bathed in serene moonlight, thought of cherished musical masterpieces and poems.

Overtired, could not sleep. Wrote postcards to several friends. Concerned about Sensei's health.

Sunday, January 6. Clear.

The fourth children's group meeting. At noon. The first meeting was held at the G. restaurant. The second, third and fourth at N. restaurant. More than twenty children's groups have grown out of the original few. Feel that the more groups are formed, the more complex and lackluster the activities will become. Keenly sense the need for freshness like that of a mountain stream as well as warm, strong unity. Many still came late. Sensei was furious. Ended at 3:00. Danced to the songs "Men of Fortitude" and "Soranbushi." Played at the amusement park with my wife and my son Shirohisa until 6:00. On the way back, I bought a phonograph for ¥8,500. Played with the children until late. Tomorrow, the New Year's holiday ends and I go back to work. Must establish a plan for our living expenses.

Monday, January 7.

Instruction from Sensei on various matters all morning. He spoke of how the flourishing of Buddhism is guaranteed by foreign invasion. In the Latter Day of the Law, during the Daishonin's time, the Mongol invasion fulfilled this function. During the Latter Day of the Law, the time of the kosen-rufu of substantiation, World War II fulfilled this role. Buddhism's great mission lies in its ability to save people from suffering.

Sensei looked extremely tired. He ended by saying, "Young people must never kowtow to others." In the evening, went with A. and the chapter chief to N.'s. Discussed for at least an hour a variety of things, including the crane emblem of Nichiren Shoshu, the Treasure Ring of the Dai-Gohonzon, Nikko Shonin's turtle-shell (hexagonal) emblem and Nichimoku's pine-bamboo-plum emblem.[1] On the days I meet Sensei, I am happy; on days I cannot meet him, I am melancholy. This is a function of my life. Sincerely praying T. will go home early.

1. The crane emblem...pine-bamboo-plum emblem: The crane is a symbol adopted by Nichiren Shoshu during Japan's Edo period for purposes of protocol in government-related matters. It represents peace and longevity. The Treasure Ring, or Wheel Treasure, was an Indian symbol for the Law expounded by the Buddha. The turtle shell was the symbol for Nikko Shonin's family and also represented longevity. The pine-bamboo emblem was the symbol for Nichimoku's family; its various components represented celebration.

Thursday, January 10. Fair.

Health extremely poor. It does not improve—frustrating.

In the morning, went alone to purchase a Japan Airlines ticket for the Hokkaido guidance trip. Sensei said, "Check into the base supply of currency issued by the Bank of Japan, its holdings of foreign currencies and the velocity of circulation." At 6:30, a youth division leaders conference in the president's office. This year's basic direction and budget were announced. Dragged my exhausted body home from the station. Have spent my youth in exhaustion. Stopped on the way home to eat a bowl of *oden* [a kind of hotchpotch] at an all-night shop. Thought about Sensei. When I look back, I have been thinking about Sensei for already more than ten years.

Saturday, January 12. Cloudy, then clearing.

Cold all day. My life lacks common sense—I constantly overtax myself. This is my unstoppable course of destiny. Severe, uncowed by raging waves of diversity—the challenging path of mentor and disciple. I absolutely cannot die.

To Myoen-ji in the evening. Attended a Third Corps leaders meeting. Old friends, new friends. Will have to ask them to undertake painstaking struggles until the day we score a shining victory for the common people. N. is a good friend. A good-hearted friend. Tomorrow, I go alone to Hokkaido. The winds are cold. My finances are also bleak. Each day I spend building good fortune and wisdom is glorious.

Sunday, January 13—Wednesday, January 16.

Hokkaido—the snowy town of Yubari; the open fields of Sapporo. An enjoyable, meaningful and deeply memorable trip.

Monday, January 28. Cloudy.

On Saturday, January 19, and Sunday, January 20, I gave guidance and lectured in Osaka. Next, I embarked on a guidance tour to:

Mon.	1/21	Iwakuni City	guidance
Tue.	1/22	Tokuyama City	guidance
Wed.	1/23	Hofu City	guidance
Thu.	1/24	Ube City	guidance
Fri.	1/25	Shimonoseki City	guidance
Sat.	1/26	Hiroshima City	guidance
Sun.	1/27	Osaka City	lecture
Mon.	1/28	Returned to Tokyo on the *Swallow* express	

Will pour all my ability and effort into struggling to transform my destiny and lay the strategic groundwork for kosen-rufu. Concrete proof will be apparent one day.

Thursday, January 31. Cloudy with occasional snow.

January has gone by all too quickly. The battle is long and severe. Yet, the results will all become apparent in the course of a moment. Want to do the kind of gongyo, morning and evening, in which I can practice the profound meditation of the Lotus Sutra. Reflecting deeply upon my life, which lacks the power of concentration. There are times I feel impelled to cross the oceans, soaring into the air to boldly advance global kosen-rufu—traveling to the mysterious developing nations of Southeast Asia; to the advanced civilization of America; to the tumultuous, newly developing communist countries; to the Christian democracies of Europe; to Africa and South America—the continents of the twenty-first century; and to Australia, the land of the future. Dreams! Never die!

An evening Study Department professors meeting in the headquarters reception hall.

Resolved again to:

1. Continue reading the Gosho.
2. Establish a habit of reading good novels.
3. Write articles for *The Daibyakurenge* magazine.

Left with the board of directors. Extremely fatigued. My room is fragrant with daphne scent. Happy.

Wednesday, February 13. Fair.

Lately, I have been reflecting upon my lack of proficiency in Buddhist study. Need unremitting effort. This is the most essential requirement for leaders from now on. Want this year to be a year of reading.

Troubled over T.'s problem. Will approach it according to Sensei's guidance. M. has been very helpful. Grateful.

To the president's office in the evening. U. and I went together to report in. Afterward, Sensei treated us to tempura in Shinjuku. Another memorable day. Returned home a little before 9:00. K. and Z. came over. We talked about many things.

My quiet home, my warm home; a home overflowing with good fortune. My pure, clean home; home of youthful poetry. While it is small, this home is my great pride.

Sunday, February 17. Cloudy, then clearing.

In Numazu since yesterday for guidance. Rested my weary body at the T. Inn. The weather was cold, as was my body and mind. Boarded the 9:16 train. Arrived in Tokyo at noon. Went directly to a meeting to plan the second part of the Study Department entrance examination. Next, commenced the promotional exam for lecturers applying as assistant professors. My group had three examiners: S., Z. and myself. We administered the exam to about thirty candidates. A professors meeting in the president's office until 8:00. Many new assistant professors were determined. Read *The Politician and the Businessman*, by Y. Uninteresting. Tidied up my bookshelf for a while. My books are like my children.

Wednesday, March 6. Fair.

The cold wind blew ceaselessly. Hope winter will pass and spring will arrive as soon as possible. Feel I'm catching a cold. Slight fever continues. Read *Japan's Prime Ministers* and *How to Lead People*. Uninteresting. Abe Isenokami Masahiro was councilor to the shogun at twenty-five. In England, William ("the Younger") Pitt became prime minister at twenty-four. This accorded with the solution of national crises. The power of youth. Lately, have come to a vivid awareness that faith and human revolution are one, and human revolution and social revolution are one.

The social standard for what constitutes good and bad people contains unresolved contradictions. Must become one who can deeply and keenly perceive good and evil based upon the standard of the Mystic Law. In leading people, it is important not to make mistakes. Must fairly and objectively perceive and understand the strong points and shortcomings of people's characters, their hearts and minds and their actions. Want to protect the disadvantaged. Want to enable good people to arise. Want to support people of justice and integrity.... Toward the final victory.

Tuesday, March 19. Scattered clouds.

Heavy fatigue from last night's train trip. Suffering from physical exhaustion all day. I don't like uneventful days. It is a difficult problem to change one's destiny. Want Sensei to see the wondrous stirrings of new life. Attended A.'s afternoon wedding ceremony with Sensei. May there be a blessing on their union. After the ceremony, there was strict instruction about various matters concerning the upcoming Osaka House of Councillors election. Like a strict father's scolding. Afterward, went with Z. and others to see the movie *Flowers Do Not Grieve* playing in Shibuya. Not very interesting.

My quiet, rich and happy home. Powerful thoughts emerge as I chant daimoku.

1. Lead a life for which I need make no excuses.
2. Lead a sound and steady life.
3. Lead a healthy life.

Another day of my youth has passed.

Wednesday, March 27. Fair.

Stomach cramps kept me in bed in the morning. My wife was extremely worried; she said I should see the doctor. Went to work in the afternoon. The devil of illness.... Sorry to worry Sensei. At 4:00, attended the completion of shop B. with Sensei. Afterward, attended T.'s wedding at Myoko-ji in Shinagawa. A lonesome ceremony. Home just after 8:00. While lying down, carefully polished the Osaka House of Councillors election campaign strategy. Statistically speaking, we cannot win. Our only choice is to fight with the spirit to "lodge an arrow deep into a rock."[1] Pray, fight, open the way; forge a path.

1. "Lodge an arrow....": A reference to the story of General Stone Tiger, whose simple arrow penetrated a boulder he had mistaken for the tiger that had mauled his mother to death.

Wednesday, May 1. Cloudy with occasional sudden showers.

A warm day. Already the green month of May. Green barley grass and lotus grass. My dearest season. The spring of my twenty-ninth year. Rather than quiet pondering, my thoughts of late give rise to action. Sensei fell ill on April 30. The Gakkai's future is extremely important. This year so far has been agonizing—fierce storms of 'the three obstacles and four devils' have arisen. The House of Councillors election in Osaka was a great loss.

> No matter how many times I stand on the field of battle,
> I shall never forget today's sadness.

One day we shall definitely defeat the establishment's corrupt influence. Definitely. Attended the opening of the S. industrial plant. Another day of my youth has passed. An uneventful day.

Thursday, May 2. Overcast, with rain later on.

Relieved to see Sensei's health seems to have improved.

Light rain has fallen since afternoon. Regarding my own happiness, cannot help thinking of Tolstoy's spirit to judge illness and regret as evils.

Beginning at 8:00, a rehearsal for the sixteenth spring general meeting at Tokyo International Stadium. It went on until 10:00.

What magnificent energy—like a mighty river.

Everyone possesses hope, confidence, joy. Keenly aware of my own weakness.

Friday, May 3. Clear.

Went with my wife and her father to Tokyo International Stadium where the meeting was to be held. The power of these valiant Bodhisattvas of the Earth arose like clouds.

Sensei's health has improved. Relieved. Want him to live on and on and on—for ten or twenty more years. Praying for this in my heart—for kosen-rufu, for our sake and for humankind.

The opening ceremonies began exactly at noon. The meeting was over at 3:00.

A very exuberant, flawless general meeting.

Afterward, a follow-up gathering at G. in Meguro. A magnificent banquet attended by two hundred.

A planning meeting until late with top youth division leaders.

Was supposed to meet my wife at Kamata Station to take her shopping but did a terrible thing—made her wait for more than two hours.

Saturday, May 4. Overcast.

An emergency chapter chiefs conference at N. at 10:00 a.m. All twelve chapter chiefs and designated individuals assembled at the appointed time.

The following topics were discussed:
1. Publication of the Gosho.
2. A general pilgrimage to commemorate the completion of the Grand Lecture Hall at the head temple.
3. Sponsoring candidates for city and ward assembly elections.

Sensei kept a serious look.

Because we could not go shopping yesterday, promised to meet my wife again in the evening...but again, she had to wait for me for more than an hour in the cold. She was angry; sorry for her. From now on, I must be more careful.

Y. came by the house with her child late in the evening. A good person.

Excellent individuals are needed in the various locales. Read and pondered until late.

Sunday, May 5. Overcast.

Children's Day. Lively, pure-hearted children. Angels of humankind, treasures of the present and the future.

Played cheerfully with Shirohisa and the others all morning. Proofread the Gosho in the afternoon; lacking confidence.

Peaceful days. Society changes with each moment. Must strive hard again tomorrow, throwing my body into the battle.

Monday, May 6. Overcast.

Felt down all day, physically and spiritually. Could it be the result of missing gongyo this morning? Seriously reflected.

Faith, the Gakkai, people, the future, reality...economics, politics, culture, science, education...I sometimes randomly ponder many things.

Sensei has begun another "Orally Transmitted Teachings" lecture. My heart pounds when I listen to his fine lectures. The power of insight and foresight that derives from a grand philosophy. Words and expressions that derive from an enlightened state of life. Ashamed of myself; can only lament my own lack of ability. Left with the top leaders, feeling forlorn. Faith is not to be found in sentimentalism. Must use Shijo Kingo's faith as a mirror for myself. Rather, unless I surpass him as a leader, kosen-rufu will be impossible. Must not lose. Must never lose to obstacles and devils. Challenge myself.

Tuesday, May 7. Rain.

Light rain all day. Was told Mercury passed in front of the Sun's disk. Difficult, troubling days. In the evening, chatted with Sensei in the president's room. Received instruction on various matters. Simply amazed at his keen insight.

Attended the second student division general meeting at 7:00. Offered guidance on the following three points:

1. Awareness as Gakkai pioneers.
2. Concrete direction concerning schoolwork and Gakkai activities.
3. Kosen-rufu and the student division's future.

Returned home, talking with M. along the way. Finished reading *Autumn Window Diary* by Jiro Abe.

Wednesday, May 8. Rain.

More rain. The train was packed. My strength is all but gone. Could not even read the paper while on the train. Neither society nor my life affords me any slack. The stock market declined violently. Have lately been humming the song "Kawanaka Island." At 6:00, a farewell gathering for Chapter Chief B., who is being reassigned. Attended with Sensei. The dinner lasted until 10:00. Is M. a person of backbone? Fed up with a life of criticism. Must forge a firm, dauntless character. Returned home alone, without the company of friends.

Saturday, May 11. Rain.

Suddenly cancelled the lecture in Osaka. Spending the night in Nagoya. Informed of the strange posture of the Osaka Prosecutor's office. Talked with F., the attorney, and the Osaka senior leaders. It's been five years since I've been in the Chubu [Japan's central] region. Nagoya has a wonderful rural atmosphere. Must exert myself deeply in giving guidance here. Traveled with S., a fine person. Held a question-and-answer session at the home of T., the chapter chief, for two hours. Exhausted. A youth division leaders meeting was held afterward. Some two hundred attended.

Steady rain. Strongly sense the presence of obstacles and devils. Stayed with several leaders from Osaka at an inn located in front of the train station. Sensei is attending the First Hokkaido General Meeting. Heard he was extremely concerned about my going to Osaka. It pains me. Grateful to have such a mentor. T., the chapter chief, is a good-natured man.

Struggle; improvement; study; character; bonds among comrades. Wealth; power; factionalism.

Sunday, May 12. Rain.

Up at 8:00. Staying at the Sugitaya Inn. A dismal rain, like that of the summer rainy season — like the contents of my heart. Discussed various matters with the attorneys. A person's goodness or badness becomes apparent at a critical moment. When a critical situation occurs, I want to take an excellent stand. At 6:00, we all went to see the film *Wings of Wild Eagles*. Everyone enjoyed themselves immensely for the first time in a while. Yet, they are unaware of my own frame of mind. Took the early-morning train *Moonlight*, which left for Tokyo at 2:23 a.m. Cold inside the train. Couldn't sleep a wink. Thought about many things; pondered.

Will this year be another series of struggles with obstacles?

Monday, May 13. Cloudy.

Thinking about Sensei. Thousands of thoughts. In particular, I cannot help worrying about the Gakkai's future. Is no one aware of Sensei's sublime state of mind? Arrived in Tokyo at 9:23 a.m. Discussed several things with O., the lawyer in Tokyo. Must advance with hope. Faith; full-fledged faith.

My wife and I attended the theater at the invitation of Sensei's wife. The play, *Noren* (Shop Curtain), was the life story of a kelp merchant who displayed the indomitable Osaka spirit. This serious drama, about a man who persevered along a single path, gave rise to beautiful tears.

Utterly exhausted in body and mind. Took a taxi home with my wife. Even keeping a diary is difficult. My handwriting is getting sloppy.

Tuesday, May 14. Partly cloudy.

Physical condition very poor. My temperature is about 100° F. Happy to see my brother has found a job. Great people always make great efforts. If he would just put forth effort, then he, too, would be a great person. Sensei returned to Tokyo from Hokkaido, arriving in Ueno at 2:15. Accompanied his wife to greet him. He seemed extremely fatigued. Though we kept commenting we were tired, Sensei didn't utter a word. Spent one hour making various reports in the president's office. Clearly sensed that Sensei has made some kind of determination. Felt apprehensive and alone. Attended an evening division chiefs meeting. Thirteen new YMD corps were formed and five new YWD corps. Youth! Be solid!

The pain in my back is intense. What slander could I have committed? If I could only be healthy. Must reveal my true potential; do human revolution. I read the Gosho for a while. Very, very difficult to comprehend.

Wednesday, May 15. Fair.

The first warmth of summer. Grateful to live in a country with four seasons. People's nature varies greatly according to the changing seasons. In the afternoon, Z., Hiromasa and I went to see the Japan International Trade Fair. Surprised at the large number of people. Science is rapidly increasing its importance in society. People must not fall behind. To know the times, to live with the times and to create the times—forgetting this will lead to grave problems. Sense the arrival of the "Age of Automation" more keenly than ever before. Reported what we saw at the fair to Sensei. A scientist himself, he listened with apparent interest. "We must think about science and religion" were his only words of guidance.

Saturday, June 1. Scattered clouds.

Had a fever again this morning. 100.4° F. The past ten years or so have been filled with intense, death-defying struggles. Must do something for my health. It finally feels like summer has begun. The year is already half over. Must grow...must strengthen my faith.

In the evening, went to To'o District to give guidance. A precious gathering of ordinary people. The world of faith is the most pleasant and beautiful of realms. To give guidance is ultimately like receiving guidance myself.

Heard Sensei is resting at home. Miss him. Tomorrow is Sunday. Perhaps I can see him on Monday. Praying.

Sunday, June 2. Cloudy.

Stayed in bed until after 10:00. Slept well. My wife seemed happy, saying: "You slept well. Good! Good!" Spread out the books *Japanese History* and *World History* in the living room. The tea my wife made was particularly tasty.

Attended a Shinjuku Chapter guidance meeting in the late afternoon. How refreshed I feel after attending a meeting! The Gakkai must begin a second development period. What is needed are new capable people, a new organization and a fresh breath of air. Some critics have charged that the "Gakkai stands at a turning point." I think so as well. Yet I can only be amused at such critics, who understand nothing of the Mystic Law's profound rhythm.

Monday, June 3. Clear, becoming cloudy.

Felt pressure in my heart all day long. Terrible. Wonder if I'm aging at an extremely rapid pace. Worrisome.

Sensei came to the headquarters in the afternoon. His physical condition has worsened, and he seems to be suffering. Because his life is so important, everyone should be more concerned about him. What are his closest aides doing? Am I the only one aware of his agony? It's heartbreaking.

An evening lecture on the "Orally Transmitted Teachings." Overexerting himself, Sensei poured all his energy into the lecture. Ashamed of my own shallow learning. Home a little after 10:00.

Tuesday, June 4. Cloudy, then clear.

My fever subsided a little this morning. This is good. Cannot die until kosen-rufu is achieved. That is, I do not want to die, so long as I have a mission...or because I believe in my mission.

Proofread the Gosho in the afternoon at the headquarters. Spoke to the division chief about the inaugural student division meeting. Prime Minister Kishi returned from Southeast Asia. His words, representing the nation responsible for the war, were empty. People! What has happened? Are you wise, or are you foolish?

Youth of the Gakkai! You must forge onward! To spread the Mystic Law — to Asia. Only we possess this mission. The people of Asia await us!

Wednesday, July 17.

July 3 was the anniversary of President Toda's release from prison.

At 4:00 p.m. on this very significant anniversary, I entered the Osaka Prefectural police headquarters. The charge: door-to-door vote solicitation. I was held for fifteen days for interrogation by the prosecutors — the first few days in various cells at the police headquarters, then for ten days at the detention center.

It is clear the charges are groundless. Yet, I had no choice but to take responsibility for the actions of those under my charge. But I am outraged at the vote-buying activities of N. and the others from K. Chapter and the irresponsible attitude of the chapter leaders. They have forgotten Sensei's spirit and the Gakkai's lofty tradition. It's deplorable.

I was released today, the 17th, at 12:10 p.m. Several hundred Osaka members greeted me. Overjoyed. The Gakkai is strong. The Gakkai is right. The Gakkai is the most beautiful of organizations.

For the rest of my life, I shall never forget my friends from Tokyo who rushed to Osaka out of concern for me. There was M., W., B., F. and H.; M. from Osaka, S., T. and Y. and the others. At 1:30 p.m. went to Itami Airport to greet Sensei. Shed tears deep in my heart at my mentor's profound compassion. Aware that the concern and worry Sensei has felt for me on this occasion have been deeper than the ocean. Must, by all means, spend the rest of my life repaying my great debt of gratitude to him.

At 6:00, a special Osaka area general meeting at Nakanoshima Civic Auditorium. Some twenty thousand members gathered. I was greeted by thunderous applause, whereupon I stated my determination to advance kosen-rufu. A day I will not forget as long as I live. I offer thanks for the protection I have received.

Thursday, July 18. Rain.

Stayed at the Kansai headquarters building in Osaka. Very tired. Many people were there; thought vaguely about various matters.

Listened to Sensei's lecture for the first time in a while. Worry alone about how long Sensei will live.

Sensei! Sensei! My only wish is that you survive in good health until kosen-rufu is achieved.

I thought seriously about Sensei and about the Gakkai headquarters. I am willing to sacrifice myself. The prosecutors' interrogation was laden with schemes. Angry feelings are growing steadily stronger. We will by all means create a time when truth will win over all. Must accurately record the facts.

Wednesday, September 25. Cloudy, then rain.

It's been a little more than two months since my release from jail.

Lately, keenly sense how profoundly important an experience it was. Someday, I will record what happened for posterity. To do so, must jot down my memories.

September 22: The last sports festival of the year (in Kansai) is completed.

September 23: Stayed in Osaka.

September 24: Spent the night in Atami to attend a Traffic Control Group conference.

Thursday, September 26. Rain.

A gloomy light rain fell all day. Physical condition still very poor; my slight fever continues. Waited for S. at the headquarters in the late afternoon, but he never came. Too bad. Have now practiced this faith for ten years. What will my destiny hold over the next ten years? Life is win or lose. Cannot help sensing the approach of new storm-driven waves of difficulty.

Attended an evening Bunkyo Chapter group chiefs meeting. Discussed:

1. Human relationships.
2. Reading.
3. The spirit of offering.

A family conference at S.'s home concerning M. Everyone seems happy. Is M. also preparing to marry this spring? The arrival of spring will be a joyful occasion.

Friday, September 27. Cloudy, then clearing.

Physical condition extremely poor. My temperature is about 100.5° F. Rested at home the first half of the day. Have been polishing my

ability for ten years. Nevertheless, health is basic. Need a strong constitution. In the afternoon, received guidance on various matters from Sensei.
Ultimately, just meeting him is the most fundamental guidance in faith.

Sensei lectured on the Gosho "Letter to Toki Jonin" at the Shinagawa
Civic Hall. A youth division executive conference followed.

Afterward, met my wife who was waiting for me at Oimachi Station
and bought her a winter raincoat. ¥3,500. She looked as happy as a
child. Returned together to our quiet, happy home. At the same time,
thought about the conditions under which the Daishonin lived.

Sunday, September 29. Rain.

Tolstoy defined unhappiness as having regrets. Must make efforts to
live each day meaningfully. Lately, I am thoroughly aware of the joy of
chanting daimoku. Had better think carefully about laying the foundation for my life, my direction and planning my living expenses. Returned
in high spirits to Fuji Station with my friends. An enjoyable pilgrimage.
Leaving the others behind, I headed for Numazu to give guidance at
4:00. The members there are extremely bright. Astonished at the development they have achieved. Attended a unit leaders meeting, a group
chiefs meeting and a district chiefs meeting before returning home just
after midnight. Felt I had exerted myself diligently.

Monday, September 30. Rain.

The snow piled up upon my hat,
And the wind whipped my sleeve.
How young I was, still seeking the breast, yet alone.
Years later, this very voice commands an entire army
From the summit of Tekkai Peak.

A poem by Minamoto Yoshitsune,[1] one of my favorite historical figures. Have been reading quite a few historical war accounts.

Tomorrow, October begins; the month of clear skies.

Light rain fell all day. Went to the headquarters to make a request of
Sensei on M.'s behalf. Sensei gladly consented. Very happy.

The headquarters leaders meeting was held at 6:15 at Shinagawa Civic
Hall. A remarkable display of progress. Afterward, T., the chief of Sakai
Chapter, visited my home with his wife. Joyfully discussed the chapter's
future development. Explained various aspects of the battle plan.

My wife will become the mother of three children. As she grows heavier, so does her responsibility: striving for social and religious revolution while raising her children to be excellent individuals.

1. Minamoto Yoshitsune: See note on p. 302.

Tuesday, October 1. Cloudy.

Autumn has arrived. Ideal weather. A serene blue sky. The air is profoundly refreshing. For a moment this autumn morning, felt a genuine love for all living things.

It's becoming necessary to plan out our monthly finances. Must think about setting guidelines to provide for the children's education. Conducted the first lecture of the month in the evening. In the meeting hall at the headquarters. On the section of Nichikan's "The Threefold Secret Teaching" that enumerates the three thousand worlds in a single moment of life. Since I had received direction on the material from Sensei, I could lecture confidently. Went to M.'s house after the lecture, though I should have gone home early. I wish to help people, but I'm astonished at how easily I let others take advantage of me. Stayed up late discussing the family budget, among other things, with my wife.

Thursday, October 3. Clear.

Went to the Tokyo Gymnasium to check into "An Evening with the Youthful Supporters of Mr. K." The meeting began at 6:40. Inside the venue was confusion. A gathering of the elderly would have been preferable. Left before it was over to attend a Suginami youth division leaders meeting. While both meetings were billed as "youthful gatherings," how shallow was the former—an assemblage for fame and profit, falsehood and conservatism. The latter—a pure-hearted gathering of conviction, ideals and power like the sun. Afterward, attended a banquet with top youth division leaders at D. in Shinjuku. Returned home by taxi a little before 12:00. The children are sleeping peacefully. Their faces are so cute. Their father and mother are young. Very young. Hope they live long.

Saturday, October 5. Clear.

Left Ueno Station at 9:30 a.m. on the *Sado* express. A guidance trip to Niigata. A pleasant trip on a clear autumn day. My wife came with Shirohisa to send me off. When I see her pregnant form, I feel sorry for her. At Nagaoka Station, the members had placed a large banner reading "Welcome Chief of Staff Ikeda." Forced a smile. Feel their childlike, honest attractiveness.

Arrived at Niigata Station at 3:15. Went to O.'s house. Immediately began to talk with young men's, young women's and men's division leaders. A very small chapter. Thought everyone cannot freely exert themselves as things are. Also thought they have yet to understand the Gakkai's great ideals.

Conducted a guidance meeting for men and women at the temple at 7:00. A serious question-and-answer session that lasted close to two hours. Keenly sensed the need to reflect upon my inadequacy at verbal expression. Afterward, held a discussion with district chiefs and chapter leaders at O.'s. Spent the night, along with a few of the leaders. Talked all evening about "The Threefold Secret Teaching" and other topics, forgetting the time.

Sunday, October 6. Rain.

In the morning, woke up at 8:00 and did gongyo. My back hurt from lack of sleep. Caught the 9:00 a.m. train to Nagaoka.

Checked into Aoki Inn. Held a guidance meeting there.

The rain intensified. Held a small banquet for the group-level leaders. Danced to "Kuroda-bushi" for the first time in quite a long while. Fine people. Comrades I shall never forget as long as I live.

Departed Nagaoka Station on the 2:16 p.m. train for Ueno. Rain and more rain. Read the Gosho "On the Ten Worlds" and "On Revealing Slander." A meaningful train ride.

Arrived at Ueno Station at 7:00. My wife greeted me alone. Like a shadow is attached to the body, she appears quietly to see me off and to greet me upon my return to Tokyo—whether in rain or snow; early in the morning or in the middle of the night.

Monday, October 7. Cloudy.

Mentally and physically drained all day. Prime Minister Nehru of India is now visiting Japan. At Keio and Waseda universities, he spoke of his love of world peace and humanity and declared, "Youth are the world of tomorrow." Want to visit India, the land from which Buddhism sprung, at the earliest possible opportunity.

An "Orally Transmitted Teachings" lecture at the headquarters at 6:30. On the parts that cover the Lotus Sutra's "Devadatta," "Encouraging Devotion" and "Peaceful Practices" chapters. Sensei's excellent lecture applied to daily life from an objective standpoint, and, from a subjective standpoint, to life itself. He said that when one steadfastly embraces the Mystic Law, living itself becomes a true pleasure.

Went home early. My wife met me at Kamata Station. Wrote the fifth installment of "The Way of the Young Men's Division."

Tuesday, October 8. Cloudy with partial clearing.

Didn't see Sensei all day. Could I feel any more lonesome? Went to the head temple and visited retired High Priest Nissho. There was a news report that the Soviet Union has successfully launched a human-made satellite. With the advancement of science, leaders must always consider things from a lofty perspective.

Study. I must study. To forge the most ideal way, I must study. To Hongyo-ji at 3:00 p.m. W.'s wedding. Sent them off in grand fashion.

A youth division executive conference at 6:30.

Discussed:

1. Hokkaido youth division guidance.
2. Guidance for leaders in Kyushu and Kansai.
3. The status of the brass band.
4. The general pilgrimage in March.
5. The block system and its implementation.

Got home just after 10:00. Talked with my wife over dinner for the first time in half a year. Took a short walk, only a few steps, in our small garden.

Wednesday, October 9. Clear with scattered cloudiness.

Must take care of my health. Lately cannot store up energy for the future.

Spent the morning at Korakuen Bicycle Racing Grounds to prepare for the autumn headquarters general meeting. Lately, have felt that for the seven years since Mr. Toda was inaugurated as president, we have been facing storms of persecution by the third of the 'three powerful enemies' (those who appear wise and lofty but who out of jealousy persecute the votary of the Lotus Sutra). There was a Gosho study meeting at the headquarters at 8:00. "Essential Points on the True Object of Devotion" and "A Sage Perceives the Three Existences of Life."

Unable to meet Sensei again today. Lonesome. Heard that retired High Priest Nissho's condition is not good. Returned with some of my younger juniors. A pleasant group.

The autumn evenings are peaceful. My wife and I talked on the veranda until late. Would like to play the flute. Want to listen to the koto.

Finished writing "The Way of the Young Men's Division."

Thursday, October 10. Clear.

The moon was full tonight. When I think about the satellite flying through space, what a profoundly poetic evening it was. With my tired body, it reminded me of listening to an exquisite, mysterious melody. The joy of living. Let it always be so. Read the Gosho:

> However great the good causes one may make, or even if one reads and copies the entirety of the Lotus Sutra a thousand or ten thousand times, or attains the way of perceiving three thousand realms in a single moment of life, if one fails to denounce the enemies of the Lotus Sutra, it will be impossible to attain the way.
>
> — "ENCOURAGEMENT TO A SICK PERSON" (WND, 78)

Ultimately, the spirit of propagation, a life of propagation, is the source of the greatest, most powerful life force and vitality.

Saw Sensei today. Happy. Listened to him talk on various topics as I was embraced in his compassion.

Participated briefly in the youth division leaders conference. Afterward, attended a YMD leaders meeting at the Shinko Center in Ikebukuro. Everyone was lackluster. They appear not to be getting enough sleep. In giving guidance, leaders of the youth division must be aware of such essential points. Unless they understand their members' basic rhythm of daily life, the members will suffer. I feel as if I am the one receiving guidance.

My wife greeted me at Kamata Station. Headed for our pleasant home, where our children await.

Friday, October 11. Clear, becoming cloudy.

Overdid it today. Perhaps why I feel so out of sorts, mentally and physically. An evening lecture by President Toda at Toshima Civic Auditorium. Moved by my mentor's effortless and magnificent lecture as well as his sublime behavior. His state of life is like that alluded to in the Lotus Sutra passage that reads, "Since I in fact attained Buddhahood, [countless eons have passed]" (LS16, 225).

Came home and worked on my manuscript. Keeping meticulous notes so I can write extensively in the future. A quiet evening. Spent a long time thinking.

Saturday, October 12. Fair.

Took the 1:30 p.m. express from Tokyo Station to the head temple. Sensei, Division Chief I., Chapter Chief T., my wife and me. My thoughts turned to the Dai-Gohonzon "bestowed upon the entire world" enshrined in the Hoan-den, on this, the anniversary of its inscription. When, conjectured Sensei, will the day come that it will be enshrined in the Sho-Hondo, completing the first step in securing the foundation for kosen-rufu?

In the evening, a question-and-answer session in the head temple's reception hall. Sensei's answers were splendid. Afterward, went to the lodging where the Suginami Chapter members were staying. Then, back to the reception hall to attend a YMD meeting. Gave guidance, incorporating the lyrics of "Gojogen."

Later, attended a meeting of Osaka and Sakai chapters. Was joyfully received by everyone. Fortunate to have such friends. Gazing up at the moonlight from this Eagle Peak, will remember the happiness I feel right now for the rest of my life. *Ushitora* gongyo was conducted at 2:00 a.m. Joyfully participated. Was received by the retired high priest, Nissho, in the afternoon. A high priest of magnificent virtue. He has treated me with great fondness, and my visit with him will be my lifelong joy.

Sunday, October 13. Clear.

Fine autumn weather. The ceremony of chanting before the Dai-Gohonzon was held at 8:30 in the morning. The trial begins on the 18th. Offered a prayer for a not-guilty verdict. Have no choice but to entrust everything to the Gohonzon.

Through this, I will truly expiate my bad karma.

Attended a unit chiefs meeting in Numazu on the way back from the head temple. Along with the chapter chief, I poured my full effort into fostering the growth of capable individuals. Where the sun shines brightly, grass and trees will flourish. Convinced that where there is guidance in faith, a procession of able people will develop.

Fatigue accumulates with each passing day. If *myo* means "to revive," then how can I fail to be revitalized?

[T]his, my land, remains safe and tranquil,
constantly filled with heavenly and human beings.
The halls and pavilions in its gardens and groves
are adorned with various kinds of gems.
Jeweled trees abound in flowers and fruit

where living beings enjoy themselves at ease.

—(LS16, 230)

Monday, October 14. Fair.

Want to congratulate N. on the news of her wedding. Yet, hearing of her husband's lack of faith, I truly worry whether she will become happy.

Attended the evening Gohonzon-enshrining ceremony at F.'s. Accompanied Priest T. as far as Yokohama. Got my wife to help edit my manuscript. Worked until late. Moonlight glistens through the window. Ah! Youth's emotions and passion shine all the more brilliantly! And my wife's face is so beautiful. Both, so young. Will never forget our youth together.

Tuesday, October 15—Wednesday, October 16. Fair.

Yesterday, the retired high priest, Nissho, died. Received communication there would be an evening service for him. Sensei came directly to the head temple from Osaka, and we, from Tokyo. Severely rebuked by Sensei, who said all communication had been poor. Reflecting, I realize he was right.

The evening memorial service was held at the Renyoan at 7:00. Countless emotions. Was moved to tears watching Sensei eulogize Nissho.

Attended *ushitora* gongyo. A private funeral service was held at 10:00 a.m. on the 16th. At 11:00, the casket was removed. Can imagine what it must have been like when the Daishonin died.

Gazed upon High Priest Nissho's face one last time. Amazed at his sublime and venerable Buddha-like countenance. Returned to Tokyo with Sensei on the steam train, which left just after 3:00. In the train, received profound guidance concerning the future of the priesthood and the Gakkai.

Thursday, October 17. Cloudy, followed by light rain.

Light rain. Left Tokyo Station for Osaka on the 9:00 a.m. *Swallow* express.

Tomorrow, the trial begins. My wife accompanied me to pay her respects to the Osaka members. Though we rode third-class, it was perhaps a trip I shall never forget.

In the evening, called on A., who is ill, at home, then offered greetings at T.'s, S.'s and Y.'s.

The devilish nature of authority; the impartiality of the court; the integrity of the lawyers—had better etch all these in my mind.

Bitter cold. Was told the weather is more like December for this area. Talked with the members until late at night. They are people I will remember always.

Slept alone in the president's room at the Kansai headquarters. Close to 2:00 a.m.

Friday, October 18. Fair.

A day I will remember as long as I live. The first court session began at 2:00. It ended with the verification of the defendants' identity.

Dashed to Kobe in the evening to give guidance. Two thousand and several hundred members gathered. The battle has finally begun.

Know that now is the opportune time to advance in faith!

My friends! Advance resolutely, toward the next victory!

I, too, will fight!

Saturday, October 19. Cloudy.

Spent the night at the Kansai headquarters. Woke up early. Left Osaka Station on the 10:25 train for Kyoto. Went sightseeing to the Uji area with H. and others. Took commemorative photographs together. Returned to the Kansai headquarters on the special express.

Participated in a YMD leaders meeting, followed by a YWD district leaders meeting. Next, attended a Senba area district leaders meeting and offered guidance. Afterward, personal guidance with youth division members. A busy evening.

Faith is to exert oneself selflessly and seriously. Visited Y. at home late. An exhausting evening in Kansai. Many hundreds of thousands of members will nobly arise from here in the future. Close to 2:00 by the time I retired, totally exhausted. My wife's concern showed on her face.

Sunday, October 20. Clear.

Spent the morning meeting with friends from Kobe. Relieved to know they have been receiving benefit. In the afternoon, we all went to Takarazuka to see "The Dance of Autumn." Felt personally encouraged by this youthful, beautifully exquisite dance. Dreamt of a carefree dance of culture in the future. Made various plans with leaders at the Kansai headquarters in the late afternoon.

In the evening, boarded the 9:00 *Venus* express. Paid my respects to those kindhearted people who saw me off.

When we arrived in Kyoto at 9:30, surprised to see that many YWD members had come to greet me. They are really sweet. Praying each of them will become happy.

Boarded the sleeping car. My wife took the top bunk. Forgot about my fatigue on my first third-class sleeper.

Monday, October 21. Cloudy, then clearing.

Arrived at Tokyo Station at 7:30 in the morning. When all is said and done, riding the night train is tiring. My wife must be exhausted, too.

Ate breakfast together. Our first, memorable, four-day excursion together. Began to study *The History of Japan* with Sensei in the morning. Started with the Fujiwara Era. Reported to Sensei about various matters. My mentor's composed and dignified demeanor increases my courage a hundredfold. Want to spend my life as a person of truth and justice.

In the evening, met with Public Relations Department members in conference room #3 at the headquarters. Resolved to fight earnestly to make the seventh general meeting a meaningful one. Went home early. My wife met me at Kamata Station with the children. They are precious. Happy.

Tuesday, October 22. Fair.

In the morning, Sensei cautioned me, asking me to help F. with his work. Finished reading *The Third Eye* in the train. Sensei repeatedly advises me, "Read books!" He often says, "You should read this book," or, "Have you read that book?"

Next year, I will become the father of three. My responsibility grows steadily heavier. Now thinking about many things.

Patience — the times.

In the evening, Sensei explained that the "Expedient Means" chapter of the Lotus Sutra is like a child's castle built upon sand [when compared to the true teaching hidden in the "Life Span" chapter] and clarified the benefit of the character *ge* of *renge* in terms of attaining Buddhahood. He deeply elucidated the difference between Shakyamuni's Buddhism, its history and ideas, and the Daishonin's supreme philosophy of Nam-myoho-renge-kyo. Went to the chapter chief's house late in the evening. Discussed the appointment of chapter leaders and district chiefs. Home after midnight.

Wednesday, October 23. Clear, then cloudy for a time.

Ah! The 23rd, the day (in August) on which Zhu-ge Kong-ming died in the battle of Gojogen. Kong-ming, one of Sensei's favorite literary characters. Who can understand his state of life? I, too, wish to live my life like Komei.

A wise saying goes: "A healthy spirit dwells in a healthy body." Because such wisdom must be applied to one's actions, the principle of 'the oneness of body and mind' is correct. Did not see Sensei today. How truly lonesome I feel.

Attended a Katsushika block meeting in the evening. A problem area. First, attended a meeting of block #1, then on to a greater block chiefs meeting at K.'s home. Because our relationship is too familiar, I could not move them. Too bad. Returned, exhausted and alone, via Ueno Station. Nevertheless, the ideals and passion burning in the depths of my heart are another matter. Though it was late, my wife greeted me at Kamata Station. She is a warmhearted woman.

An article in the paper said tomorrow is United Nations Day. Some day soon, we will appear on the international stage. My fellow members! Nam-myoho-renge-kyo.

Prepared for bed; after 12:00.

Thursday, October 24. Cloudy.

A memorial vigil for High Priest Nissho at the head temple. Left Tokyo Station on the 12:00 train with Bunkyo Chapter members. Sensei and his wife arrived after leaving on the 1:30 express.

Held a leaders meeting at the Rikyo-bo lodging, which had been set up as a headquarters. Deeply moved by Sensei's consideration toward me. Vividly aware of his greatness. Overjoyed. Want to be a frank and honest youth.

Beginning at 7:00, a memorial vigil at the Reception Hall. High Priest Nichijun presided. The person leading daimoku was changed every hour. Gongyo and memorial prayers conducted until 5:00 the following morning. Some fifteen hundred attended. District-level leaders and up.

A youth division executive conference at the Jakunichi-bo lodging for the generation of youth who will play a central role. What is needed is the insight to perceive the nature of the times. Slept next to Sensei in the Rikyo-bo.

Friday, October 25. Light rain.

Was severely admonished by Sensei in the morning. Confucius said, "Nine thoughts to one word," but I haven't been putting this into practice. Had better watch myself.

At 12:10, the ceremony to bring out the casket was held in the Reception Hall. Then, the main funeral ceremony was held before the Sutra Repository. Was moved by the service, which lasted more than two hours and was held in accord with ancient tradition.

Heartbroken to see Sensei and his wife in tears, purely bidding their final farewell to Nissho. They are true children of the Daishonin. Because Fuji Station was extremely crowded, took a car with some of the senior leaders to Numazu.

Oh, how things change. Common mortals reflect the general principle that all is transient, nothing is permanent. In light of the Mystic Law, this principle becomes the four virtues—eternity, happiness, true self and purity. I, my wife, my mentor and my friends—several decades from now, we will all have passed from this world. Impermanence.

Saturday, October 26—Sunday, October 27. Rain.

Overslept.

Rushed to Ueno Station with my wife, Hiromasa and Shirohisa. To Kanazawa, Takaoka and Toyama for the first time for lectures and guidance. As members of group #3, we traveled to the Shin'etsu and Hokuriku areas.

Arrived in Kanazawa at 7:15 p.m. Went directly to a guidance meeting. About three hundred attended.

A guidance meeting was held in Takaoka at 1:00 p.m. on the 27th. With three hundred participants. Another guidance meeting in Toyama began at 6:30. Really disappointed that I could not conduct a lecture.

I am a messenger of the Tathagata[1]—a great honor. Must not be arrogant. Must not become bigheaded. Must have a state of life and patience like flowing water.

Gazing out the train window, pondered what it would be like to travel along the Chikuma River.

Thought about the dreams of the rugged young men who fought in the battle of Kawanaka Island.[2]

Recalled the fourteen-generation history of Maeda family rule in Kanazawa. Thought about poets, shoguns, warrior generals, politicians.

The Hokuriku area has also begun to reverberate with the sounds of kosen-rufu.

1. Tathagata: (Skt) "Thus Come One." One of the ten honorable titles of the Buddha. See glossary.

2. Battle of Kawanaka Island: A series of inconclusive engagements fought between the armies of two of the most prominent lords of the Sengoku period (1467–1568).

Monday, October 28. Cloudy, then clearing.

Arrived in Ueno at 7:31 in the morning. Just when I thought no one was there, I saw my wife. The third-class sleeper is great. Will use it from now on.

To the headquarters in the afternoon to report to Sensei. While he appeared in good spirits, I sensed he was preparing himself fundamentally for something. Want to be of excellent service to him until the very end.

"I will leave such matters as personnel decisions to the general director and others," he said. A good plan; yet, it saddens me.

Attended a youth division guidance meeting at night. Everyone had a gloomy complexion. Must let them rest well. They are great warriors of the future. Leaders.

Afterward, met over dinner with executive leaders, the general director and other directors.

Tuesday, October 29. Rain.

Overslept. Was it from taking the night train yesterday? Every joint in my body aches.

"I've been waiting for you," Sensei said with a stern look when I arrived at the morning study session. As his disciple, I have absolutely no excuse. Reflected seriously. He told me a story of bravery by a lone samurai during the Battle of Yamazaki. Is Sensei using this example to describe his own state of mind?

To Jozai-ji at 4:00 to attend M.'s wedding. As a senior in faith, must earnestly consider the marital plans of many youth. An important first step in life. To Byakuren temple afterward for a group chiefs meeting. Everyone is bright and cheerful. The power of these pivotal leaders is the power of kosen-rufu.

Stopped at a stand on the way home from the station where I ate eighteen barbecued beef skewers. My stomach hurts. Had better control my appetite.

Wednesday, October 30. Cloudy.

Bothered by a stomachache all morning. Wanted to go home.

An afternoon executive conference at N. Discussed the general meeting and other subjects. Did not enjoy the meeting, due to my poor physical state.

Borrowed N.'s bicycle in the evening to go to Katsushika block. Lectured on "Letter from Sado" in one location and offered guidance to the block chiefs in another. Want it to become an excellent, happy block organization.

This month, my living expenses are in the red. Never any time to rest.

Friday, November 1. Clear.

Clear skies —

Boarded the *Sparrow* special express at Yokohama Station. To Wakayama for guidance.

Finished reading *Record of the Taiko*. Tokugawa Ieyasu's military discipline and organization were like the autumn frost. Considered Hideyoshi's fresh, familylike approach, like the open sky. Perhaps I am more like the latter. Nevertheless, Hideyoshi's family reign lasted only one generation, while Tokugawa rule endured for fifteen generations. Cannot forget both men's strong points.

The special express left Nanba at 5:00, heading for Wakayama. Arrived at 6:10. Rested about a half hour, then went to Wakayama Junior High School auditorium. About eighteen hundred attended, I was told. It has the qualities of an excellent chapter. Need to build a temple here as well. Stayed at an inn along the beautiful Wakayama coastline, a national park. Spent the night there. Had an intimate dinner with the local leaders.

Saturday, November 2. Clear.

Took a bath in the morning. A clear autumn day; the sunlight sparkled on the vast ocean expanse. Repeatedly taken in by the magnificent spectacle of waves shimmering gold and silver in the sun. Rented a boat and made a trip along the shoreline. Everyone seemed to be truly enjoying themselves. I, too, was happy.

Paid a visit to T.'s afterward; then, on to M.'s. They are both indispensable people for Wakayama. Visited Tanabe and Shirahama with Chapter Chief A. Heard this is Japan's oldest hot spring resort. Held a question-and-answer session at 7:00 in Tanabe. Was told the attendees numbered one thousand and several hundred. With the feeling, "Now is my last moment," I poured all my power and energy into giving guidance. Afterward, spent the night in Shirahama. Many leaders visited.

Sunday, November 3. Fair.

Day of culture. A superbly clear autumn day. Strolled along the Shirahama shoreline in the morning. Rejuvenating. Went to the wharf at 9:30 to board a sea plane. Took off from the water ten minutes later. There were six on board, including the pilot. Looking down from the cloudless sky upon the greenery of Kii peninsula set against the blue of the ocean, it was like viewing a picture postcard. Set down at a landing strip in Sakai just before 11:00. Surprised and embarrassed at the large number of members who came to greet us. Headed directly for the Kansai headquarters.

Very busy until evening. Lectures, interviews and guidance to the YMD, the YWD and Kyoto Chapter. A fulfilling day.

An Osaka Chapter general meeting at Nakanoshima Civic Auditorium at 7:00 p.m. Angered at their outmoded way of speaking and managing activities. Took the night train *Venus*, reluctantly leaving my beloved Kansai behind.

Monday, November 4. Cloudy.

Arrived at Tokyo Station at 7:30 in the morning. Taking the night train is certainly exhausting. Went with M. and N. for a morning bath at Tokyo Hot Springs, then had breakfast. My exhaustion eventually caught up with me and became a problem. Wanted to sleep.

Sensei left at 3:00 for Osaka on Japan Airlines. My wife and I saw him off. The headquarters building seemed somehow desolate. Keenly feel the need to create a new, strong organizational structure. Is no one capable of accomplishing this at present?

Dinner with leaders in Shinjuku. It included a planning meeting. Today again, my wife came with Shirohisa to greet me in the evening. Grateful.

Tuesday, November 5. Clear, then cloudy later.

Heard Sensei has been extremely fatigued while in Kansai. Very sorry. He has lead a tumultuous life. We, his disciples, have it too easy. I must, by all means, repay the debt of gratitude I owe my mentor.

Attended M.'s wedding in the afternoon at Jozai-ji. Heartily offered my congratulations.

An evening meeting for Study Department lecturers. Studied four passages from Nichikan's "Teaching for the Latter Day." All were serious.

Afterward, attended the Johoku District general meeting at Jozai-ji.

An enjoyable day. To become healthy, it is most important that I get enough sleep. Had better get to sleep early tonight.

Wednesday, November 6. Partly cloudy.

Overdoing it every day. To gain abundant life force, morning and evening gongyo and chanting daimoku are basic. Is my personal faith powerful enough to encompass both practice for oneself and for others? Afraid that it is not.

Have now entered the Kamakura period in the morning study sessions. Must not forget to study throughout my life. Sensei returned to Tokyo on an afternoon flight. He looks very fatigued. Day by day, the Gakkai is entering an important period of rapid growth. No one realizes this. They are all too carefree.

Many gossip or denounce me behind my back. Nevertheless, I have my own convictions and standards. This cannot be helped. In the future, the truth will become apparent.

Thursday, November 7. Cloudy, then clearing.

At 6:00 p.m., a run-through for the seventeenth fall headquarters general meeting at Korakuen Bicycle Racing Grounds. Though the moonlight was beautiful, there was no time to gaze at it and compose poetry. Enjoy thinking about the limitless cosmos.

Commemorating the Russian Revolution's fortieth anniversary, the Soviet Union has launched an artificial satellite. Nature is magnificent; humankind's power and ability to create an artificial satellite is also magnificent.

Home after 11:00. Getting cold. Admonished Chapter Chief M. and H. about M.'s failure. It could not be helped. Want them definitely to change poison into medicine. Without realizing it, I have now filled an entire notebook with random notes.

Friday, November 8. Fair.

The seventeenth fall headquarters general meeting. Tokyo—Korakuen Bicycle Racing Grounds. The meeting began at noon, with opening words and an entrance procession. YMD, YWD, headquarters flag and chapter flags—in that order. About seventy thousand participants. A great success.

Sensei seems extremely exhausted. His face is pale. I, too, am terribly fatigued. The pain in my back is like fire.

A follow-up meeting was held at N. at 4:00, with priests and top leaders attending. Afterward, attended a YWD district leaders meeting and a YMD district leaders meeting. Everyone's spirits seem to soar to the sky. Trust them. It is reasonable to expect that such physically and spiritually dynamic youth will be capable of creating a bright future. They grow splendidly with each moment.

The moonlight is pure; the wind, bitter. A mysterious painting upon this moment of my life's canvas. My house is quiet.

Must not allow elitist or privileged groups to emerge within the Gakkai. Particularly, within the Culture Department and the women's division.

Saturday, November 9. Clear.

A typically clear Japanese autumn sky. Want to live with strength. Left Tokyo Station at 1:30 p.m. on the express to Taiseki-ji. To spend my life with the greatest leader in the world, talk with him and live alongside him, makes me the happiest person in the world. Met T. in the train. Sensei said, "Introduce us!" then assuredly said: "If you are an expert on roads, then, focusing on roads in Japan alone is still thinking too small. Please link together as one the roads of the Orient—Korea, China and India." T. said, "I will rely on you for the realm of the metaphysical, but I will attend to the concrete realities myself," to which Sensei replied, "Yes, but one can only begin to accomplish things in the physical realm when firmly grounded in the metaphysical."

Conducted a question-and-answer session at the head temple—no vitality at all. Caught a cold. Attended a meeting of members from Bunkyo, Tsukiji, Osaka and Sakai chapters. Deeply aware of my limitations as a common mortal. Astounded by the unfathomable depth and breadth of Sensei's life force.

Slept at the Rikyo-bo lodging. To bed at 12:00. Did not attend *ushi-tora* gongyo.

Sunday, November 10. Rain.

Awoke at 6:40. Feeling feverish. Talked with Sensei at the Rikyo-bo. Can anyone help shedding tears at the depth of his compassion?

Ah! He is like Zhu-ge Kong-ming[1] facing his final battle. Deep autumn night.

The ceremony of chanting before the Dai-Gohonzon was held at 8:30. I did gongyo directly behind Sensei. While High Priest Nichijun visits Kansai, Priest Nittatsu Hosoi is filling in. A strong, mysterious sense of the future. Must become a great asset for kosen-rufu.

Climbed to the roof of the Grand Lecture Hall. A magnificent view. Visited Nissho's tomb. Fondly remember him. Received a talk from Sensei for one hour over lunch at the Rikyo-bo.

Eternal life. The fundamental principle for living in this world. The power of the Mystic Law and the Buddhist principle that we can be born wherever we wish.

On the way back from the head temple, attended a Thirty-fifth Corps meeting in Tsurumi. The meeting ended at 10:00. Returned home, exhausted. Study. Must study.

1. Kong-ming: See note on p. 219.

Monday, November 11. Rain.

A slight fever in the morning. My wife is very worried. When I think about the future, it is clear there will be many hardships. Left for Ajiro in Ito from in front of the headquarters at 1:00. The fall staff outing. Everyone seemed to enjoy themselves. I was in agony. From the head temple, Sensei went directly to Atami to recuperate. He was not on the bus with us.

The sights along the coast of Izu. Tangerine fields; beautiful scenery. The freshness of nature. Neither planned nor artificial. Spontaneous, innate.

We arrived just before 5:00. A dinner began at 7:00. There were quizzes and the like. Everyone seemed to have a good time.

Took a hot-spring bath for the first time in a while. Below my room is the raging sea.

The following day: Arrived back in Tokyo at 8:00 in the evening. Along the way, we picked tangerines, and I took many photographs. If they come out OK, I'll give them to everyone. Last night Sensei danced at the reception, but this morning he looked very out of sorts. Was extremely worried on the train. How will he be a year from now? Praying for him with the spirit "let them live out their lives" (LS16, 228).

Wednesday, November 13. Clear, becoming cloudy later.

Missed gongyo in the morning. Very tired. Could not meet with Sensei. Was told he was resting all day in conference room #1. He seems to be growing weaker. Such desolation, sadness.

Feel a tautness in my heart when I think of the Soka Gakkai's future. Above all, must enable the Gakkai to develop. Must forge ahead, placing faith first and foremost. Strong faith and the power of practice.

To the headquarters at 5:00. Missed Sensei. Truly miserable. To Katsushika block in the evening. Made rounds to two meeting places.

Guidance devoid of life force does not move people. Guidance in faith has nothing to do with intellectual knowledge or learning. The state of one's life; the dynamism of one's life—this is fundamental. Must care for my health, as my mission grows heavier and heavier.

Friday, November 15. Clear, then partly cloudy.

Met with Sensei in the afternoon in the headquarters conference room #1.

Heard his thoughts on the following:
1. Shakyamuni, the founder of Buddhism.
2. Capitalism.
3. Communism.
4. Politics in the future.

Cannot help feeling that Sensei's guidance has become all the more mysterious and profound.

"I have emerged victorious from my two years in prison. We have now accomplished a membership of 750,000 households," he told me.

"Daisaku, about your future…," he said, "It is shameful for a man to be defeated in battle."

The last day of the block campaign in Katsushika. Visited Block #1 and Block #2. Took a commemorative photo with youth division members. Returned home via Arakawa, arriving around midnight. Yaguchi's mother was visiting. Talked with her about the future. She is kind-hearted.

Sensei said, "When I was in jail, I wrote to my mother, saying 'As long as I exist, you are rich; Mother, don't despair!'"

I, too, am a disciple of Sensei.

Saturday, November 16. Clear; cloudy later.

Sensei's health is poor. I, too, am in poor shape, both physically and spiritually. When will I enjoy the fresh breezes of spring? In the evening, a YWD unit chiefs meeting and interviews for YMD leaders. Want to spend my life living and fighting beside the youth. In this life, I will follow a golden path. Together with seeking, creative and pure young people.

Practice. Study.

Home close to 1:00 a.m. Hiromasa and Shirohisa sleeping soundly.

How will they grow up? What will they be like in ten or twenty years? Who can tell? Only the Gohonzon knows.

The "Life Span" chapter reads:

> In order to save living beings,
> as an expedient means I appear to enter nirvana
> but in truth I do not pass into extinction.
> I am always here, preaching the Law.
> —(LS16, 229)

Sunday, November 17. Rain.

Felt chest pains this morning. Woke up early. At 5:00, my wife said. Went back to sleep. Worked on my article without eating. Felt nauseated, perhaps from smoking too much. Lately, have been thinking about how I will live the next fifty or so years of my life. The difficulty of living vibrantly and energetically, day after day and month after month. Worked on the continuation of my article until after 2:00. My wife said she doesn't feel well. Worried.

Monday, November 18. Rain; then cloudy with no rain.

The ceremony commemorating the fourteenth anniversary of President Makiguchi's death. The place: Jozai-ji in Ikebukuro. Sensei's condition suddenly became worse. Regret I did not stop by to check on him at home.

Participated in a panel discussion for the *Seikyo Shimbun* on the theme of block-oriented activities. It is easy to tell the difference between someone living within the Soka Gakkai mainstream and someone who has departed from it.

> *Through Sensei's power, we have grown this much.*
> *Through Sensei's power, we have opened the life-condition of the*
>   *Mystic Law.*
> *Through Sensei's power, we can manifest our own power.*

The debt of gratitude I owe Sensei as my mentor is higher than a mountain. Deeper than the ocean. I must not forget this. Will leave a historical record of my superb mentor for the entire world. This, I firmly pledge.

After leaving Jozai-ji, visited the Yaguchi household. A bright and cheerful family, though they are unaware of my intent. Must polish and discipline myself. Must do battle with my own weakness.

Tuesday, November 19. Cloudy.

My mentor's health has weakened extremely. Is it the devil of illness, or is it the devil of death? He has become excruciatingly thin.

Rushed to the headquarters in the afternoon. Met with Sensei. Tried to persuade him, from the bottom of my heart, to cancel his plan to attend the opening and Gohonzon-enshrining ceremonies for the new temple in Hiroshima. Undaunted, he reproached me:

"As an emissary of the Gohonzon, I cannot cancel something I have agreed upon. As a man, I must go, even if it kills me. Isn't this, Daisaku, what is meant by genuine faith?"

My tears flow at his strict guidance.

"The high priest is coming, and four thousand members will be waiting. Dai, even if it kills me, you must let me go. If I die, then take care of things with everybody afterward. If I return alive, then, with a fresh determination, we'll create a new organization. What happens next depends only on the Buddha's wisdom."

Someone came in, and the conversation between mentor and disciple ended amid tears.

Attended a Fortieth Corps meeting at Jozai-ji in the evening. Low spirits. "I understand the suffering of youth more than anyone," I said. Talked about problems with time and finances. Passionately instructed them to challenge themselves for the next five years.

Returned home just before midnight. The house is quiet.

Wednesday, November 20. Mostly clear, scattered clouds.

The cold has intensified. Has winter finally arrived? Sensei is resting at home. Extreme illness has prevented him from going to Hiroshima after all. I wonder how he is taking it. Rather, I think it is for the best. Nevertheless, his resolute guidance will remain in my life forever.

Happy to hear that Dr. H. came by last night to examine him. Can only chant to the Gohonzon for Sensei to live long. Read *Collected Works of Chikamatsu Monzaemon*. Though he is not a favorite of mine, I am surprised at the excellence of his style and descriptiveness. He may be one of Japan's great literary masters.

A sense of mission and hope is welling up from deep within me that sometime during my lifetime, I will record for posterity a record of President Toda's life. Want my mind to become clear and precise. In the quiet of the late night, my wife, beautiful in her Japanese kimono, brings me tea. The clock reads 1:10 a.m.

Thursday, November 21. Fair.

Worried about Sensei all day. When I consider the Gakkai's future, I realize I, too, have hit rock bottom in terms of health, nerves and fatigue. Visited barber shop in the early evening. Somewhat refreshed.

Day after day is a battle of human revolution. Like a human projectile, I will throw myself into battle again today and prevail while chanting daimoku. This is my entire life; the ultimate essence of faith.

6:30 p.m.—a youth division leaders meeting. Toshima Civic Auditorium:

1. Aiming toward next year's youth division general meeting.
2. Promoting an increase in division membership.
3. Developing mid-level leaders.

The spirit of the youth division is robust. The future is sound. The Gakkai is right and just. Throughout my life, I will face the storms with these youth. Do not fear the storm!

Saturday, November 23. Fine weather.

The YWD general meeting held at the Kawasaki Civic Auditorium. The meeting began at 1:00 p.m. Sensei did not attend. A sad, forlorn general meeting. Is this evidence that the Gakkai has entered an important new stage? During the meeting, heard a report that the retired high priest Nichiko Hori has died. He was ninety-one, the report said.

The general meeting centered on the theme of President Toda's "Declaration for the Abolition of Nuclear Weapons." I also talked about the atomic bomb.

Resolved during my opening words that next year's general meeting will be held in the Tokyo Gymnasium at the Meiji Shrine Outer Garden, the finest such garden in Asia, where we will welcome Sensei. The meeting ended at 3:30.

An executive conference at F. until late in the evening. My wife went to Sensei's home in Meguro to check on him. His condition did not seem good, she told me. Greatly concerned. Deeply regret not having gone to Sensei's home to report. Extremely exhausted.

Monday, November 25. Clear.

Morning gongyo is difficult, both spiritually and physically. Received a message from Sensei saying, "Look after things well while I'm away."

Sensei! Please don't die until kosen-rufu is achieved! I, too, must survive. Deeply, powerfully determined. Quietly, naturally reflected on Sensei's guidance: how to view the times; how to raise able individuals; how to judge a person's character; the merits and weaknesses of Nobunaga's leadership; of Hideyoshi's and Ieyasu's.

An evening Bunkyo Chapter leaders meeting. There are many leaders there now whom I do not know. Amazed. Clearly sense the crucial need for one-on-one guidance in faith.

To T.'s home afterward. A bright and happy family, as always. Ten years from now, fragrant flowers of benefit will surely blossom. Gave them a copy of the Gosho.

Wednesday, November 27. Clear.

Left for Hatake yesterday at 3:00. Attended a private funeral service for Nichiko Hori. Spent the night at the Takahashi Inn. My stomach is upset, perhaps from smoking too many cigarettes. This may be part of building a foundation during my youth, but I must not destroy my health.

High Priest Nichijun led gongyo at 1:00 p.m. at Sessen Manor. Later, there was gongyo and daimoku led by General Administrator Hosoi.

At 2:00, the casket was brought out.

His sublime countenance at death is that of a great philosopher of this century who, throughout his ninety-one years, devoted himself to an exhaustive study of the profound principles of this great Buddhism. Boundlessly moved. It is clear-cut proof of the power of Buddhism. We recently bid farewell to Nissho, and now we pay our last respects to Nichiko. It's as if the grand stage is changing in preparation for kosen-rufu. I have one request [of Nichiko]: that you continue to encourage and guide me until the day of kosen-rufu, and when I die, that you will take my childish hand and welcome me.

Arrived in Tokyo at 6:00. Fatigue prevented me from attending the youth division meeting in Katsushika Ward; went straight home. Decided to go to bed, feeling downcast at having missed the meeting.

Thursday, November 28. Clear.

A funeral service at 9:00 a.m. at the home of N. in Urayasu. The death of N.'s mother. She displayed the superb countenance of Buddhahood.

K. visited in the afternoon. Though he has been critical in the past, he is now extremely friendly. Tens of thousands of people who were once our enemies are now our friends. In the future, as well, millions of our critics will definitely become our allies and join the ranks of kosen-rufu. This is a great universal principle.

Attended a YMD district leaders meeting, a chapter leaders meeting and a corps chiefs meeting in the evening. The time is coming for the youth division to reveal its true potential. Resolved to ponder deeply the next stage of the organization's development. The youth division leaders themselves have stopped growing. One reason is they lack direction. The second is that they lack dialogue with their mentor. The third, among others, is that their seniors don't instill them with confidence.

My mentor's physical condition is not good. Yet no one is concerned about the gravity of Sensei's illness. They simply view his recovery as a foregone conclusion. Cannot help thinking of this as shallow. Can only sense the future, the prospects for kosen-rufu, the placement of personnel and the deadlock we now face. Frightening. Sad. I never forget Sensei's guidance, even in my sleep.

Saturday, November 30. Clear.

The monthly headquarters leaders meeting at Shinagawa Public Auditorium. Sensei did not make an appearance. We must now stand up to fulfill our great mission. We must hold aloft the torch of kosen-rufu Sensei has lit for us. Leaders must never look upon the Gakkai as their personal possession.

Went to Sensei's home in Meguro after the meeting to check on his condition. Relieved to find him in high spirits. His powerful life force, however, which usually seems capable of moving the earth, now seems to be waning. Profoundly sad. Touched by how diligently his wife nurses him and the modesty of his living quarters. Returning home, my wife and I talked until late about Sensei's circumstances. Pureheartedly, like children.

Sunday, December 1. Cloudy.

Left Tokyo Station on the *Swallow* express for Osaka to give a lecture. Traveled with H. and a few others. A dreary trip; no one spoke. We attended a leaders meeting in Kyoto. Everyone seemed sincerely happy to see us.

I love Kyoto. Afterward, enjoyed listening to records at S.'s house. Youthfulness and vibrant hope showed on everyone's face.

Monday, December 2. Cloudy.

Woke up early. Is there not a single day's rest for my nerves? I can do nothing about it amid such continuous responsibility and hard work.

The Kyoto leaders came over at around 9:00. They are all good people. The women are all very refined and dignified.

Y., too, is a really fine person. Had an earnest discussion.

Left for the Kansai headquarters a little before 1:00. Lectured on Nichikan's "Teaching For the Latter Day" in the headquarters meeting room. Gave a strict interpretation directed toward leaders. The leaders, however, seemed bewildered.

Attended an evening Sakai Chapter leaders meeting. Went to an Amagasa leaders meeting immediately afterward. Rushed off to a general block meeting when it was over.

Today was another regret-free battle for the Law. After the meeting, arrangements were made for a dinner party. Strictly admonished them, saying that at Gakkai meetings, it absolutely is not necessary to give special treatment to leaders, no matter who they are. Their faces turned pale. Felt sorry for the leaders and the women's division members.

Want next year to be a "year of victory." Many criticize the Gakkai.

Carl Hilty said: "Arrogance is always commensurate with foolishness. Pride always goes before a fall. An arrogant person is already defeated."

Youth who live to change society must never fear storms of obstacles. Stayed the night alone at the Kansai headquarters.

Tuesday, December 3. Clear, then cloudy.

A slight fever all day. Cannot bring forth any vitality, physically or spiritually. Today's ride on the express back to Tokyo was extremely tiring. Received a report Sensei's condition has not improved at all. Worried. Worried.

A general lecture at 6:00 p.m. There were protests that my lecture differed from the explanation in *The Daibyakurenge*.

Extreme care is necessary in writing explanations. The written word is frighteningly powerful.

It's getting cold—at the headquarters, in the street and in my house as well. On the other side of winter the bright sunshine of spring awaits. Life always faces the bitter north wind and awaits the coming of spring.

Life and society are complex. But life is long, and society, vast. Without fear of failure, must polish my body and mind while being buffeted by the great north wind. While walking or riding on the train, I ponder such principles as 'all is changing, nothing is constant' and the four virtues—eternity, happiness, true self and purity.

Sensei, I can only await your recovery. In my heart, I hear my mentor's words, "Fight boldly again today, and then again tomorrow!" and "Spur yourself on, advance!" To bed—is it already 1:00?

Wednesday, December 4. Clear, then cloudy.

Want to hear Sensei's voice. Haven't seen him for some time. Such a lonely feeling.

My only life is to fight, advance and survive alongside my mentor. I know I owe my life to my mentor.

An evening conference at the headquarters. I feel the Gakkai is falling behind in its pace. Is this acceptable?

Until ten:	My childhood, as the son of a seaweed farmer.
Until twenty:	Developed self-awareness, battled the devil of illness.
Until thirty:	Buddhist practice and study; fighting to destroy the devil of illness.
Until forty:	Perfect my Buddhist study; perfect my Buddhist practice.
Until fifty:	Make my declaration to society.
Until sixty:	Complete the foundation of kosen-rufu in Japan.

Many thoughts. Signposts for the future.

Now that I am approaching my thirties, I ponder alone how many of my life's goals I have completed.

Thursday, December 5. Rain.

A slight fever. A dark and gloomy day.

Spent the whole day battling myself; fighting for kosen-rufu. Way behind in writing my article. Very troubling.

Keenly aware of the excellence of President Makiguchi's and President Toda's scholarship. Lament my own lack of ability. Have no choice but to do human revolution.

Attended a YMD group chiefs meeting in the evening. Talked about Eta Benzo, the pioneer of Obihiro.

> *Boldly, I set my heart on the Northern Sea.*
> *Let the wind blow!*
> *Let the waves rise!*

This verse speaks of our destiny. Afterward, attended a YWD leaders meeting. Told them, "Whether a woman has achieved happiness in life will be apparent in her forties."

Arrived home just before 11:00. Worked on my manuscript until 2:00. Regret my lack of endurance.

Proficiency in Buddhist study and eloquence in discourse are the greatest weapons.

Friday, December 6. Cloudy.

A warm day. Like spring.

Sense the approach of a great turning point for the Gakkai. Is anyone aware of the important course we shall embark upon?

Attended an evening Bunkyo Chapter district chiefs meeting. All in high spirits. Trust them. Must take good care of these important Gakkai leaders.

Gave a Gosho lecture. All listened earnestly. Tonight, will go to bed early. Will rest well. To prepare for the campaign.

Monday, December 9. Clear, with occasional clouds.

A cold day. When Sensei is not active, the Gakkai is somehow quiet. Asking myself whether this is acceptable.

Must increase my life force with daimoku. "*Myo* means 'to revive.'"

In the morning, a *Seikyo Shimbun* panel discussion titled "Perspectives on the 705th anniversary of the establishment of True Buddhism."

To Y.'s in the evening to bring a year-end gift. Talked until late. On the 12th, the main funeral service for High Priest Nichiko Hori will be held at the head temple. My last pilgrimage this year. Wish to offer him a heartfelt send-off to Eagle Peak. Did a fulfilling gongyo. Read.

Tuesday, December 10. Clear.

The news of the double suicide of young lovers shocked society. They were both nineteen. A bitter end to their passionate and sensitive youth. Unfortunate.

Went to Sensei's house in the morning. Stayed almost an hour and a half. Dr. H. had just arrived. The doctor said Sensei appears to be doing very well. Tears of joy.

Treated to two rice cakes from Hokkaido. My mentor's simple abode.... The sharpness of Sensei's eyes, the strength of his life force to live on, are frightening.

In the afternoon, went to Myoko-ji in Shinagawa to make an offering on the first anniversary of my father's death. Went with my brother, my wife and our two children.

In the evening, a corps chiefs meeting in preparation for the Sixth Youth Division General Meeting. The meeting, a meaningful one, lasted until after 8:00. If they maintain the same degree of earnestness as today, then, according to the concept of 'consistency from beginning to end,' the general meeting ought to be a great success.

An important cause for victory is determined by the progress of the planning phase. Returned home a little before 11:00 p.m. My quiet home. My warm home — where my fatigue is naturally relieved.

Wednesday, December 11. Clear.

A board of directors meeting from early evening. Discussed next year's events, the status of pledged contributions as well as the reinstatement of members expelled from the organization.

Afterward, went to a skewered chicken restaurant in Meguro with the general director and other directors. An insipid gathering. Dislike those who let themselves go after a few drinks.

Got home just after 10:00. Z. came to visit. He stayed until late. Tired. Little time left to read. Too bad.

Read about the battle strategies of the Chinese Communist Party:

> *If the enemy advances*
> *   we retreat.*
> *If the enemy holds its position*
> *   we harass.*
> *If the enemy is tired*
> *   we attack.*
> *If the enemy retreats*
> *   we pursue.*

To bed, nearly 3:00. Want physical stamina. This is what I want.

Sunday, December 15. Cloudy.

On December 12, took the 1:30 p.m. express from Tokyo to the head temple for High Priest Nichiko's main funeral service. The service began at 7:00 p.m.

Spent the 13th and 14th at the head temple. Was granted a ceremony of chanting before the Dai-Gohonzon at 1:30 p.m. Prayed for

Sensei's health, for the youth division and for my family.

On the evening of the 14th, attended a meeting in Yoshihara City in Shizuoka Prefecture—a group of members connected with Bunkyo Chapter.

No spirit or vigor. Need to dispatch a capable leader to this area.

Returned home late at night. My wife waited up for me, sewing.

A beautiful night. Want to build a family vulnerable to no one, dependent upon no one.

Yes! Will advance tomorrow again, even if only an inch or two.

Monday, December 16. Clear.

Less and less frequent are the days I can meet Sensei. Lonely.

A strict phone call from Sensei this afternoon. He had been waiting for various reports.

The Sixth Youth Division General Meeting was held at 6:00. Sensei did not attend after all. Too bad. Disappointing. Some twenty thousand youth gathered at the Tokyo Sports Arena.

The meeting place was a crucible of thunderous enthusiasm. Here lies the future of the youth division, whose members will shoulder the next era. At 8:30, the meeting ended. Feel all the more responsible to protect and watch over these young people. Exhausted.

Because it's already too late today, will report to Sensei first thing in the morning.

Encouraged a youth being browbeaten by his superiors at work and by his seniors in the organization. Signed a book and presented it to him as a gift. Relieved to see his cheerful expression. Must strengthen my power to protect and support such young people.

Home at 11:00.

Tuesday, December 17. Mostly clear with occasional clouds.

The general director stopped by in the morning. He brought his dog with him. Left for Sensei's house in Meguro at 8:00. He talked with us for about an hour. Reported on yesterday's general meeting and other matters. Sensei treated us to strawberries. He said, "Daisaku, I want to fight for the next seven years until we attain a membership of two million households." "I will fight resolutely, with a hundred times the courage," I replied.

Nevertheless, in the depths of my life I feel a hint of loneliness. My sadness will not disappear. How long will Sensei live? What is his condition? Ah, how distressing. How miserable. How terribly regrettable. Sensei, I know. I do.

A dinner meeting with youth division leaders at H. I treated.

Back to my happy, quiet home. Wanted to begin reading early, so I hurriedly wrote replies to three letters.

Wednesday, December 18. Showers, then clearing.

Finished rereading *Record of the Taiko*. Do the principles contained here apply to our modern society?

Had a fever all day. A daily battle against the devil of illness. Decided to reread *Collected Works of George A. Gamow*. Transcending my past preconceptions about Buddhism, I steadily realize the greatness of this Buddhism of sowing.

As my mentor always says, "The more science advances, the easier it will be to prove the profound significance of this great Buddhism."

An early evening chapter administrators meeting at my house. A serious conference attended by the chapter chief.

Tired. Truly exhausted.

1. Discussed the basic direction for the coming year.
2. To be a leader means to have confidence.
3. The mysterious nature of life, which is in a constant state of flux.
4. The necessity of the Gakkai accomplishing great change in this seventh year since Sensei assumed the presidency.

Discussed the above topics openly and frankly. All are good and precious members.

Thursday, December 19. Clear.

A fever again today. Physically and mentally weary. Coughing. Must take care.

Read the Gosho:

Iron, when heated in the flames and pounded, becomes a fine sword. Worthies and sages are tested by abuse.

—"Letter from Sado" (WND, 303)

Read the following in a book: "A person who lives to seventy has spent nineteen years working, twenty-three years sleeping, four years sick, nine years enjoying some form of amusement, two years getting dressed or changing clothes and three years eating." Think of it! How many years of our lives are spent in a valuable way?

In the evening, attended a Toyoko District discussion meeting. An evening so beautiful it might be described as enchanting.

Cautioned district members not to overextend themselves. Told them, "In life, you cannot achieve complete victory if you are fatigued." I wish happiness for these dear district members. To bed, close to midnight.

Friday, December 20. Clear.

To Sensei's home in Meguro in the early evening, to offer year-end greetings. My wife and I were treated to dinner. Sensei seemed rather jittery. Think the report from the Secretariat chief has had an adverse effect on his condition.

My slight fever did not subside; returned home early. Took time to think; read.

Saturday, December 21. Fair.

To M.'s in the afternoon with my wife to offer year-end salutations. Was treated to quite a feast.

Attended an evening meeting of the Thirty-seventh Corps at Jozai-ji in Ikebukuro.

1. Pure unity, centering on the corps chief.
2. Correctly understand and put into practice even one Gosho passage.
3. Long-term, persevering faith yields a happy life.

Determined next year to pour my entire heart and soul into developing the youth division. Without this, there will be no future Gakkai development.

Returned to my bright and happy home, 11:00.

Sunday, December 22. Cloudy, thick fog.

Attended H.'s mother's funeral in the morning. Went to their home in Magome. Surprised at the small number of people attending. Said, "Let's have a good turnout for the memorial service marking the 49th day [since her passing]."

Personal guidance at the headquarters in the afternoon. Now that Sensei is away resting, the headquarters has become unusually quiet. Just as waves exist in water, waves of vital energy and determination exist in life as well. Lately, since Sensei has been away, there have been no such waves. Strange.

Rested for a while in the late afternoon. My strength returned. Getting rest is also important. Physical strength and energy are the source of power for waging a campaign.

Though winning and losing are normal events in the course of a person's life, I pray to the Buddha for my final victory.

I will engrave in my life this *waka* poem I received from Sensei; I shall not forget it.

In the evening, my wife and I discussed our plans for the coming year. Hope rises. The future opens.

Monday, December 23. Fair.

The crown prince celebrated his twenty-fourth birthday. A symbol of the dawning of a new era. The same is true of the progress of the young men's division.

A Bunkyo Chapter leaders meeting in the evening.

1. About reality.
2. About power.

Afterward, attended a year-end get-together at the K. chapter house. A raucous gathering. Unpleasant. To talk, eat, suffer and live beside pure-hearted youth is my greatest joy.

Tuesday, December 24. Fair.

Not feeling well again today. A year-end gathering at D. with seven leaders. Samurai who always live in the midst of battle. Enjoyable conversation.

Returned to the headquarters. Hearing that the top youth division leaders were at my house, headed home quickly. Talked sincerely and honestly until late at night. Future warriors, trusted heroes. How could I utter a careless word? Want to embrace and protect them—these youth.

Sensei phoned late. Regarding the purchase of land for the head temple.

Wednesday, December 25. Clear, with clouds later on.

The headquarters leaders meeting at Toshima Civic Auditorium. Sensei did not attend. We have finally achieved a membership of

750,000 households. Our goal has been brilliantly achieved. President Toda's conviction has clearly become a reality. Lots of thoughts, stemming from a realization in the depths of my life about the strict, exacting nature of the Buddhist Law. A message from Sensei containing next year's direction.

1. Faith to establish family harmony.
2. Faith to enable each individual to obtain happiness.
3. Faith to overcome obstacles.

Our magnificent religious revolution advances. Following was a chapter and division chiefs meeting at Jozai-ji. A year-end celebration was included. The meeting ended at 9:30. Headed home. Read the Gosho alone. It is shameful for a leader be deficient in study. How could I, as a seeker of the way, fail to do so. Must never become an arrogant person. Strictly admonished by my mentor's eyes.

Thursday, December 26. Cloudy, with rain later.

Took a taxi from home. Think of the cab fare as a medical expense for maintaining my health.

Sensei is profoundly ill. I, too, am ill. Regrettable

A YMD corps chiefs meeting at K. in Shinjuku. Talked about the time, as YMD Corps #1 chief, I was severely scolded by Sensei at a New Year's youth division corps chiefs meeting at S. in Shinjuku. It was a period when I received much strict guidance from Sensei. I now long for those days. Determined to have sixty-five corps next year.

It has been seven years since Sensei assumed the presidency, and his goal of 750,000 member households has been fulfilled. What should be the youth division goal? As a first step, it is our destiny to gather 100,000 young men, as Sensei stated in his essay, "Youth, Be Patriotic." It's up to me. Until then, I will resolutely battle the devil of illness. Can only pray for Sensei's recovery. In the desolate cold of winter, the fresh sprouts of spring appear. This is the simultaneity of cause and effect. The growth of the "Ikeda Library" is my greatest delight. These stacks of books are like my children. My sleeping children's healthy faces. I will continue into the future, always.

Friday, December 27. Thick haze and fog, then rain.

In the afternoon, a *Daibyakurenge* panel discussion in the conference room at the headquarters. The topic, "Remembering High Priest Nichiko Hori." My voice was weak, perhaps due to fatigue. Had difficulty speaking.

Our voices reflect the state of our bodies and minds. Our speech reveals the power of our lives. The voice is important. Ancient texts speak of demons and evil spirits that devour people's voices. I believe such [vocal] problems cannot be solved by medicine alone. I think they are problems of our entire being.

Read in the newspaper that President S. died and that Y. has fallen ill. Could it be a sign we are moving from an era of the aged to a new age of youth.

Youth should march forth, their heads held high with the pride that "Tomorrow is ours!" Always, scaling mountains, crossing valleys, boldly, unceasingly.

Caught another cold. Congested. Received a report Sensei is feeling a little better. Relieved. Happy.

Saturday, December 28. Cloudy, intermittent rain.

I will only be twenty-nine for a few more days. Soon I will be thirty. I can no longer go on being a spoiled child. Must study. Must develop true ability. Must fight. In the afternoon, visited the S. family to bring a year-end gift. A fine family. A model for others to follow.

Sunday, December 29. Fair.

With each year's passage, I feel my responsibility deepen. Another year of Sensei's lectures and of advancing my own study has ended. As I look back, I keenly sense my growth this year. Deeply, powerfully, toward revealing the actual proof of the inconspicuous benefit of Nichiren Daishonin's Buddhism. Will climb the coming year's new slope.

Rested all morning. To Sensei's home in the afternoon to pay my respects. Then, visited my parents, my brother and the general director to offer year-end gifts. Returned home late. Enjoyed gongyo with my family.

Monday, December 30. Fair.

Stayed home all day. Read a book in the afternoon. Read the Gosho, too. Visited I.'s at 6:00 p.m., where the top youth division leaders and their spouses had gathered. We all talked until late. On the way home, stopped in Shinjuku with my wife to shop for New Year's decorations.

Tuesday, December 31.

An eternal goodbye to my twenty-ninth year. May I live gloriously in my thirties. It has been a difficult year. It may have been a losing battle. This coming year, I will definitely win and make a fresh start toward a splendid life. Farewell, 1957! Mount Fuji stands undaunted, as always, against the bitter wind.

PRESIDENT TODA turned 58 on February 11, 1958, and a celebration was held in light of the recovery of his health.

On March 1, the completion ceremony for the Grand Lecture Hall at the Taiseki-ji took place. The construction project was the last major project of President Toda's after the accomplishment of his 750,000 household membership goal. Some two thousand chapter leaders and four thousand youth division members attended the ceremony. In his congratulatory speech, Josei Toda expressed his deep appreciation for the sincere contributions of so many Gakkai members and said: "By putting our faith in the power of the Gohonzon first, we must save the nation of Japan, which is experiencing the calamity of internal strife." Throughout March, more than 200,000 participated in commemorative pilgrimages. During this commemorative event, on March 16, about six thousand youth gathered on the head temple grounds and together with Toda conducted the "Ceremony of Kosen-rufu." March 16 is celebrated today as Kosen-rufu Day. Despite his failing health, Toda remained at the head temple all through the month to take full leadership for the commemorative events.

On March 17, Fidel Castro declared war against the Batista regime. On March 27, Soviet Premier Bulganin resigned and the Communist party's first secretary, Nikita Khrushchev, took over.

The early morning of April 1, President Toda left the head temple for Tokyo and was hospitalized at Nihon University Hospital. The next day, at a little after 6:40 p.m., he died, after accomplishing all his goals for kosen-rufu. The news of his death was brought to the Soka Gakkai headquarters just as a joint conference of the board of directors and planning board was concluded. The YWD and YWD corps chiefs were also gathered at the headquarters then.

On April 3, a headquarters leaders meeting was held at the Toshima Civic Auditorium. At the beginning, the Soka Gakkai general director announced Toda's passing. Chief of Staff Ikeda encouraged those in attendance to continue advancing as disciples of the late president, putting to good use all the training they had received from him. The same day, Toda's body was placed in a coffin, and a vigil was conducted. On April 8, a funeral ceremony was conducted by Nichijun, the sixty-fifth high priest. More than 120,000 Soka Gakkai members offered incense and prayers at the front gate of Jozai-ji. On April 20, an official Gakkai memorial service was held with 250,000 members attending from throughout the nation. Some critics commented that the

Gakkai would disintegrate now that Toda had passed.

On April 11, Daisaku and Kaneko Ikeda's third son, Takahiro, was born.

May 3 saw thirty-two thousand representatives gathering for the eighteenth spring general meeting. A huge photo of President Toda was hung above the stage along with a banner bearing the calligraphy "unity." At this meeting Chief of Staff Ikeda spoke of "The Seven Bells," a series of guidelines based on successive seven-year periods after the establishement of the Soka Gakkai in 1930.

On May 10, in Tripoli, Lebanon, an armed anti-American uprising triggered a civil war. Urban warfare broke out next in Beirut on June 25, followed by the arrival of the U.S. Marines on July 15. The British sent troops to Jordan on July 17. On August 21, the U.N. General Assembly passed a Middle-East Peace Resolution, and the U.S. and British forces withdrew from the area.

In July, cemeteries in various areas of Japan, operated by other Buddhist schools, began to refuse to bury Gakkai members as a way of discouraging their own parishioners from leaving their

Wednesday, January 1.

Woke up, 7:00. Physically and spiritually exhausted. Yet, I am throbbing with the awareness and determination that I am about to embark upon my thirties.

My first gongyo of the year, at Myoko-ji. The morning sun sparkled as if to congratulate us. At 9:00, greeted Sensei at his home in Meguro. Nothing could be greater than the youth division leaders' pride and joy upon welcoming the new year with their mentor.

Sensei seemed in high spirits. Want to develop such faith that I will never leave him throughout my life. There is no other life for me.

To the Gakkai headquarters at 10:00. A lecture on the 'three mystic principles' — true cause, true effect and true land. Unfathomably profound. Afterward, Sensei presented three poems. To the youth division, he wrote:

> What a cause for celebration!
> A seven-year history of fierce struggle,
>   by pure-hearted youth.

Took the 1:30 express to the head temple for the first pilgrimage of the year. Nothing compares to my happiness at accompanying Sensei.

Thursday, January 2. Cloudy with clearing later.

My thirtieth birthday. The new year's first ceremony of chanting before the Dai-Gohonzon at 8:30. Sensei spent the entire day at the

Rikyo-bo. I, too, stayed there. Sensei spoke to me on a variety of matters. Used the second camera I have ever owned. Took two or three shots of Sensei as he stepped into the hallway.

Friday, January 3. Fair.

Fuji, Mountain of the Great Sun Lotus of Many Treasures — is the most purely beautiful mountain in the world. Deeply sense this is the finest location. "'Since the Law is wonderful,...the land is sacred'" (WND, 1097). It is natural that this be true of the place where the Dai-Gohonzon, which was inscribed for the entire world, exists. Attended a ceremony of chanting before the Dai-Gohonzon in the afternoon again with Sensei. Prayed to fulfill my resolutions for this year. My heart is filled with passion.

Played *shogi* [Japanese chess] with Sensei at the Rikyo-bo. Won one and lost one. I think this will be a deeply meaningful memory. Attended an evening discussion meeting with Osaka members. Must summon my life force — for the members, for my juniors — and earnestly dedicate myself for their sake. If I fail to do so, there is no reason for me to be with my mentor.

Saturday, January 4. Cloudy then clear.

Left the head temple at noon. The first time I have spent four days there. Happy, but also thinking about the future. Left on the 1:08 *Western Sea* express. Heard the prime minister and his party were traveling on the same train. Seems they got off at Atami.

Talked with members about the present state of politics. Strongly emphasized that without realizing a new society based upon Buddhist ideals, genuine politics, real peace and true happiness will be impossible. Thought deeply about the devilish nature of authority and financial power not illuminated by the Mystic Law. Home for the first time in several days. Received guests. Nothing interesting. Ultimately, Gakkai activities are the greatest enjoyment, because they encompass the worlds of Bodhisattva and Buddhahood.

Sunday, January 5. Fair.

Had a fever all day. Troublesome — 99.9° F, I was told. Why do I always have this sort of fever? Lamentable. It always causes my wife to worry.

Attended a chapter New Year's party in the evening. Afterward, went to a New Year's party with youth division leaders. Later, went to T.'s home in Arakawa to offer New Year's greetings. Home after midnight.

Must take care of my health. This year, I want to forge a body and mind as strong as steel. Must build myself physically. Create a strong body.

This year—whether active, quiet or intense—will be a year to continuously face my destiny. My gaze is set straight ahead.

Monday, January 6. Fair.

At 6:00, a New Year's Culture Department dinner at N. Having been invited, I attended. Made a congratulatory speech. K. gave words that contradicted what I had said. A small-minded person. Home, close to 10:00. Earnestly did gongyo. Will go to bed early.

From tomorrow, I will study Buddhism. Must study. Must not lose. One who doesn't study will definitely be defeated. One who continues to study will definitely win. Listened to a record. To bed, 11:50.

Tuesday, January 7. Hazy.

To the headquarters in the evening. Saw Sensei briefly. His condition seems extremely poor. Heartbreaking. Times have changed. Lamentable, regrettable. I, however, have long to live before kosen-rufu is achieved. Sensei, please watch! The youth division will grow and will definitely carry on. A dinner at N., priests invited. Sensei looked very ill. Sixteen priests and thirty senior leaders. After Sensei left, things were truly sad. I hope all his disciples will stir themselves to further action.

To bed early. Cannot fight if I am exhausted. All that interests me is our battle for the Law.

Wednesday, January 8. Clear, with occasional clouds.

The national budget for this year is ¥1.3 trillion. Are we gradually moving into a period of inflation? Deeply sense the economy is becoming the focus of our political and social system.

An evening meeting. Worried about Sensei's condition. Received a late report he is OK. Relieved.

The movements of prosperity and decline,
Sorrow mingles with joy,
One person's history, a nation's history.

> *Behind the smile, there are tears,*
>   *and in your darkness, there is light.*
>   —MORNING BELL: SONGS OF THE GREAT WALL, BY BANSUI DOI

Left the Gakkai headquarters building just after 10:00.

Thursday, January 9. Cloudy.

My health has returned, somewhat.

The world's greatest castle of practice—the Gakkai headquarters. It is the power source for kosen-rufu; the abode of great eagles—the Bodhisattvas of the Earth; a home to years of accumulated experience in the battle to spread the Mystic Law; the birthplace of great generals and able people for world kosen-rufu.

Will advance again this year. Illuminated by the Mystic Law, I will create a supremely meaningful history.

Friday, January 10. Clear.

Attended a traffic control conference. It was about the general pilgrimage commemorating the completion of the Grand Lecture Hall, which will involve the movement of 200,000 participants. Until late, we discussed the companies involved, along with other matters.

Thursday, January 16. Fair.

January 11: Lectured at Kyoto Chapter—"Reply to Shijo Kingo." Questions and answers; guidance.
January 12: Guidance in Maizuru.
January 13: An Osaka Chapter leaders meeting and a YMD and YWD leaders meeting.
January 14: Guidance meetings for Sakai and Senba chapters.
January 15: To Okayama for a lecture and question-and-answer meeting.
January 16: Took the *Dove* special express back to Tokyo.

Wherever I go, I am astounded by the members' abundant passion for Buddhist study. If I do not study, I will fall quickly behind. Y. and S. took good care of me. Nothing is more beautiful than the human heart. Yet, people's hearts can be ugly, too. Doesn't the Mystic Law reveal the coexistence of good and evil?

On the train, read *The Sociology of Religion* by the German sociologist Max Weber. Will ponder the contrast in nature between German philosophers on the one hand and French and British on the other. Will take note of this book with the feeling of engraving a Gosho passage in my life.

The unlearned scholars today cannot even dream of the doctrine [of three thousand realms in a single moment of life].

—(GZ, 1339)

Friday, January 17. Clear.

Apricot blossoms…
The bright yellow blossoms of golden bell.

Took an injection in the morning. Met at length with Sensei after a long lapse. At the headquarters, he said, "Dai, it's been a while." My mentor's warm eyes — I miss them. Deeply moved by this greatly compassionate teacher.

Youth! Oppose all evil forms of authority. From tomorrow, I am determined to set aside time to read.

Saturday, January 18. Fair.

A traffic control conference at 2:00 p.m. The top leaders are unaware of the reality of the situation. Concerned it will be difficult for the youth at the scene to carry it out.

When Sensei is not around, the general director and the board of directors must take responsibility. The urge to become angry is intense.

Saw Sensei in the evening. "Though it may seem like an onerous task, you all must continue to support the Gakkai," he instructed us strictly.

In Sensei's heart.…

Went to H.'s housewarming party in the evening. Talked until late. A discomfiting atmosphere. Stopped by the K. chapter house afterward. Very discouraging. Amazed at the arrogance of Chapter Chief K. and other leaders. Feel sorry for the rest of the chapter members. Home early; read a book.

Sunday, January 19. Clear, then cloudy.

Rested all morning. Always thinking I must take care of my health. My wife's mother came over. It was about the children's education, our living expenses and other matters. She, my wife and I talked. Peacefully, warmly.

Tomorrow, I will have to bother Sensei at home. Took my children to the public bath in the evening. Wrote until 1:00.

Monday, January 20. Clear.

Visited Sensei at home in Meguro. Talked intimately for about an hour and a half. Could only express my appreciation for his deep compassion and concern for the future and beyond. Received guidance on the upcoming general pilgrimage and the Gakkai's cultural movement, including my own personal affairs. Must become even more deeply and powerfully conscious of Sensei's instructions; must put them into practice and prove their validity.

Will be 31 next year; 32 in 1960, 33 in 1961, 34 in 1962, 35 in 1963, 36 in 1964. I am young; I am young.

A youth division leaders meeting, the first this year, was held at the Shinagawa Civic Auditorium. A productive meeting, focused on the general pilgrimage slated for March. Want to attend a leaders meeting each month without fail.

Concerned about my relationship with the chapter. My instructions and actions determine everything. Must focus on faith and on the goal. The Gohonzon will be my witness.

Tuesday, January 21. Clear, with occasional showers.

An uneventful day. Had a temperature of 100.4° F. Neither read nor wrote. Ashamed to have spent the day unproductively.

In the afternoon, attended H.'s wedding at Jozai-ji. Offered heartfelt congratulations. On the way home, stopped at a movie theater in Shinjuku. It was dull. Left immediately.

Felt listless. Home early. Couldn't see Sensei. Lonesome—lonely beyond description.

Wednesday, January 22. Clear, with occasional clouds.

There are three ways to live. Some people live in the past, some in the present and some in the future. The same principle applies to the Gakkai, as well as to society and politics.

Youth live for the future. The board of directors, therefore, should live actively for the present while watching over the youth who live for the future.

In the afternoon, attended a directors meeting with the top youth division leaders. The agenda focused on the March general pilgrimage. The meeting lasted for four long hours. Discussion is important. Consensus is important as well. But implementation is most important of all. Who will do this? The top leaders had better know.

Home near midnight. On the way, stopped at a street vendor and ate *oden* [a kind of hotchpotch]. A taste savored by ordinary people.

Thursday, January 23. Fair.

Took an injection in the morning. Sensei's condition, too, is not good. He has often said, "The source of energy for our struggle lies in building iron bodies, life force and good health." Yet this mentor and his disciple both suffer from weak health. Resent this trick of fate.

Decided to hire M. and W. as headquarters staff. Taking a broad perspective, there was no other choice. Earnestly praying for their successful efforts. On the way back from the headquarters, my wife and I had a New Year's dinner party alone at the F. restaurant in Shinjuku. It was a cold night. Thousands of stars sparkled. It reminded me of several years ago.

Even the eagle and the lion take time to rest. Are those who fail to rest reckless in their valor? Some say Tokugawa Ieyasu had rested well before he won the Battle of Sekigahara, while Ishida Mitsunari, who was defeated, could not rest.

Home shortly before midnight.

Friday, January 24. Fair.

A fever in the morning. Forced myself to go to work. My wife told me that I look sick.

An executive leaders conference, which doubled as a New Year's banquet, at the Y. restaurant, in the afternoon. Discussed the following:

1. Concrete direction for the March general pilgrimage.
2. The next generation of corps chiefs.
3. Appointment of Culture Department members.

Returned to the headquarters in the evening. By myself, made a clean copy of the notes I had accumulated of Sensei's guidance.

Home a little before 11:00 p.m.

Saturday, January 25. Fair.

To say *nam* is to express one's heart of respect and praise. Unable to do gongyo and chant daimoku with a rich heart. Reflected deeply.

To an evening Bunkyo Chapter leaders meeting. Lecture and guidance mainly based on the Gosho "Letter to Nanbu Rokuro." Felt listless. Regret not being able to give guidance as I had wished.

On the way home, discussed the appointment of the next district chiefs with the chapter chief and others. Thought about how many able individuals would emerge in ten more years. No one seems to be thinking about this yet.

Boarded a Yamate Line train at Mejiro Station. Met some youth division members on board. Talked until Shinagawa Station. A song of young pioneers.

Sunday, January 26. Clear, then cloudy.

Deeply fatigued in the morning. A slight fever of 100.4° F. Took an injection. Read lightly in bed all morning.

In the afternoon, received news that O. had died suddenly. Shocked. He was hit by a train while riding his bicycle. Heartbreaking; brutal. Immediately rushed to the accident scene and then to the hospital. Reported to Sensei. He was extremely concerned. Mysteriously, no wounds were visible on the body; his countenance was peaceful, as if asleep.

An intense day. The weather turned bad. Weather changes from moment to moment, and the human mind, anyone's mind, is in a constant state of flux—from the beginningless past on through eternity.

Monday, January 27. Fair.

The color of the winter camellias deepens, perhaps symbolizing the flower of a woman's perseverance.

In the morning, interrupted Sensei at home to report about O. and other matters. Amazed at Sensei's broad compassion. He spoke about accidental death and karma.

Attended a top leaders conference at the Gakkai headquarters. Discussed the following, among other topics:
1. Youth division leaders' roles as revolutionary pioneers.
2. Guidance with substance.
3. Development of the Gakkai's core.

To an evening unit chiefs meeting at the Toshima Civic Auditorium. Everyone was in low spirits. Afterward, attended a district chiefs meeting. Are they all tired?

A cold, cold night. Our religious and cultural reformation is like the severe cold of winter.

Home just before 11:00 p.m. The north wind rattles the windows of my humble, yet precious, home. Read the Gosho for a while, then did gongyo.

> The five universal elements of heaven, earth, water, fire and wind are Buddhas who represent the five kinds of wisdom. Since they dwell in the bodies and minds of all ordinary people without leaving them even for an instant, the realm of delusion and the realm of enlightenment exist fused within one's mind. There is no law that exists apart from one's mind. When people listen to this teaching, therefore, they will very naturally attain Buddhahood, immediately and without hindrance.
> —(GZ, 573)

Tuesday, January 28. Cloudy, then snow and rain later.

Visited Sensei at home in the morning. Had a heartwarming talk for about two hours. Deeply appreciative. In the innermost depths of my heart, realized intuitively the solemn day is approaching. Heartbreaking.

Was told that Sensei wrote a message of condolence for O.'s wake. Wept to see the mentor's consideration for his disciple. Received Sensei's condolence message in the evening and went to O.'s wake in Omori.

Many members attended. Friends are precious. Led the recitation of the sutra and daimoku with utmost sincerity. Saw O.'s wife for the first time. They had no children.

F., who was most closely connected to O., did not attend the wake after all. Such an unfeeling man. Felt indignant about his behavior and worried for him. Reminded of the admonition that a person's heart becomes clear at a crucial time.

A cold day. A frigid, dark night.

Thursday, January 30. Cloudy.

A communication conference between priests from the head temple and Gakkai representatives regarding the ceremony commemorating the Grand Lecture Hall completion. It was held at 3:00 p.m. at Jozai-ji in Ikebukuro.

This great event will be recorded in the annals of kosen-rufu. Earnestly pledged to ensure it will end up a complete success, without any mishaps.

After the conference, returned to the headquarters to write an article. Completely forgot I had called my wife and promised to meet her at

Kamata Station at 10:00 p.m. Made my pregnant wife wait for more than one hour in the cold. Terribly sorry for her. On the way home, the two of us stopped at a street vendor and ate grilled tripe to warm our chilled bodies.

Saturday, February 1. Clear, with occasional clouds.

Left at 7:30 in the morning from Yokohama Station for the head temple via the *Eastern Sea*—to resolve some problems with the purchase of land near the head temple before the Grand Lecture Hall completion ceremony. Went with top youth division leaders, the general director and others. Progress was made toward the settlement of all issues.

Welcomed Sensei to the head temple. He has become even more gaunt and emaciated. He immediately began issuing directions with a dauntless demeanor. At Sensei's instruction, went to the land owners' home and to M.'s to reconfirm land purchase matters. Discussed until late.

Sunday, February 2. Snow, then rain.

Fever in the morning. Have I caught a cold?

At 9:00 a.m., attended ceremony of chanting before the Dai-Gohonzon with Sensei. Had many thoughts as I chanted. It began to rain at the head temple, grew warmer.

Left the head temple at 1:40 p.m. Left the others at Shinagawa Station and headed home. Had dinner with my family for the first time in a while. My wife and children seemed happy. My wife's father came over. He is in good spirits. Chanted for his longevity. All of us did a resounding gongyo and chanted daimoku together.

Read *Collected Children's Stories* to my children. Could not do a good job of reading.

Monday, February 3. Overcast with thin clouds.

A slight fever since morning. Sensei phoned from Atami, where he is resting. Received instructions on various matters.

Lectured on the "Orally Transmitted Teachings" at 6:30 p.m. at a Study Department assistant professors meeting. Covered sections on the "Universal Gateway of the Bodhisattva Perceiver of the World's Sounds" and "Dharani" [the twenty-fifth and twenty-sixth Lotus Sutra] chapters. Profound teachings.

Afterward, attended a YMD and YWD joint corps chiefs meeting in the large meeting room at the headquarters. Spoke on the following matters, among others:

1. O.'s death and the nature of life.
2. The general pilgrimage scheduled for March.
3. Personnel and other issues.

After the meeting, treated the top youth division leaders to buckwheat noodles with tempura. They are brave warriors who have climbed the slopes of hardship for the last ten years. Told them, "I believe that great glory in life awaits those who persevere through this training."

Home after 11:00. My wife looks beautiful in her kimono.

Tuesday, February 4. Fair.

A fever in the morning. Could not get out of bed. Rested quietly all day. My cold seems to be getting worse. A doctor who lives in the neighborhood came over. He looked to be around thirty. He said he has recently opened a clinic.

My wife's father, T. and Z. came over to see me. Talked with them while resting. Enjoyed sweet bean soup with rice cake.

Reflected alone on the following:

1. The outcome of the Osaka trial.
2. The third and fourth presidents of the Soka Gakkai.
3. Compiling the sequel to [Toda's] *The Human Revolution*.
4. Construction of the Gakkai headquarters building.
5. Financial planning for my family.

Asked my wife to play some records. Listened to recordings of Michiya Mihashi and others until late.

Late in the evening, Sensei's wife called to convey that Sensei, who is also sick, has asked. "How is Daisaku's illness?" Grateful.

Friday, February 7. Snow, then rain.

Snow in Tokyo. Freezing. Took the 12:30 express from Tokyo Station for a guidance trip in Kansai. The train ran straight along Tokaido, the eastern seaboard, in continuous rain.

With a feverish body, forced myself to go on the trip. Opened the Gosho, but it didn't sink into my head. Traveled alone, blankly looking out the window.

Is it a turbulent time when the bold and daring will win? Or does true humanity lie in warmth and sensitivity? Confusing for a youth.

Thought about the stout heart of faith, the pure practice of faith. Also pondered revolution, selfless devotion, common sense and wisdom. Must seriously consider a method and vision for 'the kosen-rufu through positive relationship' and 'the kosen-rufu of substantiation.'

Stayed one night in Osaka, holding dialogue with many warm-hearted friends.

Saturday, February 8. Cloudy.

Took an express from Osaka to Himeji. Attended a guidance meeting, a group chiefs meeting and a district chiefs meeting. My first visit, so I put my whole heart and soul into it. Happy to hear everyone was saying afterward, "I'm filled with confidence."

Visited the Himeji Castle [literally, the castle on the "road of princesses"]. It is also called the Castle of White Herons. Heard that in the ancient struggle between the Minamoto and Taira clans, the Taira princesses and Emperor Antoku fled on this road.

The beautiful, piteous castle of white herons. Its majestic appearance gives rise to a touch of poetry rather than the image of a battlefield. The ruins of the shattered dreams of warlords: Hideyoshi of the Tensho era, Terumasa of the Keicho era, Honda of the Gen'na era, Matsudaira of the Kan'ei era, and Sakai Tadataka of the Kan'en era — the fearsome transition of the times without a sovereign.

Stayed one night in Himeji. Could not sleep until late. Many thoughts came and went.

Sunday, February 9. Fair.

In the morning, returned to Osaka on the 8:27 from Himeji Station.

Talked with S. and other leaders over a meal at the Kansai headquarters while concerned about Sensei's condition.

At 1:00, lectured on Nichikan's "Teaching for the Latter Day."[1] Difficult.

In the evening, attended a youth division leaders meeting at S.'s. Many earnest questions. Sensed the true potential of Kansai for further growth.

One youth division member had a fight with two or three people in the dark in front of the headquarters. Cautioned that he should never harm his precious life over trivial matters. Presented the young man a book.

Did gongyo with many friends to the great Gohonzon.

1. "Teaching for the Latter Day": See note on p. 249.

Monday, February 10. Cloudy, then shower.

Arrived in Tokyo at 9:23 a.m.

Frigid, ash-gray Tokyo. My wife alone greeted me. She looked cold.

Tomorrow is Sensei's fifty-eighth birthday. Top leaders are invited to N. restaurant. I was asked to give words on behalf of the youth division.

Stayed all day at the headquarters where Sensei was absent. Discussed various matters with the general director, directors and top youth division leaders. Also had an informal talk with them. Wrote a manuscript.

Spring is near.

Tuesday, February 11. Cloudy.

Visited Sensei's home at 9:00 in the morning. Relieved to see his spirited face. Today is his fifty-eighth birthday.

Ate red-bean rice and sweet bean soup together with Sensei. My lifetime memory and honor. He spoke about economy, stocks, politics as well as directions for a new era.

Attended with several dozen top leaders a celebration for Sensei's recovery at N. restaurant at 5:30 p.m.

Sensei loves the "Dormitory Song of High School #1" and the "Song of the White Tiger Corps." Could not help being concerned about how emaciated his body is. But my heart leapt with joy to see him asking everyone to sing and giving resolute guidance. Everyone seemed to have refreshed their spirit. Wonderful. Happy.

Quoting the Gosho passage "The farther the source, the longer the stream" (WND, 940), Sensei expounded a philosophical Buddhist principle and gave strict guidance that remains in my heart: "Leaders' determination is fundamental. It is not the responsibility of general members. Leaders' faith and growth determine the entire organization's development."

Wednesday, February 12. Cloudy, then clear.

In the morning, visited Sensei's home to express my appreciation for last night. In bed upstairs, Sensei was pleased to see me. To sum up, received guidance regarding:

1. The appointment of the next corps chief in Chubu.
2. Ways to recognize capable individuals.
3. Studying the materialistic conception of history.
4. Being fully aware of the movement of labor unions.

Sensei's complexion was pale. But his attitude was resolute, and his words were powerful.

Freezing. One plum blossom, two plum blossoms — spring has not yet come.

Attended an evening Gosho study meeting. Moved by earnest seekers of the Buddhist way. These juniors will surely surpass their seniors. As my mentor often says, "Be watchful of their future existences."

Home just after 10:00. Read "The Teaching, Capacity, Time and Country."

> Fourth is the consideration of the country. One must never fail to take into account the kind of country in which one is spreading the Buddhist teachings. There are cold countries, hot countries, poor countries, rich countries, central countries, and peripheral countries, large countries and small countries, countries wholly given over to thieving, countries wholly given over to the killing of living things, and countries known for their utter lack of filial piety.
>
> —(WND, 50)

My wife made *amazake* [a sweet beverage made from fermented rice]. Enjoyed it while looking forward to a March full of peach blossoms.

Thursday, February 13. Clear with occasional clouds.

A corps flags exchange ceremony at the Toshima Civic Hall at 7:00. Because of O.'s sudden death, his corps flag was handed to W. The general director and others attended.

Visited Sensei's home to report late at night. Received guidance on:
1. Developing the youth division's potential for the future.
2. Principles Gakkai leaders should adopt.
3. Buddhism and its view of society.
4. The ultimate mission of the Gakkai.

Home at 11:50. Had many thoughts. My wife cautioned me that my complexion is pale. Feel a slight fever.

Made a clean copy of the notes of Sensei's guidance until late.

The bathtub is leaking. The whole family cannot take a bath.

Wednesday, February 19. Cloudy then clearing later.

Warm in the day, cold in the evening.

To Sensei's home in the morning.

Received cautions, instructions and guidance on the following:

1. "You seem to have become a little healthier."
2. "Walk along the path of hardship for the next ten years."
3. "It is your destiny to join the headquarters."
4. "At last, I will bring a fresh breeze into the board of directors."
5. Daily life and the economy.

Strong determination. Firm realization.

Chilly gusty winds on my way home. Had a fever today too. 100.9° F. Pain in my chest.

Saturday, February 22. Fair.

Took the noon train to the head temple with top leaders. Warm winter, just like spring.

The completion ceremony for Ryosho-bo and Jakunichi-bo lodging temples was held. Sensei, too, attended in high spirits. He is pushing himself. Hoped he would take some rest.

Sensei strictly stated, "Within this year, I will give top leaders guidance and instructions intended for the next ten years." He then stated, "I will remove all those who grovel and curry favor." Yes, I agree. He also stated, "The same holds true of those who disturb the organization and take advantage of faith." I cannot agree more.

Afterward, made preparations for the transfer of the Grand Lecture Hall and other various matters.

Monday, February 24. Rain.

My fever does not go away. Exhausted.

A traffic control conference at the headquarters from 6:30 p.m. till past 11:00. The youth division, especially H., did truly well. Appreciative. The Gohonzon will surely praise them. No doubt, the actual proof will validate the causes and effects these people created in several decades.

1. Today the preparation for the Grand Lecture Hall completion ceremony is done.
2. Tomorrow will have to turn the documents over to bus and railroad companies.
3. Staff personnel appointments were decided.

Relieved these are accomplished. Hope Sensei rests assured as well.

Home just after 1:00. Took a bath. Decided to sip whisky a little bit although I don't drink. The clock pointing to shortly before 2:00. Felt fulfilled and proud in my sense of mission.

Wednesday, March 19. Fair, then cloudy.

Nerves and body truly fatigued from overseeing transportation for the monthlong pilgrimage commemorating the Grand Lecture Hall completion. For the remaining ten days, want to fulfill my mission honorably, with renewed resolution and without any regret. My life's most noble work is to sincerely guide those awakened to the True Law.

Sensei's condition is extremely poor. He called an urgent conference of top leaders on the 22nd.

Must seriously consider the Gakkai's future and how I will contribute. Yes—after all, there is no other way than to chant to and entrust everything to the Gohonzon.

Saturday, March 29. Snow, then clearing.

Sensei is exceedingly weak.

I told him: "Just a few days to go. There have been no accidents or mishaps. Please rest assured. The top leaders are also arriving steadily."

Sensei said, "Is that right?" with a reassured look. Then he strictly appealed to me, "Never slacken in your pursuit [against evil]." Could only nod in agreement with this great general's command.

Sunday, March 30. Fair with occasional snow.

Left the head temple with Chapter Chief I. on the 11:55 a.m. train. Crowded to capacity. Couldn't sit until Shinagawa Station. A warm day. But agony and exhaustion persisted in my heart's innermost core. A day shrouded in darkness.

Visited Sensei's home in Meguro after 2:00. Discussed his hospitalization with his son. His wife said, "I want him to come home." But the son suggested hospital care. We also recommended Sensei check into a hospital. In my heart, though, I hesitated about whether I should be responsible to honor Sensei's wish to "return to the headquarters."

Feel as if I am falling into a bottomless abyss. Lament my lack of strength as a disciple. Ah...will I gain it in this lifetime? Must take a strict look at myself. To make up for this, I have no choice but to carry through with Sensei's spirit throughout my life.

Stayed at Sensei's home until after 7:00 taking pains to prepare for his hospitalization. Tired. Exhausted, spiritually and physically.

Home after a long absence.

Pondered my destiny to live on the battlefield and struggle for the Law.

Monday, March 31. Fair.

To Sensei's home in the morning. Immediately took a taxi with Sensei's wife to the Japan University Hospital in Surugadai. The room was not very good. Negotiated again and again. Earnestly requested the best room possible, but to no avail. Truly regrettable. Dr. H. also asked for our understanding, calling it only temporary. An unavoidable choice. But sincerely urged the hospital to provide its best possible treatment.

Went back to the head temple aboard the 1:30 *Western Sea*. Arrived shortly before 5:00. Immediately reported to the board of directors and the general director.

Sensei's condition is quickly worsening. Expressed my wish to delay his scheduled return to Tokyo. Dr. H. agreed.

Did not sleep all night. Stood by Sensei from downstairs. The song "Gojogen" came to mind. Sat waiting with the general director, directors, other top leaders and a few youth division members. Everyone was quiet.

Tuesday, April 1. Clear.

At 1:40 a.m., began preparing to transport Sensei to Tokyo. During the *ushitora* gongyo. Can only imagine how High Priest Nichijun and Sensei are feeling. Could it be their final parting for this life? Was told the high priest finished gongyo earlier than usual to see Sensei off.

High Priest Nichijun has been toiling for the development of Nichiren Shoshu. President Josei Toda, a leader of the Bodhisattvas of the Earth, fought to protect the high priest at the risk of his life. Cannot help ponder, with deep awe and respect, the profound relationship shared by these two, spanning past, present and future. Ah, how mystic. How worthy of respect.

Departed from the second floor of Rikyo-bo at 2:00 a.m. sharp. Carried Sensei in his futon. Said to him, "Sensei, I will escort you." He replied, "Oh?—Where are my glasses?" Regret I did not have time to hand him his glasses. Once downstairs, we placed him on a stretcher and carried him to the car. 2:20.

Riding with Sensei were his wife and a doctor. The directors and I followed in another car, and the youth division members in the last car.

Headed down the quiet country road, lit by a hazy moon, to Numazu Station. We stopped three or four times to check on Sensei's condition or give him an injection.

Arrived at Numazu Station at 3:45. Boarded the *Izumo* express at 4:15. When I said, "Sensei, now you can rest assured," he replied "Is that right?" with a faint smile, which I shall remember for all eternity.

Arrived at Tokyo Station at 6:45 in the morning. Did not sleep at all. Feeling pain and sorrow, brought Sensei off the train on a stretcher. Thanks to the station officials' consideration, we could use an elevator to transfer him into an ambulance. We immediately hurried to the Japan University Hospital and waited in front.

Sensei's fatigue and his critical condition were apparent in his face. Heart-rending. Ah, would this be the world's greatest man's last return to the capital? Could only chant daimoku in my heart. Could only pray for his full recovery.

Dr. K. and Dr. H. began treating him immediately. All procedures were finished after 9:00. Left things to Sensei's family and returned to the office.

A myriad of feelings. Could only offer a prayer for his complete recovery. All the disciples feel the same.

Warm all day. But none of Sensei's disciples can escape the dark cloud that shrouds their hearts.

We should strive further to polish our faith. We must develop ourselves. The day passed with countless verses coming and going through my mind.

Wednesday, April 2. Cloudy.

Called an emergency morning corps chiefs conference. Urgent. Sensei's condition is critical. All corps chiefs resolved to do gongyo at the headquarters for one week.

In the afternoon, received a report from the chief secretary that Sensei's condition was improving. Overwhelmed with joy.

Held a joint conference of the board of directors and top youth division leaders at 5:00.

At 6:45, the elderly H. of the building management section told me with a serious look that Takahisa, Sensei's son, was calling from the hospital. Swiftly went to the building manager's office and picked up a phone. With a composed tone, Takahisa told me the sad news: "My father just died."

This moment defies all description. Could not possibly describe my inner shock. No choice but to keep it forever in the depths of my life.

A serious conference followed immediately.

Prayed that Sensei's intent will continue to flow like a pure stream until kosen-rufu is accomplished. Admonished myself to be strong.

The directors and top youth division leaders immediately rushed to the room at Japan University Hospital.

Infinitely moved by his tranquil countenance and smile. My tears flowed ceaselessly.

Oh — April 2. This day will be recorded forever in the history of the Gakkai, in the history of my life and the lives of his disciples.

Immediately sent a telegram to High Priest Nichijun. Communicated to Priest Hosoi. Contacted the relatives.

Accompanied Sensei's body back to his Meguro home. A light rain fell.

Priest Hosoi came by. Recited the sutra and chanted daimoku. The directors and top youth division leaders took turns moistening Sensei's lips.

The life of a great hero of the Mystic Law, a towering figure of kosen-rufu, has ended. But Sensei has left behind an extension of his life, and it is about to open the second act in the decisive battle to actualize Buddhist principles in society. I will stand up.

Tuesday, April 8. Cloudy.

Have watched over Sensei's body for one week, in accord with his wishes. Today is our final parting. How sad. How mournful. Savored the golden words, "'Those persons who had heard the Law dwelled here and there in various Buddha lands, constantly reborn in company with their teachers'" (WND, 217).

One of my seniors came by to get me in the morning. Declined to accompany him. Today, I bid my final farewell to my mentor. Want to visit his home alone, as I see fit. No disciple is as grief-stricken and sad to part from Sensei as I am.

A strict father; a kind father. Owe everything I am today to my beloved mentor. Revere him.

Thirty disciples, all youth, gathered at the mentor's home at 8:30. At 9:00, Priest Hosoi recited the sutra and we removed the casket. Director I. and myself were the leading pallbearers. Left Sensei's home in Meguro at 10:00. Believe he would definitely be pleased.

"Sensei, please rest well. You must be tired." After I accomplish his will, want to quickly rush to his side. Pondered in silence.

Arrived at Jozai-ji in Ikebukuro at 11:00. Approximately 120,000 people came to offer incense today. Sincere people who heartily respect Sensei. Determined that I must guide them further from here on, limitlessly, toward happiness. On behalf of my "father."

At 11:40, High Priest Nichijun took his seat before the altar, recited the sutra and delivered a eulogy. Takahisa, Sensei's son, gave words on behalf of the family, and finally there were brief words from the funeral committee chief. Some sixty priests, top leaders, youth division corps chiefs and Sensei's family, relatives and friends — about three hundred people — took turns offering incense.

At 3:10, carried out the casket to bid a last farewell. Fulfilled Sensei's will to keep his body for one week. Accompanied him to the end. Convinced he surely would be happy.

At 3:30, all left for the Ochiai Crematorium. Youth division leaders in the first car, followed by priests riding in two cars and Sensei's family in another car. Next was the car carrying Sensei's casket. The relatives, top leaders and the board of directors followed.

A gust of wind blew as Priest Hosoi recited the sutra for the last time at Jozai-ji. The deep crimson skies above the crematorium left a very strong impression. Overcast has continued since April 2.

Tuesday, April 29. Thin clouds.

The season of greenery has arrived. Cherry blossoms scatter; magnolia flowers fall. Jonquils in bloom, unfolding their golden-colored petals. Deep and noble, dreamlike colors.

On the 25th: Took the *Swallow* express to Kobe to administer the Study Department examination for the Kansai area. My first visit since the death of my beloved mentor. Though the mentor has departed, Gakkai members are refreshed and in high spirits. Confident about their future.

Gave strict guidance to the S.s.

Deeply moved to see the several tens of thousands of sincere examinees. Is this a sign of the Gakkai's solid latent power? No mishaps or accidents. Relieved.

28th: Finished grading all written and oral exams. Arrived at Tokyo Station at 4:30. Returned forlorn to the headquarters, the site of the lion king's empty throne. A conference until 10:00, then a planning meeting.

29th: Rested in the morning. Must become healthy. My physical health becomes all the more important for the completion of my mentor's work. Vexing.

May 3, a day of profound significance, is just round the corner. This will be the day I take the Gakkai leadership in reality, will it not?

My heart is troubled. A heavy load to carry.

Will fight to prove my mentor's greatness to the world. Will advance, straight ahead. Will fight resolutely, riding over the violent waves of obstacles and devils. Have entered the essential part of my youth.

To G. restaurant at 5:00 p.m. Invited by Priest K. of Myoko-ji. To commemorate the twenty-third anniversary of the death of Daiji'in, Myoko-ji's second chief priest. Several dozen priests and leaders attended.

Home after 8:00, earlier than usual, because of fever. My beautiful wife was waiting quietly. While lying down, listened to records — for the first time in a while.

Wednesday, April 30. Clear, then overcast with thin clouds.

Still have a slight fever. Listless all day. If I don't become healthy within this year, it will be a great problem. My human revolution is a serious, life-or-death struggle.

Read Sensei's essay — for publication [in *The Daibyakurenge*]. He writes: "You must give what benefits others." To provide what supremely benefits others means to carry out propagation, does it not? Aren't we convinced the Mystic Law is the greatest source of benefit? Throughout his life, he was a mentor whose actions always accorded with his words.

Things are getting busier at the headquarters each day. Until I die, want to spend each day fighting for revolution based on the Mystic Law.

Interviewed youth division corps chief candidates at 5:00 p.m. with the general director and others in the president's office. The YWD has developed into fifty corps. The YMD has grown to fifty-six corps. My dear youth division — I will definitely protect them.

The April leaders meeting was held at 6:30. The Gakkai shall always advance. On the way home, thought about what the Gakkai will be like twenty years from now. Felt concern, anguish.

Home after 10:00. A warm spring breeze.

Monday, May 12. Rain.

After the great May 3 general meeting, the Gakkai has entered its second phase. A leader thanked me, saying, "Your address 'Toward the Realization of Kosen-rufu' set forth clear guidelines for the Gakkai."

My battle begins. Sensei, please watch over me. Pray for my

protection and for my righteousness. Am prepared to die for kosen-rufu, the noble and glorious path toward peace for humanity.

Yesterday, on the 11th, a general meeting was held in Osaka in the rain. Gave an address titled "Hopes for the Gakkai Members of Kansai."

Feel feverish. Unwell both in body and mind. Regrettable. Rest, health; progress, value.

Read "On Curing Karmic Disease":

The Nirvana Sutra reads, "There are three types of people whose illness is extremely difficult to cure. The first is those who slander the great vehicle; the second, those who commit the five cardinal sins; and the third, icchantikas, or persons of incorrigible disbelief. These three categories of illness are the gravest in the world."

It also states:

"One who creates evil karma in this life...will surely suffer in hell.... But by making offerings to the three treasures, one avoids falling into hell and receives the retribution in this life, in the form of afflictions of the head, eye, or back."

—(WND, 631)

Life's ultimate revolution.... Have I any recourse but to chant daimoku?

Tuesday, May 13. Clear.

A fever in the morning. Want to be healthy.

Stayed at the headquarters in the morning. Attended T.'s wedding in the afternoon. To an evening unit chiefs meeting in Nakano. All were in high spirits. Do I alone lack vitality?

Returned to the headquarters to organize Sensei's lectures.

The significance of "On the Three Great Secret Laws":

1. They do not exist in Shakyamuni's Buddhism.
2. Their relationship to the three types of learning: precepts, meditation and wisdom.
3. Modern interpretations of Theravada, provisional Mahayana, and the theoretical and essential teachings of the Lotus Sutra.
4. Regarding the qualifications of those who receive precepts.
5. The significance of the Jetavana Monastery.
6. What are precepts?
7. The entity of the precepts.
8. One's age and the acceptance of the precepts.
9. Regarding the violation of the precepts.

Regarding the Three Great Secret Laws of the Daishonin's Buddhism:

1. Improved education enables people to perceive the Three Great Secret Laws.
2. Because they are based on cause and effect, they are understandable to anyone.
3. The interpretations of the Three Great Secret Laws in terms of the Three Mystic Principles—true cause, true effect and the true land.
4. The meaning of the High Sanctuary of True Buddhism.[1]
5. On the high sanctuary (it is for the sake of the world).
6. The True Law and the changing times.
7. The transition to propagation abroad.
8. The errors of Chigaku Tanaka[2] and others.
9. The errors of Nichiga, Nisshin and others.
10. "Commentaries on 'On the True Cause'" by Nichiu, the ninth high priest, and other writings.

Read "Letter to Lord Matsuno":

In the past, a child called Tokusho Doji made an offering of a mudpie to Shakyamuni Buddha. Thus he was later reborn as King Ashoka and became a lord of Jambudvipa and eventually attained enlightenment.
— (GZ, 1380)

Bed after 1:00. Tranquil.

1. High Sanctuary...: See note on p. 298.
2. Chigaku Tanaka: See note on p. 308.

Wednesday, May 14. Cloudy.

Forced myself to go to work today again. Had a mild fever. Difficult, both physically and spiritually.

Now that my mentor, who was like the sun, is gone, my guidepost in life is shrouded in the darkness. My own development must become my guidepost. Stayed in the headquarters conference room all morning and afternoon. Talked with the guidance division chief and the chief secretary for a little less than an hour. Surprised and saddened by their narrow perspectives.

Does anyone understand Sensei's far-reaching goal? Concerned.

My mission is to continue to pioneer the path of my mentor. Feel the weight of my responsibility. Severe times.

Monday, May 19. Cloudy.

16th: Took the *Swallow* express to Kansai for a guidance trip.

17th: Attended the third public hearing at the Osaka District Court.

18th: Took a Japan Airlines flight at 9:50 to Kyushu for a guidance trip. Arrived at a meeting place in Kurume at 1:00 p.m.

A general meeting for two thousand YWD leaders. Successful. Bursting with vigor.

From 5:00, a general meeting for fifteen hundred YMD leaders at the same location. These great pioneers' spirits are high. Will these events go down in history? They appear to be responding to their mentor's words, "I wholeheartedly trust the youth of Kyushu." Reassuring. Happy.

Checked into the T. Inn in Hakata a little after 9:00 and spent the night.

19th: Took a 12:40 Japan Airlines flight to Tokyo. The weather was bad; felt airsick.

On the eve of the forty-ninth day since my mentor's passing, a memorial service was held in the large Gohonzon room at the headquarters.

All chapter leaders gathered. Finished at 9:00. Worked alone until midnight, organizing my mentor's guidance. Home at 12:50.

A youth, a disciple of Toda, advances alone, resolutely against the north winds, amidst the storm.

Tuesday, May 20. Rain.

Started to read *Record of Great Peace in the Yoshino Dynasty*. Not very interesting.

In the evening, from 5:00 to 7:00, went to my beloved mentor's home in Meguro to attend a memorial service commemorating the forty-ninth day after his passing with the board of directors and youth division leaders.

Sutra recitation and daimoku led by Priest Hosoi. Then the offering of incense. A sense of nostalgia. The entrance hall, his room, the framed calligraphies that read "Lord Kusunoki" and "Rissho Ankoku."

Spoke with Takahisa, Sensei's son, on various matters. A parent by blood; a teacher of Buddhism.

Home at 10:00. Conducted a memorial service for my mentor with my wife as well. Talked with her until late about Sensei. Before going to bed, read a Gosho passage, "As I have often mentioned before, it is said that, where there is unseen virtue, there will be visible reward" (WND, 907).

Wednesday, May 21. Cloudy.

"Good fortune." There are people who have fortune and others who do not, both among those who practice faith and those who do not. The mysterious essence of life.

Effort, intellectual capacity, education, heredity…. Pondered how these relate to fortune.

Kusunoki Masashige had three sons: Masatsura, Masatoki and Masanori. I am now also a father of three: Hiromasa, Shirohisa and Takahiro. What path of destiny will these three take? Lately, as a father, cannot help thinking about these things.

From 5:30 p.m., a joint conference of the board of directors and top youth division leaders. Discussed the following:

1. Planning for the cultural movement.
2. Examining the headquarters organizational structure.
3. Other matters.

Rather than being assigned to a specific department or section, I am becoming a core of guidance and administration over all. Few are aware of Sensei's capacity. Lonesome. Regrettable. Must solidify myself.

Vowed to myself: "Sensei, please watch over me. I will definitely extol your greatness to the world and return to your side."

Home at 10:00. The YWD planning board members were there waiting. Gave appropriate guidance and sent them home early. Prayed for the good health of those earnest young women.

Thursday, May 22. Cloudy.

My health has returned, somewhat.

Visited K.'s home to pray for the repose of A. Talked about my childhood memories of her with her mournful-looking parents, who are Christians. They looked extremely pleased afterward. The sudden death of their young daughter was devastating to them, as it would be to any parents.

Took a 3:30 p.m. train from Shinbashi Station with a chapter chief to attend a meeting in Numazu. Slept all the way on the train.

Friday, May 23. Cloudy, then rain.

Stayed one night in Atami after completing the guidance trip in Numazu with the chapter chief and others. Could not sleep well. Spent the time reading. My home, after all, is the best place to rest.

The Lower House election ended. Gradually beginning to develop interest.

To Kinshi-cho. Thanked the Traffic Control Group members—those who support the pilgrimages behind the scenes—for their efforts. Everyone was deeply pleased. I was happy.

Home after sending off the general director. As each day goes by, my actions carry more responsibility.

Saturday, May 24. Clear.

From 3:00 p.m., went to the National Sports Arena with several youth leaders to watch the Third Asian Athletic Meet. Thought it would be helpful for future Gakkai youth division athletic and cultural festivals.

Youth from twenty nations. Will they usher in the dawn of Asia? Their ideal to transcend politics, national boundaries and philosophy is good. But when will this ideal be lastingly realized? The magnificent passion, power and talent of youth. Watched until 5:30 and returned to the headquarters. Definitely want to hold an athletic and cultural festival for the youth division next year.

Later, went to a barber near the headquarters. Home feeling refreshed. My home is gradually becoming more orderly. Can now fight with peace of mind. Happy.

Read a book.

Sunday, May 25. Clear.

Got up at 7:00. Three of us—my wife, Shirohisa and I—went to the head temple for the first time in two months. Left Hiromasa at home.

The first pilgrimage after Sensei's passing. These have been extremely busy days. Agonizing days. But a disciple cannot remain sentimental forever. Must charge ahead once again amid the storm.

Attended the ceremony of chanting before the Dai-Gohonzon. Chanted seriously. More than ten thousand people visited the head temple. A great transition of the times.

Sometimes feel indignant at many of the leaders. Have they forgotten Sensei's death? Regrettable. On the way home, got off the train at Yokohama with several leaders and had a planning conference. Want them to do their best.

Received a call from K. Pity him.

Monday, May 26. Cloudy.

Told the family finances are tight. Must do something. Should minimize expenses first of all.

Sensei—the pillar and mainstay that we relied upon—is no longer in this world. I must take care of everyone. This is not a dream—it is reality. Must spur myself on.

Discussed the entire Gakkai organization with the general director. Spent a long time. Top leaders should not be obsessed with one chapter. They must protect and support the entire Gakkai and all members equally and fairly. Feel sorry for the members if their leaders are narrow-minded.

Home, exhausted. The flowers in the room are fresh and vivid. The noise of cars passing in front of the house is growing more intense. Feel like the house is shaking.

Tuesday, May 27. Clear.

An unpleasant day throughout. Woke up to a nightmare in the morning. Perhaps from exhaustion. Dreamed I was reproached and scolded by someone. Felt like someone was telling me, "Daisaku, you are a coward."

To Jozai-ji in the evening. A banquet to celebrate the inauguration of a new chief priest. The general director, the board of directors and top youth division leaders attended. Not enjoyable at all. Now that Sensei is gone, many became arrogant and haughty. Shameful.

Many thoughts. Many worries.

Writing a diary is like being in a dream. My mentor's image is deeply etched into my heart and does not leave me. Is it true he is still alive? Or is it reality that he is dead? Confused in the middle of the night.

Wednesday, May 28. Cloudy with occasional clearing.

In the morning, met with A., a Ph.D. in literature, at the headquarters. An arrogant person. Discussed the value-creation theory in conference room #1.

In the evening, attended a Katsushika block meeting, my first in a long while. Lectured on "Letter from Sado." Keenly sensed that as I practice more and my faith and practice deepen, my understanding also becomes more profound.

Overexerting myself. Must take care of my health. But I will fight. Home a little after 12:00.

Pondered. The Gosho states:

[The Great Teacher Dengyo writes that] the dove takes care to perch three branches lower than its father, wild geese keep perfect formation when they fly together, and lambs kneel to drink their mother's milk. He asks: if lowly animals conduct themselves with such propriety, how can human beings be so lacking in courtesy?

— "LETTER TO NIIKE" (WND, 1031)

I, my seniors, my elder brothers;...people in society.

Sunday, June 1. Cloudy.

Yesterday, May 31, left on the 10:00 a.m. *Mount Unzen* express from Tokyo Station to attend a Kyushu Headquarters general meeting. Traveled with eight others, including Miss K. The long trip gave us a good opportunity to unite our hearts. Arrived at Hakata Station a little before 8:00 a.m. Headed immediately for the T. Inn.

At noon, the procession of leaders entered. Some fifty thousand members gathered at the Kashii Stadium. It was a splendid general meeting. Want to praise the Kyushu members for their hard work and success.

My speech was titled "The Gakkai's History and President Toda's Magnificent Vision."

In the evening, a dinner meeting with the top leaders of Kyushu. Everyone was troubled by the arrogant and overbearing attitude of K., a leader from Tokyo assigned to Kyushu. Especially now that Sensei is gone, it is a time to warmly embrace the members. Concerned. Those who lack a good leader will be unhappy.

Who truly cares about the Gakkai members?

Who is truly grieved at Sensei's death?

Who is truly thinking of kosen-rufu?

Monday, June 2. Clear.

Took the 10:00 a.m. *Sea Gull* special express to Kyoto for guidance. A long trip. It would have been much quicker and easier by plane. Deeply felt the necessity of establishing financial strength.

In the evening, gave a lecture at S.'s home. Astonished to see how much more my friends in Kyoto have grown.

Exhausted, canceled my plans to check in at an inn; borrowed a futon and slept at S.'s. Fell asleep reading a magazine.

Tuesday, June 3. Cloudy.

Got up early in the morning. Did the five prayers of morning gongyo and chanted to my heart's content.

Expressed my deep appreciation for their hospitality.

Left Kyoto Station at 9:30 a.m. for Maizuru.

A question-and-answer session at T.'s home until 3:00 p.m. Everyone was pleased by my unexpected visit. Took a 3:20 train back to Kyoto. Attended a Kyoto leaders meeting.

In contrast to those who joyfully gathered at the civic auditorium, I lacked spirit, due to exhaustion. Led a Gakkai song for the first time in a while.

The "Song of Majesty" originated in Kyoto.

Wednesday, June 4. Clear then cloudy.

Left Kyoto Station for Tokyo on the 1:07 a.m. special express. Traveled third class. Completely worn out, both physically and spiritually. Could not even think straight.

Arrived in Tokyo just before 8:00. Went to the headquarters immediately. Did morning gongyo.

An image of Sensei gazing strictly through his glasses came to my mind. His large, warm face seemed to be encouraging me. Sensei's image lingered with me for a moment.

Let me raise my spirits and fight this month again.

Will struggle resolutely again this year.

Home after 10:00. Read *Hashire Merosu* (Run, Melose) again.

Saturday, June 7. Cloudy then rain.

Left Yokohama Station at 9:30 a.m. for Kansai to lecture. Read a book on the train. It did not sink in.

Arrived at Osaka Station at 4:30 p.m. Greeted by friends. Appreciative.

Lectured and gave guidance on the *Propagation Handbook*. Kansai is my second home town.

Sunday, June 8. Rain.

Rested in the morning.

It was hot. Osaka does not have much greenery.

In the afternoon—gave a lecture on "Meanings Hidden in the Depths."[1] Finished the chapter on the object of devotion in terms of the Law.

"Be watchful of youth" [Confucius].

In the evening, attended a Senba Chapter group chiefs meeting.

The passion of the common people.

On the way back, stopped by at Y.'s to offer a greeting. Always a bright, solid family.

Until late, talked casually with leaders at the Kansai headquarters.

1. "Meanings Hidden in the Depths [of the Lotus Sutra]": One of the six theses that make up Nichikan's *Six-volume Writings*. It clarifies that the ultimate Law secretly transmitted by means of the threefold comparison is Nam-myoho-renge-kyo of the Three Great Secret Laws. See note on p. 82.

Monday, June 9. Clear.

Rested in the morning.

The YWD leaders came over to talk. Wondered what the lives of these young women will be like ten years from now.

In the evening, attended a Kansai YWD leaders meeting at the Korean Community Center with YWD Chief M.

Bright and cheerful. Afterward, attended a unit chiefs meeting for Hokusetsu District. Many familiar faces.

Kansai is growing.

Tuesday, June 10. Cloudy.

Stayed at the Kansai headquarters. Thankful for their fine hospitality.

Hot. Heat doubles one's fatigue.

Went to Osaka Station to greet Sensei's wife. Attended a dinner meeting with her.

Thursday, June 12. Cloudy.

Five years have passed since June 12, 1953, the day we received our large, specially inscribed Gohonzon. Looked back on my faith — strictly.

Cool all the day.

Cannot forget K., who broke his promise to Sensei. I will definitely achieve kosen-rufu and avenge Sensei.

Wait. Wait with patience; perseverance.

Sensei is watching with his steady gaze. Sensei, Sensei, please keep watching over me.

Attended a planning conference for next year's campaign. Difficult to create harmony.

H. is serious. This will be a battle for vindication; will resolutely take the lead.

"Under a courageous general there are no cowardly soldiers." Also, "unity."

Friday, June 13. Cloudy.

Those who do gongyo assiduously are always improving.

It is becoming more enjoyable to meet with members and offer them guidance and encouragement.

Sunday, June 15. Cloudy.

On the 14th, at 12:30, took a trip to Karuizawa with staff members. All seemed to be enjoying themselves, but I was tired. Only the Gakkai's future was on my mind.

Stopped to rest briefly at Kumagaya and then Takasaki. Arrived at the Shiotsubo hot spring at 6:00 p.m. Was told the hot spring is alkaline and good for ailments of the stomach and skin.

Everyone enjoyed themselves playing cards and the like until late. They seemed to be happy. But when can I visit this land filled with memories of my mentor with a fresh and tranquil state of mind?

Left the inn at 10:30 a.m. on the 15th.

We went to the Onioshidashi lava field by way of Tsutsuji-ga-hara. An unearthly sight. One entire village was destroyed by the eruption of Mount Asama. Is this the burning hot hell described in Buddhism?

Fondly reminisced about my visit to this place with Sensei last summer. The severe transition of the past year is, rather, like a dream. That day, Sensei was already so deeply fatigued he had difficulty walking. Nevertheless, he troubled himself to take us, his disciples, on a tour, even though he had seen it once before.

Arrived at Tokyo Station at 7:00 p.m. A memorable day.

On the way back, treated everyone to tempura at T. restaurant in Shinjuku, where Sensei often took me to dinner.

Monday, June 16. Cloudy.

Attended a general conference of S. company at their invitation. The company is run by a dear friend. Seeing how desperately they struggle, I want to see them prosper. Keenly aware of the deficiencies of capitalism. Often think government should support and nurture small business growth.

Dropped by M.'s house on the way home. Want to support him. Talked with him until late about:

1. The Gakkai's mission.

2. His financial planning.
3. His marriage and future.
4. Trust in his business.

Wednesday, June 18. Rain.

At 10:00 a.m., a member of an old aristocratic family dropped by the headquarters. Said he wanted to pay his respects since he lives in the neighborhood. The general director and I greeted him. The secretary seemed to want to talk with him more.

A joint conference from 1:00 p.m. The top youth division leaders are serious. Hoping for such earnestness from the board of directors. Want them to open their eyes to the times and to our grand long-range plan.

In the evening, compiled Sensei's guidance, working with a few sincere members. Also took care of some of my late mentor's possessions.

Now, I must follow the way of a disciple expounded in Buddhism. My solitary, sublime resolve.

Thursday, June 19. Clear with occasional clouds.

The hundred-day anniversary of my beloved mentor's passing has yet to come.

Unsettling feelings every day. What are others feeling? I must win. Otherwise, my mentor will be saddened.

In the afternoon, gave personal guidance at the headquarters. Resolved to fight for those who are suffering.

The crystallization of noble faith. Must continue, always and forever, to make steady, unseen efforts. This is a guiding principle for our revolution.

In the evening, attended a Bunkyo Chapter meeting and a youth division meeting. Their sparkling eyes are fixed on the future.

Home after midnight.

Scheduled to depart for vast Hokkaido the day after tomorrow.

Salaries for staff members—the most vital source of their sustenance, a driving force for their battle of the Law.

Saturday, June 21. Clear.

Left for Hokkaido from Haneda Airport aboard a 10:20 a.m. Japan Airlines flight. Traveled with the general director.

After soaring through tranquil, clear skies, the plane landed smoothly at the airport in Chitose.

Arrived at the M. Inn at 2:30 p.m. Had a conference with local leaders to discuss various issues.

Hokkaido, land of great natural beauty. Hokkaido, the land of youth. It is also a land of poetry and romance, a historic place where my mentor once lived. Hokkaido also brings back memories of my father, who worked to develop the land. I love Hokkaido.

Climbed to the television broadcasting tower observation deck. It is almost 300 feet high, I was told, and commands a sweeping view of the city of Sapporo.

Sunday, June 22. Fair.

The first Hokkaido YWD general meeting was held with two thousand attending. The first Hokkaido YMD general meeting was also held with an attendance of three thousand. Invigorating, joyful meetings.

This expansive land where President Makiguchi and President Toda once frolicked as youth is the pride of those who live here.

At night, deeply pondered the following:
1. The Gakkai's direction for the first hundred days, one year, three years and seven years after my mentor's passing.
2. To whom the core of the Gakkai should be entrusted and how.
3. His surviving family.
4. Proper attitude of top leaders in giving guidance.

My thoughts continue endlessly.

Friday, June 27. Clear.

The temperature surpassed 86°.

Recalled last year's Coal Miners Union Incident, memories of Sensei and the Osaka Incident.

In the afternoon, gave individual guidance at the headquarters. My health is fine. As long as I am healthy, there is nothing to fear.

Attended a conference in the evening. A serious, life-or-death battle.

On the way home, strolled with friends through the pine-lined Imperial Palace Square, bathed in the moonlight.

Saturday, June 28. Cloudy.

Gakkai criticism will not cease. My heart throbs with my mentor's admonition, "Never slacken in your pursuit against evil." This is a battle for justice. Carefully pondered plans for the next seven years.

The temperature rose to almost 90° today again. Heard this was a record high. It was really hot.

Gave strict guidance to top youth division leaders: "Let's resolutely protect the headquarters!"... A dinner meeting afterward.

Sunday, June 29. Cloudy.

In the morning, read *Tales of Suiko* in bed.

Feel like I am exhausting my mind and my body—to realize my boundless imagination. Want to live each day with composure, but perhaps true composure in life can be established only through hard work and severe upheaval.

The water shortage is becoming serious. This is a year of the three calamities.[1]

At 1:00 p.m., the first student division general meeting was held at the Meguro Civic Auditorium with 800 attending.

Offered congratulations. Wondered how well everyone grasped the intent of Sensei's speech at the third YMD general meeting.

Told myself: I will spend the rest of my life just continuing to proclaim my late mentor's spirit. Sensei, please pardon me for doing so.

1. Three calamities: Disasters said to occur at the end of a kalpa. They include two sets—the three lesser calamities, which are, briefly, warfare, pestilence and famine; and the three greater calamities, which are fire, wind and water. Nichiren Daishonin attributes the fundamental cause of these calamities to be ignorance of the Law of Nam-myoho-renge-kyo, which gives rise to the three poisons—greed, anger and stupidity—the fundamental evils inherent in life.

Monday, June 30. Cloudy.

Exhausting work again today. A painful day.

Received many guests. Discussed the future with Sensei's family.

Regrettably, many leaders lack a guiding principle. It seems they can think only of themselves.

Simply want to be a person of pure faith who lives out my life courageously for an ideal.

Friday, July 4. Cloudy.

It's already July. Last July, I was confined at the Osaka Detention House. This year, though my body is free, my heart is bound. Last year, though immersed in the struggle to spread the Law, I was filled with joy because Sensei was here. This year, though the campaign for kosen-rufu is moving ahead, I am sad, because Sensei is gone.

My tooth has been aching lately. Must see a dentist.

Took the 2:40 p.m. Japan Airlines flight to Hokkaido to attend a general meeting. Travelled with A.; N. and O. met us on our arrival.

Attended a guidance meeting for Sapporo Chapter. Urged the senior leaders, who lack caring and compassion for their juniors, to reflect on themselves.

Saturday, July 5. Clear.

A very hot day. Hokkaido seems to be as hot as Tokyo.

Went to a barber with Department Chief U. in the morning. Talked with him on the way.

Attended a guidance meeting at I.'s home in the afternoon. Did gongyo.

> *Gen kai e renbo.*
> *Ni sho katsu-go shin.*
> *Shujo ki shin-buku.*
> *Shichi-jiki i nyunan.*
> *Isshin yokken butsu.*
> *Fu ji shaku shinmyo.*

> All harbor thoughts of yearning
> and in their minds thirst to gaze at me.
> When living beings have become truly faithful,
> honest and upright, gentle in intent,
> single-mindedly desiring to see the Buddha,
> not hesitating even if it costs them their lives,...
>
> —(LS16, 230)

In the evening, attended a run-through at Maruyama Field.

President Toda's disciples are serious—as if preparing to welcome Sensei himself to their meeting. The senior leaders, however, arrogantly think the members are working hard to welcome them. How foolish.

Talked casually with the top youth division leaders until midnight.

Dream of tomorrow.... This is my second visit to Hokkaido this year. Let me rest well. Good night, Sensei.

Sunday, July 6. Clear.

The Second Hokkaido General Meeting. It began a little before noon.

Hot all day. I gave a speech titled "Toward Realizing Kosen-rufu."

My entire life is dedicated to declaring and fighting to realize President Toda's vision—his last will. This is my only mission in this world.

Let those who laugh do so. Let those who are angry with me be so.

It is only natural that I live my life as a disciple, true to my belief. To fulfill this mission throughout my life is absolutely correct from the standpoint of faith. May all bodhisattvas and Buddhas of the ten directions and throughout past, present and future watch over me.

Attended a banquet at the railroad company's office.

I adore the breeze, the moon and the greenery of Hokkaido. I love it.

Monday, July 7. Clear.

Hot in Hokkaido again today.

Went to Sapporo Station to see off the high priest at 8:00 a.m. To see him in good health is reassuring.

Rode a tramway in the morning with others. Told that it was recently completed.

Stopped by U.'s home before returning to Tokyo aboard an evening JAL flight.

Tuesday, July 8. Cloudy.

Feeling completely out of sorts. Rested in the morning. Is it fatigue from the trip—in spite of my young age? Regrettable. My temperature was 100.4°.

Any society is complex, and things do not go as one wishes. Conflicts in the human world. There seems to be nothing as beautiful or as ugly as the of human realm.

Buddhism transforms the realm of impermanence into that of eternity, happiness, true self and purity.

Cool all day. Want to live for ten or twenty more years. Want to show the clear actual proof of my mentor before I die.

> *I ses^shuju ho.*
> *Mai ji sa ze nen.*

> I preach various doctrines for them.
> At all times I think to myself....
> —(LS16, 232)

Wednesday, July 9. Cloudy.

Slight fever—100.4°. Feel some pain in my internal organs. There is no choice but to advance with earnest faith.

Took the 1:30 p.m. express to the head temple to attend the memorial service commemorating the hundredth day since my mentor's passing and to lay his ashes to rest.

Arrived at the head temple with the Toda family shortly before 5:00. The stately memorial service was held at the Grand Lecture Hall at 7:00.

The high priest led the sutra recitation and offered words of reminiscence.

Quietly renewed and solidified my profound resolve.

Thursday, July 10. Clear.

Stayed at the head temple.

Completed memorial services commemorating the hundredth day after my mentor's passing. Finished the ceremony in which his ashes were laid to rest.

Thus ends the entirety of Sensei's life. Ah—Sensei no longer exists in this world.

Due to the oneness of life and death, however, Sensei is here now. Tears of warm emotion—Sensei, please watch over me.

His ashes were placed in the grave, and I said, "Sensei, please rest well." Offered five sticks of incense, one each from my wife, Hiromasa, Shirohisa, Takahiro and me.

Saturday, July 12. Cloudy.

Took the *Swallow* special express to Kansai to attend a general meeting.

The last regional youth division general meeting to be held this year.

Boarded the train at Yokohama Station with division chiefs and top youth division leaders.

Felt it getting hotter as we approached Kansai.

The top youth division leaders have grown splendidly. I. needs a little more improvement.

Members at the Kansai headquarters are strenuously preparing for the general meeting. Truly thankful for their hard work. Firmly believe such efforts in practice will be a cause that will definitely bring about their development and contribution as capable individuals.

Sunday, July 13. Clear.

The First Kansai Youth Division General Meeting.

Place: the Osaka Prefectural Gymnasium.

The YWD meeting was held at 12 noon.

The YMD meeting began at 4:30 p.m.

Attending were seven thousand YWD members and eight thousand YMD members.

Truly a splendid general meeting. Excellent. Kansai did very well. Afterward, ate sushi with the top leaders. Delicious.

Want to spend my life actively, with the vigor of youth.

Wednesday, July 16. Clear.

Stayed in a reception room at the headquarters. Talked with President Toda's family for half the day. They were extremely pleased. Nothing gives me more joy. My greatest happiness is seeing that they have overcome their sorrow and understood my heart. Want to be a person who understands the hearts of others.

A joint conference from 5:00. The meeting turned into heated discussion—we are only human. This may be good, since we are in the process of new construction. Yet I am the only one to protect Sensei's main castle.

Went home, alone. A hot day.

Must stand up with a resolve of *fu ji shaku shinmyo*, "not hesitating even if it costs them their lives" (LS16,230), aiming seven years ahead.

Thursday, July 17. Clear.

Solidified my resolve for the next battle for the Law. Excited all day —like a young lion.

Sensei's family, their faces cheerful, came to the headquarters to offer greetings. Happy.

Gave personal guidance and encouragement to members in the afternoon. Put my entire being into it.

Afterward, spoke with I. until late. He does not easily understand my intent. Can only pray our beautiful friendship continues the rest of our lives.

Went to M.'s home to offer a greeting and gift for the summer holiday.

Amid a confused battle, what a young reformist needs most is fortitude.

Saturday, July 19. Cloudy then rain.

My temperature was above normal again this morning.

M., having recovered, came to the headquarters in the morning. Truly wonderful. Faith will determine the rest.

Took the 1:30 p.m. express to Niigata. Rain began to fall from the area around Takasaki. Felt a cool breeze. Very refreshing.

Arrived in Niigata at 7:30. Immediately headed for the temple to attend a chapter leaders meeting. Our friends from Echigo are in high spirits.

Tomorrow will be the first athletic meet for Niigata Chapter.

Sunday, July 20 — Monday, 21. Rain.

Rain. Felt sorry. So did everyone else.

Another guidance meeting at the temple in the morning. Eventually announced the cancellation of the athletic meet.

Took the 12:00 p.m. steamship to Sado Island with quite a few others, crossing amid giant waves. Many became seasick from the rolling of the ship. We finally arrived after being sprayed by the waves for more than four hours. All ferry service after ours was cancelled. An unforgettable day.

Checked into an inn and slept deeply from fatigue. Woke up with a start and headed immediately to a leaders guidance meeting.

Spoke on the Buddhist view of life. The four kinds of wheels the wheel-turning kings[1] possess are gold, silver, copper and iron, which represent the sufferings of birth, aging, sickness and death.

The "Orally Transmitted Teachings" state:

> With regard to the [wheels of] gold, silver, copper and iron, gold indicates life; silver resembles bleached bones, and thus indicates death; copper gives the appearance of old age; and iron indicates sickness. Thus they signify the Buddha's four acts of enabling all people to open, show, awaken to and enter the Buddha wisdom.
>
> —(GZ, 733)

Visited Ichinosawa and a temple at Tsukahara on the next day, the 21st. Became aware of the enormous difference between the real history of these places and what they represent now. In any case, enjoyed walking and reminiscing about the Daishonin's history. Spent a meaningful half day.

My very first visit to Sado. Resolved to visit again and spend more time.

1. Wheel-turning kings: Ideal rulers in Indian mythology. In Buddhism, they are regarded as kings who rule the world by justice rather than force.

Wednesday, July 23. Rain.

The eleventh typhoon of the year hit the mainland.

From around 8:00 a.m., the typhoon rampaged the Kanto area, including Metropolitan Tokyo. It created a great inconvenience for those commuting to the headquarters. A dreadful downpour. It was reported that it is the first large-scale typhoon in nine years.

In the afternoon, a joint conference with the board of directors was held in the headquarters reception room. Discussed were:

1. Events in August.
2. Personnel appointments.
3. Analysis of each chapter.

Also, voices expressed hope for the earliest possible appearance of a responsible leader rather than continuing with collective leadership.

Attended a block meeting in Katsushika in the evening.

My own unceasing action.

Went home singing "The Song of Wu Chang Yuan." Home after midnight.

My wife's bright, calm face.

Thursday, July 24. Cloudy.

Bad weather. Hot and humid all day. In the morning, attended a *Daibyakurenge* editorial conference. The fan was ineffective. Everyone was sweating. We need an air-conditioning system installed soon, I thought.

Told the editorial staff: "Our magazine is not just for a few individuals. Don't forget that it's a guidebook for the entire Gakkai."

Afterward, talked with Director H. An easygoing person.

Be strong, everyone.

In the evening, went to the home of attorney H. to discuss the cemetery issue and other matters. Few lawyers stand up for justice. Because of this, the underprivileged remain miserable. In the power politics realm, the common people's sufferings are the same as in the days of the Tokugawa shogunate.

Religious revolution. Social revolution. The people must rise to create their own society. Must become the detonator to spark this change.

Friday, July 25. Cloudy.

The July headquarters leaders meeting was held at the Toshima Civic Auditorium at 6:00 p.m.

Without Sensei as the pillar, it was a forlorn gathering. Afterward, a top leaders meeting was held at Jozai-ji. They are out of step with one another.

Is self-preservation human beings' ultimate nature? Lamented — where are President Toda's disciples?

I will fight. Sensei, please watch over me.

I will struggle — never being praised by the foolish.

I will strive amidst the storm — only to be praised by Sensei.

Took a train home from Ikebukuro Station. Saw many friends in the crowded station.

Saturday, July 26. Rain.

A melancholy day.

Talked with Miss K. in the headquarters reception room about various aspects of the Gakkai's future. She told me her concern was growing each day. Emphasized to her the importance of unity among President Makiguchi's disciples.

From 5:30 p.m., invited student priests from the head temple to dinner at G. restaurant. They will determine the future of the priesthood.

Left for Lake Kawaguchi at 6:20, while the dinner was still under way. Arrived at the K. Inn at 10:00.

The Suiko Group. Spent a night with one hundred comrades, reminiscing about President Toda. We pledged to one another to become capable individuals for kosen-rufu. Guidance to all about taking practical action.

The members' joyous faces, concealing their resolve.

Looked at the name list of the first graduating class of the Suiko Group for the first time in a long while.

Sunday, July 27. Cloudy.

Arose early in the morning.

After breakfast, we all boarded a motorboat for a cruise around the lake. Felt refreshed.

In the morning, we engaged energetically in sports such as dodge ball and sumo wrestling.

Left at noon. Stopped by Lake Yamanaka. Enjoyed ourselves horseback riding and bicycle racing.

Arrived at the headquarters at 6:00 p.m.

Stopped by the home of my wife's parents in Yaguchi with K. We were treated to dinner. Got home early.

My wife told me I was pretty sunburned.

Monday, July 28. Cloudy.

Went to the Nakano Community Center in the evening. Concerned about the neighbors; it is located in the middle of a residential area. Want to build many community centers that members can use freely.

Attended a youth division meeting and a district chiefs meeting. They have a greater seeking spirit than I do. Respect them.

Resolved to further deepen my Buddhist study beginning in August. Those who seriously exert themselves in study during this age of stagnation will show, after a few years, a remarkable difference from those who do not. Must be careful.

Ate in Shinjuku on the way home.

Home just before 11:00. My tranquil, happy home.

Thursday, July 31. Clear.

Met with K. at 8:30 a.m. for just under an hour.

When I handed him my business card, he immediately said, "I've already heard your name from President Toda." Astonished at Sensei's foresight and initiative.

Hoping for a drastic change of the times, I returned to the headquarters. Watch what we will accomplish in twenty years!

In seven years, will build the Grand Reception Hall. In another seven, we will build the Sho-Hondo—the Grand Main Temple. And after another seven years, in 1979, will take a great step forward toward kosen-rufu. During the next seven-year period, what raging waves will arise before us?

My thoughts are limitless. My ideas are unending.

Informal evening discussion with YMD and YWD corps chiefs.

Sunday, August 10. Clear.

Left for Kyoto on the 8th aboard the *Swallow* special express. Traveled third-class. Not so bad.

Discussed several matters with local leaders.

To Arashi-yama afterward. Kyoto—its picturesque scenery, brimming with poetry—a spiritual home for the Japanese people.

Hot again on the 9th. Got up early. Stayed in Kyoto.

Took the 7:10 p.m. *Unzen* train to Kyushu with Miss K. and others. Studied and discussed Buddhism on the train.

Arrived at Hakata Station just after 8:00 on the morning of the 10th. Hot. Attended the completion and enshrinement ceremony for the Kyushu headquarters building.

Visited the ruins of a famous fortress. Imagined the winds that must have gusted through the pines there. The stone wall conjures images of soldiers in a fierce battle.

A huge coal sludge mound vividly depicted the poor's stark social reality. Genkai Sea clam fishermen remind me of my Haneda boyhood.

A disjointed meeting. Is it because the Gakkai lacks strong leadership now that our mentor is gone?

Wednesday, August 20. Cloudy.

Returned from the Nagano and Suwa areas, where I have been traveling to give guidance since the 16th.

Took the *Swallow* to Kansai, and then to Kyushu today. My promise to Sensei.... At last my battle has begun.

To Kagoshima and Sakurajima, and then on to Miyazaki for guidance. Will exert myself even more, with the "power of an attacking lion." Joyful faces, especially those of the youth division, flash though my mind one after another. Will fight for the sake of these pure-hearted members.

A history of toil amid the heat of Kyushu.

Wednesday, August 27.

Arrived at Tokyo Station at 4:30 p.m. My wife and children, and friends from Bunkyo and Katsushika greeted me.

Went straight to the headquarters. Reported to the general director and others. A usual day at the headquarters.

Hot all day.

Attended an evening Katsushika general block meeting.

Home a little after 11:00.

Opened the Lotus Sutra before going to bed:

"The father understood his sons and knew what various toys and curious objects each child customarily liked and what would delight them. And so he said to them, 'The kind of playthings you like are rare and hard to find. If you do not take them when you can, you will surely regret it later. For example, things like these goat-carts, deer-carts, and ox-carts. They are outside the gate now where you can play with them. So you must come out of this burning house at once. Then whatever ones you want, I will give them all to you!'"

—(LS3, 57)

Thursday, August 28. Clear.

Exhausted all day.

As I begin to charge ahead, cannot help my own turbulent feelings. Anger can be either good or evil. It cannot be helped in the battle to spread the Law.

Now that the lion king is gone, have no choice but to roar as a young lion.

Gave strict guidance to N. of Hokkaido, R. of Kamata and S. — because they are so dear to me.

Sat alone on the porch and pondered how the priesthood, the Gakkai and kosen-rufu will have developed ten years from now.

Enjoyed the taste and aroma of the tea my wife made.

Friday, August 29. Cloudy.

Attended the August headquarters leaders meeting at the Toshima Civic Auditorium.

Some leaders are serious; others move merely by force of habit. Some interpret things shallowly, for their own convenience; others live with perseverance. Due to the law of cause and effect, clear proof will reveal itself one day.

A top leaders meeting at Jozai-ji. The existence of one arrogant leader hampers the growth of many other people. They become as miserable as children without parents.

Ate sushi with some friends on the way home.

Home after 11:00.

Sunday, August 31. Cloudy.

My toothache has not let up since yesterday. Felt feverish all day.

Have not seen a dentist in half a year. What am I doing?

From 4:00 p.m., conducted interviews with youth division leadership candidates at Omori Beach. There are people of intellect and people of passion. Such bright, youthful junior members are truly dear to my heart.

To the Ota Ward Civic Center at 6:35. Attended Kamata Chapter meeting commemorating its achieving a membership of 100,000 households. Heard the meeting was attended by group-level leaders and above.

Decided to go home early to get some rest.

Must read seriously. Autumn is a season for tranquil contemplation. I will read.

Tuesday, September 2. Cloudy.

It's been getting cooler each morning and evening. The scorching heat is gone. Autumn is deepening.

How many springs and autumns will I see in my lifetime? What will the future hold in ten or twenty years for those now exerting themselves with youthful energy?

Is impermanence the essential aspect of all things? Or is it permanence?

Read! Think! Get physically fit!

Talked for three hours with the general director in reception room #1. Afterward attended a dinner meeting with the board of directors. Had informal talks with them.

Extremely busy. Home at almost midnight.

Wednesday, September 3. Clear.

The governor of Metropolitan Tokyo requested a meeting for tomorrow. The general director told me he intended to honor the governor's request.

There are many media reports critical of the Gakkai. Most are based on prejudice and ignorance, but we must also self-reflect.

We must naturally respect society, while challenging its irrationality. This is the essence of Buddhism and of religious reformation.

Attended a joint conference at 5:30 p.m. Deepened my resolve toward next year's turbulent battle. Will take the lead, trusting only those willing to fight and advance together.

At tonight's conference, again, participants were out of step with one another.

Monday, September 8. Clear.

Yesterday, attended a sports festival sponsored by the Kansai youth division in Kobe City. The sight of progressive youth.

At 7:30 a.m., departed from A. Inn in Kobe. Boarded the *Swallow*.

Cooler than yesterday. Refreshing autumn.

A gathering of YMD and YWD leaders at the headquarters. Offered guidance until late at the headquarters.

On the way home, stopped by the Kamata Chapter center. Discussed issues concerning the future with the general director and others.

Tired...must build a solid road for others to follow.

Tuesday, September 9. Clear.

Five months have passed since President Toda's death—long, truly agonizing months. What course will my life take from here on? Is it my destiny to continue this life-or-death struggle?

Attended a YMD and YWD joint conference at the headquarters at 7:00 p.m. Spoke about the significance of our sports festivals.

Will never forget, for the rest of my life, those youth who are now fighting beside me. Must impart philosophy to youth. Must keep the promise I have made to them.

Friday, September 12. Rain.

The anniversary of the Tatsunokuchi Persecution.

Have come to understand, of late, my mentor's heart when he said, "Return to the days of the Daishonin!"

In the evening, attended a youth division sports festival staff meeting. May have asserted my opinion too strongly. Should better trust and foster the creativity of youth.

The headquarters building is getting too small. When will we build a new, solid headquarters building?

Yet to be known are: the Gakkai's progress, my own future, the strength and future of youth division leaders.

Wednesday, September 17. Rain.

An interminable downpour. Heard it was due to Typhoon #21.

In the morning, accompanied the general director to find him a new home. Must look after everyone.

Attended an afternoon joint conference at the headquarters. Deeply troubled by the leaders' lack of reason and sensibility. 'Consistency from beginning to end.' Must focus first on developing leaders.

Decided on the formation of new chapters. The ship of the Gakkai is sailing ahead steadily on its course. Happy.

Constantly overtaxing my body and mind.

Thursday, September 18. Rain, then cloudy.

Typhoon #21 wreaked havoc this morning. It was at its fiercest around 8:00 a.m., like an angry *asura* demon set loose in the air.

Eventually, blue skies emerged. Autumn is deepening. Refreshing. At dusk, the skies were magnificent, like a painting of unparalleled beauty.

The issue of Taiwan was discussed at the U.N. General Assembly. The level of anxiety about the world situation risies moment to moment. We are entering an era of unprecedented turbulence for humanity. How grave our responsibility will become as we move closer to the twenty-first century.

Tranquillity has finally returned to the headquarters after quite some time. Sensei's headquarters. We will protect it.

Went with M. and A. to bring an invitation to the sports festival to Sensei's family in Meguro.

My wife came to Kamata Station to meet me.

The constant autumn breeze sinks deeply into my life. It quietly permeates my heart.

Friday, September 19. Clear.

Attended T.'s second daughter's funeral at Jozai-ji. Ended at 4:00 p.m.

Waited for K. and H., expecting to meet with them. Was told they went somewhere else. Waited for them in vain. Inconsiderate people.

After a while, received a call from K. Told him of my desire for closer communication. "I'll go alone," I told him.

Saturday, September 20. Clear.

Hot all day; the lingering heat of summer.

Concerned that without a clear purpose, people's seriousness will eventually wane. Am I alone in thinking this way?

Thought how important are those who offer guidance and encouragement to others, giving them direction. Worried. Am I the only one?

Stayed at the headquarters until late. Few leaders remained there, probably because most went out to meetings.

Took a taxi to Gotanda and caught a train home from there. Saw a group of those disgruntled with the Gakkai walking in front of the station. What are they thinking? Where are they going?

Tuesday, September 23. Cloudy.

On Sunday the 21st, attended a joint practice at the National Athletic Field. Was moved by the seriousness of the members who practiced until late. Is this what is meant by intensive practice? Power, strength, energy for the future. So long as we have these youth, I thought. Felt profound joy and resolve arise within me.

Was extremely busy all day on the 22nd. Thanked the top youth division leaders for their hard work.

Got up at 7:00 on the 23rd. Attended the sports festival—with the conviction that Sensei was also in attendance. A festival of youth. Spectators numbered more than seventy thousand. A magnificent spectacle. Excellent.

Greatly missed Sensei's presence.

It was President Toda alone who always watched over us youth with love and compassion. We found lives truly worth living. We were happy.

Tired. Scheduled to leave for Osaka tomorrow to attend the trial.

Wednesday, September 24. Rain.

Took a 9:00 p.m. express to Osaka to appear in court. Traveled in a second-class sleeping car with several friends. Acted cheerfully on the train but was deeply fatigued.

Thanked them for their sincerity.

Thursday, September 25. Cloudy.

Arrived at Osaka Station at 7:27 a.m. Greeted by the familiar faces of the leaders on our arrival. It's wonderful to have such comrades. Immediately headed for the Kansai headquarters.

Attended the public trial from 10:00 a.m. to 4:00 p.m. at the Osaka District Court. The session ended without me saying a word. Felt the proceedings went very unfavorably.

On the way back, went to Seikyo-ji to pay my respects. Also stopped by the home of Chapter Chief T.

In the evening, attended an enshrinement ceremony for A. Chanted for his development.

Rested alone in Sensei's room after midnight.

Friday, September 26. Rain.

Slept until late—so late I almost missed my train.

Jumped on the 9:00 a.m. special express at Osaka Station.

Traveled alone, reading and resting. It was drizzling outside. It was slightly chilly inside the train.

The train stopped at Fuji Station at 2:20 p.m. because of Typhoon #22. Our departure time was yet to be announced.

Saw some believers connected to Hongyo-ji. They told me they were on their way back from the head temple where they had lain ashes. Forty of them were waiting for a train at the station. It was good to see them, but felt sorry for them. Bought some sushi and ate together. Everyone was pleased. Happy.

Sent telegrams to my home and the Gakkai headquarters about my delay.

The headquarters sent me a telegram at Fuji Station: "The leaders meeting has been canceled."

By midnight, all the food was gone from both inside the train and the station. Ceaseless, torrential rain. A tedious but memorable night.

People's hearts are changeable. One can believe in and rely on only those who uphold the objectives of faith and exert themselves in practice.

What is victory in life?

What is a life of justice and integrity?

Tuesday, October 7. Rain.

Autumn is deepening. A serene day.

Autumn is a time to read. Today, began reading *A Complete Anthology of Japanese Literature*.

Attended M.'s Gohonzon-enshrinement ceremony. A happy gathering. The people of Bunkyo have beautiful hearts.

They have my deep appreciation.

In November, we will begin expanding and reorganizing the chapters. A tortuous road lies ahead of me again.

Must deepen my faith. Must strengthen my resolve. More daimoku?

Wednesday, October 8. Clear.

Full of vitality in the morning; exhausted by evening.

My life feels small at times and expansive at others.

At times, I am filled with conviction, while at others, I am overwhelmed with worries.

Lectured on "Letter to Akimoto" at the headquarters in the evening. Was not adequately prepared. It was nothing extraordinary. In giving a lecture, preparation and research are most important. Absolutely no more superficial, casual study. Strictly self-reflected.

Left for home with the general director and others.

I am a disciple of President Toda. Will resolutely advance along this path for the rest of my life.

Friday, October 10. Clear.

An autumn outing for the headquarters staff. Last year, we went to Ajiro in Izu with Sensei. His last trip. Sensei's action—to push himself despite his illness.

Today, there are seventy of us in all. The staff has grown large in number. Stayed one night at the K. Inn in Ajiro, reminiscing about Sensei. Everyone seemed to be enjoying themselves, dancing and boating. An anxious day for me. Is this natural for the one responsible?

Saturday, October 11. Clear.

Rested in the morning.

Left the inn at 11:30. Ate lunch at the K. Inn in Atami along the way —with friends from Bunkyo Chapter.

Saw everyone off at 2:30 p.m. Spent the night at the K. Inn with the general director and top youth division leaders so that we could have a joint conference.

Everyone either went to a movie or took a bath. Could not hold our conference in the end.

Sunday, October 12. Clear.

A solar eclipse. Read in an article that the next one is five years away. Woke up at 7:00. Took a morning bath.

To Odawara at 9:30. Waited there to join the Kayo Group[1] members, who arrived by bus. They all seemed listless, apparently due to fatigue from not having slept well on the bus.

Arrived at Lake Ashino at 11:00. Eighty of us in all. We enjoyed boating and table tennis until 2:30 p.m. We all gathered for a meeting afterward.

—Leaders should not succumb to obstacles.

—A youth division leader should have pride.

—Be aware of the Gakkai direction and what lies at its core.

—Seek guidance from many people.

We all boarded a sightseeing boat that cruised straight across Lake Ashino. At the other shore, we boarded a bus for Tokyo.

Everyone was in high spirits. I was exhausted. So glad it was sunny today.

Must continue day after day to cultivate my life with faith, practice and study. Must single-mindedly exert myself in faith.

1. Kayo Group: A special training group for YWD leaders, comparable to the Suiko Group for the YMD.

Tuesday, October 14. Clear.

On the 13th, a scuffle broke out during a session of the Diet. Watch for our comrades ten years from now. Will quietly await their appearance.

Took President Toda's family to Shiga Prefecture to gather *matsutake* mushrooms. They were pleased and seemed to enjoy themselves.

Bright autumn sunshine.

In the car on the way back, they all seemed content, like children.

Attended a youth division executive leaders conference, which went until late in the evening.

Spent the morning of the 14th at Seikyo Press. Attended a panel discussion about our cultural movement with the general director and Director K.

In the afternoon, met with members at the headquarters. Offered them guidance and encouragement. There are many troubled people waiting for patient, kindhearted and convincing guidance.

Attended a joint conference in the evening. Everyone seemed reserved and hesitant. When a general is foolish, his council will lose its creativity. May a new era come soon!

Wednesday, October 15. Clear.

Hot all day.

Took plenty of time to do gongyo in the morning. Felt my life stabilize. A mystic function.

Ate breakfast and went to work in high spirits.

Home just before 10:00.

Read the Gosho until 2:00.

Saturday, October 18. Cloudy.

Fair on the 17th.

Took the *Swallow* to Kyoto with President Toda's family. Stayed one night at Y. Hotel.

On the 18th, rested until 9:00. We all took an old-style Japanese bath together. In the evening, treated them to chicken pot dinner at T. restaurant.

People in Kyoto took great care of us.

Everything in Kyoto is like a set in a drama—its streets, greenery, rivers and mountains; its crimson leaves, gardens and its people.

Monday, October 20. Clear.

Each day is precious. Every day is a decisive battle.

My present mission is to protect the headquarters.

Must resolutely protect and support the Gakkai members. This is my calling.

Let persecutions assail me. I will neither fear nor hesitate.

Want to become a true leader who possesses wisdom and courage.

Brought a wedding gift to S.'s home. Did my utmost to encourage them. Talked with my brothers for about two hours.

Read a book by a famous old author. His style is interesting. But he is antiquated—a person of the past. Thought about growing old myself.

Sunday, November 9. Cloudy then rain.

The nineteenth general meeting at the Korakuen Bicycle Racing Grounds.

The place where the final roar of the lion—President Toda—resounded.

The meeting began at noon. A gathering of seventy thousand members.

It started to rain around the time a chapter chief was speaking. One of the more memorable general meetings.

Ten new chapters were formed: In Aomori, Fukushima, Kawasaki, Shizuoka, Toyohashi, Takamatsu, Nagasaki, Kumamoto, Miyazaki and Kagoshima. Expanding the number of chapters is fine. But what really matters is broad dissemination of Sensei's spirit.

Have not, in recent times, been as tired as I was today.

Attended a YMD and YWD joint leaders conference at Jozai-ji.

Discussed the future of President Toda's direct disciples. Some understood while others did not.

A dinner meeting with the top youth division leaders. The rain never stopped as I made my way home.

Sense that difficulties lie ahead.

Thought of President Toda's family and the board of directors along the way.

Monday, November 10. Cloudy.

Every day, I feel my late mentor's compassion flowing and pulsating within my being.

Need excellent, capable individuals. Many emotions.

In the evening, attended I. and M.'s wedding ceremony at Myoko-ji.

Wish them happiness. Very concerned about the future of these two, who are filled with vanity. Could not help sensing that their faith is crumbling.

Home early.

Chanted daimoku to my heart's content. Read.

Prayed people will emerge who can fight with an understanding of our mentor's heart—as many as possible.

Prayed for the great happiness of President Toda's family.

Tuesday, November 11. Clear.

A clear autumn day.

Made clean copies of Sensei's imprisonment records for the future.

Recorded his guidance for the sake of those to follow.

Tears welled at the thought of President Toda imprisoned under government persecution. The devil of the sixth heaven entered the minds of those in power and persecuted Sensei—the "Count of Monte Cristo."

Stayed at the headquarters until late.

Organized Sensei's guidance alone. My heart burns, at times, with passion at the guidance of this leader of unprecedented caliber. When can I extol him to the world?

"Buddhas! Bodhisattvas! Heavenly gods! Let me live long!" I pray. Long enough to finish recording the accurate history of kosen-rufu led by my mentor and leave it behind for eternity.

To this end, must take care of my health. To this end, as the sutra states, "Let us live out our lives!" (LS16, 228)

Home just after midnight.

A tranquil room, rich with the scents of autumn.

Tuesday, November 25. Clear.

Visited the head temple the day before yesterday.

Problems are arising constantly with other religious groups. Cannot afford to be defeated. Must not degrade the Law.

Day after day, the Gakkai stands amidst the violent storm. No other way but to stake my life and take the lead with profound resolve.

Read randomly until midnight.

Friends of falsehood are worse than public enemies. Want true friends.

Wednesday, December 10. Fair.

Slightly feverish—100°.

A struggle against destiny, against a life laden with karmic retribution. Stayed at the headquarters until late. Concerned about the salary of the headquarters staff.

Cannot help sensing that more hardships await us next year. How many are willing to take full responsibility and fight this noble battle to spread the Law? The road ahead is severe.

It was December 12—the winter of 1950.... Recalled the poem Sensei composed during the difficulties with his publishing company, the Nihon Shogakkan:

> Amidst the ferocious blizzard,
> A man, courageous and persistent, walks on,
> Gladdened by the love of his comrades.

Tonight I composed a poem, which I set down on calligraphy paper:

> From today,
> I shall arise
> as the Buddha's emissary,
> and continue until
> my pledge to my mentor is fulfilled
> and death calls.

Sensei is always watching over me with his compassionate gaze and kind expression.

Friday, December 12. Fair.

Took an injection in the morning.

My physical condition was poor all day. Miserable.

In the afternoon, went to inspect tomorrow's YWD general meeting site.

The youth are moving ahead dynamically. Will fight for them, throughout my life, sacrificing myself if need be. This is precisely what my mentor did.

Visited H.'s home to congratulate him. Had a casual dinner alone together. For how many more years will things remain this way?

"All is changeable, nothing is constant. This is the law of birth and death."

—(GZ, 1384)

Eternity, happiness, true self and purity.

—(GZ, 751)

"Its sagacious beams shine without measure."

—(LS16, 231)

Saturday, December 13. Fair.

The Sixth YWD General Meeting.

The place: The Tokyo Gymnasium.

Participants: twenty thousand.

Splendid. A great success. Outstanding progress. With this, our future victory is assured. It will be when these young women have grown into top women's division leaders; when their children have grown to become the successors of the Gakkai.

In the future, without fail, the YWD will be a gathering of several tens of thousands, or even several million members.

The sutra states: "It is just as when a great lion roars: the young lions will be emboldened and all other beasts will run far and lay low."

Read the sutra until late.

The faces of my children, sound asleep.

FIDEL CASTRO'S FORCES defeated the Batista regime on January 1. On February 16, he was inaugurated as Cuban premier. On January 3, Alaska became the fourty-ninth American state.

To commemorate the first anniversary of the March 16 "Ceremony for Kosen-rufu," youth representatives traveled to the head temple, where they visited Josei Toda's grave. At that event, Chief of Staff Ikeda suggested that the youth division hold commemorative events every year on that date.

At Korakuen Baseball Stadium, on June 25, the emperor of Japan attended his first professional game. In the bottom of the ninth inning, the Tokyo Giants' Shigeo Nagashima hit a game-winning home run and established his reputation as a national baseball hero. In this game, Sadaharu Oh also homered, beginning what was known in Japanese professional baseball as the ON era (taking the initial from both sluggers' names).

The second nationwide Soka Gakkai athletic meet, the Festival of Youth, was held at the National Athletic Stadium in Tokyo on September 13. From around the nation, seventy-thousand youth participated. Chief of Staff Ikeda said at the closing ceremonies: "The mission of the Gakkai is to construct nations of supreme culture and world peace. To realize our mentor's wish to rid this earth of misery, we have no choice but to spread Nichiren Daishonin's philosophy throughout human society." On September 26, a powerful typhoon hit the central coast of Japan, wreaking unprecedented havoc. A million and a half people were affected by the raging storms, with 5,000 dead or missing and 575,000 houses severely damaged or destroyed. While national and municipal governments were slow to respond, the Gakkai headquarters dispatched a rescue team to the affected area. Chief of Staff Ikeda, manning a rowboat, participated in the rescue operations.

The sixty-fifth high priest, Nichijun Horigome, bequeathed his office to his successor Nittatsu Hosoi, on November 15, and then died two days later. He was sixty-one.

Thursday, January 1. Rain.

This year marks the 706th anniversary of the establishment of Nichiren Daishonin's Buddhism.

My wish is to make it a year worthy of its theme — "Year of Sunrise."

Left home at 7:00 a.m. Went to S.'s home and then to Myoko-ji to offer New Year's greetings. Visited Jozai-ji later.

Arrived at the Gakkai headquarters at 11:00. Put on a morning coat given to me by my mentor. A wonderful beginning to the year.

Must take the lead this year — as a young general with unyielding, immovable resolve — if I am a direct disciple of President Josei Toda.

After reciting the sutra and chanting daimoku, listened to the tape of my mentor's lecture last New Year's Day. A profound, rigorous, wonderful lecture on the three mystic principles.

Left Tokyo Station on a 1:35 p.m. train for the head temple with top leaders.

Both the station and the train were extremely crowded.

The first rain on New Year's Day in nine years and first snow on New Year's Day in twenty-eight years, I heard.

Gathered here at the head temple, the faces of my fellow members from around the nation. They are the ones — out of the multitudes — with whom I share a karmic bond; the ones I have encountered in the present age, out of the thousands of years of human history. I will never neglect them.

Friday, January 2. Clear.

My thirty-first birthday.

Attended the year's first ceremony of chanting before the Dai-Gohonzon. Refreshed my resolve.

"Take care of everything after I die." "I want you to arrange my funeral." These last words resound in my innermost heart.

At 10:00 a.m., before our mentor's tomb in front of the Five-story Pagoda, we sang "Song of Wu Chang Yuan" along with the brass band and the chorus. Reported on the new YMD song.

At 11:00, a commemorative photo with youth division leaders.

The harder I work each day, the nobler the history I create. Want to create a glorious record this year.

Left the head temple with members of President Toda's family. Relieved to see them becoming bright and cheerful.

Thought awhile in the car. Want to accomplish ten years' worth of Buddhist study and general reading this year.

From this year, will make each entry in this diary as if it were my last will and testament. Every day will be an account of golden accomplishments and training. Must keep a record. What will my life be like from today on? Sensei, please watch over me.

The new year brims with determination and hope like sunrise; and with agonizing worries.

Saturday, January 3. Clear.

Did gongyo and chanted daimoku joyfully. The whole family had a breakfast together.

Read New Year's greeting cards. Wrote thirty replies.

Many people visited me at home in the morning. Extremely busy receiving them. Want to respond with this same spirit to anyone throughout my life.

In the afternoon, read *Prominent Figures in Business*.

When all is said and done, nothing surpasses the education, guidance, action, philosophy, character and humanity my mentor shared with me for ten years. What he gave me surpasses reading ten thousand volumes or having ten thousand leaders.

Gird myself for each day.

Sense the ground is being laid for my destined appointment—a position from which I will make a declaration for kosen-rufu. Something has started to move in response to the pulse of my inner resolve. Have no choice but to entrust everything to the Gohonzon.

My wife told me our children enjoy playing with other neighborhood kids.

Many people visited my home in the evening. Tired. My wife looked tired, too. Hoped everyone would go home feeling pleased and satisfied. Happy to see them all starting to dress more nicely.

Sunday, January 4. Clear.

The most tranquil new year I have experienced.

In the morning, had an enjoyable time with my children.

At noon, left for M.'s home in Ogikubo to offer New Year's greetings.

On the way back, attended a dinner meeting with top youth division leaders in Shinjuku. Left early.

Read *Ethics* by Tetsuro Watsuji in the evening.

Went to bed after 2:00.

Monday, January 5. Clear.

Stayed at home in the morning.

Decided to make it a day to receive and talk with guests, just as I did the day before yesterday.

Did not set foot outside. A form of meditative practice?

Rested a bit in the afternoon. Thought about Oishi Yoshio[1] and his son Chikara. The father's character; the son's pure heart. They gave their lives to avenge the death of their lord. A miserable wretched end. We are dedicating our lives to saving all people from suffering. Our battle for the Law is a billion times loftier.

I have a mission to keep fighting until I can report before Sensei's grave that I have accomplished kosen-rufu.

In the evening, continued my reading from last night.

1. Oishi Yoshio: (1659–1703) Samurai leader of a band of warriors who avenged the death of their lord in the famous Forty-seven Ronin Incident. In 1701, Oishi's lord was deprived of his domain and ordered to commit suicide after drawing his sword against a shogunate official. For two years, Oishi and his followers plotted revenge, feigning indifference and even dissipation. On January 31, 1703, they succeeded in killing the official. Oishi and the others, popularly acclaimed for their loyalty and heroism, were ordered to commit suicide.

Tuesday, January 6. Clear.

The new year allowed my body some rest.

The first day of the year to see the headquarters staff. Everyone in high spirits. One staff member gives me a headache.

In the afternoon, the New Year's banquet was held at R. restaurant in Shinbashi. Had a blowfish dish for dinner. Delicious.

Afterward, at around 6:00, we all went to the top of the Tokyo Tower.

Took in the night view of Tokyo. A chilly wind constantly blew. Not very enjoyable.

Stopped for a haircut. Went to a youth division meeting in Bunkyo feeling refreshed. Spoke about the strictness of our religious reformation.

YMD and YWD planning board members accompanied me home. These youth, who trust one another, will definitely become people of splendid capability.

> If the greatest significance of the Maurya dynasty lies in its creation of an uniquely Indian empire by Ashoka, grandson of Chandragupta and founder of the Maurya line, then we should agree upon the following: King Ashoka, through the immense power of his Maurya empire, attempted to establish rule based upon the dharma or Buddhist law, expounded by the Buddha, a principle founded on the ideals of compassion.
>
> —TETSURO WATSUJI[1]

Ate *ramen* noodles with my wife. Delicious.

To bed after 1:30.

1. Tetsuro Watsuji (1889–1960): A cultural historian and philosopher who examined the philosophical components of Japanese culture and devoted much of his work to the study of ethics.

Wednesday, January 7. Fair.

Attended the year's first joint conference at 3:00 p.m.

We decided to donate all temples built by the Gakkai to the head temple. This is only natural and correct.

On the way home, ate skewered chicken with the general director and the directors. They are growing old. Nothing progressive was discussed. Want excellent young friends. Want pure-hearted friends with a fresh spirit for the future by my side.

Thursday, January 8. Cloudy.

Attended the children's group meeting at N. restaurant at 6:00. An annual event since the days of President Toda.

Seventy-six gathered—thirty-one children and their parents, all of whom were selected by Sensei.

To prevent this meeting from becoming meaningless, talked about what I would like to propose as guidelines for the children's group.

1. Our mentor was like a father to us. It is of fundamental importance that we uphold his last words and practice them.

2. Develop responsibility and strive to one day lead the entire Gakkai.
3. Become genuine brothers and sisters to one another and exert your utmost to protect the entire Gakkai.
4. Protect and nurture children to be successors who possess the three virtues of sovereign, teacher and parent who will accomplish kosen-rufu.

Talking with top youth division leaders on the way home.
Already thirty-one. Have entered the most important period of my life.

Friday, January 9. Cloudy.

My home is bright. My family is full of life, like the early spring. The Mystic Law rejuvenates us.

The Lotus Sutra states in "The Teacher of the Law" chapter:

> "If there is someone who seeks the Buddha way
> and during a certain kalpa
> presses palms together in my presence
> and recites numberless verses of praise,
> because of these praises of the Buddha
> he will gain immeasurable blessings."
> —(LS10, 164)

Met with a group of business people at the headquarters at 2:00 p.m. A free and open discussion, befitting the new year.

Stayed at the headquarters until late at night. A day of no regrets. Home after midnight.

Saturday, January 10. Cloudy.

Last autumn, gales blew, and there was a solar eclipse. This year, we had the phenomenal illusion of two suns. At last, the omens of the calamity of internal strife are appearing.

Read a news article reporting that a black rain fell. Others reported that a comet will appear this autumn and sunspots will reach their maximum size.

We ordinary people are concerned only with social phenomenon, while remaining unaware of the universe's mystic workings. In the eyes of the Law, the present may bear a striking resemblance to the Daishonin's time. They are essentially the same. I am convinced the same equation applies to the future as well.

The time for the widespread propagation of the True Law has arrived at last. The Bodhisattvas of the Earth have entered an increasingly critical stage of action, and their mission is growing ever more important.

Want to develop faith great enough to move society, shape Japan's future and influence the direction of the world.

The "Distinctions in Benefits" chapter of the Lotus Sutra reads: "In the evil age of the Latter Day of the Law/if there is someone who can uphold this sutra" (LS17, 242).

Organized Sensei's guidance until midnight.

Thursday, January 15. Cloudy.

Coming-of-Age Day.

In my room there are several roses.

Took a 10:20 a.m. Japan Airlines flight from Haneda. Arrived at Chitose at 1:30 p.m. Many friends awaited me. Grateful. They seemed much more joyful than I am.

In this, the "Year of Sunrise"—the 706th anniversary of Nichiren Daishonin's Buddhism—I have decided to launch my campaign from my late mentor's home town.

Conducted a lecture on the Gosho "Reply to Lay Nun Nichigon" and then a question-and-answer session at the memorable Otaru Civic Auditorium. A thousand people attended.

Friday, January 16. Clear.

Left Otaru for Asahikawa at 8:35 a.m. My health is good.

Arrived in Asahikawa at 1:30 p.m. Many members were waiting.

At 2:30, gave a Gosho lecture on "Reply to Lord Nishiyama" and then a question-and-answer session at Daibo-ji. A full house.

At 6:30, another Gosho lecture on "The Meaning of Faith" and then a question-and-answer session at N.'s.

Afterward, a youth division leaders meeting.

Fully enjoyed Hokkaido's winter scenery.

Asahikawa—cannot forget the snow, the fresh air of this pastoral town.

Saturday, January 17. Cloudy.

At 12:35 p.m., took the train from Asahikawa Station to Yubari.

Hokkaido is a truly magnificent land. Determined to cultivate the spiritual realm, making it unsurpassed in all the world.

Someday, innumerable leaders will emerge from this great land. When will that day come?

At 5:30, arrived at Yubari Station.

A grand welcome. Thankful. As long as there are such steadfast fellow members, we will never lose our struggle. Must stand up for these people. The decisive moment is steadily approaching. It cannot be helped. Is it the current of the times, the demand of the people, or my destiny?

Went to Chapter Chief T.'s home as snowflakes danced in the twilight.

In the evening, lectured on "Reply to Shijo Kingo" and held a question-and-answer session at a rented movie theater.

The passion and energy in the densely crowded hall transformed into the spirit to seek Buddhism. My resolve became all the more solid.

This was the flash point of the Coal Miners Union Incident; the place where my dear mentor taught school as a youth; and where my friends of Bunkyo built their history.

Until midnight, talked with leaders about the past, present and future at T.'s house. I love this land, my friends here and the times we have spent together.

Wednesday, January 21. Fair.

M. dropped by this morning. He's been tormented with relationship problems to the point of contemplating suicide. How pathetic. Reminds me of the strict reality of cause and effect. Sincerely guided him toward human revolution.

Attended K.'s wedding ceremony this afternoon.

In the evening, gave guidance in high spirits at a headquarters leaders meeting in the Toshima Civic Auditorium.

Home by 10:30.

Read *Bach* by Schweitzer.

Today was a very warm day.

Tatsukichi Minobe, who advanced the "emperor as an institution" theory and vehemently criticized the emperor's sovereignty, established his theory in only three years at age twenty-seven. Is it true that only in youth can one create something great and valiantly struggle to establish justice?

Wednesday, February 11. Fair.

February 1: Attended a meeting commemorating the seventh anniversary of the Kansai Soka Gakkai's establishment. The Nakanoshima Civic Auditorium was packed to capacity. Sensed a rising tide there, surpassing Tokyo and the Kanto region. Happiness for glorious Kansai!

February 2: Went to the courthouse. Finished soon. Then attended a top leaders conference at the Kansai headquarters. Gave my all at an evening lecture with thoughts on raising competent individuals for five and ten years from now. Those young in faith who stick around with joy and patience always grow. They fill my heart with respect, contentment and joy.

February 3: Guidance trip to Takamatsu.

February 4: Guidance trip to Kochi.

February 6: Returned to Tokyo aboard the *Swallow*.

February 11: Today would have been my mentor's fifty-ninth birthday. Felt nostalgic. My wife served red-bean rice this morning to celebrate. Warmed by my beautiful family and memories of my mentor. A heart of gold surpasses all material treasures and shines more brilliantly.

On this great day, held a youth division leaders conference. Wrote on a square piece of calligraphy paper:

> *With a catalpa bow in hand,*
> *Always resolved never to return,*
> *I now count myself amongst those perished in the battle*
> *And leave behind my honorable name.*
> —KUSUNOKI MASATSURA[1]

How many among them can dedicate their entire being to the human revolution called kosen-rufu throughout their lives? Felt confident...then doubtful.

1. Kusunoki Masatsura: See note on p. 74.

Thursday, February 12. Fair.

Clear days continue. Spring is near.

The headquarters was dull. It has been a quiet election. I wonder if everything is all right.

Good deeds, when accumulated, lead straight to Buddhahood. Evil deeds, when accumulated, lead directly to hell. Want to maintain faith like flowing water and lead a meaningful existence throughout my life.

Must develop strict faith like Nikko Shonin's.

Remonstrate with the nation like High Priest Nichimoku.

Wish all priests were like them.

My glorious six-tatami—mat room. So quiet that the ticking of my clock gets on my nerves. Ate a bowl of sweet red-bean soup my wife prepared for me. Went to bed after 1:00.

Must leave again the day after tomorrow for Nagoya and then off to Kansai again. Will set out valiantly, embracing my mission close to my heart.

Sunday, February 15. Cloudy.

February 14: Boarded the *Swallow* at Yokohama Station. Brought my whole family to visit our relatives. Arrived in Nagoya before 2:00 p.m.

Held a group chiefs meeting and a women's division group leaders meeting in the afternoon and evening.

Chubu area members were in high spirits. The Gakkai is solid. Must focus on Chubu after Kansai. Chubu is a place where the entire Gakkai —not just one chapter—should pour its energy. Must not make a mistake in holding the helm.

February 15: Went to the Higashiyama Zoo. Hiromasa and Shirohisa were so happy. They were like little birds.

Visited O.'s. Discussed my brother-in-law's business for nearly an hour.

Attended an enshrinement ceremony at the Aichi Community Center at 4:00. A youth division leaders meeting at 7:00.

Parted from my children and left for Kansai aboard the *Echo* special express at 8:30 to attend the trial.

The one-year anniversary of my mentor's passing is approaching. Our faith is expressed in our behavior. Resolved anew to strive assiduously. I had so many passing thoughts on the train. My ideas are limitless.

Friday, February 20. Clear.

Had a slight fever. Rested well in the morning.

Went to the hospital for an X-ray. Met a nurse who said she was an Adachi Chapter member. She was so surprised to see me there.

In the afternoon, conducted guidance sessions at the headquarters. Did my best to offer humanistic, patient encouragement.

Had a planning meeting with K. and others over dinner at the Diamond Hotel. I don't like K. very much.

The cry that issued from the life of my mentor must not be allowed to fade as the days pass. It must never die out.

We have the organization, doctrinal study, social standing...but what's important is compassion—people of compassion; unflagging seeking spirit, individuals whose resolve to seek the Law knows no bounds.

Tuesday, February 24. Snow.

Snowed this morning.

Took a taxi to the headquarters through silver, snow-covered Tokyo streets.

Each moment shines like a gem in the early morning sunshine.

Listened to a tape of President Toda's lecture on the "Ten Blessings" chapter of the Sutra of Infinite Meanings, held at the reception hall, October 1956. Made a resolve to listen to one tape each day. Decided to make all the tape recordings into phonograph records.

Keenly sense the spiritual support for leaders waning after President Toda's passing.

Felt the urgent need for unbiased personnel appointments and warm encouragement. Feel concerned lately.

Must pave the way for those trusted by Sensei to grow freely in our organization. The Gakkai will decline if arrogant people behave as they please.

We cannot accomplish kosen-rufu unless our Gakkai family is a warmer, more solid place for its members than any other place.

Home late. Exhausted.

Friday, March 6. Cloudy.

Did gongyo with this prayer in mind: to develop faith that releases abundant life force to advance kosen-rufu.

March 1: A guidance trip to Hitachi. Focused mainly on a Gosho lecture, "Reply to Kyo'o."

March 2: A guidance trip to Mito. Gave a lecture on "The Difficulty of Sustaining Faith."

March 4: To Omiya. Gave a Gosho lecture on "Many in Body, One in Mind."

If I do not fight now, then when?

Must make it known that by exerting great effort in the present we can create value hundreds of times greater in the future.

Yesterday, gave a general lecture on "Letter from Sado" at Toshima Civic Auditorium.

Conducted a lecture and offered encouragement with my entire being while appealing to all of President Toda's disciples to rise.

Want to satisfy all those who come seeking. Gakkai members are so dear to my heart.

Monday, March 9. Clear.

My emotions are becoming difficult. Is it due to my passion? Everything I see and hear in this defiled Latter Day is repulsive.

Youth who advance with absolute disregard for personal profit and fame are those I like most. The wellspring of our movement's flow can be found nowhere else.

The old and cunning are everywhere. Cannot stand them.

Listened to the recording of Sensei's lecture on the Gosho "The Actions of the Votary of the Lotus Sutra." For a half day, stayed at the headquarters to organize Sensei's guidance as well as his personal items. Shed unexpected tears.

In the evening, had a dinner meeting at H. with President Toda's family and relatives, including M. Dialogue on our faith and future is great nourishment for me. Don't want to hear complaints for now.

In the evening, wrote a manuscript regarding the one-year anniversary of my mentor's passing for *The Daibyakurenge*.

If we forget about propagation, there would be no reason for the Soka Gakkai to exist.

Tuesday, March 17. Rain.

March 15: To the head temple aboard the 1:30 p.m. express from Tokyo Station. An overnight trip with M. In the evening, lectured on "Reply to Shijo Kingo" at the Reception Hall. The head temple was quiet.

March 16: [blank]

March 17: In the morning, continued to organize my mentor's guidance at the headquarters. Received some guests later on.

In the evening, offered encouragement and guidance to the Bunkyo Block members at Jozai-ji in Ikebukuro, mainly focusing on "Reply to Shijo Kingo."

I get a headache from some self-centered leaders who twist the Gosho. Leaders should never be obstinate or narrow-minded. Felt so sorry for the members. Felt indignant. Wanted to ask them if they have already forgotten the guidance and training they received from our mentor.

Read until late *The Elementary Forms of the Religious Life* by Emile Durkheim. Complex.

Thursday, March 19. Clear.

Busy gathering and compiling Sensei's guidance all day.

Want to maintain a pure heart like youthful Sessen Doji[1] throughout my life.

Felt regretful many times. Few records exist due to our carelessness. Very sorry.

Attended an evening Adachi Chapter leaders meeting. Gave guidance while lecturing on the Gosho.

Abdominal pain on my way home. Was it from exposure to the cold?

1. Sessen Doji: A young man said to have been willing to jump into the mouth of a flesh-eating demon (actually the Buddhist god Taishaku in disguise) in order to pursue the knowledge necessary for enlightenment. According to the Chinese version of the Nirvana Sutra, Sessen Doji was later reborn as Shakyamuni.

Saturday, March 28. Clear.

Returned from a guidance trip to the outlying areas yesterday.

Visited Toyohashi, O'otsu, Fukui, Fukuchiyama and Gifu. Had no regret over my five-day schedule of serious struggle.

Wanted to dedicate my utmost efforts before the one-year anniversary of my mentor's passing. Sensei, please watch over me.

We will develop a new era and society.

In the evening, exerted all my efforts to collect Sensei's guidance.

Wednesday, June 24. Cloudy.

It was reported that the Soviet Union's Central Committee has convened. A new, powerful country capable of moving the entire world. Should one start thinking that world affairs revolve around this country as one of their axes? An unapproachable nation. But I understand that the people there are bright and pure.

The Gakkai also held an emergency leaders meeting. The new appointments of directors and the reshuffling of leaders were announced. Will they become a driving force to influence the future?

Thursday, June 25. Cloudy.

Tired both physically and spiritually. Just exerting myself in chanting daimoku.

A newspaper reported the demand for resignation of Socialist Party executives. The times change with each passing moment. Are we entering a warring period in both religion and politics? If so, then Japan is in grave danger. Must accomplish kosen-rufu as soon as possible for the sake of our nation and the entire world.

Feel Sensei's greatness from the depths of my life these days, more and more. I must become an honorable, capable leader whom everyone can trust. To repay my debt of gratitude to my mentor, must develop myself into a compassionate, youthful leader.

Monday, July 6. Clear.

Returned from an outing with the headquarters staff. Tired. Good health is foremost.

In the evening, a Study Department professors meeting. Focused on President Toda's audiotaped lectures. Those who actualize their mentor's teachings are worthy of being called disciples.

The Gakkai is approaching a steep ascent. Must develop forbearance for this important time. Few are willing to dedicate their lives to our goal. Like-minded friends are scarce. Is this the epitome of the Daishonin's Buddhism?

Wednesday, July 8. Clear, then cloudy.

Visited K.'s home yesterday for a party.

The Soka Gakkai is forlorn without a mentor. Only pray the leaders' tenderness and love can effectively permeate the organization in his stead.

Worked out some new multidimensional plans for kosen-rufu.

Thursday, July 9. Clear, then cloudy.

The appointment of a new youth division chief conducted in the main hall of the headquarters. The youth division leaders pledged to advance kosen-rufu into the future.

Now is a crucial time for youth division leaders to courageously break through.

Attended an evening YWD leaders meeting at Nakano Civic Auditorium.

Will do my best at any meeting to inspire even one or two people to deepen their faith and stand up with a sense of mission. This is the essence of expansive propagation.

Friday, July 10. Cloudy.

Wicked people are devilish functions that destroy the order of harmoniously united believers. We must see them for what they are. In Buddhism, causing disunity among believers is said to be one of the five cardinal sins. In this sense, fostering and protecting unity is one of the greatest acts of good.

We must never allow anyone to destroy the Gakkai. Strong, young people must protect the Gakkai with their impartial, pure hearts.

In the evening, went to Taito Gymnasium for the inaugural Koiwa Chapter meeting.

What fundamentally moves people's hearts is nothing other than faith; it is neither eloquence, nor schemes, nor money. Here, *faith* has limitless meaning, including strength as a human being and influence in society. *Faith* means to become a "supreme hero of the world," another name for a Buddha. Since faith is reflected in all phenomena, victory or defeat in everything rests upon faith.

Friday, July 17. Cloudy.

Chanted daimoku to my heart's content—as always.

My mentor's compassion gradually permeates my heart. The love between father and son, the feelings between mentor and disciple—these bonds defy words. Who else knows this inseparable lifeblood?

A dinner meeting with the general director and Z. at B. restaurant. They are good people, but could not help praying that they would deepen their love and compassion for others.

When a leader's capacity is small, those who trust his or her leadership will be led to unhappiness.

On my way home, walked through the Imperial Palace Square with my friends, discussing the future of kosen-rufu.

Monday, July 20. Clear.

My physical condition has turned for the worse again. Suffered all day.

Want to develop an ironlike state of life. Fate, destiny, karma. Opening, breaking, changing.

Phonograph records of President Toda's lectures and speeches have been completed. Very happy. Repaying my debt of gratitude.

On the way home, treated the directors to sushi. Returned late.

N. is entering politics with his new persona.

The course of history. The movement of society. When will our time to appear on the stage arrive?

Tuesday, July 21. Cloudy.

It's been hot for days.

Heard air-conditioning is very bad for the body. Let me experiment with it myself.

Personnel appointments and organizational operations are both going smoothly.

In the evening, attended a Tsukiji Chapter inaugural meeting. Gave my all in the Gosho lecture.

Faith expresses itself in our lives.

Wednesday, July 22. Clear, then cloudy.

It's hot today as well. It's been hot for a while.

Must develop a strong body. Pensive.

Congressman N. came over. An impudent character. A shallow politician. Praying that K. of the Gakkai will stop associating with such petty people. For the Gakkai's sake as well as his own.

In the evening, went to see the Katsushika Block members to tell them I would no longer be assigned to their organization. Everyone looked sad. Must continue to protect and embrace them warmly and magnanimously.

Many people came to my home late at night to receive guidance, discuss plans and report on things.

No space for contemplation.

Thursday, July 23. Cloudy.

It was boiling hot today as well.

The headquarters was packed to capacity for a regular leaders meeting. Must think about building a new headquarters building.

My thoughts on the leaders meeting: The top leaders should think more seriously about our members. They should abandon their own interests in order to serve the members. Only then will others follow them gladly. Our leaders musn't become sly or calculating. It would be unfortunate for the members.

Suffered alone. Could not help thinking about how things were when Sensei was alive.

How happy-go-lucky so many people are! Must be resolved for a life-or-death battle.

Advance! Throughout my thirties....

Friday, July 31. Clear.

To Kyushu, Chugoku (Okayama) and Osaka to offer encouragement and guidance and give lectures.

Returned to Tokyo at 11:00 last night. Exhausted.

Enjoyed dinner with a couple of friends at D. in Shinjuku. K. said he's moving back to his home town. Our gathering was also a send-off party for him. He is a pitiful man. Why can't he live by his own strength and faith? He is an exceedingly sly character, a weak-minded youth who only knows how to get by relying on his friends. President Toda's angry expression flashed through my mind.

It was hot even at night.

Tuesday, August 4. Cloudy.

August 1: Left for Sendai.
August 2: Attended a Tohoku athletic meet.
August 3: Returned to Tokyo.
Thoroughly acquainted myself with Sendai Chapter, a Tohoku-area hub.

Had a nice time around Aoba Castle. We all composed poems together. A castle of poetry, a castle of music, a castle of the moon and a castle of grass and trees, it brings back many memories.

Attended a directors meeting tonight. With blood and sweat, we must toil in both the headquarters organization and the front-line organizations. Concealed my indignation toward my cold, ignorant seniors.

Tuesday, August 11. Rain.

Returned at 5:00 from a summer training session at the head temple. Went straight to the headquarters.

Was told everyone else went home. Protecting the headquarters is the same as protecting the entire Gakkai. Protecting the Gakkai leads to protecting the head temple and to advancing kosen-rufu; it corresponds to protecting the Daishonin's golden teachings—this I firmly believe.

Home late. Had many thoughts:

1. Resolved to start writing more than ten volumes of *The Human Revolution*[1] when we observe the six- or twelve-year anniversary of President Toda's passing.

In my childhood, wanted to be a news reporter. This wish was fulfilled with the publication of the *Seikyo Shimbun*, the Soka Gakkai's organ. In my boyhood, resolved to become a man of letters. Can I fulfill this wish by writing *The Human Revolution*? Thought about making preparations, including gathering materials.

"This cluster of unsurpassed jewels has come to us unsought."

—(LS4, 87)

2. Reflected on the contents of the training sessions. [President Toda's treatise] "The History and Conviction of the Soka Gakkai" is just as ardent and impassioned a treatise as "The Opening of the Eyes." "On Propagation" (a short essay by President Toda) expounds our strict practice. From reading "On the Buddha's Prophecy" and "The Teaching for the Latter Day," I sensed the Daishonin's declaration and prediction of Asian kosen-rufu. It is amazing that Lord Ueno donated a tract of prime land for Taiseki-ji to be built.

1. *The Human Revolution*: Daisaku Ikeda's twelve-volume novelized history of the Soka Gakkai, the title of which is borrowed from an earlier work by Josei Toda.

Wednesday, August 12. Rain.

A cool day.

Wish autumn would come soon.

People are struggling to take hold of society's reins, including in politics and religion, in Japan as well as throughout the world.

Along the path of justice and truth, those who have emerged from the earth are making powerful strides.

Sunday, August 30. Clear.

A Hokkaido athletic meet at Maruyama Field in Sapporo City.

Applauded the serious, pure-hearted youth for their group performances and competitions. Leaders who use such young people's vigor and sincerity to secure their own authority are evil.

Wished President Toda could have been there. My only regret.

In the evening, a conference attended by the general director.

So many people with wretched hearts simply cannot love youth!

Tuesday, September 1. Cloudy.

Heard today is the thirty-sixth anniversary of the Great Kanto Earthquake. It was a devastating disaster. Was it an omen of the cruelty and devastation during World War II?

Natural disasters are miserable. War—human-made disasters—are also tragic. There is no other way of resolving natural disasters than relying on the Mystic Law. Human-made disasters can be prevented only through each individual's human revolution.

Courage and intellect—which is more important? Both are essential.

Good and evil—it is critical to grasp a standard for judging these.

Wednesday, September 2. Cloudy.

97.5° — a record-breaking temperature!

An evening board of directors meeting was held for the first time in a while. It was carried out merely by force of habit. Was it because of the heat? Or because of lack of self-awareness and responsibility? The gap between young and old widens with each passing day. Wanted to express indignation to my seniors: "Have you already forgotten presidents Makiguchi and Toda?"

Must place our foremost emphasis on realizing kosen-rufu, on establishing a society rooted in Buddhist ideals and on demonstrating our mentor's success. We must consider everything from this viewpoint.

Tuesday, September 8. Cloudy, then clear.

Sometimes, we criticize or disparage others; at other times, we are criticized or disparaged.

We must hold one another's character in utmost respect. We must always polish ourselves. Criticizing or disparaging one another without polishing ourselves is foolish.

Life is long. Must strive in faith and in building my own humanity.

Must fear not the words uttered by deluded common mortals but the Daishonin's golden words.

Thursday, September 10. Cloudy, then clear.

Talked with President Toda's family for a long while. They were so pleased. Happy.

Been having many dreams lately.

Strictly cautioned O. and others. Although they once used the Gakkai for their own benefit and turned against Sensei, they have been reinstated. Admonished them for attempting to pollute the pure Gakkai once again.

Wise leaders! Leaders of staunch faith befitting disciples of President Toda! Protect the Gakkai! Fight resolutely against anyone who attempts to undermine the Gakkai!

Our mentor was a teacher of propagation. Accordingly, his disciples must forever advance in propagation. Do not retreat even a step no matter who slanders you, no matter what persecution befalls you!

The Gakkai's fundamental role is to guide people in faith. Therefore we must offer compassion-filled guidance and encouragement to those who embrace the Gohonzon so they may receive immense benefit.

Friday, November 20. Clear.

On the 17th, the sixty-fifth high priest, Nichijun Horigome, died.

High Priest Nittatsu Hosoi's new era has begun. Determined to realize kosen-rufu without fail during the tenure of this new high priest.

Each day is becoming busier.

Sense the dawn of kosen-rufu is near.

Friday, November 27. Cloudy.

A headquarters leaders meeting for November at Taito Gymnasium.

Autumn deepens.

As the nightly darkness shrouding the Gakkai ebbs day by day, the important time nears for us to raise the curtain of our daybreak. Must I bear such hardships because we have no genuine leader?

Some twenty thousand people demonstrated at the Diet Building, like raging billows, seeking reform. When will we witness a tranquil and peaceful society? When will a land of peace and happiness emerge with its lush greenery so serene, its vast oceans so blue and its sun so brilliant?

Our responsibility is momentous. Must develop myself in both body and spirit.

Deeply sense President Toda's vision recently.

My allies are few. Have no other destiny but to fight a solitary battle with the image of my mentor in mind.

Since I decided to devote my life to spreading the Mystic Law in this lifetime, how could I allow a slight whiff to sway me? The powers of my faith and practice shall bring forth the powers of the Buddha and the Law.

Buddhist gods — protect me! Rejoice for me! Celebrate the future of our march as Bodhisattvas of the Earth!

Saturday, November 28. Clear.

Bicycled to Kamata Station. It was cold.

Lectured on Nichikan's "The Threefold Secret Teaching" in the evening. Painfully aware of the need for lifelong study. Will never be arrogant and remiss, filled with regrets.

The headquarters has gradually settled down. Next year will probably be all the busier and more significant. Must be more resolute, attentive and prudent than anyone.

Faith leads to the study of Buddhist teachings, that is, the study of being human.

Dedication to the Mystic Law while young creates a genuine, noble time of youth; it gives rise to joy and excitement in everything.

The seventh YWD general meeting will be held tomorrow, the 29th, from noon at Ryogoku's Nihon University Auditorium.

Monday, November 30. Fine.

Felt exhausted physically and spiritually all day.

The chapter-sponsored funeral for former Chapter Chief B. was held at Josen-ji at 4:00 p.m.

Only a few leaders attended. Was it because of their busy schedules? Saddened. Shed tears at the death of this old veteran. Offered my heartfelt prayer for his peace and happiness.

My recollections of President Toda are limitless. Presumptuous leaders use Sensei only for their own interests, glory and popularity. Deeply concerned about the Gakkai's future at the sight of such arrogant leaders.

On my way home, stopped at the barber shop. Disturbed by the words of cunning elder leaders. Wonder if such people exist everywhere in society?

In any case, resolved never to become a despicable man oblivious to the debt of gratitude owed to his mentor. Will not deviate even the slightest from my mentor's last will and testament. If we are content with fulfilling only our own selfish desires, how can w possibly claim to be true disciples?

Friday, December 4. Fair.

Went to Yokohama to give a general lecture at the Harbor Memorial Hall. Covered the latter half of "Letter from Sado."

Keenly sense the greatness of Sensei's lecture. Wish to give an outstanding lecture brimming with life force and wisdom.

The next four years—1960, 1961, 1962 and 1963—will be the most important, decisive years for the Gakkai's future.

Concerned about my senior leaders' lack of seeking minds. Troubled by their growing arrogance.

There will be no progress of kosen-rufu if we neglect outstandingly capable young people. Youthful talent will make the Gakkai grow. Want to warn them never to become incompetent leaders.

Saturday, December 12. Cloudy.

Left for Sendai by train at 12:30 p.m. to lecture and offer guidance and encouragement.

Thought Sendai was a large chapter, but it's not. A leader must never overestimate.

Stayed a night at S. Inn. Spoke to my heart's content with local leaders. All good people—renowned Tohoku-area generals. Must treasure them.

It is quite natural to seek Buddhist guidance in the Gosho and to put it into practice based on the guidance of our mentor, President Toda. Nonetheless, many members are confused and suffering because of a leader who fashions his guidance to win popularity. How absurd!

Sunday, December 20. Rain.

Left Tokyo Station for the head temple at 1:30 p.m.

Cold. The last group pilgrimage this year for which I am responsible.

Held a question-answer session at the Grand Lecture Hall. Exerted all my strength.

Returned to my lodging temple and laid down. Dead tired. Thought about many things.

Must accomplish the harmonious unity between priesthood and laity as soon as possible. We should have a communication conference between representatives of the head temple and the Gakkai every month.

After President Toda's death, the head temple, too, seems lonely. Rained until midnight, very cold.

Monday, December 21. Clear.

Pondered the future of the priesthood and the Gakkai all night long. Slept little.

Attended the 8:30 ceremony of chanting before the Dai-Gohonzon. It was delayed five minutes. Was told they could not locate the key. How lax they have become in the high priest's absence!

After the ceremony, visited my mentor's grave. Recited the sutra and chanted daimoku.

Clear skies. Isn't it always clear after a rain? Hope the same holds true after facing life's "rainy days."

Arrived at the headquarters a little after 3:00 p.m. Worried deeply about M.'s family in the car on the way.

Lonely.

In the evening, attended a youth division leaders meeting in Shinjuku. Have begun training the next generation of Gakkai leaders. Every one of them is dear to me—their black eyes, firm muscles and faith like a pure stream. Have great hopes for these youth to put the finishing touches on kosen-rufu.

Home by 8:30.

My children and our maid have colds. Am told it's not serious.
Read until late.

Tuesday, December 22. Fair.

The day before yesterday, met with the wife of a Tokyo University assistant professor. She told me that after taking faith, she overcame her frail health and is now exerting herself in spreading the Buddhist teachings. Today, I presented her with a book.

We began challenging the J. Society, which is critical of the Gakkai.

Worried about my children's sickness. Our home seems to be getting chilly from drafts coming through the cracks.

Thursday, December 24. Fair.

Very cold last night. Have I caught cold too? Had a fever of a little over 100°. Rested in the morning. Asked my wife to call the headquarters immediately. While laying down, read *A Biography of Bokudo Inukai*.

Went to the headquarters in the afternoon.

Wrote three works of calligraphy upon returning home:

"Simple and Innocent."

"Pure and Awakened."

"Uncrowned Emperors."

Friday, December 25. Fair.

Good weather continues.

The Demonstration Restriction Act is being discussed in the Diet. Seems our society is gradually becoming more complex and absurd.

Gave instructions on various matters at the headquarters all day. With President Toda's passing, enemies both within and without grow in number each day; they laugh at us, anticipating the Gakkai's weakening and collapse.

In the evening, went with some friends to M.'s home to offer a year-end greeting and gift.

Upon returning home, relaxed in the small bath. Thought about many things concerning my future. So much to think about. I am but an ordinary man, and it's hard to make concrete decisions. So many things to worry about.

Since I walk the path of ordinary people and live as a common man, my circumstances may be understandable. After all, human beings are foolish.

Ultimately, I have no choice but to strive in my own human revolution through steadfast faith.

Saturday, December 26. Fair.

Good weather continues.

Fatigued in both body and mind.

With this year coming to an end, I have extended by one year the life span doctors predicted would be only thirty years.

Life must be lived thoroughly. Our source of energy is our daimoku and never-ending, steady practice to accumulate benefit from the Mystic Law. "We beg you to cure us and let us live out our lives!" (LS16, 228).

Will treasure this life I have received from the Mystic Law. Shall live a long life and do my best. Must live resolutely through each day of my life, like a son of the proud, noble king of the Law.

In the evening, had a conference with young directors and youth division leaders. Had little appetite at dinner.

Sunday, December 27. Fair.

The last Sunday of the year.

In the morning, cleaned the yard for the first time in a long while. Few flowers in the garden, but my home is like a flower garden of happiness.

Of late, I can deeply sense the benefit of the Gohonzon.

The Gosho states: "'The words of the Dharma King contain no falsehoods'" (WND, 654). I have a palace in my heart, and it permeates my small home.

From 2:00 p.m., attended an inaugural ceremony for a new chief priest at Jozai-ji in Ikebukuro. Since Nittatsu Hosoi became high priest, Study Department Chief S. is succeeding him in this position. After the ceremony was completed, a banquet was held.

Looks like I'll be busy again tomorrow.

Monday, December 28. Clear.

Felt under the weather this morning. Took a taxi to work, though I felt wasteful in doing so. Could not help it.

Was extremely busy offering guidance and encouragement at the headquarters. Many came — men, women, youth.

Attended a Mukojima Chapter leaders meeting at Josen-ji at 7:00 p.m. It was my last Gakkai activity for this 707th year since the establishment of the Daishonin's Buddhism. On the way back, stopped by the Mukojima Community Center and talked with fellow members until midnight about our memories of President Toda.

Home late. My peaceful, bright home.

Tuesday, December 29. Clear, then rain.

The year is almost over. A year of worries, development, effort and earnestness.

I miss Sensei. Every year, on New Year's Eve and New Year's Day, I was moved by Sensei's encouraging words, which were like those of a parent appreciating his child's efforts.

In the evening, discussed a number of issues with top leaders in a headquarters conference room. A united gathering of good people.

Confusion abounds in politics, in our country, and in the minds of the people. Sense that future prospects are frightening.

My back aches badly.

Wednesday, December 30. Fair.

Last day of work at the headquarters this year. Everyone worked hard. Appreciative. Yet, as those who must protect the main camp, they still lack courage, I feel. Must begin training from next year.

Only one day left in this 707th anniversary of the Daishonin's Buddhism. This year will soon be gone forever. It was like a grand epic and a masterpiece in our struggle to perpetuate the Law.

Saddened by my seniors' laxness. Prayed for them to be in high spirits from now on.

Thursday, December 31. Cloudy.

The 707th anniversary of the Daishonin's Buddhism has passed and the 708th year has come.

Rested at home. Thought about many things.

"Friends are few, foes are many"—somehow my mentor's song rings in my heart on this New Year's Eve. Must advance with conviction in the Buddhist deities' protection for us. Made solitary resolutions for the next year.

As tears fill my eyes, feel like singing my mentor's song for the sake of humanity, peace and kosen-rufu.

1 9 6 0

ON NEW YEAR'S DAY, commemorative gongyo meetings were held throughout the nation where Gakkai members listened to recordings of addresses by the late President Josei Toda.

France conducted its first nuclear testing in the Sahara Desert on February 13. The nation was roundly criticized by the international community.

March 8, the Ministry of Health and Welfare issued a memorandum regarding the interpretation of cemetery and burial laws and regulations. The ministry clarified that no one could be refused burial in their pre-owned plot because of conversion to a different religion. With this official statement, the Gakkai's assertions regarding this

legal matter were supported. This issue prompted the Nichiren Shoshu priesthood to begin the installation of facilities for burial and maintaining custody of remains.

On the fifth anniversary of the Otaru Debate, March 11, some one thousand YMD members from Tokyo held a street rally in Minobu and passed out special editions of *Seikyo Shimbun* featuring the doctrinal errors of the Minobu sect.

At an emergency board of directors meeting on April 9, Chief of Staff Ikeda was unanimously recommended to be the third president of the Soka Gakkai. After expressing his initial reluctance on several occasions, Daisaku Ikeda eventually accepted the appointment and was inaugurated officially in a ceremony on May 3 at the auditiorium of Nihon University in Tokyo, with twenty thousand members in attendance. Among his acceptance speech remarks, he said: "From today onward, on behalf of President Toda's disciples, I will take leadership to move a step forward toward the substantiation of kosen-rufu." He also expressed his resolve to achieve a membership of three million households and the construction of the Grand Reception Hall at the head temple by the seventh anniversary year of President Toda's passing. He also expressed his determination to reform the religious world. The goal of three million households was accomplished within two-and-a-half years.

Friday, January 1. Rain.

Woke up at 6:00 a.m. An extremely cold morning.

My whole family sat together before the Gohonzon.

Could not hold back my appreciation for the Gohonzon's protection of my entire family: myself; my wife; my eldest son, Hiromasa; my second son, Shirohisa; and my third son, Takahiro.

Made a deep resolution for this new year to my mentor, Josei Toda. My wife seems to know what is in my heart.

The 708th anniversary of the Daishonin's Buddhism has begun. How will it unfold? Could not help praying for every Gakkai member's steadfast faith, happiness and dynamic progress. Especially hoping for top leaders' self-awareness and earnestness.

A little after 7:00, visited Myoko-ji. The general director, H., M. and I received celebratory sake from Priest K. On the way back, we spoke about the earliest possible realization of unity between the priesthood and laity.

After visiting President Toda's home in Meguro to offer New Year's greetings to his family, went to the headquarters.

Attended a New Year's gongyo at 10:00 at the headquarters with approximately two hundred representatives.

The sutra recitation and chanting of daimoku were followed by the general director's words. Then we listened to the record of President Toda's question-and-answer session at the group pilgrimage in 1957. Top leaders must have felt Sensei's spirit is still here. A simple banquet afterward. President Toda's *waka* poems were recited. A solemn silence fell over the meeting place.

Afterward, spoke with headquarters staff in a conference room. We sang a Gakkai song and signed our names in a signature book before going home.

Received many guests. Put down some clumsy haiku on calligraphy paper:

> *The dawn of New Year's Day*
> *Shines upon youthful hearts*
> *Giving off morning's first light.*

> *New Year's Day*
> *More in eve than morn*
> *Is enjoyed at my home.*

Saturday, January 2. Cloudy.

Got up late this morning. My wife was concerned because I looked pale even though today is my birthday. Have no idea why I get so exhausted. Smiling, told her I would never succumb to the devil of illness.

My thirty-second birthday. Thought about my mother. Imagined her growing old. No, she is already getting old, I thought.

Left for my first pilgrimage of the year aboard a 10:00 a.m. express from Tokyo Station with H. and Mrs. M. and her daughter.

Recalled my departed mentor while on the train, gazed at Mount Fuji. No matter when I look at it, it is always a beautiful mountain. It is the foremost mountain in the world. Want to live as solid as this mountain.

A great sage and thinker, Nichiren Daishonin, in his boyhood, traveled the road along the eastern seaboard to Mount Hiei to study. What did he think of Mount Fuji when he saw it? Thought about his emotions at that time.

At 2:00 p.m., attended ceremony of chanting before the Dai-Gohonzon. A pure sense of rebirth permeated the entire head temple grounds.

From 6:00 p.m., a lecture on the "New Year's Gosho" was held at the Grand Lecture Hall.

The hall was filled to capacity. Reassuring. Felt that the dawn of humanity is breaking from this land.

The power of the Mystic Law and the spread of Buddhism—these are workings of the great Law, unstoppable by any race, or all of humanity.

The meeting concluded with a question-and-answer session by the general director. All the top leaders talked cordially until midnight on the second floor of the Rikyo-bo.

Could not sleep at all until *ushitora* gongyo. Afterward, could not sleep until morning—maybe because it was so cold. Lying in bed, seriously pondering building and donating a Grand Reception Hall.

Happy and proud to struggle and strive alone at the forefront of kosen-rufu. This year will be important for both the Gakkai and me. Must rely upon the guidance of the Gohonzon.

Sunday, January 3. Cloudy.

Stayed at the head temple. Early in the morning, received a message that High Priest Nittatsu would grant us an audience. Together with top Gakkai leaders, saw the high priest, who appeared in good health.

Afterward, with some youth division members, took a leisurely walk around the head temple grounds. Everyone was lively and cheerful, hopeful for the future. Reliable people. Glad. Prayed from the depth of my heart they would advance and spread the Daishonin's Buddhism together with me for the rest of their lives, sharing both happiness and suffering.

We cried out: "We are youth! We are young!" Our voices rang out high in the skies, resounding clear and serene and fell and sank into the white snow atop Mount Fuji.

From 9:30 a.m., attended a question-and-answer session for the participants of a one-day pilgrimage group. Felt I exerted my utmost.

Left the head temple with H. a little after 10:00 a.m.

On the way back, we rode the train with President Toda's family. Talked with his son, Takahisa, about many things until Yokohama Station. He has grown into a splendid young man. How happy Sensei would be! Nam-myoho-renge-kyo!

Saw clearly my mentor's virtue and benefit passed onto his son. Wondrous. Mystic.

Home shortly after 3:00 p.m. So tired. Nearly collapsed face down on my bed.

My campaign hasn't ceased over the last ten years. Will dream on toward the next ten years.

Monday, January 4. Fair.

Rested until a little after 10:00 a.m. Woke up exhausted. My wife, Hiromasa, Shirohisa and Takahiro were all in high spirits. Felt like I was seeing my family for the first time in a long time.

We ate lunch together. My wife cooked. Felt relieved and satisfied seeing my children's good appetites. My wife's cooking is more pleasing and delicious than meals served at any hotel or inn.

Read until midnight. Thought about many things.

Resolved to make earnest efforts to solidify my faith and improve my health this year.

With regard to politics, will this year see the next prime minister?

In our school, High Priest Nittatsu has been appointed. In politics, will Hayato Ikeda be the one?

Is this the year for the Gakkai to choose a leader as well?

Does anyone realize the foundation of kosen-rufu is gradually solidifying in accord with the great principle of the Mystic Law?

Tuesday, January 5. Fair.

Stayed at home in the morning.

Physically fatigued all day. Read while lying down.

Did not have a chance to play with my children during New Year's vacation. Could not be helped.

In the afternoon, went to a barber in Shinano-machi near the headquarters.

Stopped by the Gakkai headquarters to greet the great Gohonzon.

1. Must develop capable individuals this year.
2. Must strengthen the organization this year.
3. Must clarify goals this year.

There is a great need for restructuring the current weak organization to make it solid.

Attended the seventh children's group meeting at 4:00 p.m. at N. restaurant. Eighty people attended. On behalf of everyone, presented Mrs. M. a silver compact and an excellent album. She was happy.

Sang Gakkai songs together. The meeting ended at 6:00.

Went home with my wife. Chanted serenely.

Wednesday, January 6. Fair.

The temperature at noon yesterday was almost 70°.

Prayed for no earthquakes. Japan and the rest of the world must be free from calamities and disasters. No matter what wonderful constitutions, laws and treaties we make, what good do they do if a great earthquake or flood strikes? Know how important the fundamental law of the universe is.

Today was the first day of work at the headquarters. We gathered at 10:00 a.m. and did gongyo. Then some greetings were offered. The meeting ended at 10:40.

Greatly pleased to see how wonderfully made the new altar is. Our faith will always manifest itself in reality before our eyes.

Came home late. Greeted by his bright, beautiful wife, this young revolutionary's stress is relieved. Our home is rather simple, but it is my proud, noble place of great happiness.

The Gakkai exists because of President Toda. Without Sensei, the Gakkai would not have come into existence. So when we start viewing the entire Gakkai from Sensei's standpoint, we can come to understand its current condition as well as its future.

It is dreadful how some people try to use Sensei and, from their selfish standpoints, assert positions to further their own interests. Have seen this tendency more often in women.

Thursday, January 7. Fair.

Left home at 8:00 a.m.

Annoyed by the crowded train. Spent all my pocket money during New Year's vacation. No money was left for a cab. From today on, cannot waste money any more.

Must exert myself at work more earnestly from today on.

In the afternoon, along with the general director, met with lawyers about the court case regarding N.[1] and others at the headquarters.

Nothing tormented my mentor and injured the Gakkai more than this incident. Must clearly prove the Gakkai's purity, justice and tradition in court. But how can genuine Gakkai members forgive N.'s and others' base desire to be promoted and gain distinction, not to mention their unseemly conduct?

Spoke with several senior directors about the essence of the Gakkai and our departed mentor's heart. Want them to understand his heart so they will not become egoistic—for the sake of my dear Gakkai members.

In the evening, top youth division leaders came by my home. We dined together. Talked about my vision seven years and fourteen years from now. Did they understand or not? Did they believe or not?

1. Court case regarding N.: Refers to a case in which some Soka Gakkai members unilaterally broke election laws in an Osaka House of Councillors election. This was contrary to the ethics advocated by the Soka Gakkai and President Toda throughout the election campaign.

Friday, January 8. Clear.

What I must accomplish this year:
1. Promotion of the Grand Reception Hall construction project.
2. The self-awakening and unity of all leaders.
3. Nichiren Shoshu priests' self-realization for kosen-rufu.

Some people live one year's worth in ten years; others live ten years' worth in one year. How precious it is to live each day to create value!

At 3:30 p.m., the entire board of directors went to Josen-ji to offer New Year's greetings.

They served us a variety of dishes. Maybe it was OK this time since it is the New Year. But felt troubled they did not understand the Gakkai spirit toward accomplishing kosen-rufu.

Everyone appears to think they are right. This must be people's essential nature. It will require considerable effort to help them, one by one, cultivate "a land spotless and good" (LS11, 181) within them, thereby leading them to a supreme state of life. After all, have no choice but to call out continuously my faith and conviction.

Became painfully aware of my immaturity and of my weakness stemming from my pure-hearted and honest nature. Everyone seems to try to take advantage of me. But I shall walk along my own path as a youth, resolute and unperturbed, experiencing boundless joy from the Law.

Saturday, January 9. Clear.

It is a warm winter.

Twelve government officials, including Prime Minister Kishi, are leaving for the United States on the 16th to sign the new security treaty. Opposing their trip, the All-Japan Student Federation will mobilize five thousand people. Japan is a tiny, storm-tossed Asian island. What fate awaits this island country ten years or thirty years from now?

Thought of impurities of the age and of the people.

In the evening, attended a Bunkyo leaders meeting.

Senior leaders seem to hold themselves above all. They move in the direction most advantageous for themselves. In many instances, junior members find it difficult to trust their senior leaders, even those they thought they could trust in the beginning.

No members are more pitiful and sad than those whose seniors are not trustworthy and lack responsibility.

In any case, rather than criticize others, I myself must first become a great senior to the members. Will extend my love to everyone. Must expand my capacity. Must become as all-encompassing as the vast expanse of an ocean.

Never forget that we become worthy to be called true practitioners of faith only when we, as Gakkai members, live up to the Daishonin's golden words: "However wretched a beggar you might become, never disgrace the Lotus Sutra" (WND, 824).

Returned to the headquarters a little after 8:00. Discussed plans to build the Grand Reception Hall and the Grand Main Temple (Sho-Hondo), which our mentor willed in his last testament. Gave strict guidance to get serious.

Some are serious, yet others are irresponsible.

It has been only two years since our mentor departed, but the spirit he left us has already begun to decay. Must stop this.

Sunday, January 10. Cloudy then clear.

Stayed home in the morning. Rested for a while. Yet my body does not feel very rested.

In the afternoon, went with my wife to a gathering of Sensei's family and relatives.

Came home in the evening. Read quietly until midnight.

Browsed through the biographies of Marx, Yukichi Fukuzawa, Wang Yang-ming, Lenin, Hegel and Bach.

Lenin's life force at fifty-four, directed toward the revolution, is astounding and deserves some respect, the good or bad and high or low of his philosophy aside. In any case, we should learn something from those who carried through with their beliefs and creed.

Stayed up until late. Clock hands never seem to keep up with my thoughts. My wife, concerned about my health, suggested I go to bed early.

From yesterday on, decided to chant one thousand more daimoku each day. This is my new resolution, a springboard toward the next step.

Thought about how my friends have been doing since I joined. Thought about my brother.

Will advance again tomorrow. To take one more stride forward, will dig deeper into the earth of my own life and challenge myself.

Monday, January 11. Cloudy then clear.

"You must strive with all your hearts/and remove yourselves from indulgence and laxity" (LS1, 20).

How is the engine of my ship for the important embarcation into my thirties?

Discussed the staff's salary at the headquarters.

Considered carefully the harmony among all the staff, their family circumstances, their abilities and so on. Although their work is in the realm of faith, I must give serious thought to the foundation of their living in the reality of society.

In the evening, met with associates of N. at K. We discussed various issues regarding paper stock for the newspaper.

No matter what meeting I attend, I feel Sensei's heart, his image, is reflected in my mind's eye.

On my way back from the headquarters, finished reading Sensei's *The Detailed Commentary on the "Expedient Means" and "The Life Span of the Thus Come One" Chapters of the Lotus Sutra*. Felt infinitely nostalgic.

Chanted one thousand daimoku.

Inscribed "Dawn" and "Boundless joy from the Law" on calligraphy paper as mementos.

Couldn't go to bed until a little after 2:00.

Tuesday, January 12. Cloudy.

Woke up feeling fatigued.

My home is a mess because of the three brave warriors. No place to rest in this castle of mine. This may be proof of their vigor and good health. Hopeful. Happy.

Under the cover of my futon, recollected my boyhood and youth. The moment of birth, existence from birth to death, the moment of death, and existence from death to next birth—the reality of life. Now I exist in the phase from birth to death, in my youth, embraced by the Mystic Law. Must realize this is the greatest kind of life one can lead.

In 1947, took faith at nineteen. On that day, that is, August 24, did gongyo, received a precept, and heard Priest Horigome's words. Recall the time was approximately between 1:00–3:00 p.m.

My family was not rich. It could not be helped, since four of my brothers were drafted and sent to the front. My father and mother are warm and upright. Tears come to my eyes when I think of their hardships.

Lately, deeply realize my parents' greatness. My respect is all the more profound because my parents are so ordinary and honest.

In autumn 1947, decided to attend Josei Toda's lecture in Kanda. I was serious. Further solidified my resolve, thinking, "As long as I am with this mentor...." My friends were jovial, but my heart remained tranquil and constant.

On January 3, 1949, joined the editorial staff of the Nihon Shogakkan, President Toda's company. It was the first step I took as his disciple. Served him with all my heart. Gradually became aware of the strictness of life, society and the Gakkai and began to study seriously.

On August 22, 1950, the Tokyo Construction Credit Union failed. Should it be called his second persecution? Fought with all my might and made strenuous efforts as I had promised myself when I chose him as my mentor. Now recollect I accomplished my human revolution to the greatest degree at that time.

When I think of how much this single year of life-or-death struggle alongside him, during which I forged a causal relationship with him, has brought me good fortune and enabled me to change my karma, I deeply realize the mystic workings of the True Law.

Those without practice are not qualified to criticize Buddhism.

Home after 11:00. My wife awaited me with her tranquil, gentle gaze.

Wednesday, January 13. Fair.

Each day feels longer in January than in other months.

The first board-of-directors meeting of this year was held at 3:30 p.m. We discussed various agendas, including the collection of President Toda's articles and other issues like group pilgrimages, large, specially inscribed Gohonzon, publications [the Gosho and the collection of President Toda's essays], etc.

Feel sad about the senior directors' lack of comprehensive visions, of passion and of alternative planning. We should not hesitate to select the next generation of directors from among much younger people.

Buddhism teaches there should be no discrimination among people with regard to their potential to attain enlightenment. As the Daishonin states: "These sutras have two flaws. First, because they teach that the Ten Worlds are separate from one another" (WND, 235). All measures we take should be naturally based upon this.

Attended a Study Department professors meeting at 6:00. Had preliminary discussions about "The Fourteen Slanders" and Nichikan's

"Teachings for the Latter Day." Since Buddhist study is for lifetime, I need to study with patience and composure.

Chanted fifty-five hundred daimoku. Felt my inner strength naturally welling forth.

Friday, January 15. Cloudy.

Left for Nagoya aboard the 12:30 p.m. special express from Tokyo. Traveled alone.

The purpose of my trip is to lecture and offer guidance and encouragement. The first guidance trip to outlying areas this year. These shall be days to remember for Chubu-area members. Lectured on "The Fourteen Slanders" at the Nagoya Civic Auditorium.

Found out that about four thousand people stood outside in the cold. Though I am young and immature, unless I offer guidance and encouragement to these many seekers of Buddhism with seriousness and humility, it would be a terrible shame.

Stayed overnight at the Aichi Community Center. Went to bed at 1:00.

Saturday, January 16. Rain.

Headed for Osaka aboard the 2:00 p.m. *Kintetsu* special express from Nagoya. The train cars were double-decker. If we had this in Tokyo, my children would be so eager to ride on it. Y. and Mrs. S. boarded with me. Owe them a great debt of gratitude. Will never forget them for the rest of my life.

My first trip to Kansai this year. The train arrived at Ueroku Station in Uehonmachi. The general chapter chief and others were there to greet us. Went to my dear Kansai headquarters and relaxed.

The general chapter chief is a good person, yet he remains behind the scenes. He is still young. Want him to grow further.

Mrs. K. and others came here, too, from the headquarters to join this guidance trip. Everyone is serious. They are working earnestly. There is no other organization or group so deeply rooted in society where women take such an active role as in ours.

The world's greatest women's organization, cultural group, women's liberation organization, group of people expressing their individuality and modern humanism, and organization dedicated to the improvement of people's living—these are all other names for the Soka Gakkai women's division.

Some people are narrow-minded, some arrogant, some self-centered and others who disliked President Toda. Just looking at them upsets me.

Gave a lecture at the Amagasaki Civic Auditorium.

Couldn't give such a great lecture. Was it my fatigue or my lack of study?

Sunday, January 17. Fair.

In the morning, stayed at the Kansai headquarters.

In the afternoon—a Kayo Group meeting, a Suiko Group meeting, a district chiefs meeting, a district women's division chiefs meeting and a general block chiefs meeting. I attended them all.

Did my utmost despite fatigue. Do I have bronchitis? Feel pain in my chest. Must strain even to utter a sound.

At 6:00 p.m., a Kansai General Chapter leaders meeting was held at the Nakanoshima Civic Auditorium. Heard more than ten thousand people came, including those who were outside. Held two question-and-answer sessions.

Realized that more important than principles, abstract theories and idealized faith are concrete answers and guidance. Reflected upon myself.

From 9:00 p.m., attended an enshrinement ceremony for T.

Went to bed after 2:00.

Monday, January 18. Fair.

Headed back to Tokyo. Took a special express from Osaka.

Many leaders saw me off despite the cold weather. Appreciative. Admonished myself not to expect such a sendoff in the future.

Slept on the train until the area around Shizuoka. It looks like I am coming down with bad cold.

Picked up Sarton's *Introduction to the History of Science* from where I left off before. Want to use this book as my reference when I write about science and religion some day.

Took a taxi home from Yokohama Station. Telephoned the headquarters to report.

Tuesday, January 19. Clear.

I'm losing weight. Lost about twenty-five pounds since last April. Feel troubled. The devilish workings of sickness and death are harsh and fearful.

As long as I have faith in the Mystic Law, I can view my sickness as an intrinsic aspect of my life and in no way fail to transform great evil into great good. Will definitely recover my health within this year. Eradicating one's bad karma is no easy task.

Dragged my heavy body to the headquarters. Felt as if carrying a dozen pounds of weights on my back.

Attended a meeting to plan a group pilgrimage. Gave guidance to the leaders of the Traffic Control Group. Always self-reflect after being strict with them while not sharing their actual struggle.

You young leaders of the Traffic Control Group—do your best! Strive with all your hearts! Have no choice but to give my dear youth strict training and ask them to protect the Gakkai in the future.

From 6:00 p.m., attended a YMD and YWD leaders meeting. Shared my overall view on the signing of the revised security treaty.

Home earlier than usual to get some rest.

Chanted three thousand daimoku. My progress in faith leads to progress in my own human revolution.

Wednesday, January 20. Clear.

It was reported Japan's fully empowered delegation, including Prime Minister Kishi, received a grand welcome in the United States. Heard he is even being considered for a Nobel Peace Prize. Ridiculous! Gradually beginning to understand the world's average intellectual level. Sense the gears of a vicious cycle starting in Japan, Asia and the rest of the world.

The Gakkai headquarters has begun displaying more spirit lately— as if things have started moving toward something, wishing for something unspoken.

Began to collect mementos of President Toda. Want to preserve them for a long time, thus leaving behind the Gakkai spirit forever.

Invited President Toda's family to a play at the Chiyoda Theater. Afterward had dinner together. They were deeply pleased.

Have been thinking seriously of late; the long march of a human being's life is a truly formidable undertaking. My boyhood and youth were relatively easy. But my 30s, 40s, 50s and 60s will be more significant as my responsibility grows.

Is life a survival of the fittest? Is it the strong feeding upon the weak? Is it the triumph of the superior and the defeat of the inferior? Is it cruel? Is it cause and effect? How strict life is!

My mentor, President Toda, led a wonderful life in many aspects— in his humanity, in his enterprise and in the concluding phase of his life.

Thursday, January 21. Fair.

Gave a lecture at Josen-ji in Mukojima.

On the way back, treated several friends to tempura in Kanda.

Friday, January 22. Clear.

Left for Kyushu aboard the 11:00 a.m. Japan Airlines flight from Haneda Airport to give a lecture in Yame. My wife alone saw me off. A quiet sendoff.

Saturday, January 23. Cloudy.

Gave a lecture in Fukuoka. Feeling good.

Sunday, January 24. Cloudy.

Attended a successful Fukuoka Chapter leaders meeting in Kokura.

Led the "Song of Kyushu's Youth" for the first time in a long while.

Was told fifteen thousand people participated.

It has been very cold for the last three days.

Seeing is believing. My expectation of warm weather has proven futile. My cold has returned. Will care for Kyushu as I do Kansai.

Monday, January 25. Clear.

In the morning, held a haiku contest among all leaders. Many were very good.

Composed the following:

> *In the advancement*
> *Toward Asian kosen-rufu*
> *Our mentor lives on.*

Returned to Tokyo on a 4:00 p.m. Japan Airlines flight.

Tuesday, January 26. Fair.

Possibly due to fatigue from the trip, felt out of sorts today as well.

In the morning, chanted daimoku to improve my physical condition.

In the afternoon, a planning session for a headquarters leaders meeting in reception room #1.

Among the directors, some are old and others young. Some are only concerned with self-preservation while others are selfless. Felt presidents

Makiguchi and Toda were watching them, perceiving their innermost minds rather than their appearance.

The first headquarters leaders meeting was held at the Taito Gymnasium from 6:00. It was a spirited meeting brimming with enthusiasm to spread Buddhism.

Young warriors cry out earnestly, themselves becoming flag bearers. Senior directors seem to gradually express more confidence.

On the way home, ate in Kanda with directors. Everyone had bright expressions.

My mother came over late at night. My mother's feelings for her child are unchanging. Within her ordinary existence lies her greatness — far surpassing that of any philosopher, politician or great scholar. Must cherish her. Must protect her.

Wednesday, January 27. Fair.

Cold days continue.

Winter camellias are blooming. Their vitality is sturdy and robust.

Regret I forgot to give my mother some spending money yesterday.

The head temple announced the new high priest's inaugural ceremony. The Gakkai sent 100,000 members on pilgrimage to the head temple. Nichiren Shoshu is prospering.

Thought of the Gakkai's present condition. Plums will blossom soon, then cherries will be in full bloom.

In the evening, over dinner, discussed the Gakkai's future with H. and several other friends.

Young generals with serious expressions.

Overexerted myself giving instructions today as well.

The responsibility for the future of the Gakkai and kosen-rufu finally rests upon my shoulders. My friends are still easygoing in this regard.

Upon returning home, pondered the Grand Reception Hall construction including the timing of collecting donations, the spirit of making offerings, appropriate guidance in making offerings, the presentation of the plan, the personnel appointment for the committee, the date of the ground-breaking ceremony, the deadline for the completion, the selection of an architectural company, etc. Alone, thought of my grand vision for kosen-rufu.

In accord with the law of cause and effect, the good fortune deriving from such efforts must be great. Just want to make my mentor happy.

As long as my mentor watches over me, everything will be fine.

My children are growing and are in good health. Their sleeping faces and their snoring are....

Feel sorry my wife always has to go to bed so late. Want her to take good care of herself.

Thursday, January 28. Clear.

A cold day.

Feel I'm coming down with a cold. My weak constitution is weakening.

In the evening, went to a barber.

Stayed at the headquarters until late.

Gave guidance and encouragement to leaders of various divisions.

Cannot afford to give heed to criticism in society.

The Gakkai now has no choice but to move forward.

It is important to produce evidence.

It is important to show results.

In the evening, read *Marxism and Religion*. This book is thirty years old.

Have written a short essay on Eastern and Western philosophy. Made sure to do it before I forgot Sensei's methods of instruction and guidance.

Friday, January 29. Fair.

In the morning, had a discussion with Sensei's family.

In the evening, attended an informal directors meeting.

Felt sick with a cold.

The meeting ended a little after 9:00.

The top Gakkai leaders should understand the times and respond to them.

Will protect the Gakkai leaders and my juniors for the rest of my life. Concerned about the health of young directors.

Read *Songs of Han Shan*:

> *A poor man loves to gather riches*
> *as an owl cares for its young.*
> *Many a child eats away his mother*
> *as wealth ruins its owner.*
> *Fortune shall rise when riches are scattered;*
> *misfortune shall befall when riches are gathered.*

Without wealth, one is free from misfortune
*   as he flies on beating wings aloft in blue skies...*
Though my years have yet to count one hundred,
I constantly worry about the next one thousand years.
My illness is beginning to lessen...

Heard that *The Collected Songs of the Three Hermits* is the compilation of poems by Han Shan, Feng Gan and Shi Dei. Prefer Tu Fu's poetry much better.

Saturday, January 30. Fair.

Had a planning meeting with the headquarters leaders.

Gave guidance, instructions, warnings and encouragement. I am extremely busy.

Left for Atami aboard the 4:35 train from Tokyo. At the invitation of my father-in-law.

Three of us—myself, my wife and Shirohisa.

My child said he liked our home better than D. Inn.

Next morning, went to Atami Castle. Not interesting at all. Some said it is a fourth-rate amusement park.

Since I was feeling ill, we took a taxi home. On the way home, felt like vomiting. My child did, too.

Got home a little before 6:00. Rested immediately.

Must exercise. Read a little of *The Tale of the Taira Clan*.

The fall of the Taira clan was tragic. Where does its fundamental cause lie? Need to analyze it deeply. Some people, despite hardship, retain their grace and composure. Tadanori, the Lord of Satsuma province, was such a person. Of the Taira clan he was an outstanding, youthful general and also a poet. Want to become such a man in the midst of turmoil and raging waves. The meeting between this poet, who was prepared to die in battle, and Count Toshinari is like a vivid masterpiece, like a miniature of life's drama. His calmly composed verse, his free and noble state of mind, and his resolute manner as he was leaving his camp for the battlefield are moving.

Monday, February 1. Cloudy.

Stayed at home in the morning. Received several guests.

The realm of politics is laden with much trouble. News reports about it never end. Japan's destiny appears to be closing in from moment to moment. The nation needs a new light of strength.

In the afternoon, a board of directors meeting at the headquarters. Although we discussed various matters, sensed we are lacking a pillar. Feel bereft. Sorry for Sensei.

In the evening, attended a Kamata Chapter leaders meeting at the Ota Ward Civic Center in Ikegami. At the end of the meeting, instead of giving guidance, offered a greeting. Saw many dear faces.

Very difficult physically. Must wage a battle to break through my karmic deadlock.

Must not lose no matter what.

Those aware of the nature of life do not resent the heavens.

Those who know themselves hold no grudges against others.

It is stated in *An Account of My Hut*: "The flow of a river is ceaseless, and its water never remains as before. The bubbles in a pool come and go, and they never stay long. It is the same with people and their dwellings."

Wednesday, February 3. Clear.

Today I felt a little better.

Everyone seems to be thinking only he or she is right in life.

In the evening, talked with the general director until a little after 8:00.

Afterward, visited M.'s to check on his son's injury. Stayed late. They are good people. But hope they do not decide everything only thinking of their own family. Want them to understand others' feelings as well.

My mind would not rest. Fell asleep after 3:00.

Thursday, February 4. Cloudy.

The Diet session moves along sluggishly.

Heard the Socialist Party is maneuvering to change its chairperson. The Liberal Democratic Party is also moving vigorously toward appointing its next general secretary.

In the evening, lectured on "The Fourteen Slanders" at Ryogoku Civic Hall. Struck by the earnestness and seeking spirit of those who came. Keenly felt my lack of study. Resolved once again to never grow arrogant.

It was cold on my way back. Took a cab home.

S. visited me at home. He is in high sprits, but cannot conceal his age.

Opened *Collected Essays of Lu Xun*, which reads: "What is a road? It is trodden where there was not a road; it is blazed through brambles. There was a road before, and there will be one forever."

My wife is so beautiful. Is she mending clothes for our children?

Friday, February 5. Clear.

Arrived at Shizuoka Station. Was it around 4:20 p.m.?

Received various reports at the inn. Many people came and went. We might have caused some inconvenience for the inn. Must be careful.

Attended a leaders meeting at 6:30. Exerted all my energy.

As long as leaders remain steadfast in faith with the spirit of "We care nothing for our bodies or lives" (LS13, 194), our Gakkai will soar aloft for all eternity. But the Gakkai will only come to a dead end if leaders start to act out of obligation or out of their desire to be promoted.

My left lung ached all day. Felt nauseated.

President Toda once said to me with deep emotion: "What good can those who aspire to study Buddhism do if they cannot resolve problems in their own lives?" These words are excellent, superb, precious. Must exert myself in constant self-discipline.

Saturday, February 6. Clear.

Arrived at Kyoto Station at 4:00 p.m.

Discussed various matters with some friends on the train.

People's faces, their clothing, their minds and dispositions—are all different. People are mysterious; no animals are as complex as humans.

Lectured on the latter half of "The Fourteen Slanders" from 6:30. Self-reflected in light of this strict writing of Nichiren Daishonin. We should take this writing as the backbone of the Gakkai spirit.

Want some time to think.

Must genuinely cherish those spreading the Daishonin's Buddhism. For only in them lies the foundation of kosen-rufu.

Sunday, February 7. Fair.

Left for Kyoto on a night train.

Along the way, many members greeted me at Tsuruga and other stations. Asked H. to strictly caution them not to trouble other passengers.

Our guidance, propagation and faith must accord with social common sense.

Monday, February 8. Clear.

Arrived in Kanazawa a little before 6:00 a.m.

Stayed at an inn during the morning. Felt great pain in my neck and shoulders.

In the afternoon, the Study Department promotional examination was held. It was for assistant lecturers to be promoted to the lecturer level.

Afterward, took a leisurely walk in Kenroku Park. Walked around the back hills to see Mount Hakusan. Its grace and majesty inspired poetic feelings in me.

Strongly sensed the influence of Lord Maeda.[1]

Attended a group chiefs meeting at the district chief's home. Exhausted.

Returned to the inn early.

Attended Kanazawa's general meeting at 6:00 p.m.

Came to understand their dynamic progress. The meeting was held on the fourth floor of the Kanazawa Agricultural Center. The participants numbered about two thousand.

Lectured on "On Practicing the Buddha's Teachings." Herein pulsates the life of the votary of the Lotus Sutra, should I say, the original Buddha of the Latter Day, Nichiren Daishonin. Frightening but pleasing. For I am his disciple.

The spirit of kosen-rufu is alive in Hokuriku. Deeply sensed President Toda's greatness. Hokuriku was dark. But through the power of the Mystic Law, many now show actual proof of their human revolution. My conviction deepened all the more.

There is no greater strategy than the Mystic Law.

Lately, many people are trying to use me. Troubling. Must self-reflect as well. Although I'm not sure if there is much value in taking advantage of me, they are indeed frightening. So many shallow people!

Will advance resolutely. Will stride forward as a man of responsibility.

Will move ahead with a sense of equity like that of a renowned general.

Will charge on, upholding Buddhism as a supreme guide, never turning back.

1. Lord Maeda: Rising from obscure origins, Maeda Toshiie was awarded Noto province by Oda Nobunaga in 1581. Based at Oyama Castle in the city of Kanazawa, the Maeda family controlled the provinces of Kaga, Noto and Etchu (now Toyotama Prefecture).

Tuesday, February 9. Clear.

Left Kanazawa for home.

Spoke with my friends on the train, rested and read. In my mind's eye I could see the beautiful sight of Zhu-ge Kong-ming[1] serving Liubei. Wept alone.

Must read books this year as well, at least fifty or sixty.

My wife came alone to the station to greet me. Her gentle face eased this young revolutionary's tension.

On our way home, ate tempura together. It was expensive. My wife explained why. Astonished by the brilliant intelligence of women.

The time is past 1:30. Decided to go to bed.

Must take care of my health. Will exercise this year.

1.   Kong-ming: See note on p. 219.

Wednesday, February 10. Cloudy.

In the evening, met with O., F. and M., all Diet members.

Outraged by their wicked scheming toward the Gakkai.

Their insidious language and conduct angered me.

Must pray for the success of our seniors' efforts in politics. Pray our seniors who struggle to establish Buddhist ideals in government shall never, throughout their lives, compromise with those who only seek to hold the reins of the nation. Pray they will remain as heroes of the Mystic Law. Came back feeling angry at my seniors who do not uphold President Toda's magnificent, strict guidance.

Will create a new era. For the next twenty years, will grit my teeth and raise new capable people and build a new organization. Will work steadily for the next twenty years.

Read the "Orally Transmitted Teachings":

The "Emerging from the Earth" chapter states: "And in order that day and night with constant diligence / they may seek the Buddha way." This passage indicates that when we exert 100 million eons of effort in a single moment of life, the innate, unaffected three enlightened properties of a Buddha will arise from moment to moment. That is to say, Nam-myoho-renge-kyo is a practice of constant diligence.

—(GZ, 790)

The quantity of daimoku is important.

Thursday, February 11. Clear.

Today is President Toda's birthday. If he were alive, he would be celebrating his sixtieth birthday.[1] My wife and I talked about this as if we were Sensei's son and daughter.

Almost two years have passed since Sensei died. Time flies, but it feels like a long time all the same.

Fearful thoughts weigh heavily on my mind—thoughts about my responsibility, my seniors and my accomplishment.

In the afternoon, went to Myoko-ji to attend the wedding in M.'s family.

On my way home, stopped by Sensei's relatives' home. Chilly winds blew ceaselessly on the way.

Home after 9:00. My wife made sweet rice cakes to celebrate Sensei's birthday. The two of us enjoyed eating them together. We talked about how Sensei would rejoice most at our family's celebration.

Together we are happy. Together, our hearts are beautiful.

1. Sixtieth birthday (Jpn *kanreki*): In the ancient Japanese calendar system, each year has a name, and there are sixty names that make up a cycle of sixty years. Thus, on one's sixtieth birthday, one full cycle has been completed, and one is said to be born again as a baby. On this birthday one is given a red sleeveless kimono jacket and hat, symbolizing a baby.

Friday, February 12. Fair.

It was somewhat mild today unlike yesterday's cold winds.

The morning paper reported on what appeared to be two suns in the sky on the 11th.

Sensed a tragedy in the reshuffling of the cabinet. From their factional infighting comes people's unhappiness. Japan's politics have degenerated to profit-seeking and factionalism as opposed to being for the sake of the Japanese people.

It is the people who are suffering. Arouse your anger! And start a grand movement for new politics and society in order to win your own happiness.

Attended an Adachi Chapter leaders meeting at the Asakusa Civic Auditorium. People are pure and joyful while I am plagued with worry.

Saturday, February 13. Fair.

Thought about the future of the head temple:
1. Wish priests will sincerely protect people toiling to spread the Daishonin's Buddhism.
2. Became responsible for the group pilgrimage.
3. Was asked to supervise the construction of the lodging temples. Felt honored.

Regretfully postponed today's scheduled head temple visit until tomorrow because of M.'s problem. Must protect the bereaved family, embracing them with a magnanimous heart although I may be the only one.

In the evening, went out to eat at I. in Shinjuku with my wife and children. Because it has been a long while, my children were very excited.

Went home by taxi. It was cold.

Sunday, February 14. Clear.

Went to the head temple aboard the 1:30 p.m. *Western Sea* from Tokyo Station. Traveled with the family and relatives of Sensei and M. Felt confident Sensei would be pleased.

In the evening, led a question-and-answer session.

Theory and technique are important. But one's powerful life force truly touches people's hearts. After all, doesn't everything depend on faith?

An enjoyable, fulfilling night at Eagle Peak.

Did not attend *ushitora* gongyo. No excuse for a young man like myself. Must soon develop a healthy physical condition as solid as a diamond.

Monday, February 15. Clear.

Attended the twenty-fourth ceremony of chanting before the Dai-Gohonzon this year.

Chose a gravesite for M. Mystically, it happened to be in front of S.'s tomb.

Received a phone call from the high priest when I returned to Rikyo-bo. He expressed his discontent, saying, "The previous president came to visit me often, but you, who are carrying out his will, did not come to my quarters."

Immediately went to receive an audience with him. Spoke with him on various matters. He appears pleased, trusting me as if I were his own child. How fortunate!

On the way back, saw Mount Fuji soaring in magnificent beauty.

Mount Fuji stands in pristine white. Mount Fuji in crimson hue. Mount Fuji in dignity. Mount Fuji in swirling clouds.

On my way home from Tokyo Station, stopped by the headquarters. Home after 10:00. Tired. Will read a book in bed.

Tuesday, February 16. Clear.

Today is Nichiren Daishonin's birthday.

Stayed in the headquarters building all morning.

Talked with directors H. and I., then met with the general director.

Attended the wedding ceremony of our younger friends at Jozai-ji in the afternoon. Offered some celebratory words to the happy couple. May all our friends, without a single exception, become happy.

Later, at the reception, sang solo "Song of Majesty."

The Gakkai's next stage of advancement is close at hand. Who is aware of it? Who is rejoicing about it? Who is waiting for it?

Wednesday, February 17. Clear.

Good weather continues.

Seems that the Kishi Administration will remain in power for awhile.

Within the Gakkai as well, a gap between the old and new ways of thinking is becoming apparent. I can distinguish among those leaders who are progressive and those who are stagnant, those who are improving their faith and those who are idle. It is very obvious.

Went to the Byakuren temple to attend another friend's wedding ceremony this afternoon.

On the way back, met with a lawyer at Y. So many lawyers are more concerned about making a lot of money than protecting people.

It rained in the early evening. Quite refreshing.

Stayed at the headquarters all evening long.

Discussed a leaders meeting coming up this month of February, also some personnel decisions.

Thursday, February 18. Clear.

For our future development, must place steppingstones behind the scenes, one by one, toward realizing our vision, no matter what hardship it entails. A ship's engine and propeller are invisible to most people. In the future, I will continue to treasure those working behind the scenes the most.

In the evening, met some friends in Shinjuku for dinner. Discussed many things.

Friday, February 19. Fair.

Took an express from Yokohama Station to Kansai at 9:26 a.m., to conduct lectures. Traveled alone. Traveling alone is the best time for me to think in peace.

Ran into N. on the way. Invited him to the dining car with me. He told me he feels encouraged every time he sees me.

After giving a lecture, rested at the G. hotel. Nice to hear a lot of Gakkai members work at this hotel.

Pondered many things. Could not fall asleep until very late. Must take good care of my health.

Important to live life surrounded by good people.

Saturday, February 20. Clear.

Headed for Hofu in the Chugoku area aboard an 8:15 a.m. train from Osaka Station. My third visit to the area. An unforgettable place. The site of our Yamaguchi Campaign. The land here seems to reflect my life, as I'm sure it will as long as I live.

Resolved to promote Hofu to a chapter at the coming headquarters general meeting on May 3.

Led a question-and-answer session at 6:30 p.m.

Wherever I go, young people are so enthusiastic. Must respond to these pure-hearted youth. Want to help them make their dreams come true.

Youth—where else can we find such a noble, powerful and robust-sounding word, filled with visions for the future?

Sunday, February 21. Fair.

Fair weather continues. Just like spring. Spring is certainly near.

Arrived in Okayama around 6:00 p.m.

Inspected a parcel of land for the general chapter's headquarters building.

Gave a lecture and held a question-and-answer session at a gymnasium.

The members were very sincere and responsive. Is this a reflection of the character of this area's central figure? A person in charge or who takes a central role can influence in any way millions and tens of millions of people. What an awesome concept.

Stayed overnight at the general chapter chief's home. Appreciative to him for taking such good care of me.

Monday, February 22. Fair.

Left Okayama a little after 1:00 p.m. Headed for Tottori to offer some guidance and encouragement.

My first guidance trip to the San'in area. Traveled across Japan's main island. Passing the brooks, mountains and fields of early spring, it felt like I was traveling through the realm of poetry.

Not even a cloud in the sky. On the train, read *Three Kingdoms* to my heart's content. Need more capable people. Want my seniors to read this book as well. Everyone is lacking in study. For the future, we should all study hard.

In the evening, arrived in Tottori, the center of the San'in area. From 7:00, lectured and held a question-and-answer session at a gymnasium. The audience was somewhat boisterous and unsettled. Compared to Tokyo, I think they are about three years behind in their level of faith and discipline.

Determined to form a chapter in this area as well.

Will give them my full support. Must help them.

Tuesday, February 23. Fair.

In the morning, went along with other leaders to a great sand dune and stood atop it. Heard that area is designated as a national park. We looked out over the Japan Sea and composed *waka* poems. Each person read his or her poem. It was quite a memorable time.

Left Tottori for Kyoto aboard a train called *Izumo* at around 2:00 p.m.

At 4:15, heard about the birth of the emperor's grandson. An auspicious event for the royal family.

Stayed one night in Kansai.

Received a call from home. My third son, Takahiro, fell into the pond in our yard, which was surrounded by the walls of a filled-in well. Laughed about it heartily. Yet worried he might develop a fever.

Let me fight more battles tomorrow with hope.

Helen Keller said hope is the faith that leads people to success. She also said that without hope nothing can be accomplished.

Wednesday, February 24. Fair.

Returned to Tokyo aboard the *Echo* special express at 10:20 p.m.

Traveling alone was very lonely. Wished I had been with some friends. My common, foolish mind is exhausted.

Am no match for President Toda's sharp intellect and his clear understanding of Buddhism.

I am happy I associate with good people, speak with good people, live with good people and advance with such good people. I am a man of truly good fortune.

Feel exhausted physically and spiritually from this six-day trip.

My wife and her parents from Yaguchi came to greet me at Yokohama Station.

I am the happiest man in the world, in every respect.

Thursday, February 25. Fair.

Stayed in the headquarters all day, attending meetings, offering guidance and encouragement and writing manuscripts.

Fear I may forget President Toda's guidance. Whenever I recall certain things, I record them in my notebook.

In the evening, met the families of S. and I. for dinner at O. in the Ginza.

My father-in-law is a good person; I pray for his longevity.

My mother-in-law is a good person; I pray for her long life.

My wife is a good person; I pray for her happiness.

My children are good, too; I pray for their health.

Returned to the headquarters. Talked with H. and M. about the Gakkai's future until around midnight. Felt pleased at H.'s sincerity.

My seniors need to learn from his seriousness.

Seniors should have ability and a sense of mission and responsibility befitting a senior leader. This is precisely why they are called seniors.

Friday, February 26. Clear.

There are many news reports these days showing Prime Minister Kishi's absurdity and forcefulness. Is this a sign of the shameless arrogance and authoritarianism of the power hungry? How despicable.

Will the madness of the Diet lead to the eventual insanity of the land and people of Japan? How frightening. How sad.

The other day, I read a report about red winds and black winds[1] gusting at 47 mph in Tokyo. There was also a report about similar phenomena in Tottori yesterday. Are these bad omens? What does our future hold? Wish for no calamity or disaster in Japan's future. Must change poison into medicine through the Mystic Law.

In the evening, attended a February headquarters leaders meeting at the Taito Gymnasium.

Felt compelled to bow to the members in honor of their earnest efforts. They are far more capable than I am. Must never overestimate myself as a top leader of the organization. Nor should I allow myself to be overestimated by others.

The guidance of Director H. was quite good.

On the way back, ate a hot meal with my wife.

1. Red winds and black winds: This is a reference to "On Establishing the Correct Teaching for the Peace of the Land," where red, black and green winds are defined as the winds that stir up clouds of sand.

Saturday, February 27. Rain then cloudy.

Attended the completion and Gohonzon-enshrinement ceremonies of the Yokohama Community Center and Myoju-ji starting at 1:00 p.m. Severely cold.

Saw High Priest Nittatsu was in good health. Made me truly happy.

In the evening, attended the Suginami Chapter leaders meeting. Exerted all my energy in giving guidance and encouragement. All chapters have different natures and characteristics as their various missions are unique. That is a good thing.

Went home. My home is modest, yet pure. My tranquil home is a dwelling place of Buddhahood; it is the most relaxing place for me. I am truly happy. I am truly fortunate.

Takahiro, my third son, is growing gradually. We slept together tonight.

Sunday, February 28. Cloudy.

A joint conference was held tonight. We all talked, ate and listened, making preparations for our next battle.

On my way home, stopped by the barber. My heart is so lonesome. I have few people of strong character with whom I can share my thoughts.

Spring is near. I love spring. Want to fill my small yard with all kinds of flowers this year.

The flower show at the Shinjuku Imperial Garden or my home adorned with all kinds of flowers bought from street vendors — which most resembles the artwork in my heart? Which best resembles my dialogue with nature?

The Land of the Eternally Tranquil Light[1] exists within us for all eternity.

Will begin reading again in March. How many books can I read?

1. The Land of Eternally Tranquil Light: A land where a Buddha lives. One of the 'four kinds of lands,' a classification established by the T'ien-t'ai school of the types of lands mentioned in the sutras.

Monday, February 29. Cloudy.

February is over. Farewell to the cold winter. Spring will begin from tomorrow. Sense the vibrant energy of life.

Spring is a season of youth, a song of youth. Let me live with vigor, as a youth, as a genuine youth.

Heard about the death of H.'s wife tonight a little after midnight. Tried to encourage him. My friend, my comrade, be strong!

Are these words by Eiji Yoshikawa? "There is no government more foolish than that which flatters the people who are seeking frankness." Do these words suggest what good and fair government is? This is an important issue. Thought this may also apply to the development of truly capable people in general.

Tuesday, March 1. Clear.

Springtime, springtime has finally arrived. This evening at 4:50 shafts of sunlight appeared across the Tokyo sky.

There was a major earthquake in Morocco.

Talked about many things with H. and the others. Asked them, my seniors, to muster their strength and do their best.

Decision to purchase land near the headquarters building was made today. Very happy about that. The new *Seikyo Shimbun* building will be constructed there. A stronghold in the war of words. In the war of words and thoughts, this will become a great driving force for kosen-rufu.

Spoke with H., A. and others. They are all my good friends as well as my juniors. I'm sure in ten years' time they will all be great leaders in society.

Wednesday, March 2. Clear.

Ate at N. with an executive from A. & Co. He is a good person, a capable individual with backbone. I have great hopes for his lasting faith and his company's prosperity.

Came home early today. Took a bath. Refreshed.

Sorry to be going to sleep so early while others are seriously working. I press my palms together in respect.

Thursday, March 3. Clear then cloudy.

The Girls' Festival.

In our Buddhism, New Year's Day corresponds to *myo*, the Girls' Festival (March 3) to *ho*, the Boys' Festival (May 5) to *ren*, the Star Festival (July 7) to *ge*, and the Chrysanthemum Festival (September 9) to *kyo*.

I'm reminded of my early childhood. Peaceful, fun days, running and playing in fields of greenery and flowers. This day is filled with the fragrance of my mother, the fragrance of my young siblings. Innocence.

Board of directors meeting at the headquarters, 3:00 p.m. A planning meeting for President Toda's second memorial ceremony and the formation of new chapters.

In the evening, gave a general lecture at Suginami Civic Auditorium on one of the letters to Lord Ueno. A truly profound writing. Must study.

Finished reading the second volume of *Romance of the Three Kingdoms*. Have read it three times now. Wish I could have all the top leaders read it. Especially my seniors.

To sleep after 2:00 a.m. Thought of my mother. As an apostle of the Mystic Law, I left my home to find my own way. To a place without my mother, without a wife. I must stand on the front lines of kosen-rufu throughout my life.

Friday, March 4. Cloudy.

Had dinner at Azabu with F. and some others. They remind me of the passage "To discard the shallow and seek the profound is the way of a person of courage" (WND, 402).

Intensively discussed Japan's future, world trends and politics.

Until midnight, talked about our vision for the next ten, twenty, thirty years and preparations to achieve it.

It seems there are two types, or, more broadly, four types of young people. Those of knowledge, those of effort, those of faith and those of emotion.

Some are serious but get carried away, and others are quiet but have a strong backbone. There are those who are eloquent but lack backbone, and those who are reticent but have deep faith.

Returned on a full stomach. Ah, my home. What a quiet, happy home.

Sunday, March 6. Clear.

Stayed at the headquarters in the morning on the 5th. High Priest Nittatsu, the general director and others went to Okinawa for the Gohonzon-enshrining ceremony of the nearly completed Komyo-ji.

If President Toda were still alive, we would have attended together. Oh, how I miss him.

My wife went to Haneda Airport on my behalf and saw the high priest off.

Took an express train from Ueno at 3:00 in the afternoon bound for Takasaki to give a Gosho lecture. Everyone was so earnest.

Today, the 6th, spent the morning at M.'s place offering members one-on-one guidance and encouragement.

In the afternoon, attended a group leaders meeting at Shomyo-ji. Will give my all to raising the mid-level leadership. For whether we take decisive action in this area or not will decide the Gakkai's future development. Wish all top leaders would realize this point from the bottom of their hearts.

To race around and get nowhere is a truly frightful thing.

Walked to the top of Mount Takasaki on the way back. Took a 4:00 train to Tokyo.

Arrived home early. Ate too much.

Monday, March 7. Clear then cloudy.

Spring is moving in quickly.

Spring, spring, like youth, spring is a jewel of life.

Youth must be noble at heart and energetic in action, transcending ideology, putting aside position, circumstances, poverty and wealth.

Youth, trembling with anxiety as they face an unknown future. Youth of little experience, scared, surprised, hearts racing. Bold youth, recklessly striding forward.

The Gakkai as well, day by day, enters an important phase.

Others, unaware of this, seem so nonchalant.

Wish that I. would set his sights on a higher objective and come to talk with me from that perspective. It puts me at a loss. No matter how much advice one is given, sometimes that person's character never changes.

A sweet daphne tree my wife planted last year is flowering now. She left a branch of it on my desk. Ah, what a sweet smell these flowers have.

Tuesday, March 8. Cloudy then clear.

Stayed at the headquarters all day long.

Gave guidance to my juniors throughout the evening. Continually praying for the youth division to produce even one more capable person —my continuing prayer.

People, capable people, young capable people. This alone determines the Gakkai's future.

Must expand my life and give my all to guiding them.

Those who criticize, do as you please. Those who are jealous, feel as you please. Those who laugh, those who ridicule, take a look ten years from now—at the solitary youth who shoulders the Gakkai.

The Gakkai leaders, across every part of the organization, must study more and more. Must make deeper inroads into society.

486 D A I S A K U   I K E D A

Ate at T. with some friends on my way home. The food was really good. Felt happy.

Enjoyed a quiet, solitary stroll back home.

Wednesday, March 9. Clear.

Received visitors all morning.

The Gakkai is young. There is an energy of construction. Progress, ascent. Like the rising sun.

Construction of the new *Seikyo Shimbun* office building has officially been decided. It has a budget of ¥100 million. A castle of discourse.

Started reading *The Accounts of Nikko Shonin*.

Stayed at the headquarters until late. Spoke with some executive leaders about a number of topics. They are all good people. Feel their lifestyles need to be elevated a notch.

"The Road"—a poem by Kotaro Takamura.

> *There is no road before me*
> *The road will be built behind me*

Thursday, March 10. Clear.

Physically exhausted all day. I wonder why I get so tired? Maybe it's expiation of my negative karma. How frightful.

There are so many problems one cannot resolve in this lifetime. Life's mysteries, the inexplicable contradictions of sickness and health, and so on. The fundamental resolution of such problems lies in the practice of faith.

Went to a Study Department professors meeting in the evening.

The Gakkai is strong. The Gakkai is growing. Afterward, attended a youth division leaders meeting until 10:00.

Society is getting worse all the time. Newspaper articles are filled only with misery. Heard there was a robbery in my neighborhood.

Decided to chant three daimoku and go to sleep.

Feel exhausted, truly exhausted.

Friday, March 11. Rain.

Raining today. Lonely.

At noon, ate lunch at N. with T., a company president.

Spent all day at the headquarters. Keep thinking I should visit

America, India and Taiwan to find building materials for the Grand Reception Hall.

To the youth who will fight in the coming age, who will live on the next stage, may you be in good health and be happy.

Saturday, March 12. Cloudy then clear.

An outing for headquarters staff. Left for Atagawa, Izu.

Happy, but fatigued. My physical condition is not good.

Met the bus along the Second Tokyo–Yokohama State Highway, where my mother, wife and children saw me off. Hope I didn't put anyone out.

Had fun with everyone on the bus. Joined them in singing songs.

Will advance with the people, with ordinary folks, with youth. Always and forever.

Stressed to everyone that the headquarters staff—in all areas of endeavor—must become a driving force behind the Gakkai and kosen-rufu. Then told them to enjoy the rest of the evening to their hearts' content.

The bus drove by Ippeki Lake and passed through Ito. Got off at Gotanda.

Overexerted myself. Exhausted.

Monday, March 14. Clear.

When I precisely and assiduously recite the five prayers in the morning and three in the evening, I feel refreshed all day. How mystic. My extremely busy schedule has not allowed me to do so lately. Felt disgusted with myself over this. No matter how many beautiful words I speak to others, cannot conceal my inner life-condition. This is the law of cause and effect.

I am in my thirties. Want to live my thirties meaningfully, without any regret.

Must be aware of myself and my mission. Must be resolved to develop and improve myself.

Thought about the concept of the eightfold path: right way of life, right action, right speech, right views, right meditation and so on.

Had made an appointment to meet my wife on my way home in Shibuya. We stopped by a florist and bought peach and plum plants. Took a taxi home.

Read more of *Romance of the Three Kingdoms*. Kuan Yü was killed.

Chang Fei died. Now over sixty, Liu Pei falls, putting his trust in Kong-ming's loyalty and, in silence, departs for his journey to the netherworld. It is thirty years after the Peach Garden Oath. Beautiful and dramatic.

Wish for my comrades in the Gakkai to be like this. We must be. Something about this story strikes a chord in my heart, for I too have in my heart the memory of one to whom I have made a vow. Will never forget my mentor's words, filled with love and compassion. My comrades and my friends, never forget them, even in your sleep!

Bereaved disciples, arise with courage and advance! Move forward alongside me to put his words into practice and make them a reality.

Now is the time to take up courage.

Wednesday, March 16. Fair.

Two years ago, today, we conducted at Taiseki-ji what President Toda referred to as a ceremony commemorating the kosen-rufu of substantiation.

Profoundly significant.

Told the youth division leaders we must start fresh today toward accomplishing kosen-rufu for all eternity.

Felt deep significance in holding this important ceremony on such a sunny spring day. Yet the grand celebration of the kosen-rufu of substantiation will not end with this day. We should choose another important date within the next half-year and strive toward it to achieve further development.

In the evening, attended a YWD guidance meeting at the Meguro Community Center. Then went to a YMD guidance meeting at the headquarters.

Saw passion and intellect in their eyes, solid belief in the look of their mouths and purity in their complexions. These were noble gatherings of youth filled with hope yet anxious about reality.

Read until late. Feel slight pain in my eyes.

Thursday, March 17. Fair.

Attended a wedding ceremony at Kankiryo temple at 3:00 this afternoon. My junior members' departure toward happiness. May they enjoy great fulfillment together!

Studied the *Six-volume Writings* with youth division leaders at the temple. Surprised at their remarkable study progress. Will be watching their future. "Meanings Hidden in the Depths" states:

The object of devotion functions as an objective reality with which to form a relation. The object with which one forms such a relation arouses wisdom, which in turn leads one to action. Therefore, if the object with which one forms a relation is not true, neither will one's wisdom or action be true. The Great Teacher Miao-lo states: "Although one's aspiration for enlightenment may not be true, if he forms a relation with the objective reality of truth, he then will gain much merit and virtue. If the object with which one forms a relation is not true, although his aspiration for enlightenment is free from falsehood and delusion, it will not become a seed for his enlightenment."

Returned to the headquarters at 6:00.

Youth division leaders are fighting gallantly day in and day out. How can I alone rest? Now is the time to give my all to protect our main camp.

Received a report about the Akita area from H. Want to go there as soon as possible to offer encouragement and guidance.

The day draws near when we will set sail from Tokyo Bay into the high seas of the Pacific Ocean.

Must human beings live through the crashing waves of destiny— whatever they may be?

Friday, March 18. Clear.

Attended a wedding ceremony at Byakuren temple.

The reality of whether youth are progressing toward their happiness corresponds to the nation's development toward its happiness.

Wish my seniors would try to study and learn more.

Those who do not practice the words and ideals of our mentor cannot be called his disciples.

Read the Daishonin's writing "The Entity of the Mystic Law" by myself at the headquarters:

In essence, the entity of Myoho-renge-kyo is the physical body that the disciples and followers of Nichiren who believe in the Lotus Sutra received from their fathers and mothers at birth. Such persons, who honestly discard expedient means, put faith in the Lotus Sutra alone, and chant Nam-myoho-renge-kyo, will transform the three paths of earthly desires, karma, and suffering into the three virtues of the Dharma body, wisdom, and emancipation. The threefold contemplation and the three truths will immediately become manifest in their minds, and the place where they live will become the Land of Eternally Tranquil Light.

—(WND, 420)

Extremely profound. Don't these words express the ultimate truth of Buddhism, the essence of faith, the way to revolutionize our lives and a fundamental guide to daily living?

My seniors, please become people of true courage. I, too, will become a courageous, yet ordinary, man. This is my responsibility to my juniors.

Saturday, March 19. Clear.

Left for Wakayama to give a general lecture. Boarded the *Echo #1* express at Yokohama Station.

Enjoyed watching the beautiful spring flowers through the train window. Peach blossoms bloomed in white and pink, magnolias in white. Cucumber trees in bloom, as well. How beautiful, the yellow fields of March mustard blossoms.

Some seven thousand members gathered, I was told. Their passionate spirit far exceeded my expectations. Felt strongly that a new dawn of the Gakkai is rising.

Spoke with several friends until late in the evening in my room, named the "Fuji" room, at an inn in Wakayama. Such dear friends.

Visited the ruins of Wakayama Castle the next day. Wakayama Prefecture is a tranquil land dear to my heart. I adore it.

Sunday, March 20. Cloudy.

On my way back from Wakayama in the afternoon, met with a professor from Osaka University. For almost two hours, we discussed Y.'s doctoral dissertation and academic career. A rather stubborn professor. Became aware that the feudalistic relationship between a professor and his students, like that of a boss and his underlings, is deeply entrenched in the realm of medicine and other fields of scholarship.

He is ignorant of religion. Heard he practices some new religion.

Realizing that to help one person achieve great success requires the support of many people, much time and great patience.

Spent the night at Y.'s. Spoke with his father about his future.

Youth division activities in both eastern and western Japan are flourishing. Is it not the passion and power of youth that create the new era?

Monday, March 21. Rain, then cloudy.

Returned to Tokyo aboard the 4:00 p.m. *Echo #2* express from Osaka Station. Read and slept well on the train.

May 3 draws closer with each passing day. Others await it nonchalantly. My thoughts, however, should not leave my lips for now. For they are of grave importance and seriousness.

This April 2 will mark the beginning of the third year since my mentor's passing. What have I accomplished over the past two years? What can I, as my mentor's direct disciple, report to him? Lacking in courage, I deserve only his reprimand on many accounts.

Cherry trees in the outer garden of the Meiji Shrine will soon bloom as will the cherries in Aoyama Cemetery. These places are so close to the headquarters they are like our own gardens.

Tuesday, March 22. Clear.

The cemetery problem [in which cemeteries run by other sects refused to inter Gakkai members' ashes] is getting out of hand. How can any religion be so cruel as to refuse the ashes of the deceased? A sign of the times—of the Latter Day of the Law. Such an act is tantamount to a religion denying its fundamental mission and thus its failure as a religion. Told those who have cemetery plots at Taiseki-ji, no matter what religion they belong to, can freely bury ashes there.

In the evening, thanked our lawyers and senior leaders for their hard work.

After our mentor's passing, some have been lording it over others, flaunting their own status and authority. The wives of those individuals have displayed the same behavior. How foolish! How thoughtless! It's troubling for everyone.

Must be steadfast myself. Deeply concerned. My worries double and triple.

Am I coming down with a cold? My temperature is 100.4°. Will go to bed early. I feel sick.

My eldest son, Hiromasa, graduated from kindergarten.

Friday, March 25. Clear.

On the 23rd, felt out of sorts all day.

My temperature was around 101 in the afternoon. By evening, it went up further, so I went home. Nothing was pleasant.

Rested at home on Thursday and Friday. Had some time to think about various things for the first time in a long while. Saw a newspaper article saying a comet will appear toward the end of March and again around April 28.

Was told several people phoned concerned about my health. Appreciative.

Saturday, March 26. Rain.

Went to the headquarters in the afternoon. Still had a slight fever. Rode the train for the first time in a while. Saw cherry trees in bloom here and there through the window.

Everyone is concerned about my health. Thankful. Appreciative to those who truly care about me.

Until late in the evening, gave advice and encouragement on various matters.

On my way home, ate with M. and H. at D. restaurant in Shinjuku. Felt feverish again. What can I do?

Sunday, March 27. Clear.

Rested in the morning. Felt listless.

My wife's father came over out of concern for me. He has grown old. Want him to take good care of his health.

A Coal Miners Union disturbance reported in Mi'ike, Kyushu. Such an unfortunate, gloomy nation, Japan—when will it settle down and become refreshing as a fragrant breeze? Why do Japanese have to kill one another? Their misfortune arises from differences in ideology, a cause for humanity's fundamental unhappiness. How foolish! How stupid!

Went on an overnight pilgrimage to the head temple aboard a 1:30 p.m. train from Tokyo. Concerned about H.'s health. Told him, "It is you who must take care not to overexert yourself."

Had a private audience with High Priest Nittatsu.

The head temple was peaceful and calm.

Monday, March 28. Fair.

Chanted before the Dai-Gohonzon at 9:00 a.m. Why do I feel my life force well up from within when I chant to the Dai-Gohonzon of the High Sanctuary of True Buddhism, which was bestowed upon the entire world?

Visited my mentor's grave. Pledged to him I would accomplish all my goals before attending his second memorial service.

Afterward, attended a ceremony in which twenty-two men entered the priesthood. May there be great blessings and good fortune for those young disciples of High Priest Nittatsu who will shoulder the priesthood's future.

In the afternoon, exited the head temple with everyone else.

Attended a planning meeting that lasted until midnight.

Who will be the driving force behind the Gakkai's next stage of development? Only the youth division? If so, fine. The time has come; the tide is shifting.

H. is seriously exerting himself. If one person stands up, then ten thousand and more will follow.

Everyone must have been tired. Sorry there wasn't even any tea for them.

Tuesday, March 29. Clear.

The March headquarters leaders meeting was held at Taito Gymnasium. Relieved to see the meeting was enjoyable yet serious.

Had dinner with the T.s in Shinjuku on my way home.

Must advance with the people throughout my life.

Must continue to talk with ordinary people and live my life for ordinary people.

The second anniversary of President Toda's passing approaches. People both within and outside our religion will gradually come to understand his greatness. But it is his disciples' responsibility to make that happen. Those oblivious to this task are not his true disciples. How many real disciples are there?

Aren't some intent only on using our mentor's name to secure their personal interests? Because our strict teacher is no longer around, aren't there those who have succumbed to the lure of cunning and authority?

Wednesday, March 30. Clear.

In the headquarters reception room #1, met with the general director, who related his desire for me to become the third Soka Gakkai president. He said it was the consensus of all the other leaders and that the time is right. Our conversation took place beneath the stern yet kind gazes of the first president, Makiguchi, and the second president, Toda, whose photos hang on the wall.

Though it might have been selfish of me, I turned him down. I am tired.

Told him I would take responsibility for leading the Gakkai. Regarding my presidency, however, I asked that he discuss it with me again after the sixth anniversary of President Toda's passing.

Every day I feel I'm being buffeted by tidal waves. It is my responsibility alone to protect the Gakkai. Painful.

Thursday, March 31. Cloudy.

In the evening, attended a question-and-answer session at the Suginami Civic Auditorium.

The memorial service for the second anniversary of President Toda's passing will begin tomorrow. We'll be leaving for the head temple on a 9:30 train.

Torrential rain late tonight. So many things to think about. Tossed and turned in bed. If I could just be healthy…

Friday, April 1. Rain, then clear.

Light rain. A cold day.

Boarded a train at Shinagawa Station at 9:30 a.m. with President Toda's family. K., H. and M. were also with us.

We drove to the head temple from Fuji Station, where we arrived shortly before 1:00. Immediately attended the completion ceremony for the Dai-kejo Hall.

My eyes did not notice any cherry blossoms at the head temple. Is it because of the cold weather or because of my sorrow? Nor did my heart sense any peach or plum blossoms. Only weeping golden bells were in bloom; their forlorn, deep yellow color struck my heart.

At 4:00 p.m., attended the service marking the eve of the second anniversary of my mentor's passing, conducted by High Priest Nittatsu in the Grand Lecture Hall. At 7:00, we chanted daimoku and eulogies were read.

Happy that I, as an immediate disciple, could arrange such a grand memorial service for my late mentor. Renewed my resolve, aiming for the sixth anniversary of President Toda's death.

Attended a planning board meeting at the Rikyo-bo at 8:00 to decide on new chapter chief and women's division chapter chief appointments.

Had many thoughts, alone in the tranquil night.

Saturday, April 2. Clear.

Today was so refreshing, a 180 degree turn from yesterday.

Reflected on my mentor's great virtue. Have been thinking endlessly lately about the mysterious workings of the cosmos.

At 10:00 a.m., High Priest Nittatsu again led the sutra recitation at the Reception Hall.

At 11:00, we all left to visit President Toda's grave. The high priest led the procession, which included many priests and all Gakkai top leaders.

By the Five-story Pagoda, in front of the grave of my mentor, who was posthumously named "the Great Layman of the Castle of the Sun, the Guardian and the Supreme Proclaimer of the Law" (Daisen-in Hogo Nichijo Dai-koji). The song "Gojogen" was sung in his memory. My eyes filled with tears.

On the way back, chanted daimoku and offered incense before President Toda's and President Makiguchi's family graves.

Left the head temple at 1:00 p.m.

The graceful summit of Fuji soared behind the red Sanmon Gate[1] and above the giant cedar trees that have stood tall for hundreds of years. The sight of it is etched in my heart like a masterpiece.

Sense a new era close at hand. There is no responsibility more serious than that for the sake of Buddhism.

1. Sanmon Gate: The main gate on the grounds of the head temple, donated to Taiseki-ji by a believer associated with the Tokugawa shogunate in the Edo period.

Sunday, April 3. Rain.

Traveled to Shizuoka on business. So cold. The weather has changed completely since yesterday. Astonished by the drastic contrast.

Heard snow fell in Hakone. The weather is like February.

Got off the train at Shinagawa Station in the evening. It was raining in Tokyo, chilling my body.

Read the literary magazine *Cuckoo* for the first time in a long while.

Have lost almost 17 pounds since last April.

Monday, April 4. Rain.

In the morning, my wife and I visited the home of President Toda's family. His son Takahisa's wedding ceremony will be on the 9th. Happy to hear this.

"If he were alive…," President Toda's wife said, looking weary.

In the evening, attended a YWD leaders meeting at the Taito

Gymnasium. The venue was packed. A standing-room–only crowd—a dynamic gathering of youthful energy. Here strife, position, authority, hatred and jealousy are crushed into dust. To foolish or arrogant leaders, this would surely be a blinding spectacle.

Tuesday, April 5. Cloudy with occasional rain.

Went to the Kodaira area in the afternoon to survey a parcel of property for purchase by the Gakkai.

The scent of earth and the vivid sight of oaks, mustard blossoms, lily magnolias, evergreen magnolias, peach trees, apricot trees, narcissus, willows and camphor trees—a grand vista of nature in ceaseless motion; a peaceful and pastoral scene that purifies my heart. Musashino is a dear place to me.

Decided to purchase about eight acres of land for the future site of Soka University or Soka Junior and Senior High Schools.

From 4:30, offered advice on composing a Gakkai song to younger youth division leaders.

In the evening, attended a YMD leaders meeting at the Taito Gymnasium. Pioneers of a new era, aiming for the future, my dear friends displayed the vigor of youth.

Here is the power to create a new beginning for Japan's future. Is anyone aware of us? Is anyone expecting us?

Confirmed the importance of the power of faith, practice and the Law—the three primary elements for promoting kosen-rufu.

The general meeting on May 3 gets closer day by day. Everyone's expectations of me weigh heavy, too heavy, upon my heart. Is this young general destined to lead the way and take the brunt of the attacks in the course of our eternal struggle for kosen-rufu?

Wednesday, April 6. Fair.

This morning, several executive priests came by, including the general administrator and the executive advisor. We spent about three hours in the conference room, discussing various issues, including the problem of burial plots [for the members]. Some of the priests were serious about resolving the topics on the agenda, while others only looked down on us, like arrogant monks. My hope is for a profound bond between the priesthood and laity. Longing for the day the priesthood and laity can work together, becoming "as inseparable as fish and the water in which they swim." Regrettable.

Afterward, a board of directors meeting was held. Almost like having no meeting at all. Strictly admonished the senior directors.

I'm a little tired of struggling so strenuously in the world of "adults." Want to go to Hokkaido in May and stand amid a vast, open field.

My eldest, Hiromasa, has entered elementary school. Time really flies. If President Toda were alive, how happy he would be! I truly miss him. He was our father, our sovereign and teacher.

My wife put a daffodil in the vase on my desk.

Resolved again to read more.

Thursday, April 7. Clear then cloudy.

Lectured on the entire text of "On the Treasure Tower" at the Toshima Civic Auditorium. Difficult to understand. Our lives are composed of the five universal elements of earth, water, fire, wind and *ku*, says the Daishonin. He continues: "Abutsu-bo is therefore the treasure tower itself, and the treasure tower is Abutsu-bo himself" (WND, 299).

The true aspect of life—the actual manifestation of the essence of 'the three thousand realms in a single moment of life'—the real identity of the individual.

Feel a keener sense of mission as each day passes. Leaders who act from force of habit assume an easygoing attitude. But leaders who ponder their mission to be pioneers and creators seek to develop courage; tricks or tactics are the furthest thing from their minds. Troubling.

My slight fever continues. Am I coming down with cold? Want a strong body.

There is a single flower in my room. Don't know what it's called, but in it I can see my wife's loving heart. May the Gohonzon illuminate our home with good fortune for all eternity.

Friday, April 8. Fair.

Left home at 8:00. A hectic morning.

From the train, could see trees here and there with new spring buds —cherries, lilies, magnolias and green willows. It would be perfect, were the train not so crowded.

Encouraged leaders to self-reflect. I, too, self-reflected on various matters. Must become a person with capacity as vast as the ocean, someone who truly loves and protects all leaders. The Gakkai must be built upon the foundation of compassionate action and humanistic behavior.

In the afternoon, went to Josen-ji to say hello to Priest T. Concerned about the health of this elderly priest.

Discussed many issues with youth division leaders. There were some of whom I had no choice but to scold strictly.

My cold is not going away. Physically exhausted. Without relying on anyone else, must think about the Gakkai's future—ten and twenty years from now.

Saturday, April 9. Fair.

My physical condition is not good. Was told I had a temperature of 100.4.

Attended Takahisa's wedding at the Imperial Hotel from 5:00 p.m. About 150 people came. A time to celebrate. Prayed for the great happiness of the family. On the way back, my wife and I stopped at a flower shop near Hibiya Park and bought a potted African lily. Took a taxi home.

An emergency board of directors meeting was called at the headquarters. It went until very late. Received a call saying the board of directors had decided to propose me as the third Soka Gakkai president.

Politely declined.

The stormy winds of my destiny are raging through the innermost recesses of my heart. My mission is like a series of raging waves repeatedly buffeting my entire being. The thick rope of my karma binds me strongly, harshly and tightly.

Myoho-renge-kyo—my mentor Josei Toda; let me live and fight with composure until the beginning of the sixth anniversary of my mentor's passing. I am thirty-two—too young.

On that anniversary of my mentor's death I will be thirty-six, beginning the thirty-seventh year of my life—the same age at which Nikko Shonin succeeded the Daishonin.

Ah—is there no one else who can take leadership in place of my tired, worn-out self? Have no one to talk to. My wife quietly watches over me in my agony.

Sunday, April 10. Cloudy.

A miserable morning. Could do nothing about it. Although I did a powerful gongyo, I felt as if there was an iron plate in my chest. Must fuse with the ultimate reality....

In the afternoon, took a drive to the Musashino area with President

Toda's family. Wanted them to enjoy some rest and recreation. Miss K., H. and M. accompanied us.

Drove to Higashi-murayama. Spring winds swayed the orchids and blew dust into the air.

Cherry blossoms momentarily soothed my heart. So did the Japanese roses, rhododendrons, spireas, pear blossoms, apricot blossoms, weeping willows and orange blossoms; the camphor trees, fir trees, peach trees, oak trees and trees whose names I do not know.

This is my dearest Shangri-La of Tokyo; it is Japan's great plain, the land I love. On the way back, Miss K. treated us to dinner at her home.

Home after 8:00.

Could not sleep until 2:00 a.m.; the gusty winds kept making noise, banging on our tin roof. My modest home is sometimes troublesome. But this home is the fortress of my honor and pride, from where I venture into the world; it is my castle of glorious history. Thinking in this way, I feel limitless joy.

Monday, April 11. Clear.

An emergency board meeting was held in the headquarters conference room at 3:30 p.m. It was to discuss the important issue of who would become the third president. I may be unable to continue turning it down and ultimately have to accept this great responsibility as my destiny. Though I have declined several times, will I have no choice in the end but to make up my mind and accept?

This must be due to the Buddha's wisdom, but it is truly tormenting. I feel tension that defies expression.

The Gohonzon is as vast as the universe; it is infinite and eternal. All I can do is to keep my faith in it and take leadership.

I am a youth! I am a man! Advance boldly over mountains and deserts, through raging waves and storms.

Physically exhausted. Must take care of my health for the sake of all the Gakkai members.

1. From May, will put more energy into Buddhist study.
2. From May, will place top priority on discussion meetings.
3. From May, will base everything on gongyo.

Tuesday, April 12. Cloudy.

Not feeling well.

In the afternoon, met with directors H. and Z. at N. They related everyone's strong desire for me to become the third president. Declined once again.

Deep in my heart I have already decided to succeed President Toda. But could not formally express my feeling. My heart and mind contradict one another.

Conveyed my wish to postpone my presidency until the beginning of the seventh year after President Toda's passing. They have been holding board of directors meetings repeatedly. I am well aware of their dilemma. Sorry for them.

In the evening, went to Shinjuku on my way home to buy my son a gift for his entrance to elementary school. But went home without buying anything for him. Sad.

Thursday, April 14. Rain, then clear.

It rained in the morning but cleared up later, although the forecast said it would rain all day.

Left home at 8:30 a.m., my feet feeling heavy.

In reception room #1, the general director and three other directors conveyed their desire for me to become the third president. It was 10:10 a.m. Could not refuse, and they naturally took my inability to decline as an acceptance. So this is my destiny. A wave of joy washed over everyone. Everyone seemed to dance with delight.

The directors said they had been waiting, along with President Toda's family and everyone else, for me to accept. Now, it's finally over. This day will be a great turning point in my life.

It can't be helped. There is no other choice. Thought of President Toda and made a solitary determination.

Friday, April 15. Cloudy.

Contemplated aligning ourselves for our next decisive battle.

This will be my true departure, aiming for the year of my mentor's seventh memorial service. The next four years will be a succession of victories.

It will be 1964. Want to aim for victorious April 2 and May 3 general meetings that year.

I was raised by President Toda as his direct disciple. He trained me continually and repeatedly. How could I fear any battle? The time for me to repay my debt of gratitude to him has come.

Ours is a battle to create history for Japan and the rest of the world. There is no greater honor in life. No one could be prouder.

Josei Toda is my mentor, and I, Daisaku Ikeda, am his disciple.

The inauguration of the third president has been set for May 3.

Things are getting more hectic at the headquarters.

Canceled a lecture in Omiya. Returned home earlier than usual.

I, Daisaku Ikeda, son of a fisherman, at last stand at the battlefront of kosen-rufu. Must realize the karmic importance in this. May all the Buddhas throughout time and space and all the Buddhist gods and bodhisattvas protect me!

Never before have I deeply contemplated the work of a Buddha. My practice in this lifetime has become so gravely important that the depths of my life are filled with awe.

Must uphold the great Gohonzon no matter what may happen. Must always exert myself in faith and practice. Strong faith is everything. The power of this Buddhism will determine everything.

Monday, April 25. Cloudy.

On both the 23rd and 24th, traveled to the foot of Mount Akagi to entertain my mentor's family.

There was a great waterfall. Frolicked in the mountains and ate fish by a natural mountain stream. Heard the place was once a training ground for young soldiers.

The headquarters is quietly in motion.

Read halfway through *The Collected Writings of Nichiren Buddhism*. Must earnestly exert myself in Buddhist study. How can a leader be called a leader without upholding a great philosophy? How can a practitioner of philosophy be called such without studying?

Walked home from Kamata Station amid a fresh, fragrant breeze.

My home is tranquil, bright and happy.

Tuesday, April 26. Cloudy.

My physical exhaustion is growing.

The headquarters is calm but not lax. Each day, leaders are becoming more serious.

Must give my all to ensure our victory over the next four years. Will take the lead resolutely.

The headquarters leaders meeting for April was held at the Taito Gymnasium. Started at 6:00 p.m.

Offered formal greetings as the new president.

My fellow members, my brothers and sisters, were delighted for me. Told them, without any affectation, that I would take leadership as a human being, as a youth, precisely in the same way I have been doing so until now.

On my way home, met over dinner with the T.s.

Keenly felt the importance of training both my mind and body.

From May I shall begin the essential stage of my life.

Tuesday, May 3. Clear.

Inaugurated third president of the Soka Gakkai.

The general meeting at which this took place was held at 12:00 noon in the Nippon University Auditorium.

Was a little fatigued from last night.

Pictured my mentor rejoicing.

Solemn, serious.

Shall begin my lifetime battle to spread the Law, transcending life and death.

My fellow Gakkai members, my friends, were truly happy for me.

Must take leadership for kosen-rufu in a way that befits a general, a human being and a youth.

Wednesday, May 4. Cloudy.

Tired.

Thought about my objectives for the first phase of my battle.

Honing my vision for the next four years, until the beginning of the seventh year of my mentor's passing.

Will move straight ahead toward 1964.

Deeply realize the protection of the Buddhist gods. I am a Bodhisattva of the Earth.

Attended a top leaders meeting. Everyone seemed happy.

The Gakkai has started to move once again with a roaring sound; it is a living, moving entity.

A fresh breeze. Walked alone from Kamata Station.

Finished reading most of *The Collected Writings of Nichiren Buddhism*.

Thursday, May 5. Rain, then cloudy.

The Gakkai headquarters office was closed for the holiday. Serenity in the midst of activity.

Went to T. with my entire family and the S.s. Had dinner together on the way back. Exhausted.

Want to develop the strength and good health to maintain my love for all Gakkai members and all people.

Wore a kimono all day, for the first time in a long while.

Friday, May 6. Cloudy, then rain in the evening.

Tomorrow, I will go on my first guidance trip outside Tokyo as president.

Decided to go to Kansai, where I have shared both joy and suffering with the members.

Can picture their happy faces.

Read the Gosho for a while to prepare myself to give encouragement.

Will treat each and every person in a friendly manner. Will talk with every person, hold dialogues and ask that we share one another's happiness and sufferings for the rest of our lives. This is my credo.

I shall advance, fight and suffer as an emissary of the Buddha, an uncrowned hero and an honorable ally of the ordinary people.

Friday, May 13. Fair.

Attended a garden party from 1:00 p.m. at the head temple, at the invitation of High Priest Nittatsu.

Under clear skies, I and the other top leaders enjoyed many delicious foods served at booths set up on the head temple grounds. The high priest told us he will invite us there each spring.

Affirmed my commitment to the head temple. The high priest and I erected a plaque together on the site where the Grand Reception Hall will be built.

Strongly believe the dawn of a great new religious school and the time for the Gakkai's dynamic development have arrived.

All is changeable, nothing is constant See Sessen Doji.

asura (Skt) A type of demon in Indian mythology, contentious and belligerent by nature, who fights continually with the god Shakra, or Indra. The world of *asuras* constitutes one of the six paths of existence.

Avichi hell Also, the hell of incessant suffering. The most terrible of the eight hot hells. The Sanskrit word *avichi* was translated into Chinese as 'incessant,' indicating that, in this hell, pain and suffering continue without interruption. It is said that one who commits any of the five cardinal sins or slanders the correct teaching is reborn in the Avichi hell.

bodhisattva (Skt) A being who aspires to attain Buddhahood and carries out altruistic practices to achieve that goal. Compassion predominates in bodhisattvas, who postpone their own entry into nirvana in order to lead others toward enlightenment.

Bodhisattvas of the Earth Those who chant and propagate Nam-myoho-renge-kyo. *Earth* indicates the enlightened nature of all people. The term describes the innumerable bodhisattvas who appear in the "Emerging from the Earth" chapter of the Lotus Sutra and are entrusted by Shakyamuni with the task of propagating the Law after his passing. In several of his writings, Nichiren Daishonin identifies his own role with that of their leader, Bodhisattva Superior Practices.

Bonten (Skt Brahma) A god said to live in the first of the four meditation heavens in the world of form above Mount Sumeru and to rule over the *saha* world. In Indian mythology he was regarded as the personification of the fundamental universal principle, and in Buddhism he was adopted as one of the two major tutelary gods, together with Taishaku (Skt Indra).

Buddhist gods Also, heavenly gods and benevolent deities. Gods who protect the correct Buddhist teaching and its votaries. These gods also work to protect the people and their land and bring fortune to both.

consistency from beginning to end The last of the ten factors mentioned in the "Expedient Means" chapter of the Lotus Sutra. It is the integrating factor that unifies the other nine in every moment of life.

daimoku (Jpn) Literally, 'title.' 1) The title of a sutra, in particular the title of the Lotus Sutra, Myoho-renge-kyo. 2) The invocation of Nam-myoho-renge-kyo in Nichiren Daishonin's Buddhism.

Daishonin (Jpn) Literally, 'great sage.' In particular, this honorific title is applied to Nichiren to show reverence for him as the Buddha who appears in the Latter Day of the Law to save all humankind.

devil king of the sixth heaven The king of devils, who dwells in the highest of the six heavens of the world of desire. He works to obstruct Buddhist practice and delights in sapping the life force of other beings. He is also regarded as the manifestation of the fundamental darkness inherent in life. Also called the heavenly devil.

Eagle Peak (Skt Gridhrakuta) Also, Vulture Peak. A mountain located to the northeast of Rajagriha, the capital of Magadha in ancient India, where Shakyamuni is said to have expounded the Lotus Sutra. Eagle Peak also symbolizes the Buddha land or the state of Buddhahood. In this sense, the 'pure land of Eagle Peak' is often used.

fundamental darkness Also, fundamental ignorance. The most deeply rooted illusion inherent in life, which gives rise to all other illusions and earthly desires.

four bodhisattvas Various kinds of four bodhisattvas appear in Buddhism. The four leaders of the Bodhisattvas of the Earth described in the "Emerging from the Earth" chapter of the Lotus Sutra are Superior Practices, Boundless Practices, Pure Practices and Firmly Established Practices.

Fuji school Also, Nichiren Shoshu. The school of Nichiren Buddhism founded by Nikko Shonin at the foot of Mount Fuji.

Gohonzon *Go* means 'worthy of honor' and *honzon* means 'object of fundamental respect.' The object of devotion in Nichiren Daishonin's Buddhism and the embodiment of the Mystic Law permeating all phenomena. It takes the form of a mandala inscribed on paper or on wood with characters representing the Mystic Law as well as the Ten Worlds, including Buddhahood. Nichiren Daishonin's Buddhism holds that all people possess the Buddha nature and can attain Buddhahood through faith in the Gohonzon.

gongyo Literally, 'assiduous practice.' In the Daishonin's Buddhism, it means to chant Nam-myoho-renge-kyo and portions of the "Expedient Means" and "Life Span" chapters of the Lotus Sutra. It is performed morning and evening.

Gosho Literally, 'honored writings.' The individual and collected writings of Nichiren Daishonin.

Hokkeko A lay organization of believers who practice at temples under the priesthood.

human revolution A concept coined by the Soka Gakkai's second president, Josei Toda, to indicate the self-reformation of an individual—the strengthening of life force and the establishment of Buddhahood—that is the goal of Buddhist practice.

icchantika (Skt) Persons of incorrigible disbelief who have no aspiration for enlightenment and thus no prospect of attaining Buddhahood. Many sutras say that *icchantika* are inherently incapable of attaining enlightenment, but some Mahayana sutras hold that even *icchantika* can become Buddhas.

ichinen Literally, 'one mind.' The life-moment, or ultimate reality, that is manifested at each moment in people.

kalpa (Skt) An extremely long period of time. Sutras and treatises differ in their definitions, but kalpas fall into two major categories, those of measurable and immeasurable duration. There are three kinds of measurable kalpas: small, medium and major. One explanation sets the length of a small kalpa at approximately sixteen million years. According to Buddhist cosmology, a world repeatedly undergoes four stages: formation, continuance, decline and disintegration. Each of these four stages lasts for twenty small kalpas and is equal to one medium kalpa. Finally, one complete cycle forms a major kalpa.

kalakula (Skt) Imaginary insects whose bodies were said to swell rapidly in a strong wind.

kosen-rufu Literally, to 'widely declare and spread [Buddhism].' Nichiren Daishonin defines Nam-myoho-renge-kyo of the Three Great Secret Laws as the law to be widely declared and spread during the Latter Day. There are two aspects of kosen-rufu: the kosen-rufu of the entity of the Law, or the establishment of the Dai-Gohonzon, which is the basis of the Three Great Secret Laws; and the kosen-rufu of substantiation, the widespread acceptance of faith in the Dai-Gohonzon among the people.

ku A fundamental Buddhist concept, variously translated as non-substantiality, emptiness, void, latency, relativity, etc. The concept that entities have no fixed or independent nature.

Latter Day of the Law Also, the Latter Day. The last of the three periods following Shakyamuni Buddha's death when Buddhism falls into confusion and Shakyamuni's teachings lose the power to lead people to enlightenment. A time when the essence of the Lotus Sutra will be propagated to save all humankind.

Lotus Sutra The highest teaching of Shakyamuni Buddha, it reveals that all people can attain enlightenment and declares that his former teachings should be regarded as preparatory.

mahasattva A 'great being.' Another term for bodhisattva.

Mahayana One of two main branches of Buddhism. It calls itself Mahayana or the 'Great Vehicle' because its teachings enable all beings to attain Buddhahood. It lays particular emphasis upon the bodhisattva.

many in body, one in mind Also, unity in working together for a common goal, when individuals with a common mind pursue that goal with each person's originality respected.

Mystic Law The ultimate law of life and the universe. The law of Nam-myoho-renge-kyo.

Nam-myoho-renge-kyo The ultimate law of the true aspect of life permeating all phenomena in the universe. The invocation established by Nichiren Daishonin on April 28, 1253. Nichiren Daishonin teaches that this phrase encompasses all laws and teachings within itself, and that the benefit of chanting Nam-myoho-renge-kyo includes the benefit of conducting all virtuous practices. *Nam* means 'devotion to'; *myoho* means 'Mystic Law'; *renge* refers to the lotus flower, which simultaneously blooms and seeds, indicating the simultaneity of cause and effect; *kyo* means sutra, the teaching of a Buddha.

Nembutsu A generic term for those sects that seek to attain rebirth in the Pure Land by worshipping Amida Buddha.

never begrudging one's life Refers to the fundamental attitude in the practice of Buddhism; specifically, to seek the Law and propagate it unsparingly. Implies the effect of ridding oneself of the superficial ego.

Nichiren Daishonin The thirteenth-century Japanese Buddhist teacher and reformer who taught that all people have the potential for enlightenment. He defined the universal Law as Nam-myoho-renge-kyo and established the Gohonzon as the object of devotion for all people to attain Buddhahood. *Daishonin* is an honorific title that means 'great sage.'

offerings of the Law Offerings comprising our efforts to propagate the Law.

offerings of wealth Material offerings.

oneness of body and mind A principle explaining that the two seemingly distinct phenomena of body, or the physical aspect of life, and mind, or its spiritual aspect, are two integral phases of the same entity.

sensei Literally, 'teacher.'

Sessen Doji The name of Shakyamuni Buddha in a previous lifetime when he was practicing austerities in the Snow Mountains (Jpn Sessen) in pursuit of enlightenment. Sessen Doji had not yet heard of Buddhism. The god Taishaku appeared before Sessen Doji in the form of a hungry demon and recited half a verse from a Buddhist teaching: "All is changeable, nothing is constant. This is the law of birth and death." Sessen Doji begged the demon to tell him the second half. When the demon agreed but demanded his flesh and blood in payment. Sessen Doji gladly consented, and the demon taught him the latter half of the verse: "Extinguishing the cycle of birth and death, one enters the joy of nirvana." Sessen Doji scrawled this teaching on the rocks and trees for the sake of others who might pass by, and then jumped from a tall tree into the demon's mouth. Just at that moment, the demon changed back into Taishaku and caught him. He praised Sessen Doji's willingness to give his life for the Law and predicted that he would attain Buddhahood.

shakubuku A method of propagating Buddhism by refuting another's attachment to heretical views and thus leading him or her to the correct Buddhist teaching.

Shakyamuni Also, Siddhartha Gautama. Born in India (present-day southern Nepal) about three thousand years ago, he is the first recorded Buddha and founder of Buddhism. For fifty years, he expounded various sutras (teachings), culminating in the Lotus Sutra.

shoju A method of propagating Buddhism by leading another to the true teaching gradually without refuting his misconceptions.

simultaneity of cause and effect The principle that cause and effect exist simultaneously in a single moment of life. Because the Mystic Law is the law of the mutual possession of the Ten Worlds and 'three thousand realms in a single moment of life,' it simultaneously possesses both the cause, or the nine worlds, and the effect, or Buddhahood. In terms of the practice of Nichiren Daishonin's Buddhism, when one chants Nam-myoho-renge-kyo with faith in the Gohonzon (cause), his latent Buddhahood simultaneously emerges (effect).

Soka Group A group of young men charged with planning and implementing the safe movement of people at Soka Gakkai events.

Taishaku Also, Indra, one of the two main tutelary gods of Buddhism, together with Bonten.

ten demon daughters The daughters of the demon Kishimojin; also known as the ten goddesses. In the Lotus Sutra's "Dharani" chapter, they pledge to protect the sutra's votaries.

ten directions North, south, east, west, northeast, northwest, southeast, southwest, up and down. That is, the entire dimension of space. It is said that there are Buddha lands in all directions throughout the universe, each with its own Buddha.

Ten Worlds Ten life-conditions that a single entity of life manifests.

Theravada 'Teaching of the Elders.' One of two main branches of Buddhism, together with Mahayana. It teaches that since Buddhahood is almost impossible to attain, one should aim for the lesser goal of arhat, or worthy. Emphasizes a strict adherence to discipline and a literal interpretation of doctrine.

three assemblies in two places A division of the Lotus Sutra according to the location and sequence of the events described in it. The three assemblies are the first assembly on Eagle Peak, the Ceremony in the Air and the second assembly on Eagle Peak. The two places are on Eagle Peak and in the air.

three obstacles and four devils Various obstacles and hindrances to the practice of Buddhism. The three obstacles are: 1) the obstacle of earthly desires; 2) the obstacle of karma, which may also refer to opposition from one's spouse or children; and 3) the obstacle of retribution, also obstacles caused by one's superiors, such as rulers or parents. The four devils are: 1) the hindrance of the five components; 2) the hindrance of earthly desires; 3) the hindrance of death, because untimely death obstructs one's practice of Buddhism or because the premature death of another practitioner causes doubts; and 4) the hindrance of the devil king.

three thousand realms in a single moment of life Also, *ichinen sanzen*. A philosophical system set forth by T'ien-t'ai in his *Great Concentration and Insight*, clarifying the mutually inclusive relationship of the ultimate truth and the phenomenal world. This means that the life of Buddhahood is universally inherent in all beings, and the distinction between a common person and a Buddha is a phenomenal one.

Thus Come One One of the ten honorable titles for a Buddha, meaning one who has arrived from the world of truth.

Traffic Control Group The precursor of the Soka Group.

True Law Nam-myoho-renge-kyo.

YMD Acronym for young men's division.

YWD Acronym for young women's division.

ABOUT THE AUTHOR

DAISAKU IKEDA was born in Tokyo on January 2, 1928. A graduate of Fuji Junior College, he joined the Soka Gakkai in 1947 and became its third president in May 1960. He became president of the Soka Gakkai International in 1975.

Mr. Ikeda has founded several institutions, including Soka University, Soka Women's Junior College, Soka Junior and Senior High Schools, Soka Elementary School, Soka Kindergarten, the Min-On Concert Association, the Institute of Oriental Philosophy, the Boston Research Center and the Fuji Art Museum.

Mr. Ikeda has received awards and honorary degrees from institutions and universities around the world, including the United Nations Peace Award. He has made numerous proposals on peace, disarmament, culture and education, and is also the author of many books ranging from Buddhist studies, novels and poetry to essays and travel diaries. His writings have been translated into nearly thirty languages.

SELECTED TITLES BY DAISAKU IKEDA

The following Middleway Press books are available through your favorite neighborhood or On-line bookstore, or at www.middlewaypress.com:

Buddhism Day by Day, by Daisaku Ikeda, Santa Monica, Calif.: Middleway Press, 2006, ISBN-13: 978-0-9723267-5-9; $15.95

Buddhism For You: Courage, by Daisaku Ikeda, Santa Monica, Calif.: Middleway Press, 2006, ISBN-13: 978-0-9723267-6-6; $7.95

Buddhism For You: Determination, by Daisaku Ikeda, Santa Monica, Calif.: Middleway Press, 2006, ISBN-13: 978-0-9723267-8-0; $7.95

Buddhism For You: Love, by Daisaku Ikeda, Santa Monica, Calif.: Middleway Press, 2006, ISBN-13: 978-0-9723267-7-3; $7.95

Buddhism For You: Prayer, by Daisaku Ikeda, Santa Monica, Calif.: Middleway Press, 2006, ISBN-13: 978-0-9723267-9-7; $7.95

Soka Education: A Buddhist Vision for Teachers, Students and Parents, by Daisaku Ikeda, Santa Monica, Calif.: Middleway Press, 2001, ISBN-13: 978-0-9674697-4-4; $25.95

Unlocking the Mysteries of Birth & Death...and Everything in Between, by Daisaku Ikeda, Santa Monica, Calif.: Middleway Press, 2003, ISBN-13: 978-0-9723267-0-4; $15.00

The Way of Youth: Buddhist Common Sense for Handling Life's Questions, by Daisaku Ikeda, Santa Monica, Calif.: Middleway Press, 2000, ISBN-13: 978-0-9674697-0-6, $14.95

The following World Tribune Press books are available through any local SGI-USA community center, or from our Web site at www.sgi-usa.org:

Faith into Action: Thoughts on Selected Topics, by Daisaku Ikeda; M/O # 354-4135, $12.95

The Human Revolution (boxed set), by Daisaku Ikeda; M/O # 4182; $45.00

The New Human Revolution, by Daisaku Ikeda; M/O # 4601 (vol. 1); M/O # 4602 (vol. 2); M/O # 4603 (vol. 3); M/O # 4604 (vol. 4); M/O # 4605 (vol. 5); M/O # 4606 (vol. 6); M/O # 4607 (vol. 7); M/O # 4608 (vol. 8); M/O # 4609 (vol. 9); M/O # 4610 (vol. 10); M/O # 4611 (vol. 11); M/O # 4612 (vol. 12); $10.00 for vols. 4, 5 and 6; $12.00 for all other volumes

The Wisdom of the Lotus Sutra, vols. 1–6, by Katsuji Saito, Takanori Endo, Haruo Suda and Daisaku Ikeda; M/O # 4281 (vol. 1); M/O # 4282 (vol. 2); M/O # 4283 (vol. 3); M/O # 4284 (vol. 4); M/O # 4285 (vol. 5); M/O # 4286 (vol. 6); $10.95 each